NATIONAL ACADEMIES Scie Eng Mec

NAL MIES

n, DC

Community-Driven Relocation

Recommendations for the U.S. Gulf Coast Region and Beyond

Committee on Managed Retreat in the U.S. Gulf Coast Region

Board on Environmental Change and Society

Committee on Population

Division of Behavioral and Social Sciences and Education

Consensus Study Report

NATIONAL ACADEMIES PRESS 500 Fifth Street, NW Washington, DC 20001

This activity was supported by the Gulf Research Program of the National Academies of Sciences, Engineering, and Medicine. Support for the work of the Board on Environmental Change and Society is also provided by a grant from the National Science Foundation (Award No. BCS-2055602). Any opinions, findings, conclusions, or recommendations expressed in this publication do not necessarily reflect the views of any organization or agency that provided support for the project.

International Standard Book Number-13: 978-0-309-70872-2
International Standard Book Number-10: 0-309-70872-9
Digital Object Identifier: https://doi.org/10.17226/27213
Library of Congress Control Number: 2024934365

Cover image: Copyrighted by the Louisiana Sea Grant College Program.

This publication is available from the National Academies Press, 500 Fifth Street, NW, Keck 360, Washington, DC 20001; (800) 624-6242 or (202) 334-3313; http://www.nap.edu.

Printed in the United States of America.

Suggested citation: National Academies of Sciences, Engineering, and Medicine. 2024. *Community-Driven Relocation: Recommendations for the U.S. Gulf Coast Region and Beyond*. Washington, DC: The National Academies Press. https://doi.org/10.17226/27213.

The **National Academy of Sciences** was established in 1863 by an Act of Congress, signed by President Lincoln, as a private, nongovernmental institution to advise the nation on issues related to science and technology. Members are elected by their peers for outstanding contributions to research. Dr. Marcia McNutt is president.

The **National Academy of Engineering** was established in 1964 under the charter of the National Academy of Sciences to bring the practices of engineering to advising the nation. Members are elected by their peers for extraordinary contributions to engineering. Dr. John L. Anderson is president.

The **National Academy of Medicine** (formerly the Institute of Medicine) was established in 1970 under the charter of the National Academy of Sciences to advise the nation on medical and health issues. Members are elected by their peers for distinguished contributions to medicine and health. Dr. Victor J. Dzau is president.

The three Academies work together as the **National Academies of Sciences, Engineering, and Medicine** to provide independent, objective analysis and advice to the nation and conduct other activities to solve complex problems and inform public policy decisions. The National Academies also encourage education and research, recognize outstanding contributions to knowledge, and increase public understanding in matters of science, engineering, and medicine.

Learn more about the National Academies of Sciences, Engineering, and Medicine at **www.nationalacademies.org**.

Consensus Study Reports published by the National Academies of Sciences, Engineering, and Medicine document the evidence-based consensus on the study's statement of task by an authoring committee of experts. Reports typically include findings, conclusions, and recommendations based on information gathered by the committee and the committee's deliberations. Each report has been subjected to a rigorous and independent peer-review process and it represents the position of the National Academies on the statement of task.

Proceedings published by the National Academies of Sciences, Engineering, and Medicine chronicle the presentations and discussions at a workshop, symposium, or other event convened by the National Academies. The statements and opinions contained in proceedings are those of the participants and are not endorsed by other participants, the planning committee, or the National Academies.

Rapid Expert Consultations published by the National Academies of Sciences, Engineering, and Medicine are authored by subject-matter experts on narrowly focused topics that can be supported by a body of evidence. The discussions contained in rapid expert consultations are considered those of the authors and do not contain policy recommendations. Rapid expert consultations are reviewed by the institution before release.

For information about other products and activities of the National Academies, please visit www.nationalacademies.org/about/whatwedo.

COMMITTEE ON MANAGED RETREAT IN THE U.S. GULF COAST REGION

JANICE BARNES (*Co-Chair*), Founding and Managing Partner, Climate Adaptation Partners
TRACIE T. SEMPIER (*Co-Chair*), Coastal Resilience Engagement Specialist, Mississippi–Alabama Sea Grant Consortium
KAYODE O. ATOBA, Associate Research Scientist, Institute for a Disaster Resilient Texas, Texas A&M University
GARY S. BELKIN, Director, Billion Minds Project, Columbia University Mailman School of Public Health
DEBRA M. BUTLER, Executive Director, American Society of Adaptation Professionals
CRAIG E. COLTEN, Professor Emeritus, Louisiana State University
KATHERINE J. CURTIS, Associate Director and Professor of Community and Environmental Sociology, Center for Demography and Ecology, University of Wisconsin–Madison
HARRIET FESTING (Resigned December 2022), Executive Director and Co-Founder, Anthropocene Alliance
LYNN R. GOLDMAN, Michael and Lori Milken Dean and Professor of Environmental and Occupational Health, Milken Institute School of Public Health, George Washington University
E. BARRETT RISTROPH, Owner, Ristroph Law, Planning, and Research
CATHERINE L. ROSS, Regents Professor and Harry West Professor of City and Regional Planning, and Director, Center for Quality Growth and Regional Development, Georgia Institute of Technology
GAVIN P. SMITH, Professor, Department of Landscape Architecture and Environmental Planning, North Carolina State University
NATALIE L. SNIDER, Science Integrator, University of Maryland Center for Environmental Science Integration and Application Network
COURTNEY S. THOMAS TOBIN, Associate Professor of Community Health Sciences, Associate Dean for Equity, Diversity, and Inclusion, Fielding School of Public Health, and Faculty Associate, Ralph J. Bunche Center for African American Studies, University of California, Los Angeles

Study Staff

JOHN BEN SOILEAU, Study Director
CHANDRA MIDDLETON, Study Co-Director (until December 2022)
THOMAS F. THORNTON, Board Director
GRACE BETTS, Associate Program Officer
SITARA RAHIAB, Senior Program Assistant
HANNAH STEWART, Associate Program Officer (until October 2023)

BOARD ON ENVIRONMENTAL CHANGE AND SOCIETY

COMMITTEE ON POPULATION

Reviewers

This Consensus Study Report was reviewed in draft form by individuals chosen for their diverse perspectives and technical expertise. The purpose of this independent review is to provide candid and critical comments that will assist the National Academies of Sciences, Engineering, and Medicine in making each published report as sound as possible and to ensure that it meets the institutional standards for quality, objectivity, evidence, and responsiveness to the study charge. The review comments and draft manuscript remain confidential to protect the integrity of the deliberative process.

We thank the following individuals for their review of this report:

RENEE COLLINI, Gulf Center for Equitable Climate Resilience; The Water Institute of the Gulf
TISHA J. HOLMES, Florida State University
MAUREEN LICHTVELD, University of Pittsburgh School of Public Health
BONNIE J. McCAY, Rutgers University, New Brunswick
MARLA K. NELSON, University of New Orleans
JACQUALINE QATALIÑA SCHAEFFER, Alaska Native Tribal Health Consortium
LINDA SHI, Cornell University
MARK J. VANLANDINGHAM, Tulane University School of Public Health and Tropical Medicine
MARY C. WATERS, Harvard University

Although the reviewers listed above provided many constructive comments and suggestions, they were not asked to endorse the conclusions or recommendations of this report, nor did they see the final draft before its release. The review of this report was overseen by **HOLLY REED**, Queens College of the City University of New York, and **CHRIS D. POLAND**, Consulting Engineer, Canyon Lake, California. They were responsible for making certain that an independent examination of this report was carried out in accordance with the standards of the National Academies and that all review comments were carefully considered. Responsibility for the final content rests entirely with the authoring committee and the National Academies.

Contents

Boxes, Figures, and Tables

BOXES

FIGURES

TABLES

Preface

With increasing numbers of climate-related disaster events in Gulf Coast states (232 events occurring between 1980 and 2023, with twice as many per year from 2018 to 2022 as in the previous years) and extraordinary human and capital impacts (deaths of 10,838 people and costs on average of 1 billion dollars *per disaster* from 1980 to July 11, 2023), the consideration of how to reduce such impacts must grapple with the question of whether and how to relocate people and assets out of harm's way. Frequently termed "managed retreat," the topic of relocation receives scant attention in post-disaster recovery, when building back is prioritized; even less attention in pre-disaster mitigation planning; and almost no attention from regional planning organizations. This is not surprising, as the nation currently lacks consistent policy or programmatic guidance to enable communities and their governing bodies to tackle the uncomfortable issue of retreating from the coasts.

Recognizing the need for guidance, the Gulf Research Program (GRP) of the National Academies of Sciences, Engineering, and Medicine empaneled a committee of experts to study the issue of managed retreat in the Gulf Coast. The committee approached the study by reviewing the history of the region, by examining the science that characterizes the region's future and helps to explain its disaster record, and by considering the overall impact of chronic stressors on community well-being. This study offers new guidance meant to improve our understanding of the intersectionality of community well-being, planning processes, government policy, and implementation funding.

Managed retreat remains an emerging area of research with few practical examples to date. Of the examples that exist, many lack coordination, large-scale support, or buy-in from the community. Important to understanding this context, the task challenged the committee to tackle not only the issues surrounding managed retreat but also the very language of managed retreat. Through the study process, this term evolved to become "community-driven relocation."

We appreciate the range of perspectives, the depth of knowledge, and the ongoing efforts of members of the committee whose constructive debates and meaningful challenges to the very systems propagating disadvantage and the public health construct of well-being broadened the process to one of recognizing the need for transformative relationships between disciplines as much as transformations in participatory planning, funding, and regional collaboration. Thank you to the members of the committee.

The National Academies hosted workshops with frontline community members and municipal leaders from each of the Gulf Coast states whose stories echoed so many others in telling of the types of chronic stress that stems from the repetitive experiences of such disasters. We are grateful to those who participated in the workshops, sharing their lived experiences and raising questions to help guide the committee in the consensus study. We also extend heartfelt thanks to *all* workshop participants. We encourage each of you to continue to share those stories as your powerful voices help others to better understand the essence of the challenge.

With such challenging topics and range of activities, the committee relied heavily on the expertise of the National Academies staff who guided the process according to the National Academies standards and offered resources throughout the study to help the committee better characterize the issues for various audiences. Thanks to the National Academies staff whose commitment to this study and whose patience enabled the committee to tackle such a complex issue.

Community-driven relocation across the Gulf Coast is difficult to envision, even as sea level rise and subsidence combine to make the Gulf one of the most vulnerable areas in the nation. We thank the GRP for investing in such a challenging topic and, in doing so, catalyzing discussions that may in turn reduce risks while encouraging new collaborations and offering hopeful futures.

We wish to express our deep appreciation to the members of the committee for their diligent and dedicated contributions to developing this report. The diverse expertise and experience offered by the members of the committee were indispensable to the formulation of the report.

Janice Barnes, *Co-Chair*
Tracie Sempier, *Co-Chair*
Committee on Managed Retreat in the U.S. Gulf Coast Region

Acronyms and Abbreviations

100RC	100 Resilient Cities
ACS	American Community Survey
AEMA	Alabama Emergency Management Agency
ANCSA	Alaska Native Claims Settlement Act of 1971
BCA	benefit-cost analysis
BPSOS	Boat People SOS
BRACE	Building Resilience Against Climate Effects
BRIC	Building Resilient Infrastructure and Communities
CBO	community-based organization
CDBG	Community Development Block Grant Program
CDBG-DR	Community Development Block Grant Program-Disaster Recovery
CDBG-MIT	Community Development Block Grant Program-Mitigation
CDC	Centers for Disease Control and Prevention
CDC/ATSDR	Centers for Disease Control and Prevention's Agency for Toxic Substances and Disease Registry
CERCLA	Comprehensive Environmental Response, Compensation, and Liability Act of 1980
CEQ	Council on Environmental Quality
CI	confidence interval

C-LEARN	Community Resilience Learning Collaborative and Research Network
CLT	Community Land Trust
CMRC	Climate Migration and Receiving Community
CPRA	Coastal Protection and Restoration Authority
CRI	Coastal Resilience Index
CRS	Community Rating System
DOI	Department of the Interior
DOT	Department of Transportation
DTA	Building Resilient Infrastructure and Communities' Direct Technical Assistance
EAL	expected annual loss
EDF	Environmental Defense Fund
EJI	Environmental Justice Index
EJScreen	Environmental Justice Screening Tool
EPA	U.S. Environmental Protection Agency
EWP	Emergency Watershed Protection
Federal Plan for ELTRR	Federal Plan for Equitable Long-Term Recovery and Resilience
FEMA	Federal Emergency Management Agency
FMA	Flood Mitigation Assistance grant program
FRM	flood risk management
GAO	Government Accountability Office
GCCDS	Gulf Coast Community Design Studio
GLO	Texas General Land Office
GOMA	Gulf of Mexico Alliance
GOSR	New York Governor's Office of Storm Recovery
GRP	Gulf Research Program
GRPC	Mississippi's Gulf Regional Planning Commission
HCCSD	Harris County Community Services Department
HCFCD	Harris County Flood Control District
HCLT	Houston Community Land Trust
HHS	Department of Health and Human Services
HI	hazard index
HMA	Hazard Mitigation Assistance
HMGP	Hazard Mitigation Grant Program
HMP	hazard mitigation plan
HUD	Department of Housing and Urban Development

ICDBG	Indian Community Development Block Grant
IDJC	Isle de Jean Charles
IDMC	Internal Displacement Monitoring Centre
IHP	Individuals and Households Program
IIJA	Infrastructure Investment and Jobs Act
IPCC	Intergovernmental Panel on Climate Change
ITEK	Indigenous traditional ecological knowledge
LA-OCD	Louisiana's Office of Community Development
LA SAFE	Louisiana's Strategic Adaptations for Future Environments
LVRC	Lockyer Valley Regional Council
MEMA	Mississippi Emergency Management Agency
MHP	mental health practitioner
MOU	memorandum of understanding
MPO	Metropolitan Planning Organization
NACo	National Association of Counties
NCVHS	National Committee on Vital and Health Statistics
NDRC	Department of Housing and Urban Development's National Disaster Resilience Competition
NFIP	National Flood Insurance Program
NOAA	National Oceanic and Atmospheric Administration
NRCS	U.S. Department of Agriculture's Natural Resources Conservation Service
NRI	National Risk Index
NY Rising	New York Rising Buyout and Acquisition Program
NYC Build It Back	New York City Build It Back Program
OMB	U.S. Office of Management and Budget
OSTP	The White House Office of Science and Technology Policy
PA	Public Assistance Program
PAR	participatory action research
PARP	participatory action research and practice
PDM	Pre-Disaster Mitigation
PDRP	Post-Disaster Redevelopment Plan
PROTECT	Promoting Resilient Operations for Transformative, Efficient, and Cost-Saving Transportation

QRA	Queensland Reconstruction Authority
RAPIDO	Lower Rio Grande Rapid Recovery Re-Housing Program
RCP	Representative Concentration Pathway
RftR	Room for the River Programme
RMP	Risk Management Plan
RPA	Regional Plan Association
RPC	Regional Planning Commission
SARF	State Acquisition and Relocation Fund
SARPC	South Alabama Regional Planning Commission
SLR	sea level rise
SVI	Social Vulnerability Index
TBRPC	Tampa Bay Regional Planning Council
T-CRI	Tribal Coastal Resilience Index
TEK	traditional ecological knowledge
TMC	Texas Medical Center
TPC	Transportation Policy Committee
TUBs	Riverine Targeted Use of Buyouts Program
TWDB	Texas Water Development Board
UCS	Union of Concerned Scientists
UNDP	United Nations Development Programme
URA	Uniform Relocation Assistance and Real Property Acquisition Policies Act of 1970
USACE	U.S. Army Corps of Engineers
USGCRP	U.S. Global Change Research Program
USGS	U.S. Geological Survey
WHO	World Health Organization
WIN	Well Being in the Nation
WPA	Works Progress Administration

Summary[1]

Between 1980 and July 2023, 232 one billion-dollar disasters occurred in the U.S. Gulf Coast Region, with the number of disasters doubling annually since 2018. These included drought, flooding, freezes, severe storms, tropical cyclones, wildfires, and winter storms. Such events amplify displacement risks, whether short-term or permanent, and in some cases challenge the possibility of communities remaining in place as the sea rises and the land subsides across the region. These climate-related disasters also interact with chronic stressors stemming from both historic injustices and ongoing exposures to environmental pollutants from the very industries that employ many Gulf Coast residents. Compounding events, such as a hurricane coupled with a chemical spill, are threat multipliers. Yet year after year, disaster after disaster, housing and infrastructure are rebuilt in these same areas for reasons that range from deep cultural attachments and economic incentives to a lack of relocation options, among others.

As disaster recovery costs escalate, state and local governments cannot keep up, while federal recovery programs fall short of state requests for assistance. As households struggle to recover from one storm before the next one hits, families experience chronic stress with few opportunities for respite. Stress exacerbates other pre-existing health conditions even as exposure to flooding and extreme heat aggravate those same conditions. These circumstances present an untenable long-term cycle of cumulative, compounding, and cascading risks, markedly increasing vulnerability.

[1]This summary does not include references. Citations for the information presented herein are provided in the main text.

Addressing these growing challenges requires new ways of planning in anticipation of disasters and their growing potential for displacement. While disaster displacement is not a new phenomenon, the rapid escalation of climate-related disasters in the Gulf increases the urgency to develop pre-disaster policies to mitigate displacement and decrease suffering. Moreover, climate-related displacement amplifies other types of disparities, including ongoing inequities and the histories of hostile displacements over the settlement of the region. This history coupled with the need to address climate-related disasters and their growing impacts on Gulf communities presents a need to improve relationships among people and institutions through participatory planning processes that emphasize trust building and center community well-being and community priorities.

Neither the region nor the nation has a consistent and inclusionary process to address risks, raise awareness, or explore options for relocating communities away from environmental risks while seeking out and honoring communities' values and priorities. Even with the recently released *National Climate Resilience Framework* from the White House in 2023, there is a systemic gap in understanding these issues (e.g., risks, equitable relocation options) as well as lack of procedural justice as the need for relocation options and resources has rapidly outpaced regional and national planning capacities. Herein is the dilemma at the heart of this study: given the need to act quickly and given the history of distrust and inequities in the region, how might we co-create a just process while simultaneously growing trusting and sustaining relationships between the entities and the communities who need to collaborate?

In 2021, the Gulf Research Program of the National Academies of Sciences, Engineering, and Medicine initiated a consensus study to examine and analyze the unique challenges, needs, and opportunities associated with managing the relocation of people, infrastructure, and communities away from environmentally high-risk areas. The Board on Environmental Change and Society in the Division of Behavioral and Social Sciences and Education convened a committee of experts to provide in-depth analysis and identify short- and long-term steps necessary for community stakeholders to plan and implement relocation in ways that are equitable, culturally appropriate, adaptive, and resilient to future regional climate conditions (see the full statement of task in Chapter 1, Box 1-1). As part of its charge, the committee held public workshops in the Gulf region that focused on policy and practice considerations, research and data needs, and community engagement strategies. Elevating the voices of individuals and communities on the front lines of climate change was a central focus of these workshops. Testimonials from workshop participants guided the committee's findings and are interspersed throughout the report. The committee's work covers the coastal and peri-coastal counties and parishes along the U.S. Gulf Coast, spanning the states of Florida, Alabama, Mississippi, Louisiana, and Texas (see Figure S-1), and draws from case studies and research from other parts of the United States and abroad.

PART 1: INTRODUCING COMMUNITY-DRIVEN RELOCATION

Part 1 delineates the scope of the report and the committee's interpretation of the study charge (Chapter 1), gives an overview of the complex climate change–related threats to the Gulf region that will continue to compel individuals and communities to relocate for the foreseeable future (Chapter 2), and concludes with national and international case studies of relocation strategies (Chapter 3).

Terminology about relocation is important. Communities have emotional, symbolic, and physical attachments to place. These attachments, therefore, deserve consideration in the use of terminology that describes adaptive solutions, such as relocation. In describing adaptive solutions to reduce displacement, some researchers and policy makers have used the term "managed retreat" for organized efforts to relocate and resettle

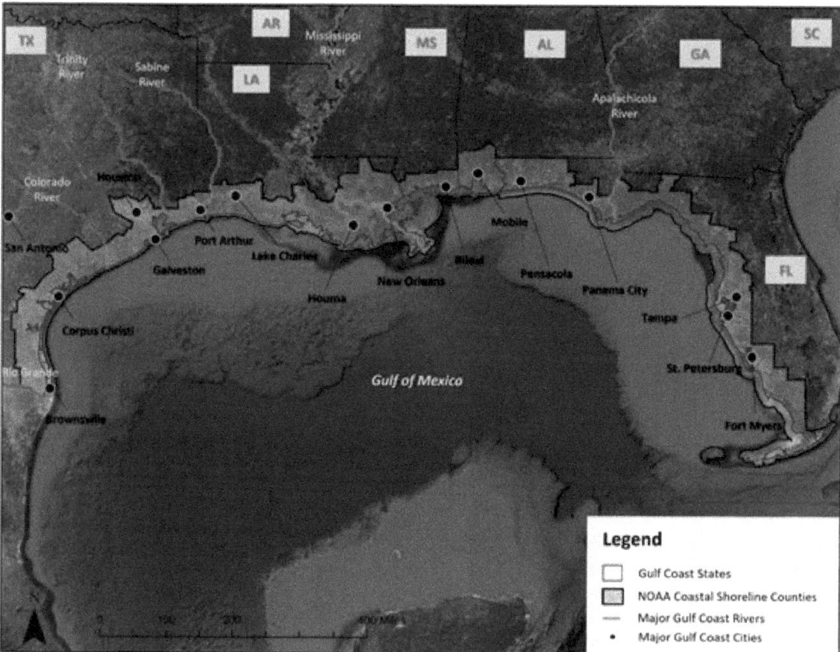

FIGURE S-1 The primary focus of this report: the U.S. Gulf Coast Region.
SOURCE: Committee generated from https://www.fisheries.noaa.gov/inport/item/66112

individuals and communities threatened by climate change and to move infrastructure away from hazardous areas (Chapter 1). The committee does not believe this term captures the key element of any adaptive solution, which is the equitable and effective involvement of the affected communities at every stage of the relocation and resettlement process.

The term "managed retreat" may trigger emotion and trauma because it is associated with intergenerational memories of violent relocations like the Indian Removal Act of 1830. Furthermore, some communities interpret "retreating" as a loss of homeland, while others see it as a movement toward safety. Because the term and concept of "managed retreat" have different assumptions for different communities, this report uses "community-driven relocation" to encompass both the abstract concept and key social dimensions that illuminate opportunities and practices that implement relocation in equitable, culturally appropriate, adaptive, and participatory and empowered ways. A community-driven approach contrasts with the largely ad hoc and post-disaster reactionary approach to mitigation and adaptation. Ad hoc approaches impede the fostering of trust and create barriers to genuine collaborative engagement and decision making. Instead, community-driven approaches could address what may be entrenched perceptions of government and institutionalized factors underpinning vulnerability. To denote the communities that people are leaving, this study uses the term "originating community"; to denote communities where people are relocating to, the committee adopted the term "receiving community." The committee recognizes the importance of shared decision making in any policy-supported and institutionalized process of community-driven relocation, meaning

- the originating community is at the center of decision making about relocation and needs for well-being;
- policy and material supports are provided for optimally enlarging a community's option for a safe landing in the receiving community or relocation destination; and
- supports are provided for the receiving community, including land-use planning, economic investments, and social resilience.

The U.S. Gulf Coast Region is experiencing increasingly intense tropical cyclones, which bring strong winds, heavy rain, storm surge, and high waves, as the sea level rises with global warming. Chapter 2 begins with an overview of the complex climate change–related threats to the Gulf region that will continue to compel relocation and concludes with displacement projections and the disproportionate impacts on minoritized and at-risk groups.

The report does not focus on climate thresholds or any one hazard but instead examines processes for how, when, why (and why not), and where people and infrastructure relocate, which could be from a variety of hazards. In other words, the committee chose to acknowledge the drivers of migration and displacement, specifically in the Gulf Region (e.g., coastal hazards), but to focus the study on relocation challenges, opportunities, policies, lessons learned, and processes (e.g., decision making). To this end, Part 1 concludes with a brief history of relocation efforts in the United States from the late 1800s onward and a selection of case studies of recent relocation efforts in the United States and abroad (Chapter 3).

> *Conclusion 2-1: Future Gulf Coast displacements are difficult to project because few models exist to fully characterize the extent of regional risks from climate changes, subsidence, and industrial impacts. Lacking more accurate exposure and risk estimates at the scale of population displacement, the Gulf Coast currently fails to hold a shared understanding of its risks and the enormity of the planning challenges that it faces. Recognizing the scale of threat warrants the equivalent of a regional displacement vulnerability risk assessment and resulting preparations for region-wide population and industry relocations.*

PART 2: UNDERSTANDING RELOCATION IN THE U.S. GULF REGION

Part 2 contains Chapters 4 through 8. Chapters 4 and 5 principally focus on the U.S. Gulf Coast Region, including its history (Chapter 4), socioeconomic demographics and recent/projected in-migration patterns, and "community profiles"—compendiums of quantitative data from federal agency datasets (e.g., Federal Emergency Management Agency's National Risk Index, U.S. Environmental Protection Agency's EJScreen) of communities the committee engaged during the study. The datasets are accompanied by first-hand testimonials from coastal residents, which give ground truth to the quantitative datasets and articulate community needs in terms of climate services and other support. The committee's approach to understanding community experiences and how risks influence relocation decision making underscores the utility of pairing quantitative and qualitative information (Chapter 5). Chapter 6 then broadens out from the Gulf region to discuss the significance of community well-being in the context of relocation and the importance of communication, participation, and engagement in discussing, planning, and implementing community-driven relocation (Chapter 7). While originating and receiving communities are discussed throughout the report, Part 2 concludes with a more detailed focus on their considerations and needs (Chapter 8).

The Critical Importance of History and the Current Realities of Gulf Coast Communities

The U.S. Gulf Coast is a dynamic and evolving socioecological system. Throughout history, human movement and adaptation to this system have been driven by the knowledge and expertise of Indigenous and place-based communities, the ramifications of colonization and enslavement, environmental fluctuations, the politics of development, and the ascendancy of the petrol-chemical industrial sector (Chapter 4). Indigenous people; immigrant groups from Africa, Latin America, the Caribbean, Acadia (present-day Canada), and Asia; and other traditional populations have adapted to the environmental conditions of the Gulf and exhibited remarkable community resilience under harsh conditions (Chapter 5).[2]

Conclusion 4-1: After European conquest and the extermination and enslavement of Africans and Indigenous people in the Gulf region, the Indian Removal Act of 1830 began an institutionalized process of displacement and forced migration of Indigenous people from their homelands. Other groups in the region have histories of forced migrations and displacement (e.g., people from Acadia, Vietnam, Cuba). Descendants of these groups that currently face the prospects of relocation report that historical injustices influence their response to current climatic and environmental changes on the Gulf Coast.

Conclusion 5-2: Despite environmental threats, Gulf Coast populations have increased steadily for 50 years. Movement toward the coast has increased construction and real estate values and thereby enhanced risk, while contributing to gentrification. Traditional placed-based communities with long relationships to coastal lands and waters have expertise, social networks, and skillsets evolved from local knowledge and centuries of resilient behaviors. Place-based communities are often reluctant to relocate because of their unique economic, social, and cultural attachments to place, and they also often lack access to resources if they do want to relocate.

[2]The committee defines "traditional population" as a self-identified group with long-standing residence in a particular place, with livelihoods and other cultural practices that are intertwined with the local environment and resources. It may be Indigenous or have roots in Europe, Africa, Asia, or other parts of the Americas.

Sustaining Community Well-Being: Physical, Mental, and Social Health

The study committee drew from various approaches and methodologies to conceptualize and assess well-being, and identified tools to enhance resilience, social capital, community cohesion, and collective efficacy in the context of climate change and climate-induced displacement and relocation (Chapter 6). A holistic approach illustrates how community well-being and adaptive capacities to respond to climate threats are undermined by pre-existing and enduring social and economic health inequities.

Conclusion 6-1: There are discernable linkages between health disparities (e.g., premature death, elevated levels of chronic diseases, poor mental health, inequitable access to health care) and complex socioeconomic disparities (e.g., intergenerational poverty, economic precarity). Equitable and sustained community-driven relocation planning requires agencies (e.g., Centers for Disease Control and Prevention, Federal Emergency Management Agency, Department of Housing and Urban Development) to examine these linkages within the context of originating and receiving communities.

Conclusion 6-2: The importance to communities of bolstering mental health and healing emotional distress lies not only in diminished suffering and enhanced coping but also in the social ties and associated social capital that mutually reinforce collective efficacy and social inclusion in processes of adaptation to social and environmental change.

Addressing the traumas, stressors, and dearth of resources as well as enhancing collective and individual psychological resources and strengths are critical prerequisites to providing a foundation for communities to participate in community-driven relocation projects. Therefore, bolstering capacity for well-being in climate-threatened communities is a priority for public health and climate adaptation across the nation (Chapter 6).

Communication, Knowledge, and Engagement

Relocating and resettling is a complex process of change and adaptation that involves more than the physical act of moving. It is a social process that involves the cooperation, coordination, and participation of affected people at the originating and receiving nodes. Yet, processes around relocation often exclude people, neighborhoods, and communities from problem solving and developing adaptive solutions, and often do not support opportunities for collective action. Relocation processes will only be just and equitable through a community-driven approach, of which participatory planning, access to knowledge, transparency of process and outcome, and shared decision making are core elements (Chapter 7).

Conclusion 7-3: For community-driven relocation, there is a particular need for participatory processes through which community knowledge is sought, brought forth, and used in planning and decision making. Acknowledging the importance of local knowledge and knowledge holders helps build trust and awareness of local perceptions, needs, and capabilities that can facilitate relocation planning, including the reintroduction of local and Indigenous frameworks that may have been eschewed over time.

Conclusion 7-4: Workshop input and findings validate the broad desire for far more substantive, ongoing civic participation/empowerment and leadership capacity that exceeds being "consulted" or "engaged" by considering participants as deciders and co-planners. At the same time, community members and local government leaders are not clear or prepared on how to meaningfully practice participation and incorporate people's capacity in decision-making processes.

Planning for Receiving and Originating Communities

Community-driven relocation requires significant planning on the part of receiving and originating communities, including how to adaptively manage the resulting open space (e.g., water retention, commemorative sites, wildlife habitat enhancement), the social and financial support needed for relocating communities, and the physical and social infrastructure needed in receiving communities (Chapter 8). In addition to effective communication and engagement of residents in receiving communities, effective preparation entails collaboration between government across jurisdictions (e.g., federal, state, local) and regional planning entities, including data sharing, guiding appropriate adaptation investments in receiving areas (e.g., infrastructure, energy bandwidth, schools), disinvestment in maladaptation in originating areas, and the facilitation of relationships between originating and receiving communities.

Conclusion 8-1: Receiving communities need to have the infrastructure and institutional capacity to provide essential services such as housing, water treatment and water supply, power and fuel distribution, broadband, education, health services, employment, and transportation for expected population increases. Currently, there is little planning or funding specifically for population relocation.

Conclusion 8-2: Land suitability analysis is a useful tool to help communities identify less hazard-prone areas for potential relocation sites. Although its use in directing relocating communities is so far uncommon, when incorporated into broader city planning efforts it has the potential to help direct people who are relocating to safer nearby areas that are also acceptable to them and that preserve a jurisdiction's tax base.

Originating communities and/or the land left behind after wholesale community and infrastructure relocation occurs have their own sets of challenges, needs, and opportunities. Setting thresholds is one of the first and most important parts of the relocation process and involves decisions about when to consolidate or reduce municipal services (e.g., waste, postal, fire, police) and decommission infrastructure. Thresholds acknowledge the limits to adaptive capacities—when environmental risks and change become so rapid and transformational that habitation becomes no longer logistically, financially, or safely feasible. Community-driven relocation requires residents to be active participants in discussions about the triggering of thresholds and the pace and timing of disinvestment, decommissioning, and the reduction of services.

Conclusion 8-9: Partnerships between originating and receiving communities can facilitate the collaborative development of policies and plans needed to address the complexities and long timeframes associated with community-driven relocation.

PART 3: FUNDING, POLICY, AND PLANNING

Part 3 of the report continues to broaden out from the Gulf to discuss the current landscape of policy, funding, and planning for relocation (Chapter 9); the associated challenges and opportunities (Chapter 10) of this landscape; and the committee's recommendations (Chapter 11).

Landscape of Policy, Funding, and Planning

The committee identified a complex web of federal programs, laws, and plans that communities must navigate when pursuing community-driven relocation and considered how to make these more inclusive of and responsive to the needs of originating and receiving communities. A major obstacle is that relocation is currently managed using a "disaster-recovery model," meaning that most funding and technical assistance comes episodically as a reaction to a specific disaster or in the form of annual nationally competitive programs rather than being available year-round and allocated based on risk and need to include addressing the root causes of vulnerability. The compressed timeframe in which people are required to act often hampers effective community engagement, collective decision making, and collaborative planning processes needed to address the myriad of complexities tied to community-driven relocation.

> *Conclusion 9-1: While federal agencies have many of the tools (e.g., funding, capacity) needed to help communities resettle under existing laws, and there are existing programs (e.g., the Federal Emergency Management Agency's Building Resilient Infrastructure and Communities and the Department of Housing and Urban Development's Community Development Block Grant Program) that have facilitated individual households and neighborhoods to relocate, there is currently no interagency coordination to enable community-driven relocation planning at the scale required to address the level of risks in the U.S. Gulf Coast Region. As a result, the existing programs are difficult for households and communities to navigate.*

> *Conclusion 9-7: Moving from a disaster-recovery model to an overall community relocation regime could entail evaluating the potential requirements to transition from a primarily competitive grant-making process to a process that places an increased emphasis on providing year-round funding and ongoing assistance to underresourced and at-risk communities to develop and implement risk reduction strategies, including long-term relocation planning.*

Adopting a comprehensive and coordinated adaptive governance approach would plan for uncertainty at the local, regional, and national levels through (a) local planning to ensure that infrastructure and other community needs are met in the originating and receiving communities; (b) regional entities to coordinate relocation that occurs across different jurisdictions; and (c) funding and guidance from higher-level governments to meet local and regional needs.

Overcoming Challenges and Identifying Opportunities

The committee provided an overview of the numerous challenges that households, local and state governments, and other community stakeholders might face when navigating the relocation process (Chapter 10), including shared responsibilities between governments and households; the role of insurance and its benefits and drawbacks under the current system (e.g., parametric insurance, the National Flood Insurance Program); individual and household eligibility determinations and prioritization in current relocation assistance programs (e.g., per-disaster rulemaking, heirs' property rights, renter support); and challenges related to the complex and time-consuming process of obtaining funding for a buyout.

Conclusion 10-4: Obtaining funding for a buyout is a complex, time-consuming process that often exceeds the capacity of communities, especially underresourced ones, to act. It requires communities to write an approved hazard mitigation plan, which also takes time and a certain level of capacity and funding, especially if this task is undertaken by a contractor, which is often the case. The complexity of the buyout process also greatly exceeds the adequacy of federal and state resources available to help households and communities navigate the process. Although some assistance programs exist (e.g., the Federal Emergency Management Agency's Advanced Assistance program), they tend to be underutilized.

Conclusion 10-6: Multiple sources of funding may be needed for relocation. It is challenging to combine different funding streams because different agencies and programs (e.g., the Federal Emergency Management Agency Hazard Mitigation Grant Program and the Department of Housing and Urban Development's Community Development Block Grant Program) have different rules and timeframes, and federal funds from one entity may or may not serve as the required match for another entity. Nonfederal match requirements prevent some poorer communities from being able to participate in buyout grants.

RECOMMENDATIONS FOR COMMUNITY-DRIVEN RELOCATION EFFORTS IN THE GULF REGION AND BEYOND

The committee arrived at 13 recommendations for community-driven relocation and grouped them into three domains, supported by multiple conclusions: (1) Centering Well-Being, (2) Developing and Sustaining Local Collaborations, and (3) Strengthening Preparations for Community-Driven Relocation. Chapter 11 also contains these recommendations but cross-references the relevant conclusions and chapters, and includes additional supportive text, such as examples of implementation and process.

These recommendations were identified by the committee through information-gathering sessions with Gulf Coast communities and by assessing the landscape of policy and funding. In parallel, agency-led efforts identified similar needs, lending credence to this kind of systemic change, specifically through the White House's *National Climate Resilience Framework* ("Framework"). The Framework identifies opportunities for action for funding, supporting, expediting, and evaluating community-driven relocation and centering well-being in climate resilience and adaptation.[3]

Centering Well-being

RECOMMENDATION 1: The U.S. Department of Health and Human Services (HHS) Office of Climate Change and Health Equity (OCCHE) and Office of the Assistant Secretary for Mental Health and Substance Use should support and coordinate efforts across HHS and other agencies with the following objectives:

- Accelerate adoption of task-shared approaches to community mental health care, especially in high climate-impacted areas (e.g., through establishment of payment mechanisms, such as assistance from the Health Resources and Services Administration and scope expansion of Certified Community Behavioral Health Clinics). Such approaches should use evidence-supported mental health care, prevention, and promotion methods that community members and community-based organizations can adopt and directly provide.
- Facilitate collaborations among federal agencies, programs, and policies that promote well-being and build community capacity to support mental health, effective empowerment, trust, inclusion, equity, and collective efficacy for adapting to environmental challenges.
- Facilitate regional coordination of the array of public health, health care, and social and mental health services that are required to support the well-being of originating and receiving communities.
- Establish metrics, indicators, and baselines to assess the longitudinal and cross-sectional well-being outcomes of individuals in the context of relocation. These data should be collated with existing data collected by federal agencies (e.g., Centers for Disease Control and Prevention, National Oceanic and Atmospheric Administration) and evaluated regularly to improve adaptation governance.

[3]The majority of these alignments appear in Framework in the section Opportunities for Action, under Objective #6, on pages 28–29. More information is available at https://www.whitehouse.gov/wp-content/uploads/2023/09/National-Climate-Resilience-Framework-FINAL.pdf

Developing and Sustaining Local Collaborations

RECOMMENDATION 2: Planning for community-driven relocation should incorporate local perspectives about the histories, impacts, and perceptions of displacements and forced relocations, as well as generational traditions.

- Federal and state agencies (e.g., Federal Emergency Management Agency, Department of Housing and Urban Development, U.S. Army Corps of Engineers, U.S. Environmental Protection Agency, the Centers for Disease Control and Prevention, state historic preservation and cultural resource agencies) should institute systematic, Gulf-wide community-informed local investigations on how past and current patterns of resilience and adaptation and relevant policies influence attitudes and behaviors toward relocation and resettlement.
- Emergency management and disaster recovery agencies (e.g., Federal Emergency Management Agency and regional and state counterparts), local public works agencies (e.g., water, power, drainage, flood protection), mental and behavioral health care institutes, and transportation planning entities (e.g., local and regional) should reevaluate their plans, expenditures, and strategies to account for discriminatory policies and practices that have exacerbated vulnerabilities, and should institute plans (e.g., the Justice40 Initiative) to redress inequities that have undermined the resilience of communities most likely to face relocation.

RECOMMENDATION 3: Agencies that assist communities with relocation (e.g., Department of Housing and Urban Development, Federal Emergency Management Agency, U.S. Army Corps of Engineers, U.S. Department of Agriculture, and state resilience and community development offices) should foster meaningful partnerships to develop and execute relocation plans in collaboration with communities, including decisions about timing and pace of the relocation process. These agencies should

- develop a consistent co-creation process and work with each community to establish specific communication requirements that include face-to-face interactions; and
- work with locally trusted community-based organizations to build understanding, trust, and enduring relationships with communities to carry out adaptation.

RECOMMENDATION 4: Regional planning entities alongside local public works, planning, and housing authorities, and departments involved in relocation, resilience, and climate adaption efforts should

- account for community-driven relocation (originating and receiving communities) in their planning efforts (e.g., land-use plans, hazard mitigation plans, and economic plans);
- revise and assess relocation strategies based on current and projected climate data and traditional ecological knowledge; and
- conduct land suitability analysis to identify suitable receiving areas, and in doing so, to work with communities to raise their own capacities to understand land suitability.

RECOMMENDATION 5: Federal agencies should engage with local governments and regional planning entities to support community-driven relocation planning across originating and receiving communities. Federal and local government collaborations with regional planning entities should

- work with originating communities to establish threshold agreements for consolidation and regionalization of local governments and tax bases as residents relocate;
- share data about priority receiving communities and assess the impacts of regional population shifts to aid in planning;
- modify federal grant programs (e.g., Building Resilient Infrastructure and Communities, Flood Mitigation Assistance grant program, Hazard Mitigation grant program) to include making the programming of open space an eligible Federal Emergency Management Agency-funded activity; and
- modify federal and other relocation funding guidelines to include a requirement that households relocate outside Special Flood Hazard Areas and, in turn, work with communities to broaden understanding of what Special Flood Hazard Areas mean to household-level risks.

RECOMMENDATION 6: State agencies, regional planning entities, professional associations, and academic-community partnerships (e.g., land and sea grant universities, minority serving institutions) should provide targeted capacity building and training initiatives to assist state and local governments in planning for community-driven relocation.

RECOMMENDATION 7: Federal government agencies, Gulf Coast state governments, and regional planning entities should increase investments in preparing receiving communities for new residents (e.g., infrastructure, energy system capacity, broadband, schools, water supply).

Strengthening Preparations for Community-Driven Relocation

RECOMMENDATION 8: The Federal Emergency Management Agency should, outside of a disaster timeframe, pre-approve properties for acquisition (conduct a single National Environmental Policy Act/National Historic Preservation Act clearance on all such contiguous properties in a flood-prone area) and deem relocation as "cost-effective" in pre-identified communities.

RECOMMENDATION 9: In the short term, federal agencies (e.g., Federal Emergency Management Agency, U.S. Army Corps of Engineers, Department of Housing and Urban Development) should fund application and implementation assistance through the establishment of hazard mitigation "navigators." The funding and implementation of navigators should be a part of long-term recovery plans and hazard mitigation plans. These navigators would

- provide the technical assistance needed to help communities apply for and implement a relocation strategy (e.g., through collective buyout programs); and
- provide household- and neighborhood-level planning assistance throughout the relocation process.

RECOMMENDATION 10: Federal agencies that provide relocation funding (e.g., Federal Emergency Management Agency, Department of Housing and Urban Development) should assess the benefits of annual funding to pre-disaster mitigation programs. Actions to improve adaptive capacity should include

- analyzing regulatory and programmatic barriers for converting pre-disaster mitigation programs to include annualized funding for developing adaptive capacities, including relocation; and
- evaluating potential requirements to transition from a primarily competitive grant-making process to a process that provides ongoing assistance to underresourced communities to develop and implement risk reduction strategies using a distribution formula that prioritizes the highest climate risk areas.

RECOMMENDATION 11: Agencies that offer funding for relocation planning, including infrastructure needs (such as Federal Emergency Management Agency [FEMA], U.S. Army Corps of Engineers,

Department of Housing and Urban Development), should streamline the process of obtaining relocation funding, including reimbursements, through the following actions.

In the short term:

- Agencies should coordinate eligibility criteria and timing of requests for proposals.
- Agencies should align the timing of grant delivery and the duration of grants across federal agencies so that applicants have the maximum amount of time to fulfill the grant requirements.
- FEMA should allow people with National Flood Insurance Program coverage, whose homes have received a certain level of damage, to apply directly for a buyout rather than going through the state and then FEMA's hazard mitigation program.
- Agencies should allow funds from partnering agencies to be used as matching funds to the main federal source (i.e., the disbursing agency). States should also provide funding matches to communities for grants that require a nonfederal partner.
- The Council on Environmental Quality should convene agencies to develop a memorandum of understanding to coordinate construction, utility provision, and the environmental review process under the National Environmental Protection Act for relocations at the scale of a neighborhood or larger.
- Agencies should create an interagency mechanism, such as a single relocation grant application platform (e.g., the Universal Application for Disaster Survivors), that is accessible by states, tribes, municipalities, and households, and establishes a process to triage the applications and direct them to the most appropriate agency. The process should include step-by-step communication with the applicant for transparency and tracking.

In the longer term:

- Agencies should develop and maintain, across jurisdictions, an information clearinghouse connecting users to existing and new resources necessary to conduct a relocation program. This repository should be controlled by an operations center that includes the services of skilled consultants, planners, mediators, and stakeholders who have experience dealing with diverse interests and navigating issues that arise during cross-stakeholder discussions about relocation.

RECOMMENDATION 12: The Federal Emergency Management Agency (FEMA), through the leadership and engagement of the Office of Information and Regulatory Affairs of the Office of Management and Budget, should revise its benefit-cost analysis process. This should include

- developing a rubric that accounts for a community's qualitative values, characteristics, and root causes of vulnerability, such as social cohesion, social capital, political disenfranchisement, linguistic isolation, and collective efficacy, among others; and
- extending FEMA's recent temporary revisions to the benefit-cost analysis for the fiscal 2022 application cycle of Building Resilient Infrastructure and Communities and the Flood Mitigation Assistance grant program.

RECOMMENDATION 13: Federal programs involved with community-driven relocation (e.g., Federal Emergency Management Agency, U.S. Army Corps of Engineers, Department of Housing and Urban Development) should

- increase acquisition payments to property owners so they can afford a comparable home in a safe location;
- provide relocation assistance to renters, and mobile or manufactured homes; and
- use management costs to support buyout grant offers to property owners above typical pre-disaster fair market values.

1

Introduction

Millions of people in the United States and millions more across the globe are at risk of displacement as a result of the effects of climate change (Global Report on Internal Displacement, 2023). In the U.S. Gulf Coast Region (spanning the states of Florida, Alabama, Mississippi, Louisiana, and Texas), flooding due to sea level rise and storm surge, subsidence, and land loss are increasing the potential for displacement of individuals, towns, and entire cities, including Indigenous communities. These effects compound other climate-related hazards, including damage to vital infrastructure (e.g., water, sewage, electricity, health care facilities, and roads); the release of pollutants due to storm damage; and heat exposure (Field et al., 2012; Oppenheimer et al., 2014). Such hazards have already contributed to substantial displacement.

Disaster displacement is not a new phenomenon, but addressing it equitably poses a multitude of challenges for residents and community stakeholders across sectors and jurisdictions. Displacement can change all aspects of daily living, such as housing, community and cultural ties, employment, access to health care, availability of safe drinking water and other services, food sufficiency, and household wealth (Hori & Schafer, 2010). In a region with a high potential for annual disasters, like the U.S. Gulf Coast Region, displacement, or the threat of it, often affects people who have survived the stress and accrued trauma of one or more disasters (e.g., Hurricane Katrina survivors impacted by Hurricane Harvey, see Eugene, 2017; see also Hu et al., 2021). Measures can be taken to support people who must move "out of harm's way," yet very few communities are preparing for, or managing the risk of, displacement (Siders, 2019). Some reasons include limited relocation policies and technical support, limited resources—including funding—deep-seated connections to place, or a propensity to "protect in place."

With increasing numbers of weather- and climate-related disaster events with losses over 1 billion dollars in Gulf Coast states (235 from 1980 to August 8, 2023), with twice as many events per year from 2018 to 2022 as in the previous years, and extraordinary human impacts (deaths of 15,971 people as of August 8, 2023; National Oceanic and Atmospheric Administration [NOAA] National Centers for Environmental Information, 2023), the consideration of how to reduce such impact fundamentally questions whether to begin discussions about relocating "people and assets out of harm's way" (Siders, 2019, p. 216).

In 2021, the Gulf Research Program (GRP) of the National Academies of Sciences, Engineering, and Medicine (National Academies) funded a consensus study to examine and analyze the unique challenges, needs, and opportunities associated with managing climate-related retreat in the U.S. Gulf Coast Region.[1] The Board on Environmental Change and Society in the Division of Behavioral and Social Sciences and Education convened a committee of experts to provide in-depth analysis and identify short- and long-term steps necessary for community stakeholders and government agencies to plan and implement the movement of people away from high-hazard areas in ways that are equitable, culturally appropriate, adaptive, and resilient to future regional climate conditions. Box 1-1 contains the full study charge. The committee members brought knowledge, experience, and expertise in domains including decision making, communication and public participation, governance, demography, climate adaptation, environmental science, public policy and law, urban and regional planning, environmental and community health, the social and behavioral sciences, and the humanities.[2] Committee member biographies are provided in Appendix A.

RESPONSE TO THE CHARGE

The committee's primary goal with this report is to provide valuable guidance about how to study, plan, and implement relocation efforts that are equitable, culturally appropriate, adaptive, and resilient to future regional climate conditions. The committee hopes to serve community stakeholders from across sectors (e.g., government, industry, academia,

[1]In 2013 the GRP was formed using funding from the criminal settlement following the Deepwater Horizon oil disaster and was created to "advance and apply science, engineering, and public health knowledge to reduce risks from offshore oil spills and will enable the communities of the Gulf to better anticipate, mitigate, and recover from future disasters." More information about the GRP is available at https://www.nationalacademies.org/gulf/about

[2]As noted in the front matter, Harriet Festing resigned from the committee in December 2022, reducing the current committee to 13 members.

BOX 1-1
Statement of Task

The National Academies will convene an ad hoc committee to conduct a study on the movement and relocation of people, infrastructure, and communities away from environmentally high-risk areas, sometimes referred to as managed retreat, in the Gulf Coast Region of the United States. In particular, the study will focus on understanding and responding to the unique challenges in the face of a changing climate along the U.S. Gulf Coast (e.g., coastal flooding due to sea level rise, subsidence, land loss). The study will make findings and recommendations based on information gathered about the challenges, needs, and opportunities associated with managed retreat in the U.S. Gulf Coast Region.

As a way to gather information for the report, three public workshops will be held in the U.S. Gulf Coast Region. The public workshops will focus on policy/practice considerations, research/data needs, and community engagement strategies. Elevating community voices will be a centerpiece of the workshops. Topics to be addressed across the workshops may include:

- Identifying considerations and best practices for engaging with communities about managed retreat, including effective communication and engagement methods, equity, co-production of knowledge, development of strategies, and involvement in planning and decision making.
- Understanding managed retreat efforts taking place within the U.S. Gulf Coast Region, including promising practices to preserve social cohesion and protect traditional and cultural practices as part of managed retreat planning, and what community stakeholders in the Gulf Coast region can learn from them.
- Identifying policy and practical barriers to managed retreat, including issues relating to equity (e.g., who is able to claim access to various public benefits and services, how displaced peoples are received by and integrated into another community).
- Highlighting key information and data needs and necessary timeframe(s) to plan effectively.
- Identifying research and information gaps, particularly in the social and behavioral sciences, which inhibit effective and equitable planning, communication, and implementation of managed retreat programs.

A publication will be produced by a rapporteur and in accordance with institutional guidelines following each workshop.

Following the completion of the workshop series, the committee will produce a report that:

- Synthesizes common themes identified through the public workshop series (e.g., policy and practical challenges, information needs, best practices).
- Incorporates evidence from the literature in areas such as public participation, communication, governance, and decision making.
- Identifies short- and long-term steps necessary for community stakeholders to plan and implement the movement of people away from high-hazard areas in ways that are equitable, culturally-appropriate, adaptive, and resilient to future regional climate conditions.

nonprofits, community members) and jurisdictions (e.g., local, regional, state, federal), as well as the needs of the study sponsor, the GRP of the National Academies, as it develops a research agenda for future programming and relevant fields of study, such as those that address the complex psychological and socioeconomic realities inherent in relocation as an adaptive strategy to climate change.

As discussed throughout this report, concerns of the community members the committee engaged with over the course of the study included the need for community-led decision making and engagement; the need for effective communication and outreach; the need for self-determination and tribal sovereignty; a lack of available resources to assist with decision making; a lack of an equitable process to become involved in relocation processes; and the importance of the preservation of social cohesion and the protection of traditional and cultural practices.

The committee therefore used a variety of means to solicit comments from members of these groups, and paid particular attention to ways of hearing from those who lack access to adequate resources (e.g., transportation, housing) and those whose voices are often silenced in decision-making processes (e.g., traditionally underrepresented groups). In addition to residents facing displacement or barriers to relocation, the committee also engaged with and emphasizes the diverse array of entities, groups of people, and individuals that are often the first to respond when disaster strikes (e.g., emergency managers, leaders of community- and faith-based organizations, nonprofits, local government). Many of these individuals and entities are poised to participate in shaping climate adaptation policies that can decrease the suffering of communities and decrease the loss of life and infrastructure before disasters, including preparation for the slower onset of climate change impacts, like sea level rise. The engagement process with this array of stakeholders is described later in this chapter; here, the committee highlights some of the types of groups the committee engaged with during the writing of this report and hopes to reach through its publication.

Gulf Coast Communities

This report is intended as a resource for Gulf Coast communities and individuals, not limited to but including those who are contemplating, undertaking, or facing barriers to relocation (including systemic issues such as structural racism), as well as individuals who have resettled and people in communities that have received such individuals. This audience includes Gulf Coast Indigenous communities, who are dealing with some of the worst land loss in the region, and immigrant groups from Africa, Latin

America, the Caribbean, Acadia (present-day Canada), and Asia, as well as other traditional populations that inhabit the U.S. Gulf Coast Region.[3]

Community-Based Organizations

These organizations and the people they serve are generally not well resourced unless they are associated with a national organization and often struggle to be heard; thus, the committee prioritized elevating their voices and their cause.

Regional Organizations, Commissions, and Entities

These government, nongovernment, and quasi-governmental bodies (e.g., Federal Regional Commissions) guide development of public/private resources to ensure public safety, well-being, and livability, and often play a boundary-spanning role in connecting communities and entities across jurisdictions and geographic scales. Such entities are often responsible for maintaining a variety of long-range planning projects (e.g., related to transportation, infrastructure, environment) required to keep their jurisdictions' eligibility for federal funding. These projects are prioritized based on the planning process. The committee hopes that such groups can use this report to leverage efforts for climate adaptation and planning, to help justify relocation and other long-term adaptation initiatives that span jurisdictions, to assist with large-scale infrastructure projects and have capacity to coordinate with multiple municipalities, and possibly to inform both Metropolitan Planning Organizations (which exist in urban areas where there are more than 50,000 people) and Regional Transportation Planning Organizations.

State Agencies

State agencies and offices that are responsible for housing, planning, floodplain management, resource allocation, and coastal zone management (e.g., public works, community development, resilience and sustainability offices) are a critical audience for this report. Such entities could use this report to inform land-use decisions; service implementation; the coordination of residents, businesses, and ecosystems; and plans for protecting resources in instances of climate- and environment-induced relocations.

[3]The committee defines "traditional population" as a self-identified group with long-standing residence in a particular place with livelihoods and other cultural practices that are intertwined with the local environment and resources. It may be indigenous or have roots in Europe, Africa, Asia, or other parts of the Americas.

State Legislatures

The committee hopes that state legislatures—which are responsible for researching, drafting, and passing legislation and whose members represent their districts and work to meet citizens' requests for assistance with a variety of issues—can use this report to support the enactment of policies and possibly facilitate the establishment of regional planning entities within or between states.

Municipal, Parish, and County-Level Government Officials

Officials at these levels inform community planning, including comprehensive plans, local hazard mitigation plans, climate adaptation plans, and others. These officials often have capacity constraints that prevent adequate responses to chronic disasters, yet they are among the first to notice increases in the frequency of extreme weather events that lead to increased displacement. This report is intended as a resource for those officials in developing plans and policies to support their communities, including communities that are willing to receive those who have been displaced. One reality this report could help to address at this level is the fact that counties and parishes on the Gulf coastline are more densely populated and have higher median incomes in comparison to many inland Gulf region counties and parishes (Kerry Smith & Whitmore, 2020; Mack, 2018; U.S. Census Bureau, 2020). For example, the report could inform a potential collaboration between the National Association of Counties (NACo)—whose mission is to strengthen America's counties and who advocates for county priorities in federal policy making to optimize taxpayer contributions—and municipal, parish, and county-level government officials, to plan and incentivize better building practices and reduce insurance claims, among other actions.[4]

Federal Agencies and Other Audiences

The committee also considered ways this report could support other audiences. Federal agencies have limited funds to support relocation and want to be diligent in utilizing existing funds. There is no one federal agency charged with the authority to lead relocation efforts, though a recent Government Accountability Office report (2020a) highlights the need for a "climate migration" pilot program to reduce federal fiscal exposure. In answer to this need, the White House launched a Community-Driven Relocation Subcommittee as part of the White House National Climate Task Force in August 2022. This interagency subcommittee is co-led by the

[4]More information about NACo is available at https://www.naco.org/counties

Federal Emergency Management Agency (FEMA) and the U.S. Department of the Interior (DOI; FEMA, 2022a).[5] Although the present report focuses on the Gulf region, our recommendations also apply at the national scale to the efforts of the Community-Driven Relocation Subcommittee.

This report may also assist government agencies in justifying the expenditure of taxpayer money by providing evidence-based information to support decisions and prioritization of relocation projects and initiatives. The recommendations in this report (Chapter 11) align with a series of federal reports that consider relocation as an adaptive strategy to build a more climate resilient nation while also fostering and enhancing community well-being, and the inherent relationship between well-being and climate resilience. The U.S. Congress was tasked with multilateral engagement in mitigation of, and adaptation to, climate change in *The White House Report on the Impact of Climate Change on Migration* (2021).[6] DOI's *Climate Action Plan* (2021) recognizes relocation as part of a "whole-of-government approach" (p. 2),[7] while the Department of Housing and Urban Development's (HUD's) *Climate Resilience Implementation Guide for Community Driven Relocation* provides a step-by-step guide for communities.[8] Finally, the first ever White House *National Climate Resilience Framework* identifies specific opportunities for action for funding, supporting, expediting, and evaluating community-driven relocation.[9]

Finally, the committee also hopes this report will support researchers in identifying promising future research goals, pairing research with practice, and establishing academic and community-based partnerships.

SCOPE OF GEOGRAPHY AND HAZARDS

The regional focus of this study adds a layer of complexity to its geographical scope. The primary geographic focus in this study is on the coastal and peri-coastal jurisdictions (e.g., counties, parishes, cities, towns)

---

[5]More information about this subcommittee is available at https://www.fema.gov/fact-sheet/fema-efforts-advancing-community-driven-relocation

[6]*The White House Report on the Impact of Climate Change on Migration* is available at https://www.whitehouse.gov/wp-content/uploads/2021/10/Report-on-the-Impact-of-Climate-Change-on-Migration.pdf

[7]More information about DOI's *Climate Action Plan* is available at https://www.sustainability.gov/pdfs/doi-2021-cap.pdf

[8]More information about HUD's *Climate Resilience Implementation Guide for Community Driven Relocation* is available at https://files.hudexchange.info/resources/documents/Climate-Resilience-Implementation-Guide-Community-Driven-Relocation.pdf

[9]More information about the *National Climate Resilience Framework* is available at https://www.whitehouse.gov/wp-content/uploads/2023/09/National-Climate-Resilience-Framework-FINAL.pdf

of the entire Gulf Coast (see Figure 1-1), which is an area that generally aligns with the state coastal zone boundaries of the National Oceanic and Atmospheric Administration's (NOAA's) Office for Coastal Management (NOAA, 2012) and which contains the NOAA-designated coastal shoreline counties of the Gulf Coast.[10] However, retrieving data from only this swath of the Gulf region is difficult, and data are often unavailable for some jurisdictions. Therefore, throughout this report, statewide data for the Gulf region (Florida, Mississippi, Alabama, Louisiana, and Texas), in addition to coastline data, are utilized. Importantly, places along the Gulf Coast or in the greater Gulf region operate as both originating communities (places from which people relocate), such as Houston, Texas, and Houma, Louisiana, and receiving communities (places to which people relocate; Junod et al., 2023). Additionally, communities receiving Gulf residents could be in other regions of the country and the world.

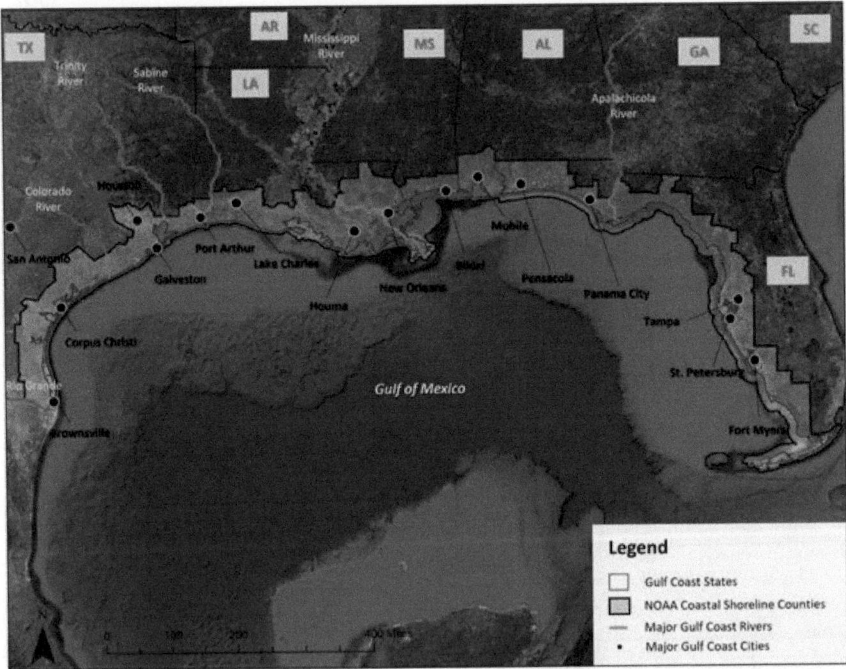

FIGURE 1-1 The primary focus of this report: the U.S. Gulf Coast Region.
SOURCE: Committee generated from https://www.fisheries.noaa.gov/inport/item/66112

[10]More information about NOAA's state coastal zone boundaries is available at https://coast.noaa.gov/data/czm/media/StateCZBoundaries.pdf

The U.S. Gulf Coast Region experiences increasingly intense tropical cyclones, which bring strong winds, heavy rain, storm surge, and high waves, and sea level rise is increasing (see Chapter 2); both of these can result in an abundance of water from various forms of flooding (e.g., pluvial, fluvial, riverine; Needham et al., 2012). Nevertheless, the committee decided against focusing the report on only an abundance of water or on any one climate threshold or hazard. Instead, we chose to examine processes for how, why (and why not), and where people and infrastructure relocate, which could be due to a variety of hazards (e.g., wildfires, land subsidence) or other environmental threats to health and well-being (e.g., airborne toxins, soil and water contamination). In other words, the committee chose to acknowledge the drivers of migration and displacement, specifically in the Gulf region (e.g., coastal hazards), but to focus the scope of the study on relocation challenges, opportunities, lessons learned, and processes (e.g., decision making, engagement, communication, transparency). Our focus is on examples from the context of environmental and climate change impacts, but we also take into account other dynamics of displacement, including broader social and economic factors. For example, at the committee's second workshop in St. Petersburg, Florida, Dr. Tisha Holmes, assistant professor in the Department of Urban and Regional Planning at Florida State University, commented on how insurance costs and other factors weigh into people's decisions to stay or leave.

> *People are juggling these decisions to stay or leave in response to a variety of things—policy incentives and mandates, having access to resources, what the employment landscape looks like, what those pressures around housing and insurance costs are, and having those strong place-based connections and social networks.*[11]

The committee sought to understand the Gulf Coast simultaneously as a region of deep and diverse cultural and social ties to community and place, a key producer of fossil fuels and petrochemical products and services, a destination for recreationists and retirees, a region with cutting-edge research centers and universities, a major source of marine resources and fisheries, and a harbinger of the nation's experience with the effects of climate change.

---

[11]Comments made to the committee on July 12, 2022, during a public information-gathering session in Florida. More information is available at https://www.nationalacademies.org/event/07-12-2022/managed-retreat-in-the-us-gulf-coast-region-workshop-2

UNDERSTANDING MANAGED RETREAT

To meet the study charge, the committee deemed it important to consider what is meant by the term "managed retreat" and thus to identify the scope of our inquiry. As the study charge notes, "managed retreat" is a phrase used by some researchers and policy makers to describe organized efforts to relocate and resettle individuals and communities and to move infrastructure away from hazardous areas (Carey, 2020; Pinter, 2021a; Siders, 2019). Managed retreat is often understood as a deliberate adaptation to a changing climate and associated altered local environmental conditions as well as the increase in environment-related risks that accompany climate change—and it is often framed as a last resort (Siders, 2019). Specifically, scholars have suggested that to count as managed retreat, an effort would include (a) intent by a significant segment of a community and/or external decision makers advising that a community relocates, (b) planning across jurisdictions and sectors, and (c) proactivity (i.e., a collective taking action in response to current and anticipated impacts of environmental hazards (Ajibade et al., 2020; Hawai'i Coastal Zone Management Program, 2019; Koslov, 2016; Pinter, 2022; Siders, 2019; World Bank, 2019b).

"Managed retreat" is most commonly used to describe a broad array of practical and policy applications associated with climate-related relocation. However, in practice, both the term itself and the concept that it denotes are often defined or applied in different ways (e.g., "managed retreat" might, in different cases, be used to indicate individual household relocation or whole community relocation). This inconsistency comes in part because managed retreat is deeply complex; it entails a wide range of decisions about public goods and policies that cannot be easily compartmentalized into an episode of a single, well-managed process of "retreat." Instead, decisions about relocation may be responses to a series of tipping points that each comprise adaptation in a local context but together, over time, result in a large-scale change. Depending on the context, a managed retreat might be constrained by degree (e.g., level of resources committed), timing (e.g., action preceding, during, or after a triggering event), and scale (e.g., individual, community, municipality, state, regional). Decisions regarding who might move, when, and to where, as well as practical questions about how the movement of people, communities, and infrastructure could actually take place, are among some of the sources of controversy within and between frontline communities and the actors involved in relocation initiatives (Anderson, 2022; Maldonado et al., 2020).

In short, "managed retreat" and related terms (e.g., individual household relocation, whole community relocation, assisted resettlement) are used inconsistently. The committee's efforts to develop a working definition of the term for the purposes of this report raised important questions that we consider throughout. The remainder of this section gives an overview of some of the key issues encountered in these efforts. The committee also found that doing this work resulted in the clarification of the report's scope—namely, its focus on the role of the community in relocation undertaken in response to climate change. In the section that follows this one, we offer "community-driven relocation" as a preferred alternate term and use this term when referring to our conclusions and recommendations throughout the report.

Who Is Doing the Managing?

One key issue the committee encountered when seeking to define "managed retreat" is the question of who (e.g., community, entity) is actually, or could be, managing the retreat of communities from environmentally high-risk areas. Much of the scholarship discusses managed retreat as some form of assistance offered from outside the community, usually by a government, that often includes financial and technical support through various mechanisms (Dundon & Abkowitz, 2021), including the private sector (e.g., the firm CSRS served as the prime consultant and lead engineer on the Isle de Jean Charles relocation project).[12] As such, managed retreat entails implicit or explicit decisions about who oversees each element of the process. Such decisions determine important things within the process: Who creates and decides the logic and scale of movement (e.g., valuation, displacement, reparation, resettlement)? Who has agency, controls decision making, and executes the process of removing and resettling communities? Who makes plans, has control over components of the process, legislates, and provides funds? What are the best processes for identifying the commonwealth interests of communities and the lands to which they are bound and connected by time, culture, and tradition?

In the United States, there is no comprehensive federal plan for how to undertake a managed retreat; there is no single federal-level funding stream, agency, or statute that directs state governments, local governments, or communities about how to begin such an endeavor. The committee notes that historically within the United States (Chapter 3) and internationally (e.g., Australia, New Zealand, the Netherlands, Japan), governments and communities have engaged with and applied the concept of managed retreat more explicitly. In the absence of federal guidance for funding, planning, and implementing managed retreat, it can be difficult to answer the questions above (i.e., deciding who is overseeing each element of the process)

[12]The Isle de Jean Charles project is discussed more in Chapter 3. More information about the firm, CSRS, is available at https://www.csrsinc.com/post/idjc-phase-2-report-now-available

in ways that result in community-driven decision making, effective use of resources, and equitable processes.

The statement of task charges the committee to identify "short- and long-term steps necessary for community stakeholders to plan and implement the movement of people," but the charge does not specify whether the committee should also consider the preconditions necessary for communities to entertain the idea of relocating as a full community (i.e., people and infrastructure) or in some other fashion. In light of the questions above, the committee determined that one critical precondition is the development of a clear and equitable decision-making process that identifies who manages portions of the retreat process at a range of levels (i.e., local, regional, state, federal).

What Is the Scale of the Proposed Retreat?

Another set of questions concerns the scale of a managed retreat. Scale raises questions around what distinguishes managed retreat from other types of migration. How many people need to be involved, for example? If a government offers a flood buyout option to an entire neighborhood, but only one household accepts the offer, is that a managed retreat, whether successful or unsuccessful? If several households decide to sell their homes and move to another town without outside financial assistance, is that a managed retreat? Similarly, could climate migrations that take place over time (e.g., atomistic, individual families moving over a decade) or a slower retreat that happens in stages (e.g., incremental retreat from the shoreline, or "up the bayou") be considered forms of managed retreat?

What are the timescales for taking action to prevent the worst consequences of the changing climate for a particular region such as the Gulf Coast (Oppenheimer et al., 2019)? While a proactive approach has been useful for prevention of hazards from acute disasters such as hurricanes or wildfires, what does it mean to anticipate incremental or slow disasters, such as sea level rise, subsidence, erosion, or rising heat intensity, accentuated by copious precipitation and floods or tropical cyclones, that have already begun to affect human health and lives? How are adaptations to anticipated environmental hazards identified? Through what processes are they implemented to ensure the equitable and culturally appropriate relocation of people? What are relevant timescales for community-level adaptation in relation to the changing climatic conditions? How does "managed retreat" align with, disrupt, or intersect with broader ongoing and previous migrations in, out, and across the Gulf region—including migration as climate adaptation that is not necessarily or neatly "managed" (e.g., evacuations, pre- and post-disaster displacement, unassisted family or community-driven relocation)?

What Is the Difference Between Managed Retreat and Other Forms of Relocation?

In developing a common definition of "managed retreat," it is tempting to use the questions listed above—who manages the retreat, what type of relocation (e.g., buyouts), at what scale—to distinguish managed retreat from other forms of migration and relocation. However, understanding managed retreat solely through the lens of these questions tends to produce a too-narrow definition that centers somewhat arbitrary metrics over community response, therefore, over community needs. For example, property acquisitions (i.e., buyouts) are the most institutionalized, the most common, and the most studied form of assisted relocation in the United States (see Chapters 3, 9, and 10 for more about buyouts). They may be carried out by any jurisdiction of government, by private nongovernment entities, or by a combination. If there is buyout assistance during property acquisitions but no support mechanisms in the receiving communities, does relocation become a managed retreat? In other words, is a set of circumstances only considered a managed retreat if support systems for successful integration in the new location are part of the assistance offered? Or is the government offering a property buyout sufficient to be considered a managed retreat?

The questions discussed in the sections above are not easy to answer, but iterating them helped the committee understand the importance of expanding and broadening the definition of "managed retreat" specifically to position it as a community-driven climate adaptation strategy. For millennia, people have been moving within, across, and in and out of the Gulf region for the purpose of adapting to both climate and non-climate factors. Thus, the committee determined that establishing arbitrary boundaries around types and scales of relocation as metrics for what does and does not qualify as managed retreat per se did not serve a purpose for the committee. Rather, the committee focuses on a definition of "managed retreat" that centers the response to climate change. On the one hand, this capacious definition allows for the development of more equitable, community-driven responses (e.g., policies) to the specific threats these groups face, and on the other hand, centers decision making about options for communities in the face of threats to habitability squarely in the affected communities.

Management of climate-related relocation could consist of assistance by an external agent, usually a government entity or entities; leadership from within the community itself; or a combination. For example, a managed retreat could include a situation where the government provides relocation funding, but the community directs how it is used, determining when retreat is considered, where residents will relocate to, and how the process is undertaken. The process might entail a move from a single home, a long-standing place-based community, or sovereign tribal lands—or all three. It might involve multiple communities, parishes, trans-state boundaries, jurisdictions, watersheds, and ecosystems. The following section discusses the need to keep affected communities at the center of decision making in any "managed retreat" scenario, including in the terminology used in discussing this complex topic, and puts forward "community-driven relocation" as a term more in line with that stance.

COMMUNITY-DRIVEN RELOCATION

Increasing numbers of U.S. inhabitants and those of other countries will need to leave home because of diminishing habitability in the face of climate change (Lee et al., 2023). Terminology about this relocation is important, not least because communities have emotional, symbolic, physical, and economic attachments to place (Chapters 4 and 5). As discussed in the previous section, the term "managed retreat" is most commonly used to describe a broad array of practical and policy approaches. However, the term and concept rest on different assumptions and evoke different associations for different communities. Moving away from specific hazards may entail loss of homeland, community, and the stability and safety therein, even as it is also a movement toward another kind of safety (i.e., an area of less environmental risk). For example, the historical legacies of the Gulf Coast—including the history of forced removal of Indigenous and African peoples from lifeways and places they were or are deeply attached to, and the broader history of their enslavement and disenfranchisement—mean that some groups and individuals regard "managed retreat" as another iteration of the economic, commercial, cultural, and political exploitation and isolation they have experienced in the past (Jessee, 2022) and continue to experience (Chapter 4).

The committee learned from workshops, information-gathering sessions, and published literature that the term "managed retreat" may trigger emotion and trauma. The committee recognizes that some Indigenous leaders consider the concept of managed retreat to be an extension of colonial and imperialist policy that extracted resources and exterminated people. For example, Chief Parfait-Dardar of the Grand Caillou/Dulac Band of Biloxi-Chitimacha-Choctaw has argued, "The only people who should be managing a retreat, if that is what they so choose, is the community and they should be in charge of the terminology and ways of thinking about their resettlement" (Comardelle et al., 2020).

The committee does not believe the term "managed retreat" captures the key element that would ideally be part of any adaptive solution—the equitable and effective involvement of the affected communities at every stage of the relocation and resettlement process. The Climigration Network[13] published a guidebook, informed by interviews with community members from across the United States, that breaks down the term's connotations: "Managed" implies top-down processes suggesting power dynamics and feelings of powerlessness over outcomes. "Retreat" left community members feeling hopeless, guilty, and inadequate (Climigration Network, 2021). For some, "retreat" is associated with intergenerational memories of violent relocations like the Indian Removal Act of 1830 (see Chapter 4 for more).[14] The committee also learned that some communities interpret "retreating" as a loss of homeland, while others see it as a movement toward safety.

Thus, this report uses "community-driven relocation" to encompass both the abstract concept and key social dimensions that illuminate opportunities and practices that implement relocation in equitable, culturally appropriate, and participatory ways. A community-driven approach contrasts with the largely ad hoc, post-disaster reactive approach to mitigation and adaptation. Ad hoc approaches impede the fostering of trust and create barriers to genuine collaborative engagement and decision making. Instead, community-driven approaches could address what may be entrenched perceptions of government and institutionalized factors underpinning vulnerability. Additionally, the term "community-driven relocation" aligns with nascent relocation initiatives by federal agencies (e.g., HUD, FEMA, DOI).[15] To denote the communities that people are moving away from, this study uses the term "originating community;" to denote communities that people are relocating to, the committee adopted the term "receiving community."

The committee recognized the importance of shared decision making in any policy-supported and institutionalized process of relocation. Specifically, shared decision making in community-driven relocation processes would mean that

---

[13]More information about the Climigration Network is available at https://www.climigration.org/mission-history

[14]Forced displacements of Indigenous peoples are not unique to the Gulf region. In Alaska, the Bureau of Indian Affairs forced nomadic Indigenous tribes to settle in coastal areas vulnerable to sea level rise and erosion (see Welch, 2019).

[15]HUD released the "Climate Resilience Implementation Guide," which provides guidance on how to scope community-driven relocation as a solution to multiple natural hazards. More information is available at https://files.hudexchange.info/resources/documents/Climate-Resilience-Implementation-Guide-Community-Driven-Relocation.pdf. Additionally, the White House established the Community-Driven Relocation Subcommittee in August 2022, which is led by FEMA and DOI. More information is available at https://www.fema.gov/fact-sheet/fema-efforts-advancing-community-driven-relocation

- the originating community is at the center of decision making about relocation and needs for well-being;
- policy and material supports are provided for optimally enlarging a community's option for a safe landing in the receiving community or relocation destination; and
- supports are provided for the receiving community, including land-use planning, economic investments, and social resilience.

The committee also found that the term "managed retreat" captured too narrow of an array of relocation circumstances because it implies a rare case of wholesale community relocation from point A to point B at a discreet point in time rather than the diversity of circumstances described above (e.g., single home, sovereign tribal lands, incremental migrations); additionally, the term managed retreat could not account for the long-game notion of adaptive governance (described below). Thus, the term "community-driven relocation" allows for consideration of how to create a fabric of policy and infrastructure that can offer a safety net for a variety of successful relocation efforts.

For the purposes of the present report, a "community" is "a geographically defined collection of people at a subnational and substate level of jurisdiction [...] that could be regions such as a metropolitan statistical area; rural villages or townships sharing similar environmental, cultural, or political ties; politically bounded places such as counties, cities, water districts, or wards within cities; or culturally defined places such as neighborhoods or street blocks that are greater than an individual household, parcel, or built project" (National Academies, 2019a, p. 13).

Disaster Recovery Model Versus Year-Round Support

A major obstacle to achieving equitable and community-driven relocation is that relocation planning is currently managed using a "disaster-recovery model" (Johnson & Olshansky, 2017; Olshansky & Johnson, 2010; Schwab, 2014)—meaning that much of the available funding, planning, and technical assistance comes episodically as a reaction to a specific disaster or in the form of annual nationally competitive programs rather than being available year-round and allocated based on risk and need, including the need to address the root causes of vulnerability. These compressed timeframes inhibit effective community engagement, collective decision making, and collaborative planning processes. In the U.S. Gulf Coast Region, communities often experience repetitive and/or annual disasters, which can result in a perpetual cycle of recovery and blur the distinction between the pre- and post-disaster state of being—for example, as in the cases of Hurricanes Zeta (2020) and Ida (2021) in southeastern Louisiana, and Hurricanes Laura and Delta (both in 2020) in southwestern Louisiana. One of the goals of this report, as discussed further in Chapters 9 and 10, and elsewhere, is to emphasize the importance of relocation funding, programming, and planning to be available and accessible year-round. A system that provides these resources regularly would enable at-risk communities to consider relocation as a viable option if they desire to move whether before or after a disaster, in addition to considering alternatives to relocation, as discussed in the next section.

Alternatives to Relocation

A great deal of emphasis in recent years has been placed on climate-induced relocation strategies, including in this report and many others (Carey, 2020; Hanna et al., 2019; Siders, 2019; Siders et al., 2019). However, along the Gulf Coast, there has been an overall lack of discussion about such strategies (see Chapter 8). Alternatives that are discussed tend to focus on avoiding development in flood-prone areas altogether or suggest that relocation is a last resort, although the latter argument has been criticized as being politically expedient rather than proactive and truly transformative (Hanna et al., 2019; Mach & Siders, 2021). It is also important to recognize that many communities are opposed to a strict reliance on relocation, often adopting measures emphasizing protect-and-accommodate strategies or a "hybrid approach" that includes a mix of protection, accommodation, relocation, and avoidance policies and associated projects (Mach & Siders, 2021; Smith, Saunders et al., 2021).

The reluctance to adopt a uni-dimensional approach to relocation (i.e., adopting and applying a too-narrow definition of managed retreat) is reflected in the comments of many of those invited to speak on this topic, particularly residents currently living in flood-prone areas. For instance, Gordon Jackson, board president of the Steps Coalition in the Biloxi and Gulfport area of Mississippi, noted that the "goal is not relocation and replacement; [it] may be a case in isolated instances, but our resources right now are going towards resilience, restoration, and revitalization."[16] While many academics and government officials emphasized the need for relocation, the option of "managed retreat" or "community-driven relocation" has not become a standard part of local government plans (e.g., hazard mitigation plans, comprehensive plans) for cities, counties, or parishes along the Gulf Coast. David Perkes, director of the Gulf Coast Community Design

[16]Comments made to the committee on March 30, 2022, during a virtual public information-gathering session. More information is available at https://www.nationalacademies.org/event/03-30-2023/virtual-focus-group-mississippi-and-alabama-gulf-coast-community-stakeholder-perspectives-on-managed-retreat

Studio,[17] has positioned his work as an alternative to a strict adherence to managed retreat. Rather, through deep community engagement and empowerment, he has focused on helping low- and moderate-income individuals become more resilient in-place by designing safer homes and communities that account for flood risk. Further research and practice-based guidance are needed to understand the ways in which communities can balance the adoption of a range of adaptation measures not necessarily limited to relocation. The focus of this report, however, is on making community-driven relocation one of the multiple adaptation measures communities may consider.

ADAPTATION AND RESILIENCE

Government entities across jurisdictions, businesses, and civil society face many challenges surrounding the prospects of single community relocations and larger climate-induced regional migrations and displacements (Hino et al., 2017). Part of this challenge is the cross-jurisdictional (e.g., interstate and intrastate) and cross-sector planning that such relocations necessitate. This report identifies these challenges and identifies strategies for civil and equitable engagement and planning, as well as policy solutions. Thus, a theme that has guided the committee's work throughout is that of adaptation and, specifically, adaptive governance.

Adaptation and Adaptive Governance

Cultural adaptation to environmental change occurs at many levels—from the individual to the family or household to the community to the state, as well as the institutions and social networks that link them—and through a variety of processes—including mobility, intensification, diversification, innovation, rationing, pooling, and even revitalization of historical practices (Thornton & Manasfi, 2010). Adaptive governance can be broadly defined as "a range of interactions between actors, networks, organizations, and institutions emerging in pursuit of a desired state for social-ecological systems" (Chaffin et al., 2014, p. 1). It is a concept that emerges from the need to intentionally shift human behavior, values, or norms at multiple levels to avoid existential threats from environmental change. Adaptive governance enables such shifts by making traditional government more agile, flexible, and continuously responsive, and thus sensitive to the complex dynamics, disruptions, and uncertainty of changing social-ecological systems. In contrast to more conventional, often rigid, governing arrangements,

[17] Ibid.

adaptive governance takes as its guiding principle the imperative to adjust and evolve across multiple organizational levels and geographic scales (Folke et al., 2005).

Adaptive governance is sometimes conceptualized as a cycle of human-environmental interactions, feedbacks, social learning, and collective response. This adaptive cycle is associated with the concept of social-ecological resilience (Biggs et al., 2015) and institutional design principles for managing commons (Ostrom, 1990), including, ultimately, Earth's systems. Accordingly, adaptive governance requires certain basic features to succeed. First are flexible and responsive institutions, both formal and informal, which must be inclusive and possess avenues for communication and participatory dialogue among actors to build trust, accountability, and a shared vision of governance (Dietz et al., 2003; Olsson et al., 2006). A second key feature is functional and durable social networks with the capacity to link and coordinate diverse actors and interests across multiple levels and scales (Sharma-Wallace et al., 2018). A third feature is organizational capacity. This includes the capacity for institutions to be flexible and responsive at different scales in order to broaden participation; monitor social-environmental feedbacks; make and enforce rules; engage in continuous learning, including through experimentation; and leverage opportunities to transition systems onto sustainable pathways (Folke et al., 2005). The magnitude and multitude of effects of environmental changes on the Gulf Coast could serve as a catalyst to develop a multi-level, multi-scale adaptive governance system for the region.

Resilience and Adaptive Governance

At the level of human communities, adaptive governance can improve resilience and well-being (e.g., social, mental, physical health) by reducing what is sometimes referred to as the climate resilience gap: "The scope and extent of climate change-driven conditions for which people (individuals, communities, states, and even countries) remain unprepared, leaving them open to potentially harmful impacts" (Union of Concerned Scientists [UCS], 2016, p. 2). In practice, this means both adapting to environmental impacts that cannot be mitigated (or mitigated in the near term) and mitigating those impacts that human actions can reduce as threats to human well-being. This two-front approach to minimizing the resilience gap works best under an adaptive governance model that is attentive to both adaptation and mitigation processes and to the requisite social capacities for resilience (UCS, 2016, p. 2).

THE STUDY PROCESS

The committee put considerable emphasis on ways to hear from and interact with residents of the Gulf region, traveling to five locations to hold hybrid public workshops (see Box 1-2). The committee also held two additional virtual information-gathering sessions. The primary goal of these activities was to elevate the voices of communities and individuals contemplating, resisting, undertaking, or facing barriers to relocation (including systemic issues such as structural racism), as well as individuals who have resettled and people in communities that have received such individuals. Each information-gathering session included community testimonials and panels of local decision makers and experts discussing processes, challenges, and opportunities that communities encounter with respect to the study's statement of task. Testimonials from workshop participants, including those from residents on the front line of Gulf Coast climate impacts, are interspersed throughout the report. The workshops in Louisiana included a closed session site visit of the Bayou Region of southeastern Louisiana. Published proceedings provide additional information about these workshops (National Academies, 2022c,d, 2023a). More information about the information-gathering sessions is available at the webpages for those events, and a complete list of people that participated in information-gathering sessions is contained in Appendix B.[18]

---

[18]More information about the information-gathering sessions is available on the event webpages (in order of occurrence):

1. Workshop 1, Part 1 (Houston): Buyouts and Other Forms of Strategic Relocation in Greater Houston: https://www.nationalacademies.org/event/06-08-2022/managed-retreat-in-the-us-gulf-coast-region-workshop-1
2. Workshop 1, Part 2 (Port Arthur): Strategic Relocation and Environmental Perception: Community Perspectives from Port Arthur, Texas: https://www.nationalacademies.org/event/06-08-2022/managed-retreat-in-the-us-gulf-coast-region-workshop-1
3. Workshop 2: Opportunities & Challenges of Climate Adaptation on Florida's Gulf Coast: https://www.nationalacademies.org/event/07-12-2022/managed-retreat-in-the-us-gulf-coast-region-workshop-2
4. Workshop 3, Part 1: Community Viability and Environmental Change in Coastal Louisiana: https://www.nationalacademies.org/event/07-26-2022/managed-retreat-in-the-us-gulf-coast-region-workshop-3-part-1
5. Workshop 3, Part 2: Assisted Resettlement and Receiving Communities in Louisiana: https://www.nationalacademies.org/event/07-28-2022/managed-retreat-in-the-us-gulf-coast-region-workshop-3-part-2
6. Virtual Roundtable Discussion: Perspectives and Approaches to Property Acquisitions: Challenges and Lessons Learned: https://www.nationalacademies.org/event/12-13-2022/managed-retreat-in-the-us-gulf-coast-region-perspectives-and-approaches-to-property-acquisitions-challenges-and-lessons-learned
7. Virtual Focused Discussion: Mississippi and Alabama Gulf Coast Community Stakeholder Perspectives: https://www.nationalacademies.org/event/03-30-2023/virtual-focus-group-mississippi-and-alabama-gulf-coast-community-stakeholder-perspectives-on-managed-retreat

BOX 1-2
Committee Outreach Activities

- Hybrid workshops in Houston and Port Arthur, Texas, June 2022
- Hybrid workshop in St. Petersburg, Florida, July 2022
- Hybrid workshops in Thibodaux and Houma, Louisiana, July 2022, including a site visit to southeastern Louisiana with stops at Isle de Jean Charles Marina, Chauvin Art and Sculpture Garden, and the new settlement for the Isle de Jean Charles Community in Schriever, Terrebonne Parish
- Virtual Roundtable—Perspectives and Approaches to Property Acquisitions: Challenges and Lessons Learned, December 2022
- Public Call for Perspectives: Managed Retreat in the U.S. Gulf Coast Region, online submission open to the public September 26–December 15, 2022
- Virtual Focused Discussion—Mississippi and Alabama Gulf Coast Community Stakeholder Perspectives on Managed Retreat, March 2023

The locations and attendees of the hybrid and virtual information-gathering sessions were selected to maximize the diversity of experiences and perspectives the committee would hear. However, time and funding limited the reach of these workshops, which could not fully cover an area as large as the Gulf region nor allow for enough time to fully hear perspectives on relocation from non-Gulf residents. In an attempt to address these constraints, the committee opened a public comment portal on the study webpage and advertised its interest in hearing from the public through National Academies listservs, social media, and the committee's own networks. Thirty comments were submitted: 23 from the Gulf region and six from outside the Gulf. These perspectives shaped and enhanced the development of this report.

In addition to the public sessions, the committee held 11 closed session committee meetings to deliberate the statement of task, review the outcomes of public sessions, and share experiences and expertise in the field as relevant to the study charge. The committee also reviewed a substantial body of evidence-based literature, including national and international case studies of community relocation. As described in Chapter 3, relocation case studies in the United States before the year 2000 were summarized primarily from the works of Pinter (2021a,b, 2022), among others. Case studies after 2000 were selected by the committee based on geographic and demographic diversity and type of hazard (Chapter 3).

During the course of the study, relocation as a climate adaptation strategy became increasingly part of national public discourse and polarizing

(Carey, 2020), as did the term "managed retreat" (Bromhead, 2022; Mulkern, 2021). Therefore, in addition to policy briefs, reports, and academic literature, the committee also collected grey literature, which is cited in this report, to understand current opinions and accounts of relocations from a diversity of perspectives.

Study Limitations

The committee feels it is also important to acknowledge several key limitations to the study. Though the committee made assiduous efforts to understand the perspectives of residents of the Gulf region through a variety of public information-gathering sessions (see below), it recognizes that these efforts could only provide snapshots of a few places and a small number of voices. Additionally, although all public meetings (e.g., workshops, virtual meetings) were hybrid, the committee acknowledges that some people could not travel and did not have the technological means to participate virtually. Another limitation is that the committee did not hear from many young people (e.g., children, adolescents, teenagers), whose perspectives are critical for the future (Moder & Otieno, 2022; Pandve et al., 2009; United Nations International Children's Emergency Fund, 2015, 2021). Additionally, the committee heard from a small number of people on the receiving end of the relocation process but found that receiving communities have been much less studied than communities whose residents are compelled to move. Recent reports by the Urban Institute did provide a useful analysis of Gulf Coast areas that became receiving communities for people displaced by tropical cyclones.[19]

Furthermore, the literature and ongoing research about relocation is vast, interdisciplinary, and dynamic, and includes research about locations across the globe (see O'Donnell, 2022). Thus, a comprehensive review of relocation is challenging. The committee did not have the capacity to cover every important element related to community-driven relocation in detail, including policies that aim to reduce the need for relocation, such as those that encourage construction outside floodplains or limit the ability of people to obtain mortgages inside a floodplain.

REPORT STRUCTURE

The report is organized in three parts. The first part, Introducing Community-Driven Relocation, clarifies the scope and the committee's interpretation of the study charge (Chapter 1); follows with an overview of the complex climate- and non-climate-related environmental threats to the Gulf

[19]More information about the Urban Institute study is available at https://www.urban.org/projects/climate-migration-and-receiving-community-institutional-capacity-us-gulf-coast

Region that will continue to compel relocation (Chapter 2); and concludes with a historical account of U.S. relocation strategies from the late 19th century to the present day and current national and international relocation case studies that illustrate various funding sources, policy adjustments, and relocation strategies (e.g., buyouts; Chapter 3).

Part 2, Understanding Relocation in the Gulf Region, begins with a history of the region, focusing on how adaptation and movement have been defining features before, during, and after European colonization, and examines historical legacies that are critical to consider in the planning and implementation of community-driven relocation strategies in the Gulf Region (Chapter 4). Chapter 5 explains prevailing demographic shifts and migration trends that are currently defining the environment in the region and provides summaries of community profiles for communities across the Gulf Coast that the committee engaged. These include St. Petersburg, Florida; Mobile County and the community of Bayou La Batre, Alabama; Harrison County and the community of Turkey Creek, Mississippi; southeastern Louisiana, including Lafourche and Terrebonne Parishes; as well as Houston and Port Arthur, Texas. Complete community profiles are contained in Appendix C. The profiles combine quantitative and qualitative analyses to illustrate how and why communities across the region are vulnerable to increasing climate change risks. Chapter 6 provides an in-depth analysis of individual and community social, mental, and physical well-being, and looks at how climate impacts, coupled with elements such as social capital and place attachment, influence the decision-making process when communities consider relocation. Chapter 7 identifies the active involvement of impacted individuals, the role of social capital through civic leadership and networking, effective risk communication, and active participation as crucial elements for successful community-led relocations. Part 2 concludes by considering the specific needs of originating and receiving communities, including the importance of partnership building between these communities and regional entities (Chapter 8).

Part 3, Funding, Policy, and Planning, broadens out from a focus on the Gulf region to examine the landscape of funding and policy associated with climate-impacted communities at a variety of jurisdictional scales and the challenges and opportunities therein. Chapter 9 explores existing legal frameworks, administrative bodies, programs, and plans that are available to facilitate relocation and considers how to make these more inclusive of and responsive to the needs of originating and receiving communities. As mentioned above, an important part of these considerations involves shifting from a disaster recovery model to a system that provides year-round support for individuals and communities who wish to consider relocation as an adaptation strategy. Chapter 10 examines numerous challenges that households, local and state governments, and other community stakeholders might face when navigating the relocation process considering the framework laid out in Chapter 9, including the role of insurance, benefit-cost analysis, and household eligibility, among others, with specific attention to the buyout process alongside other relocation strategies. Finally, the committee's recommendations are highlighted in the final chapter (Chapter 11) with additional examples and supporting text about implementation and process. Key terms and their definitions are contained in a glossary in Appendix D.

2

The Scale of the Threat

This chapter discusses the following:

- The physical environment of the U.S. Gulf Coast Region and environmental hazards, including climate changes (e.g., rising temperatures, changing precipitation), and human-induced hazards (e.g., petrochemical spills and ongoing fossil fuel extractions)
- Disruptive infrastructure and the industrial impacts on regional flood risk
- Displacement projections and population growth

THE GULF COAST PHYSICAL ENVIRONMENT AND THE SCALE OF CLIMATE CHANGE

Introduction

Changes in temperature, precipitation, and the associated sea level rise (SLR) threaten Gulf Coast communities. Compounding these hazards are existing environmental toxins and socioeconomic stressors from the very industries that sustain the region, creating tensions that threaten households and livelihoods. Yet even as risks increase, the scale of the threat of displacement is poorly understood by decision makers and communities, and the disproportionate impact on the most vulnerable communities has yet to be comprehended in ways other than quantitatively. Moreover, instead of populations withdrawing from environmentally high-risk areas, many places in the Gulf region are increasing in population as individuals, businesses, and government continue to invest in high-risk areas, where the frequency and scale of climate-related disasters are on the rise.

The Gulf of Mexico (as seen in Figure 2-1), one of the largest bodies of water in the world (Mendelssohn et al., 2017), with a watershed consisting "of 33 rivers draining from 31 U.S. states" and much of Mexico (EPA, 2022), is a vast, complex ecosystem of fresh and saltwater marshes, coral reefs, seagrasses, mangrove forests, marine algae, and marsh grasses. The Gulf is connected to the Caribbean Sea through the Yucatán Channel where sea water circulates clockwise, then exits into the Atlantic Ocean through the Florida Straits. About half of the U.S. Gulf Coast Region—spanning the states of Florida, Alabama, Mississippi, Louisiana, and Texas, and continuing south to Mexico—consists of shallow waters of the continental shelf, which has yielded evidence of human presence through anthropogenic shell deposits (i.e., middens) from over 10,000 years ago (Cook Hale et al., 2019).

The physical geography of most of the Gulf Coast is dominated by barrier islands fronting lagoons and low-lying marshy shores. Whereas in southwest Florida, mangrove forests dominate, salt marshes characterize the Big Bend and Apalachee Bay areas of Florida, and the Mississippi River enters the Gulf through a bird's foot delta (Coultas & Gross, 1975; Lagomasino et al., 2021; Ward et al., 2023).

Over time, these numerous streams and rivers, which drain a humid region, have carved the landscape of the region as they course toward the Gulf. The U.S. Gulf Coast has modest tidal ranges and is a fairly low energy area except when tropical cyclones occur. There are numerous bays, such as Tampa, Pensacola, Mobile, Galveston, and Corpus Christi, where larger rivers enter the Gulf. The bays have typically been the site for urban and commercial development.

Environmental Hazards

The coastal area of the U.S. Gulf Coast Region faces multiple co-occurring, and intensifying, environmental hazards, including climate changes (e.g., rising temperatures, changing precipitation, more intense storms, rising sea level), which in turn can lead to pluvial (surface water) flooding, fluvial (riverine) flooding, modest tidal flooding, greater reach on storm surge, and compound flooding (Sebastian, 2022). Coupled with these climate events, human-induced hazards (e.g., petrochemical spills and ongoing fossil fuel extractions) amplify risks to the area (Kühne & Koegst, 2023) and escalate land subsidence. The committee defines land subsidence as the

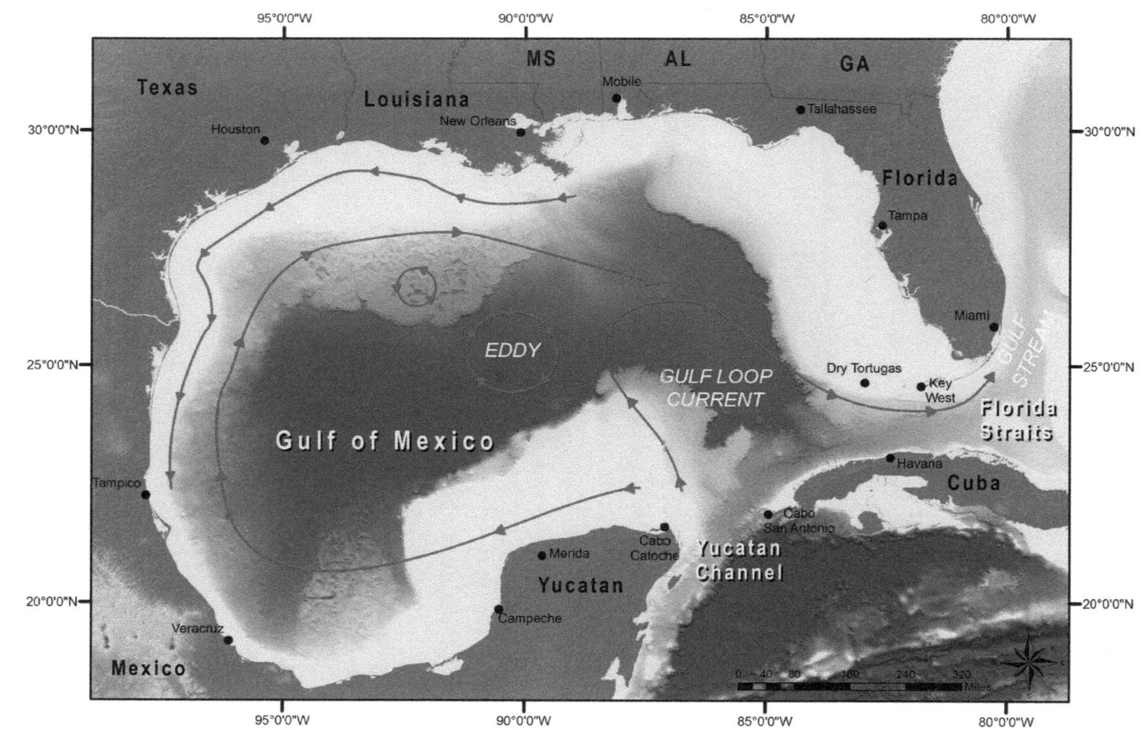

FIGURE 2-1 Gulf of Mexico region showing basic current patterns in the Gulf of Mexico, including the Loop Current.
SOURCE: Flower Garden Banks National Marine Sanctuary. (2023). *Basic current patterns in the Gulf of Mexico, including the Loop Current*. Office of National Marine Sanctuaries, National Oceanic and Atmospheric Administration. https://flowergarden.noaa.gov/about/naturalsetting.html

sinking of land due to compression of sediments, removal of groundwater or other subsurface fluids, or geologic processes such as faulting or isostatic adjustment (a section on subsidence is further below).

Although these hazards are experienced across the United States in both inland and coastal regions, research shows that the most rapid SLR in the United States can be found in the Gulf Coast (National Academies of Sciences, Engineering, and Medicine, 2018b; Lane et al., 2018). Research has also found that, based on the anticipated effect of projected tropical cyclone climatology change, projected increases in 100-year flood levels are expected to be greater than the effect of SLR for more than 40 percent of Gulf Coast counties (Marsooli et al., 2019). When storm surges are incorporated into these models' estimation of coastal risks of climate change, increased impacts are seen in the Gulf Coast (Neumann et al., 2015). To better understand the scale of the threat, the National Oceanic and Atmospheric Administration's (NOAA's) 2021 summary of billion-dollar weather and climate disasters shows an alarming cluster in the U.S. Gulf Coast Region (see Figure 2-2 below); the year 2022 tied 2017 and 2011 for the third highest number of billion-dollar disasters nationally.

Across the U.S. Gulf Coast Region, climate change,[1] combined with natural processes that shift landforms and the impacts of polluting and extractive industries, compounds regional risks and associated vulnerabilities. According to the Federal Emergency Management Agency's (FEMA's) National Risk Index (NRI), many Gulf communities have moderate to very high-risk indices, with respectively high economic risks associated (Zuzak et al., 2022). In areas where social vulnerabilities are also high and community resilience is low, according to the NRI, the compounded effect of climate change and other natural hazards challenges community readiness to prepare for, and respond to, events as they occur. Hurricane and coastal flood risks combined with social vulnerabilities estimate high or very high risks in the region. Figures 2-3, 2-4, and 2-5 show these risks, which cascade to worsen public health outcomes and overall well-being (Watts et al., 2018), emphasizing the scale of the threat to the Gulf Coast.

Climate Change and Its Impacts

Projected changes in extreme heat (including more days with higher temperatures), greater storm intensity, inland flooding (pluvial or fluvial), SLR (and associated tidal flooding and storm surge), and groundwater compound and amplify risks in the Gulf Coast.

[1]The science of climate attribution is now able to quantify not only the degree to which human-caused climate change is contributing to SLR, but also the impact of heat-trapping emissions on changes in the frequency and severity of extreme heat, drought, and precipitation (National Academies, 2016). See also Union of Concerned Scientists (2017).

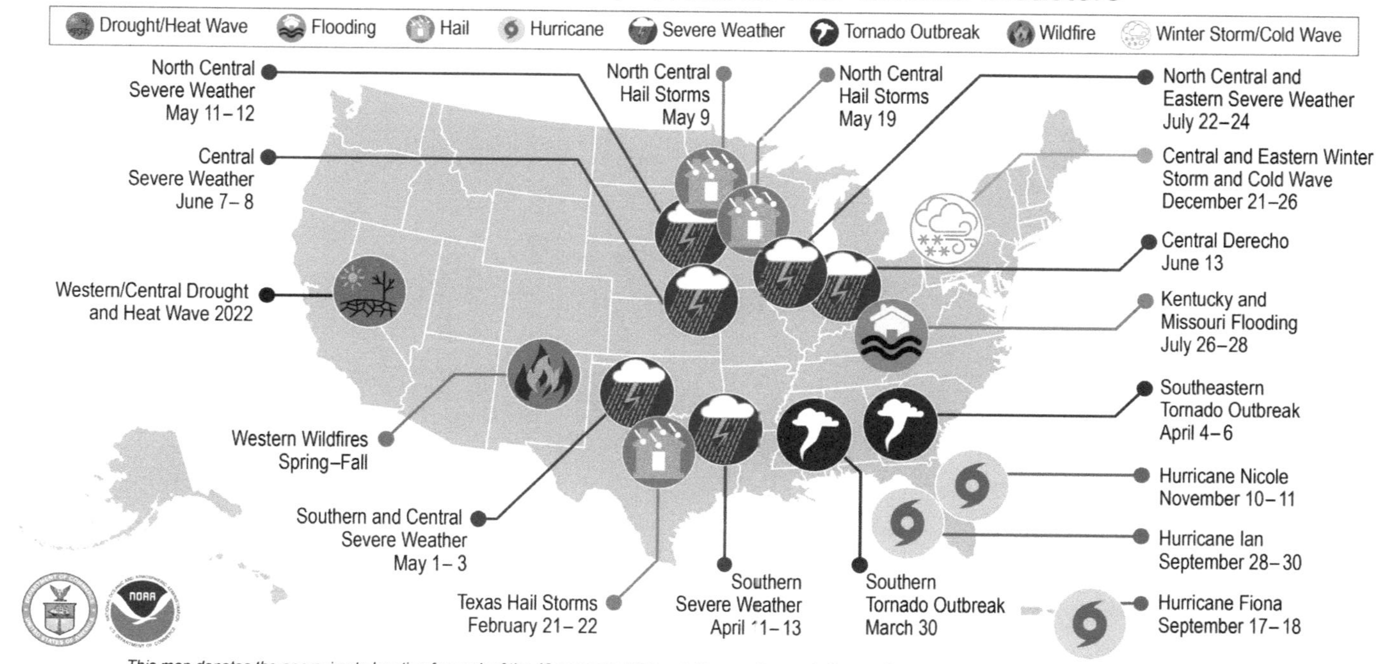

FIGURE 2-2 U.S. 2022 billion-dollar weather and climate disasters.
SOURCE: Smith, A. (2023). *2022 U.S. billion-dollar weather and climate disasters in historical context*. National Centers for Environmental Information, National Oceanic and Atmospheric Administration. https://www.climate.gov/news-features/blogs/2022-us-billion-dollar-weather-and-climate-disasters-historical-context

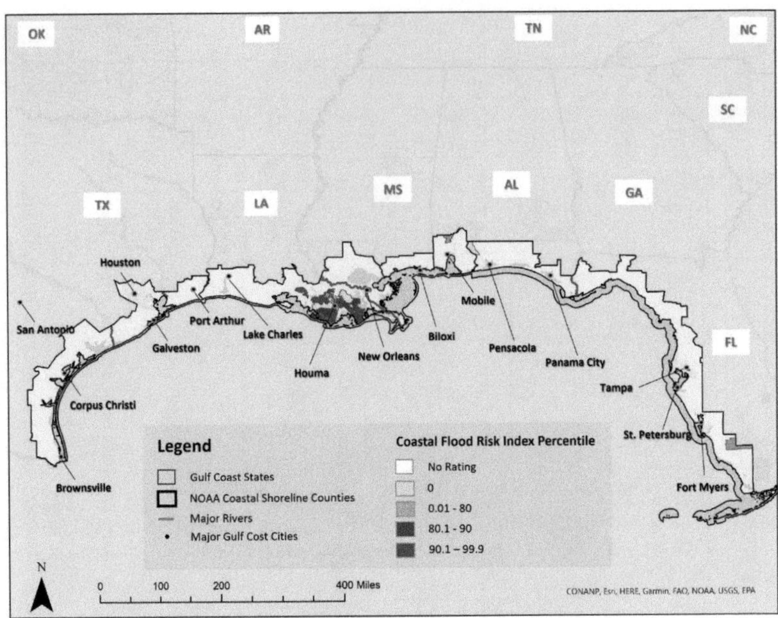

FIGURE 2-3 Coastal Flood Risk Index for tribal communities.
NOTES: FEMA obtains tribal community data from two sources: (1) "the Homeland Infrastructure Foundation-Level Data American Indian/Alaska Native/Native Hawaiian Areas shapefile that is adapted from the U.S. Census Bureau's TIGER/Line American Indian Area Geography shapefile. The shapefile includes federally recognized American Indian reservations and off-reservation trust land areas, state-recognized American Indian reservations, and Hawaiian homelands;" and (2) "the FEMA Mitigation Planning Jurisdiction Layer," which is "adapted from the Bureau of Indian Affairs geographic information system [...] data. This data includes Land Area Representations [...] and Tribal Statistical Area, among other types of tribal areas [...] Census tracts that intersect a tribal area, but with less than 5% coverage in a Census block, were visually inspected to ensure that areas of intersection arose out of natural imprecision in the boundaries rather than valid cases of small tribal areas within the Census tract" (Zuzak et al., 2023, pp. 4-9–4-10).
SOURCE: Committee generated from data at https://hazards.fema.gov/nri/data-resources

Extreme Heat

Rising temperatures introduce three types of changes in how people experience heat: (1) an increase in the average temperature, (2) an increase in the number of extreme heat days, and (3) an increase in the frequency and duration of heat waves and longer heat seasons. While increases in average temperatures allow time for behavioral and environmental changes to accommodate those increases, extreme heat days and/or the frequency and duration of heat waves present much greater challenges. For example,

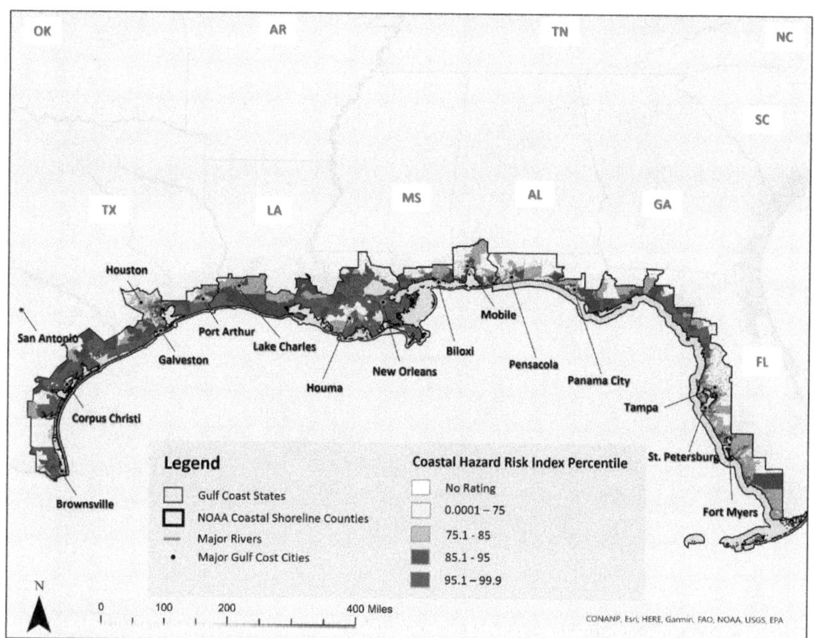

FIGURE 2-4 Coastal Hazard Risk Index for Gulf Coast communities.
SOURCE: Committee generated from data at https://hazards.fema.gov/nri/data-resources

in the U.S. Gulf Coast Region by the end of the century, many communities will experience 5–10 times more extreme heat days than 100 years prior, as shown in Table 2-1 (U.S. Federal Government, 2023).

This predicted trend is illustrated in the Climate Explorer's image of extreme heat days in Orleans Parish, Louisiana (see Figure 2-6). It charts the number of previous extreme heat days experienced from 1961 to 1990, alongside potential scenarios with lower and higher emissions.[2] From 1961 through 1990, Orleans Parish had an average of seven days over 95F. Looking forward to the middle of the 21st century, that number is expected to increase to over 46 in both the lower and higher emissions scenarios. Toward the end of the 21st century, as the emission models diverge, that number could be between 57 and 116 days per year.

Extreme heat is a serious threat on multiple levels. On average, extreme heat kills more people annually than any other weather-related hazard

[2]More information about the Climate Explorer is available at https://crt-climate-explorer.nemac.org/. The Climate Explorer uses the Representative Concentration Pathway (RCP) 4.5 to represent lower emissions and RCP 8.5 for higher emissions (van Vuuren et al., 2011).

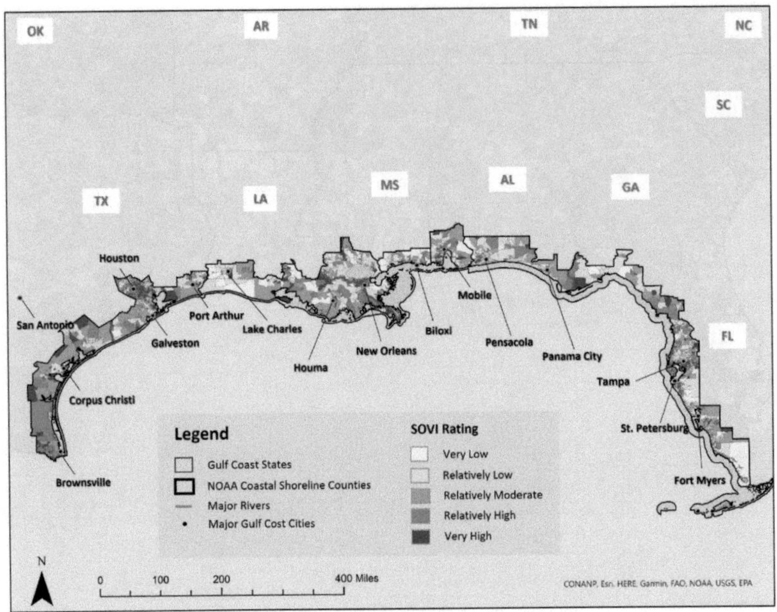

FIGURE 2-5 Social Vulnerability Index score for Gulf Coast communities.
SOURCE: Committee generated from data at https://hazards.fema.gov/nri/data-resources

TABLE 2-1 Days Over 95F (Historic and Projected) Across the Gulf Coast

Location	1961–1990 Days/Year Over 95F	2050–2090 Projected Days/Year Over 95F[a]
Houston, Texas	20	81–130
New Orleans, Louisiana	7	57–116
Gulfport, Mississippi	8	52–108
Mobile, Alabama	9	57–114
St. Petersburg, Florida	<1	60–127

[a] Under a higher emissions scenario representing Representative Concentration Pathway 8.5.
SOURCE: NOAA. (2023). U.S. Climate Resilience Toolkit Climate Explorer. https://crt-climate-explorer.nemac.org/faq/

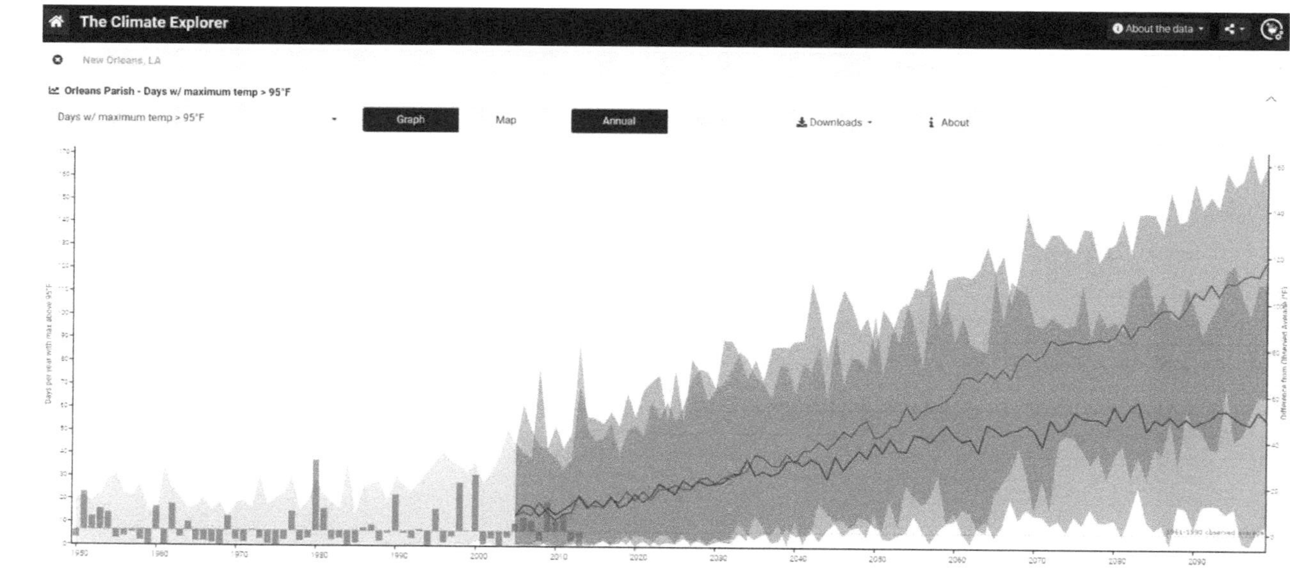

FIGURE 2-6 Orleans Parish days with maximum temperature above 95F.
SOURCE: NOAA. (2023). U.S. Climate Resilience Toolkit Climate Explorer. https://crt-climate-explorer.nemac.org/faq/

(National Weather Service, 2022). Beyond its risk to human health, particularly for those with chronic health conditions, extreme heat reduces worker productivity in unconditioned (outdoor workers) or under-conditioned spaces (factories); it also damages crops and fisheries and reduces yields (Kinniburgh et al., 2015; Parker, McElrone et al., 2020).

Extreme heat in the Gulf will continue to increase and in turn increase risks to health, demands for energy via increased cooling loads, and energy cost burdens for households. For the purposes of this study, however, extreme heat is not considered the primary risk but a precursor to the chronic flooding that is driven from increases in storm intensities, rising sea levels, and compounding issues of subsidence that have the greater immediate impact on the ability of Gulf Coast residents and businesses to sustain their existing ways of life.

Precipitation and Storm Intensity

Although net precipitation across the Gulf Coast is not projected to significantly change with either higher or lower emissions, warmer air holds more moisture and can produce more intense storm events. Increases of up to 20 percent in amounts of extreme precipitation are expected under a higher-heat scenario by the end of the century (Easterling et al., 2017; see Figure 2-7 below). Intensifying rainfall, also known as cloudburst events, contributes to inland flooding and exacerbates riparian risk (Statkewicz et al., 2021; EPA, n.d.). Moreover, such storms increase health risks in terms of both direct impacts from drowning or electrocution, for example, and indirect impacts from power loss, increased mold, or increases in vector- and water-borne diseases (Du et al., 2010).

Tropical Cyclones

A recent study simulating hurricanes in the Gulf region found that while there may be somewhat fewer hurricanes, storm intensities are expected to increase in speed of movement inland and intensification near shore, with more category 3, 4, and 5 hurricanes alongside 30–40 percent increases in precipitation (Bruyère et al., 2017). The simulations project an increase of approximately 10 percent in damage for the most intense hurricanes; this would seem manageable until compared to Hurricane Katrina losses, which were estimated based on the adjusted 2023 Consumer Price Index at approximately 194 billion dollars, and Hurricane Harvey losses estimated at 155 billion dollars (NOAA National Centers for Environmental Information, 2023).

The contribution of tropical cyclone climatology change to the 100-year flood level is highest in Gulf Coast parishes and counties, suggesting

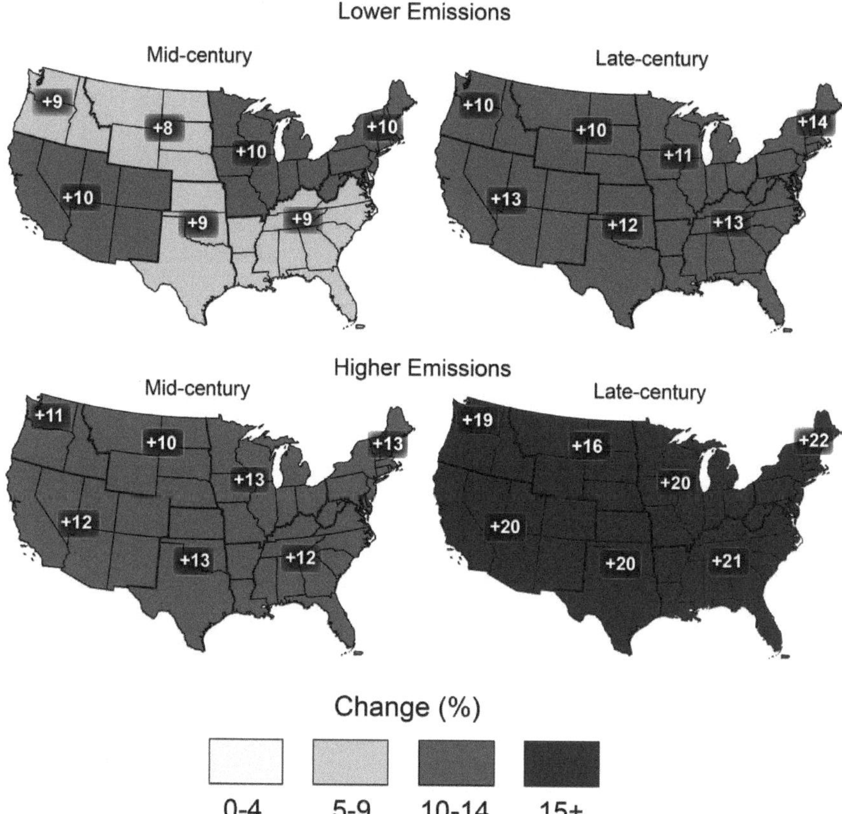

FIGURE 2-7 Projected change in daily, 20-year extreme precipitation.
SOURCE: Easterling, D. R., Arnold, J., Knutson, T., Kunkel, K., LeGrande, A., Leung, L. R., Vose, R., Waliser, D., & Wehner, M. (2017). Precipitation change in the United States. *Climate Science Special Report: Fourth National Climate Assessment, Volume I* (pp. 207–230). U.S. Global Change Research Program. https://doi.org/10.7930/J0H993CC

a potential increase in the "frequency, intensity, and/or size of [tropical cyclones] by the end of the 21st century" (Marsooli et al., 2019, p. 5). These findings are especially important given that current FEMA maps for flood risk do not account for the expected impacts of climate change on SLR and the intensity and frequency of tropical cyclones (Marsooli et al., 2019). Bates et al. (2021) estimated that the 100-year flood area (1% annual exceedance, which incorporates fluvial and pluvial flooding) is approximately double that estimated by FEMA maps (1,007,000 km^2 vs 572,000 km^2). The ability to predict weather events has improved in recent decades; however, rapid intensification of tropical cyclones approaching the coast has reduced forecast reliability and the time for effective evacuation planning (Benedetto & Trepanier, 2020).

Pluvial Flooding

Increased storm intensities introduce extreme rainfall, or cloudburst events, which means more rain falling in shorter time periods. In the U.S. Gulf Coast Region, Easterling et al. (2017) illustrate increases in such events of 9–13 percent between mid- and end of century with a lower emissions scenario and of 12–21 percent with a higher emissions scenario. In 2021, this type of rainfall event introduced significant pluvial flooding in Lake Charles, Louisiana, with a total of 12.49 inches of rain in a 24-hour period, where more than 6 inches fell in two hours (Di Liberto, 2021). Similarly, 26 inches of rain fell during Hurricane Harvey over a 24-hour period over Beaumont and Port Arthur, Texas (Di Liberto, 2021). According to a study of U.S. insurance claims, pluvial flooding is more common than fluvial, and pluvial flood insurance claims are more likely during tropical cyclone floods than non-tropical cyclone floods. This type of flooding often occurs because the volume of water far exceeds the capacities of traditional stormwater management systems (Tonn & Czajkowski, 2022).

Fluvial Flooding

FEMA's NRI illustrates the projected extensiveness of fluvial flooding in Gulf coastal counties. Also, a recent study identified previously unrecognized channels as contributors to Gulf region fluvial flood risks (Swartz et al., 2022). Figure 2-8 shows these fluvial flooding risks. Moreover, Marsooli et al.'s (2019) study of the impacts of SLR and tropical cyclone climatology change on flood hazards from the Gulf Coast and U.S. Atlantic Coast at the county level found that from 1980 to 2005, Gulf Coast counties not only had the highest 100-year flood levels, averaging 3.03m, but also saw the largest increase in 100-year flood levels, with an average increase of 2m. These historical 100-year flood levels are projected to occur every 5–30 years across Gulf Coast counties (Marsooli et al., 2019).

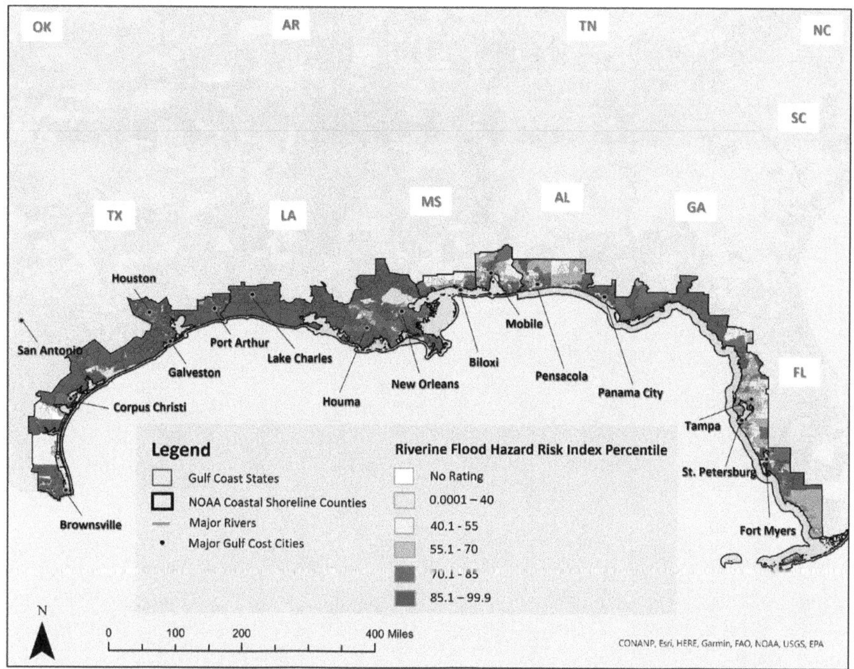

FIGURE 2-8 Fluvial (riverine) flood risk.
SOURCE: Committee generated from data at https://hazards.fema.gov/nri/data-resources

Sea Level Rise

NOAA's *2022 Sea Level Rise Technical Report* describes sea levels rising on average by 10–12 inches along U.S. coasts in the next 30 years, increasing tidal and storm surges, which in turn will reach farther inland (Sweet et al., 2022). In the Gulf Coast, this number is greater, with 14–18 inches projected. Relative sea level (land and ocean height change) is expected to be highest in the Gulf Coast due to subsidence as well as other factors such as "river sediment compaction and withdrawal of subsurface fluids" (Sweet et al., 2022, p. XII). In turn high tide flood events will "continue to occur at or above the national average frequency" (Sweet et al., 2022, p. XIII). For the Gulf Coast, this will yield an increase in the number of flood events (see Figure 2-9; Sweet et al., 2022). More frequent high tide events are also projected across the Gulf (see Figures 2-9 and 2-10). Projections suggest that by 2050, the western Gulf will see the highest number of flood events in the larger region (Sweet et al., 2022). Given that SLR escalation

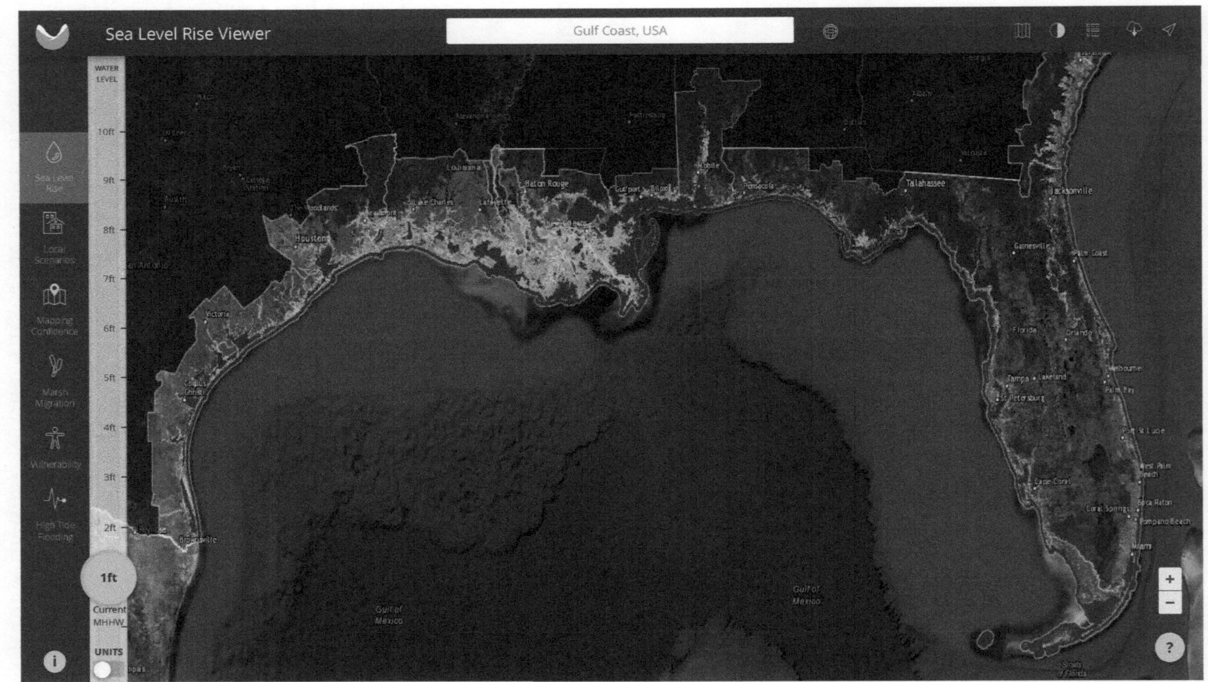

FIGURE 2-9 SLR at 1 foot.
SOURCE: Office for Coastal Management. (2023c). Sea Level Rise and Costal Flooding at 1': Gulf of Mexico. https://coast.noaa.gov/slr/

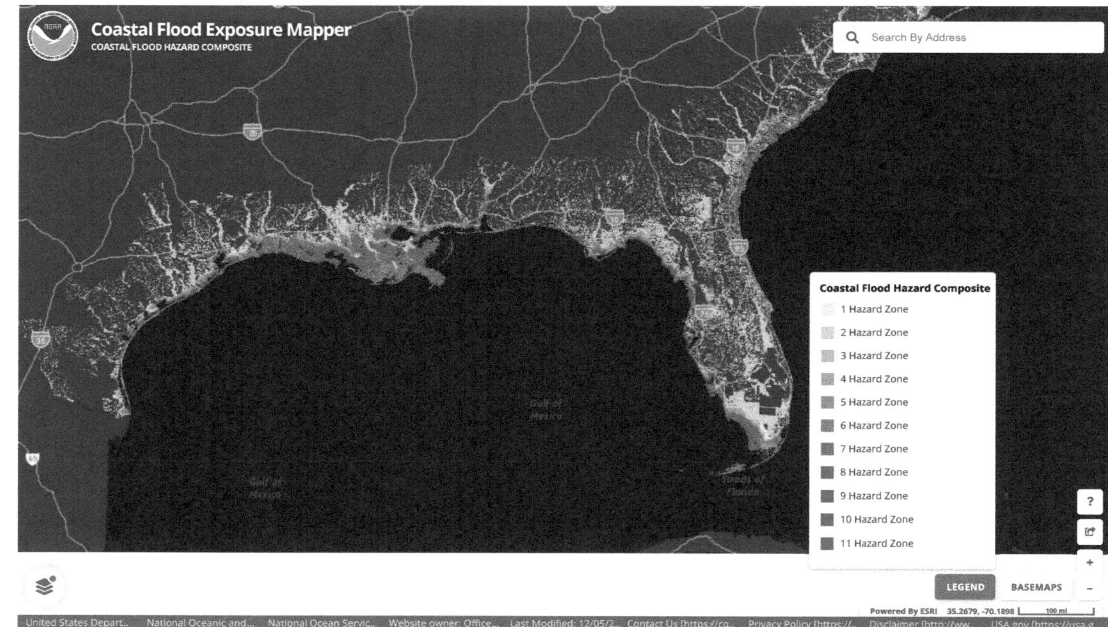

FIGURE 2-10 Gulf Coast Coastal Flood Hazard Composite.
SOURCE: Office for Coastal Management. (2023b). Coastal Flood Exposure Mapper: Gulf of Mexico. https://coast.noaa.gov/floodexposure/#-9725012,3188145,7z/eyJiIjoiZGFyayJ9

is significantly different in the Gulf and Southeast coasts (McLaughlin et al., 2018; Yin, 2023) and appears to be accelerating beyond model assumptions (Dangendorf et al., 2023), the implications for Gulf-wide population displacement warrants far more extensive review.[3]

Higher sea levels pose the risk of additional shoreline erosion; saltwater intrusion into freshwater environments and their disruption, rendering obsolete structural coastal protections; saltwater intrusion into groundwater supplies; increased flooding (storm surge and blue sky); and damage to transportation and energy infrastructure (EPA, n.d.).

Tidal Flooding

The number of days with minor (otherwise known as nuisance) flooding in the Gulf Coast (according to eight NOAA tide gauges) has been increasing over recent decades (Sweet et al., 2014). By 2050, major and moderate high tide flood events in the Gulf are expected to occur as frequently as moderate and minor high tide flood events occur today (Sweet et al., 2022). Minor high tide flooding in the Gulf is expected to more than triple from 2020 to 2050, from 3 events per year to greater than 10, and moderate and major high tide flooding will increase from 0.3 events per year to 4 and 0.04 events per year to 0.2 in 2050, respectively (Sweet et al., 2022). Projected increases in tidal flooding are important because they are expected to cause chronic flooding in the next 15–30 years, long before communities are "permanently inundated" by SLR (Dahl et al., 2017; Office for Coastal Management, 2023b,c; Thompson et al., 2021; see Figures 2-11 and 2-12 for more information).

Storm Surge

To illustrate the implications, according to the Coastal Protection and Restoration Authority (CPRA) of Louisiana, storm surge flooding will increase (due to a combination of greater storm intensities, higher sea levels, and subsidence). Figure 2-13 shows the 100 year or 1 percent Annual Exceedance Probability in Louisiana, meaning that every year there's a 1 percent chance of this type of flooding to occur. While this example focuses on Louisiana, there are data on surge trends with SLR, erosion, and marsh health changes across the Gulf, including Bilskie et al. (2018) regarding the northern Gulf; Sheng et al. (2022) for south Florida; and Kyne (2023) for the Rio Grande Valley in Texas. Notable in the consistency of storm surge

[3]A map and data viewer about the economic impacts of sea level for the northern Gulf of Mexico (Florida, Alabama, and Mississippi) are available at https://experience.arcgis.com/experience/0aa2ee3b86304fffb6b97f6dd6ffa42b

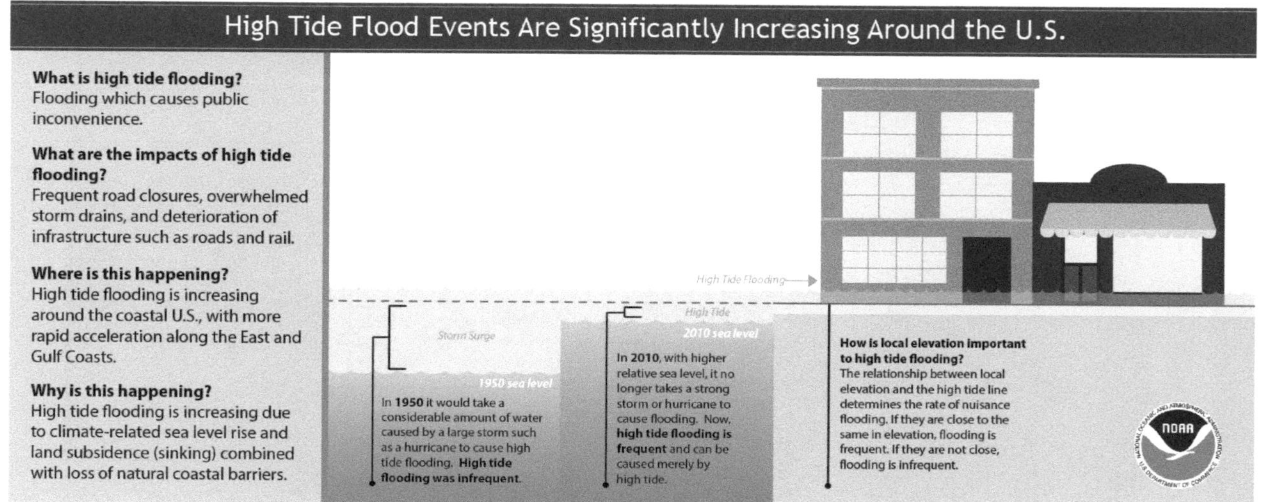

FIGURE 2-11 High tide flood events are significantly increasing around the United States.
SOURCE: National Ocean Service. (2021). What is high tide flooding? https://cceanservice.noaa.gov/facts/high tide-flooding.html

FIGURE 2-12 Visualizing high tide flooding with 12 inches of SLR in the Gulf.
SOURCE: Office for Coastal Management. (2023c). Sea Level Rise and Coastal Flooding at 12": Gulf of Mexico. https://coast.noaa.gov/slr/

impacts, these trends substantiate Gulf-wide displacement risks (Neuman et al., 2015; Del Angel, 2022).

Despite ambitious coastal restoration efforts through CPRA, Törnqvist et al. (2020, 2021) report that the Mississippi River Delta has reached a tipping point in terms of the rate of SLR surpassing the delta's ability to survive.[4] Loss of the coastal marshes will subject interior cities, infrastructure, and land uses to increased flood risk.

Groundwater

Arguably understudied, but alarming, are changes to groundwater in the Gulf Coast states. Rising sea levels alongside subsidence contribute to rising groundwater in the Gulf in two ways. First, as seas rise, salt water and groundwater (i.e., fresh water) meet along the coast; sea water is denser than groundwater and so pushes groundwater upward. Second, groundwater typically flows toward the sea as part of the natural discharge cycle. As sea levels rise and push back against groundwater, the fresh water has less ability to flow outward to the sea and instead remains inland and rises further.

Higher groundwater poses health risks beyond flooding, as it may bring contaminants (e.g., sewage, buried toxins) to the surface as it moves upward (Pierre-Louis, 2021). In an ongoing monitoring study, groundwater contaminants are notable in 30–32 percent of the Gulf Coast aquifers (Water Resources Mission Area, 2021). Higher groundwater means that there is less area to absorb increased precipitation during extreme rain events. The Coastal Lowlands aquifer system, which serves the Gulf Coast states of Texas, Louisiana, and Mississippi, already had 12 percent of study areas with high exceedances and 18 percent with moderate exceedances of inorganic contaminants; the Florida aquifer system had 14 percent high and 18 percent moderate, respectively (Water Resources Mission Area, 2021). These issues are pertinent to relocation projects in the region as groundwater and overall aquifer health relate directly to the availability of freshwater resources in the region and to the potential impacts of more extreme storms and SLR on regional flooding.

Compound Flooding

More frequent heavy precipitation events, irregular storm surges, and rising sea levels—all impacts of climate change—also contribute to an extension of coastal influences further inland along river courses. Numerous

---

[4]More information about CPRA's coastal restoration projects is available at https://coastal.la.gov/

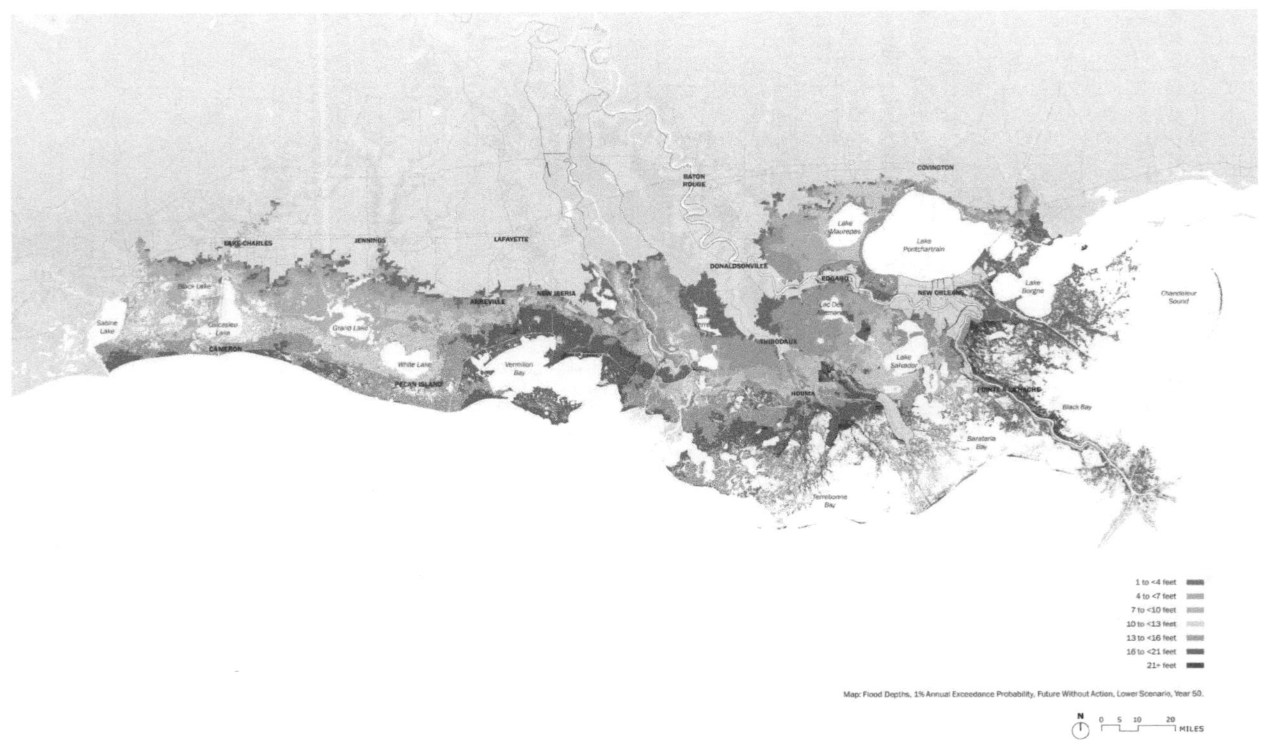

FIGURE 2-13 Projected storm surge in Louisiana.
SOURCE: Coastal Protection and Restoration Authority of Louisiana. (2023b). *Louisiana's Comprehensive Master Plan for a Sustainable Coast*. https://coastal.la.gov/our-plan/2023-coastal-master-plan/

small river basins drain the Gulf coastal plain and, in the case of extreme rain events, these river basins are prone to flooding. Communities along these waterways tend to have flood mitigation policies and practices that are oriented toward disaster risk reduction, which are often not adequate in the face of the larger threats posed by rising seas induced by accelerated climate change, and many have yet to incorporate robust and longer-term climate adaptation strategies into local and state plans (e.g., formal plans for hazard mitigation and resilience; Cowles, 2021). Furthermore, many of the federal programs that exist to help communities facing these threats provide funding only after a disaster has occurred, thereby limiting the resources available to communities during non-disaster timeframes to conduct adaptation planning (see Chapters 9 and 10).

Compound flood risks, posed by more intense rainfall events and rising seas, strain flood mitigation measures that are not oriented to coastal influences and also pose risks to residents who have moved inland to escape coastal risks. For example, families who relocated from coastal Louisiana after Hurricane Katrina in 2005 to what they thought were safe homes found themselves exposed to riverine flooding in 2016 (Colten, 2021; Cowles, 2021). Therefore, it is imperative that planning to address these risks includes inland areas that may nominally be considered receiving communities, yet that also have inherent risks of their own. The Louisiana Watershed Initiative has quantitative data that showcase how different flooding looks when only single hazards are modeled.[5]

The Causes and Impacts of Subsidence

Natural processes, such as shifting sediment patterns and subsidence, exacerbate the impacts of climate change and are in turn exacerbated by the impacts of industries that continue to extract fossil fuels and water in the region. Subsidence results from several interrelated factors, including anthropogenic causes (Lane et al., 2018; United States Geological Survey Texas Water Science Center Gulf Coast Program, n.d.). Coastal erosion, water, oil and gas extraction, canal making, and faulting contribute to subsidence and overall land loss of the Louisiana coast (Lane et al., 2018).

Recent research across the Gulf shows variable ranges of subsidence, with a number of Gulf states registering +4mm/year (see Figure 2-14; Wang, Zhou et al., 2020; Zhou et al., 2021), including areas that are densely populated (see Figure 2-16 for more on area population change).

---

[5]More information is available at https://watershed.la.gov/

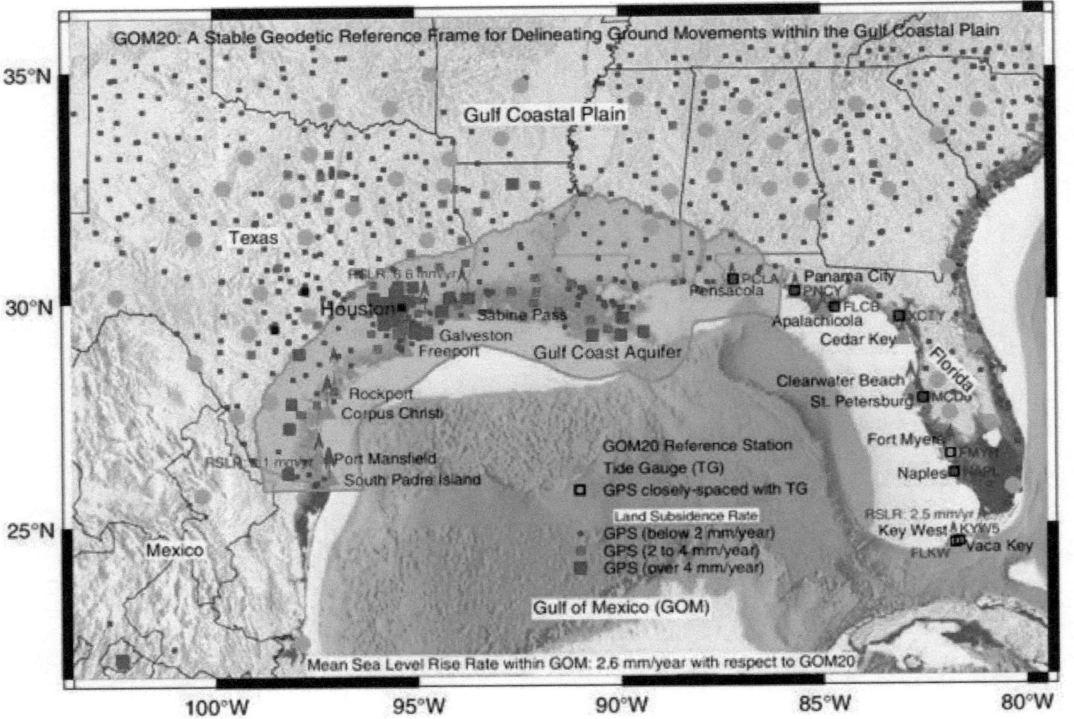

FIGURE 2-14 Gulf of Mexico subsidence rates.
SOURCE: Wang, G., Zhou, X., Wang, K., Ke, X., Zhang, Y., Zhao, R., & Bao, Y. (2020). GOM20: A stable geodetic reference frame for subsidence, faulting, and sea-level rise studies along the coast of the Gulf of Mexico. *Remote Sensing, 12*(3), 350. https://www.mdpi.com/2072-4292/12/3/350

Industrial Impacts on Regional Flood Risks

Decades of infrastructure investments that have shifted natural ecologies, introduced toxic chemical and oil spills, and amplified nutrient discharges further complicate the Gulf's flood risks.

Disruptive Infrastructure

The Mississippi River Delta is particularly at risk from storm-induced flooding and SLR. The construction of levees to protect settlements from riparian flooding since the 1700s has reduced annual sediment deposition on the floodplain and on the delta (Louisiana Coastal Wetlands Planning Protection and Restoration Act, n.d). As discussed, natural subsidence without regular rejuvenation contributes to the lowering of land surfaces. Mineral extraction and faulting also play a role. Additionally, carving canals in the coastal marshes permitted salt-water intrusion and accelerated erosion of the wetlands. All these processes contribute to land loss in the Delta region. There are active deltas, however, fed by the Atchafalaya River west of the Mississippi River's mouth (Lane et al., 2018).

Historical investments in the region have disrupted delta ecologies and amplified climate changes and natural systems shifts: the addition of the levee systems on the Mississippi River; construction of the I-10 corridor through cities, coastal lakes and rivers, swamps, wetlands, and marshes (Florida, Alabama, Mississippi, Louisiana, Texas); dredging and channeling water basins (e.g., Mobile, Alabama; Houston and Port Arthur, Texas; Lake Charles, Louisiana) and ports for shipping, shipbuilding (e.g., Pascagoula, Mississippi), and military installations and civilian airports (e.g., Mobile, Alabama; Biloxi and Gulfport, Mississippi; Chalemtte, Louisiana); and intensive development of shorelines and barrier islands, where the natural island profile has been disrupted by large-scale development on the dune berm and the back bay area, in addition to the groins installed to trap sand (Kobell, 2015). For example, over 10,000 miles of canals carved into the Louisiana coastal marshlands permit salt-water intrusion and the destruction of freshwater marsh plants, and significantly contribute to the erosion of the wetlands (Turner & McClenachan, 2018).

Toxic Chemicals and Flood Risks

The U.S. Gulf Coast faces numerous social and environmental impacts of toxic chemical pollution (Environmental Defense Fund, 2021). The Gulf Coast is especially vulnerable due to the abundance of petrochemical and oil and gas facilities on and offshore (Minovi, 2021). Approximately 97 percent of U.S. offshore oil and gas production occurs off the Gulf Coast (Bureau of Ocean Energy Management, 2023), and Port Arthur on the

Texas Gulf Coast is home to the largest petrochemical industrial complex in the country (U.S. Energy Information Administration, 2023). Like the people and wildlife who call the Gulf Coast their home, many of these facilities are located in flood-prone areas. As of 2018, 1,400 sites that handle toxic chemicals (including polychlorinated biphenyls, heavy metals like lead and mercury, and dioxin; Sharp, 2022) were in areas deemed by FEMA as having the highest flood risk, and another 1,100 more were in areas of moderate risk (Tabuchi et al., 2018). Another report identified 872 chemical facilities that are "susceptible to experiencing a hazardous substance leak triggered by climate change within 50 miles of the U.S. Gulf Coast," and showed that over 4 million people live within close proximity of these sites (Sharp, 2022). The risks to these chemical facilities grow as increasingly intense and frequent hurricanes and flooding occur. In the committee's judgment, it is worth mentioning that these assessments only consider single flood risks and not compound flood risks, so it is likely an underestimation of what is exposed.

Oil Spills

Oil spills resulting from the failure of safety systems on offshore mineral extraction have been a periodic but chronic concern since the 1930s. Spills damage ecosystems, which in turn affect Gulf fisheries; they also disrupt tourism. Early near-shore oil spills have damaged oyster populations, forcing the closure of certain beds and disrupting local livelihoods (Grismore, 2018). Larger spills since the 1970s have been disruptive to both oyster and shrimping activity, sometimes impacting harvesting activities for several years (Colten et al., 2012). According to a report by the Center for Biological Diversity, between 2010 and 2020, oil companies dumped over 66 million gallons of fracking fluid into the Gulf, the effects of which include reproductive and behavioral harm and death to aquatic species (Center for Biological Diversity, 2021). Oil spills have also been shown to reduce microbial diversity and increase degradative species in wetlands (Center for Biological Diversity, 2021). In terms of recreation and tourism, a spill near Texas in 1984 disrupted recreational activity in Galveston, and the massive BP oil disaster in 2010 produced serious declines in tourism in Mississippi, Alabama, and Florida, among its many other catastrophic consequences (Colten et al., 2012; National Academies, 2022a). Overall, the fossil fuel industry has had a negative impact on the fishing industry and tourism, which are both significant drivers of the Gulf Coast economy (Center for Biological Diversity, 2021).

Nutrient Discharge

The discharge of nutrients from agricultural practices in the upper Mississippi River basin contribute to a sizable hypoxic zone. This seasonal occurrence is an ecological stress to the shallow continental shelf area, but studies indicate it has not had a significant impact on fisheries (Diaz & Solow, 1999; Rabalais & Turner, 2019). Along the Florida Coast, harmful algal blooms and red tide events have long been increasing in size and duration and continue to do so with warming waters combined with nutrient runoff (Chapra et al., 2017; NOAA, n.d.). Warmer temperatures associated with climate change are a contributing factor (EPA, 2022a). These events can kill marine life and can cause respiratory problems for humans; consequently, they are also particularly disruptive to the tourism industry. NOAA-funded research has estimated that the direct economic impact, based on declines in Airbnb visits, of the 2017–2019 red tides was 184 million dollars in southwest Florida, with "over $45 million in total federal, state, and local tax impacts" and a loss of almost 3,000 jobs (Court et al., 2021, p. 4). Hotel and service industries, including charter fishing and diving operations, suffered most directly (Court et al., 2021).

Summary: The Scale of Climate Change in the U.S. Gulf Coast Region

In the committee's judgment, climate change increases risks to residents and businesses in the Gulf Coast. Increased temperatures introduce extreme heat exposures at far greater ranges than the region previously experienced. In turn, warming air and waters increase storm intensities, and produce greater fluvial and pluvial flooding, extending coastal influences farther inland. Sea levels continue to rise globally, and at an even greater pace in the Gulf (where ongoing subsidence contributes significantly), furthering erosion and land loss. Compound flooding from increased storm intensities and higher sea levels exposes more people and assets to potential harm. Tropical cyclones are impacting the coastal regions and inland areas with increasing intensities. SLR and other related aspects of land loss will expose more to high water and storm surge. In turn, communities across the Gulf face greater risks to households, livelihoods, and the natural resources that support them. Complicating these risks are existing environmental toxins that worsen the potential impacts of climate exposures.

THE SCALE OF THE CURRENT THREAT OF DISPLACEMENT

As evident in the preceding sections, multiple climate hazards and the number of recent disasters costing more than 1 billion dollars reinforce the ongoing outsized risks to the Gulf region. Threats from storms, various types of flooding, extreme heat, freshwater resource contamination, industrial toxicity, and subsidence combine with significant social vulnerabilities and amplify impacts to Gulf residents and livelihoods. Future climate projections will worsen the already-challenging recovery environment, rendering it difficult for local and state governments to respond to, and recover from, increasing climate threats. In turn, the scale of these risks will arguably force displacements as households lack resources to continually repair and/or to relocate. Recognizing the scale of this threat warrants the equivalent of a regional displacement vulnerability risk assessment and resulting preparations for region-wide population and industry relocations.

Displacement Tracking

At the end of 2022, the Internal Displacement Monitoring Centre (IDMC) recognized over 8.7 million internally displaced people[6] due to natural disasters (IDMC & Norwegian Refugee Council, 2023). Tracking data across the globe, from 2008 to 2022, 202 countries and territories recognized over 13,000 disaster events and 376 million internal displacements.[7] The majority of these were related to flooding and storms (IDMC, 2023). In this same period in the United States, there were over 1,000 unique disaster events reported and over 8 million internal displacements due to flooding and storms only. When including all hazards tracked, these numbers rise to 11.1 million displacements (IDMC, 2023). It is generally accepted that these displacements are likely to increase, and consequently, there is a need to better understand the receiving communities where displaced communities and households are likely to move.

In the Gulf region, flooding and storms continue to present the greatest immediate threats to household ability to remain in current locations. While other acute and chronic stressors are co-present, it is the escalating risks of total household loss from flooding or storm events that predominate the regional risk profiles. In coastal Gulf areas, the interrelationships between climate events, their projected increases, and the populations in harm's way, reveal the need for processes that first characterize the risks to understand the scale of the problem and second, that consider and support relocation planning when other options are no longer possible.

[6]"Internally displaced people" indicates the number of people "living in internal displacement at the end of the year" (IDMC & Norwegian Refugee Council, 2023, p. 135).

[7]IDMC defines internal displacements as "the forced movement of people within the country they live in." More information is available at https://www.internal-displacement.org/internal-displacement

Future Displacement

Initial small-area population projections (to account for population change, e.g., movement to coastal areas) combined with an SLR vulnerability assessment suggest that over 4.2 million Americans will be at risk of chronic inundation by 2100 with an SLR of 0.9m (Hauer et al., 2016), while other U.S. SLR scenarios range from a few million people affected to tens of millions of people (Hauer et al., 2016; Strauss et al., 2015). These predictions depend on what models account for (e.g., emission reductions, West Antarctic Ice Sheet remaining stable, immigration patterns, population projections) and how they define exposed populations (e.g., under projected sea level/permanently inundated, in projected floodplain, or in a Low Elevation Coastal Zone; McMichael et al., 2020). Another projection (based on ocean thermal expansion, mountain glacier and ice cap melting, and ice sheet decay) estimates that land occupied by 6.2 million people would be inundated by 2100 based on carbon emissions already locked in by 2015 and assuming the West Antarctic Ice Sheet remains stable (Strauss et al., 2015). If business-as-usual levels of emissions continue through 2100, based on these projections, land currently occupied by 26.5 million people would be affected. Further research is needed to understand the interactions among localized SLR and related hazards, social and political contexts, adaptation possibilities, and potential migration and (im)mobility decision making (McMichael et al., 2020; Robinson et al., 2020). Hauer et al.'s (2016) study on climate migrants notes that more than 13.1 million will be displaced in the coastal United States alone in a 1.8m SLR scenario. Bittle's (2023) work on displacement raises similar challenges given the scale of likely migration needs and the limited planning to date to prepare originating and receiving communities.

Table 2-2 shows the number of properties in Gulf states that are at risk of chronic inundation in the next three decades that could be displaced (i.e., by 2045). While noting that this table only summarizes SLR, not other flood risks nor other climate hazards, it is significant to recognize that over 5 million households, more than the population of any U.S. city besides New York, will need to consider relocation. Combined with other factors, including chronic inland flooding, the number only increases. This is the scale of the threat.

Disproportionate Impact

It is important to recognize that, as elsewhere in history and ongoing in the present, forced or unplanned migrations profoundly and disproportionately impact "communities of color, the elderly, and other at-risk populations that are already experiencing the compounding effects of

TABLE 2-2 Gulf Coast State Homes at Risk of Chronic Inundation in the Next 30 Years (i.e., by 2045)

Gulf Coast State	Number of Properties at Risk in the Next 30 Years	Percentage of Properties Statewide
Texas	1,397,757	18
Louisiana	329,176	21
Mississippi	417,644	16
Alabama	896,910	47
Florida	2,365,064	36

SOURCE: Union of Concerned Scientists. (2018). *Underwater: Rising seas, chronic floods, and the umplications for U.S. coastal real estate.* https://www.ucsusa.org/sites/default/files/attach/2018/06/underwater-analysis-full-report.pdf

climate and environmental injustices" (Marandi & Main, 2021, p. 465). For example, the impacts of toxins on the Gulf Coast are not felt equally across the population, presenting an environmental justice issue (Office for Coastal Management, 2023a; Randolph, 2021). Low-wealth, Black, and Hispanic communities are more likely to live near high-risk chemical facilities (Minovi, 2021), which can have far-reaching health effects. A study of children's physical and mental health following the Deepwater Horizon disaster found that in addition to those children with direct exposure to oil/dispersant, non-White children and those in households earning less than $20,000 annually who were also exposed were at a higher risk of physical and mental health problems, respectively (Meltzer et al., 2021).

Bisschop et al. (2018) make the case that the oil and gas industry in Louisiana, as a major economic interest, has discouraged the public at large and public authorities from adequately considering its role in coastal land loss and the harm it is causing, particularly in at-risk minority communities. Their analysis indicates that these communities are exposed to greater risk of exposure to hazardous materials, their subsistence livelihoods have been disrupted, and land loss exacerbates the impacts of SLR (Bisschop et al., 2018). Hemmerling et al. (2021) found that since 1990, the distribution of hazards associated with the oil and gas industry has become more concentrated, particularly in relation to the geography of Asian, Hispanic, and Native American populations. The lack of sufficient preparation to mitigate the stress and consequences of hazards from the industry and climate change alike only worsens community conditions and increases the likelihood of loss of life and devastation of communities and infrastructure.

NOAA's Digital Coast Tools (see Figure 2-15) illustrate the combination of projected SLR (2 feet) and vulnerable communities (Office for Coastal Management, 2023d) while Titus (2023) adds some important nuance to

FIGURE 2-15 Two feet of SLR plus vulnerable communities.

SOURCE: Office for Coastal Management. (2023d). Sea Level Rise Viewer: Gulf of Mexico Vulnerability, 2' Water Level. https://coast.noaa.gov/slr/#/layer/vul-soc/2/9785443.24747092/3371743.335002211/7/satellite/none/0.8/2050/interHigh/midAccretion

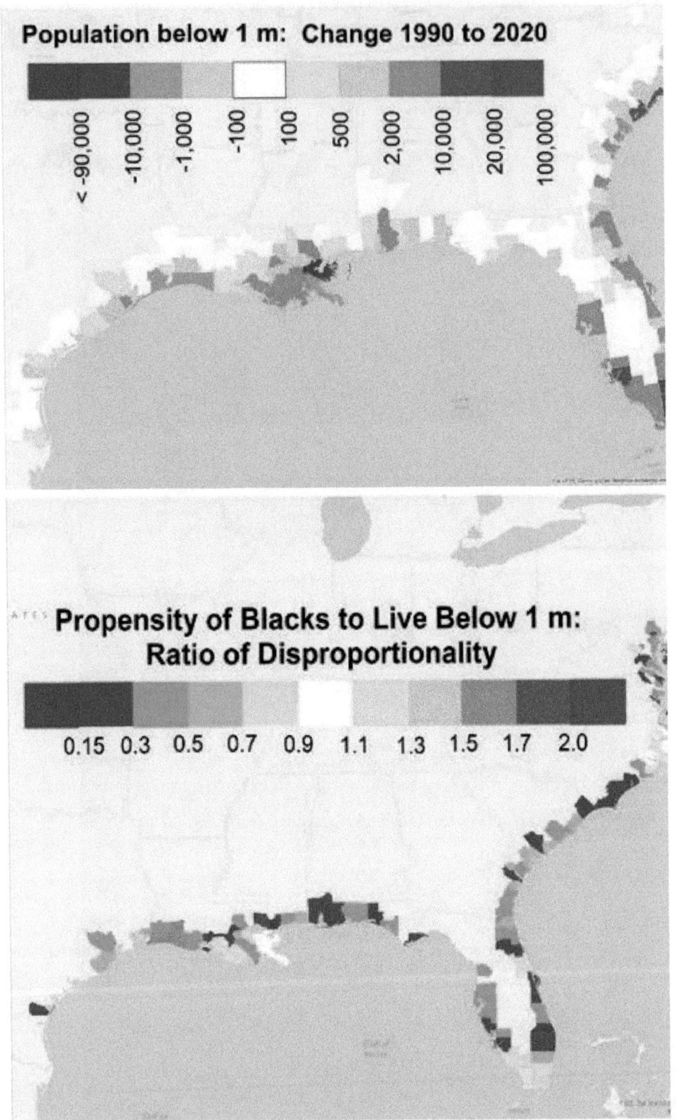

FIGURE 2-16 Top map: Change in population less than 1m above Mean Higher High Water, by county, along the southeastern U.S. coast, 1990–2020. The standard error is approximately 25 percent–50 percent of these estimates. Bottom map: Percent of Black residents who live below 1m, divided by percent of all residents who live below 1m, by county, 2020 Census.

SOURCE: Titus, J. G. (2023). Population in floodplains or close to sea level increased in U.S. but declined in some counties—especially among Black residents. *Environmental Research Letters*, *18*(3), 034001. https://doi.org/10.1088/1748-9326/acadf5

the location of people at risk (see Figure 2-16). Both maps clearly show that at-risk minority populations have been disproportionately impacted.

Growing Populations in Areas Susceptible to Environmental Hazards

Between 2000 and 2016, the Gulf Coast also had the fastest population growth among U.S. coastal regions at a rate of 24.5 percent, compared to 14.8 percent for the United States as a whole (Cohen, 2018). The region's population increased by over 3 million people, 1.2 million of whom are or were in Harris County, Texas, which includes Houston. This region (as with other coastal regions in the United States) is also more diverse than the United States as a whole, with 47.9 percent of people on the Gulf Coast identifying as something other than non-Hispanic White compared to 38.7 percent in the United States as a whole (Cohen, 2018). While varying somewhat across the Gulf, combinations of multiple hazard risks and social vulnerabilities increase overall vulnerabilities (Oxfam, 2012).

SUMMARY

Climate changes in the U.S. Gulf Coast Region are compounded by existing environmental toxins and socioeconomic stressors, while future climate impacts threaten to exacerbate these stressors. The scale of the threat of displacement looms large and will disproportionately impact vulnerable communities. However, this threat is poorly understood by decision makers and communities. As reflected in the growing literature on the importance of participatory planning, particularly community-led initiatives, addressing Gulf regional risks requires new thinking beyond traditional planning processes and creative ways of leveraging existing federal and state programs, policies, and resources. (These topics are discussed in detail in Chapter 9.) Even with limited modeling available, it is clear that the scale of the current threats to the Gulf Coast far exceeds readiness to respond. The Community-Driven Relocation Subcommittee,[8] co-led by FEMA and the U.S. Department of the Interior and launched by the White House in 2022, works across multiple agencies to address programs like hazard mitigation assistance and buyouts. However, the Gulf region lacks a more comprehensive approach, including a multi-scalar and cross-jurisdictional planning response. These challenges are not unique to the Gulf. The next chapter discusses these challenges, and more, by examining historical and current case studies of relocations from the United States and abroad and

[8]More information about the Community-Driven Relocation Subcommittee is available at https://www.fema.gov/fact-sheet/fema-efforts-advancing-community-driven-relocation

identifying lessons learned that might be applied to future community-driven relocation efforts.

CONCLUSIONS

Conclusion 2-1: Future Gulf Coast displacements are difficult to project because few models exist to fully characterize the extent of regional risks from climate changes, subsidence, and industrial impacts. Lacking more accurate exposure and risk estimates at the scale of population displacement, the Gulf Coast currently fails to hold a shared understanding of its risks and the enormity of the planning challenges that it faces. Recognizing the scale of threat warrants the equivalent of a regional displacement vulnerability risk assessment and resulting preparations for region-wide population and industry relocations.

Conclusion 2-2: As elsewhere in the United States, recent Gulf Coast displacements occur within the context of the histories of injustices in the region, requiring ever more thoughtful approaches to discussions about risks and potential plans to reduce those risks. Understanding these inequities and their continued and pervasive impact on regional investments reinforces the knowledge that community well-being must be at the center of efforts to address risks.

3

Examples of Relocation

This chapter discusses the following:

- A brief history of community relocation in the United States from the late 1800s to the late 1900s as federal involvement increased
- Challenges, opportunities, and lessons related to buyouts, including those gleaned from forced relocations with eminent domain and from the Dutch Room for the River Programme (RftR)
- Case studies of buyout programs and community relocations from the United States and abroad, including in New York and New Jersey, Alaska, Louisiana, Australia, and Japan

INTRODUCTION

The committee examined a variety of relocation efforts during the course of the study. From the late 1800s to today, several community relocation efforts have been documented in the United States. The case studies that the committee recounts in this chapter describe how approaches to relocation developed over time and included community-driven efforts, an array of funding sources and policy shifts, and the use of buyouts as one mechanism to relocate communities to areas of lower environmental risk. The literature also revealed current national and international relocation efforts. The chapter's coverage of these case studies and their relevance to this report is structured as follows: a history of relocation efforts in the United States from the 1800s to the late 1990s, followed by a high-level description of the infrastructure of buyouts in the United States and a review of the lessons learned and existing challenges of this approach. The next section covers a set of national and international case studies from the 2000s onward, including the Isle de Jean Charles (IDJC), Louisiana; Newtok, Alaska; Hurricane Sandy in New Jersey and New York; Grantham, Australia; and Tohoku, Japan. The chapter does not present a comprehensive review of relocation cases; rather, the committee chose these cases to illustrate both specific challenges and effective pathways forward for community-driven relocation. Most cases include cross-references to other sections of the report about these challenges and pathways, as relevant to the study charge.

A BRIEF HISTORY OF COMMUNITY RELOCATION EFFORTS IN THE UNITED STATES

The United States has a long history of community relocations that is often forgotten in more recent discussions about the topic (Pinter, 2021a,b, 2022; Pinter & Rees, 2021). Starting with Niobrara, Nebraska, in 1881, there have been over 20 instances of wholesale (i.e., full) or partial relocation in the United States, many of which occurred in Midwestern states such as Illinois, Wisconsin, and Indiana (Pinter, 2021a). Relocations occurring before 1993 "were largely managed by local and state authorities, by private groups such as the Red Cross, and left in significant part to the flood victims themselves" (Pinter, 2021a, p. 2). In 1992, the Federal Emergency Management Agency's (FEMA's) Hazard Mitigation Grant Program (HMGP; established in 1988) began funding floodplain property acquisitions, marking a new period of major federal involvement in buyouts and community relocation (Pinter, 2021a).

Early Cases

The relocation of Niobrara, Nebraska, in the late 1800s occurred after the village of almost 500 people was flooded under 2m (about 6 feet) of water due to an ice dam on the Missouri River (Carter, 1991; Pinter, 2021a). The decision to relocate the town was decided by community residents following "intense local debate" within a month of the flood occurring (Pinter, 2021a, p. 2). Houses and commercial structures were physically dragged by horse teams to a site on higher ground 2.4km (about 1.5 miles) away, and most were relocated within a year of the town's decision (Pinter, 2021a). Although the swiftness of this move may be impossible to achieve when larger communities are relocating and when houses cannot be physically moved but must be deconstructed and rebuilt, the timeliness of Niobrara's relocation likely contributed to its success. The multi-year process of buy-outs described by community members at National Academies of Sciences, Engineering, and Medicine workshops and in numerous reports is a major deterrent in people choosing to relocate. This topic will be discussed further in Chapter 10.

In 1937, following catastrophic flooding of the Ohio River and a suggestion from President Franklin Roosevelt to move affected towns to higher ground, both Leavenworth, Indiana, and Shawneetown, Illinois, received external funding to assist them in relocating their communities. In the case of Leavenworth, within about a year and a half of flooding, the Works Progress Administration (WPA) "built streets, sidewalks, parking, water and sewer, and a new town hall," and the American Red Cross assisted the city of about 400 in completing their relocation, assigning residential lots "in keeping with former locations" and groupings of similar type and cost (Bondy, 1938, p. 8, as cited in Pinter, 2021a, p. 6). Shawneetown (pre-flood population: 1,440), which was experiencing "successively larger flood events" and had already discussed relocating 25 years prior, began discussing relocation while still 8–10 feet under water (Pinter, 2021a). Few objected at first, but as the process dragged on, tensions grew between locals and outside engineers and designers from the WPA. Despite this, about half of the residential structures were physically relocated and the rest were rebuilt in the new location 5.6km (3.5 miles) away. The WPA did not cover commercial construction, so the town used discretionary funds to build new commercial properties (Pinter, 2021a). Questions about who pays for what and how decisions are made and by whom are critical to a successful relocation. Community engagement and leadership is discussed further in Chapter 7, and funding sources are discussed in Chapter 9.

In the early 1960s, the U.S. Army Corps of Engineers (USACE) was planning to build a dam upstream of Soldiers Grove, Wisconsin (pre-flood population: 514) and proposed an accompanying levee to protect the town. The town instead decided to relocate structures in the floodplain (about half of the town) using the money that had been earmarked for the levee. The town made a relocation plan and bought a site 800m away, but in 1977 the dam project was canceled, along with the town's relocation funding. The following year, the town flooded again; but with a relocation plan ready to be deployed, they began construction and relocation of their new town in 1979, "relocating the fire station, two other municipal facilities, 24 homes, and virtually the town's entire business district, about 36 structures" (Brown, 1993, as cited in Pinter, 2021a, p. 6). They also elevated or flood-proofed 12 homes on the margins of the floodplain and "[a]bout half of the new commercial and municipal buildings incorporated passive solar design" (Pinter, 2021a, pp. 6–7). In 2020 dollars, the partial relocation of Soldiers Grove cost 27.4 million dollars, the largest portion of which came from the

Department of Housing and Urban Development (HUD; 13.3 million dollars), followed by 8.8 million dollars in village borrowing (Pinter, 2021a). Although they lost their initial relocation funding, developing a relocation plan ahead of time allowed Soldiers Grove to act swiftly when the town was ready to relocate. Incorporating relocation options into existing plans (i.e., land-use plans, hazard mitigation plans, and other comprehensive planning efforts) is discussed further in Chapters 8 and 9. Soldiers Grove also demonstrated the potential for community relocation to enhance not only safety but also environmental sustainability (e.g., through the addition of solar panels).

Members of the Bad River Band of the Lake Superior Chippewa (Ojibwe) Nation, like many other Indigenous groups and people of color, live where they do because they were forced out of previous homes. This Ojibwe band moved west from Maine to escape European invaders in the 1800s, settling by the Bad River in Odanah, Wisconsin (Hersher, 2018). Then, a few years before the tribe began reportedly relocating to higher ground in the 1960s, the Indian Relocation Act was passed, which incentivized people living on reservations to move into cities, resulting in widespread tribal collapse. Over three decades starting in the 1960s, the Bad River Band relocated to a new site on higher ground with a majority of funding coming from HUD. The new location meant the town avoided destruction from severe flooding at the old site in 2016; while the Odanah relocation is viewed as a success from an outside perspective, a tribal historian described it as another forced relocation with federal government interference (Hersher, 2018). Understanding the history of the communities faced with the prospect of relocation is key to a just and community-centric relocation process. The importance of history is discussed throughout the report, particularly in Chapter 4.

The Great Midwest Floods of 1993 and FEMA-Supported Relocation

Following three floods between 1943 and 1947, USACE built a levee protecting the town of Valmeyer, Illinois, and 60,000 acres of nearby farmland (Knobloch, 2005). After a few decades of effective flood protection by the levee, in the 1980s, the village council adopted federal floodplain regulations, which allowed residents to purchase federal flood insurance while restricting development in the floodplain, unless it was elevated above base flood elevation (about 10 feet above the ground). Until 1993, "a group of business and political leaders" were attempting to "find a solution to the halt in new construction" (Knobloch, 2005, p. 42). These efforts ended abruptly in 1993, when persistent heavy rains caused river flooding that topped the levee and left the town (pre-flood population: 897; post-flood population: 1,300) under 16 feet of water, damaging over 90 percent of town structures (Knobloch, 2005; Pinter, 2021a). Although it was FEMA representatives and the regional planning commission who reportedly first suggested the town relocate, about a month after the flood two-thirds of residents were in favor, voting to move to a "cornfield and surrounding woodland 3.4 km away and approximately 120m higher" (Pinter, 2021a, p. 9). In the decade immediately following the move, the town dropped in population and only about a quarter of businesses survived; however, the population bounced back between 2000 and 2010 (Pinter, 2021a).

Much of the town's success is attributed to "strong leadership and community engagement," reflected by the development of citizen planning committees and a planning charrette attended by regional architects and planners along with locals (Pinter, 2021a, p. 10). Over 100 residents served on a planning committee, with focus areas including town design, infrastructure and utilities, housing, business, social services, school construction, and finance (Knobloch, 2005). The move cost 54 million dollars in 2020 dollars, with 21.8 million dollars coming from FEMA and 20.9 million dollars coming from the Department of Commerce and Consumer Affairs (Pinter, 2021a). Residents began moving to their new community in 1995, and infrastructure was completed by the end of that year. Construction had been delayed by the review process in which over 25 different federal, state, and local agencies participated following the initial environmental assessment. Delays meant long periods in temporary housing and hit business owners especially hard as they lost not only their homes but also their livelihoods (Knobloch, 2005). Many left the community as a result. Despite the considerable challenges encountered, the town's resilience was largely due to its strong leadership and engaged community. This collaborative spirit not only helped navigate the complexities of relocation but also played a critical role in building a cohesive and adaptable community in their new environment. The resulting success is a testament to the power of effective leadership and active community participation in overcoming the hurdles of such significant transitions. The importance of community leadership and engagement in a successful community relocation is discussed further in Chapter 7, and governance and policy mechanisms that can support community-driven relocation efforts are discussed in Chapters 9 and 10.

In 1993, Rhineland, Missouri (pre-flood population: 157; post-flood population: 135) and Pattonsburg, Missouri (pre-flood population: 414; post-flood population: 318) flooded numerous times following levee failures (Pinter, 2021a). Over 90 percent of residents in both towns voted to relocate, with Rhineland managing 98 percent with support from its town planning commission. Rhineland physically moved approximately 50 structures to nearby higher ground ($8,000–10,000 per structure), moving some commercial structures just to the edge of the floodplain to maintain access to Highway 94 (Pinter, 2021a). New parcels of land for residents to relocate to were transferred as a land swap: relocating residents swapped their old properties on the floodplain that were left behind for new land parcels in New Rhineland, using a lottery to identify the new parcels (Pinter, 2021a). Pattonsburg was established along the railroad, but due to frequent inundation from flooding, the population had declined from over 1,000 in the 1940s to just over 400 in the 1990s, during which time the town experienced repeated flooding. In 1993, long-time residents were already in the process of rebuilding when the second flood hit, leading to the almost unanimous decision to relocate. The town acquired 235 flooded properties with 6 million dollars and used their remaining 6.5 million dollars to develop the new site approximately 3km from the river. The old site was later used as a movie set, and energy-saving measures were incorporated into the new town school. The new site was designed with a "'Main Street' feel," and the town's relocation was deemed one of most successful examples of moving businesses and was credited with boosting the town's economic health. In 2017, the old site experienced multiple floods (Pinter, 2021a). The success of Pattonsburg's relocation highlights the importance of planning, not only for immediate needs like housing but also for longer-term needs like economic viability. Planning for relocation is discussed further in Chapters 8 and 9.

In other cases, where new sites were not developed for a community to relocate to, collective buyouts resulted in the effective removal of communities, in which people who received a buyout moved to already-existing communities in neighboring counties. In contrast to a wholesale or partial relocation in which the new site is within the same tax base, "piecemeal buyouts are often opposed by local leaders" because, with each resident who leaves, the tax base of the original community erodes (Pinter, 2021a, p. 11). In some cases, money was received for parts of the relocation process (i.e., buyout and demolition) but not others (i.e., relocation and new site development), resulting in unsuccessful wholesale moves even when they were desired by the town (e.g., Allenville, Arizona, and Olive Branch, Illinois; Pinter, 2021a). More on the importance of funding for the entirety of the relocation process can be found in Chapters 8, 9, and 10. Issues related to eroding tax bases and the need for existing cities and counties to prepare to receive people leaving a town through piecemeal or collective buyouts are discussed in more detail in Chapter 8.

Many of the issues experienced by the people in these cases can inform how community relocation is done in the present and future, and will be elaborated on throughout this report. For example, in many of these cases, the decision to relocate was made by residents immediately following a flood event, in some cases while standing water was still multiple feet high; furthermore, in some cases, sustainable design measures were incorporated into new structures. Planning for the possibility of relocation in advance of a disaster could allow communities to make the decision to relocate with more confidence while in the throes of disaster recovery and to create a more sustainable new community. On the other hand, some circumstances are markedly different for present communities than these early cases of community relocation. The examples above involved relatively small groups, and many involved moving to a new, undeveloped site within a few miles of the old site. This type of relocation is more difficult today due to the increasing number of people living in vulnerable areas and the decreasing amount of safe, open space, particularly in the Gulf region. Furthermore, because most of the new sites didn't have already-existing development, these cases do not provide much insight into preparing existing communities to be receiving communities. Additionally, earlier relocations were more often a physical relocation of structures rather than a demolish and rebuild, which brings with it a higher price tag and a need to plan for what will happen to the old site. These topics are expanded upon in Chapter 8 but warrant further investigation than this report is able to provide. Individual home buyouts, which typically facilitate ad hoc relocations and are offered after a disaster has occurred (Carey, 2020), are currently the most common form of relocation supported in the United States and will be discussed in greater detail in the next section and throughout the report.

BUYOUTS: CHALLENGES, OPPORTUNITIES, AND LESSONS

Buyouts (i.e., property acquisitions) of flood-prone properties are the most institutionalized, the most common, and the most studied type of "assisted" relocation in the United States, involving all jurisdictions of government and often the private and nongovernment sectors (Elliott et al., 2020; Environmental Law Institute, n.d.; Greer & Binder, 2017; Urban Land Institute, 2021; see Chapter 9).[1] At the most basic level, buyouts are voluntary or sometimes mandatory transactions of properties from owners to the government so that the purchased areas return to their prior undeveloped state and possibly assist in future flood mitigation and other ecosystem services, preserve or revive natural habitats, provide education opportunities,

[1]FEMA, the lead federal agency for disbursing funding for buyouts, uses the term "property acquisitions." However, the term "buyouts" is more commonly utilized by residents and local government. More information is available at https://www.fema.gov/openfema-data-page/hazard-mitigation-grant-program-property-acquisitions-v1

and serve as commemorative sites such as burial grounds, among others.[2] Most generally, the ultimate goal of this process is to decrease suffering, the loss of life, and the loss of infrastructure in areas that have repeated flooding by relocating people, communities, and livelihoods to less flood-prone areas. Governments are increasingly utilizing buyouts as a tool for climate adaptation at the local, state, and regional levels (Greer et al., 2022).

During virtual and hybrid information-gathering sessions, the study committee was presented with a broad array of existing challenges, opportunities, and lessons learned about the buyout process (i.e., planning, implementation, outcomes). Several participants with expertise in the buyout process supplemented their presentations with evidence from the literature (National Academies, 2022c, 2023a); the committee, in turn, examined evidence-based literature to develop the following key takeaways:[3]

- Buyouts take a long time to implement (Binder et al., 2020).
- Participants in buyout programs do not always move to less hazardous areas (McGhee et al., 2020).
- Counties and neighborhoods with a higher proportion of White households are more likely to receive buyout offers, but households of color within those neighborhoods are more likely to accept buyout offers (Elliott et al., 2020).
- The locations of buyouts are influenced by racialized historic housing policies, such as redlining (Zavar & Fischer, 2021).
- The use of the land after buyouts often has provided little utility for the community or city/county (Zavar & Hagelman, 2016). However, the Riverine Targeted Use of Buyouts Program (TUBs) in Harris County, Texas, is an exception. TUBs utilizes green stormwater infrastructure techniques at strategically selected places adjacent to multiple downstream waterways where buyouts have occurred in Harris County and surrounding counties. The objective of the

[2]As one example of a mandatory buyout program in the Gulf region, Harris County, Texas, operates the Project Recovery Post Disaster Relocation and Buyout Program. More information is available at https://harrisrecovery.org/post-disaster-relocation-and-buyout-program/. One example from the Gulf region of a voluntary buyout program as part of a statewide initiative is the Louisiana Watershed Initiative. More information is available at https://watershed.la.gov/buyouts

[3]In addition to the hybrid workshops (National Academies, 2022c,d, 2023a), the committee also engaged virtually with buyout experts from each Gulf state and other regions at the following event: "Managed Retreat in the U.S. Gulf Coast Region: Perspectives and Approaches to Property Acquisitions: Challenges and Lessons Learned." More information about this event is available at https://www.nationalacademies.org/event/12-13-2022/managed-retreat-in-the-us-gulf-coast-region-perspectives-and-approaches-to-property-acquisitions-challenges-and-lessons-learned

program is to increase coastal and riparian resilience, reduce sediment and erosion, and enhance hazard mitigation.[4]

- Because of the sole focus on property owners, to include a house or other buildings and the surrounding land in the exchange of ownership to the government, renters are neglected and renters' vulnerability to the impacts of climate change increases (Dundon & Camp, 2021).

Several of these issues are examined in more detail in Chapters 8 and 10 and, in the context of communication and participation, in Chapter 7, and further contextualized with testimonials from workshops participants.

Eminent Domain/Forced Relocations

The Uniform Relocation Assistance and Real Property Acquisition Policies Act of 1970 (URA) is a federal law establishing the "minimum standards for federally funded programs and projects that require the acquisition of real property (real estate) or displace persons from their homes, businesses, or farms."[5] It provides for basic human rights in the event of forced relocations, but, for purposes of FEMA buyouts, moves required by climate change and economics do not fall under the act since they are considered voluntary (Howe et al., 2021). Yet, in many situations "voluntary participants" feel forced to move (de Vries & Frasier, 2012). In interviews following past buyouts, many participants did not consider the program fully voluntary as some expressed that they felt they did not have better options due to limited savings, pressure placed on them by other participants, and a lack of communication regarding the rules by program administrators (de Vries & Frasier, 2012). The lack of effective communication may result in greater confusion and heightened frustration for all participants. As discussed in Chapter 4, many affected communities have a history in which residents have been forced by the government to relocate. This history has tinged current perceptions of relocation, particularly for Indigenous communities (Barra, 2021; Ristroph, 2021).

Instances continue in which mandatory buyouts occur through the use of eminent domain.[6] For example, USACE projects for flood control must include eminent domain if there is not a "100 percent voluntary participation

[4]More information about TUBs is available at https://houstonwilderness.org/riverinetubs

[5]More information about the URA is available at https://www.hudexchange.info/programs/relocation/overview/#overview-of-the-ura

[6]More information about mandatory buyouts through eminent domain is available at https://kleinmanenergy.upenn.edu/research/publications/climate-adaptation-strategies-how-do-we-manage-managed-retreat/

plan for acquisition" (USACE, 2016, p. 2). Some communities have agreed to USACE terms on the use of eminent domain for flood control (see Cheng, 2021).

In other cases, states have developed their own buyout programs. The committee heard from workshop participants about negative experiences and negative impacts regarding the ongoing mandatory buyout program in Harris County, Texas, which will use eminent domain if residents reject the county's offer.[7] Among workshop participants, there was an overall negative reaction to mandatory buyouts, especially in this case where residents felt that after the buyout occurred, nothing was done to restore the land, and buildings were left to deteriorate (National Academies, 2022c).

The Dutch Strategy of Bottom-Up, Integrated, and Holistic Flood Risk Reduction

The committee provides this example to showcase how buyouts can be part of a broader risk management strategy and still employ bottom-up proactive planning. Adaptation involves creating opportunities for alternative pathways that can lead to diverse outcomes, including transformational adaptation capable of forging entirely new trajectories. Managed retreat is a potential option within an adaptation pathway for the reduced impact of the effect of climate change (Siebentritt et al., 2014). One such suggested adaptation pathway is the Dynamic Adaptive Pathway Planning method, employing specific water management measures to empower policy makers to explore alternative strategies for changing environmental conditions over time (Haasnoot, 2013; Haasnoot et al., 2013). The post-Hurricane Sandy buyouts in the United States exemplify this cross-scale interaction of transformation and adaptation (van Veelen, 2016). However, the execution of Hurricane Sandy buyouts can still be characterized by a reactive approach to flood risk management.

Examining examples outside the United States provides insights into a proactive adaptive pathway toward managed retreat. An illustrative instance is the Dutch Delta program, acknowledged as a model adaptive pathway for water management (Bloemen et al., 2018). This adaptive pathway encompasses various responses to evolving flooding and sea level scenarios. These responses include dike strengthening and relocation, as well as river widening—each necessitating the relocation of homes and people from vulnerable areas.

Hazard-related property purchase in the Netherlands is managed largely as a part of a broader systematic approach integrated into the existing

---

[7]More information about eminent domain in Harris County, Texas, is available at https://harrisrecovery.org/wp-content/uploads/2021/07/If-I-Say-No-for-print.pdf

structural and nonstructural strategies for flood risk reduction (Jan Goossen, 2018). Notably, the Delta program actively supports the RftR, a major managed retreat initiative in the Netherlands, with an investment exceeding 2.4 million euros, and which is a prime example of these concerted efforts (Delta Programme Commissioner, 2014). The RftR is a bottom-up approach to the relocation of people and communities out of harm's way as part of a long-term, managed process; it is one of the most popular buyout-type projects in the Netherlands. This approach to managed retreat is proactive and part of an ongoing integrated water administration strategy rather than a post-event acquisition of properties (Atoba, 2022; Wendland, 2020).

As part of the RftR, the Dutch government spent about 2.3 billion euros to acquire flood-prone residential and agricultural land around the IJssel, Waal, Nederrijn, and Lek rivers, converting them to open space to create room for the river (Atoba, 2022, p. 306, citing Rijkswaterstaat, 2019). Particularly, the Nijmegen project, which acquired about 50 properties, has been lauded in its approach to engaging its residents to support the government's effort (European Spatial Planning Observation Network, 2017; Yu et al., 2020).

The flexibility in the RftR process, which encourages active citizen engagement, is one of the reasons for the success of the program (Jan Goossen, 2018). For example, to increase local buy-in, the program applied a less bureaucratic, bottom-up approach to determine who qualifies for a buyout rather than the strict programmatic requirements employed by the traditional FEMA HMGP programs (see Chapter 9). This approach encouraged local leadership and engagement of government leaders to cooperate with local stakeholders (Edelenbos et al., 2017). Incentives were created for the program to foster this collaboration between government officials and residents throughout the decision-making process (de Bruijn et al., 2015). Their approach was described as the case where the water management authority "would sit down at the 'kitchen table' with residents to look for individual solutions. In addition, families were offered the opportunity to sell their homes at market value (before RftR); and farmers were helped in their search for new farmland" (van Alphen, 2020; see Chapter 10 for further discussion of buyout offers and the cost of replacement housing and Chapter 8 for discussion of identifying suitable land). More discussion of active citizen engagement can be found in Chapter 7 of this report.

The RftR's management of property acquisition embeds benefit-cost analysis (BCA) in the overall integrated flood risk management strategy of the nation, thus evaluating costs and benefits to balance safety with "hydraulic effectiveness, ecological robustness, and cultural meaning and aesthetics" (van Alphen, 2020, p. 310). This is a major difference from the larger federally funded buyout programs in the United States in which BCA is mostly benefit-cost driven at smaller scales (usually at the parcel level;

Atoba et al., 2020; see Chapter 10). The overarching goal of the Dutch strategy is improving overall spatial quality and reducing flood risk (largely defined as protecting assets), creating robust ecological systems, and enhancing the aesthetics of the existing natural landscape (Klijn et al., 2013).

The Dutch approach to water management has gradually shifted from a mainly top-down approach to a more inclusive participatory planning approach, as shown in the RftR project (Edelenbos et al., 2017). Rather than adhering to a strict one-size-fits-all approach to buyouts, a localized and community-engaged approach may receive more support from residents and lead to more positive outcomes. Importantly, the Dutch approach is anchored in adaptation planning and associated adaptive delta management to reduce flood risk. Key elements of success include (a) long-term programmatic development designed to keep political involvement separate; (b) a clearly stated approach to dealing with uncertainty; and (c) an organizational strategy to allow for adjustments over time as thresholds warrant (Bloemen et al., 2019).

The United States can learn important lessons from the Dutch buyout strategy. One is that beneficial outcomes can result from incorporating flood-prone property acquisition into a proactive and integrated water management system rather than conducting a siloed acquisition of property in small patches. Another is that while BCA is important for property acquisition, the focus of successful flood risk management is to improve overall spatial and environmental quality at larger scales. A third lesson is that successfully achieving this level of incorporation requires active community engagement (i.e., sitting at the kitchen table with residents) and highlights the importance of participatory planning. Elements of longer-term planning are discussed in Chapter 9 while issues of uncertainty and thresholds are discussed in Chapter 8. See Chapter 10 for two more international examples of national policies addressing managed retreat.

CASE STUDIES

Hurricane Sandy in New York and New Jersey

Background

Hurricane Sandy, often referred to as Superstorm Sandy, made landfall near Brigantine, New Jersey, in October 2012 and was the second costliest Atlantic storm on record (Risk Management Solutions, Inc., 2013). New York, New Jersey, and Connecticut were significantly damaged by catastrophic storm surges and inundation (Blake et al., 2013). Damages were estimated to cost 86 billion dollars (Consumer Price Index-adjusted), making it the fifth costliest storm to hit the United States as of August 2023 (National Oceanic and Atmospheric Administration [NOAA] National Centers for Environmental Information, 2023). Hurricane Sandy forced 23,000 residents into temporary shelters and had a death toll of 159 (Brown, 2014; NOAA National Centers for Environmental Information, 2023). HUD allocated several billion dollars for a "Community Development Fund" to restore infrastructure post-disaster (Disaster Relief Appropriations Act, 2013, pp. 13 and 34). A coordinated effort from federal agencies allocated an estimated 1.4 billion dollars for relief to households, and approximately 1.2 billion dollars was used for housing and property assistance, repair, and temporary relocation.[8] Following this disaster, buyout programs emerged to assist residents in vulnerable and at-risk areas in New York and New Jersey, such as New York Rising Buyout and Acquisition Program (NY Rising) and New York City Build It Back Program (NYC Build It Back). In addition, existing programs, like Blue Acres in New Jersey, received federal recovery money to facilitate the relocation of numerous families out of flood-prone areas.[9] Some efforts were also sourced from nonprofits; for example, the Red Cross Move-In Assistance Program assisted residents with rent, repairs, temporary housing, and volunteer housing, especially for uninsured families (American Red Cross, 2017). The following section describes the buyout and acquisition of residences in New York City and New Jersey.

New York City

NYC Build It Back, announced by Mayor de Blasio in 2015,[10] offered options for purchasing damaged properties and resettling families (i.e., for more resilient redevelopment, for restricted future development, or for assistance in purchasing replacement housing; NYC Build It Back, 2018). Criteria for acquisition and buyout included that the property met redevelopment purposes, was located in a suitable area, was a public health or safety risk, or was contiguous with an acquired site. Because the program offered different options for interested applicants, applications were reviewed for eligibility and other considerations, such as identifying the "most appropriate end-use for the property," and then routed to the appropriate option (NYC Build It Back, 2018). (The benefit of this type of centralized system for routing interested applicants to the right buyout option is discussed in Chapter 10.) Demolition, preparation, remediation, and maintenance were paid for by Community Development Block Grant Disaster Recovery (CDBG-DR) funding (NYC Build It Back, 2018). As of October 2017, when the "Completing the Built It Back Program" report

[8]More information about federal agency relief is available at https://www.fema.gov/press-release/20210318/remembering-sandy-five-years-later

[9]More information is available at https://www.fema.gov/case-study/3-years-long-3-years-strong-new-jerseys-successful-approach-purchasing-homes-along

[10]More information about the NYC Build It Back program is available at https://furmancenter.org/coredata/directory/entry/build-it-back

was published, 600 homes (27% of the 2,200 substantially damaged homes that received assistance) were being bought out and the land returned to nature. About 200 were being acquired and redeveloped (Mayor's Office of Housing Recovery Operations, 2017).

Governor Cuomo supported a New York State buyout program as part of long-term recovery efforts, offering participants in flood-prone areas pre-storm market prices to relocate and transforming affected areas into buffers against future flooding (Binder, 2013, p. 3; Goldstein, 2013). In 2013, using a 4.4 billion-dollar grant from the CDBG-DR program, the NY Governor's Office of Storm Recovery (GOSR; established by Governor Cuomo) established such a program, calling it NY Rising (Ghorbani & Wolf, 2018).

NY Rising established "Enhanced Buyout Areas" where contiguous parcels in highly flood-prone areas were identified, and property owners could receive incentives for agreeing to a buyout (GOSR, 2015, p. 14). These included a "ten-percent incentive above the pre-storm fair market value" for residents within the enhanced buyout area who agree to a buyout and "a five-percent incentive for participants who would relocate within the same five boroughs of New York City or county to maintain local tax bases" (Spidalieri et al., 2020b, p. 3). McGhee (2017) surveyed 323 post-Hurricane Sandy Staten Island buyout participants and found that almost 82 percent relocated within New York State. Only about 22 percent relocated within their ZIP code, but almost 75 percent stayed in Staten Island.

As of 2018, NY Rising had closed or was processing the buyout or acquisition of over 1,500 properties, about 75 percent of total eligible properties. Residents of the remaining approximately 25 percent chose not to participate (Ghorbani & Wolf, 2018). Notably, instead of requiring municipalities to cover the 25 percent nonfederal match, New York State covered the match, helping to "make buyouts more financially viable for municipalities, since they need to accommodate only the loss in tax revenue" (Freudenberg et al., 2016, p. 28). Nonfederal matches came from CDBG-DR funds, which were administered via the Non-Federal Share Match Program set up by GOSR (2021, p. 13). Rental properties not considered second homes were also eligible for buyouts under NY Rising (GOSR, 2015, p. 23). However, this meant tenants could be displaced if a property owner decided to participate in a buyout. Under the URA, NY Rising was required to "take steps to minimize any displacement of residential tenants" GOSR (2017, p. 1). Thus, renters whose landlords decided to participate in NY Rising may have been eligible for assistance to cover moving expenses, deposits for temporary housing, and cost differences between temporary housing and current rent (GOSR, 2017, p. 1). Barriers caused by nonfederal match requirements and by programs providing for homeowners but not renters are discussed later in Chapter 10.

The Ocean Breeze community on Staten Island faced challenges with buyouts after Hurricane Sandy, especially when those buyouts were executed through FEMA (Misdary, 2022). The chief policy and research officer at GOSR during the Staten Island buyout program stated that "buyout programs are needed in a recovery and resiliency toolbox, but they're very expensive and can be a lengthy process [... b]ut there's also a lot of potential for climate adaptation and climate mitigation funding" (Misdary, 2022). Buyout programs are often not well advertised or communicated to residents. As a result, many residents of the Ocean Breeze community only learned about buyouts via word of mouth or spent much of their own time advocating for them.

Conversely, the Oakwood Beach community on Staten Island, which took advantage of the NY Rising program, can be viewed as a successful example of community-driven relocation largely due to strong community leadership and open communication pathways. A group of Oakwood Beach residents organized into a buyout committee to (a) educate residents about the potential for buyouts and, later, state and local officials about the community's interest in buyouts; and (b) coordinate government-funded buyout efforts and relocation assistance (Spidalieri et al., 2020b, p. 2). The community was poised to advocate for buyouts as they had a history of advocating for better coastal protection and against the continued development of nearby wetlands since at least 1992, when the neighborhood was flooded by a nor'easter (Koslov, 2016). The Oakwood Beach Buyout Committee also spearheaded the surveying of at-risk neighborhoods in their community to decide which areas should be converted back to open floodplains, rather than deferring to outside experts, which further empowered residents (Freudenberg et al., 2016, p. 31, citing Rush, 2015). (The importance of community engagement and leadership as well as risk communication and data access in community-driven relocation is discussed in more detail in Chapter 7.) Concerns from Staten Island residents echoed wider reports of difficulties with FEMA's process, including having limited windows of opportunity to apply for the buyout program and prolonged service delays up to two years post-application (Misdary, 2022).

New Jersey

New Jersey's CDBG-DR Action Plan describes the state's efforts to help cities, households, and businesses to recover following Hurricane Sandy (New Jersey Department of Community Affairs, 2013). This document does not describe a coordinated or proactive effort to relocate individuals whose homes were damaged by Hurricane Sandy to safer locations. Rather, the focus is on keeping individuals and businesses in place to preserve local tax bases. For example, the Homeowner Resettlement Program describes providing grants to households to cover increasing insurance premiums and so help them to remain in their communities (New Jersey Department of Community Affairs, 2013, p. 48). However, there are elements of this plan that would also be helpful if residents wanted to pursue community-driven relocation. For example, to bolster economic recovery, the New Jersey Economic Development Authority offered grants and "low-cost loans" to impacted small businesses, which could be used for rehabilitation, expansion, new construction, acquisition, mitigation, etc. (New Jersey Department of Community Affairs, 2013, pp. 60–61). Although these grants and loans were not specific to helping businesses relocate away from flood-prone areas, businesses often struggle to survive the long waits accompanying relocation efforts (Pinter, 2021a). Recovery funding targeted toward small businesses during community-driven relocation efforts may help local businesses survive, thus helping to bolster the local economy and preserve community ties.

After the storm, Governor Christopher Christie bolstered the fast-action state-led Blue Acres acquisition program for 1,300 properties in New Jersey (FEMA, 2021b).[11] Ten years after the storm, the program had purchased more than 350 acres and converted flood-prone land to "natural flood storage, parkland, and other community benefits."[12] As of 2021, the Blue Acres program had received 273 million dollars in acquisition funds from FEMA's HMGP, HUD's CDBG-DR, the U.S. Department of Agriculture Natural Resources Conservation Service, and additional funds from the Garden State Preservation Trust (FEMA, 2021a; Garden State Preservation Trust, 2018).

One community, Woodbridge Township, worked with Blue Acres to facilitate a 120-acre neighborhood-scale buyout with support from state and local government, private and public partnerships, and community members (Spidalieri et al., 2020a). The Woodbridge community used cooperative action, education and outreach campaigns, public meetings, Catholic Charities, and state and local partnerships (i.e., with the Land Conservancy of New Jersey) to facilitate the buyouts (Spidalieri et al., 2020a). Almost 200 households accepted a buyout. To discourage future harmful development, the mayor and City Council rezoned the buyout area to Open Space Conservation/Resiliency. This new zoning fosters recreational amenities (e.g., trails and open space) and enables the land to act as a "natural flood buffer" (Spidalieri et al., 2020a, p. 86). It also requires residents to elevate their properties if, for example, there is a change in tenancy or they do any

[11]More information about the Blue Acres program is available at https://www.fema.gov/case-study/3-years-long-3-years-strong-new-jerseys-successful-approach-purchasing-homes-along

[12]More information is available at https://dep.nj.gov/sandy-10/climate-flood-resilience/#blueacres

renovations. The community also worked with local apartment complexes to assist residents with waiting lists for relocation. After participating in the National Flood Insurance Program's (NFIP's) Community Rating System (CRS)—a point-based program that rewards communities for flood risk management actions that go beyond the NFIP—residents experienced reduced flood insurance premiums.[13] The CRS is discussed further in Chapters 9 and 10.

Follow-Up Research and Resident Testimony

There are a variety of motivations and concerns that drove residents to relocate after Hurricane Sandy, such as cost of living, employment opportunities, and retirement. A survey of 46 households after Hurricane Sandy indicated that some respondents would consider relocation if there were "relocation of job[s] as well; cheaper taxes; lower insurance rates, mortgage payments, and cost of living; retirement; suburban lifestyle; and better job opportunities" (Bukvic & Owen, 2017, p. 117). Another survey found that those who opted to relocate or were eligible for a buyout were less likely to report stress (Koslov et al., 2021, p. 14). Bukvic & Owen (2017) surveyed devastated households in New York and New Jersey communities five months after Hurricane Sandy. They found that those parties interested in buyouts attributed the decision to the promise of "economic growth and recovery" and those cascading impacts of well-being and livelihoods rather than based on "coastal risks, community ties, or [...] experienced damage" (p. 116).

The Village of Newtok, Alaska

Experiencing thawing permafrost, erosion, and frequent flooding, Alaska's Newtok Village has had the goal of relocating their entire community to Mertarvik, "the only high ground in the vicinity, situated on an island nine miles away" since the mid-1990s (Ristroph, 2021, p. 330, citing Agnew Beck Consulting, 2011). In 2003, Newtok was identified as one of four Alaska Native Villages that were "in imminent danger and were planning to relocate" (Government Accountability Office, 2009, p. 1), and in 2006, USACE projected that "the entire village may go underwater by 2027" (Ristroph, 2021, p. 330, citing USACE, 2006). Environmental threats like these are also facing Gulf Coast communities, the scale of which is discussed in Chapter 2. See Figure 3-1 for a picture of permafrost and erosion on the coast of Newtok. These environmental conditions have threatened the community's land, housing and building stock, infrastructure that provides

[13]More information about the CRS is available at https://www.fema.gov/floodplain-management/community-rating-system

FIGURE 3-1 Erosion on the coast of Newtok in 2020.
SOURCE: Ristroph, B. (2020). Coast of Newtok, Alaska [Photograph].

services like sanitation, and the resources residents rely on for subsistence and livelihoods. The effects of such environmental conditions in these villages can be compounded by social problems such as addiction, suicide, and a sense of disempowerment, stemming in part from historical trauma, which limits a community's capacity to respond (Ristroph, 2021, p. 331). The importance of community well-being and its role in implementing community-driven relocation is discussed in Chapters 6 and 7.

Like most Alaska Native Villages, Newtok is home to both Newtok Village (a federally recognized tribe) and Newtok Native Corporation (Ristroph, 2021, p. 332). Newtok Native Corporation, a landholding corporation created by the Alaska Native Claims Settlement Act of 1971 (ANCSA),[14] owns land in and around the town site. In the late 1990s, faced with worsening environmental conditions, "Newtok Village and Newtok Native Corporation sought to trade Corporation-owned land for land managed by the U.S. Fish and Wildlife Service at Mertarvik" (Ristroph, 2021, p. 332). Although ANCSA allows uneven land trades that are in the public interest (43 U.S.C. § 1621(f); c.f. 16 U.S.C. § 3192), it took seven years to negotiate an act of Congress to allow the trade due to political complications (P.L. 108–129, 2003; Ristroph, 2021, p. 332). Chapter 8 will discuss

[14]More information about ANCSA is available at https://ancsaregional.com/about-ancsa/

in more detail the multitude of considerations that must be made when a community is selecting and obtaining a new town site, or when they are instead relocating into existing communities.

A new town site was obtained in 2003, and in 2006 the Alaska Division of Community and Regional Affairs worked with the tribal leadership to form "the Newtok Planning Group to facilitate coordination assistance from agencies" (Bronen & Chapin, 2013; Ristroph, 2021, p. 332). The Newtok Planning Group worked as an informal "boundary organization" consisting of numerous governmental and nongovernmental agencies at the federal, state, and tribal levels (Bronen & Chapin, 2013, p. 9322).[15] The group met regularly, even through leadership changes, and has been successful in securing technical assistance and raising awareness among agencies about Newtok's situation (Ristroph, 2021, p. 332). The need for increased technical assistance is discussed further in Chapter 10, and the critical importance of community determination in the relocation process is the focus of Chapter 7.

Following the first structures at Mertarvik (three houses built by residents in 2006), in 2009, Newtok constructed a multipurpose evacuation center and barge landing (Bronen & Chapin, 2013, p. 9322) using 6.5 million dollars from the state legislature (Ristroph, 2021, p. 332). The evacuation center's multipurpose function has served the community well during resettlement. For example, it served as a school until the community built a new one (Ristroph, 2021, p. 332).

Around 2015, Newtok's leadership began lobbying for a congressional appropriation for relocation, and by 2018, Congress appropriated 15 million dollars to the Denali Commission for its work with Alaska villages (P.L. 115-141 2018; Ristroph, 2021, p. 333).[16] This funding, which was granted to the Alaska Native Tribal Health Consortium,[17] supported the construction of numerous facilities (including bulk fuel storage, a landfill, a temporary air strip, roads, a preliminary power plant, and preliminary water and wastewater treatment plants) and 13 houses with partial plumbing (Ristroph, 2021, p. 333; see Figure 3-2). Before and after this, Newtok has managed to piece together numerous grants from HUD and FEMA to pay for houses and infrastructure, using Denali Commission funds toward FEMA's nonfederal match (Ristroph, 2021). The experience of pulling together funding from different sources with different requirements and

---

[15]As described in the Key Terms (Appendix D), a boundary organization is "an organization that facilitates production of shared goals through capacity across different cultural knowledge systems and across the science/policy divide" (Robards et al., 2018).

[16]More information about the Denali Commission is available at https://www.denali.gov/

[17]More information about the Alaska Native Tribal Health Consortium is available at https://www.anthc.org/

FIGURE 3-2 The first few houses built in Mertarvik, the new site for Newtok Village.
SOURCE: Ristroph, B. (2019). New site for Newtok Village [Photograph].

restrictions is not unique to Newtok's relocation and is discussed further in more detail in Chapters 9 and 10.

Ristroph (2021) notes, "While each community is different, several factors that have helped Newtok may benefit other communities: strong leadership; unified community vision and policy; a local coordinator serving as a continued point of contact; strong capacity for grant writing; trusted, reasonably priced consultants controlled directly by the tribal government; professional accounting services; and a housing policy to ensure fairness" (p. 337). For example, strong leadership meant there was effective communication (discussed in Chapter 7) between community leaders, residents, and external agencies, which helped to avoid misinformation and to set priorities for the relocation process that aligned with community desires (e.g., housing before plumbing; Ristroph, 2021, p. 335). Additionally, the local relocation coordinator position, funded by the Denali Commission, was held by the same Newtok resident for several years to serve as a "single point of contact" for external entities and provide institutional and local knowledge (Ristroph, 2021, p. 336). The role of coordinators or navigators is discussed in Chapter 10.

It is important to point out that as of 2023, there are a number of households still at the original site in poor conditions, living with the threat of a storm destroying more homes.

Isle de Jean Charles, Louisiana

IDJC is an "island" in Terrebonne Parish, Louisiana, in the Gulf of Mexico's coastal marshes, about 80 miles southwest of New Orleans. IDJC is connected to the mainland by a narrow causeway called "Island Road" that was constructed in 1953, but the causeway is increasingly impassable because of high tide flooding, water surges driven by high winds, and flooding.[18] The past and present residents of IDJC are primarily of Indigenous ancestry who resettled there while fleeing the series of violent forced removals that accompanied the Indian Removal Act of 1830, together called the "Trail of Tears" (Sand-Fleishman, 2019; see Chapter 4 of this report for further discussion of this history). IDJC once consisted of about 33,000 acres of landmass but has been reduced to less than 400 acres because of the impact of tropical storms, relative sea level rise, subsidence, oil and gas infrastructure, and levee development (Carter et al., 2018; Maldonado, 2019, p. 29; Törnqvist et al., 2008). IDJC was once a protected place within a resilient ecological infrastructure, located amidst complex bayous, swamps, and marshes that mitigated the force of storms; it now is vulnerable and exposed to the nearby Gulf (see Figure 3-3).

In January 2016, through the National Disaster Resilience Competition, HUD awarded 92 million dollars to Louisiana's Office of Community Development (LA-OCD), of which 48.3 million dollars was allocated to relocate IDJC in the form of CDBG funds (LA-OCD, 2021).[19] The purpose of the funds included the development of the relocation site, which became known as "The New Isle," a 515-acre area of undeveloped rural land about 40 miles north of IDJC in Terrebonne Parish.[20] LA-OCD embarked on an extensive community engagement planning process that included interviews, community meetings, an open house, and design workshops where The New Isle would be established so future residents could discuss their vision of their new home and neighborhood (LA-OCD, 2020), as Mark Goodson, a private firm lead for the project told the committee: "[resettlement decision making] is going to take resources, and it's going to take conversations at kitchen tables to help give folks in those resettling communities the information that they need to get them comfortable with a yes or no decision" (National Academies, 2023a, p. 57). The data-gathering and engagement phase of the IDJC project also included assistance from private firms.[21] The majority of eligible households on IDJC decided to relocate (37

[18]More information about IDJC is available at https://isledejeancharles.la.gov/

[19]More information about HUD's National Disaster Resilience Competition is available at https://www.hud.gov/program_offices/economic_development/resilience/competition

[20]More information about "The New Isle" is available at https://isledejeancharles.la.gov/new-isle

[21]These firms included Pan American Engineers, Chicago Bridge & Iron Company, and Concordia. More information about this phase is available at https://isledejeancharles.la.gov/sites/default/files/public/IDJC-Final-Report-Update.pdf

FIGURE 3-3 View of IDJC facing northward. Island Road that connects IDJC to the mainland is in the top right side of the photo.
SOURCE: Google Earth. (2023). Isle de Jean Charles, Louisiana, 29°23'39"N 90°28'25"W. https://earth.google.com/web/search/Isle+de+Jean+Charles,+LA/@29.40611415,-90.47644019,-2.61320997a,9848.76718144d,35y,-10.9951822h,34.77168086t,0r/data=CigiJgokCWjLlJZQcj1AES2AkylTYT1AGWsAmkonm1bAIVIYC9IDo1bAOgMKATA

out of 42), and one household decided to move to a location separate from The New Isle (Setyawan, 2021).

In July 2022, the study committee engaged with past and current residents of IDJC during two workshops in southeast Louisiana (National Academies, 2023a). The committee heard differing perspectives on the process and outcomes of the IDJC relocation project. Some past and current residents expressed frustration at the process and outcome, while others were optimistic about their opportunity to relocate. Participants at one workshop relayed that the IDJC project was "an imperfect process, but that it can be used as a benchmark for future projects to do better with gaining increased community input" (National Academies, 2023a, p. 29). One notable policy outcome of the IDJC project, as discussed further in Chapter 8, involved negotiations with HUD and LA-OCD about the right to return to the original IDJC. A solution was reached that allows the original homes of resettled participants to remain intact and guarantees that "they are not used for residential purposes or redevelopment" but as places to use that would facilitate fishing for the previous owners.[22] This is an innovative outcome because vacated properties in traditional HUD-funded relocation

[22]More information about island homes after resettlement is available at https://isledejeancharles.la.gov/frequently-asked-questions#q55

programs must be returned to permanent open space.[23] If IDJC residents had been required to relinquish all access and the use of their old properties once they resettled in The New Isle, many would not have left (National Academies, 2023a, p. 58).

Across both workshops, the study committee learned that IDJC exposed the complexities and deficiencies of the relocation process. Conflict and disagreements were a common feature among the Indigenous residents and between specific tribes, other stakeholders, and the supervising agencies during the process, and these remain contentious and unsettled. Fundamental questions at the core of the resettlement process were raised during the workshops: How can community, communal, and sacred spaces be preserved after displacement? What economic and political impediments prevent humane and equitable retreat from familiar places to unfamiliar places? Because of this, the question of whether a similar relocation could be effective for a large urban area remains unanswered (Dundon & Abkowitz, 2021; Gibbs, 2016). Furthermore, underpinning these questions is the importance of local history, as this report addresses across the chapters, with particular focus in Chapter 4; the importance of transparency of process and outcome and effective and equitable participation, as discussed in Chapter 7; and the importance of using policy and funding to address the concerns and desires of the communities that are most impacted by relocation (Chapters 8, 9, and 10).

Grantham, Australia: 2011 Flash Flood

Grantham, a rural agriculture community situated in the Lockyer Valley of Queensland, Australia, was severely affected by a devastating flash flood in January 2011, a disaster subsequently described as an "inland tsunami."[24] The catastrophe resulted in substantial human and infrastructural losses, claiming 12 lives and inflicting considerable structural damage to approximately 150 residential buildings located within the floodplain.[25] In an attempt to address this calamity, the Queensland Reconstruction Authority (QRA) collaborated with the Lockyer Valley Regional Council (LVRC) to devise a comprehensive recovery strategy termed "Rebuilding Grantham Together." The strategy was enabled under the Queensland

[23]Ibid.

[24]More information about rebuilding Grantham is available at https://www.qra.qld.gov.au/news-case-studies/case-studies/case-study-rebuilding-grantham-together-2011

[25]More information about flash flood loss is available at https://www.iag.com.au/sites/default/files/Documents/About us/Final Appendix A_0.pdf

Reconstruction Authority Act of 2011[26]—an act of recovery and enhanced resilience that was catalyzed by the devastating 2011 flood.[27]

The LVRC's proactive leadership was instrumental in kick-starting the recovery program. They first suggested the idea of a land swap, identified the new land parcel, negotiated its purchase, and initiated its development even before any financial support from the state and federal governments was secured (Sipe & Vella, 2014). Within three months of the flood, they procured a 377-hectare parcel of elevated farmland to relocate flood affected residents (Sipe & Vella, 2014). Conventional planning regulations were circumvented in order to expedite the process through a strong collaborative framework involving local, state, and federal governments (Sipe & Vella, 2014). The planning and permitting process was greatly expedited due to the QRA designating Grantham as a reconstruction area (Sipe & Vella, 2014). This allowed the LVRC to bypass many typical land-use planning procedures to secure a safe new area for the community and avoid residents ending up in another flood-prone site (Okada et al., 2014). Further discussion of the complex and multi-level planning required for community-driven relocation is discussed in Chapters 8 and 9.

The LVRC and QRA developed two primary recovery initiatives, the Grantham Master Plan[28] and the Land Offer Program,[29] and placed a strong emphasis on community engagement. Through a series of regular community consultations, visioning meetings, design workshops, as well as personalized meetings between case managers and affected property owners, the council nurtured a strong sense of trust and confidence within the community (Sipe & Vella, 2014). This community-centric approach facilitated the smooth integration of the Land Offer Program and its lottery-based selection system—a model perceived to be equitable for determining land swap participation (Sipe & Vella, 2014). The value of, and methods for improving, community engagement during the planning and execution of community-driven relocation is discussed further in Chapter 7.

In order to effectively execute these initiatives, the LVRC developed the Grantham Relocation Policy.[30] This policy outlines the guidelines of

---

[26]More information about the Queensland Reconstruction Authority Act of 2011 is available at https://www.qra.qld.gov.au/sites/default/files/2018-10/rebuilding-grantham-full.pdf

[27]More information is available at https://www.legislation.qld.gov.au/view/pdf/2017-07-03/act-2011-001

[28]More information about the Grantham Master Plan is available at https://www.granthamnh.net/vertical/sites/%7B8E4EE0D6-AAA5-4E63-B5FA-19873AF96E35%7D/uploads/Grantham_Master_Plan_Adopted_2017.pdf

[29]More information about the Land Offer Program is available at http://www.floodcommission.qld.gov.au/__data/assets/pdf_file/0005/9599/QFCI_Exhibit_602__Lockyer_Valley_Regional_council__Grantham_relocation_policy_dated_11_May_2011.pdf

[30]Ibid.

the Land Offer Program, including eligibility requirements for participation in the land swap, procedures for randomized land allocation, and rules governing the eventual sale of the new properties on the open market. Additionally, all blocks available in the land swap were connected to the municipal water system. Identifying appropriate land with consideration for safety and connectivity to essential services (e.g., water and electricity) is an essential part of community-driven relocation and is discussed in Chapter 8. The first lottery took place in August 2011, marking a significant milestone in the community's journey toward recovery (Sipe & Vella, 2014).

The enactment of "Rebuilding Grantham Together" aligned planning regulations and infrastructure planning with the Land Offer Program, with the goal of enhancing the long-term sustainability of the communities while promoting self-contained employment opportunities and growth. Recognizing that the local economy is predominantly driven by rural industries and related activities, "Rebuilding Grantham Together" sought to preserve and grow these aspects. It supported the expansion of industries that aligned with the town's agricultural heritage, such as the processing and packaging of local produce, cottage industries, and small-to-medium-scale incubator businesses. It presented a detailed land-use plan that incorporated co-existing district zones, each designed to cater to a diverse array of community needs and preferences, with a considerable emphasis on flood risk mitigation.

The recovery strategy was further bolstered by an ambitious infrastructure program. The scope of the program included the construction of internal and external roads, establishment of water supply and sewerage systems, implementation of stormwater management strategies, creation of recreational parks, and integration of electricity and telecommunications networks. The program was designed to be self-funded by landowners, thereby ensuring that the new development was fully serviced. A new railway line crossing was constructed to enhance connectivity between the old site and the new development site. Further discussion of the infrastructure needs of receiving communities can be found in Chapter 8.

At the core of the plan was the council's Land Offer Program. Property owners from flood affected areas were allowed to exchange their land for equivalent-sized parcels in the new town area, with the understanding that they would bear the construction costs. To support this, government funding, insurance payments, and private donations were used for recovery and reconstruction, with state-provided grants available to cover moving costs, utility connections, and initial construction needs (Sipe & Vella, 2014). The LVRC facilitated the process with caseworkers assisting residents with complex legal and financial issues. Moreover, the plan was crafted with a high degree of adaptability to accommodate future changes in technology, economic conditions, sociodemographic trends, and housing preferences.

Finding a comparably sized plot of land that is affordable under the United States's current buyout system can be difficult, as was described by Houston workshop participant Perla Garcia, who relied on a large plot of land to store trucks for her business (National Academies, 2022c). While the Grantham program was tailored primarily for homeowners, the effects on renters in these areas are not as well known. This opens avenues for further research into the long-term impacts of such policies on tenant stability, relocation options, and the need for more comprehensive support systems for renters which are similar to those available to homeowners.

The LVRC team of six, including the mayor, a chief executive officer, a manager with planning and environmental engineering experience, a project coordinator, a consulting planner, and an engineer, expertly orchestrated the recovery efforts. Despite none being trained planners, their small-team approach expedited decision making and coordination. Through swift action, the LVRC harnessed corporate and community contributions, adding value to the recovery effort (Sipe & Vella, 2014). For example, a local law firm offered free property conveyancing services for the Land Offer Program. This promptness kept costs low, enabling land development to a higher standard than what existed in Grantham previously (Sipe & Vella, 2014). The success of the interdisciplinary LVRC team reflects the value of cross-sector collaboration throughout community-driven relocation, reflected in the broad content of this report from mental and physical well-being to risk communication to land-use planning and federal policy.

Tohoku, Japan: The 2011 Great East Japan Earthquake and Tsunami

On March 11, 2011, a 9.0 magnitude earthquake struck Japan's Tohoku region, triggering a devastating tsunami that resulted in approximately 20,000 fatalities; destroyed or damaged over a million buildings, predominantly in the Fukushima, Iwate, and Miyagi prefectures (Ranghieri & Ishiwatari, 2014; Reconstruction Agency, 2023); and displaced over 470,000 individuals. To aid in recovery, the equivalent of approximately 265 billion U.S. dollars was allocated to reconstruction and protection efforts; these efforts involved constructing about 145,000 homes, including the infrastructure for entirely new towns, in areas outside the tsunami hazard zone (Pinter et al., 2019).

Japan's multi-level disaster governance relies heavily on local authorities for executing relief and reconstruction, despite relying on and utilizing national financial assistance. Although not mandatory, Japanese municipalities traditionally develop recovery plans, which may vary at the district level (Thiri, 2022).[31] The Basic Recovery Policy for the Great East Japan

[31] A district is made up of one or more rural municipalities within a prefecture.

Earthquake and Tsunami disaster, established on July 29, 2011, was a pivotal step in the national response strategy (Thiri, 2022). This policy advocated a multi-stakeholder approach, in which the national government provided funding, the prefectural government mediated recovery, and municipalities played an essential role as significant participants in the recovery efforts (Thiri, 2022). The policy aimed to not only restore but also transform Tohoku's structure, industry, and energy sector into a "New Tohoku." Careful spending and corporate incentives were introduced to attract the younger generation and venture capital, with proposals for self-sustained, renewable energy sources (Thiri, 2022).

Post-tsunami Japan focused on risk reduction and disaster preparedness in its reconstruction, encompassing infrastructure restoration, livelihood support, and housing recovery plans (Miyasada & Maly, 2021; Thiri, 2022). Preserving the social fabric of affected communities was also a core value for Japan's leadership. The government's relocation strategy first provided displaced individuals with emergency shelters, followed by temporary and then permanent housing (Hikichi et al., 2017). Emergency and temporary housing provisions consisted of the construction of over 50,000 shelters and the implementation of a system to cover the rental expenses of over 70,000 private apartments designated for temporary accommodation (Miyasada & Maly, 2021). Residents were given several options while still in emergency shelters: choose between collective relocation, where entire communities moved to prefab temporary housing villages, or independent relocation, where individuals moved to public housing via a random lottery; seek accommodation in the open rental market; or build new homes (Maly et al., 2018). These choices allowed residents to choose a relocation option based on their circumstances, such as family size, convenience, or eagerness to leave the overcrowded emergency shelters (Hikichi et al., 2017). Further information on the importance of suitable land and housing for relocation is covered in this report (Chapter 8).

Japan's recovery strategy also included a significant buyout program as part of collective relocation efforts (Ghezelloo et al., 2023). "Hazardous" areas faced bans on new residential construction, allowing landowners to sell properties to the government and move to safer locations. Collective relocations received greater financial support, with the national government funding 75 percent of the costs, as compared to 50 percent for individual relocations; all are supplemented by local government contributions (Ghezelloo et al., 2023). The repurposing of acquired land played a crucial role, with some areas leased to the private sector for commercial or industrial activities, while others were transformed into green infrastructure for future tsunami protection (Ghezelloo et al., 2023). Moreover, extensive coastal land, particularly in heavily affected prefectures, was converted into memorial parks and museums to serve as places of remembrance and also to share lessons learned from the disaster and recovery with future generations (Ghezelloo et al., 2023). The study committee's findings and conclusions related to the use of land post-buyout and collective relocation are covered in Chapter 8 of this report.

To prioritize community well-being and engagement, the Japanese government's post-disaster strategy took into account local needs and aspirations. Citizens actively participated in developing master plans for each area, ensuring that the restoration of public infrastructure and the creation of safer environments resonated with residents (Pinter et al., 2019). Transparent dissemination of detailed development plans empowered affected individuals to envision their future lives (Reconstruction Agency, 2023). In Kitakami, a remarkable community-led initiative involved a local planning committee collaborating closely with government officials, architects, and researchers. They strategically planned and developed eight new communities on elevated land, located within 3–4km of the original villages. Seven of these communities served as direct replacements, preserving proximity and familiarity, while the eighth was designed as a mixed community to accommodate any tsunami-displaced residents (Pinter et al., 2019).

In service of the government's focus on preserving the social fabric, initiatives were implemented to ensure a smooth integration of residents into their new communities. Designated community members conducted wellness checks on vulnerable individuals twice a day. Inclusive spaces, like the Ibasho House in Ofunato City, were established as connectivity hubs, encouraging senior citizens to engage in community-led activities and fostering a sense of belonging (Pinter et al., 2019; Thiri, 2022).[32] An extensive network of welfare services, including trained social workers and volunteers from nonprofit organizations, was mobilized to support the overall well-being of displaced people. This collaborative effort aimed to provide ongoing comprehensive care, guiding individuals along the path to recovery until they could fully resume normal lives (Reconstruction Agency, 2023). The study committee examines the critical importance of the well-being of displaced and potentially displaced individuals and communities in Chapter 6.

To aid homeowners in the transition to higher, safer locations, a comprehensive package of donations, government subsidies, subsidized loans, and buyout payments was provided, covering approximately 40 percent of relocation and rebuilding costs (Pinter et al., 2019). Special emphasis was placed on reviving key industries like fisheries, agriculture, and tourism, which formed the region's economic backbone (Reconstruction Agency, 2023). Furthermore, extensive public housing was constructed to accommodate low-income and elderly residents who otherwise were unable to bear the additional costs. Despite political unpopularity, a 2.1 percent

[32]More information about the Ibasho House is available at https://ibasho.org/about-ibasho

income tax surcharge was accepted by Japanese citizens to aid in recovery costs (Ranghieri & Ishiwatari, 2014). This collective response was not just a reaction to the massive scale of the tsunami disaster but was also rooted in a shared national history of disaster recovery and shared cultural traditions (Pinter et al., 2019).

SUMMARY

This chapter briefly reviewed a long history of relocation efforts in the United States and took a closer examination of several more recent (post-2000) relocation efforts in the United States and abroad. A comprehensive review of past and present relocation efforts is beyond the capacity of this study; however, among others, see Bower et al. (2023) for a review of flood-related relocation cases, Pérez and Contreras (2022) for a review of relocation and resettlement initiatives with informal communities in Puerto Rico, and the Georgetown Climate Center (2020) for lessons and tools from 17 cases of relocation from the United States that were not covered in this chapter.

This chapter concludes Part 1 of this report. The next chapter starts Part 2, Understanding Relocation and the Gulf Region, by delving into the history of the region, focusing on its long history of adaptation and movement as well as the historical legacies that will shape any community-driven relocation effort in the future.

4

Understanding the Gulf Region: Historical Context

This chapter discusses the following:

- The history of adaptation and movement in the Gulf region, with an emphasis on how people's livelihoods and practices have been affected by the interplay between ecosystems and human-made infrastructure and political systems
- The effect of slavery and post-Reconstruction on migration
- Historical legacies of the region, including political disenfranchisement, economic injustice, geographic isolation, the role of place, and the preservation of culture

INTRODUCTION

To appreciate what lies ahead for the Gulf region, it is necessary to understand not only the climate- and environment-related hazards that have already begun to impact the area but also the historical circumstances of the place and its people. This chapter provides a brief overview of the rich and complicated past of the Gulf region and illuminates historical legacies anchored in this history that have implications on present-day communities as they navigate climate change. The committee has identified such legacies as particularly important to attend to in the development of hazard responses, particularly community-driven relocation efforts, that best meet the needs of the people who will be affected.

The committee came to understand the Gulf region as a complex and dynamic system in which diverse human populations have adapted (or not) to environmental and social changes over millennia. Movements to, from, and within the Gulf region have been driven by factors including the knowledge and expertise of Indigenous and place-based communities; colonization and settlement by European groups; environmental fluctuations; changing socioeconomic and political realities; and the consequences of industrial activity such as oil and gas extraction. The vibrant social ecologies that sustain this region have been consistently harmed through systemic injustices including, but not limited to, forced migration and slavery, legalized segregation and the systemic preservation of other inequities, and political disenfranchisement. The committee is keenly aware that these realities have substantially heightened the vulnerability of the region and its communities to climate, environmental, and human-made hazards but also understands that these realities are not unique to the Gulf and reflect the environmental, political, and socioeconomic history of the United States as a whole.

The committee wants particularly to highlight that Indigenous and placed-based knowledge is a critical part of the region's history and will be essential to developing climate adaptation strategies. The committee defines place-based knowledge as knowledge developed by a community in a particular location that incorporates cultural heritage as well as adaptations to the landscape and ecosystem. Throughout the report, the importance of place-based knowledge is well illustrated by many of the testimonials of individuals who made time to talk with the committee during information-gathering sessions; this topic is covered more fully in Chapters 7 and 8, which address its impact in the present day. Here, the testimonial excerpt in Box 4-1 is offered as an example and makes a direct connection between place-based knowledge and the history of human life in this region.

The first section of this chapter examines the history of adaptation and movement in the Gulf region, with an emphasis on how people's livelihoods and practices have been affected by the interplay between ecosystems and human-made infrastructure and political systems. The second section summarizes historical legacies of the region that are relevant to the challenges faced by those who have lived there. The committee particularly focuses on the legacy of profound injustices that have shaped a region that is now on the front lines of climate threats, and also highlights the strengths that Gulf Coast communities have built. The legacies highlighted here are foundational for the development of equitable, community-based, and efficacious plans in response to climate threats—work discussed in the rest of the report. This historical overview, which is by necessity abbreviated, is based on information-gathering sessions and a review of scholarship in

BOX 4-1
Community Testimonial: Elder Theresa Dardar, Pointe-au-Chien Indian Tribe, Lafourche/Terrebonne Parish

"Now, if you talk about relocation for us, where are you going to put us where we can just cross the road, get to work, and—or just cross the road and go catch a fish or catch shrimp for supper? You know, there's no other community—you can't move us to a place that would imitate this place. And like you said, 11 miles makes a difference. I'm sure it does, because when you're living on the bayou—I mean, we are bayou people. So [...] you're taking us like you would take a fish out of water and put it on dry land and just leave it there to die, because, I mean, our ancestors have been there for centuries, and none of us want to move [...] So, you know, we're trying to not only save our community where we live, but we would like to see something done where we could save, you know, the lands around our cemeteries and our mounds. And they can do this. They can protect us in place, because they build islands in the Gulfs, in open waters. It's just that they're not wanting to protect the coastal lands, you know. The people don't want to move [...and] it'll probably cost more to move everyone than for them to protect us, so why not protect the same place and keep us there? We don't want to move."

SOURCE: Elder Theresa Dardar, Pointe-au-Chien Indian Tribe, Lafourche/Terrebonne Parish. Workshop 3: Community Viability and Environmental Change in Coastal Louisiana, July 2022, Thibodaux, Louisiana. See also National Academies of Sciences, Engineering, and Medicine (2023a).

history, geography, anthropology, and related social sciences and humanities disciplines.

ADAPTATION AND MOVEMENT

Evidence suggests that perhaps as early as 30,000 years ago, humans settled and migrated throughout the Gulf region (Callaway, 2021; Dartnell, 2020; Raff, 2022). Migration has been a dynamic process, linking places to one another through streams and counter-streams and, over time, turning yesterday's receiving communities into today's originating communities (Ravenstein, 1885, 1889). The committee's examination of adaptation and movement in the Gulf region begins with a brief overview of the peoples who occupied the region for thousands of years before European conquest in the 16th century. This centers on Indigenous peoples' relationship with the land and the effects of the arrival of Europeans. The committee then examines the history of enslavement in the region, with a focus on its implications for people's attachment to place. We also consider later migrations to and from the region. A visual timeline of this history generated by the committee can be found in Appendix E.

Indigenous Peoples of the Region and European Contact

The Gulf of Mexico—its coastal habitats, islands, and tributary river valleys—has long been the home to a rich and diverse set of small and large Indigenous groups who migrated to the region prior to the first European contact. Early inhabitants found the Gulf ecologies productive and relied on their abundance to support cultural and demographic growth (Davis, 2017). These groups lived in nature-society relationships from the Yucatan peninsula to the Florida Keys and across the northern Gulf Coast, often establishing relatively stable chiefdoms. They engaged in extensive trade networks and seasonal migrations along coastal shorelines and barrier islands both to follow marine resources and to expand their communication networks. Connections among the peoples who occupied sites in the Gulf region, such as the Hopewell and Mississippian cultures, with more distant groups are evidenced by artifacts, such as large marine shells recovered from mounds as far away as the upper Midwest (Krupnik, 2022). Trading networks connected people from the Pacific coasts through the Mississippi and other rivers leading to the Gulf of Mexico and southward through the Yucatan into the Caribbean Sea.

These complex systems fostered the exchange of languages, cultures, technologies, and people (Mann, 2011). The northern Gulf Coast was among the most ethno-linguistically diverse regions in aboriginal North America (Fogelson et al., 2004; Goddard & Sturtevant, 1996). Successive migrations of people in the Mississippian Period converged with those of other Indigenous peoples who were going to lands where the Mississippi River meets the Gulf (Butler-Ulloa, 2022; Krupnick, 2022). "This place of convergence, where the great waters drain into the Gulf of Mexico, was near New Orleans, or (in Hitchiti) *Bulbancha*, the place of many languages" (Ethridge & Shuck-Hall, 2009; Klopotek, 2011; Osburn, 2014, as cited in Butler-Ulloa, 2022, p. 68). Sophisticated earthworks were a predominant feature of these peoples' settlements. It has been suggested by anthropologists as early as the 1890s that these earthworks were adaptive solutions for stabilizing coastlines against strong tides, hurricanes, and storm surge (Cushing, 1896). Prehistoric mound sites are found throughout the U.S. Gulf Coast Region, especially in the greater Mississippi Delta and the Florida Panhandle, and near the Gulf region in northern Alabama. Middens are common to riverine and coastal areas and provide evidence of the changing Gulf coastline (Helmer et al., 2023). Settlement areas were inundated as seas rose during the Last Glacial Maximum (between 19,000 and 29,000 years ago; Dobson et al., 2020; Garrison & Cook Hale, 2020; Hale et al., 2023). These ancient mounds are evidence of deep place-based knowledge developed over time by the multiple groups who lived in this region and are evidence of information exchange. Models predict that as sea level rise accelerates, Gulf waters will again move northward and ancient mound sites, originally constructed on dry land, will be endangered (Mehta & Skipton, 2019).

The lives of the Indigenous peoples of the Gulf region were profoundly affected by the arrival of Europeans, whose arrival caused widespread disruptions to communities in the region. This began in the early 16th century, with the violence and exploitation brought by the Spanish conquistador Hernando de Soto, whose army marched through territory in present-day Florida, Georgia, Alabama, and Mississippi searching for riches (Hudson, 1997; Knight, 2009; McKee & Schlenker, 1980). These disruptions throughout the region were varied and complex. The communities encountered by the Spaniards and other Europeans endured multiple disruptions and forced relocations and, with them, the loss of stable lifeways, village complexes, and their cultivated fields and farms. An example of profound loss is that of the Calusa people, or "Shell Indians." Prior to the 1500s, thousands of Indigenous Calusa people lived on Florida's Gulf Coast. They were a seafaring people with wide-reaching communication and trade networks that alerted them to the arrival of Spanish explorers in the Caribbean long before Spanish ships reached Florida in the 1630s. By the 1700s, after fighting European diseases and raids from non-Calusa people seeking to capture and profit from slavery, the Calusa disappeared as a distinct tribe (Granberry, 2011).

It has been suggested that these disruptions, more than actual colonization, were the pronounced legacy of the Spanish presence (Hoffman, 2002). For example, the Choctaw and Chickasaw groups, who were induced to fight as surrogates for warring European powers, suffered massive losses because of their involvement (Keller Reeves, 1985; Phelps, 1957). Many groups sought refuge from Europeans by retreating to swamps, wetlands, and bayous. The Acolapissa, another group that disappeared as a distinct tribe, moved to escape capture but was then decimated by European diseases (Kniffen et al., 1994, pp. 50–51). Other tribes, such as the Chitimacha, were directly attacked by European armies. In the case of the Chitimacha, this did not result in disappearance, but it did present an existential threat. Today, the Chitimacha Tribe maintains a small reservation and fosters the preservation of language, traditional cultural hunting, fishing, and foraging in local ecologies (Kniffen et al., 1994, pp. 55–56; Lee, 2022); it is one of the few federally recognized tribes in Louisiana.[1]

Following the U.S. war for independence (1775–1783), there was intense pressure from wealthy merchants, bankers, exporters, and plantation owners to transfer ownership of traditional tribal lands to settlers pushing into the southeastern coastal territories. The newly formed U.S. government

[1]A list of other federally recognized tribes is available at https://www.bia.gov/service/tribal-leaders-directory/federally-recognized-tribes

recruited European immigrants to settle on the frontier to deter resistance from Indigenous tribes, to defend against incursions from Spanish Mexico, and also to support the establishment of plantation economies. The ongoing effort to systematically displace once-stable tribal groups was official government policy, as in the Indian Removal Act of 1830, and from its earliest inception as a nation, the U.S. government showed itself willing to use overwhelming and relentless violence to achieve the goal of controlling land of the Indigenous groups (Ostler, 2015). One notorious example is a series of forced removals that are now described together as the "Trail of Tears." These were a direct application of the Indian Removal Act; begun in the 1830s, the policy resulted in a genocide and massive displacement in which thousands of Indigenous peoples were brutally forced to migrate from their homes in the southeast (Ostler, 2015). Among those displaced were approximately 5,000 Choctaw from present-day Mississippi territories to present-day Oklahoma, Arkansas, and Kansas (McKee & Schlenker, 1980, pp. 5–7, 14–15, 32–37, 76). By the mid-19th century, the Indigenous population of the U.S. Gulf Coast Region had been decimated. However, groups of Indigenous peoples—including Seminole people in Florida, the Mississippi Band of Choctaw in Mississippi, and the Houma people and other small tribes in Louisiana—remained in areas near the coast. This series of forced removals that comprise the "Trail of Tears" is seen by tribal communities as evidence that federal government-initiated resettlement may not serve the tribe's best interests.

Other groups have been affected by forced migration to the Gulf region. For example, the Acadians, a group of French immigrants to Nova Scotia in present-day Canada, were forcefully expelled from that region by British colonizers and, with offers of assistance from the Spanish government, ultimately settled in south Louisiana, where they established rural settlements in the Atchafalaya swamp and its basin, in the coastal wetlands, and in the coastal prairies in southwest Louisiana. The Spanish settlers envisioned Acadian settlements as buffers against British intrusions from upstream on the Mississippi River. The Acadian immigrants brought with them hunting and trapping skills and adapted their farming techniques to the different ecologies of semi-tropical Louisiana. Unable to raise wheat on drained fields, as they had in Acadia, they pursued small-scale agriculture on the natural levee of the Mississippi River and intermarried with Indigenous peoples (MacLeod, 2016, p. 124). They incorporated Indigenous and African foods, plants, music, languages, musical instruments, and modes of transport (pirogues) into what became one of Louisiana's most distinctive cultural and linguistic groups (Ancelet et al., 1991). This group's survival partly illustrates the power of traditional "social institutions and agricultural practices [to promote] economic self-sufficiency and group solidarity" (Brasseaux, 1992, p. 21; Faragher, 2005).

The Isleños comprise another group that has retained its identity despite forced migration. Isleños are conscripts into the Spanish army from the Spanish Canary Islands, who arrived in the late 1700s and were the most numerous Spanish speakers who arrived during the colonial period. Together, Acadian and Isleño immigrants added several thousand settlers to the population in the lower Mississippi River valley (Brasseaux, 1987; Din, 1988) and remain prominent ethnic communities. The enduring memory of forced displacements from Nova Scotia and the Spanish Canary Islands to Louisiana contributes to deeply rooted skepticism toward government-initiated resettlement discussions.

The specific fates of different groups have had effects that are evident today. One area of difference is tribal status. Federal tribal recognition can be a divisive and politically contested process. Though the U.S. government began to formally recognize tribal groups via the 1934 Indian Reorganization Act, many communities encountered political and judicial resistance to obtaining that recognition. For example, the Seminole people living in what is now Florida were able to resist the U.S. government's efforts to control their land, undertaken between 1817 and 1858. They sustained substantial losses but never surrendered or ceded lands to the United States (Perdue, 2012; Weisman, 2014). The small surviving population subsequently intermarried with other Gulf residents, and consequently, fewer individuals were officially recognized as members of the Seminole Tribe of Florida by the federal government in 1957.[2] Which is to say, because the Seminole people never surrendered or ceded lands to the United States and because hundreds of Seminole people are African-Indigenous, they are not listed in the U.S. Census as Seminole and so are not considered Seminole by the U.S. government, regardless of how their status is defined by the Seminole government.

This history of land loss—of displacement and forced relocation—is the basis for powerful cultural memories that are retained by residents throughout the Gulf region and influences responses to the climatic and environmental changes occurring on the Gulf Coast.

[2]The Seminole Tribe is a confederation of several tribal groups and was officially classified as "mixed race" by the U.S. government before being targeted by removal in three wars—the First Seminole War in 1816, the Second Seminole War in 1835, and the Third Seminole War in 1855—spurred by Andrew Jackson in 1816 (Kai, 2015). The "Dawes Rolls" determined who was eligible for tribal membership (National Archives, n.d.). Tribal rolls did not exist until the federal government instituted the recognition requirement acknowledging sovereignty status. More information is available at https://www.archives.gov/research/native-americans/dawes/tutorial/intro.html

ENSLAVEMENT

Millions of people were enslaved in the Gulf region before abolition in 1865. The institution of chattel slavery in the United States (1776–1865), the system in which people were classified and treated as legal property, transformed the region's social, economic, racial, and cultural legacy. In many Indigenous groups throughout the southeastern United States, the enslavement of war captives was customary both before and after European contact. Defeated warriors were often executed, but the young and old men were used as laborers, while women and young children were sold or traded to other tribes (Reséndez, 2016).

Unlike the enslavement of Indigenous peoples as a part of war, the enslavement of Africans was rooted in the broader economic exploitation that fueled colonization. European traders began forcibly shipping African people to the U.S. Gulf Coast Region in the 1500s, a practice that grew out of already-existing contact between European and African people: the crews of Christopher Columbus included African men, both free and enslaved (Clark, 2017). By the 1700s, French traders were bringing sizable numbers of African people to the lower Mississippi River valley (Hall, 1992).

Slavery was central to the colonization efforts of Spain, Britain, and France; each of these countries relied on the forced labor of enslaved Indigenous and African persons in the Gulf region. The most significant numbers of enslaved Africans along the Gulf Coast during the Spanish colonial era were in Louisiana (1763–1803 in Louisiana), where laborers cultivated the heavy delta soils (Hall, 1992). The French Company of the Indies brought nearly 6,000 enslaved individuals to Louisiana, relying on the knowledge of people from the Senegambia region of rice cultivation and processing techniques (Hall, 1992; Morris, 2012). Plantation slavery was essential to the success of rice, sugar, and cotton plantation economies in the areas that became Louisiana, Mississippi, and Alabama, as well as the economies of the ports that ringed the Gulf Coast.

The populations of enslaved persons grew rapidly, despite their harsh working conditions and often brutal treatment. Enslaved Africans soon outnumbered the non-enslaved population in many areas. For example, by 1763, there were 3,654 free people and 4,598 slaves in lower Louisiana, and the 1800 Census reported that the population included 19,852 free people and 24,264 enslaved people (Hall, 1992).[3] By the time of the Civil War, the numbers were substantial; see Table 4-1.

Slavery had complex effects on the people who were enslaved and those who sought to escape it; it also had countless other effects on life

[3]Categories enumerated by the U.S. Census have changed regularly since the first one was carried out in 1790. "Slave" was a category from that year until the 1860 Census; see https://www.pewresearch.org/interactives/what-census-calls-us/

TABLE 4-1 Enslaved Populations in Gulf States, 1860

Gulf State	Enslaved Population
Florida	61,753
Alabama	435,132
Mississippi	436,696
Louisiana	332,520
Texas	180,388

SOURCE: Mitchell, S. A. (1861). Map of the United States, and territories [Map]. Library of Congress Geography and Map Division. https://www.loc.gov/item/99447041/

in the region more generally. Along the Gulf and Atlantic coasts, centuries of exploration, colonization, and slavery by the Europeans created a new form of clandestine migration called maroonage, in which self-liberated African and Indigenous slaves called maroons fled plantations and found temporary, transitional, and semi-permanent refuge in the bayous, swamps, and forests (Diouf, 2014; Sayers, 2015).[4] More direct revolts against slavery also had lasting effects. The brutal *Code Noir* of Louisiana was developed in response to violent uprisings throughout the Gulf Coast (DeDecker, 2015; Din, 1980; Dormon, 1977; Lachance, 1994; Schwartz, 2015).[5] The code outlined punishments for enslaved persons who rebelled, including branding, amputation, or death, as well as restriction of communication (e.g., drums were banned) and limitations on travel, assemblage, and other forms of movement and gathering. The *Code Noir* also called for punitive isolation of communities and surveillance of men, women, and children. After emancipation (1865), these codes were adapted by so-called Sundown towns—all-White municipalities or neighborhoods that codified racial segregation, exclusion, and criminalization of non-White people (Loewen, 2005).

MIGRATION

Though forced displacement and slavery uprooted countless individuals and communities across a period of several hundred years, other kinds of migration have also affected the Gulf region. Following emancipation in 1865, Black citizens began migrating away from the southeastern United

[4]Wolf (1982, p. 156) points out how the English term "maroon" comes from the Spanish word "cimarrón," initially applied to escaped feral livestock, then to runaway Indigenous slaves, and finally to fugitive African slaves.

[5]More information about the *Code Noir* is available at https://lasc.libguides.com/c.php?g=254608&p=1697981

States, first moving toward urban centers within the region and then moving farther north in stages (Tolnay, 2003). Those who moved sought social and economic opportunities, but they were also responding to the physical, ecological, and economic devastation brought by the Civil War and to fading hopes for Reconstruction.

Similarly, the Great Migration (1910–1970) saw Black people move to northern, midwestern, and western states in order to pursue economic and educational opportunities; but the urge to move was also fueled by the urge to escape escalating racial violence and oppression in the post-Reconstruction era, the institution of Jim Crow laws, and the segregation of most aspects of daily life (Gregory, 2005; Tolnay, 2003). In the wake of Reconstruction's failure, White people quickly regained political power and imposed restrictions to prevent Black Americans from voting. Though the Fifteenth Amendment (ratified in 1870) granted Black men voting rights, efforts to exercise this right were met with literacy tests, poll taxes, or land ownership requirements.[6] Many voters who were able to meet "requirements" were threatened with loss of employment, violence to family, rape, castration, church burnings, and death (e.g., the Millican Massacre in Texas, 1868).[7] Lynching was a common tool used by White citizens to repress Black citizens' exercise of constitutional rights, including voting, in both northern and southern states. The Equal Justice Initiative (2017) report states, "During the period between the Civil War and World War II, thousands of African Americans were lynched in the United States. Lynchings were violent and public acts of torture that traumatized Black people throughout the country and were largely tolerated by state and federal officials" (p. 3). The Tuskegee Institute reported that 960 lynchings occurred in the Gulf Coast states between 1900 and 1931—years that fall within the Great Migration (American Map Company, 1931; cf. Tolnay & Beck, 1995). The failure of Reconstruction, persistent racialized violence, and the racial caste system of Jim Crow all fueled the Great Migration.

Another driver in post-Reconstruction migration was the Great Mississippi Flood of 1927, one of the largest human, environmental, and ecological disasters in the history of the United States. Responses to this flood amplified the harsh political, economic, and social realities of racism in the affected region. The flood submerged an estimated 27,000 square miles of land, and an estimated 335,000 people were displaced into Red Cross camps and subsequently to areas outside of the affected area (Barry, 1998). While the flood affected states up and down the river, the most extensive

[6]More information about requirements after Reconstruction is available at https://www.loc.gov/collections/civil-rights-history-project/articles-and-essays/voting-rights/

[7]More information about the Millican Massacre is available at https://today.tamu.edu/2022/02/23/remembering-the-millican-massacre/

damage occurred in Arkansas, Louisiana, and Mississippi. Altogether, the volume of this migration substantially altered both the cities outside the Gulf region to which people moved and the communities they left behind.

Apart from the Great Migration, it is also important to note the many groups of people moved into the Gulf region voluntarily to seek opportunity and flee disruption in their own home countries. These have included Haitian refugees fleeing both the French and Haitian revolutions in the late 1700s and early 1800s, as well as recent refugees from economic and political turmoil in Haiti. Many others have come from Central and Latin American countries. Various phases of immigration reform and restriction have influenced the immigration of Mexicans to Texas and other destinations. Following the overthrow of the Batista regime in 1959, groups from Cuba settled in south Florida and established communities (Wasem, 2009). Additionally, the banana trade, along with periodic political strife, economic turmoil, and tropical cyclones, prompted migration from Honduras. By 1990, New Orleans had the fourth largest number of self-identified Hondurans in the United States, and the Honduran community remains a distinctive enclave of the city (Sluyter et al., 2015).

The fall of the South Vietnam regime and withdrawal of U.S. forces in 1975 prompted a massive outmigration of Vietnamese citizens fearing reprisal from the North Vietnamese. This migration led to the re-formation of Vietnamese and other Southeast Asian communities throughout the Gulf Coast that have continued to grow. Over the past 50 years, Southeast Asians have become established in the region, remaining connected to original settlement locations such that concentration has enabled economic stability and mobility (Airriess & Clawson, 1991; Bankston & Zhou, 2021). As with other immigrant populations in the Gulf region, Southeast Asian culture and foodways have added to the distinctive character of the Gulf Coast. This stability has not been without challenge, however. Vietnamese communities and individuals often became targets of threats and racial violence and were wrongly accused of poaching (see community spotlight on Bayou La Batre in Chapter 5).

While the Great Migration impacted the demographics of the South and other regions where Black migrants settled, since the 1970s there has been a net in-migration of Blacks returning to the South. Dissatisfaction with urban life in the North, and improved racial, political, and economic opportunities provided motivation for this return flow, as did persistent cultural ties to the region (Leibbrand et al., 2019).

Despite this long history of violent removal and injustice, Indigenous, Black, Acadian, Hispanic, Latino, Caribbean, and Asian communities have established themselves in the U.S. Gulf Coast Region and engaged in economic activity rooted in the resources of its waterways. Although these communities are vibrant and have contributed in countless ways to the culture and economy of the Gulf region, many have also faced profound challenges in the present, such as those fleeing from Hurricane Katrina (2005) and the Deepwater Horizon disasters (2010), among others.

In this section, the committee has only been able to touch on a few key developments of the Gulf region's rich and complex history. An understanding of the unique history of each group will support successful planning for relocation and other climate mitigation efforts and the preservation of traditional and cultural practices, an issue the committee discusses further in Chapters 5, 6, and 7.

HISTORICAL LEGACIES

The history above is necessarily brief; for the purposes of this report, the committee wishes to highlight several enduring legacies that play important roles in the present. These specific historical legacies have implications today for communities that in many cases are already bearing the brunt of climate change effects: political disenfranchisement, economic injustice, and the role of place. While the focus below is on impacts within the Gulf states, the committee stresses that these legacies have occurred in their own ways in other parts of the United States.

As discussed above, the Gulf region has experienced invasion and colonization as well as the exploitation and commoditization of human beings through enslavement and land-use practices. The region's communities of Indigenous, Black, Asian, Hispanic, Latino, and Caribbean people have been underresourced and subject to discrimination, violence, forced relocation, and other injustices. This history has resulted in degraded social and ecological resources and has rendered Gulf residents vulnerable to environmental changes and, in many cases, compromised their political power when decisions were being made. These issues are an important backdrop for the remainder of the report, which discusses strategies for devising optimal relocation efforts.

Political Disenfranchisement

The starkest cause of political disenfranchisement was institutionalized slavery, a system under which enslaved people were not granted citizenship. Additionally, restriction of voting rights denied Black citizens the ability to participate in civic affairs and government decision making, which has had direct implications for their capacity to contribute to deliberations about management of land and resources and responses to environmental challenges (see above for the discussion of strategies used to keep Black people from voting). Historically, and up to the present day, state legislatures continue to pass voting laws that can limit the political representation of minority groups (Okonta, 2018).[8] With the completion of the 2020 Census, new battles have developed over the redrawing of district boundaries that decrease the number of congressional seats in Black majority districts in Georgia, Alabama, Mississippi, and Louisiana.[9]

Economic Injustice

There has been significant poverty and economic disadvantage in the U.S. Gulf Coast Region for centuries. A thorough exploration of its economic history is beyond the scope of this report, but without a doubt, the enslavement of Indigenous and African peoples was a primary factor in the economic disadvantages that have persisted to the present day in many parts of the United States. In strictly economic terms, the people who were enslaved for over 400 years were not compensated and did not have the opportunity to accumulate wealth across generations (this is further discussed in the section below on Geographic Vulnerability), resulting in high poverty rates across the Gulf Coast states. As of 2021, the estimated percentage of the population in poverty is 16 percent in Alabama, 13 percent in Florida, 20 percent in Louisiana, 19 percent in Mississippi, and 14 percent in Texas.[10]

In the Gulf region, as elsewhere in the South, employment opportunities open to Black Americans after emancipation were menial and poorly paid. Those who labored as sharecroppers found it nearly impossible to escape the economic bondage of that system (Aiken, 2003). Lack of access to jobs paying a living wage, credit from financial institutions, and opportunities to own real estate and other wealth that could be passed on perpetuated poverty. Inadequate education in substandard schools denied Black students opportunities and benefits of citizenship.

This legacy of disadvantage has environmental implications. For example, a 2006 study mapped social vulnerability to multiple hazards across most of the Gulf Coast (Cutter & Emrich, 2006). The scores were particularly high along the western coast of Florida and the full breadth of the Louisiana and Texas coasts.

[8] More information is available at https://www.brennancenter.org/our-work/research-reports/voting-laws-roundup-june-2023

[9] More information is available at "Congressional district maps implemented after the 2020 census": https://ballotpedia.org/Congressional_district_maps_implemented_after_the_2020_census

[10] More information, including the number of children in poverty in 2021, is available at https://data.ers.usda.gov/reports.aspx?ID=17826

Geographic Isolation and the Preservation of Culture

As our brief review of the history of migration demonstrates, individuals and communities have been forced to relocate for varied reasons almost as long as humans have lived in the Gulf Region. But whether a group moved long ago or more recently, whether it left or remained in place, many distinct cultural groups—especially economically disadvantaged ones—became geographically isolated and faced discrimination. Geographic isolation has generally made many communities more vulnerable to climate-related challenges; at the same time, it has often also allowed many groups to preserve their cultural heritage and resist assimilation.

Some Indigenous communities are among the most isolated and underresourced groups in the Gulf Region. Many Indigenous communities retreated into the coastal marshes during the colonial and federal removal periods to escape warfare, disease, and enslavement. While formal recognition via the 1934 Indian Reorganization Act provides autonomy over important decisions such as those about the protection and use of land and other resources, as well as access to federal services and resources, obtaining recognition was often difficult if not impossible for myriad reasons.[11] The territory that many Indigenous groups occupy is composed of coastal wetlands that have been threatened by land loss. In Louisiana, this includes Indigenous groups such as the Isle de Jean Charles Band of Biloxi-Chitimacha-Choctaw, the United Houma Nation, the Pointe-au-Chien Indian Tribe, and the Grand Bayou community. The Isle de Jean Charles, a narrow island that is disappearing into the coastal marshes of Louisiana, has been home to members of several of these tribes and is currently undergoing a relocation project (see Chapter 3). Additionally, many tribal groups have also faced the desecration and destruction of sacred sites and graveyards by academic institutions, commercial development, and infrastructure projects.[12]

In general, cultural insularity increases group identification, even as it tends to diminish residents' political influence and constrain their participation in deliberations about the places they live (Arreola, 2002; Leong et al., 2007). The committee considers it important to emphasize the benefits that often come with the establishment of distinct communities that have a geographic home. These benefits include not only increased group identification but also the preservation of language, customs, foodways, and economic practices that interact with the ecosystem, such as the utilization of marine

[11]Although the National Congress of American Indians has advocated for a speedier process, the process of obtaining federal recognition as a tribe can take many years and requires groups to meet complex criteria.

[12]More information is available in the article "The Nation's Top Universities and Museums Still Have the Remains of Thousands of Native Americans": https://www.wnycstudios.org/podcasts/takeaway/segments/museums-and-universities-native-americans

resources. Other groups have historically been forced into cultural enclaves in remote places; for example, as discussed above, Acadian immigrants and their descendants adapted their housing, foodways, livelihoods, and methods of agriculture to the local Indigenous ecologies of southern Louisiana (Comeaux, 1978). Alongside this adaptation, however, the Acadian community's isolation from other European groups was critical for retaining the French language and Catholicism in a region increasingly populated by English-speaking Protestants after 1812. Although persecuted for speaking French in Louisiana's public schools during the early 20th century, Acadian communities have retained cultural traits, foodways and lifeways, and self-identify as a distinct population. Similarly, the Vietnamese fishing families who migrated to this area in the wake of the Vietnam War have established ethnic enclaves in coastal communities from Texas to Florida, where they live among others who speak their language and share their cultural traditions (see community spotlight on Bayou La Batre in Chapter 5).

Minority and ethnic groups have also often experienced cultural isolation in urban areas, which, as above, has led to a stronger sense of group identity and has also rendered them vulnerable to discrimination. As Black families moved from rural areas into cities, Jim Crow laws and redlining (systematic denial of financial resources or housing access based on race) limited access to financial markets and housing. Such discriminatory lending practices that were sanctioned by the federal government further entrenched segregation even after the earlier practices were deemed illegal by court decisions (Delaney, 1998; Zhu et al., 2022). Black residents established their own communities (Ueland & Warf, 2006). These communities often became hubs for Black entrepreneurship, churches, social institutions, and schools (Inwood, 2011). Yet, policies and lending practices in many cities contributed to a lack of public investment in Black neighborhoods (Zhu et al., 2022). Official designation of the urban territories available for Black residences and deed covenants reinforced the limitations imposed by individual developers (Colten, 2005). White flight from urban centers to suburbs in the latter half of the 20th century reinforced the residential segregation across the region. Although residential segregation is highest in metropolitan areas outside of the South (e.g., Melish, 1998; Ross, 2018), the persistence of segregation and its implications for Southern communities and their residents must be acknowledged. Within-place segregation has diminished in the United States since the 1990s (and in the South since the 1970s) while the expansion of between-place segregation has increased, thereby preserving racial segregation at a larger scale (Hwang & McDaniel, 2022; Iceland et al., 2013; Lichter et al., 2015).

Other groups, including immigrants from Cuba, Mexico, and Honduras, also established urban communities in such cities as Tampa, Miami, New Orleans, Corpus Christi, and Houston. As in Black communities, these enclaves provided a space where traditional cultures thrived but generally had poor quality housing, infrastructure, and educational facilities. These ethnic enclaves have contributed to both a psychological and institutional barrier to full participation in deliberations about relocation, even as (and because) this relative isolation has allowed for a larger degree of cultural preservation (see Chapter 7).

A community testimonial the committee heard in Houma, Louisiana, expresses the idea that benefits of cultural isolation are associated with the establishment of communities that have a stable geographic home; see Box 4-2.

Geographic Vulnerability

This history of forced migration has given rise to major social and economic injustices that have long characterized much of the Gulf region. One significant consequence is a stark disparity in the safety and security of the places people live, in terms of both environment and quality of housing. As noted above, many groups, beginning with those Indigenous to the region, have been forced to move, often to areas that were distant from traditional hunting and fishing grounds, sacred sites, foraging and gathering sites, and water or forest landscapes that would have been utilized for cultural and subsistence resources. This rendered these groups vulnerable to the loss of cultural knowledge, practices, and, ultimately, identity. Furthermore, such

BOX 4-2
Community Testimonial: Bette Billiot, the United Houma Nation

"Thank you all for being here on the land of the United Houma Nation. Indigenous peoples have called this land home for literally thousands of years, and I want you to understand how special this place is. There is human-made architecture in coastal Louisiana that is older than the pyramids of Giza. And if there are so—and there are so few places in the entire world that monumental architecture of that scale predates agriculture. Coastal Louisiana, as you may already know, was built by the Mississippi River, and as long as the land has been there, so have the Indigenous peoples. Thousands of years of history living and being in this beautiful land, the Houma, the BCCM [Biloxi Chitimacha Confederation of Muskogees], the Pointe-au-Chien, the Tunica Biloxi, and the Chitimacha are—and so many other tribes whose names have been lost to time. We the—we are the original inhabitants of this land, and while land acknowledgments are great, it would be great to give the land back."

SOURCE: Bette Billiot, the United Houma Nation. Workshop 3: Assisted Resettlement and Receiving Communities in Louisiana, July 2022, Houma, Louisiana.

relocation has often lessened physical safety. The safest real estate in settled areas, including small towns and large cities located in better-drained areas or on higher ground, has typically been acquired by White residents (Ueland & Warf, 2006), who could more easily secure clear legal title to the property. Especially in larger urban areas, the discriminatory practices described above (including deed covenants and redlining practices) led not only to geographic isolation and racially segregated neighborhoods but also to housing vulnerability. Often relegated to low-lying, flood-prone sections of Gulf-region cities, Black and other minority residents faced higher flood risks and other environmental challenges. Such policies and practices excluded Black residents from buying in safer locations until the late 20th century (Colten, 2005; Delaney, 1998). Furthermore, the lower value of houses in these segregated neighborhoods has impeded the ability of minority homeowners to assemble adequate equity to relocate inland if desired (Morris & Diaz, 2020; Van Zandt et al., 2012).

Public utilities and flood protection have excluded minority groups; for example, the Louisiana Master Plan for a Sustainable Coast has excluded some Indigenous communities (Dalbom et al., 2014) and the Mid-Barataria Sediment Diversion project threatens the livelihoods of ethnic oyster farmers and shrimp and crab fishermen (U.S. Army Corps of Engineers, 2022). This vulnerability is magnified by recent adjustments in the National Flood Insurance Program through the new Risk Rating 2.0 methodology (see Chapter 10) that will increase the cost of flood insurance premiums for some properties[13] and may make selling houses in high-risk locations more difficult, thereby reducing the value of homeowners' property. Housing in many flood-prone areas is of poor quality, and many communities have insufficient resources for evacuation when storms arrive or to rebuild after a disaster (Bullard & Wright, 2009).

One housing and community concern mentioned frequently by workshop participants is the threat of "climate gentrification"—the displacement of low-income residents and people of color for the construction of high-priced housing for wealthy families. This phenomenon, which has its roots in historical legacies and is not unique to the Gulf region (Best et al., 2023), occurred in New Orleans following Hurricane Katrina (Aune et al., 2020) and is evident in coastal Louisiana and other areas of the Gulf where modest homes are replaced by expensive "camps" used by affluent sportsmen.[14] The barrier islands across the Gulf Coast are subject to displacement of

---

[13]More information is available at https://www.fema.gov/flood-insurance/risk-rating

[14]Comments made to the committee on June 26 and 28, 2022, during public information-gathering sessions in Louisiana. More information is available at https://www.nationalacademies.org/our-work/managed-retreat-in-the-us-gulf-coast-region#sectionPastEvents

service workers and fishing families for condominiums and high-priced residences (Anguelovski et al., 2019).

SUMMARY

The Gulf region comprises varied landscapes and ecosystems that have been occupied for millennia by peoples who have moved, both willingly and through forced relocation. These peoples have continually adapted to changing environmental circumstances, despite enduring profound injustices and brutality. They have established deep and lasting relationships with the places they occupy, making livings and refining their understanding of changing climatic and environmental conditions. Legacies of economic and political injustice have increased the vulnerability of coastal communities and sapped their confidence in government motives and assistance. The committee's conclusions about the subjects covered in this chapter are below.

CONCLUSIONS

Conclusion 4-1: After European conquest and the extermination and enslavement of Africans and Indigenous peoples in the Gulf region, the Indian Removal Act of 1830 began an institutionalized process of displacement and forced migration of Indigenous peoples from their homelands. Other groups in the region have histories of forced migrations and displacement (e.g., people from Acadia, Vietnam, Cuba). Descendants of these groups that currently face the prospects of relocation report that historical injustices influence their response to current climatic and environmental changes on the Gulf Coast.

Conclusion 4-2: In Gulf communities, many of which are often poor, racial power imbalances do not reflect constituent populations and therefore undermine community agency. The long-term, historical dynamics of disenfranchisement and disengagement are at the core of discussions about relocation.

5

Current Realities of the Gulf Coast

This chapter discusses the following:

- U.S. Gulf Coast Region social and economic demographics and associated risks
- In-migration to the U.S. Gulf Coast Region and Gulf coastal shoreline communities
- Reasons why people live in this region, including place attachment and other economic and social factors
- Brief profiles of six Gulf Coast communities that include quantitative information from federal agency datasets (e.g., Federal Emergency Management Agency [FEMA], Centers for Disease Control and Prevention [CDC], U.S. Environmental Protection Agency [EPA]) about flood and other environmental hazards, social vulnerability, health, environmental justice issues, and the impacts of recent tropical cyclones interspersed; the profiles also include community testimonials about these issues

INTRODUCTION

The committee sought to understand the Gulf Coast simultaneously as a region of deep and diverse cultural and social ties to community and place, a key producer of fossil fuels and petrochemical products and services, a destination for recreationists and retirees, a region with cutting-edge research centers and universities, a major source of marine resources and fisheries, and a harbinger of the nation's experience with the effects of climate change. In many respects, the U.S. Gulf Coast is a distinctive region with unique demographic, economic, environmental, and social conditions. At the same time, it reflects processes and conditions that occur in coastal regions throughout the country. The history reviewed in the previous chapter reveals Gulf Coast communities' deep attachment to the land, even as they endured forced migration to and from the region. This chapter functions as a complement to the previous chapter's long-term historical view and will offer a more contemporary view of the present human condition along the Gulf Coast. To do this, it first reviews the current demographics and migration patterns that are presently shaping risk in this dynamic region. As the population grows mainly along the shore, despite the risks, the committee considers it essential to understand and account for the strong attachments to place that are based in histories, livelihoods, and local cultures. Additionally, this chapter examines economics and commerce as factors in shaping life and society in the region. Finally, it concludes with a series of community profiles from across the Gulf Region that couples the scale of the threat of displacement (introduced in Chapter 2) with existing socioeconomic, health, and environmental justice datasets. The community profiles are of communities the committee engaged during workshops and webinars in each Gulf state.

Gulf Coast Demographics

The Brookings Institution created maps based on 2020 Census data that reflect coastal counties with significant "non-White" populations (defined as counties with ethnic groups exceeding the national average for that group).[1] Coastal counties in Texas and Florida reflect significant Latino or Hispanic populations. Alabama, Mississippi, and Louisiana coastal counties have sizable Black populations. Southeast Texas and Terrebonne Parish, Louisiana, reflect large populations that self-identify as belonging to two or more racial groups (Frey, 2021). Data from the American Community Survey (ACS) and the 2010 U.S. Census showed that throughout the Gulf Coast, Hispanics or Latinos make up the largest racial or ancestry group after White, reported as over 29 percent in 2010 (LSU AgCenter, 2012). African Americans represent the second largest race or ancestry group at 19 percent of the total population. Asians represent almost 3 percent of the population. Indigenous peoples represent about two-thirds of 1 percent.

[1]More information about the Brookings Institution's diversity maps is available at https://www.brookings.edu/articles/mapping-americas-diversity-with-the-2020-census/

Individuals identifying as White constituted 64 percent of the population (LSU AgCenter, 2012).

Gulf Coast Economies and Associated Risks

Population distributions across the Gulf Coast are a mixture of high- and low-density communities. Major urban agglomerations (e.g., Tampa/St. Petersburg, Mobile, New Orleans, Houston) are hubs for an array of urban services, including finance, medicine, education, and entertainment. A number of smaller cities (e.g., Pensacola, Biloxi, Gulfport, Houma, Lake Charles, Galveston, Corpus Christi) depend on ports and shipbuilding, the military, gaming, and petroleum-related industries. Smaller coastal communities depend on commercial fishing and oil and mineral extraction, and have also evolved into retirement and tourism enclaves.

From the extraction of fossil fuels to the abundance of marine life, natural resources lie at the heart of many economies of Gulf Coast communities. This section details several ways in which these communities are economically impacted by and vulnerable to changes in the environment, major weather events, and climate change. A coastal economic vulnerability index noted that within the territory from the central panhandle of Florida to Galveston Bay, the coasts of Terrebonne, Lafourche, and Plaquemines parishes were the most economically vulnerable (Thatcher et al., 2013). Key factors in defining economic vulnerability were physical exposure to coastal hazards and a concentration of economic infrastructure. Lower Lafourche Parish has substantial offshore mineral industry infrastructure at Port Fourchon, plus a highly exposed physical setting. Adjacent Terrebonne Parish has both mineral and fisheries infrastructure and low-lying topography. Southeast Texas and southwest Louisiana also had elevated scores in the index with their concentration of petrochemical industry infrastructure. These locations tend to have modest economic diversity, which could accentuate vulnerability. In contrast, low vulnerability tends to exist in locations with low population density and urban development, along with lower physical exposure, such as the Mississippi and Alabama coasts (Thatcher et al., 2013).

Natural resource-based economies depend on adequate resources. Humans pursue those resources, deploy technology to gather them efficiently, and market those products. The Gulf of Mexico is productive with numerous forms of commercial marine life: shrimp, crabs, oysters, menhaden, and mullet, along with numerous types of sport fish. These marine species have supported commercial fisheries since the 19th century and have suffered overfishing in the past. Conservation policies enacted since the late 19th century sought to protect these marine populations to ensure sustainable fisheries. Policies limiting the seasons and regulating harvest gears improve the abundance and distribution of target species, although fishing families have found some regulations to impede customary practices, thus forcing adaptations to traditional livelihoods (Colten, 2014).

Environmental conditions directly impact the economic viability of coastal communities. Additionally, these conditions are often affected by human activity, both in terms of pollution and clean up. Nutrients transported into the Gulf from farm fields in the upper Mississippi River basin have contributed to a chronic seasonal hypoxic zone in the Gulf that impacts marine life. Pollution from industry and cities has disrupted fisheries in Apalachee and Galveston bays, and algal blooms and red tides are disruptive off the coast (Kennicutt, 2017; United Nations Environment Programme, 2018). Proposed coastal restoration projects in Louisiana would impact shrimp and oyster production (Parker, 2022; Schleifstein, 2023). In addition to the impacts of environmental conditions on the economic viability of coastal communities, fisher families are facing increased competition from farm-raised shrimp in Asia and high fuel costs, which makes shrimping a marginal livelihood (Bourgeois et al., 2016; Marks, 2012). Subsistence fishing of shrimp and mullet is also important to local diets and culture (Burley, 2010; Mayer et al., 2015; Zacks, 2019). These natural-resource economic pursuits are important locally and do not have an assured future.

While agriculture is a vital component of the economies of the Gulf Coast states, the coastal shoreline counties are seldom among the top agricultural counties (other than aquaculture). Ranching is found in coastal counties in Texas and Louisiana, where extreme heat can stress dairy cows and livestock (Carter et al., 2014) and water inundation can become fatally deep for some calves (Gustin, 2017). Pine plantations exist from Florida to Louisiana; however, tropical cyclones can have a profound impact on pine forests, croplands, and grazing lands. Strong winds can topple trees and destroy a slow-growing crop. Sugar cane in Texas and Louisiana can suffer destruction during hurricanes as well. Meanwhile, rising sea levels mean that saltwater intrusion threatens aquifers used by rice farmers in Louisiana and Texas for flooding their fields (McClain, 2003; Zhang, 2020).

The oil and gas industry is an important component of Gulf Coast economies, but it faces serious risks from rising seas and more intense storms. This industry includes both oil extraction, mostly offshore, and transport and processing in key petrochemical hubs near Houston, Lake Charles, and New Orleans. The combination of rising sea levels and intensifying storms can threaten operations near the coast, particularly around Galveston Bay, Port Arthur, Lake Charles, and downstream from New Orleans (Hemmerling, Barra et al., 2020). For example, tropical cyclones can damage or disrupt the petrochemical infrastructure on the Gulf Coast. They can also prompt temporary shutdowns of oil and gas platforms, including the evacuation of personnel, in order to minimize harm to personnel and facilities. Such shutdowns affect local workers and are also disruptive to the national petroleum supply chain.

In addition to its susceptibility to storm disruptions, the oil and gas industry has a record of boom and bust economic cycles (Brown et al., 2011; Gramling & Brabant, 1986). Activity soars when global prices are high and sags when prices sink. This causes economic and social stress to communities dependent on these industries (see Figure 5-1).

Oil releases from offshore operations and tanker spills, caused by natural events, have disrupted commercial fisheries since the 1930s and negatively affected recreational activities (Colten et al., 2012, 2015). Damage to industrial facilities during Hurricane Katrina released hazardous materials and petroleum, and the overall disruption to production in the region caused a spike in gasoline prices (Santella et al., 2010). Damage in the Houston/Galveston Bay region during recent hurricanes also caused damage and fires at industrial facilities (Misuri et al., 2019). Lake Charles refineries also experienced damage that contributed to the emission of chemicals due to Hurricane Laura (Schwartz & Tabuchi, 2020). Thus, while oil and gas have strong support from state governments in Louisiana and Texas, the eastern Gulf Coast states are wary of the damage this economic sector can cause to their recreational economies (Hedden, 2020; Nelson & Grubesic, 2018).

CLIMATE CHANGE AND RECENT/PROJECTED MIGRATION TOWARD AND AWAY FROM THE COAST

According to the 2010 U.S. Census, 23,802,699 people lived in coastal shoreline counties in the Gulf region (National Oceanic and Atmospheric Administration [NOAA], 2013). Florida has more than 14 million residents living in shoreline counties (Gulf and Atlantic coasts combined), followed by Texas, where over 6 million people live in shoreline counties (as shown in Table 5-1). Alabama and Mississippi have narrow coasts with multiple bays and inlets, and together they have fewer than 1 million residents in shoreline counties. Louisiana has a larger, less habitable coastline, where over 2 million people live in shoreline counties.

In-Migration to the U.S. Gulf Coast Region and Gulf Coastal Shoreline Communities

Increased population density increases risks to people, infrastructure, and ecologies. NOAA reported that coastal population growth rates outpaced those of inland areas, with 123.3 million (39% of the U.S. total) people living in coastal shoreline counties. Florida and Texas have seen the

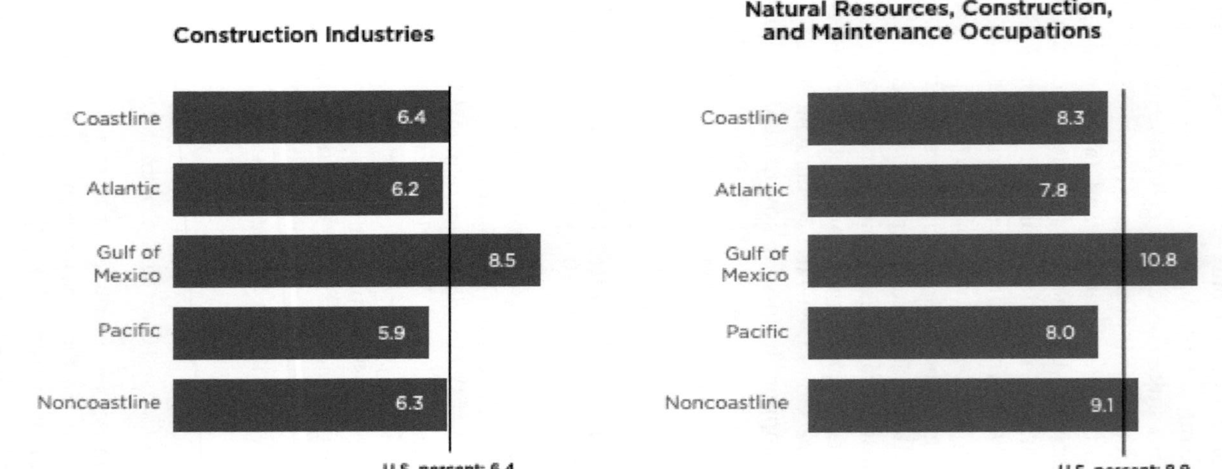

FIGURE 5-1 Among coastal regions, the Gulf of Mexico had the highest percentage of the workforce in construction industries and in natural resources, construction, and maintenance occupations.
SOURCE: U.S. Census Bureau. (2019). *Coastline America*. https://www.census.gov/library/visualizations/2019/demo/coastline-america.html

most dramatic population growth in shoreline Gulf counties (U.S. Census Bureau, 2021b; see Table 5-1). In-migration caused Florida's total population to nearly triple from 6.8 million in 1970 to 22 million in 2020 (U.S. Census Bureau, 2021b). Growth was pronounced in the coastal shoreline counties, where the growth rate was 165 percent between 1970 and 2010 (NOAA, 2013). The Tampa-St. Petersburg-Clearwater metropolitan statistical area grew from 1 million in 1970 to over 3.1 million in 2020 (U.S. Census Bureau, n.d.; U.S. Department of Commerce, 1972).

Texas' statewide population more than doubled from 11.2 million in 1970 to 29.1 million in 2020. The state's coastal shoreline counties registered a 107 percent growth between 1970 and 2010 (NOAA, 2013; U.S. Census Bureau, 2021b). The Houston-The Woodlands-Sugar Land metropolitan statistical area, which includes Galveston, grew from 2.2 million in 1970 to over 7.1 million in 2020 (Texas Real Estate Research Center, 2022).

Louisiana's shoreline population growth between 1970 and 2010 was the smallest of the five Gulf Coast states, with a high percentage of elderly residents, many of whom retired and chose to stay at their current locales.

Other coastal metropolitan areas, such as Pensacola, Mobile, Biloxi-Gulfport, and Corpus Christi, also reported significant growth (Macrotrends, 2023; Mississippi Regional Economic Analysis Project, 2023). Upward projection of current trends and the amplification of existing trends portend upward trends for other Gulf Coast cities facing more intense tropical cyclones and sea level rise.

The impact on human and ecological communities in the aftermath of tropical cyclones, in conjunction with social and economic factors, has significantly impacted coastal population growth trends. A common pattern of demographic change in the U.S. Gulf Coast Region is the continuation, acceleration, and exacerbation of current trends (e.g., urban renewal,

TABLE 5-1 2010 Population for Shoreline Counties Along the Gulf Coast and Percentage of Population Change Between 1970 and 2010

State	Shoreline County Population	% of Population Change 1970–2010	% Change Over 65 Years of Age 1970–2010	% Living in Poverty
Alabama	595,257	58	702	17
Florida	14,468,197	165	208	13
Louisiana	2,2247,053	23	89	16
Mississippi	370,702	54	202	15
Texas	6,121,490	107	198	18

SOURCE: NOAA. (2013). *State of the coast: National Coastal Population Report, Population trends from 1970 to 2020.* https://aambpublicoceanservice.blob.core.windows.net/oceanservice prod/facts/coastal-population-report.pdf

gentrification, rural depopulation) following major storms, which contributes to an increase in population in those areas that can offset short-term decreases in population immediately after the storm.

Florida, for example, has experienced short-lived population departures from coastal areas following major storms. The panhandle region registered a delayed out-migration in 1996 after Hurricane Opal in 1995, but over the course of several years, there was also in-migration, which offset the departures. The 2005 hurricane season in Florida followed multiple storms in 2004. Home sales in southwest Florida declined, but the downward trend was not long-lived (National Association of Realtors, 2006). Following Hurricane Ivan (2004), Pensacola, Florida, showed higher price trends from larger and expensive homes sold immediately after the storm and speculations of wealthy vacation owners inclined to sell and withdraw from the market (National Association of Realtors, 2006).

Population growth after major storms is not always the case, however. New Orleans had been experiencing population loss since the 1960s. In 2000 the population of New Orleans was 484,674 but fell by more than 50 percent by 2006 (Hurricane Katrina occurred in 2005; Plyer, 2016), with significant loss occurring in the city's center (Zaninetti & Colten, 2012). Importantly, population change via migration in one community suggests change in other communities, and much of the post-Hurricane Katrina movement was to and from nearby areas within the region (Curtis et al., 2015; Fussell et al., 2014). Hurricanes Laura (2020) and Ida (2021) prompted some residents to relocate, although there was not complete abandonment of towns and other factors have contributed to the chronic rural depopulation in the region (Mitchell, 2023). In southeast Louisiana, migration has occurred mostly among those with the means (i.e., wealth, job opportunities, etc.) to relocate inland. Elderly and minority populations remain as younger and more mobile individuals move away from the coast (Hemmerling, 2017).

In more extreme cases of storm impact on population, numerous coastal towns across the Gulf have been "depopulated" by storms throughout the Gulf's history. For example, the once thriving port of Indianola, Texas, fell victim to hurricanes in 1875 and again in 1886, which forced citizens to abandon the town. Cheniere Caminada, Louisiana, a small fishing village, experienced gradual abandonment effort after an 1893 storm. Galveston, Texas, however, launched a major rebuilding and fortification after a devastating 1900 hurricane. Biloxi-Gulfport, Mississippi, also rebounded after Hurricane Camille in 1969 and Hurricane Katrina in 2005 (Colten & Giancarlo, 2011). It is important to note that severe weather events alone rarely cause complete abandonment of older, larger legacy communities. However, when combined with other social, economic, and political factors, severe weather events contribute to the process of displacement.

Receiving communities often lack the support or political, social, and economic resources to prepare for influxes of displaced, traumatized families in need of social services like health care, education, infrastructure (housing, roads, etc.), and employment support. The tendency for unsustainable growth and development (e.g., St. Tammany Parish, Louisiana, building in floodplains; Hickey, 2022) is compounded by a lack of broader regional plans to help guide population shifts (Vock, 2021).

Hauer et al. have projected demographic changes for coastal locations facing sea level rise by 2100. Their research indicates that the Tampa-St. Petersburg metropolitan area (site of Workshop 3) is a U.S. Gulf Coast Region that may experience "serious levels of population impact" and risk of decline under a 1.8 sea level rise scenario (Hauer et al., 2016, p. 693). Alabama, Texas, Mississippi, and Louisiana also are projected to see populations at risk of decline. In a follow-up study, Hauer (2017) projected considerable population departures from southwest Florida and southeast Louisiana, as opposed to fewer departures from the Florida Panhandle, southern Alabama and Mississippi, and coastal Texas (with the exception of the Houston metro area). Significantly, Hauer's research suggests that not all coastal areas will see future mass out-migration, as explained below. For example, local topography and deliberate adaptation measures might offer protection in some locations, thereby potentially mitigating the need to move away from the coast. Study scenarios suggest that future inland migration will likely flow toward nearby cities. For departures from the Gulf Coast, the study projects inland cities such as Orlando, Atlanta, and Austin as receiving cities (Hauer, 2017).

Louisiana, with its exceptionally vulnerable coastline and compromised barrier islands (primarily used for recreation and fishing), is already experiencing inland migration and has been for some time. By using post office closures as a measure of depopulation, Hemmerling (2017) has shown a gradual migration since the 19th century. Notable pulses of population decline followed major storms from 2000 to 2010. Inland movement among Louisiana's coastal residents, those with deep family ties and place-based relationships, has tended to be modest shifts "up the bayou" where migrants can still live supported by familial and cultural ties (Colten et al., 2018; Hemmerling, 2017; see Box 5-1). These movements have not been coordinated or assisted by government programs. In fact, from a comparative perspective across the Gulf region, Louisiana has the lowest in-migration rates, and migration is largely within the state. Data released by the U.S. Census Bureau report that between April 1, 2020, and July 1, 2022, 67,508 residents left Louisiana (Skinner, 2022; U.S. Census Bureau, 2023b).

REASONS WHY PEOPLE LIVE ON THE GULF COAST

Several factors contribute to modern settlement along the Gulf Coast. Prior to 1900, coastal settlements were founded in areas where trade,

BOX 5-1
Community Testimonial: Migrating up the Bayou

"Migration is a part of our history. It's something that, as coastal residents, that our families have been doing for an awful long time. So, this isn't necessarily anything new. This isn't our first rodeo with this experience. Most of our people migrate one town north up the same watershed. And I'm an example of that, in my family over the past three generations. And so, my dad grew up in Cocodrie, which is the town that is the furthest down the bayou [...] And so, he grew up in a town the furthest down the bayou. He and my mom got married, and then moved to Chauvin, one town north. Hurricane Juan in 1985 put two feet of water in our house, and that's when our parents—my parents decided to look for land that was a little bit higher. So, while the water was high, they drove around and found that Bourg was the highest bit of land that they saw. And they said this is where we're going to buy property and build our home. And so, they did. But then, when it came time for me to buy a house, I went up the same watershed and moved to Houma. Now, again, in terms of those watersheds, Terrebonne Parish has five bayous. So, if I'm in Cocodrie and moving to Chauvin, then I'm moving to Bourg. If I'm in Cocodrie, I'm not moving to Montegut, and I'm not moving to Dulac, I'm moving up the same watershed, right."

SOURCE: Jonathan Foret, Executive Director, South Louisiana Wetlands Discovery Center. Workshop 3: Assisted Resettlement and Receiving Communities in Louisiana, July 2022, Houma, Louisiana.

shipping, and natural resources provided livelihoods (Davis, 2017) and local resource extraction drove economies, beginning with agricultural exports (rice, sugar, and cotton), forest resources (pine, cypress, oak, cedar, and naval stores), fishing, and oil and gas. Since the mid-20th century, beaches, recreation, and warm-weather retirement, and more recently gaming, have fueled rapid development in Texas, Mississippi, Alabama, and Florida (Davis, 2017; Meyer-Arendt, 1987). Additionally, the U.S. Gulf Coast Region broadly (i.e., coastal and inland) has the highest percentage of the workforce in construction industries and in natural resources, construction, and maintenance occupations as compared with other coastal regions in the United States (see Figure 5-1, above). In some cases, land allotments (i.e., reservations) for federally recognized tribes are instrumental for Indigenous peoples to remain on or near traditional lands in the coastal region (Parfait, 2019). This section first identifies *place attachment* as a factor in decisions to stay or move away and looks at various forms this attachment takes; it then briefly reviews other factors shown to influence decisions around relocation.

Place Attachment

Place attachment presents both practical and psychological barriers to relocation alongside obstacles such as a lack of economic opportunities and a distrust of top-down relocation options (Chapters 4 and 7). Broadly, "place attachment" refers to the relationship between people, place, and process (i.e., ways individuals and groups relate to a place; Scannell & Gifford, 2010) and can be understood in terms of an emotional bond between people and their environments (Masterson et al., 2017). Individuals develop personal connections to place, whereas groups develop social meanings associated with place via, for example, ancestral and social structural ties, religious sentiment and rituals, historic events, material and livelihood connections, and other expressive cultural forms such as names, stories, songs, and visual art, all of which comprise communities' senses of place (Amundsen, 2015; Feld & Basso, 1996; Thornton, 2008). The environment in and of itself gives form to the social meaning of place and thus informs place attachment (Stedman, 2003).

Scholars have conceptualized place attachment in multiple ways, including sense of place, place identity, place making, place dependence, topophilia, and rootedness (DeMiglio & Williams, 2008; Gurney et al., 2017; Khalil & Jacobs, 2021; Low & Altman, 1992; Tuan, 1980; Ujang, 2012). Some scholars delineate elements of place attachment (i.e., place identity and place dependence; Dandy et al., 2019; Williams & Vaske, 2003), while others assert such distinctions are artificial. The latter point often, although not exclusively, emerges in contexts of Indigenous peoples and communities (Carter, 2010). Generally, sense of place and place attachment are the principal terms used to describe how humans create and relate to places through "dwelling" or inhabitation.

Economic relationships with the environment also inform place attachment. People with livelihoods dependent on natural resources relate to their natural environment in distinct ways; additionally, they may perceive and respond to environmental risks differently (Kroll-Smith & Couch, 1993). For example, studies in the U.S. Gulf Coast and Canada have found environmental complacency (i.e., inaction in the face of climate change) among oil workers in contrast to fishers, whose well-being is dependent on a healthy marine environment (Cope et al., 2013; Milnes & Haney, 2017; Picou & Gill, 1996). Damage to the resource base results in damage to fishers' identity and way of life (Henry & Bankston, 2002; Oberg et al., 2016). However, it is important to note that both oil workers and fishers have limited influence on how their respective industries affect the environment.

Attachment to place, strong family ties, and land and water relationships are essential to quality of life, security, and cultural sovereignty (see Chapter 6). Burley (2010) and Simms et al. (2021), among others, emphasize the powerful bonds that coastal residents in Louisiana have to their home territory. Additionally, strong place identification is prominent among residents of Galveston, which has housed island communities since Indigenous migrations (Hardwick, 2002). (Chapter 6 further elaborates on place attachment in relation to relocation and well-being.) Consequently, despite grave risks such as tropical cyclones and sea level rise, many coastal residents are reluctant to move inland. Long-term residents and place-based communities are accustomed to tropical cyclones. They may "retreat" temporarily but have a high dependence on coastal resources and historically possessed the capacity to rebuild, and therefore have not considered seasonal hurricanes as a sufficient reason to migrate. Fishing communities across the coast, including those with other diverse backgrounds, share a similar connection to local livelihoods that cannot be replicated inland. Rich histories and lifeways in old settlement communities like Port Arthur, Texas, currently surrounded by petrochemical industries, are a powerful dissuasive force. In addition, participants from the Port Arthur workshop and community meeting were mindful that the unknowns of a new destination would deter retreat and departures from home (National Academies of Sciences, Engineering, and Medicine, 2022c). For legacy populations—descendants of earlier migrants, including Acadian, Black, Isleño, or Southeast Asian groups—a familiarity with the local ecology and traditional fishing practices and a strong sense of cultural and ethnic identity shared by members of the community constitute an attachment to place and contribute to the resilience and strength of community (Colten, 2017). However, even with a strong track record of adaptations to remain in place, the present and future projections of rising seas and more extreme weather could exceed the adaptive capacity of Gulf Coast residents.

Other Reasons to Remain in Place

Alongside attachment to place, there are additional anchors that bind people to their current Gulf Coast locales. Retirees from outside the Gulf region who have migrated to Florida, for example, have already uprooted themselves and are not inclined to move again. Vietnamese residents in Alabama also recall their forced dislocation from their homeland and struggles to re-establish themselves in the United States (National Academies, 2022d). The painful process of establishing strong roots and re-building "place" discourages interest in relocating.[2]

[2]Based on comments the committee heard at public information-gathering sessions. More information about these sessions is available at https://www.nationalacademies.org/our-work/managed-retreat-in-the-us-gulf-coast-region#sectionPastEvents

Familiarity with local institutions and services is another compelling reason why many seniors opt not to follow younger family members inland (Simms, 2017; Simms et al., 2021). The rising cost of flood insurance makes selling houses in coastal areas more difficult and reduces the equity a homeowner could apply to an inland home, increasing the weight of the anchor of place (Colten, 2017). While tropical weather events can have devastating impacts, long-term coastal residents often believe that they know how to cope with these storms; like people in other locations with different hazardscapes, they do not see familiar risks as sufficient reason to relocate, and indeed, many have endured many tropical cyclones and remained in place. With rising seas and more extreme weather, newer residents to the Gulf Coast are likely to be unable to adapt to these environmental changes.

COMMUNITY PROFILES

This section features comparative profiles of six coastal communities across the region facing climate threats. Communities are introduced via summaries of community profiles (the full profiles are available in Appendix C) and residents' first-hand accounts of their experiences, here called "Community Testimonials." Together, these data provide a composite portrait of the diverse communities in the region. The committee notes that when considering a community's capacity to plan for and participate in adaptive relocation, it is necessary to also consider the breadth of social, economic, and environmental issues faced by the community; the history of climate impacts and potential future climate-induced hazards on the locale; and community planning to address these issues (e.g., hazard mitigation, comprehensive plans). The following profiles combine the "scale of the threat of displacement" (as explored in Chapter 2 of this report) with datasets about hazard and health risks, and EPA's Environmental Justice Index (EJI).

To "ground truth" the sociodemographic data (Carp, 2008; National Academies, 2019a), the committee interacted with community stakeholders through public information-gathering sessions (Chapter 1, Box 1-2) and discussed risks and how risks influence decision making about relocation. Community testimonials give important context to the quantitative datasets and articulate community needs in terms of climate services and other support. The committee's approach to understanding community experiences and how risks influence relocation decision making underscores the utility of pairing quantitative and qualitative information. As we note at the end of this chapter, the committee's approach resulted in two conclusions about the utility of data.

Overview of the Following Profiles

This section includes an abbreviated community profile and data visualizations for each community in which the committee hosted a workshop, plus Mobile and Harrison Counties in Alabama and Mississippi, respectively, highlighting the communities of Bayou La Batre, Alabama, and Turkey Creek, Mississippi. Each of the community profiles in this chapter includes a brief introduction, followed by data on current and projected flood risk, social vulnerability and health, risk to 19 natural hazards included in FEMA's National Risk Index, environmental justice issues based on EPA's Environmental Justice Screening Tool (EJScreen), and a list of significant tropical cyclones affecting the community's portion of the Gulf Coast since 2000. More information on each community and the data sources used for these profiles can be found in Appendix C.

City of St. Petersburg, Florida, Including Pinellas County

Introduction

St. Petersburg, the location of this study's second workshop, is located on the Gulf Coast of Florida in Pinellas County on the Pinellas Peninsula, between Tampa Bay and the Gulf of Mexico. The city was incorporated in 1903 (City of St. Petersburg, 2023) and, as of 2020, had an estimated population of 258,356 (U.S. Census Bureau, 2023a), making it the fifth most populous city in the state. It forms part of the Tampa-St. Petersburg-Clearwater metropolitan statistical area, which has a population of approximately 3.2 million (U.S. Census Bureau, 2022).

Current and Projected Flood Risk

The Coastal County Snapshots from the NOAA Office for Coastal Management[3] reveal that almost 40 percent of Pinellas County's land is within the designated 100-year floodplain. This floodplain region is inhabited by nearly 30 percent of the total populace and 34 percent of individuals aged 65 or older, and houses 16.4 percent of crucial facilities and nearly a quarter of local businesses. The county witnessed more than 12,000 flood insurance claims between 1991 and 2020, amounting to 152 million dollars. An analysis by the Union of Concerned Scientists[4] predicts that under

[3]The Coastal County Snapshots online tool is available at https://coast.noaa.gov/digitalcoast/tools/snapshots.html

[4]More information on the national analysis from the Union of Concerned Scientists is available at https://ucsusa.maps.arcgis.com/apps/MapSeries/index.html?appid=cf07ebe0a4c9439ab2e7e346656cb239

a moderate sea level rise scenario, 256 homes in St. Petersburg, valued at nearly 130 million dollars, will risk chronic inundation by 2035. By 2100, this risk is expected to escalate to include 19,383 homes, accommodating 35,665 residents, with a value of close to 5 billion dollars. This heightened threat to housing from flooding coupled with other infrastructure loss and damage emphasizes the pressing need for elected officials to tackle these intersecting issues to guarantee the well-being of Pinellas County residents (see Boxes 5-2 and 5-3).

Social Vulnerability Index and Health

Pinellas County is classified as having a medium-to-high level of vulnerability, according to a 2020 Social Vulnerability Index (SVI) score of 0.7247 out of 1, which combines sociodemographic factors such as poverty, access to transportation, and crowded housing.[5] Pinellas County's high SVI score of 0.8444 for housing type and transportation indicates significant vulnerabilities related to housing conditions and accessibility, pointing to potential issues such as inadequate affordable housing and limited or unreliable public transportation. While St. Petersburg generally exhibits levels of asthma, heart disease, and poor mental health close to national averages,

BOX 5-2
Community Testimonial: Cascading Problems—Housing and Transportation

"What's going on with housing right now? People being forced out of their neighborhoods or their communities because of gentrification. The majority of these people are workers. If transportation is abysmal, how are they supposed to get into the city and work these 15-dollar-an-hour jobs as essential workers? People don't think about the planning that goes into making the city function and we need to see some changes from our elected officials because of all these intersecting vectors people aren't paying attention to it."

SOURCE: Getulio Gonzalez-Mulattieri, Resident of St. Petersburg, Florida. Workshop 2: Opportunities & Challenges of Climate Adaptation on Florida's Gulf Coast, July 2022, St. Petersburg, Florida.

[5]The highest SVI score is 1, meaning that all SVI scores will be 1 or lower. A location's social vulnerability decreases as the SVI decreases. The SVI represents a ranking for each tract or county, meaning that a score of 1 indicates the county or tract with the most vulnerability within the state or nation. SVIs reported in this chapter reflect rankings within the state. More information about the SVI from CDC's Agency for Toxic Substances and Disease Registry is available at https://www.atsdr.cdc.gov/placeandhealth/svi/fact_sheet/fact_sheet.html

BOX 5-3
Community Testimonial: Sea Level Rise, Flooding, and Isolation

"But really, the nature of sea level rise inundation is going to fundamentally reshape living on the coast. It's making places unlivable. It's making livelihoods unlivable. And it really is an irreversible condition. But for municipalities that are already juggling these multiple priorities with limited funding, they are seeking to strike a rational balance. They don't want to over-adapt, especially in the face of uncertainty and slow change. But they also don't want to under-adapt to the inevitability of these future risks. So, the struggle here is, at what point do the community risk of exposure and impact outweigh the benefit of being on the coast, right? When did they become salient enough to trigger commitment to a strategic and costly movement away from the coast to higher ground?"

SOURCE: Tisha Holmes, Assistant Professor, Department of Urban & Regional Planning, Florida State University. Workshop 2: Opportunities & Challenges of Climate Adaptation on Florida's Gulf Coast, July 2022, St. Petersburg, Florida.

"I live in Clearwater, and my home is about 15 feet above sea level. There is good drainage, so we really have not had an issue with flooding in my specific area. However, every time we experience heavy rainfall, it becomes difficult to access or leave my area. The main roads, which are two-lane roads with one lane going and one lane coming, turn into rivers. We find ourselves isolated whenever severe water-related situations occur. And that's a main concern that we have."

SOURCE: Eliseo Santana, Resident of St. Petersburg, Florida. Workshop 2: Opportunities & Challenges of Climate Adaptation on Florida's Gulf Coast, July 2022, St. Petersburg, Florida.

underserved regions such as Child's Park, Lake Maggiore, and Pinellas Park, where over 25 percent lack health insurance, reveal heightened vulnerability within the county (see Box 5-4).[6]

FEMA's National Risk Index

FEMA's National Risk Index is a dataset and online tool that provides a "baseline risk measurement" for U.S. counties and census tracts to

[6]Health data come from the CDC Places website (https://experience.arcgis.com/experience/22c7182a162d45788dd52a2362f8ed65) using data from CDC's Behavioral Risk Factor Surveillance System (https://www.cdc.gov/brfss/index.html).

BOX 5-4
Community Testimonial: Climate-Related Health Concerns

"Air quality control is an issue here in South St. Pete, Childs Park area specifically. And we have a campaign: Smell Something, Say Something. And we've actually started putting up air quality monitors in that area, and we're in the process of putting up more. But this is a very, very important issue. We've known about it years' past in industrial areas, but unfortunately, there's still areas here today that are industrial, and there's bad air quality. Which, as we know, causes different sicknesses and illnesses, particularly in our communities [...] we have a website through the city, See, Click, Fix. So anytime somebody smells something that's out of the ordinary, they report it. So now we have data tracking the air quality issues."

SOURCE: Antwaun Wells, Resident of St. Petersburg, Florida. Workshop 2: Opportunities & Challenges of Climate Adaptation on Florida's Gulf Coast, July 2022, St. Petersburg, Florida.

"Without regards to climate, African Americans are disproportionately affected by human disease such as heart disease, which is the number one cause of death in the African American community, and in the White community as well. But African Americans have a higher incidence of heart disease. African Americans have [...] the highest incidence of prostate cancer than any other group in the world [...] Most other cancers are disproportionately affecting the African American communities [...] Then you have cerebrovascular disease, renal disease, HIV and AIDS, nine times the incidence, five times the incidence of amputations as a result of diabetes."

SOURCE: Kenneth Bryant, Founder and Chief Executive Officer of Minority Health Coalition of Pinellas, Inc. Workshop 2: Opportunities & Challenges of Climate Adaptation on Florida's Gulf Coast, July 2022, St. Petersburg, Florida.

"illustrate the communities most at risk for 18 natural hazards."[7] FEMA's National Risk Index is calculated using three components: a natural hazard risk component (expected annual loss [EAL][8]), a consequence enhancing

[7]More information about FEMA's National Risk Index is available at https://hazards.fema.gov/nri/learn-more and in the National Risk Index Technical Documentation (Zuzak et al., 2023).

[8]According to FEMA, "Expected Annual Loss (EAL) represents the average economic loss in dollars resulting from natural hazards each year. It is calculated for each hazard type and quantifies loss for relevant consequence types: buildings, people, and agriculture. As the natural hazards component of the National Risk Index, an Expected Annual Loss score and rating represent a community's relative level of expected losses each year when compared to all other communities at the same level. An Expected Annual Loss score is positively associated to a community's risk; thus, a higher Expected Annual Loss score results in a higher Risk Index score." More information is available at https://hazards.fema.gov/nri/expected-annual-loss

risk component (social vulnerability[9]), and a consequence reduction risk component (community resilience[10]; Zuzak et al., 2023).[11] The index ranks Pinellas County in the 99th percentile in the nation and 91st percentile within Florida (see Figure 5-2), meaning that only about 1 percent of counties in the United States and 9 percent of counties in Florida have a higher risk index than Pinellas County.

The National Risk Index for Pinellas County (see Figure 5-2) reflects relatively high[12] EAL and social vulnerability with very low community resilience (FEMA, 2023h). Of the 18 hazards included in the National Risk Index, Pinellas County has ratings above the 80th percentile in the nation for coastal flooding, cold wave, hurricane, lightning, and tornado. With percentiles around 99th and above, Pinellas County is one of the most at-risk counties in the United States for hurricanes, lightning, and tornadoes. The EAL from all hazards (building value, population, and/or agriculture value) for Pinellas County is over 325 million dollars.

EPA's EJScreen

According to EPA's EJScreen,[13] St. Petersburg is above the 50th percentile in the nation on particulate matter 2.5 ("fine inhalable particles, with diameters that are generally 2.5 micrometers and smaller"[14]), ozone[15] (a greenhouse gas composed of three atoms of oxygen), diesel particulate matter, air toxics cancer risk, air toxics respiratory hazard index (HI), toxic releases to air, traffic proximity, lead paint, superfund proximity, proximity

[9]Social vulnerability comes from the SVI (described previously in this profile). More information is available at https://hazards.fema.gov/nri/social-vulnerability

[10]The community resilience score in the National Risk Index represents the relative level of a community's resilience compared to all other communities at the same level. A community's Community Resilience score measures its national rank and is inversely proportional to a community's risk. A higher Community Resilience score results in a lower Risk Index score. More information is available at https://hazards.fema.gov/nri/community-resilience

[11]Community resilience measures come from the University of South Carolina's Hazards and Vulnerability Research Institute's Baseline Resilience Indicators for Communities (Zuzak et al., 2023, p. 4-4). More information is available at https://hazards.fema.gov/nri/community-resilience

[12]The National Risk Index ranks levels of risk in the following categories: very high risk is 80th–100th percentile, relatively high is 60th–80th, relatively moderate is 40th–60th, relatively low is 20th–40th, and very low is 0–20th (Zuzak et al., 2023, p. 3-3).

[13]More information about EPA's EJScreen is available at https://ejscreen.epa.gov/mapper

[14]More information is available at https://www.epa.gov/pm-pollution/particulate-matter-pm-basics

[15]High ground-level ozone (ozone in the troposphere) may cause an array of health issues that irritate the lungs, especially in individuals with lung conditions like asthma, as well as in children and the elderly. More information is available at https://www.epa.gov/ozone-layer-protection/basic-ozone-layer-science

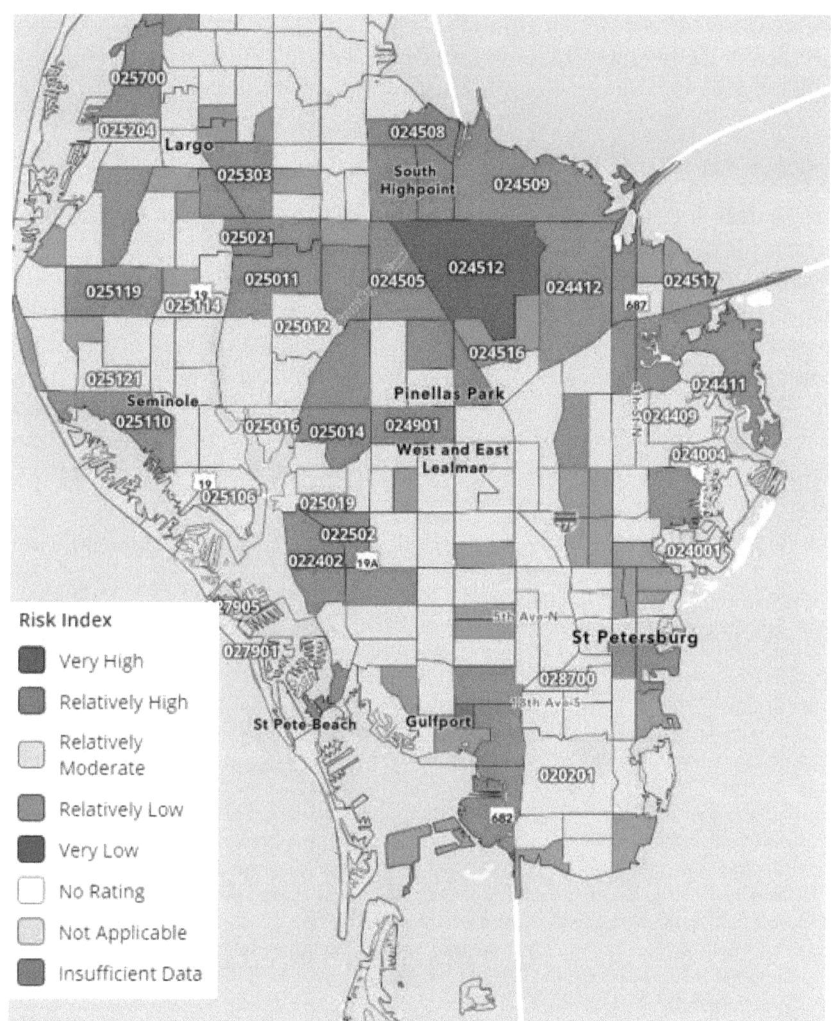

FIGURE 5-2 National Risk Index, Pinellas County, Florida.
SOURCE: FEMA. (2023h). *National Risk Index: Explore the map*. https://hazards.fema.gov/nri/map

to hazardous waste, underground storage tanks, and wastewater discharge (see Box 5-5). In general, the higher the percentile, the more vulnerable the selected area is compared to the entire state and country.

Tropical Storms and Hurricanes That Have Impacted Florida Since 2000

Florida has faced a series of notable disasters from the year 2000 to present day, including Hurricanes Ian (2022), Irma (2017), Jeanne (2004), Frances (2004), and Charley (2004), each of which were federally declared major disasters. The total financial impact from Hurricane Ian was estimated to be upward of 4.5 billion dollars to the state and individual households for loans, flood insurance, and federal grants (FEMA, 2023d), and the Florida Department of Law Enforcement (2023) reported 149 deaths in the state attributed to the storm. Other notable recent environmental disasters affecting St. Petersburg include the 2021 Piney Point Wastewater Disaster[16] and the 2018 Red Tide Event.[17] See Table C-2 in Appendix C for more information.

BOX 5-5
Community Testimonial: Recent Environmental Disasters and Community Responses and the 2021 Piney Point Wastewater Disaster[a]

"Our community does what they can from a reactionary level [...] they clear the dead fish off the beach, and they're putting them in dumpsters, but the red tide bloom is out there, and it's washing new fish and new toxins into the air all the time [...] You know, individual households [...] you close your windows, you run your air conditioning, you maybe buy a better air conditioning filter, maybe you buy filters for your home. It was particularly bad because I have a young daughter, and she would wake up in the night coughing."

[a]More information, including a timeline of the Piney Point wastewater disaster, is available at https://www.floridamuseum.ufl.edu/earth-systems/blog/a-timeline-of-the-piney-point-wastewater-disaster

SOURCE: Chelsea Nelson, Resident of Madeira Beach, Florida. Workshop 2: Opportunities & Challenges of Climate Adaptation on Florida's Gulf Coast, July 2022, St. Petersburg, Florida.

[16]More information about the Piney Point Wastewater Disaster is available at https://www.floridamuseum.ufl.edu/earth-systems/blog/a-timeline-of-the-piney-point-wastewater-disaster/

[17]More information about the 2018 Red Tide Event is available at https://oceanservice.noaa.gov/hazards/hab/florida-2018.html

Mobile County and Community of Bayou La Batre, Alabama

Introduction

This community profile supplies information about Mobile County and spotlights the community of Bayou La Batre. In addition, stakeholders from communities across Mobile County and Baldwin County contributed to this study through virtual discussions; these included Africatown (aka, "AfricaTown U.S.A." and "Plateau"), Foley, and Gulf Shores. To provide an inclusive representation of communities in the coastal region of Alabama, this profile considers Mobile County-level data. When data from Mobile were not available, the committee included data from Bayou La Batre.

Located in the southwestern region of Alabama, with a population of 414,620, Mobile County stands as the second most populous county in the state and is home to its sole seaport.[18] The county is marked by a long history of different colonial occupations. From 1702 to 1763, the area was under French occupation, followed by British control from 1763 to 1780. The Spanish took over the region from 1780 to 1813, when the United States ultimately claimed the territory. On December 18, 1812, Governor of the Mississippi Territory David Holme officially established Mobile County, envisioning it as a deepwater port along the Mobile River. The northern part is inhabited by the Mobile and Washington County Band of Choctaw, who settled in the area following the conclusion of the Creek War in 1814.[19] A portion of the southern reaches of the county is inhabited by a large population of Southeast Asian immigrants and their descendants (see Boxes 5-6 and 5-7). The county also encompasses various islands, including Dauphin Island, Gaillard Island, and Mon Louis Island. Mobile County's economy has seen steady growth in its traditional sectors such as "shipping, port facilities, shipbuilding and repair, forest products, chemicals, oil and gas production and exploration, seafood industry, and water-oriented tourism and recreation."[20] In recent times, the county has also experienced robust expansion in newer industries like aircraft production and repair, as well as steel and steel products.

---

[18]More information about Mobile County is available at https://www.britannica.com/place/Mobile-Alabama

[19]More information is available at https://www.mobilecountyal.gov/government/about-mobile-county/

[20]More information about Mobile County's economic history is available at https://www.mobile.org/things-to-do/history/

BOX 5-6
Community Testimonial: Cultural Preservation and Relocation

"When I think of [managed retreat] for the Gulf Coast, I think about how to navigate the challenges, especially with the Asian community that originally came to the Gulf Coast and became part of the seafood industry. I think about the challenge it would be to move this community somewhere that has a climate they aren't familiar with, or where they won't be able to earn a living or find the skills or education to find another job to support their family. So, there are just so many challenges when I think about managed retreat and how it would even be possible, especially for the first generation people who immigrated here from Vietnam."

SOURCE: Jane Nguyen, Program Manager, Boat People SOS. Virtual Focused Discussion: Mississippi and Alabama Gulf Coast Community Stakeholder Perspectives on Managed Retreat, March 2023.

Current and Projected Flood Risk

The Coastal County Snapshots from NOAA[21] reveal that 22 percent of the land is within the designated 100-year floodplain; that area is home to roughly 14 percent of the population in Mobile County, with 13 percent of that population over 65 years of age. These flood zones also include around 5 percent of important facilities like schools, police stations, fire stations, and medical facilities, and approximately 10 percent of businesses. The area had over 10,600 flood insurance claims between 1991 and 2020, costing over 315 million dollars. An analysis by the Union of Concerned Scientists[22] predicts that, under a moderate sea level rise scenario, approximately 3 percent of community homes collectively valued at more than 72 million dollars, including 580 people and over 300 homes in Bayou La Batre, could be at risk of chronic inundation by 2035. This risk is expected to escalate to nearly 1,800 homes, 17 percent of the community, with a collective value of more than 377.7 million dollars by 2100.

SVI and Health

With an SVI of 0.697 out of 1 in 2020, Mobile County is classified as having a medium-to-high level of vulnerability at the national level,

[21]See footnote 3.
[22]See footnote 4.

BOX 5-7
Community Testimonial: Impacts of Flooding Events and Pollution

"One problem is the gradual impact of climate change—hurricanes, severe flooding, health case access. I don't know where to begin with the Vietnamese community and issues with them relocating. Hurricane Katrina severely affected the fishing community of Bayou La Batre, where we also have an office, and where everyone's livelihood relies on the seafood industry. Severe flooding and the opening of the Bonnet Carre Spillway, which was open for over 120 days, killed off massive numbers of oyster and shrimp from the spillovers of toxins. In addition to extreme weather, healthcare access along the Gulf Coast is almost non-existent. Just in the three lower counties of Mississippi, Harrison, Hancock, and Jackson County alone, there are 10,000 Vietnamese and not one single medical physician can speak Vietnamese. Many are refused care if they don't have an in-person interpreter. So, there are so many issues with the Vietnamese community. I think one reason they don't relocate and want to remain here is because of past trauma, as many of them are refugees who escaped the Vietnam war. Before coming here, many of them were shrimpers and fishermen because many of them lived in southern Vietnam. These are the skills they brought with them to America, and this is how these communities developed along the Mississippi and Alabama gulf coast. But settling down and integrating into the seafood industry, many of them faced a lot of animosity and violence. Because they fought for their spot here and their rights and developed their livelihoods, they are resistant to just move to another area. Another issue is limited English proficiency, which means they need a lot of assistance for housing (buying, renting etc.), and reliable public transportation is almost non-existent. The seafood industry is increasingly difficult to earn a living wage to even think about relocation. So, there are many issues with remaining and also many barriers to relocating."

SOURCE: Jane Nguyen, Program Manager, Boat People SOS. Virtual Focused Discussion: Mississippi and Alabama Gulf Coast Community Stakeholder Perspectives on Managed Retreat, March 2023.

according to factors such as poverty, access to transportation, and crowded housing.[23] This ranking means that less than 31 percent of counties in Alabama are classified as more socially vulnerable than Mobile County. Mobile County's high SVI scores of 0.8272 for socioeconomic status and 0.8253 for racial and ethnic groups indicate considerable challenges related to socioeconomic inequality and racial disparities for county residents. While Mobile County generally exhibits levels of asthma, heart disease,

[23]More information about Mobile County's SVI is available at https://ucsusa.maps.arcgis.com/apps/MapSeries/index.html?appid=cf07ebe0a4c9439ab2e7e346656cb239

poor mental health, and lack of health insurance close to national averages, a few neighborhoods show levels substantially higher than the national averages.[24] This indicates that within the county there are areas of higher and lower vulnerability. Mobile County is composed of cities, such as Mobile City and Africatown, that are surrounded by various chemical and industrial plants that release toxic pollutants into the air and water[25] and have previously been connected to several forms of cancer prevalence in the surrounding communities.[26]

FEMA's National Risk Index

FEMA's National Risk Index[27] ranks Mobile County in the 98.8th percentile in the nation and in the 100th percentile within Alabama (see Figure 5-3). This ranking means that only about 1 percent of counties in the United States and 0 percent of counties in Alabama have a higher risk index than Mobile County. FEMA's National Risk Index is calculated using three components: a natural hazard risk component (EAL[28]), a consequence enhancing component (social vulnerability[29]), and a consequence reduction component (community resilience[30]; Zuzak et al., 2023). With scores above the 99th percentile, Mobile County is one of the most at-risk counties in the United States for hurricanes and lightning. The EAL from all hazards (building value, population, and/or agriculture value) for Mobile County is over 274 million dollars. Mobile County reflects relatively high EAL, social vulnerability, and community resilience (FEMA, 2023h). Of the 18 hazards included in the National Risk Index, Mobile County has ratings above the 90th percentile in the nation for heat wave, riverine flooding, and tornado.

EPA's EJScreen

According to EPA's EJScreen,[31] Mobile County is close to the 60th percentile in the nation for particulate matter, ozone, diesel particulate matter, air toxics cancer risk, air toxics respiratory HI, toxic releases to air, traffic

---

[24]See footnote 6.

[25]More information about plants in Mobile County is available at https://ejatlas.org/conflict/africatown-united-states

[26]More information about cancer risk in Africatown is available at https://www.theguardian.com/us-news/2018/jan/26/africatown-site-of-last-us-slave-ship-arrival-sues-over-factorys-pollu=share_btn_link and more information about cancer risk throughout the United States is available at https://projects.propublica.org/toxmap/

[27]See footnote 7.

[28]See footnote 8.

[29]See footnote 9.

[30]See footnotes 10 and 11.

[31]See footnote 13.

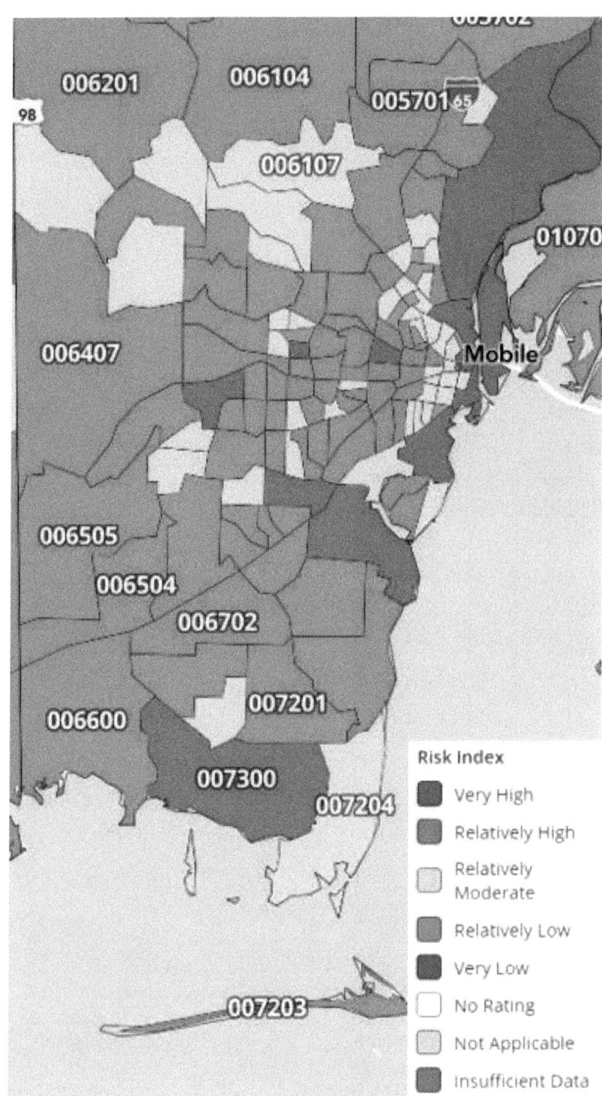

FIGURE 5-3 National Risk Index, Mobile County, Alabama.
SOURCE: FEMA. (2023h). *National Risk Index: Explore the map*. https://hazards.fema.gov/nri/map

proximity, lead paint, superfund proximity, Risk Management Plan (RMP) facility proximity, proximity to hazardous waste, underground storage tanks, and wastewater discharge (see Boxes 5-8 and 5-9).

Tropical Storms and Hurricanes That Have Impacted Alabama Since 2000

Alabama has faced a series of notable disasters from the year 2000 to present day, including Hurricanes Ida (2021), Zeta (2020), Sally (2020), Katrina (2005), and Ivan (2004), each of which were federally declared major disasters. Notable storms include Hurricane Katrina and Hurricane Ivan, which were two of the strongest and most expensive storms to impact Alabama. Another seriously damaging storm was Hurricane Sally; due to its registration as a category 2 hurricane, many residents failed to evacuate, which led to high levels of preventable damage and costs. Throughout these disasters, FEMA has worked closely with Alabama Emergency Management Agency to identify local partners to distribute funds and resources from federal programs to affected communities. See Table C-3 in Appendix C for more information.

Harrison County and Community of Turkey Creek, Mississippi

Introduction

This community profile is for Harrison County and spotlights the community of Turkey Creek (see Box 5-13). In addition, a number of

BOX 5-8
Community Testimonial: Response to Pollution

"The City of Mobile experiences floods and extreme weather events, for sure. Those are reasons why we would and should consider moving, in addition to serious pollution issues. One of our biggest examples is the community that lives around Africatown. In the 40s a bunch of really heavy industry was built all around that community. But the community wants to be there. They want to live in a place that is their history and is important to our community's story."

SOURCE: Casi Callaway, Chief Resilience Officer, City of Mobile, Alabama. Virtual Focused Discussion: Mississippi and Alabama Gulf Coast Community Stakeholder Perspectives on Managed Retreat, March 2023.

BOX 5-9
Bayou La Batre

Bayou La Batre is a small Gulf Coast city along Portersville Bay on the Mississippi Sound in the county of Mobile, Alabama, about 25 miles south of the city of Mobile. Bayou La Batre can be characterized as a fishing community and contains a processing harbor for seafood brought in on fishing and shrimp boats. It has been described as the "Seafood Capitol" of Alabama (Mississippi-Alabama Sea Grant Consortium, 2021). The bayou itself was called "Riviere D'Erbane" by early French colonizers and eventually acquired its current name (which translates into "bayou of the battery") in the late 1700s with the construction of the French-maintained artillery battery on the bayou's west bank. The bayou runs from Portersville Bay inland for approximately 5.5 miles and provides boat access to the Mississippi Sound, Mobile Bay, and the Gulf of Mexico. The city of Bayou La Batre was officially incorporated in 1955. Its population has averaged about 2,200 people since the 1950s (Kaetz, 2023). Despite having a small population, its lucrative seafood industry has more than an 80-million-dollar economic impact on the state of Alabama annually (Coastal Alabama Partnership, 2022), and it is also a place known for the design and construction of a variety of boats (Kaetz, 2023).

Bayou La Batre is also known for its multi-ethnic population, principally the result of the resettlement of displaced people from Vietnam, Cambodia, and Laos in the 1970s during the Vietnam War. About 20,000 displaced Asians were resettled in the Gulf states, from Texas to Florida, and some people that were settled in other regions migrated to the Gulf (Macchi, 2015). In 2021, 18.5 percent of the population of Bayou La Batre was Asian, compared to less than 1 percent for the state of Alabama (U.S. Census Bureau, 2021a). Like elsewhere on the Gulf, many Asian immigrants to Bayou La Batre were from southern Vietnam, where they sustained livelihoods from the seafood industry in environmental conditions similar to the Gulf Coast. After arrival to the Gulf Coast in the 1970s, Asian immigrants struggled to integrate into the local and regional seafood industry because of language barriers, animosity, and racism (Macchi, 2015). However, over time, they found a place in every part of the industry (e.g., boat construction, shrimping, fishing, processing), established themselves as dependable workers, and founded community institutions and support networks. Today, nearly a third of the seafood industry in Bayou La Batre is composed of Asian immigrants and their descendants (Mississippi-Alabama Sea Grant Consortium, 2021).

In 2005, Hurricane Katrina devastated Bayou La Batre and destroyed boats, businesses, and facilities critical to sustaining the livelihoods of residents. The storm surge was nearly 20 feet, more than 2,000 of 2,300 residents were displaced from their homes, and 23 shrimp boats were stranded on land (Gaillard, 2007). Despite barriers to recovery, such as language, literacy, cultural differences in help-seeking, and the challenges of navigating disaster recovery bureaucracy (Nguyen & Salvesen, 2014), the Asian community of Bayou La Batre exhibited resilience to the social and economic setbacks they suffered. As with Vietnamese communities in New Orleans after Hurricane Katrina (National Academies, 2023a), levels of trust, cooperation, and collaboration mitigated the damage during and after the recovery period (Nguyen & Salvesen, 2014). Additionally,

(*continued*)

BOX 5-9
Continued

the devastation of Hurricane Katrina promoted the international aid organization Boat People SOS (BPSOS) to establish a Gulf Coast branch, with offices in New Orleans, Biloxi, and Bayou La Batre, to assist with recovery; BPSOS remains a strong and supportive community institution today.[a]

[a]BPSOS is a nonprofit international aid organization founded in 1980 to rescue Vietnamese people fleeing Vietnam by boat and help them gain refugee rights in asylum camps. It has since expanded services to rescue, protect, and aid victims of persecution and trafficking in Vietnam, the United States, Russia, Ghana, and other countries. More information is available at https://www.bpsos.org/about

stakeholders from communities across Harrison County and Jackson County contributed to the study through virtual discussions; these included Biloxi, East Biloxi (see Box 5-10), and Gulfport as well as Pascagoula and Ocean Springs. To provide an inclusive relation of communities at the Mississippi coast, this profile considers Harrison County-level data except where county data were not available and the City of Biloxi was focused on instead.

Harrison County, founded in 1841, is located on the state's Gulf Coast. It is the second most populous county in Mississippi, with a population of 207,382 (Mississippi Encyclopedia, 2023; World Population Review, 2023).[32] There are a number of oil and chemical refineries located near the coastal cities of Harrison County, which are also major tourist destinations (e.g., Biloxi Beach) and the site of the Keesler Air Force Base.

Current and Projected Flood Risk

The Coastal County Snapshots from NOAA[33] reveal that almost 20 percent of Harrison County's land and over a quarter of its population resides within the designated 100-year floodplain, a region where almost a third of the residents are over the age of 65 and nearly 30 percent live in poverty (see Box 5-11). Critical community facilities, such as schools and fire stations, along with 14 percent of businesses, are also in this flood-prone area, which has had more than 1 billion dollars in flood insurance claims between 1991 and 2020. While most development within

[32]More information about Harrison County is available at https://harrisoncountyms.gov/index.php

[33]See footnote 3.

BOX 5-10
Community Testimonial: Factors Affecting Resilience in the Face of Flooding

"I call it Heartland East Biloxi, kind of like the core of the community that has long been part of the African American community [...] We have a lot of history. We want to preserve that history. We want to use it as a platform to preserve our community and continue to rebuild [...] We have our challenges. We are in the flood zone. We are looking at the sea level map and it does show that East Biloxi will be more affected in the next five [to] ten years. Whatever homes or buildings that need to be built now need to be elevated. And we've still got a low-income community that deals with high utility bills. And also deals with the high cost of flood insurance."

SOURCE: Gordon Jackson, Board President, Steps Coalition. Virtual Focused Discussion: Mississippi and Alabama Gulf Coast Community Stakeholder Perspectives on Managed Retreat, March 2023.

the floodplain predates 1996, an additional 11.6 percent of development occurred between 1996 and 2016. An analysis by the Union of Concerned Scientists[34] predicts that under a moderate sea level rise scenario, by 2035, one house (less than 1%) valued at $316,057, or two people, is expected to be chronically inundated with water. This is expected to rise to 154 homes (1%) in Harrison County, valued at over 30 million dollars and housing 348 residents, by 2100.

SVI and Health

With an SVI in 2020 of 0.6296 out of 1 within the state of Mississippi, Harrison County is classified as having a medium-to-high level of vulnerability, according to factors such as poverty, access to transportation, and crowded housing.[35] This ranking means that less than 38 percent of counties in Mississippi are classified as more socially vulnerable than Harrison County. With high SVI scores across socioeconomic status (0.9236), household characteristics (0.831), racial and ethnic minority status (0.7543), and housing and transportation (0.8568), Harrison County has notable socioeconomic, demographic, and infrastructural vulnerabilities.

[34]See footnote 4.
[35]See footnote 5.

BOX 5-11
Community Testimonial: Response to Air Pollution and Climate-Related Health Concerns

"We get industry pollution that is coming in on us. We've already proven to everyone how bad the toxic air is for us to breathe. We've lost [had pass away] 27 residents in the last five years out of 120 households. We currently have about seven active people taking chemo at this time. So, it's a major health issue, plus the flood issue and industry continues to pollute. So that's why everything here is so prominent in that we work to get relocated. So, we can basically survive and live [...] Where is my clean air? Where is my clean water? I don't have either one. We have a senior citizen that says, 'I would love to go to kind of like a condo situation where it would be like a senior citizen community. But Pasco County has no place like that for me to go,' is what her answer was. There's been several that said, 'Well with relocating, am I going to have enough funds through this relocation or through this buyout to go, relocate and live somewhere else.' Then others say, 'No, I don't want to stay here, because I know what the toxin is doing to me so I'm ready to go.' Matter of fact, right down the street we have one who has cancer that's returned, and she says, 'I just hope I could live long enough to get out of here.' That was her answer that she could live long enough to get out of here."

SOURCE: Barbara Weckesser, Head of Concerned Citizens of Cherokee Subdivision and Resident of Pascagoula, Mississippi. Virtual Focused Discussion: Mississippi and Alabama Gulf Coast Community Stakeholder Perspectives on Managed Retreat, March 2023.

FEMA's National Risk Index

FEMA's National Risk Index[36] ranks Harrison County in the 97th percentile in the nation and 100th percentile within Mississippi (see Figure 5-4). This ranking means that only 3 percent of counties in the United States and 0 percent of counties in Mississippi have a higher risk index than Harrison County. FEMA's National Risk Index is calculated using three components: a natural hazard risk component (expected annual loss[37]), a consequence enhancing component (social vulnerability[38]), and a consequence reduction component (community resilience[39]; Zuzak et al., 2023). The National Risk Index for Harrison County reflects relatively high[40] EAL and community resilience, and very high social vulnerability (FEMA,

[36]See footnote 7.
[37]See footnote 8.
[38]See footnote 9.
[39]See footnotes 10 and 11.
[40]See footnote 12.

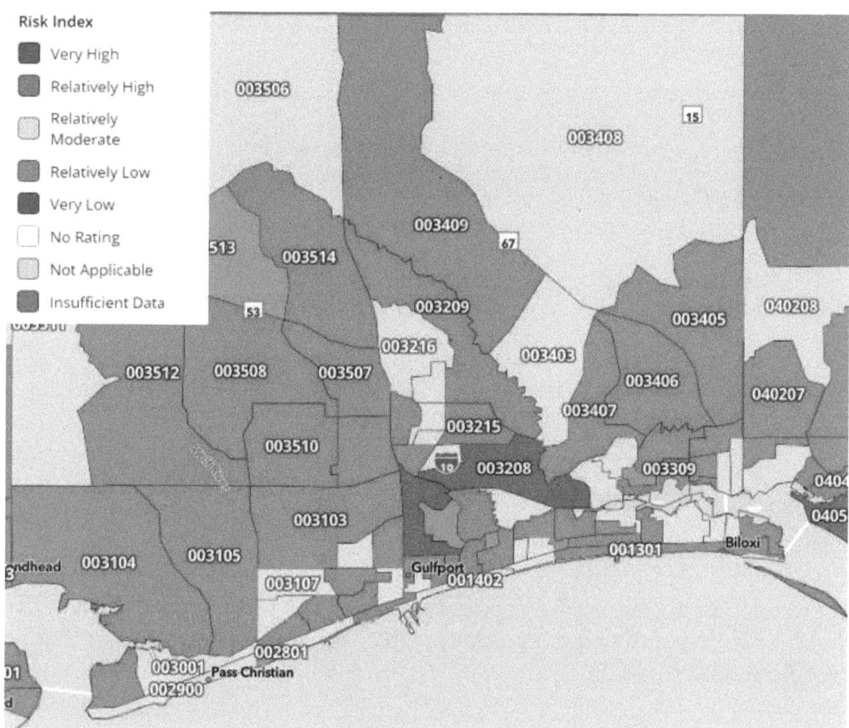

FIGURE 5-4 National Risk Index, Harrison County, Mississippi.
SOURCE: FEMA. (2023h). *National Risk Index: Explore the map*. https://hazards.fema.gov/nri/map

2023i). Of the 18 hazards included in the National Risk Index, Harrison County has a relatively high score (above the 90th percentile) in the nation for hurricane, lightning, and tornado. With scores above the 97th percentile, Harrison County is one of the most at-risk counties in the United States for hurricanes and lightning. The EAL from all hazards (building value, population, and/or agriculture value) for Mobile County is over 142.8 million dollars.

EPA's EJScreen

According to EPA's EJScreen,[41] Harrison County is approximately at or above the 50th percentile in the nation in particulate matter, ozone,

[41]See footnote 13.

BOX 5-12
Community Testimonial: Environmental Justice

"Environmental justice isn't just justice for low income and minority people in communities. Environmental justice, properly understood, is the best bar or standard that would accomplish environmental and community health resiliency for all because it's environmental justice in communities like East Biloxi, Africatown, Turkey Creek, and so forth that has most often experienced, contemplated, argued, advocated, to avail or to no avail, around these issues that increasingly cause people in communities to have to consider relocation."

SOURCE: Derrick Evans, Executive Director, Turkey Creek Community Initiatives in Gulfport, Mississippi, and Gulf Coast Fund for Community Renewal and Ecological Health (2005–2013). Virtual Focused Discussion: Mississippi and Alabama Gulf Coast Community Stakeholder Perspectives on Managed Retreat, March 2023.

diesel particulate matter, air toxics cancer risk, air toxics respiratory HI, toxic releases to air, traffic proximity, superfund proximity, RMP facility proximity, proximity to hazardous waste, and underground storage tanks (see Boxes 5-12 and 5-13).

Tropical Storms and Hurricanes That Have Impacted Mississippi Since 2000

Mississippi has faced a series of notable disasters from the year 2000 to present day, including Hurricanes Ida (2021), Zeta (2020), Nate (2017), Isaac (2012), and Katrina (2005), each of which were federally declared major disasters. The impact of these storms on Mississippi has been significant, with power outages, storm surges, heavy rainfall, and tornadoes causing widespread destruction of infrastructure, housing, and cultural institutions, and loss of life. The federal response to these disasters has varied, with assistance ranging from millions to billions of dollars to support housing, public assistance grants, and other needs. See Table C-4 in Appendix C for more information.

BOX 5-13
Community Spotlight: Come Hell or High Water—The Battle for Turkey Creek

Turkey Creek, an African American community in Gulfport, Mississippi, was established over 150 years ago following the Civil War. The environment was characterized by swamps, mangroves, lagoons, and maritime forests and has been home to Indigenous peoples and self-liberated Africans. Self-sufficient residents built their own town structures and have acted as stewards of the surrounding ecosystems. In 1926, Mississippi State Highway 49 was built, fragmenting the community and disrupting access to the creek. In the decades following, Turkey Creek has struggled to protect their community and surrounding ecosystem against practices and infrastructure that have removed native plants, destroyed wetlands and a cemetery, displaced people, and contributed to petrochemical runoff leading to water pollution (Butler-Ulloa, 2022; Mahan, 2013).

"In years past (roughly 2005–2010), I worked closely as a Gulf Coast Fund Advisor with Chief Albert Naquin and others facing the unfortunate fate of their native Isle de Jean Charles, so I know quite well how serious and ultimately imminent relocation is and will be for a growing number of coastal communities—including irreplaceable cultural enclaves akin to Turkey Creek. I am more than certain, however, that many of them (and definitely Turkey Creek or Africatown [Mobile, Alabama] in particular) will never even remotely entertain relocating until and unless they were already permanently under water (and probably not then either, lol). And given our unique historic, cultural and continuous political circumstances, even discussing the concept in theory is a very tall order. Nevertheless, relocation where adaptation is not possible or sufficient is a topic warranting deeper discussion regionally, and I would certainly be interested in contributing to a deeper analysis of both place-based and broader scientific and cultural variables that do confront Turkey Creek and similar Gulf Coast communities broadly, but also diversely. I firmly believe, for example, that the vastly needed, possible, and far from finished work of climate 'adaptation'—i.e., ambitious conservation and restoration of Turkey Creek's coastal and upland wetlands—remains the community's most important need and very best bet for confronting and surviving imminent sea level rise."

SOURCE: Derrick Evans, Executive Director, Turkey Creek Community Initiatives in Gulfport, Mississippi, and Gulf Coast Fund for Community Renewal and Ecological Health (2005–2013). Personal Email to Debra Butler, Committee Member, February 10, 2023.

Southeast Louisiana (Lafourche and Terrebonne Parishes)

Introduction

This community profile provides information about the location of this study's third workshop, held in both Lafourche Parish (Thibodaux, Louisiana) and Terrebonne Parish (Houma, Louisiana).

Lafourche and Terrebonne are coastal parishes located in the bayou region of southeast Louisiana and are connected by a network of waterways

BOX 5-14
Community Testimonial: Housing and Land Loss

"So, we have dealt with land loss and learned about land loss [...] Do we know the technical scientific terms, no. But we know we lose land. We know we lose about a football field of land a day. So, we know that, but we can't always see that. But what we can see is insurance not covering our homes and making it unrealistic to live here because you can't keep paying out of pocket every year to repair a home."

SOURCE: Cherry Wilmore, Resident of Houma, Louisiana. Workshop 3: Assisted Resettlement and Receiving Communities in Louisiana, July 2022, Houma, Louisiana.

"I think that we were some of the first to realize the land loss that Louisiana is experiencing. Every year we'd go to these shrimp growing platforms, and we could see less and less of the marshland. Louisiana has been sinking since its inception [...] As land loss and subsidence became more of an issue people kept moving further and further north to get out of harm's way. Rising sea tides and land loss are definitely having an effect on communities such as Chauvin. I feel that people who enjoy what our area has to offer are changing. More people are building camps rather than buying [...] property to raise their families."

SOURCE: Thaddeus Pellegrin, Resident of Houma, Louisiana. Workshop 3: Assisted Resettlement and Receiving Communities in Louisiana, July 2022, Houma, Louisiana.

and industrial channels.[42] The population of Lafourche is 95,890[43] and Terrebonne is 104,786.[44] The cities of Thibodaux and Houma, home to the United Houma Nation, are located within the Lafourche and Terrebonne Parishes, respectively.[45] Among others, the bayou region includes members of the Cajun and Creole cultures and high concentrations of Indigenous peoples (Yeoman, 2023). The bayou region is considered one of the most productive fishing grounds in the United States, including shrimp, oysters, redfish, and trout, and is a popular destination for wildlife and recreational tourism (Heart of Louisiana, 2023).

[42]More information about Lafourche and Terrebonne Parishes is available at https://bayouregion.com/doing-business-here/region/

[43]More information about the Lafourche population is available at https://www.census.gov/quickfacts/fact/table/lafourcheparishlouisiana,US/PST045222

[44]More information about the Terrebonne population is available at https://www.census.gov/quickfacts/fact/table/terrebonneparishlouisiana/PST045222

[45]More information about the United Houma Nation is available at https://education.nationalgeographic.org/resource/bayou/

Current and Projected Flood Risk

The Coastal County Snapshots from NOAA[46] reveal a high vulnerability to flooding in both Lafourche and Terrebonne Parishes, with over 90 percent of their land within the designated 100-year floodplain (see Box 5-14). In Lafourche, 63 percent of residents and almost 40 percent of businesses lie in this region, while in Terrebonne, 53 percent of the population and 23 percent of businesses lie in this region. Between 1991 and 2020, flood insurance claims in Lafourche totaled about 51 million dollars; in Terrebonne, the amount was significantly higher, at 270 million dollars. An analysis by the Union of Concerned Scientists[47] predicts that under a moderate sea level rise scenario, 34 percent of existing houses in Lafourche and 23 percent in Terrebonne face chronic inundation due to sea level rise by 2035 (see Box 5-15). By 2100, the figures are expected to rise to 75 percent and 60 percent, respectively (see Box 5-16).

SVI and Health

Lafourche Parish, with an SVI in 2020 of 0.3175 at the state level, is classified as having a low-to-medium level of vulnerability at the national level, according to factors such as poverty, access to transportation, and crowded housing.[48] This classification implies that less than 68 percent of counties in Louisiana have a higher social vulnerability level than Lafourche Parish. Similarly, Terrebonne Parish, with a score of 0.5079, exhibits a medium-to-high level of vulnerability, indicating comparable factors. This score means that it is as socially vulnerable as about 50 percent of the other counties in Louisiana. Within the various subcategories measured by the SVI, Lafourche and Terrebonne Parish have relatively high SVI scores, which indicates that both parishes face vulnerabilities in socioeconomic status (0.7438 and 0.817, respectively), household characteristics (0.7632 and 0.7807), and housing and transportation (0.7957 and 0.825). In addition, Terrebonne's racial and ethnic minority status score of 0.7212 suggests possible issues with racial and ethnic disparities.

FEMA's National Risk Index

FEMA's National Risk Index[49] ranks Lafourche Parish in the 94th percentile in the United States and in the 83rd percentile within Louisiana,

[46] See footnote 3.
[47] See footnote 4.
[48] See footnote 5.
[49] See footnote 7.

BOX 5-15
Community Testimonial: Community Members Understand the Risks, but Still Plan to Stay

"I've seen the Coastal Master Plan and I've worked on it in a community setting, looking at it, over the last three that they've had for the community. And if you look at it, in all three of the stages of light, moderate, and severe, and what they've shown for Terrebonne and Lafourche Parish, you know, in that 50-year plan, we're not here with the tidal surge. But people are still staying. And when it's been presented at different community events looking at it, people are still staying. And we're going to—I'm going to stay. And I know the severity, and I understand the language of what they're saying, you know, of what our future looks like. But I'm not going anywhere, you know. My people are water people. And, you know, we're going to ride it out until we can't ride it anymore, you know. And we'll go back to boats, you know."

SOURCE: Bette Billiot, the United Houma Nation. Workshop 3: Assisted Resettlement and Receiving Communities in Louisiana, July 2022, Houma, Louisiana.

"These occurrences are not new occurrences. These things continue to happen. But yet, after each event, I see the delays in receiving resources to help people get back to living, you know, in their homes and in their communities. The delays have increased exponentially. So, in my opinion, there's [sic] —I see a prevalence towards conversations to look towards the coastal zone, the coastal region to industrialization. And I think that's the big thing that we have to worry about, not gentrification, per se, although we do see some of that happening. But I think we need to dissuade those who have the perspective of thinking that we are going to let this happen and not speak out against our removals from our land because they fail to, you know, put in the resources necessary for us to continue our lives and our inhabitation that that's going to happen easily. It's not. We are determined to remain where we are. We're going to work for reforms. We're going to have the conversations for people who are like-minded and who advocate for us to find ways to live with the changes until we can find something different. But I think that gentrification is not the word that we need to start focusing on. We need to look at industrialization."

SOURCE: Elder Rosina Philippe, Atakapa-Ishak/Chawasha Tribe and President of the First Peoples' Conservation Council. Workshop 3: Community Viability and Environmental Change in Coastal Louisiana, July 2022, Thibodaux, Louisiana.

meaning that about 6 percent of U.S. counties and 17 percent of counties in Louisiana have a higher risk index than Lafourche Parish. Terrebonne Parish is in the 96th percentile in the United States and in the 89th percentile within the state, meaning that only about 4 percent of U.S. counties and 11 percent of counties within Louisiana have a higher risk index than Terrebonne Parish. FEMA's National Risk Index is calculated using three components: a natural hazard risk component (EAL[50]), a consequence enhancing component (social vulnerability[51]), and a consequence reduction component (community resilience[52]; Zuzak et al., 2023). The National Risk Index for Lafourche Parish reflects relatively moderate[53] EAL while Terrebonne Parish reflects relatively high EAL; ratings for both parishes reflect very high social vulnerability and community resilience (see Figure 5-5). Of the 18 hazards included in the National Risk Index, Lafourche Parish has a rating above the 80th percentile in the nation for hurricanes, tornadoes, coastal flooding, and lighting, while Terrebonne Parish has a rating above the 80th percentile for hurricanes, tornadoes, riverine flooding, coastal flooding, lighting, and heatwaves. With percentiles around 95 and above, Lafourche Parish is one of the most at-risk counties for hurricanes, and Terrebonne Parish is one of the most at-risk counties in the United States for hurricanes and lighting. The total EAL from all hazards (i.e., total building value, population, and/or agriculture value) for both Lafourche Parish and Terrebonne Parish is over 190.6 million dollars.

EPA's EJScreen

According to EPA's EJScreen,[54] Lafourche Parish is approximately at or above the 50th percentile in the nation for particulate matter, ozone, diesel particulate matter, air toxics cancer risk, air toxics respiratory HI, toxic releases to air, lead paint, superfund proximity, RMP facility proximity, hazardous waste proximity, underground storage tanks, and wastewater discharge. Terrebonne Parish is approximately at or above the 50th percentile in the nation for particulate matter, ozone, diesel particulate matter, air toxics cancer risk, air toxics respiratory HI, toxic releases to air, traffic proximity, lead paint, superfund proximity, RMP facility proximity, proximity to hazardous waste, underground storage tanks, and wastewater discharge.

Tropical Storms and Hurricanes That Have Impacted Louisiana Since 2000

Louisiana has faced a series of notable disasters from the year 2000 to present day, including Hurricanes Ida (2021), Zeta (2020), Laura (2020), Delta (2020), Isaac (2012), Gustav (2008), and Katrina (2005), each of

[50]See footnote 8.
[51]See footnote 9.
[52]See footnotes 10 and 11.
[53]See footnote 12.
[54]See footnote 13.

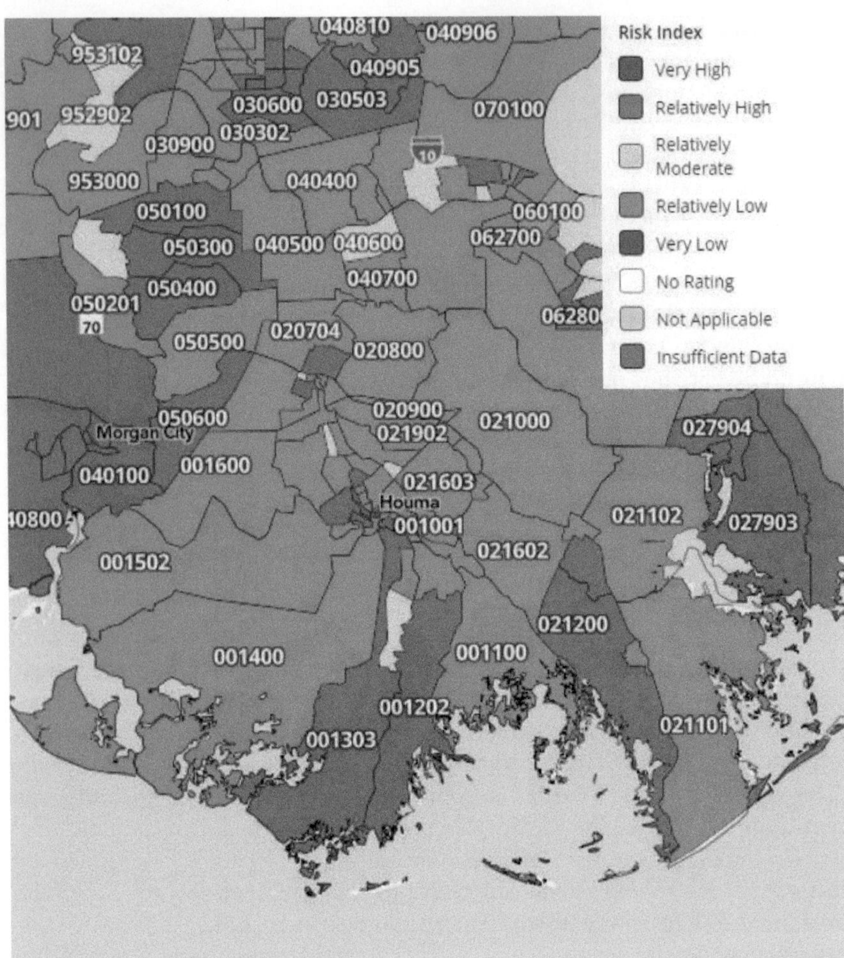

FIGURE 5-5 National Risk Index, Lafourche and Terrebonne Parishes, Louisiana.
SOURCE: FEMA. (2023h). *National Risk Index: Explore the map*. https://hazards.fema.gov/nri/map

BOX 5-16
Community Testimonial: Response to Hurricanes

"We've all just experienced Hurricane Ida, and it was a very, very hard time for all of us here, and still is. Still very difficult. And one of the things that was most difficult for me to grapple with was that I wanted my son, who's a year and a half, to be able to have the experiences that I had as a kid. And I wanted him to grow up in this culture that I found so dear to my heart. And it wasn't until the hurricane that I realized that the town I grew up in, Chauvin, in the '80s no longer exists. And that no longer existed before the storm, right. And it's because this migration took place long before the hurricane, because, again, it's a part of our story. So, my son is not going to grow up in that same way, but that's just the way that it is for different reasons."

SOURCE: Jonathan Foret, Executive Director, South Louisiana Wetlands Discovery Center. Workshop 3: Assisted Resettlement and Receiving Communities in Louisiana, July 2022, Houma, Louisiana.

which were federally declared major disasters (see Boxes 5-17 and 5-18). The most severe of these hurricanes was Hurricane Katrina, with a total of 186 billion dollars in damages and 41.1 billion dollars in insured damages in the United States (25.3 billion dollars in insured damages in Louisiana) in 2005 (Hartwig & Wilkinson, 2010; Knabb et al., 2023). The federal response to these disasters involved major disaster declarations; financial assistance for affected residents; and funding for public infrastructure projects, emergency protective measures, and hazard mitigation programs, including relocation (see Box 5-19). See Table C-5 in Appendix C for more information.

Port Arthur, Texas

Introduction

This community profile provides this information for one of the locations of this study's first workshop, Port Arthur in southeast Texas along the Gulf of Mexico. However, some datasets were only available at the county level of Jefferson County, where Port Arthur is located.

Port Arthur is a coastal city located in Jefferson County about 90 miles east of Houston in the Beaumont-Port Arthur metropolitan area. Port Arthur has a population of 55,757, with 42.2 percent identifying as Black or African American, 43.0 percent identifying as White, and 32.2 percent

BOX 5-17
Community Testimonial: Locals Are Used to Flooding, but Hurricane Ida Brought Damaging Winds, Exposing Community Vulnerabilities

"Now, the difference, for us, in past hurricanes, everybody knew what to do. So, you had a flood, and you cut out four feet of your walls, and you wainscoted it, and you moved on, because Cajun men knew how to fix their homes. And you might have had Chauvin that was affected, but Bourg not so much, and Montegut not so much. So, they came together to help the people who needed it. For Ida, it was very, very different. Very different. Whether it is climate change, a better levy system, we were spared from the flooding. But, for the first time ever, the damages were different [...] I would like to know the percentages of who lost their roofs, and those men didn't know how to fix that, nor do you really have the capability to put your own roof on. You have to hire somebody. So, I think we lost so many residents [i.e., they moved away] this hurricane because it was a different monster of a hurricane. We knew how to handle water; nobody knew how to handle what we went through for Ida. And so, it was tough. And so, yeah, I think we'll see people, I think, leave because they can't fix their homes, you know. Most of them just couldn't even fix their homes, where in the past they could have done it themselves."

SOURCE: Genie Ardoin, Resident of Houma, Louisiana. Workshop 3: Assisted Resettlement and Receiving Communities in Louisiana, July 2022, Houma, Louisiana.

"I hadn't thought about that before because I kept hearing people say this is a storm like we've never had before. And in my head, it was that it was so destructive, and it was more of a wind event than a water event because we're used to water events. But I think maybe what you just said may be more of what it's about. It's that we weren't able to help each other. And we couldn't use the storm as a unifying event, which storms in the past kind of had been. Because we'd come together, you have that experience. You're eating at somebody's house because you're helping them. And we're all helping each other. And it kind of makes you feel good. This one, we all needed help. And it didn't come and it's still not coming. And we are a people who rely on ourselves. And it's sort of like we couldn't like we could."

SOURCE: Jonathan Foret, Executive Director, South Louisiana Wetlands Discovery Center. Workshop 3: Assisted Resettlement and Receiving Communities in Louisiana, July 2022, Houma, Louisiana.

BOX 5-18
Community Testimonial: Planning for Protecting Culture Lags Behind Planning for Protecting Land

"In Louisiana we've talked about the coastal Master Plan. We are ahead of the game in restoring land because we've been thinking about that for a long time. Remaking Barrier Islands and making levies and we're really good at that but I have a feeling what we're going to talk about today is we're behind on that real important part of the formula of saving the culture and the Rougarou Fest is like a step in the right direction. Right? But there's this—everybody knows that if the people from all down the bayou communities, if they all move to Houma, it still wouldn't quite be the same. So, there's this effort—there's an idea that maybe we can save those places. So, to me there's a paradox. It's like—Chauvin is almost like—in a Hospice situation. Like if you've had someone in your family in Hospice, you know it's coming. You know it's coming but they're still alive and Chauvin is kind of like that. The paradox is I want to save the little town of Chauvin. I wish we could save it but it'd be really hard for me to tell my daughters okay, go move there. Yes, go put a house in Chauvin. It just does not make sense to build a new house in a place like Pointe-aux-Chenes or Chauvin. It just doesn't add up because it seems too dangerous. Right? So, it seems like to me we have this conflict that we're facing and so maybe state policy makers, since we put so much effort into saving the land, the next step is to come up with plans and strategies to save the culture so that we don't lose that. That's what I wanted to say."

SOURCE: Gary LaFleur, President, Barataria-Terrebonne National Estuary Foundation and Professor, Biological Sciences, Nicholls State University. Workshop 3: Assisted Resettlement and Receiving Communities in Louisiana, July 2022, Houma, Louisiana.

identifying as Hispanic or Latino. It is adjacent to the Sabine and Neches Rivers and borders the state of Louisiana. The Sabine Lake area has been occupied for over 1,500 years, when its first settlers were primarily the Atakapa tribe.[55] In 1901, the "Lucas Gusher," an oil discovery near Beaumont, led to Port Arthur serving as a hub for the emerging petrochemical industry.[56] Gulf Oil Corp and Texaco established refining plants in the city in 1901 and 1902, respectively. The Motiva Refinery, the largest oil refinery in the United States, is located in the city (Motiva, 2020).

[55]More information about Sabine Lake and the Atakapa Tribe is available at https://www.portarthurtx.gov/236/About-Us

[56]This oil discovery launched the modern petroleum industry. More information is available at https://aoghs.org/petroleum-pioneers/spindletop-launches-modern-oil-industry/

BOX 5-19
Community Testimonial: Cascading Problems—Housing and Transportation

"The only thing we wanted was guidance from our mayor [...] but then he was absent [...] The plan was [to get them] into housing and helping them [...] But yet whenever you're in a situation where there's chronic unemployment or there's chronic loss of houses and habitat, someone needs to talk to the people; someone needs to guide people. We didn't have that leadership and that guidance at that particular time, so we were really, really excited to get the mayor on the phone and one of their plans was basically [...] to house people on barges. So that plan kind of fell through. It didn't work out [and] the next thing you know they were talking to the U.S. Army about bringing in tents, and that's actually what they did. They brought in a bunch of tents, set up those tents by the public library on Highway 73, and they started housing people there."

SOURCE: Hilton Kelley, Founder and Director, Community In-Power and Development Association Inc. Workshop 1: Strategic Relocation and Environmental Perception: Community Perspectives from Port Arthur, Texas, June 2022.

"One of my big pet peeves about being on the west side is that they feel that they don't have to do certain things that they really should do because of who we are, where we are, and what they think we don't have to offer. We have people that live on the west side that are very educated that are there because they want to be there, not because they have to be there. Retirees, people that have relocated back home after retiring from other places, because the cost of living here is cheaper, but they pay the price of having to live in these areas. So, but that is what I would like to see, I would like to see Port Arthur cleaned up. I would like to see the west side cleaned up."

SOURCE: Pamela Graham, Resident of Port Arthur, Texas. Workshop 1: Strategic Relocation and Environmental Perception: Community Perspectives from Port Arthur, Texas, June 2022.

Current and Projected Flood Risk

The Coastal County Snapshots from NOAA reveal that 1.5 percent of Jefferson County's population resides in low-lying areas.[57] However, *all* critical facilities, including schools and medical establishments, are located outside these low-lying areas. An analysis by the Union of Concerned Scientists[58] projects that under a moderate sea level rise scenario, by 2035, fewer

[57]Low-lying areas are defined as "less than 2 feet of sea level rise." More information is available at https://coast.noaa.gov/digitalcoast/tools/snapshots.html

[58]See footnote 4.

than 1 percent of homes in Port Arthur, valued at $689,230 and housing 18 residents, will be chronically inundated. This risk is expected to escalate to include 62 homes (still less than 1% of the total), accommodating 141 people, with a value of close to 5 million dollars by 2100 (see Boxes 5-20 and 5-21).

SVI and Health

With an SVI of 0.8063 in 2020 within the state of Texas, Jefferson County is classified as having a high level of vulnerability, according to factors such as poverty, access to transportation, and crowded housing.[59] This ranking means that less than 5 percent of counties in the United States and less than 20 percent of counties in Texas are classified as more socially vulnerable than Jefferson County. With high SVI scores across socioeconomic status (0.9188), household characteristics (0.9112), racial and ethnic minority status (0.9233), and housing and transportation (0.8978), Jefferson

BOX 5-20
Community Testimonial: Flooding Complications

"It's a continuous spiral and you feel like you are never going to be able to recover. After Hurricane Harvey [2017], a lot of the homes that we see in Port Arthur that weren't in the floodplain are now all of a sudden in a floodplain. Now these folks are required to get flood insurance just to potentially get some help in the future if they ever do flood. So, it's like you're stuck in a corner and now the tables have turned, all of a sudden, your home is in a floodplain, and you have to purchase flood insurance that you cannot afford."

SOURCE: Michelle Smith, Community In-Power and Development Association Inc. Workshop 1: Strategic Relocation and Environmental Perception: Community Perspectives from Port Arthur, Texas, June 2022.

"It was devastating. I'm 75 years old, I felt like I was aged when finally, I found a place where I was comfortable. It was devastating to lose my home in that flood because my husband had passed away. It was just me. So, I've got to get back to trying to bring things back together and make it a home—that was devastating to me. And they've talked about buyouts. I have considered it, I really have, because I don't want to go through another storm."

SOURCE: Octavia Sanders, Resident of Port Arthur, Texas. Workshop 1: Strategic Relocation and Environmental Perception: Community Perspectives from Port Arthur, Texas, June 2022.

[59] See footnote 5.

BOX 5-21
Community Testimonial: Emissions-Related Health Concerns

"I'm a person who is quite sensitive to emissions that are in the air because there are times at night when I wake up my nose is runny, I'm coughing, I'm sneezing, [but] I know my house is clean. But still I wake up [coughing at night]. I take vitamins. I am very healthy. I've never really been sick a day in my life and I've been here 65 years. But now every morning, you're sneezing and you're coughing, you're sneezing and you're coughing. Your eyes are burning. There's nowhere to go. There's no one to talk to. What can we do? Where can we go? We're healthy people and now we're getting sick every week."

SOURCE: Marie Kelley, Community In-Power and Development Association Inc. Workshop 1: Strategic Relocation and Environmental Perception: Community Perspectives from Port Arthur, Texas, June 2022.

"The large number of emissions that were being dumped from the air, like sulfur dioxide, benzine, ethylene oxide you name it, people in West Port Arthur breathe. And we have scars to prove it, many of us have died, many of us are still suffering from cancer, respiratory problems, liver and kidney disease."

SOURCE: Hilton Kelley, Founder and Director, Community In-Power and Development Association Inc. Workshop 1: Strategic Relocation and Environmental Perception: Community Perspectives from Port Arthur, Texas, June 2022.

County possesses notable socioeconomic, demographic, and infrastructural vulnerabilities. One of the most significant challenges facing Port Arthur is the pollution caused by the petrochemical industry (Environmental Integrity Project, 2017). The city is home to several large refineries and chemical plants, which emit toxic pollutants into the air and water. These pollutants have been linked to a range of health problems, including chronic and acute bronchitis, cancer, acute myocardial infarction, emergency room visits, restricted activity days, and even adult and infant mortality (Environmental Integrity Project, 2017).

FEMA's National Risk Index

FEMA's National Risk Index[60] ranks Jefferson County in the 97.74th percentile in the nation and 95.7th percentile within Texas (see Figure 5-6). This ranking means that only about 2 percent of counties in the United States and 4 percent of counties in Texas have a higher risk index than

[60]See footnote 7.

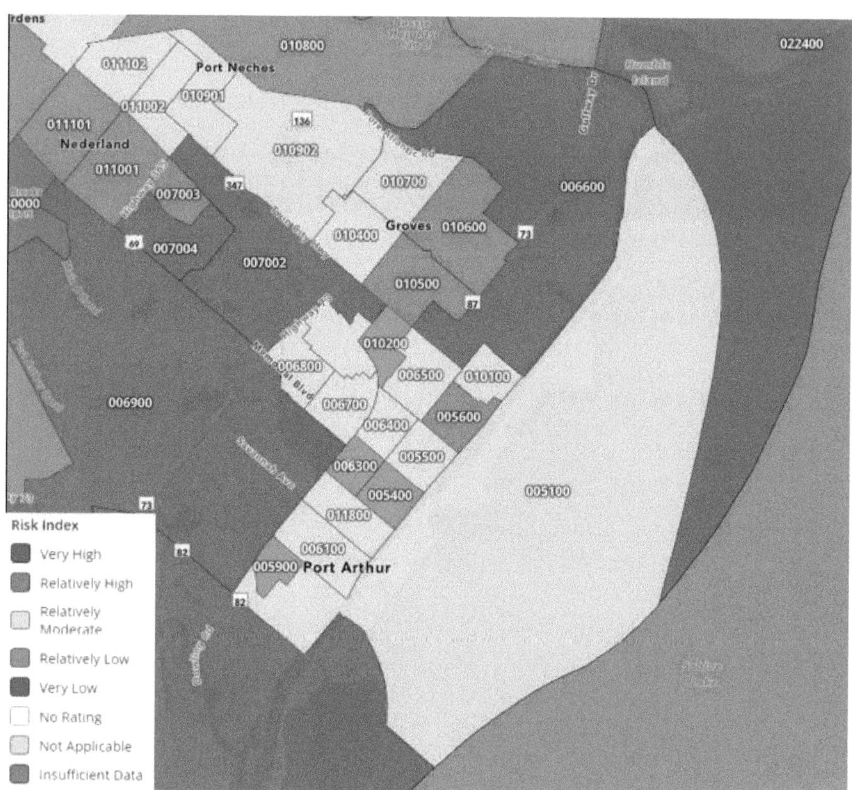

FIGURE 5-6 National Risk Index, Jefferson County, Texas.
SOURCE: FEMA. (2023h). *National Risk Index: Explore the map.* https://hazards.fema.gov/nri/map

Jefferson County. FEMA's National Risk Index is calculated using three components: a natural hazard risk component (EAL[61]), a consequence enhancing component (social vulnerability[62]), and a consequence reduction component (community resilience[63]; Zuzak et al., 2023). The National Risk Index for Jefferson County reflects relatively high[64] EAL and very high social vulnerability with relatively high community resilience (FEMA, 2023h; see Box 5-22). Of the 18 hazards included in the National Risk Index, Jefferson County is above the 85th percentile rating in the nation for hail and heat waves. With percentiles around 98th and above, Jefferson County is one of the most at-risk counties in the United States for hurricanes, riverine

[61]See footnote 8.
[62]See footnote 9.
[63]See footnotes 10 and 11.
[64]See footnote 12.

BOX 5-22
Community Testimonial: Residents Have Few Choices

"There was one woman who got ripped off by contractors. She was trying to rebuild a home and her husband needed a breathing machine just to survive [...] They were staying in a shelter that it wasn't okay for them to have [the respirator] there, that he didn't have enough to actually [... use] the breathing machine. They had mold in the house, they moved back into that home with mold and his health conditions that he had because they had no other choice. And it's plenty of people who can tell you the same story of how they had no other choice."

SOURCE: Landry Patin, Resident of Port Arthur, Texas. Workshop 1: Strategic Relocation and Environmental Perception: Community Perspectives from Port Arthur, Texas, June 2022.

flooding, tornadoes, and lightning. The expected annual loss from all hazards (building value, population, and/or agriculture value) for Jefferson County is over 161.6 million dollars.

EPA's EJScreen

According to EPA's EJScreen,[65] Port Arthur is approximately at or above 90th percentile in the nation for particulate matter, ozone, air toxics cancer risk, toxic releases to air, superfund proximity, RMP facility proximity, hazardous waste proximity, underground storage tanks, and wastewater discharge. The only EJI for which Port Arthur is below the 80th percentile in the nation is diesel particulate matter and air toxics respiratory HI.

Tropical Storms and Hurricanes That Have Impacted Port Arthur Since 2000

Port Arthur has experienced several notable disasters from the year 2000 to present day, including Hurricanes Laura (2020), Harvey (2017), Ike (2008), Gustav (2008), and Rita (2005), each of which were federally declared major disasters. These hurricanes caused widespread and significant power outages, flooding, death and injury, and temporary relocation, and widespread damage to homes, infrastructure, and businesses. FEMA and other federal assistance programs supported much of the state of Texas to assuage flooding and storm damages to businesses and infrastructure. See Table C-6 in Appendix C for more information.

[65]See footnote 13.

DATA AVAILABILITY ACROSS PROFILES

Data availability was not uniform across the places that were profiled above. Smaller communities completely lacked or had gaps in publicly available information. For example, data from the U.S. Census Bureau were not publicly available for Bayou La Batre, Alabama, or Turkey Creek, Mississippi, and summarized or "QuickFacts" were not available in communities with less than a population of 5,000.[66] In Port Arthur, Texas, some U.S. Census Bureau data were "suppressed to avoid disclosure of confidential information" or "did not meet publication standards."[67] For FEMA's National Risk Index, most case locations were only available at the parish level or at the county level.[68] The NOAA Coastal Flood Exposure Mapper did not include data for Turkey Creek at the community or ZIP code level, where all other cases were represented. Finally, there is a lack of clarity among data and statistics for notable recent disasters; some sites report damages, repairs, and deaths differently, making summarizing the damage and impacts as well as the federal response post-storms difficult.

Data scale and application context is often a barrier to accurately representing smaller communities (National Academies, 2018a). Additionally, the U.S. Census Bureau's annual ACS has high margins of error and lower response rates in less populated areas than more populated areas, creating inconsistent data metrics (Scally & Burnstein, 2020).[69] Other challenges for collecting data in rural areas include higher poverty rates, limited access to technology, higher unemployment rates, and lower high school graduation rates (O'Hare, 2017). Finally, there is a higher number of hard-to-count counties in rural areas (O'Hare, 2017).

SUMMARY

The community members' testimonials foregrounded in this chapter have provided invaluable insight into the varied experiences, desires, and concerns that people living in this region bring to decisions around how to respond to changing environmental realities. The statistics reviewed in each

---

[66]More information about the U.S. Census Bureau is available at https://www.census.gov/en.html

[67]More information is available at https://www.census.gov/quickfacts/fact/table/stpetersburgcityflorida,portarthurcitytexas,terrebonneparishlouisiana,lafourcheparishlouisiana/PST045222#qf-flag-D

[68]More about FEMA's National Risk Index information is available at https://hazards.fema.gov/nri/map

[69]ACS metrics are combined over five years to compensate for smaller sample sizes. Additionally, there has been a gradual transition to an internet-based census, which is limiting for rural areas. More information about this is available at https://www.urban.org/urban-wire/rural-communities-need-better-data

community profile add to these insights, and it is the hope of the committee that these profiles illuminate important aspects of this complex topic. In the committee's judgment, it is critical for policy makers and community stakeholders to understand and acknowledge the following:

1. Climate change projections and pre-existing socioeconomic vulnerabilities result in Gulf Coast communities of diverse geographic scale and demographics facing the threat of displacement.
2. Population is increasing in all Gulf Coast areas except in Louisiana. Increases in population place more people and property at risk in the Gulf region.
3. Resource- or amenity-based livelihoods deter residents from considering relocation. Strong attachments to place among traditional cultures also minimize the interest in relocation.

The next chapter approaches the concept of relocation from a different angle as it examines well-being frameworks in the context of climate change, displacement, and relocation. Specifically, it focuses attention on how well-being frameworks help understand, navigate, and prioritize mental and psychological health and identifies tools to enhance resilience, social capital, community cohesion, and communal/collective efficacy.

CONCLUSIONS

Conclusion 5-1: Community profiles, combining quantitative and qualitative analyses, illustrate how and why communities across the U.S. Gulf Coast Region are vulnerable to increasing climate change risks and the limits of their capacities to adapt-in-place. As climate change impacts accumulate, compound, and intensify, the analysis also suggests which areas of the region will require consideration of relocation and on what timescales.

Conclusion 5-2: Despite environmental threats, Gulf Coast populations have increased steadily for 50 years. Movement toward the coast has increased construction and real estate values and thereby enhanced risk, while contributing to gentrification. Traditional placed-based communities with long relationships to coastal lands and waters have expertise, social networks, and skillsets evolved from local knowledge and centuries of resilient behaviors. Place-based communities are often reluctant to relocate because of their unique economic, social, and cultural attachments to place, and they also often lack access to resources if they do want to relocate.

Conclusion 5-3: The combination of increasing population, growth of urban areas, economic activity, and infrastructure investment make the Gulf Coast even more susceptible to the impacts of extreme weather and sea level rise than decades ago.

Conclusion 5-4: If decisions about relocation are to be community-driven, data that influence those decisions need to be transparent to residents, accessible, and up to date.

Conclusion 5-5: Data relevant to community-driven decision making about relocation are effective and can be efficiently leveraged if they are generated by pairing quantitative information with the qualitative experiences of residents; in this report, qualitative input was obtained through dialogue with the people that live in the context that the data quantify.

6

Sustaining Community Well-Being: Physical, Mental, and Social Health

This chapter discusses the following:

- Definitions and frameworks for a holistic approach to well-being, including capacities for subjective well-being and capabilities for action
- Pre-existing, continuous, and new impacts to well-being, including mental health impacts, in the context of climate change and displacement
- Enhancement of well-being through task sharing and nurture effects
- Relocation in the context of social capital and place attachment

INTRODUCTION

Previous chapters presented an overview of historical and current injustices (e.g., enslavement, isolation, political disenfranchisement). The summaries of community profiles in Chapter 5 (and the full profiles in Appendix C) demonstrate that these injustices are compounded by a range of vulnerabilities (e.g., social, health, economic), current climate and environmental hazards, and a history of disastrous climate events. The present conditions of these communities collectively contribute to reduced adaptive capacity and resilience in response to climate change, creating a strong need for more support mechanisms to improve and ensure that communities can cope with and adapt to the additional stresses of the potential need to relocate (as well as other responses). Ultimately, heightened vulnerability compounds risks and compromises community well-being, the focus of this chapter.

Well-being has long been recognized as an essential component of health. The World Health Organization (WHO) made a critical link between well-being and health in its definition of health as "a state of complete physical, social and mental well-being and not merely the absence of disease and infirmity" (WHO, 1946). While well-being is a critical component of health, it is sometimes missing from conversations about health care and public health (cf. Eiroa-Orosa, 2020).

Well-being can be broadly defined as how people feel and how they function physically, socially, and psychologically (Jarden & Roache, 2023). In this report, we define physical well-being as maintaining a healthy lifestyle, access to health care, regular sleep, eating well, adequate housing, exercise, and avoiding exposure to harmful substances (Capio et al., 2014). We define social well-being as social connectedness, "the degree to which individuals or groups of individuals have and perceive a desired number, quality, and diversity of relationships that create a sense of belonging and being cared for, valued, and supported" (Centers for Disease Control and Prevention [CDC], 2023; Holt-Lunstad, 2022; National Academies of Sciences, Engineering, and Medicine, 2021, 2022b). Finally, we define psychological well-being as several aspects of health-related quality of life, thriving, and several psychological dimensions, including "positive emotions and moods (e.g., happiness); the relative absence of negative emotions, moods, and states (e.g., stress, sadness, loneliness); life satisfaction; sense of meaning and purpose; quality of life; and satisfaction with other life domains (e.g., work satisfaction, satisfaction with relationships)" (Feller et al., 2018, p. 137). In this chapter, the committee asserts that centering the physical, social, and psychological well-being of individuals and communities, as well as the relationships inherent in and consequential to both spheres, can foster and enhance the capacities and capabilities of communities, their institutions, and their organizations (e.g., local government, health institutions) in the context of displacement and community-driven relocation.

This chapter begins with a transdisciplinary overview of health and well-being, delineating various conceptual framings of well-being in the context of environmental threats and relocation that construct, represent, and value subjective and objective measures of well-being. Next, we review the evidence-based literature about the application of a well-being lens in the context of the pre-existing, continuous, and new climate change and displacement impacts on communities. Lastly, the chapter presents arguments of how social capital and place attachment, which are strongly linked to well-being, factor into community decision making regarding the process of relocation. Overall, this chapter focuses attention on how centering and prioritizing well-being helps to understand, navigate, and prioritize mental and psychological health, and to identify tools to enhance resilience, social capital, community cohesion, and collective efficacy. Many of these tools reside within cultural legacies; Indigenous sovereignty; and attachment to, reciprocity with, and relationship to place—all of which exist within the context of increasing climatic extremes, uncertainty, displacement, and relocation processes.

The committee engaged with Indigenous individuals and representatives of Indigenous perspectives, and acknowledges that the well-being frameworks included in this report (e.g., Seven Vital Conditions, Building Resilience Against Climate Effects [BRACE]) do not include all the distinct cultural models and dimensions of health and well-being that exist throughout the world or even in the U.S. Gulf Coast region, including the multitude of models by Indigenous groups. However, we learned that specifically Indigenous concepts and experiences of well-being can exist at the interface of elements such as identity, place, culture, and community, in concert with the surrounding world (e.g., land, water, animals, ancestors, ecosystems, vibrant matter, and cosmologies; King et al., 2009; United Nations, 2023). We hope that this chapter incorporates these elements in ways that acknowledge the interactions we shared and the information we learned from diverse models of well-being and from participants at information-gathering sessions.

A HOLISTIC APPROACH TO WELL-BEING

A holistic approach to well-being discerns linkages between health disparities (e.g., premature death, elevated levels of chronic diseases, poor mental health, inequitable access to health care) and complex socioeconomic disparities (e.g., intergenerational poverty, economic precarity). These linkages are in large part perpetuated through failures, or an inability, to address important elements of community well-being, in particular, social capital, public goods, and emotional health—elements that sustain and mutually reinforce hope and collective efficacy (Graham, 2017, 2023). A holistic well-being approach has been promoted as an important policy focus for governments and an alternative to a dominant focus on the generation of economic growth (e.g., see Dalziel et al., 2018; Sen, 1983, 1999), which may come at the expense of well-being or be undermined by conditions of poor well-being, such as high vulnerability to climate change threats. Prioritizing well-being and its outcomes as the primary aim by which economic choices are judged and by which economic investments are made has proven feasible and scalable (see Brown et al., 2017; Frijters & Krekel, 2021; Hardoon et al., 2020).

Climate change presents a multitude of challenges to the well-being of individuals and communities. A holistic view shows how community well-being and adaptive capacities to respond to climate threats are undermined by pre-existing social and economic health inequities resulting from historical racial and social discrimination and marginalization, as discussed in Chapters 4 and 5. These conditions, in turn, have placed many poor and minoritized coastal communities in harm's way (i.e., in more flood-prone areas, in housing that is less protective, and in communities where there has been a failure to invest in levees and other community-level protective measures; Morello-Frosch & Obasogie, 2023). Climate vulnerability in communities is a function of "baseline vulnerabilities (health, social/economic, infrastructure, and environment)" in the context of significant "climate change risks (health, social/economic, extreme events)" (Tee Lewis et al., 2023, p. 1); therefore, climate vulnerability is an exacerbation of already-existing challenges to community well-being.

The U.S. Department of Health and Human Services' (HHS's) efforts to recognize the interrelations between climate change, health equity, and environmental justice are visualized below in Figure 6-1, which draws from the U.S. Global Change Research Program's (USGCRP's) Fourth National Climate Assessment (Reidmiller et al., 2018) and the Climate and Health Assessment (Crimmins et al., 2016), and particularly recognizes how climate-induced health effects disproportionately affect underresourced communities and how these impacts are compounded by existing environmental and social contexts.[1] These interrelations offer a productive entry point to examine ways for the broader community of health service providers, including community health workers, to take a more active role in connecting all aspects of well-being in climate adaptation planning.

A shift to a well-being approach means departing from a pre-disaster planning and post-disaster recovery paradigm to an ongoing project of sustaining community ties, collective efficacy, and participation. These three components nurture and rely on emotional, psychological, and behavioral strengthening. Community health (including well-being) is critical to the sustaining of community agency and to being able to adequately navigate the huge range of decisions, challenges, and transformations that U.S. Gulf Coast communities increasingly face as they cope with environmental change.

Resources for this kind of participatory and holistic approach to community building are readily available to support such work. In the United States, for example, the integration of well-being science and community strengthening has been implemented at scale through the work of the Well

[1]More information about the HHS initiative for climate change, health equity, and environmental justice is available at hhs.gov/climate-change-health-equity-environmental-justice/index.html

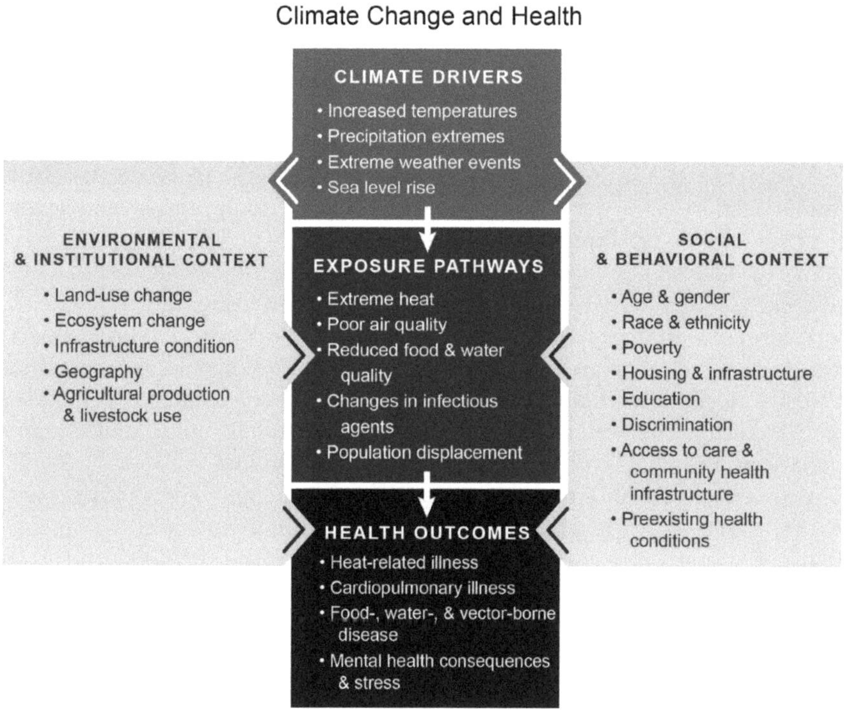

FIGURE 6-1 Conceptual diagram illustrating the exposure pathways by which climate change affects human health.
SOURCE: Crimmins, A., Balbus, J., Gamble, J. L., Beard, C. B., Bell, J. E., Dodgen, D., Eisen, R. J., Fann, N., Hawkins, M. D., Herring, S. C., Jantarasami, L., Mills, D. M., Saha, S., Sarofim, M. C., Trtanj, J., & L. Ziska (Eds.). (2016). *The impacts of climate change on human health in the United States: A scientific assessment.* U.S. Global Change Research Program. https://health2016.globalchange.gov/

Being in the Nation (WIN) Network.[2] Through an effort of more than 100 organizations and communities, with support from the National Committee on Vital and Health Statistics (NCVHS), the work of WIN has yielded comprehensive core measures that are accessible and relevant to communities, government, and other entities.[3] These core measures include the well-being of people, the well-being of places, and equity.[4] WIN created a template for community coalition-led actions for advancing population well-being through addressing "The Seven Vital Conditions for Well-Being," a framework that combines major determinants of health with the properties of

[2]More information on WIN is available at https://winnetwork.org/
[3]More information about NCVHS is available at https://ncvhs.hhs.gov/about/
[4]More information is available at https://www.winmeasures.org/

places and institutions that together advance a collaborative and cross-sector approach to well-being. The seven vital conditions included in the framework are reliable transportation, thriving natural world, basic needs for health and safety, humane housing, meaningful work and wealth, and lifelong learning, with belonging and civic muscle at the center.[5]

Together, the seven vital conditions and the WIN template for community action were the foundation for a federal comprehensive strategy, the Federal Plan for Equitable Long-Term Recovery and Resilience (Federal Plan for ELTRR), a cross-agency effort to "equitably achieve enhanced resilience."[6] Implicit within this plan is the need for engaging public health, writ large, in all aspects of community-driven relocation planning. Building on the Federal Plan for ELTRR, the first ever White House National Climate Resilience Framework (2023) uses a "people-centered principle" to "[p]osition the well-being of individuals, families, communities, and society at the center of [climate resilience] goals and solutions" (p. 7). The framework's objectives assert that both the built environment and nature-based solutions are also investments in community well-being, and that investments in a community's health care system—including outreach networks—will "improve not just the overall health and well-being of community members during normal operations, but also their capacity to mitigate, adapt to, and recover from the compounding impacts of extreme weather events and long-term climate stresses" (p. 26).[7]

CDC's framework, BRACE (see Figure 6-2), is another tool that can be used in taking a well-being approach to climate adaptation. This framework outlines a five-step process for health officials to develop strategies and programs to anticipate, prepare for, and respond to a range of climate change impacts on health and well-being (CDC, 2022) more effectively. Alongside epidemiologic analysis, the BRACE process also involves the inclusion of climatological data and projections (e.g., future temperature and precipitation) in public health planning (CDC, 2022). The inclusion of updated climatological science strengthens the process of informed risk

[5]Each of the seven vital conditions for well-being are broad categories. For example, the condition of "civic muscle" includes social support; freedom from stigma, discrimination, and oppression; collective efficacy; and spiritual life, among others. The condition of "reliable transportation" also includes efficient energy use. The condition of "thriving natural world" includes freedom from heat, flooding, wind, radiation, earthquakes, and pathogens as well as access to natural spaces, among others. More information about these conditions is available at https://winnetwork.org/vital-conditions

[6]More information about the Federal Plan for ELTRR is available at https://health.gov/our-work/national-health-initiatives/equitable-long-term-recovery-and-resilience

[7]More information about the National Climate Resilience Framework is available at https://www.whitehouse.gov/wp-content/uploads/2023/09/National-Climate-Resilience-Framework-FINAL.pdf

FIGURE 6-2 The CDC's Framework, BRACE.
SOURCE: CDC. (2022). CDC's Building Resilience Against Climate Effects (BRACE) Framework. https://www.cdc.gov/climateandhealth/BRACE.htm

communication about climate hazards for the health sector, thus enhancing a sustained assessment of current and projected risks for communities in environmentally high-risk areas.

A multitude of community resilience frameworks and models, such as BRACE, can be utilized to assess and enhance well-being. It is beyond the capacity of this report to provide a comprehensive overview of these works, but relevant examples could include a perspective on community resilience as a process that links a network of adaptive capacities (Norris et al., 2008); a place-based model for understanding disaster resilience (Cutter et al., 2008); and a reimagining of community resilience in terms of equity and sustainability (National Academies, 2023b). In the context of climate and displacement, there is also much to learn from recent critiques of the resilience concept by climate justice scholars and practitioners (see Moulton & Machado, 2019; Porter et al., 2020; Ranganathan & Bratman, 2019).

Another resource that provides a community well-being perspective on health and climate change is the U.S. Environmental Protection Agency's (EPA's) Social Vulnerability Report (2021b), which delineates six impacts that adversely affect health either directly or indirectly: (1) air quality, (2) extreme temperatures, (3) negative impacts of extreme temperature on work, (4) coastal flooding impacts on traffic, (5) coastal flooding impacts on property, and (6) inland flooding impacts on property. These impacts undermine the key conditions for well-being and adaptation (as outlined above) by degrading the physical, natural, and social capital that communities possess and rely upon to sustain themselves and effectively respond to stress and change.

Developing a holistic understanding of community well-being and centering it in climate adaptation planning processes allow for more equitable, community-driven responses. Improving well-being is a critical part of this; the next section defines and examines a *capabilities and capacities approach* to improving well-being and adaptive capacity.

Capabilities for Subjective Well-Being and Capacities for Action

Climate adaptation relies on psychological and behavioral adaptation—that is, changes in mindsets and ways of relating to others and nature, reflecting what has been detailed as competencies and strengths of needed "inner-outer transformation" (Wamsler et al., 2021). These shifts are seen as essential for shifts in how societies work in relation both to how people treat each other and to how they treat the planet. Above, we discuss the benefits of understanding climate adaptation from a holistic well-being perspective; here, we discuss how well-being itself might be conceptualized and pursued using a capabilities and capacities approach. Such an approach to the improvement of well-being means working toward social and political conditions that, as much as possible, center and support the abilities of individuals and communities to achieve well-being. This approach specifically incorporates two interrelated domains—capabilities for subjective well-being and capacities for action—that are particularly relevant to our conclusions and recommendations for communities to manage and navigate the conditions and prospects of relocation.

1. *Capabilities for Subjective Well-Being, or How People Are Feeling*. Taking a capabilities approach to the subjective well-being of individuals involves enriching and enabling opportunities for people to socially and emotionally bond, trust, engage reciprocally, and have satisfaction with their lives and their mental and

emotional states—essentially, to create conditions that allow for the improvement of how people are feeling. Conditions within this domain have critical health implications, underpinning socioemotional states including despair, optimism, emotional validation and support, distress, and trust (or lack of it). And, the fulfillment (or not) of these capabilities plays a significant role in premature death, violence, intergenerational poverty, reduced educational success, and civic conflict (Fiedler et al., 2021; Graham, 2017, 2023).

2. *Capacities for Action*. At a community level, well-being is dependent on the capacity for group action and problem-solving strengths (e.g., social capital and cohesion, collective efficacy, shared sense of place; HHS, n.d.). The importance of these capacities and actions in maintaining community well-being for equitable and effective climate adaptation highlights the need to broaden understanding of how communities can prepare for potential displacement or relocation in a socially interconnected and community-centered way. Alongside capabilities for subjective well-being, this domain rests on questions of whether individuals live in conditions that allow them to act on and realize the lives they desire: the actions that enable participation, inclusion, and individual and collective agency, and how these actions are promoted and enacted.

Understanding well-being along these two domains (how people are feeling and their capacity for action) and addressing the challenges that often comprise them is key to understanding and addressing what individuals and communities can withstand, including what actions can be harnessed when relocation is imminent. Importantly, however, strengthening well-being is not an episodic strategy only relevant when the specter of relocation looms. Rather, centering well-being can be a "new normal" for community-driven climate adaptation. In the current context of decision making about relocation, the implementation of well-being frameworks can consist of adapting policies that incorporate and strengthen a community's existing social capabilities (e.g., socioemotional bonding, trust, reciprocal engagement) and capacities for actions (e.g., social capital and cohesion, collective efficacy, shared sense of place). As Hardoon et al. (2020) have articulated, "Using a well-being 'lens' highlights complex problems that require cooperation and joint strategies to tackle. Improvements to our lives can also be bolstered when we design interventions to maximize the impact on all aspects of our well-being, rather than a narrow focus on a specific target" (p. 7).

Thus far, this chapter has defined "well-being" and described its various conceptual framings in the context of environmental threats and relocation, emphasizing the importance of a community's existing social capabilities (e.g., socioemotional bonding, trust, reciprocal engagement) and capacities for actions (e.g., social capital and cohesion, collective efficacy, shared sense of place). In the following sections, we describe pre-existing, continuous, and new impacts to well-being from climate change and climate-induced relocation, and examine practices that can promote individual and community well-being in this context.

PRE-EXISITING, CONTINUOUS, AND NEW IMPACTS ON WELL-BEING

The challenges facing communities contemplating relocation are the result of current processes of displacement and migration, including the culmination of human and ecological precedent and serial events that can exacerbate mental, emotional, and physical distress and, in this, undermine community well-being. In the realm of mental health, for example, this can be seen in the growing body of research on mental health and displacement, which suggests that the effects of climate change interact with and affect the preconditions and current conditions that determine imminent consequences of displacement, as well as impending decisions to relocate (Adams et al., 2009; Lamond et al., 2015; Lawrance et al., 2021; Shultz et al., 2019). These lived experiences underscore how climate and environmental changes profoundly impact individuals and communities in their decision making for migration and relocation. First-hand testimonials from workshop participants (see Box 6-1) attest to the intersection of climate change impacts, displacement, and well-being.

Collectively, these stressors, which operate at individual and community levels, are known as "social determinants of health"[8] and are often compounding and build on existing traumas (including historical traumas detailed in Chapter 4), vulnerabilities, and a lack of capacity to cope, such as the following:

- *Pre-existing and Long-Term Environmental Issues.* Toxins from petrochemical facilities; exposure to airborne toxins from marine, human, and construction "waste" incinerators in or near communities; contaminated food resource pools (gardening, fishing, hunting); chemical exposure to up-stream fertilizers and pesticide deposits in excavated and dredged materials; exposure to

[8]More information about the social determinants of heath is available at https://nam.edu/programs/culture-of-health/young-leaders-visualize-health-equity/what-are-the-social-determinants-of-health/

BOX 6-1
Workshop Testimonials: Mental Health

"And then you have the mental health issue. Post-traumatic stress syndrome, anxiety, and depression are very rampant in people that have to relocate from one area to another because of extreme weather events. Suicide is on the increase in people that have moved from or have been exposed to a severe weather event. Substance abuse is significantly up in people that are suffering from these events. And interpersonal violence, such as violence against women and violence against children, also increases in severe weather events."

SOURCE: Kenneth Bryant, Founder and Chief Executive Officer of Minority Health Coalition of Pinellas, Inc. Workshop 2: Opportunities and Challenges of Climate Adaptation on Florida's Gulf Coast, July 2022, St. Petersburg, Florida.

"And so, just as a community, our mental health is really suffering right now. And [...] you know, people are coping in whatever ways they're able to cope. We do need some serious programs across the board. Because I know for even me [...] because we were out there every day driving down the roads [after Hurricane Ida]. And we would say we're really going to need some counseling after this. Because we were fine, but when you talk to those people and you pull that energy in, you have no choice. I mean, it was horrifying and sad. I know I still didn't get mental help. But I probably need it because it was tough. It was tough. And you just move on. You know, you just move on, for us, helping people. We just forged on. But there were so many people that we had to refer. And we were lucky enough to have some counselors that were willing to do it for free."

SOURCE: Bonnie Theriot, Resident of Houma, Louisiana. Workshop 3: Assisted Resettlement and Receiving Communities in Louisiana, July 2022, Houma, Louisiana.

"I would like to weigh [in] on this issue [of mental health] by lifting up the name of Sharon Hanshaw of East Biloxi because she was an African-American hairdresser who found herself on a rooftop during Hurricane Katrina. The next day she became one of the most significant advocates for climate resilience and justice across the Gulf. The advocacy and community work she took up became very difficult to sustain and ultimately, I believe, it was that work that caused Sharon at a very young age to have a stroke, and then another stroke, and then to pass away. She is one example of many of people whose physical and mental health as community caretakers in an inhospitable context of not just natural disasters but manmade disastrous non-recoveries, living in toxic contamination adjacent to their communities, etc., bear the additional physical and mental assault that this advocacy work entails. So, volunteer caretakers, or otherwise, that are themselves not getting taken care of as they care for others is a worse danger than even sea level rise."

SOURCE: Derrick Evans, Executive Director, Turkey Creek Community Initiatives in Gulfport, Mississippi, and Gulf Coast Fund for Community Renewal and Ecological Health (2005–2013). Virtual Focused Discussion: Mississippi and Alabama Gulf Coast Community Stakeholder Perspectives on Managed Retreat, March 2023.

formaldehyde from the Federal Emergency Management Agency's (FEMA's) Hurricane Katrina trailers; etc.

- *Individual and Community Trauma.* Experiences of weather-related disasters that have resulted in economic damages, higher rates of physiologic (allostatic) stress, chronic diseases, and excess morbidity and mortality in communities.
- *Mental Health Impacts from Climate Change and Climate-induced Relocation.* Repeated exposure to climate harms that are simultaneously episodic, chronic, and anticipated, causing stress mediated by both allostatic load and post-traumatic stress.

Pre-Existing and Long-Term Environmental Health Issues for U.S. Gulf Coast Communities

As described in Chapters 4 and 5, and above, U.S. Gulf Coast communities have been exposed to decades of environmental injustices. Such long-term hazardous and life-threatening conditions include (but are not limited to) chemical, paper, and petroleum refineries; gas and electric production facilities (Bullard, 1983, 2000); airborne toxins from marine, human, and construction "waste" incinerators in or near communities impacted by the BP Oil Spill (Burke & Dearen, 2010); ground contamination from Superfund sites and contaminated food resource pools (e.g., gardening, fishing, hunting) resulting from Hurricane Harvey (Biesecker & Bajak, 2017; Carter, 2017; Page, 2017; Potenza, 2017); chemical exposure to up-stream fertilizers and pesticide deposits in excavated and dredged materials (e.g., from the U.S. Army Corps of Engineers' Mississippi River and Mobile Bay dredging/mitigation projects; Carse & Lewis, 2020); and exposure to formaldehyde from FEMA's Hurricane Katrina trailers (Murphy et al., 2013; Smith, 2015).

These pre-existing and long-term social, economic, and environmental traumas and stressors have negatively impacted well-being, thus depleting individual and collective capacities to cope with or respond effectively to the adverse conditions that underlie climate-induced relocation considerations. Historical traumas and stressors may compound and amplify chronic conditions and jeopardize community-driven relocation planning. During a virtual discussion with residents and stakeholders from Alabama and Mississippi Gulf Coast communities,[9] testimony from Barbara

[9]Comments made to the committee on March 30, 2023, during the information-gathering session; see https://www.nationalacademies.org/event/03-30-2023/virtual-focus-group-mississippi-and-alabama-gulf-coast-community-stakeholder-perspectives-on-managed-retreat

Weckesser of Pascagoula, Mississippi, demonstrated how the proximity to facilities with toxic emissions diminishes community well-being: "[W]e're a fenceline community and we're working to accomplish a buyout; we have flooding and industry pollution. Many residents are taking chemo and there are major health and flood issues while the industry continues to pollute. We just want to be able to survive and live."

Neighborhoods now located immediately adjacent to refineries (i.e., "fenceline communities") existed long before the industries whose toxic emissions poisoned air, water, and land (e.g., the community of Port Arthur, Texas; see White, 2018). Yet, political economies consider such neighborhoods as "sacrifice zones," or zones that, within the benefit-cost framework, present no value to corporate stockholders (Bullard, 2000; Bullard & Wright, 2012). Moreover, environmental hazard events (e.g., leaks, explosions, air pollution) often result from the impacts of natural hazards, like hurricanes, and cause multiple displacements, which, in turn, intensify mental and physical health problems, including anxiety, depression, substance abuse, and suicide (Reuben et al., 2022). For example, in 2020, during the height of the COVID-19 pandemic, Lake Charles, Louisiana, was impacted by two major hurricanes within six weeks. Hurricane Laura came ashore in Louisiana with 150 mph winds on August 27, followed by Hurricane Delta on October 9 with 100 mph winds, only 12 miles east from where Hurricane Laura made landfall. The storms destroyed homes, businesses, schools, and hospitals. Additionally, oil tanks located at multiple refineries lifted from their mooring and leaked into the river (Dermansky, 2020). Even now, Lake Charles residents still feel let down and forgotten by their government and disaster agencies. Lake Charles Mayor Nic Hunter called it "a humanitarian crisis right here on American soil" (Smith, M., 2022).

As Eliseo Santana, a resident of St. Petersburg, Florida, stated, "[Y]ou have to be aware that these individuals [residents of marginalized communities] have been traumatized and have not had a chance, [sighing] and it just keeps building up. So, just be aware of that [when we talk about managed retreat]."[10] Hence, communities already dealing with pre-existing and long-term environmental conditions need more robust support mechanisms to cope with and adapt to climate stresses, including potential displacement or relocation.

[10]Comments made to the committee on July 12, 2022, during the committee-hosted public workshop. More information is available at https://www.nationalacademies.org/event/07-12-2022/managed-retreat-in-the-us-gulf-coast-region-workshop-2

Forms of Mental Health Impacts from Climate Change and Climate-Induced Relocation

Episodic and Chronic Climate Harms

Although well-being is not yet centered in pre-disaster planning and post-disaster recovery, episodic and chronic climate-related harms are well understood (Clayton et al., 2021; Crimmins et al., 2016; Reidmiller et al., 2018). Disruption caused by episodic adverse weather events (e.g., individual storms, heat waves, and flood events) can cause acute impacts (e.g., anxiety, depression, stress; Cruz et al., 2020) and multiply levels of depression, anxiety, trauma, suicide, and substance use in the affected communities (see Box 6-2). There are similar marked escalations in mental health burdens from continued climate disruptions (e.g., drought, ongoing elevated heat and flooding, and displacement and migration), especially as they compound already-existing economic and agricultural precarity and property loss or damage (Clayton et al., 2021).

Anticipated Climate Harms: Eco-anxiety and Solastalgia

Mental health effects also result from the anticipation of future events. These may be less obvious than the ones listed above but still profoundly impact communities. For example, while nostalgia stems from a separation

BOX 6-2
Community Testimonial: Displacement and Mental Health Concerns

"I think even before the storm that [...] a lot of folks in our bayou areas were already going through mental health issues because of land loss issues. And I find in our community, and, losing our land and our homes and places where we grew up is like losing a family member. We're suffering with grief, and we don't actually understand, you know, what it is. But that's kind of—we're losing a part of ourselves, you know, as we're losing our home and our communities. And it takes a toll on us [...] So, when these events happen, you know, and Mother Nature, you know, she just has a way of kicking us when we're down sometimes. You know, it takes a toll, and then it's one thing on top of the other. And then the depression, and then being out of work, and then, you know. You find other ways to, you know, to fill those voids and all that. The mental health issue is very strong, very undertreated in Houma, in Louisiana as a whole."

SOURCE: Bette Billiot, the United Houma Nation. Workshop 3: Assisted Resettlement and Receiving Communities in Louisiana, July 2022, Houma, Louisiana.

from and longing for home, solastalgia arises while people are still physically at home, but environmental change causes distress due to an inability to draw "solace," or comfort, from one's home environment or landscape (Albrecht et al., 2007). Solastalgia starts with the recognition of environmental deconstruction or risk, which can bring a sense of impending change or displacement (Simms et al., 2021). It is accompanied by the erosion of a sense of place, a loss community resources, and feelings of powerlessness (Albrecht et al., 2007).

Eco-anxiety is common and psychometrically consequential in terms of interfering with daily function; it may in some ways be distinct from the experience of other common anxiety or depressive disorders (Hogg et al., 2021). Similarly, ecological grief, or various forms of experienced loss or threatened/anticipated loss of place, have been described (Cunsolo et al., 2020). Youth are especially vulnerable to direct traumatic effects of climate-related events. In terms of distress from anticipated consequences, survey data suggest that such distress is markedly common and impairing among youth globally and reflects an erosion of social trust and experienced intergenerational betrayal (Hickman et al., 2021).

Climate and Stress

Allostasis is the body's response to internal and external conditions or stressors to maintain physiological equilibrium (McEwen, 1998). In public health, allostatic load describes the cumulative physiological consequences of chronic exposure to fluctuating or heightened neural or neuroendocrine response, which results from repeated or prolonged chronic stress over the life course. *Chronic allostatic load* is an important variable in individual mental and physical health and well-being (Sandifer et al., 2017). People in communities that repeatedly receive displaced newcomers may experience an increase in allostatic load, for example, when community assets, such as housing, jobs, and schools, are already scarce or underfunded. Individuals who live in economically and socially marginalized conditions typically face greater exposure to social and economic stressors (e.g., discrimination; low wages; lack of access to affordable food, housing, child care, and health care; Henderson, 2022; Hernández & Swope, 2019; Taylor & Turner, 2002), and experience higher levels of allostatic load and deteriorated physical health (Geronimus et al., 2006; Thomas Tobin et al., 2019; Thomas Tobin & Hargrove, 2022). Chronic stress associated with past, present, and anticipated adverse climate events is a causal factor in several diseases via the disruption of hypothalamic-pituitary-adrenal axis relationships and other mechanisms that in turn can lead to premature mortality over many years (e.g., via increasing hypertension [cardiovascular disease and chronic renal disease]; Cohen et al., 2007; Ghosh et al., 2022).

Cumulative Climate Harms

The implications of cumulative psychological morbidity for public health are substantial in terms of premature mortality, suffering, and impairment (Case & Deaton, 2021; Compton & Shim, 2015; United Nations Development Programme [UNDP], 2021). But they are also substantial in terms of social costs—damage to a myriad of social outcomes—in the areas of sustained employment, education success, family and parenting stresses, as well as the social cohesion and collective efficacy that enable shared action and problem solving. These social costs are beginning to receive more attention, such as in the latest UNDP human development report, which found that "mental well-being is under assault" globally and connected this to the impairment of a wide range of psychological and emotional capabilities that collectively from humanity's ability to meet the demands of "shaping our future" in a world that climate change is transforming (UNDP, 2022, p. 13). The UNDP report traces in detail connections between individual, communal, and societal well-being. This acknowledgment of psychological resilience as a resource is echoed in a body of research relating mental health and emotional well-being with social capital (Almedom, 2005; De Silva et al., 2005), and being recognized as a needed component of global efforts in scaling climate adaptation.[11]

Policy Implications

The broader policy implications of climate-induced impacts are important to a region like the Gulf, where health and well-being are severely stressed by inequitable exposures to climate-related risks and public health and health care investment is relatively low (see Box 6-3).

ENHANCING RESILIENCE AND WELL-BEING THROUGH TASK SHARING AND NURTURE EFFECTS

This section examines practices that can promote individual and community well-being in a changing climate and during climate-induced relocation decision making. Psychological resources and emotional well-being are social determinants of public and individual health that need specific attention. In addition to arguments for increasing access to care to address symptomatic distress or illness, there exists a growing body of knowledge around practices of "task sharing" and "nurture effects." These practices

[11]The COP27 Sharm-El-Sheikh Adaptation Agenda is one example of recent global efforts. More information is available at https://climatechampions.unfccc.int/wp-content/uploads/2022/12/SeS-Adaptation-Agenda_Complete-Report_COP27-.pdf. More information about COP27 is available at https://unfccc.int/cop27

BOX 6-3
Implications of Health Service Availability for Relocation and Displacement

- Nationally, only 10 states have not expanded Medicaid to cover all uninsured adults, and four of these states are in the Gulf region (Florida, Alabama, Mississippi, Texas; Kaiser Family Foundation, 2023). People in the resultant "coverage gap" are non-elderly adults who are mostly working parents with Black or Hispanic race or ethnicity (Rudowitz et al., 2023).
- As has been presented in Chapter 2, several negative social and environmental determinants of health are concentrated in this region, including poverty, racial and other forms of historical discrimination, and certain sources of environmental and industrial pollution. These historical conditions continue to impact both physical and mental health in the region today.
- As of fiscal year 2019, per capita spending for public health services in Gulf states ranges from a low of $21/year/person in Florida and $22/year/person in Texas to a high of $30/year/person in Louisiana (Trust for America's Health, 2021). Historical conditions have played a role in shaping decisions about health care and public health access and resources.
- Black, Latinx/Hispanic, and American Indian/Alaska Native people in the United States face economic barriers to health access, with each U.S. Gulf Coast state in the bottom quartile for overall state health system performance for at least one non-White racial/ethnic group (Radley et al., 2021). Minority groups also face social and cultural barriers caused by the lack of a diverse and culturally competent workforce (Gomez & Bernet, 2019).
- Heath and public health systems are themselves vulnerable to climate-related emergencies. Moreover, the workforce has been repeatedly depleted by the cumulative impacts of multiple disasters as well as COVID-19 (e.g., fatigue and burnout; National Academies, 2019b).
- Relocation of communities, large numbers of uninsured individuals, and modest government budgets for public health care together have serious implications for health care provisioning and access in sending and receiving communities alike.
- Health inequity and environmental justice issues are inevitable consequences of the racial disparities in the context of severe shortages of care (Ndugga & Artiga, 2023).

can be deployed to promote mental health, build socioemotional strengths, and forge prosocial attachments that can help anchor mutually oriented and collectively effective groups and communities. The following sections describe these two practices and the ways in which they are essential to community-driven relocation efforts.

Task Sharing

Task sharing is "an arrangement in which generalists—nonspecialist health professionals, lay workers, affected individuals, or informal caregivers—receive training and appropriate supervision by mental health specialists and screen for or diagnose mental disorders and treat or monitor people affected by them" (Fulton et al., 2011; Kemp et al., 2019, p. 150). Task sharing is a growing set of innovative tools and methods that can improve a community's capacity to improve individual and community well-being, including through community skill-sharing (Hoeft et al., 2018; Patel, 2012; Stevens et al., 2020). Bolstering mental health building blocks can also be advanced through macro-social policies that promote nurture effects, such as economic stability, education and health access, and early childhood opportunities. Those effects are also achievable through "ground game" methods for spreading hands-on skills that can be adopted by a range of community members; this also has the benefit of markedly expanding sheer capacity for care and treatment (McClure et al., 2022, pp. 22–23).

Task sharing mental health skills—which can carry a whole spectrum of purposes—is an innovation largely developed in the past 15 years in the Global South. This paradigm rests on current evidence that a wide range of skills—from direct acute care to prevention and mental health and resilience promotion—can be adopted by lay people, therefore allowing much wider, credible, and scaled access and scope that at the same time build upon and reinforce other common local and social practices that provide empathy and care (Atif et al., 2022; Chibanda et al., 2016; Kohrt et al., 2020; Patel et al., 2017; Shidhaye et al., 2017; Singla et al., 2017). It is a model that was adopted at substantial scale in New York City in the initiative Thrive NYC (Belkin & McCray, 2019; Stevens et al., 2020), and it was put to randomized study through a large effort of coalition building in Los Angeles, Community Partners in Care, where almost 100 community organizations began to offer depression counseling and screening skills as a way of closing care gaps in South Central Los Angeles and North Hollywood (Wells et al., 2013a,b).

To treat depression in New Orleans following Hurricane Katrina, a task-sharing effort called REACH NOLA trained residents to help their neighbors by teaching them skills of psychological counseling and ongoing monitoring (per the widely used Collaborative Care Model), which are usually performed by clinical social workers or nurses (Bentham et al., 2011; Springgate et al., 2011).[12] This effort started as a collaboration between "local health and social service agencies" and academic partners at Tulane University, RAND Corporation, and the University of California, Los Angeles (REACH NOLA, n.d.). The effort mobilized lay community members to help with neighborhood recovery efforts and serve as the front line for a mental health system that was literally implemented in neighborhoods and homes of community members and tackled climate impacts and compounding adversities. The larger health system served as a supportive ally and backup. REACH NOLA subsequently evolved as a foundation of community member health roles throughout Louisiana and a community-partnered Louisiana State University research center on community resilience, Community Resilience Learning Collaborative and Research Network (C-LEARN).[13]

Ultimately, task sharing is about drawing on the current capabilities of different groups, such as community-based organizations (CBOs), mental health practitioners (MHPs), and lay community leaders and CBO clients, but also committing to building new capacities through collaborations and the co-implementation of well-being services (Farr et al., 2020; Stevens et al., 2020). Figure 6 3 shows the capabilities that CBOs, MHPs, and CBO clients and community members can leverage in mental health task sharing.

Adding to this approach is recent proliferation of lay support groups generated through climate activism networks. These groups often draw upon a range of psychological and eco-psychological practices, as well as Indigenous cultural and knowledge, and relevant local knowledges and practices. These groups are lay-led, and they craft responses to the psychological and social challenges of facing environmental loss and the need to generate growth, hope, and motivation in the face of daunting climate realities. Examples of many such efforts of self-formed support groups spread globally include the Good Grief Network in the United States, the Resilience Project in the United Kingdom, and SustyVibes in Nigeria.[14]

Nurture Effects

The concept of "nurture effects" also captures a wide array of well-evidenced psychological capabilities, such as mutuality, pro-sociality, psychological flexibility, empathy, affective security, and caring dispositions

[12] More information about the Collaborative Care Model is available at https://aims.uw.edu/collaborative-care

[13] More information about C-LEARN is available at https://www.c-learn.org/

[14] More information about the Resilience Project is available at goodgriefnetwork.org/theresilienceproject.org.uk/sustyvibes.org. More information about SustyVibes is available at https://sustyvibes.org/

Capabilities Leveraged in a Task Sharing Approach

CBO

Engage community members in trusted relationships

Address various types of life challenges and social determinants (e.g., housing, employment, education)

Help clients navigate social service or legal systems

Strengthen community ties and networks

Gather data and promote local voice to identify social needs, goals, and strategies

Develop and deliver culturally responsive approaches to improve social outcomes, which may include trauma-informed approaches

MHP

Identify and help people understand specific mental health issues

Provide specialized clinical care, including therapy and/or medication

Provide specialized training and supervision in mental health skills

Apply clinical expertise to design, test, implement, or improve approaches to clinical care

Gather data about mental health needs and goals and develop strategies to improve mental health outcomes

CBO Clients & Community

Identify community needs and priorities related to mental health and social outcomes

Identify trusted community resources

Provide input to design and improve services and support

Help generate responsive solutions to community history and culture

Offer social support

Take action to improve individual or community mental health and well-being

FIGURE 6-3 Capabilities leveraged in a task-sharing approach.
SOURCE: Stevens, C., Tosatti, E., Ayer, L., Barnes-Proby, D., Belkin, G., Lieff, S., & Martineau, M. (2020). *Helpers in plain sight: A guide to implementing mental health task sharing in community-based organizations*. RAND Corporation. https://www.rand.org/pubs/tools/TL317.html

and attachments (Mayseless, 2020). These capabilities are cornerstones for emotional well-being, mental illness prevention, and mental health promotion at scale (Biglan et al., 2020). They also serve as social connective tissue for what psychotherapist Sally Weintrobe described as stacking the deck in favor of dispositions across institutions and modes of daily life toward care rather than uncare (Weintrobe, 2021). In this view, foregrounding nurture strategies in community strengthening policies mutually reinforces motivation around climate adaptation and eco-sustainable action. In the context of climate change and at the front end of adaptation to it, the continuity and strength of communities in the work of adaptation markedly widens what mental health-oriented policy can include.

Thus far, this chapter has discussed well-being frameworks in the context of climate change and climate-induced displacement and relocation, the well-being impacts of such changes, and practices that promote and enhance well-being in this challenging context. A principal objective of enhancing well-being for communities faced with displacement is to bolster their capacity to effectively and equitably participate in a community-driven relocation process. Critical to a community-driven approach is the recognition of the value of social capital, community cohesion, and collective efficacy, the subject of the next section.

SOCIAL CAPITAL, COMMUNITY COHESION, AND COLLECTIVE EFFICACY

"Social capital" refers to "features of social organization, such as networks, norms, and trust, that facilitate coordination and cooperation for mutual benefit" (Putnam, 1993b, p. 2). These features of social life can have benefits for a community and its residents (Coleman, 1998). At the community level, social capital can be represented by *social connections* formed between and among a community's members (Putnam, 1993a, 1995). These social connections and resultant networks are the foundation upon which trusting relationships and solidarity among community members, or *social cohesion*, are nurtured. As the social cohesion of a community is strengthened, the likelihood that community members willingly intervene or act on behalf of each other, or *informal social control*, becomes more favorable (Cagney et al., 2016). Strong social cohesion and favorable informal social control work together to cultivate the community's perception of its capacity to achieve common goals that will improve the lives of its members, thus shaping a community's *collective efficacy* (Cagney et al., 2016). Mutual trust and expectations around action in service of collective goals are central elements to achieving collective efficacy (Browning & Cagney, 2002; Cagney et al., 2016). By extension, scholars suggest that these same elements are central to community resilience (Sherrieb et al., 2010).

All Resources Matter

A focus on social resources (e.g., social capital, social cohesion) does not suggest ignoring the significant influence of economic, structural, medical, housing, transportation, employment, and other material resources in shaping the health and well-being of communities and residents. Furthermore, emphasis on community cohesion is not a promotion of residential segregation or other projects generating or maintaining racialized socioeconomic homogeneity (Kalra & Kapoor, 2009). Scholars caution that an emphasis on social capital and community cohesion can distract attention away from the forces that generate material inequities by uncritically promoting assimilation (Lin, 2000). For instance, if we assume social capital requires homogeneity to create community cohesion, we implicitly assert that ethnoracial diversity threatens or otherwise undermines the formation of social cohesion and, ultimately, community well-being. This framing centers ethnoracial diversity (or homogeneity) as the force deterring (or promoting) well-being. Scholars have aptly characterized this approach as a diversion from addressing material deprivation and social marginalization (e.g., Kundnani, 2007; Letki, 2008). This approach enables "policy-makers seeking less costly, non-economic solutions to social problems" to place the burden on disadvantaged groups and communities to form social relations as pathways to better social and economic outcomes (Portes, 1998, p. 3, as cited in Kalra & Kapoor, 2009).

Research examining environmentally induced relocation emphasizes the varied significance of material resources for the well-being of people post-move (de Sherbinin et al., 2022). For example, residents of flood-prone communities in Iquitos, Peru, who relocated to environmentally safer areas ultimately moved back to their original community because of a lack of economic opportunities at the relocation site, despite the risk of another flood. At the same time, some parents who relocated to environmentally safer communities willingly accepted less favorable economic opportunities in their relocation site in order to provide a cleaner and safer place for their children (Wirz et al., 2022).

Research has also emphasized how the uneven distribution of material resources shapes options for relocation (whether collectively or individually pursued) with significant implications for future material well-being (de Sherbinin et al., 2022). Analyses of home buyouts in Harris County, Texas, revealed that the most probable pathway for homeowners in less economically advantaged neighborhoods was individual household relocation (Elliott et al., 2021). Significantly, individual household relocation is the most potentially disruptive pathway because it separates community members from one another and uproots individuals from their home community. As elaborated and emphasized throughout this chapter, these social and spatial fissures have significant impacts on individual health and overall community well-being.

PLACE ATTACHMENT, RELOCATION, AND WELL-BEING

The concept of place attachment, along with the broader notion of sense of place, was introduced in Chapter 5 and is elaborated here in the specific context of relocation, health, and well-being. The loss of place attachment is one of the most impactful contributors to poor mental health for the displaced (Adger et al., 2018; Burley et al., 2007; Vos et al., 2021). Place attachment informs the process of environment-related migration by constraining people's decisions to leave; prompting decisions to leave when loss becomes intolerable; informing destination choice; and shaping the post-migration experience, including loss, grief, and the (in)ability to form new place attachments (Dandy et al., 2019). In this committee's workshops, participants expressed strong attachments to place and the interrelationship between place and individual identities, as described by a workshop participant in Box 6-4.

Participants in this committee's workshops expressed the interrelationship between place, livelihoods, and individual identities. People make a life through the material and social resources provided by livelihoods (Allison & Ellis, 2001; de Haan & Zoomers, 2005; Rakodi & Lloyd-Jones, 2002). Natural resource-based livelihoods generate place attachments informed through direct social-environmental interactions. Within the U.S. Gulf Coast, for example, fishing and oil industries have shaped Cajun ethnic identity (Henry & Bankston, 2002). In the case of fishing, emplaced

BOX 6-4
Community Testimonial: Bette Billiot, the United Houma Nation

"We know what the 1830s did to our people, the Houma. Communities and places change through time. Community will continue to thrive when culture is passed down but there have been and still are structural barriers. Our fishermen cannot pass this down to the next generation. We are embedded in the land and the water, family, culture, language, customs, and rituals. Our elders want to stay in place—but what is lost if this happens? We are this place. Living here means knowing how to live. If you want to live here, you have to know how to tarp your roof [after wind damage]."

SOURCE: Bette Billiot, the United Houma Nation. Workshop 3: Assisted Resettlement and Receiving Communities in Louisiana, July 2022, Houma, Louisiana.

economic ties to natural resources link to cultural ways of life, including the significance of local food (e.g., see Box 6-4; Lambert et al., 2021; see also Nelson et al., 2020).

Environmental change alters the social elements of place, which can include material and symbolic elements of place (Stedman & Ingalls, 2014). For example, among Vietnamese American residents in the New Orleans East community, place was understood to be a "homeland" holding significant cultural resources that in the absence of material resources often took on even greater importance for individuals making decisions about managed retreat (Chamlee-Wright & Storr, 2009). Research engaging Indigenous concepts of "country" approach connections to place in terms of a living system to which people belong and are related, and not in terms of resources provided to people by the environment (Dandy et al., 2019). Within this conceptualization, features of place and entities are family, and "country" is "love of place" (Wooltorton et al., 2017, p. 58; see also Cunsolo et al., 2012).

The implications of place attachment for relocation are multiple. As a place begins to change, residents might feel stronger place attachments (Burley et al., 2007; LeMenager, 2014; Low & Altman, 1992). Intensified place attachment can generate stronger commitments to staying in place and greater resistance to migrating (Barcus & Brunn, 2010). In fact, some conceptualize place attachment as a desire to stay in place (e.g., Hay, 1998). In the U.S. Gulf Coast, a region with a long history of hurricane exposure and responses to hurricane damage, some people become increasingly tied to place over time as rebuilding efforts recommit people to place (see Simms, 2017). Research on Louisiana coastal communities found residents' resistance to relocating largely related to strong place attachments (Simms, 2017; see also Burley et al., 2007; Manning-Broome et al., 2015).

Place Attachment, Relocation, and Social Capital

While not all forms of social capital are spatially bounded (Barrios, 2014), place is one domain that fosters social relationships, social networks, and, ultimately, social capital. Places give rise to individual identities (Massey, 1994) and support site-specific beliefs, emotions, stories, and experiences (Lambert et al., 2021); for example, Convery et al. (2014) described the place of schools and their role in communities during disaster recovery, acting as structures where human experiences and the material world intersect and interact with one another (Casey, 1997). Place shapes people's lived experiences, including their "environmental conceptualizations, rootedness to place," and sense of belonging (Seamon, 2015; Simms et al., 2021, p. 317). Consequently, people changing places through, for example, an environmentally motivated migration are uprooted from these critical aspects of their lives (Askland & Bunn, 2018; Jenkins, 2016; Oliver-Smith, 2009).

Place attachment closely relates to social capital (Stedman, 2003) and contributes to community resilience (Berkes & Ross, 2013). Research demonstrates that place attachment and social capital can increase capacity to adapt to environmental change and create barriers to change, including resistance to migration (Marshall et al., 2012), by promoting a reluctance to leave family, familiar surroundings, and ways of life (Fresque-Baxter & Armitage, 2012)—especially among people who have lived in a particular place for a long time (Anton & Lawrence, 2014).

Moving to a new community inherently disrupts place-based social capital, which can directly undermine an individual's well-being as well as the origin community's well-being (McMichael et al., 2010). Whether households move as a group to a single new location or move independently to multiple new locations, the move itself affects the integrity of social capital and, consequently, sense of belonging (Albert et al., 2018). Moreover, the site-specific meaning and value of social and social-material relationships people develop in their origin community are inadequately captured or replicated in resettlement (Morrissey & Oliver-Smith, 2013; Wrathall, 2015). Maintaining ties to property in origin communities, including ancestral lands, through continued access and ownership affects the likelihood of relocating and reestablishing social capital in new places, and thus enhances the social and mental well-being of people resettling to new communities (Simms et al., 2021). This sentiment was exemplified by workshop participants who explained that "progressives" leave Houma and move to Smith Ridge but have started to restore relationships and culture through large community "reunions that re-connect people to place and to each other" (see Box 6-5).

Place Attachment and Destination

Among those who migrate, place attachment informs the choice of destination and shapes the post-migration experience (Dandy et al., 2019). In terms of destination choice, people with strong place attachments might seek places with similar and, thus, recognizable biophysical, social, and cultural characteristics. This might implicate short-distance moves within the region or even more long-distance moves to places that approximate the characteristics of the origin community. Preference for receiving communities similar to home, however, can lead people to relocate to similarly if not more environmentally vulnerable areas (Glorioso & Moss, 2007), thus unintentionally increasing people's vulnerability to environmental hazards (Anton & Lawrence, 2014; Moskwa et al., 2018; Niven & Bardsley, 2013).

BOX 6-5
Cherry Wilmore, and Sherry Wilmore, Residents of Houma, Louisiana

Cherry and Sherry Wilmore are twin sisters and residents of Houma.

"We're migrants. We migrated here as foster children." Houma was a foster care placement.

In 1991, when the twins were six years old, they entered foster care for the first time. They were placed in a group home for a few days before moving to their first foster home, located on a farm. It was there that they developed their love of knowledge, which they attribute to days spent watching *Jeopardy* with their neighbor. In addition, their foster mother taught them how to read using canned goods in the cabinet. Around age 10, Cherry and Sherry left that home and returned to their former group home for a month. Afterward, they were transferred to the MacDonell Children's Home in Houma.

For the first time in their lives, the twins would find themselves separated from one another. "We have been together since conception." The children were separated to make them more "adoptable." Cherry was sent to a foster home, leaving Sherry behind at the group home. Cherry was determined to be reunited with her sister and resisted the system of child protection services.

She fought and "acted up" in the new place, she says, "so they would send me back with my sister [...] and we were united on our 11th birthday."

Since European contact, the community has always been multi-ethnic, with people claiming Spanish, French, African, Cajun (Arcadian), Isleño, Filipino, and Asian roots. "Progressives" leave Houma and move to Smith Ridge but have started to restore relationships and culture through large community "reunions that reconnect people to place and to each other."

Sherry explained that the vernacular of place names and referring to bayou directions (i.e., up or down the bayou) is not how Black people refer to places. "We have to understand that when you talk about this area as being particularly Terrebonne or Lafourche, and you refer to [a] place like Chauvin, Black people are going to refer to Smith Ridge [...] When you speak about Houma, you may speak about 'up the bayous' [... but] African Americans are going to ask you, 'Are you from the Mechanicville area, are you from the Alley, are you from Deweyville, are you from Gibson?' because that is how they represent themselves" (National Academies, 2023a, p. 35).

Structural obstacles to community restoration and wellness are institutionalized (property taxes and insurance) and procedural (state and federal disaster responses). Slow recovery destroys communities. After Hurricane Ida, communities had no water, fuel, power, food, communication, schools, sanitation, or jobs for 60 days. "We are used to water. This was wind. Ida was in August, extremely hot. A year later, people are still living in those conditions. How can you take care of old people, sick people? How do you take care of children?"

SOURCES: Cherry Wilmore, and Sherry Wilmore, Residents of Houma, Louisiana. Workshop 3: Assisted Resettlement and Receiving Communities in Louisiana, July 2022, Houma, Louisiana.

Connections with place inform an individual's identity, feelings of self-efficacy, and attitudes about the future (Adams, 2016). Disruptions to this social-environmental relationship can have negative health consequences (Brown & Perkins, 1992), including those associated with loss and grief (Cunsolo & Ellis, 2018). Similar disruptions to health equilibriums are experienced by people who remain in close and intimate living and working "cultural relationships with the natural environment," especially in rural areas; this includes Indigenous peoples, farmers, oystermen, shrimpers, and fishermen (Cunsolo & Ellis, 2018, p. 275; see also Bukvic et al., 2022). The material and social character of place is changed not only by climate but also by the economic, commercial, and political deconstruction of lands, culture, and home; this can ultimately lead to psychological and emotional distress (Albrecht et al., 2007; Jacquet & Stedman, 2014; Sorice et al., 2023).

Place attachment, therefore, provides a foundation from which to consider the various cognitive-emotional factors influencing how people and communities engage in change processes, including relocation (Adger et al., 2009, 2013; Clayton et al., 2015). Differences in place attachment underlie disagreements among residents and nonresidents regarding measures aimed at altering, preserving, or restoring a particular built environment (Kianicka et al., 2006). Willingness to relocate can be slowed by a strong sense of place attachment as well as a lack of community consensus on whether and where to move, lack of job opportunities, and distrust of government (Dannenberg et al., 2019; Davenport & Robertson, 2016). As a result, failure to understand differences in meanings assigned to place by people, state actors, and nongovernmental organizations can create barriers in communication and generate conflict between parties (Masterson, 2016; Sorice et al., 2023). In contrast, processes that allow and engage multiple, diverse place meanings may generate more resilience and greater health (Adger et al., 2013; Stedman, 1999).

SUMMARY

In the Gulf region, individuals and communities faced with pressures to relocate have already experienced a range of traumas and stressors from other environmental "events" that impact well-being and deplete social capital. Concurrently, individuals and communities may lack the necessary support mechanisms to ensure well-being, a crucial prerequisite to access to and participation in the decision-making processes that lead to mitigation and adaptation. Acknowledging, addressing, and acting on individual and communal trauma are the first steps toward increasing well-being, social capital, community cohesion, and collective efficacy; re-establishing trust between all stakeholders; and guaranteeing opportunities and resources for community agency at levels of decision making and policy in both short- and long-term goals.

CONCLUSIONS

Conclusion 6-1: There are discernable linkages between health disparities (e.g., premature death, elevated levels of chronic diseases, poor mental health, inequitable access to health care) and complex socioeconomic disparities (e.g., intergenerational poverty, economic precarity). Equitable and sustained community-driven relocation planning requires agencies (e.g., Centers for Disease Control and Prevention, Federal Emergency Management Agency, Department of Housing and Urban Development) to examine these linkages within the context of originating and receiving communities.

Conclusion 6-2: The importance to communities of bolstering mental health and healing emotional distress lies not only in diminished suffering and enhanced coping but also in the social ties and associated social capital that mutually reinforce collective efficacy and social inclusion in processes of adaptation to social and environmental change.

Conclusion 6-3: Mental health is a critical aspect of community-driven relocation planning and demands greater breadth in scope and capacity, levels of support, resources, long-term commitment, and capabilities. Yet, mental health supports are inequitably distributed, further hindering historically marginalized communities from optimally coping, acting, and being empowered to make community-driven decisions. One way to address this situation is through the task-sharing paradigm, which intentionally leverages social capital and mutually reinforces community collective efficacy, shared action, and empowerment.

Conclusion 6-4: In the current context of decision making about relocation, the implementation of well-being frameworks can consist of adapting policies that incorporate and strengthen a community's existing social capabilities (e.g., socioemotional bonding, trust, reciprocal engagement) and capacities for actions (e.g., social capital and cohesion, collective efficacy, shared sense of place).

Conclusion 6-5: One's identity, well-being, and lifeways are tied to one's sense of place. Place attachment critically informs decisions to relocate and can constrain decisions to leave; prompt decisions to leave when impending loss becomes intolerable; inform destination choices; and shape the post-migration experience, which includes loss, grief, and the long-term process of forming new place attachments. Place attachment is also related to social connections and social capital because shared place attachment facilitates collective identities, especially in contexts where subsistence and commercial-based activities are practiced in groups. A lack of understanding and valuation of place attachment can create tensions between residents, state actors, and economic and nongovernmental entities and organizations involved in relocation planning and implementation. A failure to recognize the importance of place attachment can undermine communities' trust in relocation.

7

Communication, Participation, and Knowledge

This chapter discusses the following:

- The lack of discussion about relocation in the Gulf Coast region of the United States and a distrust of government
- The challenge of communicating the idea of relocation (e.g., terminology, purpose, process, outcomes), including issues of transparency, language, and culture
- Lessons learned from the communication of scientific information around climate change that are relevant to communicating risk in the context of relocation
- Linking of social capital to participation, civic leadership, and power sharing
- Co-production and participatory action research and practice (PARP) as guiding principles for engaging communities about relocation
- Local and Indigenous knowledge in participatory planning, including traditional ecological knowledge (TEK)

INTRODUCTION

Climate adaptation ultimately depends on and profoundly affects people, neighborhoods, and communities, yet they are often left out of processes around problem solving, developing adaptive solutions, and taking collective action (see Box 7-1). There are instrumental methods and tools for organizing and facilitating community-driven relocation processes that can build on existing community capacities and processes of engagement, including the co-production of knowledge and decisions relating to climate action, as well as participatory action approaches to research. Successful climate adaptation necessitates opening new spaces for community engagement in the face of increasing risks from climate change impacts.

Community engagement requires trust building and power sharing through outreach, consultation, involvement, collaboration, and shared leadership in decision making (see Clinical and Translational Science Awards Consortium; National Institutes of Health, 2011). This chapter discusses some of the key actors and constituencies that need to be engaged and looks in depth at tools of communication, participation, and knowledge-building that support communities' co-production of their relocation plans, where relocation may be necessary.

BOX 7-1
Community Testimonial: Elder Chief Shirell Parfait-Dardar

"So, when we hear talk of managed retreat, and we've seen some of the things that have happened with communities facing resettlement, it's quite scary because of the examples we have to look at. They do not include the voice of the community. The community is not the one that is guiding these efforts. You don't see them involved from the start to the completion of the project. And all it does is remind me of how these communities have constantly been forced because someone either thinks that they have a better plan, that they have more knowledge, you know, whatever their agenda is [...] The community knows their community, their landscape, and everything, better than any other outsider. So, I think they should be brought to the table to where they could discuss if anything is going to be—any work—done in their community, it should be discussed with the community. So, for anyone that is considering partaking on this managed retreat, managed by whom? If the people that are having to retreat are not the ones guiding, are not the ones determining, if they're not at the table, then you're not helping them. You're simply causing more harm."

SOURCE: Elder Chief Shirell Parfait-Dardar, Grand Caillou/Dulac Band of Biloxi-Chitimacha-Choctaw, and Chair, Louisiana Governor's Commission on Native Americans. Workshop 3: Community Viability and Environmental Change in Coastal Louisiana, July 2022, Thibodaux, Louisiana.

Chapter Overview and Outline

For effective communication and outreach, the committee heard that messaging has to clearly outline purpose and need for relocation, while providing comprehensive and comprehensible information to potential movers. To alleviate uncertainties, participants noted, it is important to use personalized interactions and provide extensive details about potential receiving communities. Using information that comes from trusted sources and is consistent with other sources makes planning more accessible and understandable to community residents.

There was a general sentiment among workshop participants that government cannot be trusted to support communities—that politicians were not acting on the desires of the communities that they represent because there is a revolving door and discontinuity of government staff at the community interface level—and so the only real leverage is to vote local government out of office. However, many people are unaware of who their local elected officials are, and/or they are politically disengaged (Knight Foundation, 2020; Luchi & Mutter, 2020). When they are recognized, elected officials are often seen as ineffective in helping the communities most in need (Pew Research Center, 2018; Schneider, 2008).

Another theme workshop participants raised that is closely connected to the overarching message of disaffection and distrust toward largely unresponsive governments is the principle that community residents need to lead planning and relocation efforts from the outset, with government "assisting," not "managing," relocation. That is, there is the basic need for self-determination. The affected communities need to be involved from the outset in all aspects of planning and the implementation of relocation efforts.

Lastly, workshop participants talked about the lack of resources and the lack of equity in planning and implementing relocation. Residents need adequate and accessible information on future environmental and health risks at both their current locations and at possible future locations, as well as information about the costs of relocation, in order to participate in their own and their community's futures.

This chapter explores these issues around communication and participation, dividing the work into five sections. The first section considers the relative lack of discussion of relocation in the Gulf region, including the lack of participation by the people most affected and how this can instill a general lack of trust in the government. The second section turns to the broader issue of communication, including risk communication, which is the subject of the chapter's third section. In the fourth section, we look broadly at participation and knowledge, perhaps the most critical parts of any relocation process. Here, we revisit the idea of social capital canvassed in Chapter 6 by considering how it is intrinsic to civic leadership, power sharing, and participatory decision making, which are critical elements when planning and implementing community-driven relocation. We then briefly examine the themes of co-production and PARP as guiding principles for engaging communities about relocation, followed by a discussion about the importance of local and Indigenous knowledge in participatory planning.[1] The chapter concludes with section five, the committee's summary and conclusions.

A LACK OF DISCUSSION ABOUT RELOCATION AND A DISTRUST IN GOVERNMENT

Communication is one of several barriers to managed retreat (Bragg et al., 2021; Siders, 2019). There are many ways to confront the situation, and at the core of these are the ways in which people have access to, and can equitably and effectively participate in, relocation and resettlement decision-making processes (Climigration Network, 2021). Along the U.S. Gulf Coast, there has been an overall lack of discussion about climate-induced relocation strategies, especially between U.S. Gulf Coast residents who likely will have to relocate and the government entities and nongovernment stakeholders that would need to facilitate relocation, compounded by the fact that existing government frameworks do not include relocation as a viable option. When the topic of relocation (often in the form of buyouts) does arise, there is limited meaningful involvement of U.S. Gulf Coast residents in discussions (National Academies of Sciences, Engineering, and Medicine, 2022c). This includes a lack of transparency and communication from the entities managing the buyout programs (National Academies, 2022c).

When efforts *are* made to engage communities, the mechanisms are not effectively facilitating participation (Gosman & Botchwey, 2013). For example, public meetings are inaccessible for a number of reasons, including being held at inopportune times, not providing child/elder care, and not always using terminology understood by those affected (Bower et al., 2023; Spidalieri & Bennett, 2020d); key documents are often not translated into the primary languages of vulnerable communities (National Academies, 2022c). In addition, community capacity to engage is generally limited (Barra et al., 2020; Hemmerling, Barra et al., 2020) and varies within communities. Moreover, distrust of government can prevent community

[1]As discussed below and defined in the Key Terms (Appendix D), "co-production" in the context of community-driven relocation is the process of developing and implementing knowledge, plans, and strategies through the iterative engagement of at-risk communities, researchers, practitioners, and other groups, whose participation is necessary to the relocation process (see also Armitage et al., 2011; Meadow et al., 2015; Wamsler, 2017).

members from believing the messages they are receiving. As a result of these issues, decisions are made predominantly by people who are not affected by those decisions, and programs are established without understanding or accounting for cultural variability (e.g., large families, community connections, renters; National Academies, 2022c, 2023a).

Consideration of, or planning for, community relocation is not included in required planning exercises for U.S. Gulf Coast communities (i.e., local hazard mitigation plans [HMPs], longer-term comprehensive plans, disaster recovery plans) as there are no federal mandates to do so. The topic is polarizing for any mayor or elected official to take on during a four-year term and is therefore rarely considered as a mitigation solution. In general, if something is not required, then it is often left out of these plans, as local governments have limited time and resources. For example, most local HMPs do not include a commitment to climate adaptation or include mechanisms on how to incorporate new climate data into plan revisions (Stults, 2017). Additionally, HMPs are often developed to meet minimum federal standards rather than serving as a key decision-making tool that includes the identification of specific climate threats and adaptation projects (Berke et al., 2014). Some would also argue that politicians are not talking about relocation due to the economic and political ("blame the messenger") ramifications of asking people to leave their homes (Teirstein, 2021). In the case of the U.S. Environmental Protection Agency (EPA) Superfund program, it has been found that listing of a site on the National Priorities List has resulted in a decline in housing values, which in turn reduces the local tax base, thus fueling opposition to government action (though often values go up again post cleanup; see Chapter 9 for more on EPA Superfund relocations; Kiel & Williams, 2007).

In addition to the committee's decision to use the term "community-driven relocation," there have been previous suggestions to rebrand the term "managed retreat" since retreat can be negatively associated with loss of property (Bragg et al., 2021). Notably, effective communication may help to establish relocation as a potentially viable option even if community members have not considered it before. In instances when there may not be direct experience with the forces driving relocation, it may be helpful to provide readily understandable local information about the scale and nature of risks to community members' livelihoods, well-being, and property (see Figure 7-1). Vandenbeld and MacDonald (2013, p. 166) stress the "importance of ensuring [...] emotional support when this information [is] conveyed."

Distrust of Government

A general distrust of government (Chapters 4 and 5) coupled with a lack of transparency in the process of relocation (including criteria for a buyout) limit residents' confidence in the need for relocation (see Box 7-2)—residents want to better understand why locations are being singled out for relocation (National Academies, 2022c). Barbara Weckesser, head of Concerned Citizens of Cherokee Subdivision and resident of Pascagoula, Mississippi, spoke of the lack of trust in government officials that can impede relocations: "So we're trying to pull in and bring in city and county and state [for relocations]. But again, there's so much mistrust. So how did you build that trust up?"[2] The interplay of trust and transparency issues can also result in the residents' lack of understanding about the government's specific reason for issuing mandatory relocations. Some groups feel targeted and believe acquired land is not to reduce flood risk but for other vested government interests such as oil extraction or new development for wealthier groups (National Academies, 2022c, 2023a).

During the workshops in Texas (National Academies, 2022c),[3] the committee heard from community members that trust issues can be reduced by

- engaging communities through a trusted third party (e.g., community leaders) who has no financial interest in the outcome;
- improving transparency in who is funding the relocation process; and
- communicating to relocating communities on the use of land post-buyout or post-relocation.

Establishing trust between residents and government will enable discussions of relocation in a transparent and two-way context. The next section discusses some of the challenges and opportunities surrounding the broader issue of communication and relocation.

COMMUNICATION

Communicating the idea (e.g., terminology, purpose, process, outcomes) of relocation is a challenge. Residents often have difficulty relating to complex, technical, or larger-scale plans, such as the Louisiana Coastal Master

[2]Comments made to the committee on March 30, 2022, during a virtual public information-gathering session. More information is available at https://www.nationalacademies.org/event/03-30-2023/virtual-focus-group-mississippi-and-alabama-gulf-coast-community-stakeholder-perspectives-on-managed-retreat

[3]Comments made to the committee during the committee-hosted public workshops. More information is available at https://www.nationalacademies.org/our-work/managed-retreat-in-the-us-gulf-coast-region#sectionPastEvents

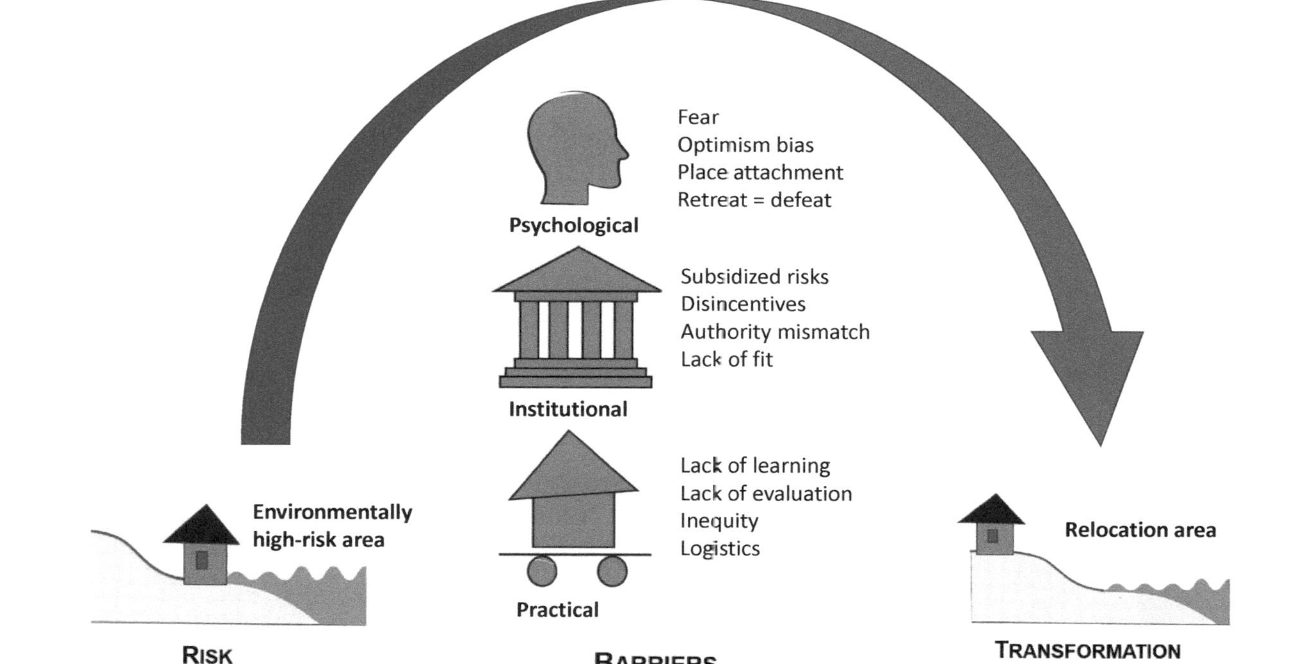

FIGURE 7-1 An example of the psychological, institutional, and practical barriers to relocation from environmentally high-risk areas.
SOURCE: Siders, A. R. (2019). Managed retreat in the United States. *One Earth*, *1*(2), 216–225. https://doi.org/10.1016/j.oneear.2019.09.008

BOX 7-2
Community Testimonials: Distrust in Government

Derrick Evans, executive director of Turkey Creek Community Initiatives in Gulfport, Mississippi, and of the coast-wide and grassroots community-focused U.S. Gulf Coast Fund for Community Renewal and Ecological Health (2005–2013), shared his sentiment about lack of trust in government, saying that disaster response has not "been equitable, fair, [or] trustworthy," and this has to be considered "before you get to relocation." He later said that "lack of trust in the government is not the problem. Lack of trust is the result of past government behavior." Casi (KC) Callaway, chief resilience officer, Mobile, Alabama, responded, "Knowing that we're not trusted is a big challenge. And how do we overcome it? And that's probably what I want to say [more] than anything else [...] we have to be able to provide real and accurate and solid information [...] I can't imagine most of us wanting anything more than that. But if we or the data isn't not trusted, we gotta fix that."

SOURCES: Derrick Evans, Executive Director, Turkey Creek Community Initiatives in Gulfport, Mississippi, and Gulf Coast Fund for Community Renewal and Ecological Health (2005–2013) and Casi Callaway, Chief Resilience Officer, Mobile, Alabama. Virtual Focused Discussion: Mississippi and Alabama Gulf Coast Community Stakeholder Perspectives on Managed Retreat, March 2023.

"While there are numerous programs available, the lack of trust, knowledge, and accessibility poses a significant challenge. It has been mentioned before that there are no individuals knocking on our doors, offering support. In reality, even if someone were to approach me, I wouldn't trust them. So, we need trusted individuals in the community who can introduce the programs to the community. Then, the community can open up and have access. It's not that we don't have an overwhelming number of programs, but we need to give them access to our community for better use, and trust plays a huge role in that."

SOURCE: Eliseo Santana, Resident of St. Petersburg, Florida. Workshop 2: Opportunities & Challenges of Climate Adaptation on Florida's Gulf Coast, July 2022, St. Petersburg, Florida.

"So, I—as an organizer, I have been completely unsatisfied with the political response to these issues. Like, currently I'm working on an electrical school bus campaign to transition every school bus in the state of Florida to electric. While that's—you know, that's important. When it comes to finding funding from municipal and local governments, county governments, to develop charging infrastructure, for example, there's no political will to do that and there just isn't a compromise. Nobody is willing to come together to see that done. So, yeah, I believe that it's going to take more involvement from academia, from frontline communities, people coming together and demanding more of their elected officials [...] I'd also like to mention that in 2021, I was doing disaster resilience work in the Town and Country area, and we had collected about 3,000 surveys. And three in 100 people who were surveyed knew who their elected officials were.

So, you have entire communities who don't know who their city council person is. They don't know who their state house representative is. They don't know who their state senator is. So, if our elected officials can't be trusted to go out into the communities that they represent and inform these people of what's going on, we have to hold them accountable. We have to expect more from the people that we elect to represent us. That is their duty. That's the reason we put them into office. If they can't do something as simple as making sure that the community is safe from climate change, I'm sorry, you shouldn't be in office."

SOURCE: Getulio Gonzalez-Mulattieri, Resident of St. Petersburg, Florida. Workshop 2: Opportunities & Challenges of Climate Adaptation on Florida's Gulf Coast, July 2022, St. Petersburg, Florida.

"So, one thing we saw negatively when the government interacted with communities when it came to the land was their claims of eminent domain to claim a lot of the lands in the coastal region. And another thing they did, they did not gather our people altogether as a group. They went homestead to homestead, you know, and they had intimidating tactics where they had the local official, the sheriff's department with them, men from the government, and they had people sign papers. Well, the concept of landownership and paper did not translate, you know, with the people. They didn't really grasp that concept of when they were signing these documents that they were losing their land, giving their land away, because they were told that, you know, the government was going to use it, that they had more beneficial use of the land than the people but that they wouldn't—their actions would not interfere with the people's lifeway."

SOURCE: Elder Rosina Philippe, Atakapa-Ishak/Chawasha Tribe and President of the First Peoples' Conservation Council. Workshop 3: Community Viability and Environmental Change in Coastal Louisiana, July 2022, Thibodaux, Louisiana.

"Being a practicing journalist, I understand the importance of getting the right information from the right sources, and I think maybe I could best answer by saying that I don't want to get the information from the city government or the state government because of their attempts—I don't think they have our best interests at heart. We need to get direct information from the organizations or the agencies so that we know that the information is authentic and accurate."

SOURCE: Gordon Jackson, Board President, Steps Coalition. Virtual Focused Discussion: Mississippi and Alabama Gulf Coast Community Stakeholder Perspectives on Managed Retreat, March 2023.

Plan (National Academies, 2023b).[4] Messages need to clearly indicate need and purpose with adequate information that is clear and comprehensible at the community and household scale (Harrington-Abrams, 2022; Spidalieri & Bennett, 2020d). One-on-one interaction can reduce uncertainties and foster trust. People need more information about their potential destination (i.e., receiving place) to eliminate uncertainties (Hino et al., 2017).

It may be useful to foster partnerships and knowledge exchanges between originating and receiving communities (or the community that holds customary title to the receiving area). More discussion of partnerships between originating and receiving communities can be found in Chapter 8. Ministries, academics, and nonprofit groups with expertise in social services, cultural preservation, and local languages may be helpful in fostering communication and bridging knowledge (Connell & Coelho, 2018, p. 48), and ultimately in "linking" social capital across hierarchies. External facilitators should spend time in dialogue with originating and receiving communities and their trusted leaders to facilitate building trust (Dumaru et al., 2020). Additionally, longer planning timeframes can help build relationships among the various actors, allowing for more meaningful community participation (see Box 7-3; Boege & Shibata, 2020; Campbell, 2022; National Academies, 2023a).

Communicating Relocation as an Option

Community-driven relocation means that the decision to relocate is community-led, a process that rests on effective communication. Early and consistent communication is essential to facilitating awareness and understanding that relocation is even an option (see Box 7-4). Communication and engagement strategies may need to be tailored to a given community; working with community members through co-production (see below) and scenario methods may be helpful for understanding the culture and identity of a community (Bragg et al., 2021; Lemos & Morehouse, 2005; Wollenberg et al., 2000).

When co-producing such strategies, it is important to keep in mind that community members may utilize a variety of perspectives and values to assess a relocation strategy. Alexander et al. (2012) found that few community members make decisions related to relocation using a political perspective, most respondents appeared to draw on more than one worldview, and there were a variety of viewpoints about the risks of sea level rise. Because of the difficulty of reaching consensus amidst this diversity of perspectives, the authors "propose that the goal of community engagement processes should

---

[4]More information about Louisiana's Coastal Master Plan is available at https://coastal.la.gov/our-plan

BOX 7-3
Community Testimonials: Community-Led Decision Making and Engagement

"I'd also like to say also that's—that about relocation. Sometimes we're—you know, given our history in the south, given our history of how we do things and how long it takes to do things, relocation is pretty much not a option, because what we're thinking is, because we don't have the influence in our communities and then people, the powers that be, that has the decision-making power, we want to be able to be inclusive in that so that I'm not moving because you're not doing nothing. You know, we want to make sure that everybody has a—that we have a fair option, that we're putting resources in the community, so you don't have to relocate."

SOURCE: Trevor Tatum, Resident of St. Petersburg, Florida. Workshop 2: Opportunities & Challenges of Climate Adaptation on Florida's Gulf Coast, July 2022, St. Petersburg, Florida.

"Earlier I said 'assisted retreat,' when people choose. In other words, the community takes the lead by saying, 'We want to do this' or 'I as an individual want to do this.' The government responds to the initiation of the individual or the community. So, no one's managing. Someone's assisting in doing something that both groups agree is the direction to go [...] and do it with the idea that it is assisting people to do the will that they hope to do."

SOURCE: Windell Curole, General Manager, South Lafourche Levee District. Workshop 3: Community Viability and Environmental Change in Coastal Louisiana, July 2022, Thibodaux, Louisiana.

"More or less people coming in with ideas, and their studies, or whatever, tend to view what the local population had to contribute as being anecdotal or just nonscientific, you know, something that was not of value to the whole. We have made some strides and made some changes. But I think sometimes we still run into these concepts. And that's the perspective that we have to change. Come in, sit at the table, invite, you know, people to have those conversations and let it be a true collaborative effort, you know, where I'm learning from you, you learning from me, because our objectives should be the same, the best for the region that we're hoping to work in and to live in. And I think the more that we foster those kinds of concepts and ideas, we all would come out for it in the better. But, you know, that's a long road to go [...] So, you know, we just need to have those conversations. Those conversations need to begin with the at-risk communities. You know, not coming in as an afterthought or, you know, or even inviting—sometimes we're invited to the table just to get your opinion. But at the end of the day, we see that whatever you share doesn't make it to the end product."

SOURCE: Elder Rosina Philippe, Atakapa-Ishak/Chawasha Tribe and President of the First Peoples' Conservation Council. Workshop 3: Community Viability and Environmental Change in Coastal Louisiana, July 2022, Thibodaux, Louisiana.

be to encourage the underlying messages of competing interest groups to be understood by all stakeholders [... A]lthough efforts should continue to communicate with science and economics, a broader dialogue is required to address community concerns about the complex topic of managed retreat" (Alexander et al., 2012, p. 429). In other words, it is important that various groups are transparently engaged and respected, even if consensus cannot be achieved. Bragg et al. (2021) encourage the use of "surveys or workshops to understand the predominant worldviews, priorities, and values" of involved communities.

Effective communication may require building trust among community members and leaders. Key to this process is understanding how relationships form in a given community, including knowing "the ways people connect culturally and create spaces for conversation," which can then be incorporated into meetings with community members (Climigration Network, 2021, p. 26). Ryan et al. (2022) also emphasize the importance of allowing space for residents to tell stories, voice concerns, and provide local knowledge. When engaging in communication, the messenger is also a relevant consideration; "when residents learn about plans from a trusted local source who supports the changes, they are more likely to be accepting" (Bragg et al., 2021). Outside messengers should reflect on their positionality and acknowledge that some community members may not be willing to share information with outside individuals (Climigration Network, 2021). This may be particularly true when community members have had negative experiences when sharing their stories previously, making "trauma-informed" work essential when interacting with impacted communities (Climigration Network, 2021).[5]

Transparency

A key communication issue for residents facing relocation is transparency (Shadroui, 2022; Siders, 2018; Tucker, 2018). Throughout the Gulf region, there has been a lack of transparency about what is planned or contemplated with regard to relocation. For example, there is variance in the scope and administration of buyouts across communities wherein buyouts are mandated in some locations and not others. The reasons for this variation often are not transparent and may seem arbitrary or even discriminatory in communities where there is limited understanding of the

[5]The Climigration Network (2021, p. 30) defines "trauma-informed" work as "realizing the widespread impact of trauma, recognizing its signs and symptoms, and integrating knowledge about it into policies, procedures and practices."

BOX 7-4
Community Testimonials: Challenges for Effective Communication and Outreach

"The Hispanic community in Pinellas County presents a unique situation. Unlike other neighborhoods, we are integrated across different socioeconomic levels, from the poorest to the richest. We lack concentrated pockets within specific neighborhoods. Therefore, we require a central location, like a magnet, where community members can come together for cultural celebrations and receive assistance. This location would serve as a hub to connect individuals with the resources provided by local government, organizations, and institutions, and that requires a sense of community. Once we're connected as a community, we can amplify our voice in the political realm and advocate for increased resource allocation from our politicians."

SOURCE: Eliseo Santana, Resident of St. Petersburg, Florida. Workshop 2: Opportunities & Challenges of Climate Adaptation on Florida's Gulf Coast, July 2022, St. Petersburg, Florida.

"So, what I'm saying is, is there an initiative that we got going on that we haven't disseminated all the information in the communities, so that we can make good decisions, you know, about these things. And I think that, not only that, but there's also a lot of things—the information problem is really there. And I don't know who's giving up the information, but I think that that's one of the things that we should address. Is the information getting to everybody, so that everybody has an equal opportunity to deal with whatever they have to deal with?"

SOURCE: Trevor Tatum, Resident of St. Petersburg, Florida. Workshop 2: Opportunities & Challenges of Climate Adaptation on Florida's Gulf Coast, July 2022, St. Petersburg, Florida.

"So, when you talk about the—if I didn't go to Leadership Terrebonne last year, which is the—a group of leaders that they do every year, I would have never known about the Coastal Master Plan [...] I'm not going to lie, the language was a lot for the average person to understand. I do believe that if you want people to truly understand what you're talking about, what it entails, that has to be broken down for the average person to understand [...] We have to realize that in Terrebonne Parish we are actually working to build up our educational level. Most people have a high school diploma and that's just about it. We are 22 percent, 22 percent of a higher, post higher education here in this community. So, we have to make it more so people can understand what that entails and what it means, break that down to the ordinary person, so somebody can understand what that plan entails, what does it look like. And save the scientific terms, no offense to you and your studies and your research. But for the average person, they should know—break it down to them."

SOURCE: Sherry Wilmore, Resident of Houma, Louisiana. Workshop 3: Assisted Resettlement and Receiving Communities in Louisiana, July 2022, Houma, Louisiana.

(continued)

BOX 7-4
Continued

"[I]n the coastal communities, too, there's a bit of distrust just because of past experience. You'll have forecasters that say, 'This is going to be a terrible, terrible, terrible storm,' and it comes, and nothing materializes. And so, the next one, they're not as worried about it. And then you have something like a couple of years ago when we had Tropical Storm Eta. It hardly made the news. There wasn't an emergency declared, and Madeira Beach got walloped. I mean, we got flooded. We had 75 water rescues in the middle of the night, no power, streets flooded up to chest level. The next day, it looked like the world's worst yard sale out there, just people hauling carpets and furniture from their homes, cars getting towed out. We had no warning. By the time we were offered sandbags, the roads were flooded and impassible. So, there's a real disconnect sometimes with what is being said with what is happening."

SOURCE: Chelsea Nelson, Resident of Madeira Beach, Florida. Workshop 2: Opportunities & Challenges of Climate Adaptation on Florida's Gulf Coast, July 2022, St. Petersburg, Florida.

different criteria for buyouts and how they will be implemented for local households.[6]

However, transparency issues with the buyout process are not limited to the Gulf region. For example, at the committee's information-gathering session on property acquisitions, Courtney Wald-Wittkop, program manager of New Jersey's Blue Acres buyout program, described a lesson learned:[7]

> *I think one of the other things is transparency. We realized that in the past we were treating buyouts like simply a real estate transaction. We were really focused on making sure that the homeowners had all the information, and we had case managers whose job it was to walk the homeowners through the process, one-on-one. But really there wasn't as much concern about making sure that the communities where these buyouts were happening were as engaged or informed. Elected officials change and buyout programs span a couple of years, [so we] have to keep building the vocabulary of local government officials so they understand what is going*

[6]Comments made to the committee on June 8, 2022, during a public information-gathering session in Texas. More information is available at https://www.nationalacademies.org/event/06-08-2022/managed-retreat-in-the-us-gulf-coast-region-workshop-1

[7]Comments made to the committee on December 13, 2022, during a public virtual information-gathering session. More information is available at https://www.nationalacademies.org/event/12-13-2022/managed-retreat-in-the-us-gulf-coast-region-perspectives-and-approaches-to-property-acquisitions-challenges-and-lessons-learned

on, what the end goal is, and what the driving philosophy was from the buyout planning process through the implementation and into the post-buyout restoration phase.

Issue framing affects communication between government and residents, and highlights differing perspectives and priorities. For example, climate change issues may be received differently when framed as a health problem compared to another type of problem (e.g., economic or environmental; Badullovich et al., 2020; Dasandi et al., 2021). Transparency around the framing of issues around relocation can affect outcomes. This could also apply to transparency around eligibility to participate in the process, including issues such as the geographical boundaries of buyout zones (Binder & Greer, 2016; Martin et al., 2019). For example, migrants and minoritized groups have been disproportionately affected by a lack of communication about relocation (Shi et al., 2022). Strategic communication can contribute to improved transparency, especially in underserved communities, in several ways:

- allowing for meaningful input from residents about alternative approaches;
- enabling potential relationships between the community leaders involved in disaster recovery and relocation professionals (e.g., planners, local government) that advise on the process and logic of the relocation process;
- providing time for people to become prepared psychologically and to prepare their families for possible relocation; and
- allowing for people to make their own decisions about where they wish to go.

Participation and transparency mean full community engagement in all discussions.

Language, Literacy, and Cultural Considerations

Workshop participants in Houston explained that letters sent through the U.S. Postal Service are the main way that they have received information regarding buyouts (National Academies, 2022c), but that this critical information was not available in other languages (e.g., Spanish, Vietnamese), engendering a sense within those communities of being excluded from the process. Language coupled with limited connections to elected officials, staff turnover, and the lengthy process result in many people being left out (National Academies, 2022c). The impact of turnover can be prevented by local community leaders, through employment or other means, with knowledge and access about the relocation processes to facilitate communication and, in turn, deliver residents' concerns back to the government—a process that could foster a more participatory and culturally relevant approach (see Box 7-5). Underresourced groups can be included by working with trusted leaders in vulnerable towns and cities to act as communicators about buyout options and to help design and promote locally meaningful and community-led models of relocations that have been shaped by residents. Those involved with relocation efforts need to understand not just the physical topography but also the social and ethnic topography of communities to assure meaningful engagement and action (e.g., language, and sociocultural values that underlie choices about where to live; National Academies, 2022c, p. 38, 2023a; Spidalieri & Bennett, 2020a).

Systemic inequalities also create practical barriers to participation in relocation. The COVID-19 pandemic has illustrated both the promise of connection through technology and the large and enduring gaps in who has

BOX 7-5
Community Testimonials: Lack of Resources and Equity

"So, the feeling of feeling stuck I believe comes from people who don't have resources. So, they don't know which way to go, what to do, or how to solve the problem. And if there is not a resource that is available or one that they can qualify for, collect the data, present it to the city and let them know what the needs are."

SOURCE: Antwaun Wells, Resident of St. Petersburg, Florida. Workshop 2: Opportunities & Challenges of Climate Adaptation on Florida's Gulf Coast, July 2022, St. Petersburg, Florida.

"I wanted to say also that there has been a trend that's been going on in our five bayous for a long time. And we noticed, you know, as the people are moving, as the resources are leaving, you know, it's the small businesses, it's the mom and pops. And then they come for the schools and then the schools are closing. You know, they're taking away or we're losing, you know, all these things that brought people together, you know, all these things where people gathered at, like the fairs that happen on all the bayous through the churches, slowly all of these things are being taken away from each of these areas. You know, and then to where's just, you know, there's just the people and then the people are not coming out and communicating as heavily as they were back in our days, you know. It's just been a trend that has been growing over, you know, the last several years and it's just, it's growing strong and that is also a huge contribution to the disconnect that is taking place, you know."

SOURCE: Bette Billiot, the United Houma Nation. Workshop 3: Assisted Resettlement and Receiving Communities in Louisiana, July 2022, Houma, Louisiana.

access to that promise (Parker, Menasce, & Minkin, 2020; Vogels, 2021a,b; Vogels et al., 2020). It is well known that traditional news media—newspapers, radio, and television—are no longer consumed universally and that local print news sources in many communities have dried up (Pew Research Center, 2019). The Internet itself is not a reliable way of reaching people in communities universally. Moreover, even in the presence of strong online networks, broadband is often not an option in rural areas (Vogels, 2021b) and on tribal lands (Howard & Morris, 2019). Access to broadband also affects the ability of people in many communities to participate via the ability to attend online community meetings, conduct online research, and fill out online applications. Participating is difficult when lower-income households have difficulty affording child care (National Academies, 2022c; see also Bhattarai & Fowers, 2022). These factors have significant implications for who can participate in community meetings and other activities concerning less immediate needs, such as future options for relocating their community. Outsiders coming into the community to build capacity or otherwise engage community members might not be sensitive to these barriers, or cognizant of their effects on community involvement or decision making (see Box 7-6).

Communicating relocation as an option for those who wish to move entails communicating why the option is even on the table. In other words,

BOX 7-6
Community Testimonial: Lack of Communication

Workshop participants did not feel they had been communicated appropriately with about the mandatory buyouts affecting their homes.

"I am one of the people who has tried to stay very active in the communication with them, trying to have contact with the directors or superiors because it is not easy. Also, because the information at times does not reach people, and they are not doing everything possible to ensure that it reaches people who have not even been visited by one of them. There have been various communication problems and a lack of preparation in the program. It became apparent that the staff were not prepared for this type of program because many people had come and gone in the program area. We had very little access to communication with them; they did not answer calls and we had to fight to get emails answered, since there are also many elderly people who speak mostly Spanish. They were not prepared at all for this type of situation."

SOURCE: Perla Garcia, Coalition for Environment, Equity, and Resilience. Workshop 1: Buyouts and Other Forms of Strategic Relocation in Greater Houston, June 2022, Houston, Texas.

communicating risk in locally understandable terms and learning from residents about their perceptions and their local knowledge are critical to a community-driven relocation process. The next section discusses the importance of local risk perception, as well as models and strategies for risk communication and messaging.

RISK COMMUNICATION

Lessons learned from the communication of scientific information on climate change are relevant to communicating risk in the context of relocation efforts. A recent National Academies report (National Academies, 2022b, Box 2, p. 1) suggests 10 practical strategies for communicating about climate risks to vulnerable communities:

1. Use simple, clear messages by paring down technical information.
2. Understand how messages are interpreted by different communities.
3. Repeat messages often.
4. Enlist caring messengers trusted by both decision makers and local communities.
5. Articulate clear objectives for climate- and disaster-related actions.
6. Move beyond the abstract and describe risks in terms that are psychologically near in space and time.
7. Trigger affect-driven responses but use emotional appeals judiciously.
8. Emphasize emerging social norms around adaptation and resilience.
9. Frame climate change–related hazards and risks strategically.
10. Convey the available risk management options and their effectiveness.

Among these generalized strategies, strategy two makes clear that effective risk communication also necessitates an understanding of risk perceptions in the specific communities one is engaging. Recognizing how people perceive risk can thus help improve the two-way communication needed for major adaptations like relocation to be discussed, planned, and implemented effectively and equitably.

Risk perception "generally refers to how individuals cognitively and emotionally evaluate risks and their vulnerability" (Lim, 2022, p. 3; see also Grothmann & Reusswig, 2006; Lindell & Perry, 2012; van Valkengoed & Steg, 2019) and is influenced by local values and mental models (see below) of what is important to community residents (Bostrom, 2017; Kempton et al., 1995; Leiserowitz, 2006). Both past experiences and personal values determine a person's acceptable level of risk (Siegrist & Árvai, 2020; Zammitti et al., 2021). In addition, it is important to recognize that humans have a finite number of things they can emotionally process before they become overwhelmed. Therefore, people prioritize issues and actions that seem most urgent, which can affect risk perception.

Understanding this threshold can help communicators comprehend an individual's perception of and response to that risk. Friends, family members, and other actors within an individual's social network play a strong role in cues about risks and values, and also influence an individual's social learning (Haer et al., 2016). To improve risk communication of potential relocation, all of these factors must be taken into consideration. Once an appropriate message has been co-developed with community partners, it is important to offer realistic solutions, use trusted messengers to deliver the message, and respect different viewpoints while also acknowledging the emotions the message may trigger (Bard Center for Environmental Policy, 2012; Hayes et al., 2018; United Nations, n.d.).

Effective messaging about relocation does not mean presenting the same facts over and over again. It means that leaders or outside authorities develop a dynamic, strategic, and intentional way of meaningfully conveying risks based on an understanding of how individuals and the community perceive risk in general. This sort of communication must happen while working alongside community members, to alter the message as needed to support better risk perception and address concerns expressed by those affected.

For a relocation effort to become community-driven, effective communication strategies, especially in places where place attachment runs deep, are critical (Hanna et al., 2020). Risk communication in general is challenging, especially when it involves an often-uninformed or under-informed public. For example, in climate change–related risk communication, communication and engagement between stakeholders and residents can be hampered by common cognitive barriers, such as the relevance of climate change impacts to one's life; a disagreement with the vision, plan, or solution (e.g., relocation); or the framing of the issue and the language around it (Moser, 2007; Moser & Dilling, 2007). The uncertainty resulting from risk mitigation is also very much at the heart of the relocation dilemma (Hanna et al., 2020), making risk and potential mitigation measures difficult to communicate to locals who are often the ones impacted by this gap.

An expected outcome of effective risk communication to the community is an increased knowledge of the risk and the associated mitigation measures. For climate-related policies to succeed and gain support, this sort of knowledge and awareness is critical (Khatibi et al., 2021; Madumere, 2017). In a synthesis of articles on participatory environmental monitoring, participant outcomes included knowledge gain, increased community awareness, attitude and behavior change, and support toward natural resource management policies (Stepenuck & Green, 2015). Whether the knowledge acquired by an individual is local knowledge in an informal setting (Semali & Kincheloe, 1999) or traditional/Indigenous knowledge with a code of ethics guiding environmental use (Craig & Davis, 2005; Mazzocchi, 2006), the context of the knowledge-gathering process is critical as to whether it is used effectively. In communicating the nature and risks of climate change to the public, it has been suggested that a coordinated process of using both local knowledge and scientific information can increase people's understanding of critical issues (Bulkeley, 2000). Such a coordinated approach can also improve the trust between and among community members (Khatibi et al., 2021).

For information to be perceived as credible and usable to influence policy outcomes, a more active, iterative communication approach is critical (Cash et al., 2003). A well-crafted public engagement process where stakeholders and community residents participate in the (co)production of plans and strategies is an essential step to ensuring that knowledge created can be useful and beneficial to community members (Lemos & Morehouse, 2005). Such an approach of active public engagement has been seen to be a critical component of successful managed retreat exercises, and it provides a valuable lesson about the intersection of risk communication and community knowledge creation (Spidalieri & Bennett, 2020d). The next section discusses mental models, which is another tool that can be utilized to access cultural understandings of risk and climate in the context of relocation.

Mental Models for Risk Communication

Morgan et al. (2002) explain the need for a systemic approach to communicating risk. In many cases, rather than conducting an assessment of what the audience believes and what information they need to make the decisions they face, communicators will often turn to technical experts to ask what people should be told. When confronted with a wealth of information that is not tailored to specific needs or understandings, the target audience can become confused, miss the point, or become disinterested. To overcome this dilemma, a five-step method, known as the mental models approach, was developed for creating and testing risk messages: (1) create an expert model, (2) conduct mental models interviews, (3) conduct structured initial interviews, (4) draft risk communication, and (5) evaluate communication (Morgan et al., 2002).

Photo sorting, open-ended interviews, and confirmatory questionnaires are a few methods by which data can be collected to better understand shared mental or cultural models (cf. Kempton et al., 1995). Comparing expert mental models with those of the target audience can reveal different ways of understanding the same issue, gaps in knowledge and confusing terminology for both sides, as well as linkages to misconceptions for both sides. This information can then be used to co-produce both more accurate and more culturally relevant messages about risk. This process can be time-consuming but is necessary to properly understand and communicate risk.

PARTICIPATION AND KNOWLEDGE

Relocating and resettling is a complex process of change and adaptation that involves more than the physical act of moving. It is a social process that involves the cooperation, coordination, and participation of affected people at the originating and receiving nodes, as well as various stakeholders that could cross sectors and jurisdictions, as evident in case studies in Chapter 3. Critical to the engagement process is the inclusion of local knowledge, such as place-based knowledge systems or TEK, as described below.

A public lack of trust in entities managing relocation (e.g., government) and a lack of communication and transparency in information about relocation (e.g., buyout criteria; post-buyout land use), compounded by a lack of access to decision-making spaces, also limit the fostering of social capital. The next section takes a closer look at how particular types of social capital might alleviate issues of access, transparency, and participation in the context of relocation.

Linking Social Capital to Participation and Civic Leadership

The well-being of a community is both a contributor to and an outcome of building social capital. In this section, we continue the discussion of social capital and community well-being in Chapter 6 by considering how social capital is critical to enabling effective civic leadership, which is, in turn, a contributor to and outcome of community well-being. To do this, we look at three different types of social capital, as identified by researchers: bonding (within networks), bridging (between networks), and linking (across hierarchical networks of power; Adger, 2003; Aldrich, 2012; Frankenberger et al., 2013; Kawachi et al., 2004; Putnam, 1993a, 1995). Each type of social capital "identifies variation in strength of relationships and composition of networks and thus different outcomes for individuals and communities" (Aldrich & Meyer, 2015, p. 258). These categories are particularly useful in considering the role of social capital in participation and civic leadership, as described below.

Bonding refers to emotionally connected members of the same network, such as friends or family (Adler & Kwon, 2002). Bonding is essential for fostering trust, solidarity, and reciprocity, and can be especially useful in disaster contexts and during other times of dire need (Hurlbert et al., 2000). *Bridging* refers to connections between more demographically diverse networks, such as between groups that are united through institutions (e.g., sports, religion, civic or political unions, parent-teacher associations; Aldrich & Meyer, 2015). Bridging between these different groups is essential for the exchange of novel information and pooling of resources. *Linking* social capital refers to connections that cross sociopolitical hierarchies and link communities to institutions and political structures, connecting "regular citizens to power" (Aldrich & Meyer, 2015, p. 259). Linking is essential for political representation, the mobilization of resources, and the enhancement of civic leadership.

Focusing on social capital in conceptualizing resilience reveals the importance of social relations in a community's capacity to respond to challenges (Eder et al., 2012; Marré & Weber, 2010; Osborne et al., 2007; Riabova & Skaptadóttir, 2003). Research examining disaster response asserts that relevant social relations include those among local governments, aid organizations, and affected populations or community members (Barrios, 2014), including religious and co-ethnic social capital and networks spanning geographic scale (Airriess et al., 2008). Linking social capital, which connects hierarchies, can create feedback loops between otherwise independently operating entities (e.g., community members, grassroots organizations, scientists, government planners) working on thematically or geographically overlapping projects (Frankenberger et al., 2013; see also Aldrich, 2012; Woodson et al., 2016; see Figure 7-2). Feedback is important for entities that are potentially in conflict with one another, depending on material (e.g., subsistence) and symbolic (e.g., identity, sense of security) attachments to place (Dandy et al., 2019; Masterson, 2016; Masterson et al., 2017).

A key takeaway from our committee's workshops was that people do not feel involved in the discussion and decision-making processes about relocation or relocation options or do not know about these processes and, therefore, feel they have little to no influence on them (see Box 7-1, above). If social capital connects "regular citizens to power" (Aldrich & Meyer, 2015, p. 259) and engenders political representation, focusing on bridging social capital among communities and then linking that social capital across sociopolitical hierarchies can provide access to decision-making spaces and promote participatory decision-making processes that can, in turn, draw on local knowledge and enhance community resilience and well-being (Aldrich, 2012; Woodson et al., 2016).

Examples of linking social capital include collaborative governance strategies that integrate citizen science (McCormick, 2009, 2012), community science (Charles et al., 2020), participatory action research (PAR; Baum et al., 2006), Indigenous and local knowledges (Renn, 2020), and strategies that engage a collective response to such change (Boonstra, 2016). These strategies draw on emotional and behavioral strengths that can be positively nurtured by mental health systems and other core social anchoring

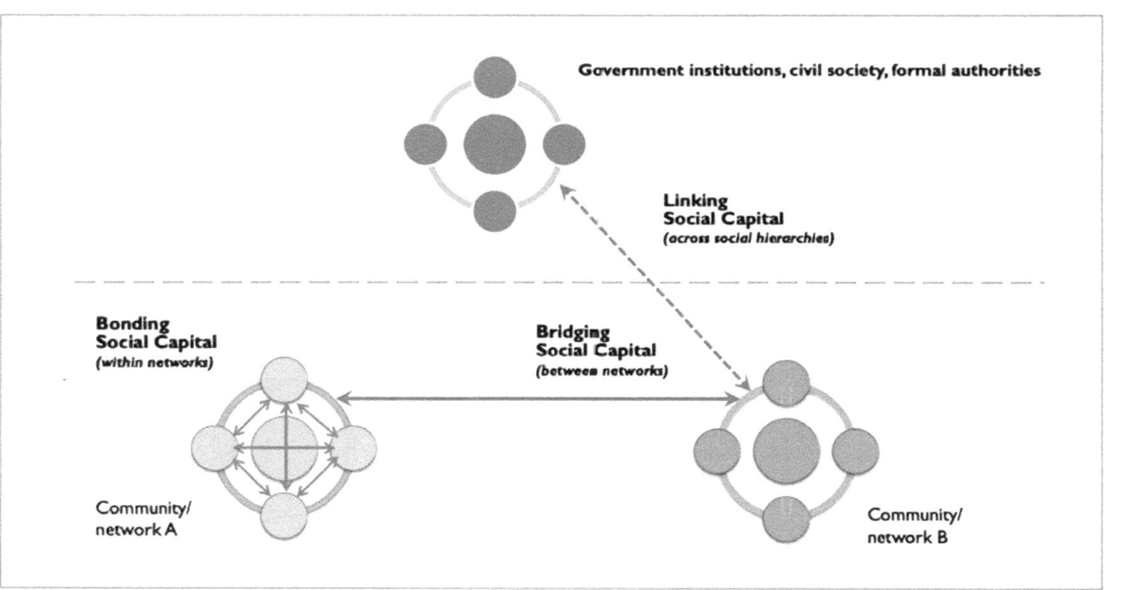

FIGURE 7-2 Bonding, bridging, and linking social capital.
SOURCE: Aldrich, D. P. (2012). *Building resilience: Social capital in post-disaster recovery*. University of Chicago Press.

institutions, as discussed in Chapter 6 (Belkin, 2020; Wamsler & Bristow, 2022; Wamsler et al., 2021). Importantly, a focus on social capital and civic leadership does not diminish the importance of material resources in shaping community well-being while managing adaptation (see "All Resources Matter" in Chapter 6).

Other approaches that show the range of thinking about linking social capital to civic leadership and policy participation include empirical work about voluntary collaboration and cooperation in managing shared environmental resources and harms, such as Ostrom's key design principles for managing commons resources (Dietz et al., 2003; Ostrom, 1990; see also applications of Multilevel Evolutionary Framework; Waring et al., 2015). Such approaches pull on certain emotional and behavioral strengths and attributes identified as foundations of emotional resilience, and can be positively nurtured and learned by mental health systems as well as other core social anchor institutions, as described in Chapter 6 (Belkin, 2020; Wamsler & Bristow, 2022; Wamsler et al., 2021). These combined elements of participation, social cohesion, and emotional well-being are interconnected and essential for realizing transformational adaptation (Intergovernmental Panel on Climate Change [IPCC], 2014b; Shi & Moser, 2021).

Similarly, studies of participatory decision making draw attention to innovation in how knowledge relevant to these decisions is packaged in a way that is coherent to residents and other stakeholders. To achieve this coherence, there is a need for novel transdisciplinary and locally generated approaches, such as citizen science and tacit, cultural, and Indigenous and local knowledge (Renn, 2020).

Power Sharing and Participatory Decision Making: Who Decides?

The multiple dimensions of power that affect levels of community engagement in decision making for social change have been analyzed by Gaventa (2006). There are several examples and methods of empowerment and participation that can enhance and rely on social capital and collective governance. In the Gulf region, the Louisiana's Strategic Adaptations for Future Environments (LA SAFE) initiative provides one such example.[8] LA SAFE took a holistic and regional (i.e., cross-sector, multi-jurisdictional) approach to addressing climate-induced risks and enhancing resilience by enlisting the support of, and training, trusted community leaders to help lead the engagement process. Key lessons from LA SAFE include the importance of the program in acknowledging the inherent limitations of its data and "communicating the need and opportunity to augment preacquired

[8]More information about LA SAFE is available at https://lasafe.la.gov/

data and science with locally sourced experiential knowledge" (National Academies, 2023b, p. 38).[9]

There is also increasing adoption of activities, both nationally and internationally, for more community-involved decision making on matters of policy through relationship-building and active collaborations between community members (e.g., residents) and other community stakeholders (e.g., local government, community-based organizations; Boothroyd et al., 2017). These collaborations have taken a range of formats, often described as "deliberative" or "participatory democracy" (Curato et al., 2017; Gilman, 2019). They can also take many forms and exist at multiple scales, including citizen assemblies, citizen juries, public utility ownership, and participatory budgeting. Collaborations have the capacity to cover a diversity of geographies and a range of scopes and mandates, and involve communities of differing populations. For example, citizen panels or juries might focus on a more bounded question of policy and/or place for action (e.g., Citizens Initiative Review Commission).[10] These are examples of more systematic ways of positioning more collective and participatory deliberation and decision making in discussions about relocation.

The basic logic underpinning these approaches to collaboration is that a random but representative set of community members can make good decisions that might be credible to the larger community if some key parameters are in place. Those parameters tend to include a sequencing of steps along the lines of deliberation: facilitated group learning, group propositions, and coming to consensus. Ideally, throughout each step of the process, a set of subject matter experts prepares trusted, objective background information and responses to member questions (Curato et al., 2017; Dryzek et al., 2019; Gilman, 2019; Le Strat & Menser, 2022).[11] In many ways, these practices capture some of the ground rules of collaborative governance of commons resources described by Elinor Ostrom (1990) in her Nobel prize-winning work and, relatedly, in principles of prosociality, which mutually reinforce social cohesion, ties, and well-being (Atkins et al., 2019).

Longer planning timeframes can help build relationships and trust among the various actors, allowing for more meaningful community participation. For example, in the Carteret community relocation in Papua New Guinea, the community-based nonprofit organization Tulele Peisa reached

[9]More lessons learned from LA SAFE and other community-centered Gulf region and national resilience-building efforts from a National Academies study are available at https://nap.nationalacademies.org/read/26880/chapter/5#37

[10]More information on the Citizens Initiative Review Commission is available at https://olis.oregonlegislature.gov/liz/2019R1/Downloads/CommitteeMeetingDocument/173979

[11]More information about examples of approaches in the United States for other health and public health uses are available at https://healthydemocracy.org/what-we-do/local-government-work/oregon-assembly-on-covid-recovery/

out to families facing relocation several years before starting relocation, and likewise invested much time in outreach to the receiving communities and relationship-building between hosts and settlers (Ristroph, 2023; United Nations Development Programme, 2016).

Co-Production of Community-Driven Relocation

There is a growing recognition of the importance of involving multiple stakeholders, including community residents, in the co-production of climate adaptation strategies (Conde & Lonsdale, 2005). In the context of this report, co-production is the process of developing knowledge, plans, and strategies through the iterative engagement of at-risk communities, researchers, practitioners, and other groups, whose participation is necessary to the relocation process (see Armitage et al., 2011; Meadow et al., 2015; Wamsler, 2017). The literature on co-production has been growing since the 1970s and has been applied across fields and contexts (Norström et al., 2020). It is beyond the capacity of this report to specify which disciplinary form or interpretation of co-production is ideal for relocation planning and implementation. However, the climate adaptation strategy of community-driven relocation, as recommended by this committee, shares co-production's guiding principle of equity in participation and knowledge (Yua et al., 2022)—which may involve broadening engagement with Indigenous knowledge systems (Carlo, 2020) and the "prioritization of Indigenous voices, experiences, knowledge, reflections, and analyses" (Zanotti et al., 2020; see also White House, 2022, p. 12).

PAR and Practice

PAR differs from conventional research in that it focuses on how to enable action, it pays considerable attention to power relationships, and it blurs the line between researcher and those being researched (Baum et al., 2006) in the (co)production of actionable knowledge. Self-reflection is a key component of this research process. Similar to co-production, PAR is an iterative approach that cycles between research, action, and reflection. It uses both qualitative and quantitative data collection to better understand a problematic situation while bringing to light the views of local people, their reality, their challenges, and their ideas for solutions.

Schneider (2012) outlines the key goals of PAR: (a) to produce practical knowledge, (b) to take action and make the knowledge actionable, and (c) to be transformative both socially and for the individual(s) who take part in it. This requires a commitment to the co-production of knowledge by researchers and ordinary people (White, 2022). It also implies a mutual learning among participants and respect for the different types of knowledge shared by participants. PAR typically pays attention to the needs of marginalized groups or people and promotes social justice for these groups (Cornish et al., 2023).

A recent consensus report by the National Academies (2023b) about strengthening equitable community resilience in U.S. Gulf Coast and Alaskan communities utilized the PAR framework. However, the study committee decided to add the word "practice" to the term and thus coined PARP. As the study committee noted, "[T]he inclusion of the term practice underscores the practical applications of PAR and how the PAR approach can be applied beyond pure research projects to include capacity-building projects that may or may not include a research component" (National Academies, 2023b, p. 3).

Local and Indigenous Knowledge in Participatory Planning

> *Communities want to determine their own climate change adaptation strategies, and scientists and decision makers should listen to them—both the equity and efficacy of climate change adaptation depend on it. (Pisor et al., 2022, p. 213; see also Forsyth, 2013)*

Increasingly, local and Indigenous knowledge[12] is being sought out in scientific studies, land-use decision making, and planning to gain a more detailed understanding of how climate and other environmental and sociocultural changes are interacting and affecting communities on the ground. These place-based knowledge systems are diverse, distinct, and highly attuned to local conditions. They also may reveal how residents have in the past responded to similar environmental change or events, as well as how they are responding now or may respond in the future. Thus, the engagement of local and Indigenous knowledge along with scientific knowledge is increasingly being promoted and accepted as best practice in addressing diverse and intersecting climate challenges, especially when communities need to adapt or otherwise respond urgently to environmental changes (see Boxes 7-8 and 7-9; Lazrus et al., 2022; Thornton & Bhagwat, 2021; Wildcat, 2013).

Recent National Climate Assessments have emphasized the importance of engaging with Indigenous peoples. As summarized in the Fourth U.S. National Climate Assessment (Ch. 15),

---

[12]According to the IPCC (2019), "Indigenous knowledge (IK) refers to the understandings, skills and philosophies developed by societies with long histories of interaction with their natural surroundings. Local knowledge (LK) refers to the understandings and skills developed by individuals and populations, specific to the place where they live." More information is available at https://www.ipcc.ch/srccl/faqs/faqs-chapter-7/

> *Indigenous peoples in the United States are diverse and distinct political and cultural groups and populations. Though they may be affected by climate change in ways that are similar to others in the United States, Indigenous peoples can also be affected uniquely and disproportionately. Many Indigenous peoples have lived in particular areas for hundreds if not thousands of years. Indigenous peoples' histories and shared experience engender distinct knowledge about climate change impacts and strategies for adaptation. Indigenous peoples' traditional knowledge systems can play a role in advancing understanding of climate change and in developing more comprehensive climate adaptation strategies. (Reidmiller et al., 2018, p. 105)*

In November 2021, the White House Office of Science and Technology Policy (OSTP) and the Council on Environmental Quality (CEQ) issued a memorandum on Indigenous traditional ecological knowledge (ITEK) and federal decision making, identifying the relevance and importance of the former in environmental decision making and committing to elevate its role in federal scientific and policy processes (OSTP, 2021). In this context, this report uses the term, ITEK (Lander & Mallory, 2021), as defined in the Key Terms (Appendix D).

A year later, on November 30, 2022, OSTP and CEQ together issued Guidance for Federal Departments and Agencies on Indigenous Knowledge (OSTP, 2022). The seventh principle is to "[p]ursue co-production of knowledge," defined as "a research framework based on equity and the inclusion of multiple knowledge systems," including those of the 574 tribes recognized by the U.S. Bureau of Indian Affairs[13] (Prabhakar & Mallory, 2022, p. 12). The new guidance aims to "promote and enable a Government-wide effort to improve the recognition and inclusion of Indigenous Knowledge," and offers guidance for collaborating with tribal nations and Indigenous peoples (Prabhakar & Mallory, 2022, p. 3). This position is consistent with that of U.S. tribes for whom Indigenous knowledge recognition in co-production has become a key pathway for affirming Indigenous worldviews, rights, and responsibilities, including among tribes who may not have federal recognition but may be state-recognized or seeking federal recognition (Latulippe & Klenk, 2020; Zurba et al., 2022).

Earlier chapters have shown that local and Indigenous knowledge has been an important component of understanding and adapting to coastal conditions on the U.S. Gulf Coast, including extreme events such as

[13]More information about the list of all tribal entities that are recognized by the federal government, as of January 2021, is available at https://www.federalregister.gov/documents/2021/01/29/2021-01606/indian-entities-recognized-by-and-eligible-to-receive-services-from-the-united-states-bureau-of

hurricanes and storm surges. Indigenous adaptations included earthworks to complement natural levees and seasonal, or in some cases permanent, relocations to avoid life-threatening conditions. Yet, many communities in threatened coastal areas today, such as the U.S. Gulf Coast, are not able to maintain local knowledge to previous degrees, nor to share it effectively with other governments. Furthermore, these Indigenous communities are marginalized and underserved and often have been made more vulnerable by loss of lands, mobility, and resources, and to industrial development and pollution, and other environmental stressors, thus undermining their capacity to cope or adapt (Cottier et al., 2022). All of these hazards threaten the existence of community and individual knowledge and practices. This has been pointed out in community meetings by local Indigenous groups, both as a part of this study and in previous studies going back at least a decade (Felipe Pérez & Tomaselli, 2021; Siders & Ajibade, 2021). For example, a member of the Isle de Jean Charles Band of Biloxi-Chitimacha-Choctaw made the following statement in 2012:

> *We are historically fishermen and trappers. We have maintained this life well for hundreds of years, probably longer. Now our waters are contaminated by the industries that increase global warming and the layer of pollution in the atmosphere, which brings with it an increase in storms that has led to salt water intrusion of our lands. This is also destroying the vegetation that has been plentiful and abundant for generations, destroying the opportunity for us to be a self-supporting people and to share our bounty with the rest of the planet. (Maldonado et al., 2014, p. 602)*

Local and Indigenous knowledge and adaptive capacity, then, must be considered against the backdrop of historical circumstances, including marginalization and inequality, which may have affected crucial relationships to local lands, waters, and other critical resources, as well as the rights of recognized tribes to exist and determine their own futures as sovereign entities (see Box 7-7). Two subsequent boxes highlight two other aspects of Indigenous knowledge within the realm of climate adaptation. Box 7-8 discusses the concept of TEK[14] while Box 7-9 details a self-assessment tool for communities, the Coastal Resilience Index (CRI).

[14]As defined in the Key Terms (Appendix D), TEK is "a cumulative body of knowledge, practice, and belief that evolves by adaptive processes, is handed down through generations by cultural transmission, and centers on the relationships of humans with one another and with their environment" (Berkes et al., 2000).

BOX 7-7
Community Testimonials: Self-Determination and Tribal Sovereignty

Community-led planning and relocation is vital, promoting an "assisted" approach rather than a top-down managed retreat. This highlights the need for self-determination and active involvement of impacted communities in every stage of the process—from planning to implementation and conclusion.

"If resettling communities is not done with a sense of responsibility and accountability to the people that are having to experience it, then we have lost much more than just our land. And part of the reason why we participate in these talks and discussions is because we know what our future holds if nothing is done. If we are not fully included, if our voices are not valued, we will cease to exist. And that process has been in the making for many generations. So at least we have something that we can leave behind. So that, if we no longer exist, we can be remembered."

SOURCE: Elder Chief Shirell Parfait-Dardar, Grand Caillou/Dulac Band of Biloxi-Chitimacha-Choctaw, and Chair, Louisiana Governor's Commission on Native Americans. Workshop 3: Community Viability and Environmental Change in Coastal Louisiana, July 2022, Thibodaux, Louisiana.

"It seems—one of the issues that tribes deal with in this country is the issue of recognition. We've subdivided recognition into state recognition and federal recognition, and each stage of recognition offers a certain level of funding and support. In Louisiana, we don't see any funding or support for state-recognized tribes. And often when we try to work with state governments or state agencies, there are conversations that are had and people [state officials] say, 'Well, you need to be federal. We can't really do that because you need to be federal, even if it's a state-level issue.' So, even though it's not a specific project, on a broader, more systemic level, when tribes try to engage with state agencies or engage with the state overall, the problem is that people aren't exactly recognizing tribal people as sovereign people or people in general."

SOURCE: Chief Devon Parfait, Grand Caillou Band of Biloxi-Chitimacha-Choctaw. Workshop 3: Community Viability and Environmental Change in Coastal Louisiana, July 2022, Thibodaux, Louisiana.

"And I'm here to say that there is no such thing as management of that process unless the people who have come to the determination that they need to relocate to another area are in charge of that process. If anyone, at the end of the day or the beginning of the day, thinks that, you know, they know better how to and where to relocate people, and I think that's a flaw. That's a flaw in the whole plan. So, it's the people that have come to that determination, they need to be the ones in charge of the entire process. Because you are not just moving from one location to the other, you have to have considerations for how that move will translate into the future."

SOURCE: Elder Rosina Philippe, Atakapa-Ishak/Chawasha Tribe and President of the First Peoples' Conservation Council. Workshop 3: Community Viability and Environmental Change in Coastal Louisiana, July 2022, Thibodaux, Louisiana.

BOX 7-8
Case: TEK Used to Aid Restoration Decisions

TEK—that is, local knowledge of an area gathered and held by Indigenous residents—has been successfully incorporated into decision making for coastal restoration in some instances (Bethel et al., 2014). Matthew Bethel and his team blended geospatial technology with the social sciences to assist the Atakapa-Ishak Tribe of southeast Louisiana in Grand Bayou. The locals involved in the project took Bethel's team out on boats and showed them places where they had seen the largest changes in the marshland that impacted their ability to provide for their families. In turn, Bethel introduced them to other scientists working in the field in a systematic engagement process, so that residents could ask questions and offer input about ongoing projects. Bethel's efforts, in addition to being scientifically valuable, created a feeling of mutual respect between those living in Grand Bayou and others also working to save it. His team integrated the knowledge in a format that state coastal restoration planners could understand and use. For example, they created mapping products that combined scientific and TEK-based datasets to identify specific geographic locations and features in need of focused restoration by government agencies. The Coastal Protection and Restoration Authority of Louisiana saw the value in this project for decision support and secured funding to broaden the scope of the study, both geographically, to include the entire Barataria Basin, and in types of data collected. Having TEK in a format that the state could use as an overlay onto existing restoration layers allowed it to easily be used in the decision-making process (see also Hemmerling, Barra et al., 2020; Mississippi-Alabama Sea Grant Consortium, 2021).

Community Knowledge and Protocols

There may be cultural protocols that should be followed for collecting knowledge, such as approaching community elders to get their permission (Boege & Shibata, 2020; Mercer et al., 2010). Community knowledge holders could be drawn from all groups, including village and church officials, elders, youth, and women (Anisi, 2020); and external knowledge should not be privileged over community knowledge (Mcleod et al., 2019).

Drawing on the knowledge of elders is particularly important. It may also be helpful to involve the larger diaspora of those who have left a community but still support it (Dumaru et al., 2020). Depending on the cultural norms of the community, it may be important to have separate forums for different groups of people, so each can speak freely (Mercer et al., 2010). While knowledge collection may occur in a segregated manner, it could be helpful to have some sort of community-wide knowledge-sharing forum so that knowledge is not held only by a certain group (Walshe & Nunn, 2012).

There is still much to learn about how to best use community knowledge in the relocation process, and what works well in some communities

BOX 7-9
Case: Tribal Coastal Resilience Index (T-CRI)

The CRI is a self-assessment tool communities can use to assist them in identifying their vulnerabilities and strengths prior to the next coastal storm. Developed in the aftermath of Hurricane Katrina, the CRI has been utilized in over 60 communities in the Gulf of Mexico. During the recent revisions and updates to the CRI (Sempier et al., 2021), it was apparent that tribal communities needed a different version of the tool in order to more adequately assess their risks and assets. Climate stressors (subsidence, coastal erosion, saltwater intrusion, rising water levels) have had a disproportionate effect on the Pointe-au-Chien Tribe in coastal Louisiana. The tribe still farms, fishes, and hunts on the land, but climate change is threatening their way of life. The tribe is co-producing the T-CRI with Louisiana Sea Grant, EPA, the National Oceanic and Atmospheric Administration, and other partners in anticipation of using it to set tribal priorities in the face of shifting coastal conditions (EPA, 2021a, p. 13). The T-CRI will emphasize the importance of ITEK in the process of prioritizing threats, developing solutions, and implementing future projects. Once completed, the T-CRI will be available for other tribes searching to assess their current resilience and looking for a long-term pathway of building capacity to withstand the next natural or technological disaster (National Oceanic and Atmospheric Administration, 2022; Setyawan, 2022).

may not work well in others. Thus, external relocation facilitators need to be willing to adapt policies and procedures to learn from past experiences, pursue innovation (White, 2022), and consider cultural diversity. For example, a special government task force in Fiji has been trying to relocate communities since 2018. A document that is guiding the relocation process, Standard Operating Procedures for planned relocations, is considered a "living document" that is updated regularly in response to lessons learned with successive relocations and ongoing dialogue (Lyons, 2022; Office of the Prime Minister, Republic of Fiji, 2023).

SUMMARY

This chapter has identified the need for strong efforts to shift decision making from government agencies (at all levels) to the communities that are most directly affected by relocation. The challenge is a complex one, given that community relocation touches on all aspects of people's lives. Currently, relocation decision making is occurring against a backdrop in which there is a lack of recognition by many across the Gulf region that relocation is imminent or, in some areas, already underway. Moreover, there is a lack of consistent planning and communications by governments, and there is a desire by most communities to stay in place. Only a handful of efforts in the Gulf region and beyond are underway that engage deep participation beyond consultation. These efforts are usually not consistent, generally do not empower communities to make decisions, and have failed to address numerous barriers, such as communication barriers, knowledge gaps, and legal and financial obstacles. Most existing efforts are not leveraging the knowledge, perspectives, and social capital that are present in affected communities to drive adaptation.

More comprehensive and robust approaches are needed for civic engagement and community-level knowledge to guide and improve processes around relocation. All communities, including tribes and other historically marginalized populations, need to be included and their knowledge incorporated. Potential barriers need to be identified and addressed one community at a time. Only after learning about a community and beginning to interact with it, through co-production or PAR models, for example, can an effective two-way communication process be developed. Overall, governance processes around relocation need to be fundamentally reexamined and, in some cases, overhauled, to shift the balance of expertise and information sharing to a two-way process and to re-balance decision-making power in the direction of communities most affected by relocation projects, including the communities that will be receiving relocated people.

CONCLUSIONS

Conclusion 7-1: Effective risk communication is a dynamic, strategic, and locally attuned way of meaningfully conveying the dangers posed by climate change in specific communities, while working alongside residents. Messages may need to be adjusted to reach diverse populations according to their perceptions, cognitive models of climate and risk, and previous experiences with similar threats.

Conclusion 7-2: Participatory and comprehensive approaches to mental health and well-being care and promotion, as well as participatory and deliberative practices, call for new levels of civic participation for policy making, consistently and over the long term. Making such connections is, however, at an early stage of knowledge, application, and effectiveness that challenges usual disciplinary lines and knowledge generation. An important step in empowering community knowledge can occur through implementation of ongoing decision sharing with community members and the routine adoption of participatory and deliberative democracy methods. These methods cultivate an ongoing and credible dialogue and continuous evolution of trust, participation, co-production of knowledge, and consensus-building.

Conclusion 7-3: For community-driven relocation, there is a particular need for participatory processes through which community knowledge is sought, brought forth, and used in planning and decision making. Acknowledging the importance of local knowledge and knowledge holders helps build trust and awareness of local perceptions, needs, and capabilities that can facilitate relocation planning, including the reintroduction of local and Indigenous frameworks that may have been displaced over time.

Conclusion 7-4: Workshop input and findings validate the broad desire for far more substantive, ongoing civic participation/empowerment and leadership capacity that exceeds being "consulted" or "engaged" by considering participants as deciders and co-planners. At the same time, community members and local government leaders are not clear or prepared on how to meaningfully practice participation and incorporate people's capacity in decision-making processes.

Conclusion 7-5: Faith-based and community-based organizations, universities, and nonprofit groups with expertise in social services, cultural preservation, and local languages may be helpful in bridging knowledge between the entities involved in the relocation project, and trusted facilitators should spend time in dialogue with the community to build trust between external entities (e.g., local government, private consultants) and residents. Longer planning timeframes can help build relationships and trust among the various actors, allowing for more meaningful community participation.

8

Receiving and Originating Communities

This chapter discusses the following:

- Receiving community considerations
  - Characteristics of receiving communities
  - Methods to identify suitable receiving areas
  - Resource needs for receiving communities, including topics such as housing, transportation, and ecological services
- Originating community considerations
  - Planning for when to disinvest (Thresholds)
  - How to accommodate financial impacts of population relocations and loss (Consolidation and Regionalization)
  - What to do with land left behind (Decommissioning and Restoration)
  - Issues related to providing continuing access to land left behind
- Need and potential for partnerships between originating and receiving communities

INTRODUCTION

Community-driven relocation may be ultimately driven by environmental change circumstances, but there are myriad other factors that affect both the decision to relocate and where to move. Given the complex, multidimensional nature of moving to a new community, community-driven relocation requires significant planning on the part of receiving and originating communities, including how to thoughtfully manage the social and financial support needed for resettlers, the physical and social infrastructure needed in receiving communities, and the resulting open space in originating communities. This chapter looks in depth at those two communities and their needs in the face of community-driven relocation, acknowledging that there may be no clear distinction between originating and receiving communities in many cases, especially when relocation takes place within the same city, or when it occurs at the household or neighborhood level.

The first section of this chapter comprises a discussion of receiving communities, an often-neglected aspect of community-driven relocation in its current form. The *National Climate Resilience Framework* calls explicit attention to the need to support receiving communities in community-driven relocation, "such as by directing funding and capacity for social services or expediting development of additional affordable housing" (White House, 2023, p. 27). These elements are discussed in further detail throughout this chapter and in the recommendations in Chapter 11. This chapter then shifts attention to the originating communities with a discussion that focuses on planning for and managing the land people will move or have moved away from.

Before looking more at these communities below, we offer definitions of five key terms for understanding the process: receiving community, originating community, land-use planning, regional planning, and infrastructure. Receiving community (or destination community) is a broad term used to describe locations where people are resettling away from a hazardous area (Spidalieri & Bennett, 2020a), either moving to a new jurisdiction or moving within the current jurisdiction to a new location. Ideally, receiving communities have a lower climate risk and the necessary physical, economic, institutional, and social infrastructure to accommodate resettlers, although this is not always the case. The term refers to both the jurisdiction to which resettlers move and the social communities into which they integrate.

Originating community—also known as origin or sending community—refers to a location deemed to be unsafe and from which the populations need to leave, either following a disaster or preemptively in the face of either immediate or looming threats in their area. It is the point of departure for individuals or communities who relocate. "Sending community" is a term that has been used for more than 125 years, beginning with

Ravenstein (1889); however, the committee decided to use "originating" to avoid implying that people are being sent away and do not have agency over their decision to relocate or not.

Land-use planning is a process used to manage "a variety of influential human activities by controlling and designing the ways in which humans use land and natural resources" (Ramkumar et al., 2019, p. 6). Land-use planning emphasizes collaborative problem solving, process-based techniques, and spatially oriented processes. Plans include comprehensive land-use plans, economic development plans, hazard mitigation plans, climate change adaptation plans, and capital improvement plans.

"Regional planning may be defined as the integrated management of the economic, social, and physical resources of a spatially bounded area" (Johnson, 2015, p. 141). For example, regional planning may be used to address watershed protection that affects more than one local jurisdiction. In this report, regional planning refers to both intrastate and interstate issues.

Infrastructure includes both physical infrastructure (e.g., utilities, roads, municipal buildings, health clinics) and social infrastructure. The latter involves "the policies, resources, and services that ensure people can participate in productive social and economic activities. This includes social services, public education, and healthcare" (Gould-Werth et al., 2023).

RECEIVING COMMUNITIES

This section characterizes the spectrum of receiving communities, explains the need to identify suitable land for resettlers, and describes both the natural and built infrastructure and social infrastructure and resources needed to accommodate resettlers.

While the topic has been the subject of academic research, little has been done at any government level to specifically assess the capacity of communities to receive resettlers from a community-driven relocation. Regional planning, which might help receiving communities anticipate an influx of resettlers, inherently requires consideration of density, resources, and overall population support; failure to consider these needs when planning relocation can have cultural, educational, financial, and infrastructure effects, particularly in terms of housing shortages (Marandi & Main, 2021). Many communities across the Gulf region already lack affordable housing, and the shortage could be aggravated by resettlers (Butler et al., 2021; Cash et al., 2020; Housing Matters, 2022; Ortiz et al., 2019). Especially during a disaster, receiving communities may rapidly incur increases in the cost of providing municipal services, housing, water, police, utilities, medical services, transportation, education, and related services (Braga & Elliott, 2023).

Characteristics of Receiving Communities

Receiving communities come in many forms. On one end of the spectrum is a "recipient city," which Marandi and Main (2021, p. 468) define as those "that serve as unsuspecting, unwilling, or unprepared recipients following sudden-onset disasters." Recipient cities are often close in proximity to originating communities (Eyer et al., 2018), more urban with more job opportunities (Junod et al., 2023), and have already received many resettlers but are often less buffered from climate hazards than "climate destinations" (described below) due to their close proximity to the originating community. Some U.S. Gulf Coast examples include Orlando, Florida; St. Tammany Parish, Louisiana; and Houston, Texas. In many cases, counties adjacent to those along the U.S. Gulf Coast have higher rates of poverty than coastal communities, with very little access to discretionary resources (Economic Research Service, 2022). For example, during the committee's workshop in St. Petersburg, Florida,[1] Joseph Ayala, assistant program manager of the CLEO Institute,[2] said,

> *When people immigrate because of natural disasters they tend to come to areas that are already underresourced. So, food and security is a problem in the neighborhood and you add five families, it just gets worse. You know, you could think of all these things as compounding, but I think it's kind of A to B. It's very if and then. Very logical in that way that, you know, we're talking about transportation issues. We're talking about things like CO_2 and how that contributes to bigger natural disasters. Well, what happens when you don't have public transportation in an underresourced neighborhood with now more families who have to drive farther to go to grocery stores, who have to send their kids to different schools because they will want them to do well, but those schools don't exist in that neighborhood? So, all these things work together to create a more unhealthy environment.*

On the other end of the spectrum is what Marandi and Main (2021) call "climate destinations," or "cities seeking to rebrand their communities as climate havens, ready to welcome climate migrants through equitable planning and preparation." These cities face less, or more manageable, climate hazards but, unfortunately, tend not to be in close proximity to originating communities on the U.S. Gulf Coast. Examples include Buffalo, New York (City of Buffalo, 2019; Vock, 2021); Cincinnati, Ohio (Swartsell,

---

[1]Comments made to the committee on July 12, 2022, during a public information-gathering session in Florida. More information is available at https://www.nationalacademies.org/event/07-12-2022/managed-retreat-in-the-us-gulf-coast-region-workshop-2

[2]The CLEO Institute is a nonprofit, nonpartisan organization exclusively dedicated to climate crisis education and advocacy. More information about the CLEO Institute is available at https://cleoinstitute.org/

2021); and Duluth, Minnesota (Pierre-Louis, 2019; Rossi, 2019). While review of these types of climate destinations is outside the scope of this study, it remains an important task.

Recent work by the Urban Institute in its Climate Migration and Receiving Community (CMRC) study highlights key considerations for receiving communities using case studies of Houston, Texas; Orange and Osceola Counties, Florida; and Terrebonne and Lafourche Parishes, Louisiana (Junod et al., 2023). Based on their research, Junod et al. (2023, pp. v–ix) make the following recommendations to receiving community institutions so that they can better "prepare for, receive, and support climate migrants": "(a) strengthen coordination across institutions, agencies, and community populations now, (b) understand community population trends and strengthen networks between sending and receiving communities, (c) apply lessons from resilience and sustainability planning, (d) plan for population gains and losses, and (e) develop integrated response plans for both 'fast' and 'slow' climate migration."

Identifying Suitable Receiving Areas

One crucial step in ensuring that residents who relocate move to less hazard-prone areas is identifying appropriate and safe relocation sites (or receiving areas). One method of doing so is through land suitability analysis. This includes the identification of land suitable for existing or proposed infrastructure (e.g., water, sewer, roads) and critical public facilities (e.g., police and fire stations, schools), and areas zoned for residential construction (Smith & Nguyen, 2021). Land suitability analysis is often used in land-use plans to help identify environmentally sensitive areas that should be preserved or where development should be restricted. Its use as a tool in comprehensive plans to direct the relocation of at-risk communities to less vulnerable locations (within a jurisdiction's borders) remains uncommon, although places like Norfolk, Virginia, are employing this tool for that purpose. The city has adopted a Coastal Resilience Overlay Zone, where new development must comply with additional flood resilience standards, as well as an Upland Resilience Overlay, which encourages new, more intensive development in parts of the city facing lower risk of flooding (City of Norfolk, 2023; Smith, Anderson, & Perkes, 2021).

Once suitable, less hazard-prone land is identified, land-use planning and zoning tools can facilitate development in these areas. For example, King County, Washington, uses a Transfer of Development Rights Program to allow developers with rights in originating areas (areas that should not be developed) to transfer rights to receiving areas. In King County the focus is on land conservation and avoiding urban sprawl,[3] but the same type of program could be used to guide development away from hazard-prone areas. This concept could be applied to designate hazard areas as originating areas and safer areas not slated for conservation as receiving areas.

An example of using land suitability analysis to assist with relocation comes from North Carolina following Hurricane Matthew, when the state Division of Emergency Management collaborated with faculty at the University of North Carolina at Chapel Hill and North Carolina State University to assist six hard-hit rural communities (Smith & Nguyen, 2021). Specific projects included undertaking land suitability analysis to identify areas outside of the floodplain but adjacent to supporting infrastructure, including roads, water, sewer, schools, and land zoned as residential; the creation of possible replacement housing prototypes that could be built as replacement housing; and the development of open space management strategies to identify possible uses of the resulting open space after a buyout (Smith & Nguyen, 2023). One of the six communities the team worked with was Princeville, North Carolina,[4] in which a five-day design workshop was held with town officials and residents; design professionals; and federal, state, and local officials. The workshop goal was to develop preliminary design ideas for the partial relocation of critical facilities, new housing, and supporting infrastructure to a 52-acre site purchased by the state, located outside the floodplain and adjacent to the town's existing boundaries (Smith & Nguyen, 2021). An important caveat regarding this work is the reality that the team provided direct assistance to the six communities for more than two years and found that this was an insufficient length of time to address several key relocation issues given that the buyouts had not begun during this time (Smith & Nguyen, 2021).

Another example of proactively identifying receiving areas can be found in Hillsborough County, Florida, which adopted a sending and receiving area strategy in its Post-Disaster Redevelopment Plan.[5] In the plan, waterfront communities and homes severely damaged may consider relocating inland to identified receiving jurisdictions. Although the plan has been adopted by the county government, it has not been "tested" in a post-disaster setting. Furthermore, it remains unclear whether Gulf-front residents would be willing to relocate to more rural inland areas.

---

[3]More information about King County is available at https://www.georgetownclimate.org/files/MRT/GCC_20_King-3web.pdf

[4]More information about Princeville, North Carolina, is available at https://www.adaptationclearinghouse.org/resources/annexing-and-preparing-higher-ground-receivingareas-in-princeville-north-carolina-through-post-disaster-recovery-processes.html

[5]More information about the Post-Disaster Redevelopment Plan is available at https://www.hillsboroughcounty.org/en/residents/public-safety/emergency-management/post-disaster-redevelopment-plan

In Louisiana, Haley Blakeman, associate professor of land architecture at Louisiana State University, conducted research funded by the Coastal Protection and Restoration Authority to identify communities within Louisiana that could receive households that wish to relocate from the coast (Blakeman et al., 2022).[6] Blakeman's research included the following methods to identify potential receiving communities:

- identifying communities in south Louisiana (which have a similar culture to coastal Louisiana communities) with populations of more than 1,000;
- removing from this list communities with high risks of flooding;
- selecting communities that have resources to provide for the current and future well-being of residents, using the Child Opportunity Index (e.g., education, health, environment, social, and economic);[7] and
- identifying communities with sufficient economic, social, and environmental resources (e.g., proximity to social services, job training, quality affordable housing).

Although Blakeman's work is ongoing, findings underscore the importance of affording people time to consider when it is right for them to move, and that without proper planning for receiving communities, vulnerabilities may increase for those who relocate (Blakeman, 2023).

Where possible, developing receiving sites in proximity to originating neighborhoods so that residents still have familiar access helps to "reduce relocation stress because social and economic ties help residents re-establish their lives" (Iuchi, 2023, p. 14). In many communities, particularly smaller, more rural jurisdictions, local officials may be concerned with the associated loss of tax base and so prefer the identification of solutions that emphasize the relocation of buyout participants within their jurisdictional boundaries (Smith & Nguyen, 2021).

A less visible, but still important, component of a suitable receiving community, described by workshop participant Dee Knowles, community liaison for the nonprofit micah 6:8 mission, during the committee's third workshop in Louisiana,[8] is a welcoming atmosphere:

---

[6]Report to be published in Fall 2023 based on the cited presentation; Blakeman et al. (2022).

[7]More information about the Child Opportunity Index is available at https://www.diversitydatakids.org/child-opportunity-index

[8]Comments made to the committee on July 28, 2022, during a public information-gathering session in Louisiana. More information is available at https://www.nationalacademies.org/event/07-28-2022/managed-retreat-in-the-us-gulf-coast-region-workshop-3-part-2

> *I got the chance to [...] interview with people here [in Sulphur, Louisiana] during both storms. And it was amazing how much the community, just the people of the community, came together. If they would have had more resources, it would have been so much better. But what the community did have, they put into their community. And [...] I just fell in love with this place because of that type of community. So, if you're looking to see what you need to make a place more attractive, then give it that community. Give it the whole love, just love, and show people that you're there for them. That will make a city so beautiful to any outsider looking in.*

Sustained Assessment

Climate change will require planners to revise assumptions that inform housing, infrastructure, and service needs tied to relocation. Past decisions linked to the analysis and mapping of natural hazards risk—such as riverine flooding and tropical-storm-induced storm surge—have been connected to modeling assumptions that the history of natural hazards provides an accurate means to assess future hazard risk (stationarity). As discussed in Chapter 9, flood maps from the Federal Emergency Management Agency (FEMA), for instance, are often outdated, inaccurate, and do not account for future flood risks (Government Accountability Office [GAO], 2021; Kuta, 2022; Lehmann, 2020; Marsooli et al., 2019). In an era of climate change, the concept of stationarity is no longer valid: the 1 percent chance flood event and the intensity of coastal storms are changing, and planners need to adopt strategies to plan for this uncertainty.

The suitability of receiving areas will need to be assessed relative to hazard risks not only today but also well into the future, reducing the likelihood that receiving areas will be located in harm's way at a later date (Chakraborty et al., 2011; Quay, 2010). Yet this need to plan for uncertainty is exposing the lack of connection between knowledge and action, as well as weak standards for adaptive planning. The result has been consistent failures to fully address climate projections and to monitor or sustain assessment of those projections over time. As part of conducting a land suitability analysis, a future-oriented assessment may be needed to include creating climate projections that account for future hazard risk and to adopt design and land-use standards that account for these changes.

The practical application of sustained assessment applies to conditions in both sending and receiving communities. As part of this process, local governments could remap and rezone areas while adjusting capital expenditures over time to accommodate for more intense rainfall events; differing predictions associated with sea level rise; and more intense, water-laden coastal storms. Furthermore, federal-, state-, and locally funded programs tied to the purchase of hazard-prone housing could modify eligibility determinants like benefit-cost analysis to account for an evolving understanding of risk and the need to better address equity concerns. Finally, updates could complement standing planning practices, such as 10-year comprehensive plan updates, five-year hazard mitigation plan updates, or Intergovernmental Panel on Climate Change (IPCC)-led climate science updates. Re-evaluation would ideally occur following major events and/or when new externalities are introduced.

Relocation Site Planning

Among the complexities of identifying a suitable receiving area, it can be difficult for a relocating community to secure the environmental and historical clearance needed to construct a new site (GAO, 2009; Howe et al., 2021). In 2014, based on the Sandy Recovery Improvement Act of 2013 (42 U.S.C. § 5189g), FEMA, the Department of Housing and Urban Development (HUD), and nine other agencies signed a memorandum of understanding (MOU) to create the unified federal review process to expedite and unify the process for completing environmental and historic preservation reviews and reduce duplication of effort for program applicants (GAO, 2022b). But the MOU did not establish a single review process in cases where multiple agencies fund a single project, nor did it supersede existing requirements. Thus, it did little to reduce the time and costs of these reviews (GAO, 2022b). Agencies could adjust their regulations to clarify that the MOU supersedes conflicting resolutions. Examples of such MOUs for infrastructure and utility relocation include the Great Falls, Montana, MOU for the Relocation of Water Main in Clara Park to Make Way for NorthWestern Substation Improvements;[9] Portland, Oregon's MOU for the Design and Construction of Relocated SE Water Avenue;[10] and the state of Maine's MOU for Overhead Utilities/MaineDOT/Associated General Contractors of Maine.[11]

---

[9]More information about the MOU for the Relocation of Water Main in Clara Park to Make Way for NorthWestern Substation Improvements is available at https://greatfallsmt.net/sites/default/files/fileattachments/city_commission/meeting/packets/94441/ar20160719-20-mou_relocate_water_main_clara_park.pdf

[10]More information about the MOU for the Design and Construction of Relocated SE Water Avenue is available at https://www.portland.gov/sites/default/files/2020-06/se-water-avenue-mou-011811-exhibit-a-336066.pdf

[11]More information about the MOU for Overhead Utilities/MaineDOT/Associated General Contractors of Maine is available at https://www.maine.gov/mdot/utilities/documents/AerialutilityMOU_02_25_09.pdf

Resource Needs for Receiving Communities

The ability of a receiving community to meet the immediate needs of resettlers (e.g., housing, employment, health care, education, transportation) is a critical component of community-driven relocation (Junod et al., 2023). In addition to conducting a land suitability analysis, receiving communities must also review physical resources and associated carrying capacities, evaluate availability and capacity of social programs, and highlight an overall equitable approach to resource allocation.

Receiving communities are often already growing communities, and, as with any planned growth, the availability of necessary resources is a central criterion for suitability. In reality, many receiving communities do not have sufficient resources and infrastructure to meet the needs of resettlers: even in communities with currently sufficient resources, rapid growth patterns challenge the adequacy of those resources. For example, in DeFuniak Springs, Florida, officials noted sewer and water services that were inadequate to support current and future neighborhoods. As a result, county and city officials worked together to secure the funding for a system update (WMBB, 2021b). In nearby Freeport, they are proactively upgrading their septic and sewer system in anticipation of future growth (WMBB, 2021a). In other cases, dwindling supplies limit future development: due to water shortages, authorities in Phoenix recently issued a moratorium on new housing development until 100-year water resource access could be demonstrated (Flavelle & Healy, 2023). A lack of financial resources can likewise limit infrastructure development. For example, a lack of funding was identified as a barrier to creating an integrated transportation system and developing a "stormwater system with low impact on [the] natural system" in a report about the Mississippi Gulf Coast (Gulf Regional Planning Commission et al., 2013, p. 43). Furthermore, inland communities not far from the coast are generally at a lesser economic advantage than coastal communities that may need to relocate inland (see Uhler [2015] for an example from California and Table 8-1 for poverty rates of U.S. Gulf coastal resettlement destinations).

Moreover, population increases and resulting demand on resources have to be carefully identified and planned for to reduce the inadvertent displacement of current residents while also providing adequate support to resettlers. Community-based organizations and government institutions are often a primary source of support for both current residents and resettlers arriving in receiving communities, but they may have insufficient resources, staff, and knowledge to meet the often extensive and changing needs of those displaced by disaster or other climatic events, as well as understand their cultural preferences, all while continuing to support the needs of current residents.

For these reasons—sustaining growth and preventing displacement of current residents—it is critically important that receiving communities prepare before the need emerges, strengthening collaboration among governmental agencies, community-based support groups, faith-based organizations, first responders, social services, and transport service providers (Junod et al., 2023).

Research from Enterprise Community Partners,[12] a long-time HUD support team, identifies eight practical approaches for governmental preparations for receiving communities (Drew & Temsamani, 2023, pp. 8–15):

1. Encourage and provide resources for potential receiving communities to build capacity in advance of a migration event.
2. Allocate disaster relief to receiving communities when a migration occurs.
3. Set up a centralized system for migrants to access available services and resources.
4. Increase transportation options and availability for migrants.
5. Provide cash assistance directly to migrants.
6. Bolster coordination between key stakeholders.
7. Expand data collection during climate migrations to identify and address both current and future needs for migrants.
8. Plan for a long-term recovery.

Neighborhoods and the Built Environment

Although some communities may be able to scale up their capacity to become receiving communities in some ways, they may lack the existing infrastructure to rapidly absorb additional population. This can result in a resource imbalance. For example, in communities with limited affordable housing, a population increase can increase housing demand, spiking prices and forcing those with less means into poorer-quality housing. These impacts can stretch to nearby jurisdictions. In Miami, for instance, "climate gentrification" is occurring in "Little Haiti," where waterfront residents are moving inland, resulting in increases in property values and causing some residents to relocate elsewhere (Keenan et al., 2018; Nathan, 2019; see Box 8-1). This can also affect other costs of living, such as property taxes, and can send poorer long-time residents to seek affordable housing that may be in less safe areas than their current homes (Graff Zivin et al., 2023). For low-income communities, the availability of affordable housing severely affects people's ability to move far from their existing homes in

[12]More information about Enterprise Community Partners is available at https://www.enterprisecommunity.org/about/where-we-work/gulf-coast

threatened areas (Li & Spidalieri, 2021). Similarly, schools that are at, or near, peak enrollment may lack capacity to support additional students who have relocated or may overburden teachers with large class sizes in efforts to accommodate families. This challenge is both temporary (i.e., workforce demands during recovery periods) and long term (as relocations occur).

To mitigate these challenges, especially in regions grappling with climate gentrification and displacement, Community Land Trusts (CLTs) offer an innovative and equitable solution. CLTs are nonprofit, community-based organizations that hold land in trust for the collective benefit, mainly focusing on providing long-term affordable housing.[13] CLTs work by owning land and leasing it for residential use, which decouples the value of the land from the cost of the homes situated on it (Grannis, 2021). This unique structure ensures housing remains affordable perpetually, as homes on CLT land are sold at below-market rates and are subject to resale restrictions to maintain affordability for future low- to moderate-income buyers.

This model also offers a powerful countermeasure to the historical injustices of housing discrimination and exclusion, particularly impacting communities of color. By facilitating more stable, affordable housing, CLTs help build resilience against the housing market's volatility and the pressures of gentrification, which often intensify with climate change impacts (Grannis, 2021). Furthermore, the CLT governance model involves residents and local stakeholders directly, embedding democratic decision making and community engagement at its core. In this model, the board typically comprises CLT residents, community members, and public interest representatives, ensuring decisions about land use, housing, and community resources reflect the needs and aspirations of the community (Grannis, 2021).

Carrying Capacity

An important concept in state, regional, and local planning is carrying capacity: the ability of a community to accommodate its populations, whether current residents or resettlers (Junod et al., 2023). The term needs to be used with caution, as it can easily be a way to shut out resettlers from communities that could, with some assistance, meet their needs. Thus, authorities may need to consider the carrying capacities of existing infrastructures and determine how to assist receiving communities in providing adequate infrastructure and services while minimizing environmental damage (Vock, 2021). For example, in this vein, the Gulf Regional Planning Commission's Metropolitan Planning Organization considers the adequacy of transportation infrastructure and could consider how relocation will

[13]More information about CLTs is available at https://www.georgetownclimate.org/adaptation/toolkits/equitable-adaptation-toolkit/introduction.html

BOX 8-1
Community Testimonials: Gentrification and the Cost of Living

At the committee's public workshop in St. Petersburg, Florida, local homeowners discussed the challenges they face with gentrification and the rising cost of living. A retired homeowner discussed the impact of gentrification on his financial stability.

"As a homeowner, and I've been retired for 10 years so I'm on a fixed income, and my interest and principal on my home is pretty fixed, but the insurance and the taxes are not, especially with gentrification. I bought my home for like $150,000 and around my neighborhood they're in the $350,000 and above range. So, the property values have gone up [...] and my monthly payments are creeping up. And so, that's one of the effects of gentrification that happens."

SOURCE: Eliseo Santana, Resident of St. Petersburg, Florida. Workshop 2: Opportunities & Challenges of Climate Adaptation on Florida's Gulf Coast, July 2022, St. Petersburg, Florida.

Another homeowner emphasized the importance of maintaining a sense of community in their neighborhoods and how gentrification disrupts this cohesion.

"We would prefer to stay where we are. Right? Prefer to stay in our neighborhoods. We build strong communities here and with gentrification, that's impacting us. It's forcing people out if they can't find a way to make it happen. They have to live in the outskirts of town in less desirable areas and have to commute in to where they work and have to put their children in different schools. So, now they have to move to a different community and go to different schools and commute which also, if your mom is commuting an hour to work, means that they have to pay for more daycare or after-school care. So, there's a million ways that that's impacting economically and personally everybody in the community."

SOURCE: Marilena Santana, Resident of St. Petersburg, Florida. Workshop 2: Opportunities & Challenges of Climate Adaptation on Florida's Gulf Coast, July 2022, St. Petersburg, Florida.

shift transportation infrastructure demand and capacity.[14] Similarly, ongoing efforts in the Gulf region to establish energy transition plans offer ways to improve energy security and reduce transition risks (Beckfield et al., 2022), while studies of regional water security identify blue water (e.g., surface water) scarcity as a growing challenge (Veettil & Mishra, 2020). These assessments acknowledge the need for ongoing evaluation of carrying capacities beyond the needs for resettlement, and perhaps, depending on

[14]More information about the Gulf Regional Planning Commission's Metropolitan Planning Organization is available at https://grpc.com/mpo-plans

the findings, a complementary driver for suitability assessments of possible resettlement areas.

Often, analysis of carrying capacity focuses on physical aspects of a community, such as housing, schools, and utilities (e.g., Keenan's [2019] analysis of Duluth as a receiving community), rather than available services and societal connections—even though the latter are essential (House, 2021). Research by Junod et al. (2023, pp. v–vi) on the institutional capacity of receiving communities (Orange and Osceola Counties region near Orlando, Florida; Houston, Texas; and inland Terrebonne and Lafourche Parishes in Louisiana) offers this key finding: "Institutional sectors with strong, existing connections across government, private sector, and civil society groups and organizations that also exhibited relevant cultural competencies and expertise were most successful in addressing the needs of climate migrant populations." Drew and Temsamani (2023) suggest that one approach to encouraging this type of preparation is for federal and state agencies to provide funding and technical assistance to potential receiving communities. This would enable communities to evaluate their capacity and "develop off-the-shelf strategies that can be quickly activated" (Drew & Temsamani, 2023, p. 8).

Housing

The availability of short-term and long-term housing at an affordable price is often among the biggest challenges in the relocation process. Suitable replacement housing needs to be identified or built in receiving communities, emphasizing characteristics that meet the needs of resettlers, such as cost, square footage, number of bedrooms, and culturally appropriate layouts or location. Authorities currently working on affordable housing issues need to plan for a future increase in demand in receiving areas, which will not only limit the inventory of housing stock but also cause an increase in real estate prices, as described above. To keep resettlers within the same tax area, jurisdictions may develop new housing in undeveloped, safer areas or annex nearby unincorporated land. Resettlers may also move into existing communities in a different jurisdiction, as renters or through the purchase of homes that are for sale or via the construction of infill[15] housing in less vulnerable locations than their current homes. Houston's proposed Buy In/Buy Out Program would be such an example.[16]

[15]"Infill development refers to the construction of buildings or other facilities on previously unused or underutilized land located within an existing urban—or otherwise developed—area." More information is available at https://www.planetizen.com/definition/infill-development

[16]More information about the Buy In/Buy Out Program is available at https://houstontx.gov/housing/hap.html

In response to such challenges, Houston has taken proactive measures through the formation of the Houston Community Land Trust (HCLT) in 2018.[17] The HCLT exemplifies an innovative approach to preserving and expanding affordable housing options. The HCLT's New Home Development Program aids residents in purchasing newly constructed homes on land owned by the Houston Land Bank, thereby ensuring a supply of affordable new homes (Kidd & Tilchin, n.d.). Complementing this, the Homebuyers Choice Program offers significant city-funded subsidies to assist residents in purchasing market-rate homes, addressing the rising home values throughout the city (Kidd & Tilchin, n.d.). In both programs, the HCLT retains land ownership, thus ensuring long-term affordability even when these homes are resold. This model not only mitigates the immediate issue of housing stock availability but also addresses the systemic challenge of escalating real estate prices, especially for low-income buyers.

In collaboration with the city of Houston and the Houston Land Bank, the HCLT highlights the potential of land trusts in managing and subsidizing the development of affordable homes. While land banks, like the Houston Land Bank, focus on acquiring and repurposing vacant properties, CLTs emphasize long-term housing affordability (City of Houston, 2016). The HCLT's efforts, in conjunction with the Houston Land Bank[18] and the city's Housing and Community Development Department,[19] have been pivotal in ensuring affordable housing options while navigating challenges like ensuring construction quality and timely completion by developers.

The long-term need for affordable housing is particularly challenging, and often the housing prices in the receiving community are costlier or experience a spike due to increasing demand and so may not be affordable to resettlers. This occurred in Baton Rouge following Hurricane Katrina (Bullard & Wright, 2009; Johnson, 2005). When newcomers are looking more for temporary housing (e.g., renting), it will first affect housing prices in those neighborhoods that traditionally serve the rental market, with impacts on the homeownership market felt later and less acutely (Drew & Jakabovics, 2023). Although the Urban Institute's CMRC study (see above) did not find "substantial changes" in the housing market due to climate migration, it did show "noticeable impact on specific neighborhoods or ZIP codes, particularly in areas with demographic and economic characteristics

[17]More information about the HCLT is available at https://www.houstonclt.org/

[18]More information about the Houston Land Bank is available at https://houstonlandbank.org/

[19]More information about the city of Houston's Housing and Community Development Department is available at https://houstontx.gov/housing/

similar to those of the migrant population" (Drew & Jakabovics, 2023, pp. 9–10).

Housing counseling is an important social service for newcomers described in the disaster recovery literature (Smith, 2014). Counseling services may include, but are not limited to, assessing an individual's financial situation (to include one's savings and value of the home to be sold), identifying a suitable replacement home (with similar square footage, number of bedrooms, etc.) or providing rental assistance, and identifying community services available (schools, churches, parks) in a receiving locale. Additional services may include providing psychological support services for family members who are relocating (including adults and children) and for current residents in a receiving community (to include garnering their input in the design of receiving areas).

Many programs and researchers tend to focus on homeownership and public housing; thus, there is a limitation in understanding issues that commonly affect renters, such as availability, flood risk disclosure, and affordability. This is significant as many flood-prone areas include a disproportionate number of rental units, including those defined as affordable housing (Lee & Van Zandt, 2019). The failure to rebuild damaged affordable housing in Galveston following Hurricane Ike (Walters, 2018) and in New Orleans following Hurricane Katrina are two instances on the U.S. Gulf Coast where this issue has arisen (University of North Carolina Center for Community Capital, 2018). During the committee's acquisitions webinar,[20] Courtney Wald-Wittkopp, Blue Acres program manager, discussed how the issue of affordable housing intersects with flood risk:

> *I think the social justice component is the other thing that really, we learned a lot after Sandy, which was that a lot of our flood-prone areas are more affordable areas. So, this has a very clear affordable housing tie for us in New Jersey, and it's one thing to make somebody a buyout offer, get clear and marketable title, and be able to buy the house. But we need to start having real pragmatic conversations about where they can go and what they can do. I think that with housing, especially with the real estate market as sort of robust as it is right now, it's hard to find replacement housing.*

[20]Comments made to the committee on December 13, 2022, during a public virtual information-gathering session. More information is available at https://www.nationalacademies.org/event/12-13-2022/managed-retreat-in-the-us-gulf-coast-region-perspectives-and-approaches-to-property-acquisitions-challenges-and-lessons-learned

Transportation

In the CMRC study, transportation was identified as playing a key role in determining whether and how resettlers are able to access economic opportunities and community resources (e.g., health care, education), as well as where they were able to live (Junod et al., 2023). In this study, many newcomers were without a vehicle due to a disaster and therefore had to rely on public transportation (Junod et al., 2023). The provision of transportation, particularly public transportation, is critical, and the lack of adequate mobility and travel options, which may already be inadequate for existing populations, can have significant effects on community-driven relocation for both originating and receiving communities (Clark-Ginsberg et al., 2023; Junod et al., 2023). Furthermore, state transportation ratings for Mississippi, Alabama, and Louisiana are D+, C–, and D+, respectively, so existing transportation infrastructure is currently deemed seriously inadequate and in need of investment.[21] Recent funds made available through the Promoting Resilient Operations for Transformative, Efficient, and Cost-Saving Transportation (PROTECT) Formula Program to help increase the resilience of surface transportation offer ways to address the deficiencies in transportation systems.[22]

Educational Access and Quality

For schools in receiving communities, educational access and quality may be affected by an influx of new students, for both newcomers and those already enrolled. Moreover, better educational access may be a factor in attracting resettlers.

Buffalo, New York, provides an interesting example response, in this case to the influx of families from Puerto Rico following Hurricane Maria in 2017 (Vock, 2021). While the city did not have a specific strategic plan for "receiving," local community-based organizations established relief efforts immediately following the disaster (due to many families connected between New York and Puerto Rico) and subsequently created local partnerships to enable immigrating families to more easily resettle in the Buffalo community (City of Buffalo, 2018). This example of societal connection and the responsiveness to resettling families drew from existing relationships between the Hispanic Heritage Council of Western New York, Inc. and other

[21]More information about infrastructure report cards is available at https://infrastructurereportcard.org/

[22]The PROTECT Formula Program provides 7.3 billion dollars from the infrastructure law to help communities build resilient infrastructure. More information is available at https://www.fhwa.dot.gov/bipartisan-infrastructure-law/protect_fact_sheet.cfm

local organizations who worked at the speed of trust[23] to initially provide disaster response and help to resettle families, including helping them find apartments, pay rent, and provide them with essential materials for new homes (Pope, 2023).

As part of any community-driven relocation strategy, planning authorities are in a position to connect school curricula between originating communities and receiving communities to foster relationships ahead of arrival. Examples from science, technology, engineering, and mathematics learning ecosystems in cross-country studies, as well as localized multi-school studies, provide demonstrable outcomes (Traphagen & Traill, 2014; Wang, Charoenmuang et al., 2020).

Employment

Job opportunities are another factor that needs to be considered in resettlement plans. In Buffalo, creating employment for displaced teachers while simultaneously helping resettle Puerto Rican families required recognizing and actively addressing job and social needs of families traumatized by loss related to Hurricane Maria. For receiving communities, where increases in populations may strain local job markets, purposeful interventions to improve job prospects and provide job opportunities are part of social infrastructure development. Skill transfers from originating communities offer opportunities to broaden job offerings; however, without purposeful planning, livelihoods may be interrupted by population gains whether via a shortage of opportunity or a misalignment in skills and need. Municipalities alongside institutional and nonprofit partners could create job training and workforce opportunities in the development of denser neighborhoods, improving job prospects for existing and new residents.

In Texas, the Walker Montgomery Community Development Corporation is an example in the U.S. Gulf Coast that focuses on trade school development training for disadvantaged youth.[24] Such a program could help with rapid job attainment and with efforts to prepare the community for population increases simultaneously.[25]

Research shows that poverty rates in evacuation and resettlement destinations within 75–100 miles of the U.S. Gulf Coast are higher than the national average: see Table 8-1. These near-coast receiving communities, which often suffer from disinvestment (in their education, affordable housing,

[23]This phrase refers to the need to build and sustain trusting collaborative relationships in order to proceed in any endeavor.

[24]More information on the Walker Montgomery Community Development Corporation is available at https://www.wmcdc.net/

[25]More information is available at https://gctc.us/WMCDC-CHDO/

TABLE 8-1 Poverty Rates of Coastal Resettlement Destinations within 75–100 Miles from the Coast of Alabama, Mississippi, and Louisiana, by County, 2020 National and State

	County/Parish	Poverty Rate (in percent)
U.S. Average		12.8
Alabama		16.1
	Washington	16.7
	Clarke	21.9
	Monroe	22.2
	Wilcox	27.4
	Escambia	23.5
	Covington	18.0
	Butler	18.2
	Marengo	22.3
Mississippi		19.4
	Pearl River	14.5
	Stone	18.5
	George	21.1
	Marion	24.4
	Lamar	11.6
	Forrest	19.1
	Greene	15.3
	Perry	21.4
Louisiana		19.6
	Cameron	8.3
	Assumption	16.4
	Lacombe[a]	16.4
	East Baton Rouge	19.2
	Evangeline	27.0
	Rapides	19.9
	Jefferson	17.3

[a]Lacombe is a census-designated place rather than a parish.

SOURCE: Adapted from Butler-Ulloa, D. M. (2022). *Climate displacement, migration and relocation in the United States: Resistance, restoration and resilience in the Coastal South* (Publication No. 29323594). [Doctoral dissertation, University of Massachusetts Boston]. ProQuest Dissertations & Theses Global. https://www.proquest.com/dissertations-theses/climate-displacement-migration-relocation-united/docview/2710980853/se-2?accountid=152665; using U.S. Census Bureau S1701 Poverty Status in the Last 12 Months, 2021 ACS 5-Year Estimates Subject Tables.

jobs, health care, child care, retail centers, etc.), will likely need long-term, sustained multifaceted investments to create social, economic, educational, and employment pathways for both current and future residents.

Ecological Services and Environmental Amenities

Environmental considerations, including habitat preservation and ecological services, are valuable planning considerations if large numbers of people move to places that have not previously been residential areas, such as open space and farmland. This type of resettlement is resource intensive and less environmentally sustainable than relocation to an already-developed area, but it is one possible outcome of relocation from coastal areas. For example, the relocation of Isle de Jean Charles (IDJC) residents to a new development in The New Isle, Louisiana, would be considered a greenfield resettlement. In contrast, strong planning, guided by sustainable development principles, could encourage urban densification, more walkable communities, and greater preservation of environmental resources. Central to sustainable development is ensuring that "ecological services" are still available, including the water filtration and stormwater capture services that are provided by wetlands as well as the environmental amenities that people desire in a community.[26] Such amenities may include not only parks, open spaces, and undeveloped land but also opportunities to carry out one's traditional culture. For example, coastal Louisiana residents who participated in the workshops for this study spoke of the importance of being able to step outside their front door and fish for their evening meal.[27] Such an amenity may not be available in a more urban setting, which can affect residents' sense of place (see Chapter 6). Windell Curole, general manager, South Lafourche Levee District, spoke on this topic at this study's third workshop in Thibodaux, Louisiana:[28]

> *There's some real general things, like your family, you can keep family. But even that experience is not as good because there's nothing like catching a whole bunch of crawfish, whole bunch of crabs, and fish, and sharing it with the larger family. I can remember as a kid taking a day off school because on alley 24 crawfish were crossing like crazy. Someone had bought a new dryer and we caught enough crawfish to fill that dryer box. And not only our family, but the neighborhood got invited. And those types of*

[26]More information on Sustainable Development Goals 11 (Sustainable Cities and Communities) and 15 (Life on Land) is available at https://sdgs.un.org/goals

[27]See footnote 8.

[28]Comments made to the committee on July 26, 2022, during a public information-gathering session in Louisiana. More information is available at https://www.nationalacademies.org/event/07-26-2022/managed-retreat-in-the-us-gulf-coast-region-workshop-3-part-1

things, like a Boucherie, those are things that are built in our communities and make them—just people—our gardens produce so much, you're always giving to your neighbor, you go red fishing, you get a lot of red fish, you share it.

Social and Community Context

Understandably, receiving communities are not always welcoming to an influx of new residents. In any location, poorer, ethnically distinct resettlers may face resistance from the receiving community. For example, during the resettlement of Pecan Acres, residents from the lower-income, predominantly Black neighborhood north of New Roads, Louisiana, faced opposition from residents near proposed sites throughout the site selection process (Jones, 2018). Many relocating residents felt this opposition was driven by racial bias (Spidalieri & Bennett, 2020b). (See Box 8-2 for comments from workshop participants about community acceptance.) This has also been seen for refugees from other countries (Coenders et al., 2017), and for U.S. residents unhoused and displaced by disasters (Hamilton, 2010; Masquelier, 2006). Aranda and Rivera (2016) describe Puerto Rican migrants facing this type of discrimination in Orlando, Florida, which in turn may blunt their "economic progress and socioeconomic integration" (p. 57). They note that "the erosion of feelings of belonging due to discrimination may, in turn, affect future settlement decisions" (Aranda & Rivera, 2016, p. 57).

It is important that receiving communities do not feel overwhelmed or overburdened by resettlers, and learning from the experience of other receiving communities is a critical step. The Urban Institute detailed how Orlando responded when more than 56,000 Puerto Ricans arrived in Florida following Hurricane Maria, serving "as a crash course in emergency coordination and collaboration" (Housing Matters, 2022). They noted the need to densify with accessory dwelling units where possible, to plan for significant growth as a receiving community, and to establish regional collaboratives to manage influx and to coordinate services. Chris Castro, former director of sustainability and resilience at the city of Orlando, Florida, and now chief of staff for Office of State and Community Energy Programs at the U.S. Department of Energy, advises that cities build capacity and governance structures that can support resilience to climate migration in advance of newcomers arriving, so that when they do, the city already has an entity in place to respond. "Orlando, for instance, helped establish the East Central Florida Regional Resilience Collaborative to coordinate climate mitigation and adaptation efforts with other cities" (Housing Matters, 2022).

One approach to easing the social and cultural transition of resettlers into receiving communities identified by Drew and Temsamani (2023) is to utilize the suggested funding and technical assistance (described in the

BOX 8-2
Community Testimonials: Community Acceptance

At the committee's third workshop, Gary LaFleur spoke about changes in a community's acceptance of resettlers:

"But you know there was a time when Bourg was being considered as a receiving community for the people of Isle de Jean Charles, and that very close Terrebonne community said to the people of Isle de Jean Charles, no, we don't want you. All right. So, when we talk about receiving communities, that sounds good at first. But [...] I think people have to get used to that idea. And the same thing sort of happened at New Isle. There were some people in that Terrebonne community that were already there, that weren't automatically inviting to The New Isle community. But I mean now I think that they are. And it ended up working out better than the Bourg community, you know, because New Isle has been built."

SOURCE: Gary LaFleur, President, Barataria-Terrebonne National Estuary Foundation, and Professor, Biological Sciences, Nicholls State University. Workshop 3: Assisted Resettlement and Receiving Communities in Louisiana, July 2022, Houma, Louisiana.

Similar thoughts were expressed by Jonathan Foret:

"So, a thing that we really have to figure out is what does, like, maybe we all need some training on what a welcoming community looks like on both sides, for the people who are receiving the people and for the people who are moving into that new area."

SOURCE: Jonathan Foret, Executive Director, South Louisiana Wetlands Discovery Center. Workshop 3: Assisted Resettlement and Receiving Communities in Louisiana, July 2022, Houma, Louisiana.

"Carrying Capacity" section) to prepare for the specific needs of resettlers, "such as cultivating cultural competency to bridge gaps in traditions and language barriers, collaborating with community partners, and developing relationships with likely origin communities to facilitate information and record sharing" (p. 8). Another method suggested by Drew and Temsamani (2023) for readying the social and community context of receiving communities is to identify partners who could bridge cultural and language differences between the receiving community and new residents (p. 13) and set up a one-stop shop for new residents to "learn about and access critical services" to address their needs (p. 10). Regulatory enforcement could help to address entrenched NIMBYism ("not in my backyard") through upzoning initiatives like providing density bonuses and requiring inclusionary zoning to encourage higher density development in areas with lower flood risk and to ensure these developments are affordable for people with low to moderate incomes (see City of Norfolk, 2023).

Another possible approach is to develop communication campaigns that promote resettlers as assets, highlighting cultural diversity and celebrating differences. This approach is one way to socialize the idea (share it with others early in planning to receive feedback) of receiving resettlers with members of the receiving community. Municipal authorities can also support stronger "development practices that minimize some effects of newcomers on local housing, community composition, and other civic resources and assets (e.g., displacement and gentrification)" (Martín & Williams, 2021, p. 17). Another method that may help preserve community ties is employed by Harris County's Voluntary Buyout Program, which offers a $19,875 incentive payment to homeowners who relocate to an area outside the 100-year floodplain but within Harris County. This incentive serves to preserve the county's tax base while also potentially enabling homeowners to find housing near friends, family, and/or members of their origin community (Lessans, 2022).

Similarly, community-based organizations, like those in Buffalo, New York, are often trusted advisors whose consistent support carries tremendous significance in low-resourced communities. For example, Catholic Charities was instrumental in the resettlement of Vietnamese immigrants in New Orleans post-Vietnam War (Bragg, 2000), and today Boat People SOS, a community-based organization, works closely with the Vietnamese community.[29] Engaging community-based organizations in the socialization of resettlers and providing support to those organizations for such work offers an important complement to municipal initiatives. Enterprise Community Partners, advice to communities includes recommendations to self-assess housing and systems capacities, leverage existing community ties, and work with current residents to set expectations and make sure that the receiving community is also prepared for climate change (Drew & Temsamani, 2023).

Health Access and Quality

An important aspect of infrastructure evaluation is the assessment of local health systems' readiness to support a larger population within its catchment area. As discussed in Chapter 6, the well-being of both the relocating community and the receiving community is critical to a successful community-driven relocation. Maintaining it requires consideration of a receiving community's capacity to offer access to health care for mental and physical needs. Broadly defined, this includes a range of child and family services necessary to support trauma-induced transitions, such as

[29]More information about Boat People SOS is available at https://www.bpsos.org/about

from Hurricane Maria and Hurricane Katrina (Hamilton et al., 2009). In Houston, this required deployment of the regional disaster plan, which led "to the activation of the Regional Hospital Preparedness Council's Catastrophic Medical Operations Center, and the rapid construction of a 65-examination-room medical facility within the Reliant Center" (Hamilton et al., 2009, p. 515). Such response differs from the type of health care planning needed to address planned growth, which is more common to traditional planning efforts. For resettlement, especially following a disaster, institutions will need to prepare for counseling for the behavioral health and grief associated with the planned relocations from one's home (Shultz et al., 2019).

Common within health care institutions is the assessment of preparedness and response (Office of the Assistant Secretary for Preparedness and Response, 2016). Health system facilities also need to evaluate their own readiness for disasters and the implications of potential relocation from disaster-prone areas. This is pertinent not only to receiving communities: a recent World Bank study noted that health systems must prepare for climate changes, recognizing the importance of regional and system-level responses and the ties to national emergency management coordination, including the system's own infrastructure demands (Rentschler et al., 2021).

Equity

The history of the Gulf region is marked by pervasive and systemic inequities and a history of forced migration, as described in Chapter 4. This history affects the planning preparations that communities will undertake. It is important to recognize past inequities and the time required to engender trust and to develop diverse networks capable of addressing resettlement in a sensitive and culturally competent manner.

Hauer's model illustrating climate-induced migration suggests that migrations from the U.S. Gulf Coast will increase even as housing affordability and job security decrease in receiving communities (Hauer, 2017). Furthermore, from 2000 to 2017, the U.S. Gulf Coast saw more population growth than all other U.S. coastlines, with Harris County, Texas, receiving the largest gain of all U.S. counties (U.S. Census Bureau, 2019). Hauer also identified the Houston-The Woodlands-Sugar Land metro area as receiving the fourth highest net migration in 2100 under a no adaptation scenario, following Orlando-Kissimmee-Sanford in second (Hauer, 2017, Supplementary Table 1). These areas each have their own challenges with sea level rise, flood risk, and affordable housing. The compounding challenges of existing inequities and supply-demand management with the volume of expected migrations underscore the importance of preparatory planning for receiving communities.

ORIGINATING COMMUNITIES

Thresholds

As people leave high-risk areas to resettle elsewhere, there is a need to attend as well to what remains of the originating community. In some cases, this means consolidating or reducing municipal services and even decommissioning infrastructure. There may be a need to set thresholds at which investment in those areas is reduced, and relocation, consolidation, decommissioning, and ecological and cultural restoration begins. Such thresholds acknowledge two important realities: that at some point in time continuing services in certain areas may no longer be possible, and that there are limits to adaptive capacities—that is, that environmental changes are so transformational that area habitation is no longer possible. Thresholds are typically identified within broader "adaptation pathways" that "map out a sequence of adaptation strategies in response to rising seas" (Collini et al., 2022, p. 29). For example, Alaskan government agencies proposed four indicators to trigger the transition from protection in place to community relocation: (1) "life/safety risk during storm/flood events," (2) "loss of critical infrastructure," (3) "public health threats," and (4) "loss of 10% or more of residential dwellings" (Immediate Action Workgroup, 2009, p. 84). Extreme weather events that cause mass displacement are not an appropriate indicator; rather, appropriate factors include erosion rates, sea level rise, and loss of drinking water (Bronen, 2014).

In regions such as the Gulf and southeast states, the challenges of rising sea levels and increased coastal flooding have prompted a reevaluation of how to manage and maintain road infrastructures. The term "abandonment" is frequently used in these areas to describe the official process of governments deserting roads, driven not only by the immediate damages but also by the economic burdens of repeated maintenance in the face of these environmental threats (Jones et al., 2019). Legal frameworks in these states emphasize that roads are held in public trust, implying that decisions around their maintenance or abandonment must prioritize the collective welfare over individual property interests. The choice to abandon is not made lightly but is based on a range of considerations including the cost implications, the degree to which the public relies on the road, and any demonstrable decrease in its usage. Such decisions reflect a broader adaptation strategy, wherein the principle of public welfare serves as a guiding force, ensuring that community resilience and safety are at the forefront.

Part of such threshold setting includes decisions about how or whether to maintain basic health and safety services in the originating areas. For example, with the IDJC relocation, it is not clear who will provide basic services such as garbage collection for those who have opted to stay behind; at the same time, it is unreasonable to expect that governments can continue to service areas that are repeatedly flooded. Logan et al. (2023) also characterize the challenge of communities becoming isolated well before chronic inundation occurs.

However, disinvestment in public infrastructure, such as roads to homes, without buy-in from residents could lead to a "takings" claim against the government for limiting access to private property. Monroe County, Florida, faces such a challenge. Monroe County studied the cost to elevate roads to serve 30 households. With a price of over 75 million dollars to elevate for anticipated 2025 sea level rise and king tides, the city initially sought to abandon those roads (Harris, 2019), but the city is now studying the design solutions that could allow residents to stay in place a bit longer.[30] Examples like this one make it more obvious why coordinated planning at the federal, state, and regional levels is needed to characterize risks in a consistent manner and to develop processes to support decision making and ensure effective use of limited government funding. Establishing adaptation pathways well in advance of decision making allows time for the co-development of solutions by community residents, planners, and policy makers that are based on science and local desires and knowledge (Collini et al., 2022).

Without specified thresholds that trigger disinvestment, small communities like the one in Monroe County will continue to try to remain even as climate science reinforces how unsustainable staying will become (Foote, 2022). Thus, it is important to have a systematic approach to address thresholds. A recent study by Hermans et al. (2023) provides a sample framework connecting sea level rise, flooding, and the predictability of the service life of flood protection investments. Combined, Logan et al. (2023) and Hermans et al. (2023) suggest that thresholds are far from definitive, but progressive, and that community-driven discussions about risk tolerance need to be central to planning for disinvestment.

Establishing thresholds is a highly sensitive topic, particularly if it appears that outside entities are determining that a particular community is no longer worth supporting. For example, after Hurricane Katrina, officials considered turning New Orleans' flood-prone, historically marginalized Ninth Ward and other neighborhoods into parkland, stamping them with green dots on a planning map of the city (Johannessen & Goldweit-Denton, 2020). The community uproar was so great that the "Green Dot Plan" is

[30]More information is available at https://www.hdrinc.com/portfolio/monroe-county-roadway-vulnerability-study

now a case in point of how not to proceed with resilience planning (Hennick, 2014; Warburg & Metcalf, 2015). Such plans can be perceived as gentrification at the cost of current residents, or even seen as a form of ethnic cleansing. Davis (2014, p. xiii) wrote, "In a nutshell, the Urban Land Institute's recommendations [regarding the Great Footprint Debate] reframed the historical elite desire to shrink New Orleans's socioeconomic footprint of Black poverty (and Black political power) as a crusade to reduce the city's physical footprint to contours commensurate with flood safety and a fiscally viable urban infrastructure." Davis (2021) further connects the regional history of racism to the post-Hurricane Katrina effects. This example also highlights how the best time for discussions of planned community relocation is not immediately following the traumatic effects of a disaster. During the post-disaster aftermath, most people just want to return to normal, so pre-disaster planning is essential to effectively engage a community in the planning process (FEMA, 2017).

Residents can be suspicious of relocation efforts, including planned buyout programs (such as those described in Chapters 3 and 9), when they see development and industrialization continuing around them. For example, residents of IDJC had heard rumors of the parish halting maintenance on the Island Road—the only route to the island. As work progressed on The New Isle community, the state invested in recreational fishing turnouts on the Island Road, which caused residents to feel that they had been misled about continued maintenance of that road (Jessee, 2021). Similar sentiments were expressed at the committee's workshops (see Box 8-3).

Thus, it is essential that neighborhoods and households not only are involved in deciding at what point they would want to relocate but also have a say in setting the threshold at which disinvestment begins (Bronen, 2021) and in deciding what happens to the land left behind (discussed in the below sections). It is important that these thresholds are set with an understanding of the fiscal constraints of continuous recovery on individuals and municipalities. This community involvement could be done in connection with regional planning entities who can provide the support needed to ensure that those in originating areas will have a place in receiving areas. Shi et al. (2023) explore Florida's St. Petersburg region in this way.[31] Planning out where those disinvestments may occur over time and where residents might relocate to is essential to giving communities the time, space, and resources to adjust. Haasnoot et al. (2019) offer coastal typological examples of such adaptation planning while Stege (2017) refers to habitability thresholds. It is also essential that this type of planning is accompanied by policies that protect and reflect resident decisions about

[31]More information about Shi et al. (2023) is available at https://cugis.maps.arcgis.com/apps/MapSeries/index.html?appid=754b615fa5db4bbea0ed393a2c730163

BOX 8-3
Community Testimonials: Relocation for Whom?

At the committee's third workshop in Thibodaux, Louisiana, Elder Rosina Philippe, Atakapa-Ishak/Chawasha Tribe and president of the First Peoples' Conservation Council, highlighted concerns about people being forgotten.

"I'd like to mention one thing, that even though some of our coastal communities are not afforded the protections of other communities in the region, we're still subjected to the same tax base and cost of living. So—you know, our living expenses don't go down because we're not protected as a citizen of these regions. We're excluded from the protections but not anything else. As far as gentrification goes, for me, I think for coastal inhabitants, that's not our primary concern. I think the word that we need to be looking at is industrialization. I believe there is a concentrated effort to continue to disenfranchise and discourage re-inhabitation of the coastal region by residential people in order to turn these regions into industrial zones. And, I see the delays after the storm events to resources getting back to help people recover and to rebuild and to reclaim their lives."

SOURCE: Elder Rosina Philippe, Atakapa-Ishak/Chawasha Tribe and President of the First Peoples' Conservation Council. Workshop 3: Community Viability and Environmental Change in Coastal Louisiana, July 2022, Thibodaux, Louisiana.

And at the committee's second workshop in St. Petersburg, Florida, Trevor Tatum, resident of St. Petersburg, Florida, pointed out a related concern.

"I don't want to be in the position where I have to relocate, and then somebody else comes and snatches up my home, and then they solve the problem. So that's an issue that we got to think about. In our heart, are we really looking for our best interest as a community? Are we just doing it for the sake of whoever has the money?"

SOURCE: Trevor Tatum, Resident of St. Petersburg, Florida. Workshop 2: Opportunities & Challenges of Climate Adaptation on Florida's Gulf Coast, July 2022, St. Petersburg, Florida.

disinvestment. In other words, if a community decides to relocate away from an environmentally hazardous location, it is important for policies to be in place that appropriately limit the type of development that may occur in that area in the future.

In setting thresholds and making adaptation decisions, it is also important for planners, community members, and other decision makers to be mindful of maladaptation, which Schipper (2020, p. 409) notes is when planning efforts "create[e] conditions that actually worsen the situation." Maladaptation is defined by the IPCC (2022, p. 2915) as "actions that may lead to increased risk of adverse climate-related outcomes, including via increased greenhouse gas emissions, increased or shifted vulnerability to climate change, more inequitable outcomes, or diminished welfare, now or in the future. Most often, maladaptation is an unintended consequence." More broadly, maladaptation impacts human capacities and may well inadvertently increase vulnerability or exposure to environmental conditions.

Reckien et al. (2023) recognize that maladaptation appears to be on the increase. Similarly, the IPCC Climate Change 2022 report notes "increased evidence of maladaptation across many sectors and regions" (Lee et al., 2023, p. 27). Most concerning is the outsize impact of maladaptation on vulnerable populations, in turn "reinforcing and entrenching existing inequities" (Lee et al., 2023, p. 27). Maladaptation sometimes takes the form of signaling safety in communities where risks continue to escalate. Such signals could include building back in increasingly flood-prone areas or encouraging development in places certain to experience chronic inundation, which conveys a message of "safe to return" while also locking in investments (Lee et al., 2023; Schipper, 2020). Juhola and Käyhkö (2023) recognize the importance of systematically examining maladaptation as part of any national adaptation policy and focus particularly on deeper understandings of distributive and restorative justice, encouraging more diverse methods, more stakeholder engagement, and more procedural justice efforts to reduce negative outcomes.

Consolidation and Regionalization

Transportation investments, affordable housing, and acquisitions are costs that typically require significant financial investments by receiving communities. However, it is also important to consider the financing needs of those communities that are losing residents and may face a loss of the supporting tax base for economic development and places of well-being for residents that remain and others who may choose to move there (Siders, 2019). Local development paradigms rely on growth in property value and developed land to finance municipal budgets. Coastal governments are also often small and have little to no land that is not in a flood zone (Deyle et al., 2008). Not only will this potential loss of tax base come from outmigration, but a recent study on the impacts of climate change on the U.S. housing market found that properties exposed to flood risk are overvalued by 121–237 billion dollars, and, as a result, those homeowners and municipalities are at risk of losing equity and property tax revenue as these prices deflate (Gourevitch et al., 2023). A study examining the impacts of sea level rise on municipal revenues in Florida, for example, found that with 6.6 feet of sea level rise, the average municipality would see almost a third of their total municipal revenues affected (Shi et al., 2023). Historically, major urban centers have created metropolitan area taxing bodies to support services such as sewerage, garbage, and library services that cross jurisdictional lines. And in the southern United States, several cities and counties/parishes have merged governments, including Columbus, Georgia; Athens, Georgia; and Lafayette, Louisiana (Leland & Thurmaier, 2005). Such actions reflect attempts to create greater economies of scale for municipal utilities as their tax bases shift from the city center to the suburbs. Consolidation and regionalization of resources and planning are also identified by Shi et al. (2023) as ways to ease people's transition away from the coast while sharing benefits that come from investments in areas of higher elevation. This model allows for more cooperation, fiscal resilience, and adaptability (Shi et al., 2023). It also creates more opportunity for planning between receiving and originating communities that fall within a common jurisdiction.

The shifting of services from city to county/parish responsibility has also occurred following population and subsequent tax revenue losses after hurricanes (Flavelle & Belleme, 2021). This has also occurred with city-county/parish mergers (e.g., Baton Rouge[32]), but inter-county mergers could be more politically challenging (Citizens Research Council of Michigan, 2020). Rural counties without cities, such as Cameron Parish, Louisiana,[33] will face challenges maintaining infrastructure as an already small population declines (Shi & Varuzzo, 2020). Inter-county authorities have been created for coastal education, restoration, and protection efforts, suggesting that similar efforts could be applied to relocation planning. For example, Louisiana created the Chenier Plain Coastal Restoration and Protection Authority to coordinate coastal restoration and protection efforts across Cameron, Calcasieu, and Vermillion Parishes, although to date it has largely focused on habitat restoration and structural protection projects.[34] Planning could consider whether and when to "regionalize" or merge government and utility services (where publicly held) in an originating area with those in a receiving area, such as with water services (Riggs, 2020), and incorporate these plans into adaptation pathways where possible.[35]

Decommissioning and Restoration

Just as it is important to avoid abandoned, unremediated oil and gas wells in relocation (Ristroph & Robards, 2019), it is important to avoid

[32]More information about the city of Baton Rouge and parish of East Baton Rouge is available at https://www.brla.gov/1062/Our-Government

[33]More information about Cameron Parish is available at https://www.louisiana.gov/local-louisiana/cameron-parish

[34]More information is available at http://www.cpcrpa.org/

[35]More information on "Utility Strengthening through Consolidation: A Briefing Paper" for an example is available at https://www.uswateralliance.org/initiatives/utility-consolidation

leaving abandoned infrastructure in originating neighborhoods and communities. When homes and infrastructure are slated for buyouts through FEMA grants, the original site must be maintained as open space in perpetuity (42 U.S.C. § 5170c(b); 44 C.F.R. § 80.19). This may include the conversion of the land to its former undeveloped state, to parks and greenways, to water retention areas, to ballfields, to commemorative sites, or other specified uses (Smith et al., 2023). Not only do these conversions provide ecological and community benefit, but they can also help to restore faith in government and generate support for future mitigation projects, unlike when buyout land is left as a vacant unattended lot (Zavar, 2022). The thoughtful reprogramming of buyout lands to include ecosystem restoration can also provide substantial economic value through improved ecosystem services, including maintaining important habitats for fish and wildlife species, improving water quality, and reducing fire and flood risk (Thomas et al., 2016).

As with oil and gas infrastructure, decommissioning needs to be planned in advance to avoid a situation in which a community with a dwindling tax base cannot afford the costs (Flavelle & Belleme, 2021). Funding for demolition and restoration is included in some, but not all, grant budgets. For instance, FEMA-funded buyouts do not include the resources (including financial and technical support) suitable for the development of thoughtful design-based open space management options, and as a result, the land often becomes a financial burden rather than an asset, particularly in underresourced communities (Ben Dor et al., 2020; Smith et al., 2023; Zavar & Hagelman, 2016). Moreover, the acquisition of properties in piecemeal approaches makes subsequent restoration efforts ever more problematic. Kathy Hopkins of the Texas Water Development Board commented at the committee's acquisitions webinar[36] that setting priority areas is key to avoiding checkerboarding buyout patterns, which end up giving buyouts a "bad taste" among residents. Acquiring contiguous properties near vacant open spaces and identifying areas that need to be conserved before the acquisition is even necessary is a more proactive approach that offers better long-term outcomes (Atoba, 2022). Harris County Flood Control District (which includes Houston, Texas) sets these priority areas so that when the county obtains funding, they know what areas to look at for continuous acquisitions.[37] Houston Wilderness, a Houston-based nonprofit organization, also works to maximize the public benefit of buyout land (see Chapter 9).

[36]See footnote 20.

[37]Presentation by Kathy Hopkins, made to the committee on December 13, 2022, during the information-gathering session. More information is available at https://www.nationalacademies.org/event/12-13-2022/managed-retreat-in-the-us-gulf-coast-region-perspectives-and-approaches-to-property-acquisitions-challenges-and-lessons-learned

In an emerging trend, grants from FEMA's Building Resilient Infrastructure and Communities program are being used in a small number of communities to improve planning for the resulting open space (Smith et al., 2023). In addition, more and more states and local governments are creating their own buyout programs, and the funds are being used in part to address current federal eligibility shortfalls, thereby better addressing local needs and conditions, to include the resources needed for restorative activities. Funding is also available from the National Fish and Wildlife Foundation's National Coastal Resilience Fund.[38] For example, outside the Gulf region, the Alaska Native Tribal Health Consortium received one of these grants for restoration of parts of Newtok as that community relocated (GAO, 2022a; National Fish and Wildife Foundation, 2018; see Chapter 3 for a discussion of Newtok's relocation process). Like many villages in Alaska powered by diesel, Newtok has a "bulk fuel tank farm" and prior to relocation, the tanks were in bad shape.[39] The tanks and other equipment needed to be removed to avoid risk of contamination to the Ninglick River, an important food source. Nonprofit organizations, including Anthropocene Alliance and Buy-In Community Planning, are now working to get similar funding for communities so buyout sites can be restored and provide ecological services (e.g., water retention) for the remaining neighborhoods in the areas (Festing, 2023).[40]

Continuing Access

Preserving the original site of a community and all of its physical aspects may not be possible in the face of climate change. Currently, previous owners of properties that have been acquired have no rights to return to the site where their homes once stood (see 42 U.S.C. § 5170c(b)(2)(B); 44 C.F.R. § 80.19), which is a deal-breaker for some (e.g., residents of IDJC). To preserve the culture and identity that are intertwined with community knowledge or sites that are culturally significant, it is important to have some way to allow residents to return to the original site, to include the purposeful creation of commemorative sites (Smith et al., 2023; Zavar, 2019). Community involvement in these decisions and those around the repurposing of land can also help to build trust in the relocation process, which is demonstrably lacking in many U.S. Gulf Coast communities (see Box 8-3). Nelson et al. (2022, p. 94), in a study including interviews with residents

[38]More information about the National Fish and Wildlife Foundation's National Coastal Resilience Fund is available at https://www.nfwf.org/programs/national-coastal-resilience-fund

[39]More information about decommissioning the infrastructure is available at https://www.commerce.alaska.gov/web/Portals/4/pub/Newtok_Mertarvik_Relocation_Energy_Plan.pdf

[40]More information about Buy-In Community Planning is available at https://buy-in.org/our-vision-for-a-better-buyout-1

from and professionals working in Terrebonne Parish, Louisiana, similarly found that residents suspected ulterior motives behind resident relocation, such as acquiring mineral rights, and that this "mistrust was grounded in past oil and gas industry land deals and the dispossession of Native lands."

The National Park Service has a program that could serve as a model for acquisitions for neighborhoods where the older generations may be very attached to the land or have limited mobility, but younger generations are ready to leave. When the National Park Service acquires land for parks, it allows residents to have life estates, giving them a right to the property for up to 25 years, at which time full ownership goes to the National Park Service.[41] This program has already been imitated in Louisiana. For the IDJC relocation after Hurricane Ida, where residents' attachment to their traditional land and homes was a barrier to moving, Louisiana negotiated with HUD to allow residents to keep their old homes at the original site as long as they wanted (Louisiana Office of Community Development, 2021). Although IDJC residents secured the right to return to their homes, effectively using them as fishing camps, they are not permitted to make substantial repairs or improvements. Outside the Gulf region, Charlotte-Mecklenburg, North Carolina, and Austin, Texas, have used "leasebacks" to allow residents to continue leasing homes subject to a buyback, giving the residents more time to move (Shi et al., 2022).

Where maintaining property rights is not feasible, there could be some sort of memorial to acknowledge the former residents and why they left. This acknowledges the attachment to place (see Chapter 6) and provides a historical marker for future generations to understand why the land remains open.[42]

There may also need to be discussion regarding how to handle cemeteries and sacred sites. For example, the relocation process of Vunidogoloa, Fiji, recognized the villagers' cultural, emotional, and spiritual ties to their traditional territory and the burial place of their ancestors: ancestor remains were exhumed, and the local church provided for the transfer of the burial site (Borsa, 2020). The old village site was left in place so villagers could continue to visit it (Tronquet, 2015). In Christchurch, New Zealand, buyout participants are allowed to go back to their former property to collectively harvest fruit trees that were left standing, as well as maintain roses and other plantings as part of a larger regeneration plan that focuses on the management of the resulting open space (Smith et al., 2023). And (as discussed in Chapter 3) in Newtok, Alaska, former owners can go on their bought-out land if they want to; it is owned by their tribe, though it

---

[41]More information about the National Park Service acquisitions is available at https://www.nps.gov/policy/DOrders/DOrder25.htm

[42]See footnote 20.

is projected by the U.S. Army Corps of Engineers to be under water by the end of this decade (Ristroph, 2021).

ORIGINATING AND RECEIVING PARTNERSHIPS

Jurisdictions in the United States have yet to develop partnerships between originating and receiving communities. In contrast, when residents from the Carteret Islands (in Papua New Guinea) were preparing to relocate to a larger island with higher ground (Bougainville), the nonprofit group Tulele Peisa brought chiefs and elders from the receiving area to visit the Carteret Islands (Boege & Rakova, 2019). The extended visit enabled Bougainville leaders to see the difficulties faced by Carteret Islanders and enabled the leaders to be more welcoming (Rakova, 2022). In addition, Tulele Peisa arranged for a group of youth from both the Carteret Islands and Bougainville to conduct outreach in the receiving area by going from household to household and spending time with families (Rakova, 2022). Also included in Tulele Peisa's work was a program to teach agricultural techniques (Boege & Rakova, 2019; Edwards, 2013; Rakova, 2022). Together, the originating and receiving communities have taken part in a number of customary practices that helped build their relationship (Rakova, 2022).

There are partnerships in the United States that could be expanded to address community-driven relocation. City-to-city networks, such as Strong Cities Network,[43] C40,[44] and Peace in Our Cities,[45] could be invested in and capitalized on to contribute to regional planning between cities (Blaine et al., 2022). Some networks, such as C40, already provide guidance on relocation (referred to as managed retreat on their website). C40 notes,

> *Establishing a regional board or working group can help to coordinate a regional strategy to address sea level rise and coastal flooding. A good example is the [bi-partisan] Southeast Florida Regional Climate Change Compact, which was established in 2009 by Broward, Miami-Dade, Monroe and Palm Beach Counties to coordinate action to increase the region's climate resilience, share tools and knowledge and increase political will.*[46]

---

[43]More information about the Strong Cities Network is available at https://strongcitiesnetwork.org/

[44]More information about C40 is available at https://www.c40.org/

[45]More information about Peace in Our Cities is available at https://www.sdg16.plus/peaceinourcities

[46]More information is available at https://www.c40knowledgehub.org/s/article/How-to-adapt-your-city-to-sea-level-rise-and-coastal-flooding?language=en_US

Specific activities in the Southeast Florida Regional Climate Change Compact include the creation of a regional climate change adaptation plan; the development of agreed upon policy statements and advocacy positions; a repository of the best available, locally relevant scientific information on the physical indicators of climate change; and a set of resources that communities may draw from to implement local actions spelled out in the regional plan.[47] Support for the idea of city-to-city partnerships also came up at the committee's Louisiana workshop, where one participant suggested the idea of creating "cousin cities" in closer proximity to one another that could mutually assist each other in times of need (National Academies of Sciences, Engineering, and Medicine, 2023a, p. 54). Another participant mentioned that something similar happened after Hurricane Laura in New Orleans, where thousands of people from the Lake Charles area were able to stay in downtown hotels (National Academies, 2023a).

Partnership organizations that are oriented toward community-driven relocation, like the ones described above, could help to match nearby communities and facilitate dialogues between them, putting this idea of "cousin cities" into practice. While it may not be possible to specifically match communities, a network could be established to connect communities who have undertaken the relocation process with those considering this complex venture. This program could include pairing communities with similar characteristics (e.g., size, rural or urban, geography, governmental capacity). Additional actions undertaken as part of this program could include the identification of communities that plan to undertake managed retreat and communities that may seek to accept those scheduled for relocation. This proposed approach may foster greater policy learning (or the sharing of policy problems with others to produce more effective policy), a recognized shortfall in the current approach taken to acquire hazard-prone housing (Greer & Binder, 2017).

SUMMARY

This chapter identified the relationship between receiving and originating communities and the importance of early and ongoing action to coordinate community-driven relocation and related community development initiatives. Given the relatively minimal work to date to acknowledge, much less address, this relationship between receiving and originating communities, the chapter first defines these key terms as well as others, including regional planning, land-use planning, and infrastructure—the latter capturing social as well as physical components. These definitions and discussions

[47]More information about the Southeast Florida Regional Climate Change Compact is available at https://southeastfloridaclimatecompact.org/

offer important nuance as the work on relocation tends to focus on leaving, and less attention is therefore paid toward the preparations needed for communities to receive arriving households or industries, including physical and social infrastructure. In these communities, the socialization of risks, the shared decision making regarding when to leave, and the possibility of continued access to former homesites share equal importance to planning for the physical environment.

The chapter also highlights the importance of sustained assessment, or monitoring over time, which acknowledges that current climate challenges will continue to evolve, and likely escalate, in terms of sea level rise, temperatures, and precipitation intensities. Such sustained assessment of risk enables communities to adjust planning should risks escalate more rapidly, or differently, than initially considered. Referred to as non-stationarity, this warrants a whole-of-government approach wherein changes in originating communities amplify the need for planning in receiving communities and the need to monitor receiving communities' carrying capacities, housing affordability, transportation availability, educational access and quality, employment opportunities, as well as ecological and environmental amenities. Social and community context, health care access and quality, and equity considerations are paramount. Moreover, as originating communities reduce populations and remove assets from risky areas, municipal governments' declining tax bases may require consolidation and/or regionalization. Within these communities, remaining open spaces need decommissioning and ecological restoration; this is true particularly in areas where permanent inundation may otherwise introduce toxins to newly aquatic environments. Determining how to care for these ecological landscapes while simultaneously reducing the tax base deserves specific planning.

Inherent in this type of coordinated planning is the need to engage, or establish, regional planning entities alongside state and municipal governments. Creating relationships between cities and sustaining them over time requires additional attention in the early stages of community-driven relocation and requires partnership building among regional collaborators. Given the work already needed in the U.S. Gulf Coast, moving quickly toward a type of interstate regional planning collaborative is an important near-term step. Within such a collaborative, receiving and originating communities could have helpful dialogues and, through networks of such dyads, grow capacities far more quickly while making progress toward the types of relocation that the U.S. Gulf Coast will inevitably see. In the next chapter, the committee will lay out the framework of funding, policies, and planning under which relocation currently happens in the United States.

CONCLUSIONS

Conclusion 8-1: Receiving communities need to have the infrastructure and institutional capacity to provide essential services such as housing, water treatment and water supply, power and fuel distribution, broadband, education, health services, employment, and transportation for expected population increases. Currently, there is little planning or funding specifically for population relocation.

Conclusion 8-2: Land suitability analysis is a useful tool to help communities identify less hazard-prone areas for potential relocation sites. Although its use in directing relocating communities is so far uncommon, when incorporated into broader city planning efforts it has the potential to help direct people who are relocating to safer nearby areas that are also acceptable to them and that preserve a jurisdiction's tax base.

Conclusion 8-3: Community relocations and individual buyouts can be slowed down by long environmental review processes, particularly when multiple agency approvals are involved and agencies are reluctant to take the lead, given the expense, time, and potential for litigation.

Conclusion 8-4: Becoming a receiving community can have numerous implications, including on housing costs and education systems. Thus, ensuring communities understand and prepare for those implications ahead of time can lead to smoother outcomes for both current and new residents. Preparing receiving communities might include "socializing the idea" with current residents, identifying suitable land, building or identifying affordable housing options, and identifying livelihood pathways for new residents.

Conclusion 8-5: A history of pervasive and systemic inequity and forced migration affects the planning preparations required for community-driven relocation. Thus, communities need to recognize past inequities and invest the time required to engender trust and to develop diverse networks for planning community-driven relocation in a sensitive and culturally competent manner.

Conclusion 8-6: As a result of resettlements, coastal cities may experience a decline in tax revenue as some properties become vacant or real estate values fall among at-risk properties that remain in use. To avoid losing real estate tax bases, county-level governments or private entities providing services, such as electricity or wastewater, can consolidate their governments or identify suitable areas for resettlement in their existing jurisdiction.

Conclusion 8-7: Authorities need to provide for systematic decommissioning of facilities on acquired sites and restoration of these areas, not only to avoid contamination and hazards to wildlife but also to protect neighboring communities from future flood events and provide appropriate ecosystem, recreational, and educational services.

Conclusion 8-8: The opportunity for people who have relocated to visit their original sites and the creation of commemorative sites that are culturally significant would help preserve the culture and identity that are intertwined with community knowledge.

Conclusion 8-9: Partnerships between originating and receiving communities can facilitate the collaborative development of policies and plans needed to address the complexities and long timeframes associated with community-driven relocation.

9

Landscape of Policy, Funding, and Planning

This chapter discusses the following:

- Nested scales of government involved with community-driven relocation and the interrelationship of funding, policy, and planning within this framework
- Federal agencies, programs, and policies that dictate or provide funding for elements of community-driven relocation, split by disaster-related agencies, agencies not primarily disaster-related, and nonfinancial technical assistance
- State buyout program examples across the United States
- The lack of and need for regional planning for community-driven relocation within the Gulf states, with examples of state planning entities in each state that could address such issues
- Local-level buyout program examples from across the United States and land-use planning for relocation
- Private and public-private funding and programs related to community-driven relocation

INTRODUCTION

The present chapter takes a closer look at the current landscape of laws, government agencies and programs, and state and community resilience and hazard mitigation plans (HMPs) that can or do play a role in facilitating (or hindering) relocation when the status quo is untenable and relocation is deemed necessary (whether as a result of discrete disasters or gradual changes). The chapter reviews this landscape at the federal, state, regional, and local levels of government, as well as nongovernmental institutions that work alongside government entities. Each section examines how agency- or program-specific mechanisms for funding shape what is actually possible in terms of relocation. The chapter describes the complex web of programs, policies, funding opportunities, and plans that communities pursuing relocation must navigate in the absence of a formal federal program focused on community-driven relocation. The ramifications of this complexity will be discussed in Chapter 10, including issues of equity, social vulnerability, and justice.

As this chapter shows, the several government entities that work in this space have different areas of focus. For example, the Federal Emergency Management Agency (FEMA) is largely focused on response, hazard mitigation, and disaster recovery, while the U.S. Army Corps of Engineers (USACE)—with some degree of involvement from FEMA and the Natural Resource Conservation Service of the U.S. Department of Agriculture—is focused on floodplain management. Meanwhile, the Department of Housing and Urban Development (HUD), the other major federal agency discussed below, is focused on housing and community infrastructure. These differences at the federal level can result in competing or contradictory goals and approaches. For example, in Fair Bluff, North Carolina, the U.S. Department of Commerce's Economic Development Administration invested in a business center while, in the same area, FEMA-funded buyouts of houses and businesses were undertaken (Flavelle & Belleme, 2021). Another example of multiple sources of funding supporting multiple courses of action is Princeville, North Carolina, where FEMA and HUD are funding buyouts, USACE is planning a new levee (Flavelle & Belleme, 2021), and the town is in the process of moving part of its community to a 52-acre site located outside the floodplain (Smith & Nguyen, 2021). Despite the existence of many laws and programs that could support community relocation, the existing legal framework does not address relocation in a coordinated, comprehensive manner that communities can easily navigate (FEMA, 2023g; Howe et al., 2021; Ristroph, 2019). In some cases, as discussed below, local and state programs can complement federal programs, especially when states and local communities are given greater flexibility in how they administer federal programs and are given the time to plan for this complex activity. (Newtok,

Alaska, is representative of this type of effort [Ristroph, 2021]; see Chapter 3 of this report for more.) However, this is not the norm and at times there are disconnects among federal and other governments, as well as between local government leadership and community members (see Box 9-1).

Legal and funding structures can be disaster-related, a reactive approach, or non-disaster-related, to include a proactive approach that involves acting based on sound planning practices. Government programs, and the agencies that run them, most commonly follow a disaster-recovery model when facilitating relocation and other courses of action around environmental threats such as increasingly destructive hurricanes, subsidence, and sea level rise. In a disaster-recovery model, much of the available funding comes episodically as a reaction to a specific disaster or in the form of annual nationally competitive programs. Furthermore, it may not be aligned with state and community policies and plans, particularly those relating to capital improvements. This stands in contrast to a model of proactive measures, where funding might be available year-round and allocated based on risk and need.

These two models of action are not the only difference in the approaches of various government agencies, programs, and plans; the intended purpose of the funding can also vary. *Resilience approaches*—which encompass a range of measures that a community can take that aim to prevent, plan for, mitigate against, react to, and recover from disasters—will continue to be important as these communities navigate the evolving threats of climate change. As shown below, that approach is much more common than relocation.

Furthermore, the notion of community relocation itself is highly varied (as discussed in more detail in Chapters 1 and 3). This is due to several factors, including a deep attachment to place, the lack of a coordinated governmental strategy within and across jurisdictions and agencies, and the narrowly defined grant programs available. In most cases, relocation is undertaken by local governments, and involves a partial movement of housing and a community's physical assets. Communities typically draw from multiple sources of post-disaster recovery funding, including grants tied to the removal of hazard-prone housing alongside funding to repair and rebuild other parts of a community. In one of the largest known examples in the United States, in the 1990s, thousands of homes in multiple Midwest communities were purchased, demolished, and relocated following floods (see Chapter 3). In most cases, less flood-prone parts of the communities remained, often protected by large levee systems.

Finally, disaster aid (financial or otherwise) is a critical factor in recovery and resilience, but the type of aid can be more important than the amount (Greer & Trainor, 2021). For example, one study found that temporary housing can slow permanent household recovery (Peacock et al., 1987, cited by Greer & Trainor, 2021). In order for aid to be effective, agencies need to align the timing of aid programs with the community's capacity to accept and manage the program(s), and ensure programs meet household needs and are designed to efficiently and effectively address these needs (Greer & Trainor, 2021). In addition, Zurich (2013) stressed the need to rebuild structures to be more flood resilient and suggested that governments and insurers can play a role in this by creating incentives and providing advice. Other effective drivers of action include economic incentives and regulatory and market drivers (Dawson et al., 2011; Suykens et al., 2019; Valois, Tessier et al., 2020; Zou et al., 2020).

Below, the focus is on federal, state, and regional levels of government. However, it is important to note that in many cases, there is insufficient attention placed on supporting local capacity building, drawing from local bases of knowledge and experience (see Chapter 7), and addressing relocation-specific challenges, such as the programming of the resulting open space, the identification of receiving areas, and the construction of replacement housing and new communities (see Chapter 8). Each of these deficiencies benefit from inclusive, collaborative planning, as the committee also discusses in Chapter 8.

BOX 9-1
Disconnects Among Federal and Other Governments

At a committee seminar for Mississippi and Alabama, Derrick Evans, executive director, Turkey Creek Community Initiatives in Gulfport, Mississippi, spoke of bottlenecks or dead ends in the system of funding that is supposed to flow between different levels of government:

"We have produced numerous federally funded, place-based, intelligent, actionable, fundable [...] community plans [...] that would benefit the entire city [...] But we can't prevent elected leadership [...] from (a) not participating on the front end, (b) being surprised that all of a sudden there's this federal windfall [of funding], (c) thinking it is meant for them [...] almost like private new development capital, or (d) don't move forward with that 8 million dollar coastal Restoration Grant. [...] Local government leadership can be a dead end, or the last stop, or the last point in a funnel that lets the resources through."

SOURCE: Derrick Evans, Executive Director, Turkey Creek Community Initiatives in Gulfport, Mississippi, and Gulf Coast Fund for Community Renewal and Ecological Health (2005–2013). Virtual Focused Discussion: Mississippi and Alabama Gulf Coast Community Stakeholder Perspectives on Managed Retreat, March 2023.

Nested Scales for Regional Planning

As was introduced above, multiple government levels come into play when a community considers or pursues relocation. Understanding the different levels of institutions and how they connect is important to understand which agencies have the ability to invest in or otherwise contribute to solutions. The FEMA Hazard Mitigation Grant Program (HMGP) buyout approach, as illustrated in a report from the Natural Resources Defense Council (see Figure 9-1) and described in more detail in the next section, offers an example of nested scales of decision making (Weber & Moore, 2019). The HMGP buyout process involves a multifaceted collaboration among federal, state, and local entities and homeowners that spans approximately five years. Initiated by a presidential disaster declaration, FEMA invites affected states and tribes to apply for funding, which is further broken down into local "subapplications." Local entities, in preparation, identify potential participants, conduct analyses, and collate necessary documentation. However, they often grapple with uncertainties around funding amounts and requirements for matching funds, leading to delays. Once FEMA approves applications and disburses funds, local jurisdictions manage property-related activities like appraisals, offers to homeowners, and demolitions. Although FEMA allows a year-long application window post-disaster, the ensuing procedures displayed in Figure 9-1—from property appraisal to demolition—are intricate (Weber & Moore, 2019). Because of this intricate web of procedures and people across multiple levels, a lack of coordination and leadership at the federal level trickles down, placing additional pressures on state, regional, and local entities to manage the coordination of resources.

Interrelationship of Funding, Policy, and Planning

In addition to the nested scales described above, this chapter discusses three interrelated elements of relocation: funding, policy, and planning. Funding is the money available to fund relocation and planning for relocation. Policies dictate how much funding is available, for whom, and for what activities. Planning defines more specifically what actions will take place with available funding within a state or locale, adhering to policy and funding stipulations. Additionally, federal policies may require that plans (e.g., HMPs) exist at the state or local level in order for a state or locale to receive funding, and funding can, at times, be used to help states and locales develop such plans, revealing the intricate connections between these three elements. As is displayed in Figure 9-1, community relocation is a multilevel process, each level with different roles and responsibilities. As such, the

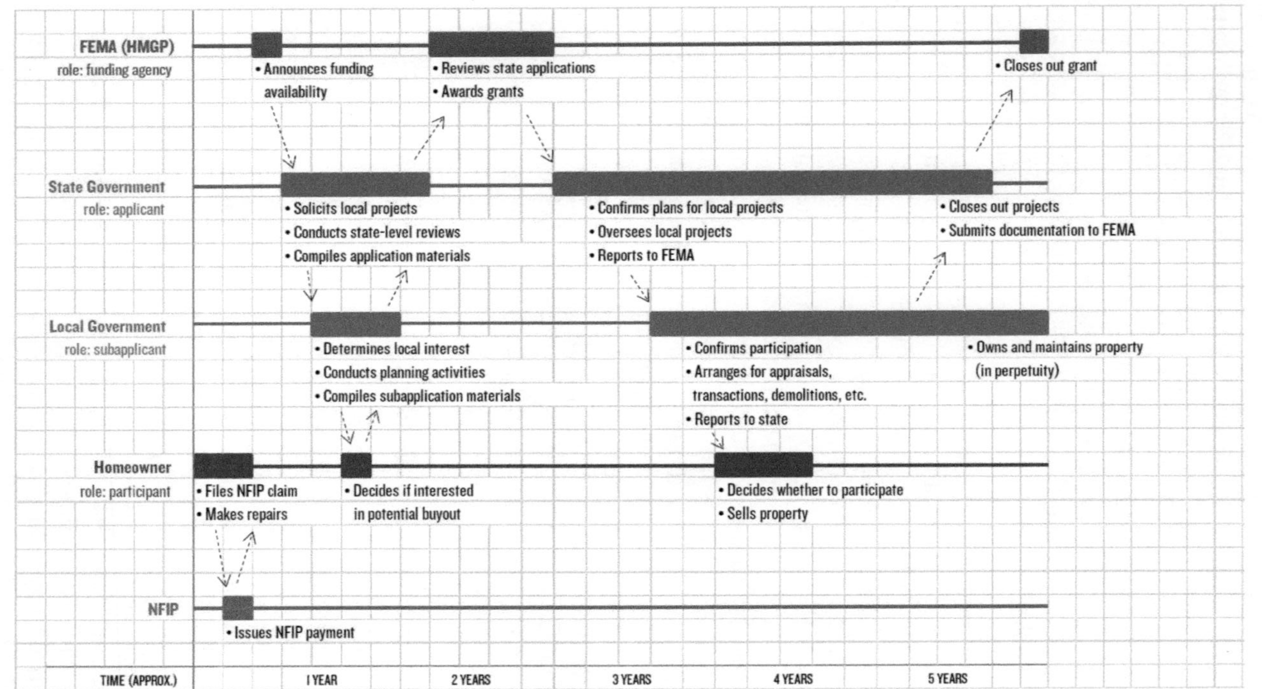

FIGURE 9-1 Blueprint for FEMA-funded buyouts.
SOURCE: Weber, A., & Moore, R. (2019). *Going under: Long wait times for post-flood buyouts leave homeowners underwater.* Natural Resources Defense Council. https://www.nrdc.org/resources/going-under-long-wait-times-post-flood-buyouts-leave-homeowners-underwater

sections of this report, broken down by level (federal, state, regional, local), cover funding, policy, and planning to different extents.

The federal section primarily discusses funding, as the federal government's main role in the current landscape is to provide funding for states and communities. Because most of the funding comes from the federal level, the policies that stipulate eligibility are also key at this level, and community actions are dictated by them. Notably, the financial costs of community-driven relocation vary greatly from case to case depending on a multitude of factors (e.g., distance of move, current price of supplies, community expectations such as for housing types). The costs of relocation for several case studies are noted in Chapter 3. At the state level, the discussion centers on state programs, which can help to facilitate relocation, particularly by connecting communities to federal and other funding and to state plans (e.g., Louisiana's Coastal Master Plan), which mention relocation as an adaptation strategy. The state-level programs discussed in this chapter vary in the amount of planning for relocation they conduct. For example, Blue Acres proactively purchases undeveloped land and works to identify contiguous parcels in order to enhance the benefits of relocation while other state programs do not. The regional coordination section covers planning on topics that affect multiple jurisdictions (e.g., counties, cities, states). The landscape of regional planning entities in Gulf states does not currently incorporate community-driven relocation but rather the structures and networks which, if desired by members, could be leveraged to plan for community-driven relocation. At the local level, there are buyout programs that may draw from local funding sources and therefore have more flexible spending guidelines and that in some instances serve a similar role as state buyout programs. At this level there is also a heavier focus on detailed land-use planning.

FEDERAL AGENCIES, AUTHORITIES, AND POLICIES

This section looks at the agencies and programs through which the federal government offers support to individuals and communities dealing with changes to their home areas. It is divided into examples of agencies and programs that follow a disaster-response model and those that follow a more proactive model; the section then briefly discusses nonfinancial technical assistance provided by these federal agencies to state and local governments.

Maze of Potential Assistance

As will be demonstrated by this section's summaries of federal agencies and programs, and the current set of laws and policies, communities have to navigate a complex maze centered mainly on funding buyouts of individual households while allowing for enough time and money to obtain replacement housing. Funding distributed through competitive grant applications is too often episodic and unpredictable, does not provide a stable base of resources for planning, is resource intensive for communities, and may unfairly privilege the communities and households with the best grant writers over those most in need (more in Chapter 10). Figure 9-2 depicts the array of federal programs that threatened communities may navigate when pursuing relocation. Each of the agencies displayed in Figure 9-2, and their relevance to community-driven relocation, are explained in more detail in this section. This "unclear federal leadership" was identified as the "key challenge to climate migration as a resilience strategy" in a recent report by the Government Accountability Office (GAO, 2020a). A discussion of specific challenges with this current framework and opportunities to overcome them is in Chapter 10.

Disaster-Related Agencies

Much of the federal-level funding for relocation has been allocated for discrete purposes as components of larger federal post-disaster efforts or efforts otherwise directly linked to the occurrence of a specific disaster (as opposed to ongoing change over time and/or proactive measures taken against the threat of that sort of change).

Federal Emergency Management Agency

With a history of providing disaster relief tracing back to 1803, FEMA's mission is to "[help] people before, during and after disasters."[1] FEMA funding is authorized through the Robert T. Stafford Disaster Relief and Emergency Assistance Act of 1988 (Stafford Act, P.L. 100-707) and its amendments.[2] As discussed below, FEMA funding is tied to a presidential disaster declaration, meaning that the programs administered by FEMA largely conform to a post-disaster funding model. This can curtail efforts to proactively prepare for anticipated hazards (including relocating away from hazardous areas). Additionally, the slow effects of climate change, including erosion and sea level rise, are not eligible to be presidentially declared disasters. Thus, FEMA funds are often off-limits to individuals or communities seeking to proactively address climate-related threats (GAO, 2009;

[1]More information about FEMA's mission, values, and history is available at https://www.fema.gov/about

[2]These amendments include the Disaster Mitigation Act of 2000 (HR 707, 106th Congress, P.L. 106-390) and the Disaster Recovery Reform Act in 2018 (HR 4460, 115th Congress).

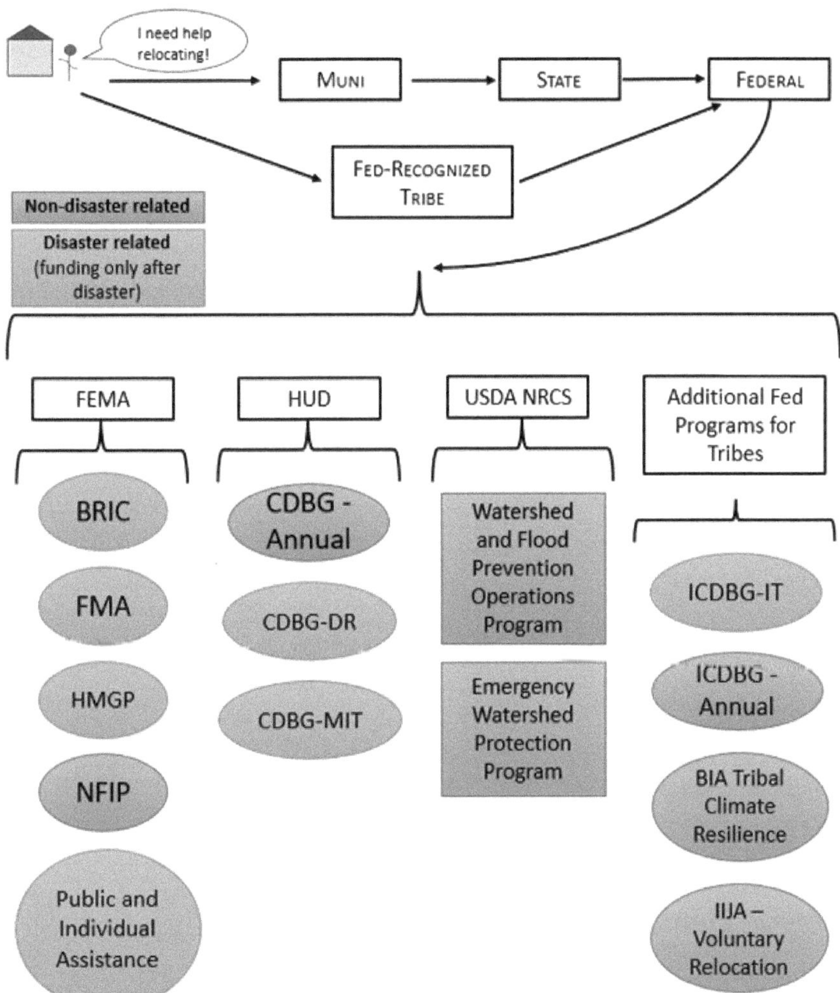

FIGURE 9-2 Sources of federal government support for relocation.
NOTES: Municipality (Muni); Federal Emergency Management Agency (FEMA); Building Resilient Infrastructure and Communities (BRIC); Flood Mitigation Assistance grant program (FMA); Hazard Mitigation Grant Program (HMGP); National Flood Insurance Program (NFIP); Department of Housing and Urban Development (HUD); Community Development Block Grant (CDBG); CDBG Disaster Recovery (CDBG-DR); CDBG Mitigation (CDBG-MIT); U.S. Department of Agriculture Natural, Resources Conservation Service (USDA NRCS); Indian Community Development Block Grant (ICDBG); ICDBG Imminent Threat (ICDBG-IT); Bureau of Indian Affairs (BIA); Infrastructure Investment and Jobs Act (IIJA).
SOURCE: Committee generated.

Shen & Ristroph, 2020). Furthermore, this type of funding model (and the annual competition model used by the Building Resilient Infrastructure and Communities [BRIC] program) does not provide the consistent predictable funding that planning for community-driven relocation warrants.

There is some opportunity, however, to use FEMA assistance programs for community-wide relocation, despite funds often being made available only in the immediate aftermath of a presidentially declared disaster. For example, Alatna Village in Alaska was able to relocate using funds from FEMA's HMGP after flooding disaster declarations in 1994 (GAO, 2009). FEMA administers several assistance programs, most of which include relocation as an eligible action. Those most relevant to this report include the Public Assistance (PA) Program, Individuals and Households Program (IHP),[3] and Hazard Mitigation Assistance (HMA) programs.[4] HMA programs include the HMGP, BRIC, and Flood Mitigation Assistance grant program (FMA). Eligibility for each program, except FMA, requires a prior disaster declaration. BRIC requires a disaster declaration in the past seven years. Thus, FMA and BRIC are formally classified by FEMA as non-disaster-related programs but are discussed in this section to keep FEMA programs together. Additionally, each of these programs (minus IHP) require applicants and subapplicants to have a FEMA-approved HMP usually at the time of application and when funds are distributed. HMGP also requires an approved plan at the time of the disaster declaration.

The PA Program is aimed at providing immediate relief to disaster-affected communities to restore disaster-damaged facilities. Unlike HMGP, which allows funds to be used for damaged and non-damaged facilities, PA funds can only be used to repair damaged facilities. Relocation is an approved project under this program if the relocation meets certain conditions including that the relocation is cost-effective and the property is subject to repeated damage (e.g., is located in a Special Flood Hazard Area; FEMA, 2020b). IHP funding is meant to help individuals and households to cover expenses related to basic needs (such as housing) and disaster recovery efforts that are not covered by insurance, including moving and expenses.[5]

HMGP funding is intended to "support mitigation activities that reduce or eliminate potential losses" and foster "resilience against the effects of disasters" (FEMA, 2023c, p. 28); however, funds are only made available after

[3]More information about the PA Program is available at https://www.fema.gov/assistance/public, and more information about the IHP is available at https://www.fema.gov/assistance/individual/program

[4]More information about HMA programs is available at https://www.fema.gov/fact-sheet/summary-fema-hazard-mitigation-assistance-hma-programs

[5]More information about IHP is available at https://www.fema.gov/assistance/individual/program

a disaster declaration. HMGP distributes an estimated percentage of federal disaster assistance, typically 15 percent of total federal disaster costs, to the applicant (state, tribal, and territorial governments, and the District of Columbia) on a sliding scale.[6] States with an approved Enhanced Hazard Mitigation Plan (a plan that exceeds the basic requirements) receive an additional 5 percent (FEMA, 2022b). Successful applicants then establish their own funding parameters within FEMA's eligibility constraints and distribute this assistance to communities (subapplicants). In the past 30 years, HMGP has obligated more than 3.6 billion dollars for property acquisition (FEMA, 2023f). In a property acquisition, typically the land is purchased and the structure is either demolished or relocated. Significantly, entities are eligible for this mitigation funding only in the wake of a specific disaster and cannot apply to use the funds for projects that might mitigate the impact of future hazards, unless they have recently experienced a disaster.

In an effort to be more proactive, FEMA established an annual competitive grants program, the Pre-Disaster Mitigation (PDM) Grant Program,[7] to support planning for and implementing measures to reduce *future* risk from natural hazards at the state, local, tribal, and territorial government levels. In 2020, the BRIC program[8] essentially replaced PDM and shifted its focus to nature-based solutions[9] rather than the large-scale acquisition of hazard-prone housing (FEMA, 2021a). BRIC is funded as a percentage of the total disaster funding allocated by Congress in the previous year, or through one-time appropriations, such as the Infrastructure Investment and Jobs Act of 2021 (IIJA). This approach perpetuates a system in which a community's eligibility is determined by past disasters rather than future need as determined by projected vulnerabilities due to climate change. Furthermore, like any competitive grant program, BRIC does not provide the predictability in future funding needed across all states and localities. Competitive processes also often exacerbate and widen gaps between need and access to funding (see Chapter 10).

---

[6]More information about the FEMA-approved HMPG is available at https://www.fema.gov/grants/mitigation/hazard-mitigation

[7]More information about the PDM is available at https://www.fema.gov/grants/mitigation/pre-disaster

[8]More information about the BRIC program is available at https://www.fema.gov/grants/mitigation/building-resilient-infrastructure-communities

[9]"Nature-based solutions are actions to protect, sustainably manage, or restore natural ecosystems, that address societal challenges [e.g., climate change, disaster risk reduction ...] providing human well-being and biodiversity benefits." Nature-based solutions are an alternative to grey or manmade infrastructure solutions. One example is planting coastal trees as a method of reducing storm impact. More information about nature-based solutions is available at https://www.worldbank.org/en/news/feature/2022/05/19/what-you-need-to-know-about-nature-based-solutions-to-climate-change

FEMA's FMA[10] is focused on flood hazards and does not require a prior disaster declaration. The program is authorized for reducing or eliminating the risk of repetitive flooding for buildings that are insured by the National Flood Insurance Program (NFIP) and thus funds buyouts only for that group of properties. In 2022, FMA launched the Swift Current Initiative[11] with money from the IIJA.[12] The intent of this initiative is to expedite money to "disaster survivors with repetitively flooded homes" to help them become more flood resilient.[13] Only NFIP-insured properties designated as Severe Repetitive Loss, Repetitive Loss, or Substantially Damaged are eligible.[14] The initiative provided 60 million dollars in fiscal year 2022 across Louisiana, New Jersey, Pennsylvania, and Mississippi, the four states with the highest losses following Hurricane Ida. Eligible projects include the acquisition and subsequent demolition or relocation of eligible properties. Non-relocation flood mitigation projects (e.g., elevation and dry floodproofing) are also options under this program (FEMA, 2022b).

NFIP also has a history of investing in efforts to lower flood risks, such as through the Community Rating System (CRS), a program designed to reward communities that take actions to better manage flood risks beyond those required under the program. CRS has led to reduced overall losses and lower flood claims in participating communities (Gourevitch & Pinter, 2023; Highfield & Brody, 2017; Kousky & Michel-Kerjan, 2017). Additionally, in 2020, Congress passed the Safeguarding Tomorrow through Ongoing Risk Mitigation Act (P.L. 116-284), which authorizes FEMA to award grants to states, federally recognized tribes, and territories so that these smaller governmental entities can establish and administer revolving loan funds aimed at promoting resilience and available to local communities. This system differs from existing HMA programs in that the state, territory, or federally recognized tribe is responsible for making funding decisions and awarding loans to local governments rather than routing local government subapplications to FEMA for approval. FEMA's program for administering these grants, the Safeguarding Tomorrow Revolving Loan

---

[10]More information about the FMA is available at https://www.fema.gov/grants/mitigation/floods

[11]More information about the Swift Current Initiative is available at https://www.fema.gov/grants/mitigation/floods/swift-current

[12]More information about the IIJA is available at https://www.whitehouse.gov/briefing-room/statements-releases/2021/11/06/fact-sheet-the-bipartisan-infrastructure-deal/

[13]Ibid.

[14]More information about Severe Repetitive Loss, Repetitive Loss, and Substantially Damaged is available at https://www.fema.gov/txt/rebuild/repetitive_loss_faqs.txt

Fund Program,[15] received an initial sum of 500 million dollars over five years, authorized by Congress via the IIJA. FEMA has initiated the first notice of funding opportunity for these grants, and eligible entities are passing legislation and applying for monies with which to establish locally focused revolving loan funds. To alleviate one of the largest barriers for states and localities, FEMA does not require the use of benefit-cost analysis to determine project eligibility for this program, and loans may be used to cover nonfederal match costs for other HMA grants. (Benefit-cost analysis and nonfederal matches will be discussed in more detail in Chapter 10.)

Department of Housing and Urban Development

HUD was created in 1965 through the consolidation of five agencies, including the Federal Housing Administration and the Community Facilities Administration, with the intent of creating one federal agency through which to address "urban problems including substandard and deteriorating housing."[16] Although HUD's primary purpose is not relocation or climate resilience, the Community Development Block Grant (CDBG) Program "supports community development activities to build stronger and more resilient communities,"[17] and funding under this umbrella can be (and has been) used for community relocation (GAO, 2020a). In addition, HUD recently released an implementation guide for community-driven relocation (HUD, 2023a). The guide details relocation mechanisms, HUD and FEMA funding opportunities, and a six-step process for community-driven relocation with examples. The CDBG funding categories most relevant for relocation are CDBG Mitigation (CDBG-MIT) Program funds and CDBG Disaster Recovery (CDBG-DR) Program funds, both of which are tied to recent disasters, and neither of which receives regular annual congressional appropriations. Components of HUD's CDBG Program may receive congressional funding after a disaster, while also having an annual competitive grants program (discussed below). Notably, funds from these two programs "have a statutory focus on benefiting vulnerable lower-income people and communities and targeting the most impacted and distressed areas" (HUD, 2019, p. 45838).

Funds for CDBG-MIT were first appropriated by Congress in 2018 for disasters that occurred in 2015, 2016, and 2017. The program provides

[15]More information about the Safeguarding Tomorrow Revolving Loan Fund Program is available at https://www.fema.gov/grants/mitigation/storm-rlf

[16]More information about the history of HUD is available at https://archives.hud.gov/hud50/hud50.hud.gov/hud_history_timeline/index.html

[17]More information about the CDBG is available at https://www.hudexchange.info/programs/cdbg/

grants to areas recently impacted by qualifying disasters to carry out "activities to mitigate disaster risks and reduce future losses" (HUD, 2019, p. 45838). CDBG-MIT funds[18] can be used for post-disaster buyouts (Smith, 2014). Grantees must develop an action plan for their proposed projects and these plans must reference FEMA-approved HMPs. Funds can be used to update HMPs and for other planning activities, including integrating mitigation plans with other planning initiatives (HUD, 2019). Thus, if a community or state decides to incorporate community-driven relocation into their HMP, the associated planning is an activity that could be covered by CDBG-MIT funds.

CDBG-DR[19] is another such program that relies on competitive grants to disburse funds. It is funded as a supplemental congressional appropriation and can be used to fund the nonfederal cost-share that is required by other federal disaster assistance programs. After Congress appropriates funding to CDBG-DR, HUD formally announces the availability of CDBG-DR awards and associated rules in the Federal Register. CDBG-DR grants are subject to laws that apply to all CDBG programs. Eligible activities that grantees have undertaken with CDBG-DR grants include relocation of displaced residents, acquisition of damaged properties, rehabilitation of damaged homes and public facilities (e.g., neighborhood centers and roads), and certain hazard mitigation activities (HUD, 2023b).

Separate funding is reserved for federally recognized tribes through two programs, the Indian Housing Block Grant and the Indian Community Development Block Grant (ICDBG) Program.[20] Notably, many U.S. Gulf Coast tribes are not federally recognized, meaning they cannot benefit from these programs. Under ICDBG, Imminent Threat Grants are available on a noncompetitive basis to recognized tribes for a problem "which if unresolved or not addressed will have an immediate negative impact on public health or safety" (Title I of the Housing and Community Development Act of 1974, as amended, 42 U.S.C. 5301, 2023, § 1003.4). For example, Newtok, Alaska, received funding from ICDBG Imminent Threat Grants to aid in its relocation efforts (Ristroph, 2021; see Chapter 3 for more). Because of the focus on the imminent nature of the threat, this report considers these grants to be disaster-related (i.e., contingent on a specific event rather than ongoing).

There is also some precedent for HUD funds, outside of those described above, being used to support community relocation in the wake of disasters

[18]More information about HUD's CDBG-MIT funding is available at https://www.hudexchange.info/programs/cdbg-mit/overview/

[19]More information about CDBG-DR funding is available at https://www.hudexchange.info/programs/cdbg-dr/overview/

[20]More information on both grant programs is available at https://www.hud.gov/program_offices/public_indian_housing/ih/grants

even though they were not labeled as such. An appropriations bill that followed Hurricane Sandy allocated 16 billion dollars[21] for HUD's Community Development Fund (the program in which CDBG sits) to be used for "disaster relief, long-term recovery, restoration of infrastructure and housing, and economic revitalization" (P.L. 113-2, 127 Stat 36, January 29, 2013). These funds were limited to jurisdictions with presidentially declared disasters from 2011 to 2013. For example, through HUD's National Disaster Resilience Competition (NDRC), Louisiana received 48 million dollars in CDBG funds to relocate the community of Isle de Jean Charles (see Chapter 3).[22] Additionally, with NDRC, state funding, and innovative partnerships with philanthropic organizations, such as Foundation for Louisiana, a total of 47.5 million dollars was available for Louisiana's Strategic Adaptations for Future Environments (LA SAFE)[23] (Spidalieri & Bennett, 2020c).

Although the majority of the HUD programs described above are tied to disasters, it is worth noting the range of resilience actions that HUD has undertaken, including addressing issues of housing, transportation, education, community centers, and implementing flood risk reduction measures to multiple hazards, including tidal flooding, stormwater, and episodic storm events. By doing so, HUD has demonstrated the ability to provide a more comprehensive approach to resilience in comparison with other federal programs whose funding might be used for relocation. This is important considering the numerous elements (e.g., housing, transportation, and education) that must be considered in community-driven relocation.

Agencies Not Primarily Disaster-Related

A number of other federal programs are generally proactive, unlike disaster-related programs, but they do not have sufficient funding for community relocations that are needed now or to prepare for future climate conditions (Howe et al., 2021).[24]

U.S. Army Corps of Engineers

The Civil Works Program of USACE is the main federal agency in charge of flood risk management (FRM), which stands as one of its three

[21]Which was reduced to 15.2 billion dollars as a request of sequestration (GAO, 2014).

[22]More information about the Isle de Jean Charles resettlement is available at https://islede-jeancharles.la.gov/

[23]More information about LA SAFE is available at https://lasafe.la.gov/

[24]As noted above, although BRIC and FMA are designated as pre-disaster grant programs, they are included in the previous section because their funding is tied to past disasters.

core missions.[25] Authorized through the 1960 Flood Control Act (P.L. 86-645) and subsequent amendments, USACE statutes require various authorizations through the Water Resources Development Act to work on individual or multiple water projects.[26] The Rivers and Harbor Act of 1968 (P.L. 90-483) authorized USACE to assist states and localities with water resource development projects and beach erosion control and to conduct flood control surveys. It is also the authority under which USACE conducts nonstructural projects, which have included community relocation. However, the requirement that USACE seek congressional authorization to address flood risk in a specific locality, with no organic statute governing overall authority of USACE to determine its own agenda, has resulted in piecemeal and inequitable distribution of FRM projects.

USACE's FRM program does evaluate, recommend, and fund nonstructural measures, including buyouts and relocations, to reduce the risks of flooding from fluvial or coastal sources, and it authorizes "relocation with a view toward formulating the most economically, socially, and environmentally acceptable means of reducing or preventing flood damages" (33 U.S.C., § 701b-11). To this end, USACE's National Nonstructural Committee advises USACE internally on policies and processes to increase the capacity of USACE to implement nonstructural measures.[27]

Although used sporadically in the past, USACE's use of nonstructural measures is growing, as indicated by the designation of 296 million dollars largely for elevating and floodproofing structures through the Southwest Coastal Louisiana Project[28] (through IIJA; Renfro, 2022). However, notably, relocation is not identified as one of the nonstructural measures that will be pursued in this project. Furthermore, the Coastal Texas Protection and Restoration Feasibility Study final report (USACE & Texas General Land Office, 2021, p. 35) finds that "managed retreat" was "determined not to be a practicable and standalone solution" to reduce impacts from a wide array of coastal hazards but that "managed retreat" could "work in combination with a structural system to manage residual risk and address changes in future conditions." These examples show that while there may be increasing attention on nonstructural flood management measures, community relocation is not a predominant option.

[25]USACE's two other core missions are core missions support commercial navigation and the restoration of aquatic ecosystems. More information about the FRM mission is available at https://www.usace.army.mil/Missions/Civil-Works/Flood-Risk-Management/

[26]More information about the Water Resources Development Act is available at https://www.usace.army.mil/Missions/Civil-Works/Water-Resources-Development-Act/

[27]More information on the role of the National Nonstructural Committee is available at https://www.usace.army.mil/Missions/Civil-Works/Project-Planning/nnc/

[28]More information on the Southwest Coastal Louisiana Project is available at https://cims.coastal.louisiana.gov/outreach/Projects/SWCoastal

Natural Resources Conservation Service (NRCS)

The U.S. Department of Agriculture's NRCS administers several programs related to flooding and erosion control projects and watershed planning. The Watershed and Flood Prevention Operations program[29] and the Emergency Watershed Protection (EWP) program[30] both allow for structural measures, buyouts, and relocations to prevent erosion or reduce risk exposure. For a community to receive funds or technical assistance from NRCS watershed programs, a local sponsor (e.g., city, county, federally recognized tribe), working through their local NRCS office, must first demonstrate project feasibility. Once feasibility has been assessed, NRCS may authorize the proposed project, and then resources are made available to sponsors. EWP does require that an NRCS State Conservationist declare a "local watershed emergency," but it does not require an official federal or state disaster declaration.[31] Additionally, individual landowners who would like assistance from EWP must apply through a local sponsor. Funding from NRCS was used in the purchase of flood-damaged properties in Pecan Acres, a neighborhood in Pointe Coupee Parish, Louisiana, that had flooded almost 20 times in the past three decades (Louisiana Office of the Governor, 2023).

U.S. Department of the Interior (DOI)

The Bureau of Indian Affairs of DOI has small funding streams specific to tribes, inducing annual competitive grants awarded by the Tribal Climate Resilience Annual Awards Program.[32] Previously, this program only provided limited funds for planning, travel, and capacity building, but the Bipartisan Infrastructure Law enacted as the IIJA (P.L. 117-58) in 2021 provided 216 million dollars for climate resilience programs, with 130 million dollars for community relocation (DOI, 2022a; Flavelle, 2022). This funding has enabled Alaska tribes, including Newtok Village and the Village of Chefornak, to plan and carry out relocation efforts in a proactive way (Bureau of Indian Affairs, 2022). However, there are only 11 federally

[29]More information on the Watershed and Flood Prevention Operations program is available at https://www.nrcs.usda.gov/programs-initiatives/watershed-and-flood-prevention-operations-wfpo-program

[30]More information on the EWP program is available at https https://www.nrcs.usda.gov/programs-initiatives/ewp-emergency-watershed-protection

[31]Ibid.

[32]More information on the Tribal Climate Resilience Annual Awards Program is available at https://www.bia.gov/service/tcr-annual-awards-program

recognized tribes in the Gulf states,[33] so many Indigenous communities in need were not eligible to apply for these funds, and no tribe in the Gulf states has yet received funding (DOI, 2022b).

In partnership with FEMA, DOI also leads the new Voluntary Community-Driven Relocation program to assist tribal communities severely affected by climate-related environmental threats. At the November 30, 2022, White House Tribal Nations Summit, the Biden Administration committed the government to providing noncompetitively awarded funding to various federally recognized tribes, including the Chitimacha Tribe in Louisiana (DOI, 2022a).

U.S. Department of Transportation (DOT)

In contrast to several disaster-related programs, the Highway Trust Fund of DOT is distributed to all states annually for state and local priorities.[34] Although also inadequately funded in relation to needs, this consistent source of funding has allowed state and local governments to build and maintain the staffing capacity and expertise needed to implement and maintain infrastructure over time. Adopting a funding model wherein funds are distributed annually to be used for state and local priorities provides a consistent source of funding that allows states and local governments to strategically pursue their own policies and plans, particularly those relating to capital improvements, in a way they might not be able to do with disaster-based funding, which is episodic. Which is to say, adopting a funding model that more closely resembles the DOT Highway Trust Fund might be beneficial for disaster and relocation planning.

The IIJA designates several DOT funding sources for transportation improvements, in addition to the governmental funding for the relocation of tribal communities via the Bureau of Indian Affairs described above. Although these DOT programs are not directly related to relocation, they could be relevant to receiving communities for building up more sustainable and resilient transportation systems in anticipation of growing populations. One of these funding sources is the Rebuilding American Infrastructure

[33]This list includes tribes that do not reside along the Gulf portion of Gulf states (e.g., Ysleta del Sur Pueblo, El Paso, Texas): Poarch Band of Creek Indians (Alabama), Seminole Tribe of Florida, Miccosukee Tribe of Indians (Florida), Coushatta Tribe of Louisiana, Jena Band of Choctaw Indians (Louisiana), Tunica-Biloxi Indian Tribe (Louisiana), Chitimacha Tribe of Louisiana, Mississippi Band of Choctaw Indians, Alabama-Coushatta Tribe of Texas, Ysleta del Sur Pueblo (Texas), and Kickapoo Traditional Tribe of Texas.

[34]More information about the Highway Trust Fund is available at https://www.fhwa.dot.gov/policy/olsp/fundingfederalaid/07.cfm

with Sustainability and Equity Discretionary Grant program.[35] This is not a new source, but 1.5 billion dollars was allocated in the IIJA.[36] The IIJA also created a new Rural Surface Transportation grant program, allocating 300 million dollars[37] to "increase connectivity; to improve the safety and reliability of the movement of people and freight; and to generate regional economic growth and improving quality of life" (§11132, IIJA). The IIJA also increases DOT's funding for the Transportation Alternatives Program that supports "pedestrian and bike infrastructure, recreational trails, safe routes to school and more."[38] Again, this funding could be relevant in preparing receiving communities to offer sustainable transit options to new and current residents.

U.S. Environmental Protection Agency (EPA)

In an effort to mitigate a different set of environmental risks than those related to climate change, EPA grants the authority to fund permanent relocations of residents, buildings, and community facilities as a remedial action[39] to protect against the effects of pollution through its Comprehensive Environmental Response, Compensation, and Liability Act of 1980 (CERCLA; P.L. 96-510), also known as its Superfund Program. A presidential determination is required to the effect that relocation is more cost-effective and environmentally preferable to alternative management strategies to protect public health from exposure to hazardous substances. Similar authorities exist under the EPA National Contingency Plan,[40] and implementation of EPA's relocation policy is governed by the Uniform Relocation Assistance and Real Property Acquisition Policies Act of 1970 (P.L. 91-646), which provides "for uniform and equitable treatment of persons displaced from their homes, businesses, or farms by Federal and federally assisted programs and to establish uniform and equitable land acquisition policies for Federal and federally assisted programs."[41] EPA uses the

[35]More information about the Rebuilding American Infrastructure with Sustainability and Equity program is available at https://www.transportation.gov/RAISEgrants/about

[36]More information about IIJA is available at https://www.transportation.gov/bipartisan-infrastructure-law/fact-sheet-equity-bipartisan-infrastructure-law

[37]Ibid.

[38]Ibid.

[39]More information about EPA grants to support permanent relocation is available at https://www.epa.gov/superfund/superfund-relocation-information

[40]More information about the National Contingency Plan is available at https://www.epa.gov/emergency-response/national-oil-and-hazardous-substances-pollution-contingency-plan-ncp-overview

[41]More information about the Uniform Relocation Assistance and Real Property Acquisition Policies Act of 1970 is available at https://www.govinfo.gov/app/details/COMPS-1432#

services of USACE and the Bureau of Reclamation to assist in conducting relocations.

As of October 2019, permanent relocations of businesses or residences had only been implemented by EPA at "33 of the more than 1,700 final and deleted sites on the Superfund National Priorities List" (EPA, 2019a, p. 1). "Of those 33, only 11 sites" were due to human health concerns; 19 of the remaining 22 relocations "were for engineering solutions" required for a cleanup remedy (EPA, 2019a, p. 1). This is reflective of CERCLA's preference for cleanup solutions over permanent relocation (Scott, 2014).

Under CERCLA, the decision to conduct a relocation is made following an EPA technical analysis of available remedies. EPA has created several opportunities for community involvement and provides extensive information on its residential relocation policies on its Superfund relocation information website.[42] EPA stresses that community involvement must occur early and frequently throughout the relocation process. When a permanent relocation is under consideration, EPA offers access to an independent relocation technical expert or advisor to assist residents and businesses.

The consequences of EPA's relocations have not been well documented. Documentation that does exist shows mixed results, with a need for further attention to the consequences of these relocations. In the case of the Escambia Wood site in Florida, the EPA Office of Inspector General conducted a follow-up survey of a subset of homeowners who were relocated (Office of Inspector General, 2004). Respondents reported a number of concerns, including inadequate compensation for properties and a lack of transparency on how appraisals were carried out. Of note, people who identified their own new homes rather than moving into the homes that the government provided were more satisfied.

It has been suggested that a legal framework analogous to the CERCLA provision could be developed in the context of relocating communities affected by climate change (Scott, 2014). CERCLA can be used to support relocation for communities that face climate hazards *and* are near a Superfund site or other affected sites, such as areas close to chemical spills during disasters. Scott (2014) suggests that such a law applying to environmentally displaced persons could be funded through a tax or fee on greenhouse gas emissions. This example demonstrates an existing relocation framework from which lessons can be drawn and applied to making community-driven relocation an achievable adaptation strategy.

[42]More information about Superfund community involvement tools and resources is available at https://www.epa.gov/superfund/superfund-community-involvement-tools-and-resources

Justice40 Initiative

The Justice40 Initiative is an unprecedented commitment by the federal government, established through Executive Order 14008 in 2021, to make "40 percent of overall benefits of certain federal investments flow to disadvantaged communities that are marginalized, underserved, and overburdened by pollution."[43] As the committee heard during the study's workshops across the U.S. Gulf Coast, perhaps most starkly in Port Arthur, many of the communities facing environmental threats, such as increasingly destructive hurricanes, subsidence, and sea level rise, are also overburdened by industrial pollution (see Chapter 5). Thus, the White House's push to increase the flow of federal funding to disadvantaged communities through Justice40 could also help to increase funding available to help these communities relocate if they choose to do so. Hilton Kelley, founder and director of Community In-power and Development Association Inc., spoke on this issue at the committee's first workshop:

> *The large number of emissions that were being dumped from the air, like sulfur dioxide, benzine, ethylene oxide—you name it and people in West Port Arthur breathe it. And we have scars to prove it. Many of us have died. Many of us are still suffering with cancer and respiratory problems like liver and kidney disease.*

Every federal agency has been tasked with "identifying which of their programs are covered under the Justice40 Initiative, and to begin" reforming these programs so that they deliver benefits to marginalized communities and those overburdened by pollution.[44] Under FEMA, these programs include BRIC and FMA (including the Swift Current Initiative); under HUD, they are CDBG-DR and ICDBG. Additionally, FEMA has been tasked with the oversight of the Community Disaster Resilience Zones Act, which seeks to identify and designate underserved communities and provide targeted assistance to help them reduce their risk to natural hazards and disasters.[45] Although this is not a part of the Justice40 Initiative, it is recommended that when designating these zones, FEMA align with the initiative.[46] At

---

[43]More information about the Justice40 Initiative is available at https://www.whitehouse.gov/environmentaljustice/justice40/

[44]Ibid.

[45]More information about the Community Disaster Resilience Zones Act is available at https://www.fema.gov/flood-maps/products-tools/national-risk-index/community-disaster-resilience-zones

[46]More information about public input into the implementation of Community Disaster Resilience Zones is available at https://www.fema.gov/fact-sheet/summary-request-information-implementation-community-disaster-resilience-zones

the time of this report's publication, FEMA was developing a method to identify these areas and determine the types of assistance it might provide.

Federal Nonfinancial Technical Assistance for Flood Events

In addition to funding, federal agencies provide important resources to state and localities before, during, and after flood events (Smith, 2011; Snel et al., 2020, 2021). These resources include the provision of technical assistance or "programs, activities, and services provided by federal agencies to strengthen the capacity of grant recipients and to improve their performance of grant functions" (GAO, 2020c, p. 3). Technical information is provided through training and education related to, for example, how to reduce disaster damage and develop and assess mitigation plans,[47] and the delivery of useful localized information, such as flood maps. However, there are problems with some of the information. For instance, many of FEMA's flood maps are outdated and inaccurate, and they do not account for future flood risk (Kuta, 2022; Lehmann, 2020; Marsooli et al., 2019). The work to identify future climate predictions from the National Oceanic and Atmospheric Administration (NOAA) is not integrated into other agencies' decision-making processes and funding allocations.

In some instances, a lack of data and information-sharing requirements from governmental agencies has opened the door for other stakeholders to step in and provide information about the scale or nature of potential environmental threats. For example, the United States does not have a federal requirement for home sellers to disclose information to prospective buyers about a property's flood risk, flooding history, or previous flood damage (Scata, 2019). In the absence of a federal requirement, flood risk disclosure has become available on real estate market and other websites, which may incentivize people to move away from or not purchase properties in flood-prone areas.[48] This information on flood risk does little to help those located in these areas who seek to move, however, and in fact, may further hamper their ability to do so. For example, if one's home is identified as being in a high-risk area via the Zillow app and such data lack connection to planned capital projects to reduce local flood risks, one's home is still devalued. Additionally, risk information coming from multiple entities without clearly defined roles and uses, and with varying levels of robustness, can cause confusion for users. While raising risks is a valuable

---

[47]More information about examples of technical assistance provided by FEMA is available at https://www.fema.gov/grants/mitigation/building-resilient-infrastructure-communities/direct-technical-assistance/communities

[48]One such organization is Risk Factor; more information is available at https://riskfactor.com/

contribution, risks without context and optionality present more challenges for the very communities already facing those risks. Without more federal support to contextualize risk data, organizations seeing market demand for this information will continue to provide resources without federal or state coordination on the implications of those data.

In another case, the Gulf Coast Community Design Studio (GCCDS) realized that many coastal residents devastated by Hurricane Katrina's storm surge were unsure of the cost of reconstruction. GCCDS sought to reduce this uncertainty for residents in Biloxi, Mississippi, by creating a map of affected areas at the parcel scale that visually depicted the projected heights to which houses would need to be rebuilt to comply with FEMA's advisory base flood elevation maps; see Figure 9-3. Such advisory base flood elevation maps are often created following a major disaster as an update to pre-existing flood insurance rate maps, so that community officials and residents have the most recent information available to inform post-disaster reconstruction standards. The image in Figure 9-3 was created by overlaying planimetric data at the parcel level and projected elevation estimates to provide more useful information to residents as they sought to determine how high they would be required to elevate their homes, something an advisory base flood elevation map does not provide. Communities, however, cannot depend on regional institutions to provide pro bono services to understand risks and associated costs of risk reduction. More substantive investments in risk awareness, preparedness, and community-driven decision making are necessary.

In addition to gaps in the provision of locally contextualized data to improve decision making, significant problems exist relative to the creation of federal disaster assistance policies that are flexible enough to better reflect unique localized conditions. Several studies have suggested methods of improving federal flood mitigation policies, including strengthening partnerships between relevant actors; considering bottom-up and participatory processes for policy making and resilience planning and implementation; and recognizing key social factors (i.e., factors that influence where households decide to locate) to foster community acceptance, avoid administrative burdens on individuals, and prevent unfavorable socioeconomic outcomes (Greer & Trainor, 2021; Hemmati et al., 2021; Suykens et al., 2019). Evident within these studies is the need for more, and more specific, federal assistance to establish collaborative structures and to substantiate the coordination required for the degree of risks and likely needs for mitigation measures.

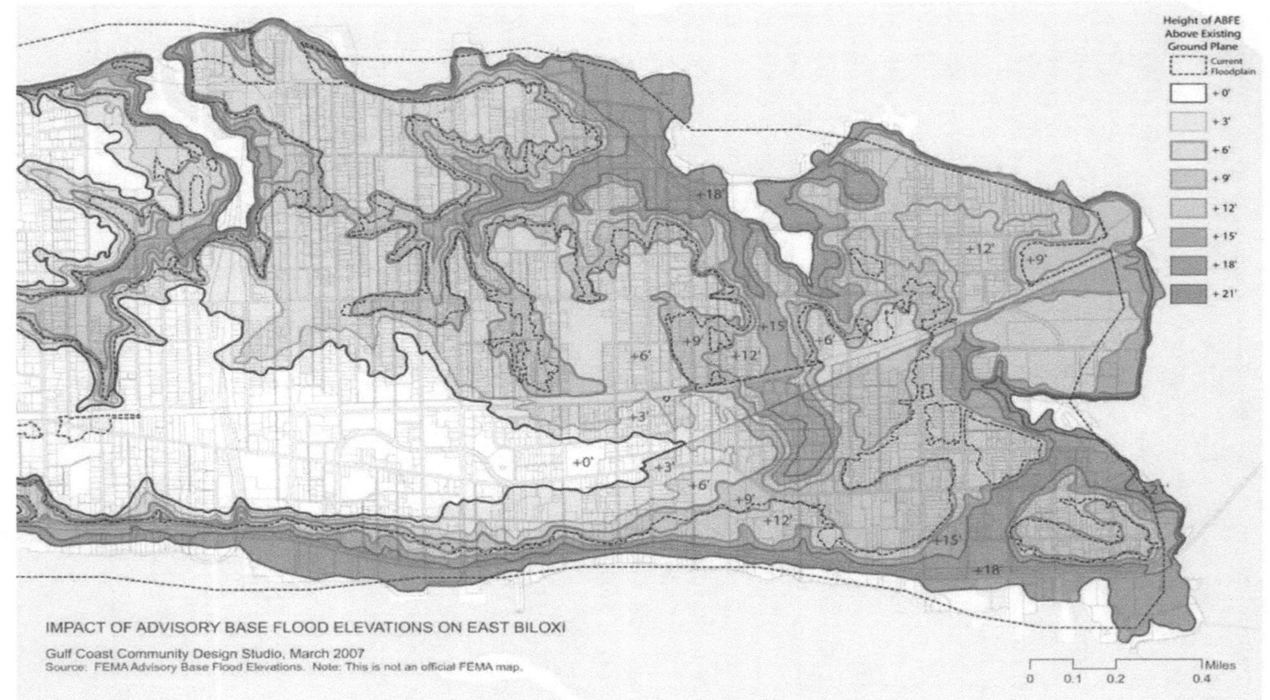

FIGURE 9-3 Impact of advisory base flood elevations on elevation requirements during post-disaster reconstruction of the Biloxi, Mississippi, peninsula.
SOURCE: Gaspar, C. (2007). *GISCorps volunteer teaches GIS to Gulf Coast community design studio team in Biloxi, Mississippi.* GISCorps. https://www.giscorps.org/biloxi_022/#

STATEWIDE RELOCATION AND PLANNING EFFORTS

This section first looks across the United States at what several states have done to address the need for relocation in the face of climate change. It then discusses in detail a range of efforts in Texas.

National Overview

Several coastal states and local governments outside the Gulf region have developed long-term buyout programs or offices such as Blue Acres in New Jersey and ReBuild NC in North Carolina to administer federal buyout funding and conduct related long-term planning (e.g., identifying high flood risk areas). In 1995, New Jersey's Department of Environmental Protection created the Blue Acres program, a revolving grant program that is designed to relocate families whose homes are at risk of flooding and to convert these lands to parks, natural flood storage, and open space.[49] The program has two primary aims: to provide post-disaster funding to assist flood-damaged homes, and to proactively acquire land that has been damaged in the past or to acquire land that is prone to future damages and can serve as a means to protect adjacent communities (see Chapter 3). Much of the program's funding comes from FEMA's HMGP and HUD's CDBG-DR (see Chapter 3 for more information about Blue Acres funding).

The North Carolina Office of Recovery and Resiliency, or ReBuild NC, was created following Hurricane Florence to lead the state's recovery efforts. The office manages almost a billion dollars in HUD CDBG-DR and CDBG-MIT funding through several long-term disaster recovery programs that assist homeowners affected by disasters.[50] Through grants and loans, it supports rebuilding, replacing, relocating, or elevating damaged homes, while collaborating with local governments and organizations to enhance resilience, including infrastructure, ecosystems, and the well-being of residents. One of ReBuild's NC's programs is the Strategic Buyout Program, allowing eligible homeowners in flood-prone areas to sell their homes and relocate to safer areas, with purchased properties transformed into green spaces maintained by the local government. The primary funding for this program comes from CDBG-MIT, but CDBG-DR funds may also be used for "housing counseling activities and future program costs" (North Carolina Office of Recovery and Resiliency, 2023, p. 9).

State programs like Blue Acres and ReBuild NC's Strategic Buyout Program are unique because they are able to address shortfalls in federal programs. These ongoing programs facilitate buyouts across the state by pulling together funding from, at times, multiple federal (and state, in

[49]More information about Blue Acres is available at https://dep.nj.gov/blueacres/

[50]More information about ReBuild NC is available at https://www.rebuild.nc.gov/about-us

the case of Blue Acres) agencies and partnering with local organizations to address the numerous elements of relocation. For example, Blue Acres partnered with local nonprofits to help individuals cover moving expenses and legal fees (FEMA, 2021a). This continuous funding allows for more long-term planning surrounding relocation than is often possible in the traditional federal buyout process, which also tends to take much longer to implement. For states without such programs, community organizations have emerged to fill gaps. For example, Buy-In Community Planning (a nonprofit founded in 2020) helps households with "planning for and relocating to safer areas."[51] (See Private and Public-Private Funding and Programs section below for more information.)

Some states have also developed programs to address more specific shortfalls of federal funding, including limitations tied to the provision of pre-disaster fair market value for prospective applicant housing—a limitation that hampers the ability of low-income homeowners to identify housing options of comparable size and good condition in areas of lesser hazard risk. To address this issue, North Carolina created the State Acquisition and Relocation Fund (SARF), which provides up to $50,000 in state money on top of a federal buyout offer through HMGP (North Carolina Department of Public Safety, 2019; Smith, 2014). Funding for SARF also comes from HMGP funds distributed following Hurricanes Matthew and Florence and is administered by the North Carolina Division of Emergency Management (Pender County, 2019). As such, in addition to being "located in a Special Flood Hazard Area" and being an "owner-occupied primary residence at the time of the event," for a property to be eligible, it must have been approved for acquisition by FEMA HMGP during one of these two hurricanes (North Carolina Department of Public Safety & North Carolina Emergency Management, 2023). If SARF funds are used, the recipient is required to purchase a home in the county in which they resided but outside the floodplain (Smith, 2014). The stipulation tied to moving within the county sought to lessen the economic effects to the community and region tied to the loss of local tax base. In Rocky Mount and Kinston, North Carolina, this stipulation resulted in an estimated 90 and 97 percent of participants, respectively, staying within their municipality (Salvesen et al., 2018). The program's ability to track the movement of residents and the ability of residents to maintain their new homes given their limited financial resources proved challenging in many circumstances (Salvesen et al., 2018). This state program, as well as several others, was codified by the North Carolina legislature to include the development of triggering mechanisms that will result in their application based on the severity of the disaster (Smith, 2014).

[51]More information about Buy-In Community Planning is available at https://buy-in.org/aboutus

Most states have not historically planned for relocation, although this is slowly changing. Existing state plans tend to acknowledge the risks posed by climate change but offer limited funding and programmatic solutions to address the challenges. For example, the 2023 Louisiana Coastal Master Plan refers to the need for residents to move due to increasing flood risks and dedicates 11.2 billion dollars out of the 50-billion-dollar 50-year plan to implementing "nonstructural" measures (elevations, floodproofing, and voluntary relocation; Coastal Protection and Restoration Authority [CPRA], 2023b). However, since the original dedication of the funding in the 2012 Coastal Master Plan, the state implementation agency, CPRA, had not dedicated actual funding or staff capacity to develop this program. In the Fiscal Year 2024 Annual Plan, CPRA is funding nonstructural measures, with 3 million dollars a year for the next three years to develop the nonstructural program, in addition to funding 2.6 million dollars in Jefferson Parish and 13.7 million dollars over two years in Southwest Louisiana for home elevation projects (CPRA, 2023a). Although CPRA is now funding projects, the implementation of these measures will largely depend on other agencies, such as Jefferson Parish government or USACE, while CPRA works to develop its own implementation program in coordination with other state agencies. Furthermore, the 2024 Annual Plan does not include relocation or buyouts in any project descriptions (CPRA, 2023a).

States also set the priorities for federal HMGP funding (Smith et al., 2013)[52] and have substantial flexibility in doing so (FEMA, 2016), assuming the states meet FEMA-codified requirements. Problematically, the entities and criteria used in setting these priorities are not always easily accessible or easily understood. For example, in Alaska, the State Hazard Mitigation Advisory Council sets priorities, but nothing is available on the state's website about this entity or what it does for households. In Louisiana, the Governor's Office of Homeland Security and Emergency Preparedness offers examples of eligible HMGP activities and lists regional liaisons, including State Applicant Liaisons to help subrecipients develop grant applications.[53] In Texas, the Division of Emergency Management identifies priorities such as most impacted jurisdictions, vulnerabilities addressed, cost-effectiveness, and population served.[54] In Florida, the Division of Emergency Management's website notes that selection is delegated to

[52]More information about the acquisition of property by a state using FEMA allocated HMGP funding after a flood event is available at https://www.fema.gov/press-release/20230502/fact-sheet-acquisition-property-after-flood-event

[53]More information about HMGP in Louisiana is available at https://gohsep.la.gov/divisions/hazard-mitigation-assistance

[54]More information about HMGP in Texas is available at https://statutes.capitol.texas.gov/Docs/GV/htm/GV.418.htm

each county's Local Mitigation Strategy Working Group.[55] However, there remains little transparency into how priorities are set and by whom, and the same types of information are not readily available in Alabama[56] or Mississippi (although a direct contact with the Mitigation Officer is provided for both). Moreover, one important contextual consideration is that the rules associated with congressional and supplemental appropriations change in each federally declared disaster, making the process more challenging as states and local governments cannot always rely on past precedent.

State-level efforts to identify areas that could receive people who move are nascent. One example is the Bayou Culture Collaborative[57] of Louisiana; this working group considers the transition of coastal residents and their culture to other communities and how communities can be better prepared to receive them. Although CPRA seeks to engage with these types of groups, these efforts have not yet been incorporated into state-level planning.

In contrast, the Blue Acres program in New Jersey is entwined with other state-level planning and is involved with both planning and implementing relocation in the state. Blue Acres emphasizes the use of housing counselors and the purchase of contiguous parcels to foster the preservation of community. Blue Acres buyouts are part of both the state's disaster recovery and climate resilience strategies. To advance climate resilience, the program purchases undeveloped land as a proactive measure, using the land purchase to buffer adjacent communities from current or projected flooding, including flooding tied to sea level rise. Tenant relocation assistance was added to the program in 2017 to provide relocation assistance for renters being displaced by an acquisition of their rental property (Senate Bill 3401, 220th Legislature).

Another example can be found in North Carolina, where the governor's office, the State Director of Emergency Management, and the state legislature provided one-time funding to support a team of faculty and students at the University of North Carolina and North Carolina State University to assist six underresourced communities in attending to a range of issues not addressed by federal and state programs. These issues include conducting

[55]More information about HMGP in Florida is available at https://www.floridadisaster.org/dem/mitigation/hazard-mitigation-grant-program/

[56]More information about HMGP in Alabama is available at https://ema.alabama.gov/hazard-mitigation-grant-program/

[57]The Bayou Culture Collaborative is an informal group involving the Louisiana Folklore Society, the Center for Bayou Studies at Nicholls State University, the South Louisiana Wetlands Discovery Center, the Barataria-Terrebonne National Estuary Program, the Louisiana Division of the Arts Folklife Program, the University of Louisiana at Lafayette Center for Louisiana Studies, and other nonprofits. More information about the working group, Preparing Receiving Communities, is available at https://www.louisianafolklore.org/?p=1351

land suitability analysis to identify areas more appropriate for resettlement (see Chapter 8; Smith & Nguyen, 2021).

A Case Study of State Agencies and Buyouts: Texas

In Texas, the state provides funding support to local communities based on federal government allocations. Two significant state agencies in Texas that oversee buyout-related assistance to local communities are the Texas General Land Office (GLO) and the Texas Water Development Board (TWDB). These agencies are involved in buyout funding separately through both FEMA and HUD, and they both channel funds to local Texas communities. Harris County, which includes Houston, is the largest beneficiary of buyout funding from these agencies due to the scale of flood risk in the county. In Harris County, both TWDB and GLO work with various local agencies to implement buyout funding, obtaining support from different funding streams. In this way, TWDB and GLO help to reduce the burden on local entities to navigate the complex web of federal relocation funding.

GLO is responsible for administering and managing buyouts on behalf of HUD. Its main role is to act as a custodian of disaster recovery funding from HUD's CDBG-DR Program and distribute these funds to local communities in need to execute buyout programs. Currently, GLO is disbursing funds through its Local Buyout and Acquisition Program[58] specifically for the recovery efforts after Hurricane Harvey.

While GLO serves as the funding agency overseeing the buyout programs, the actual implementation of these programs is carried out by local agencies. In Harris County, this responsibility falls to the Harris County Community Services Department (HCCSD), which is accountable for various areas, including housing assistance, community development, and disaster recovery within the county. Within this department, the HCCSD Project Recovery program is responsible for implementing GLO's buyout program in Harris County.[59] The Project Recovery program is specifically designed to assist residents in recovering and rebuilding their homes following major disasters. It provides funding assistance that covers buyouts and relocation to support affected residents in their recovery efforts.

TWDB is a state agency that focuses on water resources planning and management. It plays a key role in addressing water-related challenges, including flood management, by providing financial assistance, technical support, and expertise to communities and agencies across the state. One

---

[58]More information about the Local Buyout and Acquisition Program is available at https://recovery.texas.gov/grant-administration/grant-implementation/buyouts-and-acquisitions/index.html

[59]More information about Project Recovery is available at https://harrisrecovery.org/

program administered by TWDB is the Flood Infrastructure Fund, which offers funding for various flood management initiatives, including property acquisition.[60]

To implement buyouts in Harris County, TWDB collaborates directly with the Harris County Flood Control District (HCFCD), a local agency responsible for managing flood control infrastructure and drainage systems in the county. Its primary objective is to mitigate flooding risks and safeguard lives and property from the impacts of severe storms. Under the Home Buyout Program of HCFCD, the agency submits applications to FEMA through TWDB and receives buyout funding from FMA (HCFCD, 2023). Through HCFCD, Harris County has the largest number of buyout properties in the most recent study (Mach et al., 2019).

The distinction between the roles and funding sources of HCCSD and HCFCD in Harris County highlights the fact that the fragmentation of relocation efforts at the federal and state levels trickles down to local communities. For example, the Project Recovery program by HCCSD specifically notes on its website that "[t]he Flood Control District also has a buyout program, but it is not the same as the Project Recovery program, and not everyone who qualifies for the HCFCD program will be eligible for the Project Recovery program."[61] Understandably, the two agencies focus on different issues (i.e., housing assistance and flood mitigation), but their separateness is not ideal. The decentralized approach and varying eligibility criteria among different agencies and programs underscore the confusion and administrative burdens of the lack of coordination and highlight the need for improved coordination and a more cohesive strategy for community-driven relocation at all levels of government.

REGIONAL COORDINATION IN THE GULF REGION

The Need for and Lack of Regional Coordination

For U.S. Gulf Coast states—Texas, Louisiana, Mississippi, Alabama, and Florida—there is no interstate or intrastate jurisdictional authority for planning. Such an authority could offer collective support between the existing Gulf Regional Planning Commission[62] (Mississippi); the Emerald

[60]More information about the Flood Infrastructure Fund is available at https://www.twdb.texas.gov/financial/programs/FIF/index.asp

[61]More information about the Project Recovery program by HCCSD is available at https://www.harrisrecovery.org/

[62]More information about the Gulf Regional Planning Commission is available at https://grpc.com/about-grpc/

Coast Regional Council[63] (Northwest Florida); and similar entities in Texas, Louisiana, and Alabama. The Gulf of Mexico Alliance (GOMA), a non-profit, emphasizes the need for such collaboration with representation from all five Gulf states and an Integrated Planning Cross-Team Initiative that "supports the implementation of adaptation, conservation, and resilience activities at the local community and regional scale" and includes team leads from Louisiana, Texas, and Mississippi.[64] By contrast, in the North-east, New York, New Jersey, and Connecticut coordinate interstate and intrastate planning efforts through the Regional Plan Association (RPA).[65] Although the geographic scale of the RPA's scope is much smaller than that of the Gulf states, both these regions have shared systems, whether economic, environmental, social, or otherwise. RPA informs policy makers and decision makers about economic development and public works through "independent research, planning, advocacy and vigorous public engagement effort"; it also convenes experts to develop long-range plans that shape "land use, transportation, the environment, and economic development."[66] In the Gulf region, similar regional strategies could identify opportunities for receiving communities and address the challenges of originating communities, readying the states and municipalities for more detailed efforts. While regional authorities can play an essential boundary-spanning role, there are myriad challenges associated with community-driven relocation that would require a multi-scalar planning approach spanning regional (i.e., watershed), county, municipal, neighborhood, and site scales in both areas from which people are moving and the ones to which they are moving.

As an example, the Texas Medical Center (TMC) is located near Buffalo Bayou in Houston. The bayou and the watershed that feeds it begin well upstream of TMC, yet TMC has to address bayou flooding in order to continue to provide health services during extreme rain events. Recognizing that watershed planning begins with the San Joaquin River and cascades through Texas, reaching Houston and eventually the bayou, TMC has to monitor upstream improvements and encourage promising flood management practices while also recognizing localized flooding risks that remain. Understanding those risks and the scale of the challenge, TMC invested in a pedestrian bridge system, a coping strategy, to manage floodwaters while upstream efforts to improve watershed management are underway (Fang et al., 2014).

---

[63]More information about the Emerald Coast Regional Council is available at https://www.ecrc.org/

[64]More information about GOMA is available at https://gulfofmexicoalliance.org/priority-issues/integrated-planning/

[65]More information about the RPA is available at https://rpa.org/our-region

[66]More information is available at https://rpa.org/about/about-rpa

Several important lessons were learned following Tropical Storm Allison, which struck in 2001. TMC sought to retrofit several buildings and infrastructure that were hard hit by the flooding rains, which caused over 2 billion dollars in damages to the medical campus (Minemyer, 2017). The retrofitting included the addition of berms, flood walls, and submarine doors protecting at-risk medical equipment and lab research (George, 2018). Health officials also took steps to mitigate risk. They purchased high-water vehicles; improved emergency response plans; and elevated emergency generators, switch stations, and laboratory research facilities that were formerly located in basements that were flooded during Tropical Storm Allison. As a result, when Hurricane Harvey hit, TMC was better prepared (George, 2018). While this work was going on, the Texas Watershed Planning Commission,[67] the HCFCD,[68] the city of Houston,[69] and the Buffalo Bayou Partnership[70] were all simultaneously working on watershed management and overall resilience approaches.

Gulf-Wide and State Planning Agencies and Organizations

State law can enable regional planning entities. For example, the 2013 Mississippi Code (MS.C. 17-1-33) identifies, as a responsibility of regional planning commissions (e.g., the Mississippi River Regional Planning Commission), the advising of counties, municipalities, and local areas in the state regarding planning matters to include zoning, planning, and subdivision regulations. Water resources management, highways and interstate transportation planning, public schools, recreational areas, urban development, and other areas concerning the acquisition and planning of land, building structures, and facilities are included under the purview of regional planning commissions working with local communities.

Regional planning commissions could collaborate to address changes to infrastructure and resource efficiency (including social services) in anticipation of or response to population shifts and growth in receiving communities. They could also leverage existing watershed planning initiatives to reprogram resulting coastal and riverine open spaces, advancing watershed performance alongside passive recreational strategies and restorative ecologies in the areas communities choose to leave. These efforts in high-risk areas could contribute to reducing the impacts of climatic and

[67]More information is available at https://www.tsswcb.texas.gov/index.php/programs/texas-nonpoint-source-management-program/watershed-protection-plan-program

[68]More information is available at https://www.hcfcd.org/About/Harris-Countys-Flooding-History/Hurricane-Harvey

[69]More information is available at https://www.rebuildhouston.org/drainage-utility-charge-faqs

[70]More information is available at https://buffalobayou.org/our-work/

environmental hazards (more details in Chapter 8). The following examples of the existing regional planning commissions within each state illustrate these possibilities.

Gulf-Wide Entities

GOMA was formed in 2004 by the governors of Alabama, Florida, Louisiana, Mississippi, and Texas to work collaboratively on priority issues, such as water resources, habitat restoration, wildlife and fisheries, and coastal community resilience. This partnership network includes "state and federal agencies, tribal governments, communities, academic organizations, businesses, and nongovernmental organizations" (GOMA, 2021). The coastal community resilience team's goals are to (a) "Increase communication, awareness, and knowledge of tools and resources to assist coastal stakeholders in becoming more resilient and sustainable"; (b) "promote the assessment of coastal risks and the availability of resilience and restoration products for those who live, work, visit, and do business in the Gulf of Mexico"; and (c) "promote adaptation, mitigation, and restoration as strategies to preserve heritage, conserve natural resources, and support the economic viability of the coast" (GOMA, 2021, p. 12). GOMA's mission is determined based on the Gulf states' interests, and partnerships such as these exist to accomplish shared goals and visions. Thus, if there is interest and need indicated by the states, GOMA's mission could be expanded to cover matters related to community-driven relocation within and across the Gulf states. Conversely, if community-driven relocation is not a priority of multiple Gulf states, it would not become a part of GOMA's mission.

The Gulf Caucus of the National Association of Counties (NACo) is another entity that has the potential to influence the coordination of community-driven relocation within U.S. Gulf Coast states. It is open to all elected officials in Alabama, Florida, Mississippi, Texas, and Louisiana. It was established after the Deepwater Horizon Oil Spill to promote a clearer understanding of problems that Gulf counties face.[71] Members have voting privileges in their respective city, county, or parish governments and therefore could have greater local impact on issues related to community-driven relocation than regional planning commissions. However, like GOMA, the NACo Gulf Caucus focuses on issues that all members agree are a priority. In the past, these have included federal assistance for flood control and coastal erosion mitigation, hurricane preparedness, tourist opportunities, and healthy coastal ecosystems and economy.

[71]More information is available at https://www.naco.org/articles/building-coastal-resilience-gulf-mexico

Florida

An example of a regional planning entity that could expand its focus to address community-driven relocation within Florida is the Tampa Bay Regional Planning Council (TBRPC), one of 10 regional councils in Florida, which covers six counties and multiple municipal governments. "The region's six counties, Citrus, Hernando, Hillsborough, Manatee, Pasco, and Pinellas are required by law to exercise regional cooperation through membership on the Council."[72] TBRPC[73] has the potential to address community-driven relocation more actively as it has planning and oversight responsibilities, which specifically include

> *environmental management, water quality and emergency preparedness planning, protection and restoration of the Tampa Bay estuary, economic analysis, coastal zone management, housing and infrastructure analysis, hurricane evacuation and recovery planning, development of regional impact review, local government comprehensive plan review, cross acceptance, dispute resolution, and review of transportation plans.*[74]

Although its recently released Regional Resiliency Action Plan[75] currently lacks mechanisms to address community-driven relocation, the structural capacity of the organization, connected as it is with many collaborative partners, is in place to do so. Moreover, the state's Department of Environmental Protection now requires "a coordinated approach [...] to improve the state's resilience to flooding and sea level rise"[76] so the pathway to orchestrate managed retreat discussions is in place.

Alabama

The South Alabama Regional Planning Commission (SARPC) "helps facilitate the deliberation and resolution of common problems and issues of member government representatives, elected and nonprofit officials and private-sector leaders throughout the South Alabama region."[77] The

---

[72]More information is available at https://www.tampa.gov/city-planning/citywide-vision/partners

[73]More information is available at https://tbrpc.org/

[74]See footnote 72.

[75]More information about the 2022 Regional Resiliency Action Plan is available at https://tbrpc.org/resiliency-planning/rrap/

[76]More information is available at http://www.leg.state.fl.us/statutes/index.cfm?App_mode=Display_Statute&Search_String=&URL=0300-0399/0380/Sections/0380.093.html

[77]More information about the SARPC is available at https://sarpc.org/

SARPC 2022 comprehensive economic development strategy includes this recognition:

> *[T]he 120-mile coastline of the Region's Coastline Warning Area (CWA) has historically been impacted and will continue to be impacted by tropical storms and hurricanes which will continue to disrupt the local economy due to either residents being displaced due to evacuations, businesses closing either temporarily or permanently, jobs and incomes being lost. Planning and being more [prepared] for disasters will make our Region more resilient and will substantially alleviate these negative economic impacts. (SARPC, 2022, p. 94)*

While SARPC primarily focuses on economic resilience, its role as a coordinating body could be adapted to address the issues of community-driven relocation. More holistically, as in the other U.S. Gulf Coast states, coastal planning commissions like SARPC could partner with other regional commissions, such as the Central Alabama Regional Planning and Development Commission or the East Alabama Regional Planning and Development Commission, to link assessments of coastal risk, population displacement, and receiving community readiness.

Mississippi

Mississippi's Gulf Regional Planning Commission (GRPC) provides general planning support to 15 member governments, 12 cities, and the three coastal counties.[78] Although GRPC is focused primarily on transportation, as a standing convener of a board of commissioners from across the coast and as liaisons to local public agencies and community members, the commission represents the type of collaborative network that could address issues related to community-driven relocation.

Louisiana

The New Orleans Regional Planning Commission (NORPC), composed of the Regional Planning Commission (RPC) and the Transportation Policy Committee (TPC), addresses regional issues on transportation, environment, and economic development.[79] While RPC represents the New Orleans metropolitan area, it is the governing board of one of Louisiana's eight

---

[78]More information about the GRPC is available at https://grpc.com/about-grpc/grpc-overview/

[79]More information about the New Orleans Regional Planning Commission is available at https://www.norpc.org/about/

multi-parish planning and development districts and functions as a part of the New Orleans region's Metropolitan Planning Organization (MPO). NORPC's TPC is the MPO for New Orleans, Hammond-Ponchatoula, Mandeville-Covington, and Slidell. All members of RPC are members of TPC, including mayors and other elected officials representing local areas and municipalities. Other members of TPC include representatives from freight, maritime, public transportation, and aviation industries.

RPC is "acting as the fiscal agent for Region 8 during the duration of the LWI Regional Capacity Building Grant. As fiscal agent, the RPC will facilitate the establishment of the Region 8 watershed coalition. Currently the Region 8 watershed coalition is in the planning phase under the Regional Steering Committee" (New Orleans Regional Planning Commission, n.d.). The state Louisiana Watershed Initiative was formed in May 2018 by Louisiana Governor John Bel Edwards' executive order (JBE 2018-16), which "called for several state agencies to form the Council on Watershed Management (Council) and develop a program that would support a regional approach to floodplain management."[80] The Initiative provides funding to programs to focus attention on watershed planning needs. They include a Watershed Projects Grant Program for local and regional projects; a State Projects Grant Program to facilitate the statewide flood mitigation strategy; a Regional Capacity Building Grant Program to grow staff capacity; and a statewide modeling effort to assess flood risk and risk reduction, to build on the state's data and modeling of coastal flooding, and to support education and outreach to build resilience. Such an initiative offers a replicable model for one that focuses on community-driven relocation, recognizing originating and receiving communities as part of a system or network, much like watersheds, and establishing funds to support a range of efforts to understand risks more fully, to grow risk awareness, and to engage communities in managed retreat discussions.

Texas

The Houston-Galveston Area Council already supports regional planning in numerous regional and sub-regional initiatives. For example, its recently released *Our Great Region 2040* emphasizes the importance of addressing resilience, specifically in the face of sea level rise (Houston-Galveston Area Council, n.d.).[81] While the plan does not identify relocation

[80]More information is available at https://www.adaptationclearinghouse.org/resources/louisiana-watershed-initiative.html

[81]More information about *Our Great Region 2040* is available at https://www.adaptationclearinghouse.org/resources/louisiana-watershed-initiative.html

per se, it does require "innovative adaptation strategies that help communities prepare for potential environmental changes, such as severe weather events and sea level rise" (Houston-Galveston Area Council , n.d., p. 16). The Houston-Galveston Area Council and the regional planning entities in other U.S. Gulf Coast states hold similar roles and thus similar potential to address managed retreat at a regional scale.

LOCAL GOVERNMENTS AND COMMUNITIES

Local-Level Buyout Programs and Planning

In addition to state programs, local buyout programs have been developed in some areas to address recognized shortfalls in federal initiatives (Smith et al., 2023). These programs are less common in the Gulf region, but they do exist. As described above, one is Harris County, which combines different funding sources to provide for both voluntary and mandatory buyouts (HCFCD, 2023). Participants in the committee's June 2022 Houston workshop who had been part of a mandatory buyout criticized the program on grounds that they did not receive adequate, clear, and timely information; such lags in the program led to low offers as housing values declined (National Academies of Sciences, Engineering, and Medicine, 2022c). Locally funded buyout efforts outside the Gulf region include Charlotte, North Carolina,[82] and Tulsa, Oklahoma.[83]

Local programs are not constrained by narrowly defined federal rules. Stormwater management fees are often used to support these programs (Smith et al., 2023). Charlotte/Mecklenburg County, North Carolina, has used a locally funded buyout program (drawing from CDBG-MIT funds and stormwater fees) to address multiple community goals identified in their parks and recreation, hazard mitigation, economic development, and environmental plans. More specifically, goals and objectives include reducing flood hazard vulnerability, improving recreational opportunities through greenway expansion, enhancing water quality in creeks and streams, and enhancing economic development in areas adjacent to the resulting greenways (Smith et al., 2023). Achieving these goals has benefitted from the targeting of geographically identified parcels, including homes, apartments, and vacant lots that may connect existing greenways, provide unique water

[82]More information about Charlotte, North Carolina's Floodplain Buyout Program is available at https://stormwaterservices.mecknc.gov/floodplain-buyout-program

[83]More information about flood mitigation in Tulsa, Oklahoma, is available at https://headwaterseconomics.org/wp-content/uploads/Tulsa-Report-R5.pdf, and more information about its buyout program is available in Smith et al. (2023).

retention areas, and serve as environmental education venues for adjacent schools (Smith et al., 2023). Houston Wilderness, a nonprofit organization based in Houston, Texas (described in more detail in the section below on private and public-private funding), also works to strategically identify priority buyout properties that will provide the most protection against catastrophic storms and heavy rainfall events. Furthermore, the creation of an ongoing source of funding provides county and municipal officials the time required to engage with prospective buyout participants over long time periods rather than the short time periods typically found when assessing the type of community engagement used to determine eligibility and initiate federally funded post-disaster buyout programs.

Tulsa, Oklahoma, began a locally funded buyout program prior to the codification of buyouts under the Stafford Act in 1988. It was supplemented with FEMA funding following a series of federal disaster declarations, including three in one year (Smith et al., 2023). Drawing from a local stormwater management fee, local sales tax, and bond revenues, the city has embarked on an ambitious program to acquire flood-hazard properties and convert the land into greenways, water retention areas, and ballfields. In addition, the city linked the buyout program to the adoption of higher codes and standards, joining the CRS, and zoning practices that address flood risk reduction (Smith et al., 2023). Gaining the public's support was crucial, and an extensive outreach effort has resulted in widespread public support. Following the acquisition of 900 properties, the city has not faced a federal flood disaster, and its CRS score of 1 (the highest possible) has resulted in a 45 percent reduction in flood insurance rates for all policyholders in the city (Smith et al., 2023).

A local government's planning department can also play a vital role in community-driven relocation efforts through the application and management of both land-use planning tools and processes, typically overseen by a town's land-use planner. One important example is the creation and administration of a comprehensive land-use plan itself, which is adopted by a local government and used to regulate and manage land use in a community. Typically, embedded in this kind of plan are several techniques directly relevant to the relocation process, including but not limited to land acquisition authorities, zoning, cluster development, tax increment financing, and open space management. Smaller jurisdictions may not have a land-use plan and may therefore benefit from assistance provided by regional planning entities described earlier in this chapter.

In many states, municipal governments are granted land use and zoning authority by state legislatures (known as home rule states); this authority has the potential to shape relocation strategies within a municipality, limit development in hazard areas, and ensure adequate resources outside of hazard areas for resettlers. Municipal governments in these states are given greater autonomy, and the states have limited power to interfere in local affairs. In other states, the legal principle known as "Dillon's Rule" limits the powers of local governments to what is expressly granted, implied, or essential by state legislatures or constitutions (Richardson et al., 2003). The differences in a state's regulatory control of land use exemplify the importance of recognizing state-local relationships, including how they can shape varied local managed retreat strategies.

One example of state law designating land use to municipalities is Texas' zoning enabling statute (Title 7, Chapter 211 of the Local Government Code) that provides for municipalities to adopt zoning regulations in accordance with a comprehensive plan. Another approach is to provide incentives for metropolitan planning efforts to conduct vulnerability assessments, which Florida does.[84] Such incentives can help communities develop land-use plans to facilitate and assist both receiving communities and people who need or want to relocate. For example, Florida's Hillsborough County has identified sending and receiving areas, to include waterfront and inland communities, in its Post-Disaster Redevelopment Plan (PDRP)[85] (see Chapter 8).

Another example comes from Charleston, South Carolina, which uses land elevation to map development guidance and where future development should be avoided.[86] Similarly, Carey (2020) notes that Kaua'i, Hawaii, requires setbacks based on expected shorelines at the end of the century, and Rhode Island uses "triggers" requiring structural removal at certain thresholds of sea level rise. Carey (2020) also shows how national policies that withdraw support for development in risky areas, which would likely be politically challenging in the United States, are now underway in Gatineau, Canada, where property recovery is capped at 50 percent damage, beyond which relocation is required (Carey, 2020). An example of a land-use plan that provides for resettlers is that of the Yellow Springs, Ohio, Comprehensive Land Use Plan.[87] Another example comes from Zebulon, North Carolina, which specifically provides for welcoming "newcomers."[88]

[84]More information about incentives is available at https://floridadep.gov/sites/default/files/VA%20Scope%20FINAL%202_0.pdf

[85]More information about the PDRP for Hillsborough County is available at https://www.hillsboroughcounty.org/en/residents/public-safety/emergency-management/post-disaster-redevelopment-plan

[86]More information about Charleston, South Carolina, is available at https://www.charleston-sc.gov/DocumentCenter/View/31227/Final-City-Plan-Adopted-October-12-2021

[87]More information about the Village of Yellow Springs, Ohio's Village Comprehensive Land Use Plan is available at https://www.yso.com/egov/documents/1426784623_42902.pdf

[88]More information about the town Zebulon's newcomer policy is available at https://www.townofzebulon.org/sites/default/files/uploads/planning/Documents/zebulon_comprehensive_land_use_plan.pdf

Land-use planning may also be required to qualify for—or at a minimum increase a locality's competitiveness for—federal funding. Whenever possible, FEMA advocates a consistent approach for hazard mitigation in a community, and it favors projects that are included in or closely align with, among others, the community's local HMP, comprehensive plan, transportation plan, stormwater management plan, and land-use plans, as applicable (FEMA, 2023e). While land-use planning is encouraged by FEMA as part of a community's set of strategies found in its HMP, the degree to which local governments adhere to this voluntary element of the planning process is limited (Lyles et al., 2014b). Furthermore, research has also found that few communities were coordinating HMPs with the emerging development of climate change adaptation plans (Lyles et al., 2014a). Incorporating climate adaptation strategies, such as community-driven relocation, across a jurisdiction's suite of plans could increase opportunities for relocation grants. Additionally, one study, which compared and evaluated cities' resilience and adaptation plans, concluded that resilience plans could be improved "by strengthening the fact base, addressing uncertainty, and including additional implementation guidance" (Woodruff et al., 2018, p. 65). As described below in the Norfolk case study, it is also critical that relocation plans clearly consider all the aspects needed to address the needs of resettlers and receiving communities. The inclusion of receiving communities in planning for and funding community-driven relocation is also emphasized in the National Climate Resilience Framework (White House, 2023; see Chapter 8 for more on receiving communities).

In practice, research has shown that the network of plans developed by communities can contain contradictory policies and investment strategies that may hinder community-driven relocation. For example, HMPs may guide development away from hazardous areas while comprehensive land-use plans, economic development plans, and capital improvement plans simultaneously encourage more development in areas known to be at significant risk to natural hazards, including those influenced or caused by climate change (Berke et al., 2015, 2019, 2021). Berke et al. (2019, p. 901) discuss the utility of a plan integration for resilience scorecard to identify "conflicts between plans" and "whether plans target areas that are most vulnerable." This information is intended to show communities that these contradictions are present and to take action to remedy the discrepancies, leading to more resilient communities.

Case Study of Applying Land-Use Planning to Address Relocation: Norfolk, Virginia

The city of Norfolk is one of the most vulnerable locations in the United States to the effects of rising sea level (Kramer, 2016). As a result of this threat, the city has incorporated resilience into its zoning ordinance to include several land-use tools to manage the need for some people to relocate by guiding new development to higher ground.[89] The ordinance includes a coastal resilience overlay zone that establishes explicit regulations for new development and redevelopment, as well as an upland resilience overlay, which incentivizes greater urban density in areas less prone to flooding. In addition, the city has adopted a resilience quotient system, which provides incentives for developers, who can earn points for the adoption of varied resilience-related activities that advance flood risk reduction across development types, including residential, commercial, and mixed uses (City of Norfolk, 2016). The number of points accrued is based on the size of the proposed development. The ordinance also provides points if development rights are extinguished or densities are reduced in the coastal resilience overlay district (see Figure 9-4).

A system that rewards receiving communities through a point system or other incentives to act has the potential to motivate these communities to be more receptive to accept those that need to relocate. In practice, an incentive-based system operationalized through ordinances and local laws has the potential to go beyond "encouraging" specific actions by providing concrete rewards to those participating in the process. However, this example incentivizes developers, not necessarily residents. More research is needed to understand how residents and receiving communities might be incentivized to welcome resettlers. This research would benefit from drawing from the existing literature that unpacks the motivation behind why people agree to relocate or stay in hazardous areas, as well as research that describes the need for more flexible policies that reflect local needs and conditions and the value of collaborative planning and problem solving.

PRIVATE AND PUBLIC-PRIVATE FUNDING AND PROGRAMS

Recognizing that local, state, and federal governments cannot address managed retreat on their own, there is a potential for major philanthropic programs and community organizations to play a role. (Note that the role of private insurance companies is discussed in Chapter 10.)

[89]More information about land-use tools is available at https://www.norfolk.gov/4542/Land-Use

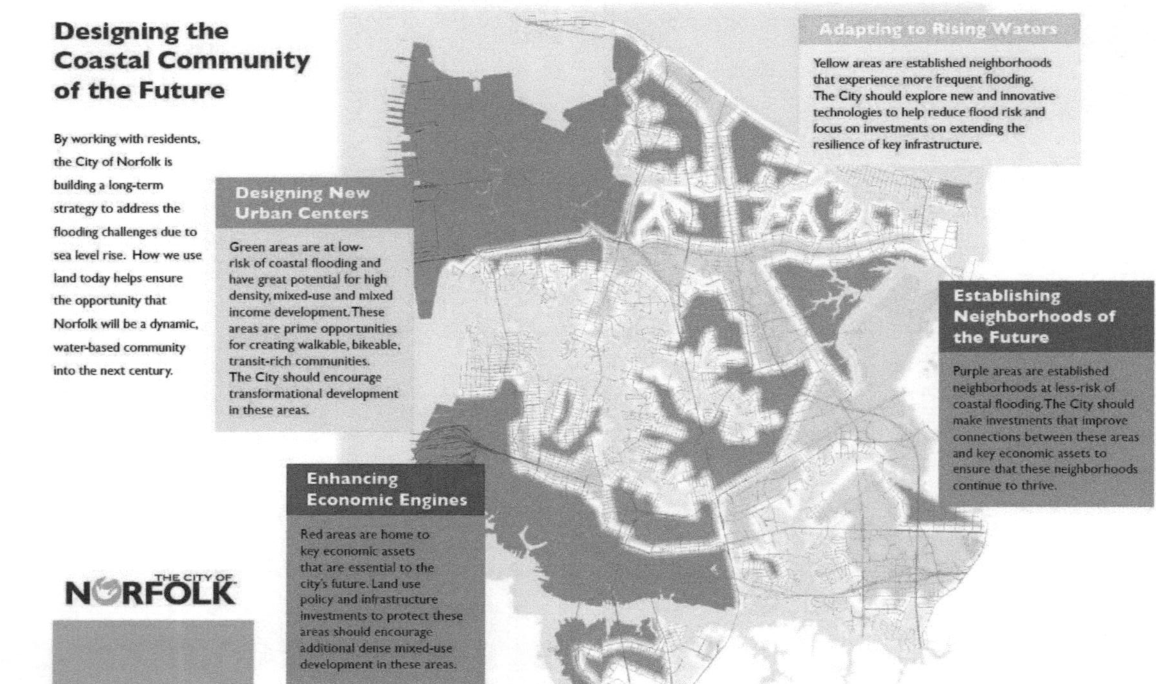

FIGURE 9-4 A community plan for reinvestment and disinvestment.
SOURCE: City of Norfolk. (2016). *Norfolk Vision 2100*. https://www.norfolk.gov/DocumentCenter/View/27768/Vision-2100---FINAL?bidId=

Following Hurricane Katrina, numerous philanthropies, including the Rockefeller Foundation, assisted the greater New Orleans metro area in its extended recovery effort. The foundation convened practitioners alongside financial resource providers to create a new type of coordinated conversation about recovery.[90] These efforts evolved into 100 Resilient Cities (100RC), a global program to help cities develop resilience strategies and to be able to consistently compare approaches while continuing to grow together.[91]

The Rockefeller Foundation also provided significant anchor funding to complement HUD's NDRC, which used funds from the appropriations bill that followed Hurricane Sandy toward this one-time competition, and implemented successful funding strategies developed in the Rebuild by Design competition.[92] Additionally, the Rockefeller Foundation provided technical assistance to applicants, helping them "identify recovery needs and innovative solutions."[93] The state of Louisiana received funding for LA SAFE (see above) and the relocation of the community on Isle de Jean Charles (see Chapter 3; HUD, 2016).

In 2019, the 100RC program came to a close, but the chief resilience officers continued their work by forming the Resilient Cities Network, which continues to this day.[94] The model that 100RC represented, which is well documented in its archives referenced and in the standing resilience plans developed, is based on a collective network of collaborators who continue to work in this space even as the Rockefeller Foundation reduced its funding and redirected its own programs toward global health. Additionally, although 100RC focused on city-level intervention, a report by the Urban Institute noted "increasing attention on the importance of national policy environments that enable coordination across levels of government" and the recent emphasis on improved national and regional coordination (McTarnaghan et al., 2022). McTarnaghan et al. (2022, p. 6) found that 100RC had mixed results in transforming city-level outcomes (e.g., in constructs such as transparency and accountability and government structure) but was successful in "[catalyzing] a movement around urban resilience." One

---

[90]More information about the Rockefeller Foundation is available at https://www.rockefellerfoundation.org/insights/perspective/what-the-rockefeller-foundation-has-learned-from-new-orleans/

[91]More information about 100RC is available at https://www.rockefellerfoundation.org/100-resilient-cities/

[92]More information about the Rebuild by Design competition is available at https://rebuildbydesign.org/hurricane-sandy-design-competition/

[93]More information is available at https://www.rockefellerfoundation.org/news/hud-awards-1-billion-through-national-disaster-resilience-competition/

[94]More information about the Resilient Cities Network is available at https://resilientcitiesnetwork.org/

of the challenges the program faced was a timeline that did not allow for the realization of long-term resilience goals (McTarnaghan et al., 2022); however, many cities are still in the process of delivering actions identified in the program.

In Texas, the Kinder Foundation[95] provides complementary resources to Houston's resilience program. The Center for Disaster Philanthropy[96] provides similar support. The Robert Wood Johnson Foundation and Kresge also support related activities, though in each of these cases the funding provided is primarily for planning, not for construction, particularly for convening to do the preliminary planning.[97] In parallel, and often in collaboration, other large-scale nonprofit organizations offer additional community support. For example, the Nature Conservancy works extensively with the U.S. Gulf Coast states[98] as does the Trust for Public Land.[99]

The intent is not to recognize each philanthropy active in the Gulf region but to recognize that many are active, have a history of responsiveness to regional crises, and have resources to significantly increase the capacities of local and state governments. However, at this time, there are no major philanthropic efforts to address the basic issue of relocation in the U.S. Gulf Coast, much less any effort to coordinate their collective power.

Smaller philanthropies, such as the Gulf Coast Community Foundation,[100] frequently pair up with the larger donors who vet the value of proposed programs or run their own localized programs. There are also notable efforts by other small nonprofit organizations, such as Climigration Network,[101] Anthropocene Alliance,[102] and Buy-In Community Planning,[103] which are working directly with communities in the Gulf. The Climigration Network seeks to assist coastal communities confronting the range of challenges associated with sea level rise. It seeks to build relationships between

[95]More information about the Kinder Foundation is available at http://kinderfoundation.org/about-us/mission/

[96]More information about the Center for Disaster Philanthropy is available at https://disasterphilanthropy.org/

[97]More information about the Robert Wood Johnson Foundation is available at https://www.rwjf.org/en/insights/our-research/2020/06/the-intersection-of-health--equity--and-climate-change.html and https://kresge.org/initiative/climate-resilience-and-urban-opportunity-cruo/

[98]More information about the Nature Conservancy is available at https://www.nature.org/en-us/about-us/where-we-work/united-states/

[99]More information about the Trust for Public Land is available at https://www.tpl.org/resource/trust-public-land-joins-partnership-gulf-coast-land-conservation

[100]More information about the Gulf Coast Community Foundation is available at https://www.gulfcoastcf.org/

[101]More information about the Climigration Network is available at https://www.climigration.org/

[102]More information about the Anthropocene Alliance is available at https://anthropocenealliance.org/

[103]See footnote 51.

practitioners and community organizations to "co-create new community-led, safe and equitable models for assisted relocation."[104] It organizes community dialogues and provides tools for community groups through its website. In addition, it offers small innovation grants to launch community-led projects to contend with questions surrounding relocation. Buy-In Community Planning seeks to facilitate a "holistic approach to buyout programs" that centers people, housing, and land, asking "Who wants to move?" "Where will they go?" and "What happens to the land that gets left behind?" Acknowledging limited government capacity, Kelly Main, executive director, described Buy-In Community Planning as aiming to become a "one-stop shop" for individuals and local governments who need assistance in applying for and keeping up with federal grant requirements and funding opportunities.[105] Additionally, a new and ongoing effort by the Coastal States Organization and the Association of State Floodplain Managers, in partnership with Annika Tomson, a NOAA Digital Coast Fellow, aims to "develop technical guidance resources to support local communities in planning for and managing residential coastal properties acquired or vacated due to erosion, inundation, and flooding worsened by climate change."[106]

Nonprofit organizations also leverage the use of buyouts for such activities as planting trees or using nature-based solutions in areas where buyouts have occurred. For example, Houston Wilderness has a program called Riverine Targeted Use of Buyouts Program.[107] This program implements a dual-strategy aimed at transforming flood-prone properties. Local and county government officials voluntarily acquire these properties. Once acquired, these properties undergo restorative enhancements using Green Stormwater Infrastructure techniques to enhance sustainability and encourage habitat restoration, such as introducing native plant species and implementing nature-based infrastructure; these are then managed either by the respective counties, municipalities, state agencies, or nongovernmental organizations. The program also supports policy and practice changes to maximize public benefit from the buyout land, including creating contingency plans for potential future flooding that may necessitate further buyouts of surrounding properties and fostering increased involvement of community-based organizations. Incorporating nature-based infrastructure

[104]More information is available at https://www.climigration.org/our-story

[105]Comments made to the committee on December 13, 2022, during the information-gathering session. More information is available at https://www.nationalacademies.org/event/12-13-2022/managed-retreat-in-the-us-gulf-coast-region-perspectives-and-approaches-to-property-acquisitions-challenges-and-lessons-learned

[106]More information about the NOAA Digital Coast Fellowship 2022–2024 project summaries is available at https://coast.noaa.gov/fellowship/digitalcoast/22_fellows.html

[107]More information about the Riverine Targeted Use of Buyouts Program is available at https://houstonwilderness.org/riverinetubs

onto contiguous buyout properties has proven beneficial in reducing flood risks to surrounding communities (Atoba et al., 2021; see Chapter 8). This implementation demonstrates not only the feasibility of such efforts but also the effectiveness of including additional ecological criteria in the flood buyout selection process. This approach can offer strong economic benefits without any compromise.

AN OVERVIEW OF THE MULTI-LEVEL CHANGE NEEDED

Federal agencies have many of the tools needed to help communities resettle under existing laws but are not proactively putting them into place with regulations, protocols, and cross-agency cooperation and collaboration, and no one agency is currently responsible for overseeing interpretation and coordination. As a result, although some have managed to do so, communities have no clear way to navigate the programs that *are* available to support relocation. Furthermore, the level of coordination for equitable community-driven relocation is currently insufficient among individual agencies operating within their current regulatory silos. For example, it is not within the capacity of state governments to enforce a seamless mode of collaboration among the various federal agencies and programs that may provide funding. Additionally, because programs are siloed, they can be at odds with each other, with one agency investing in redevelopment or protection (e.g., a levee) and another investing in buyouts of the same area. Notably, compared to federal funding assistance, which is application-based, private systems of small and large developers are the reality of how day-to-day operations function for households and municipalities. They drive whether we are intensifying development on the U.S. Gulf Coast, sustaining costly life there, or relocating, and for the most part the public and the public has no input on this process (Shi & Moser, 2021).

In the longer term, legislative change is needed. In the more immediate term, much can be done by capitalizing on existing programs—such as improving the utilization of local and state HMPs as decision-making tools—including capitalizing on land use as a risk reduction strategy and incorporating resettlement into these plans, while adapting FEMA's interpretation of cost-effectiveness, particularly when targeting clusters of buyout properties (see Chapter 10).

Much of the funding for relocation is associated with disaster recovery programs rather than programs that plan for community development and well-being whether pre- or post-disaster. Such an approach is insufficient. Programs also have to address the root causes of vulnerability, such as poverty, bad land-use choices and investments, and poor levels of community empowerment (see Chapter 6). While the presence of post-disaster funding may coincide with an individual, community, or local government's increased awareness of risk and an enhanced willingness to consider relocation (though the opposite may also be true), the compressed timeframe in which people are required to act often hampers effective community engagement, collective decision making, and the use of planning processes needed to address the myriad complexities tied to community-driven relocation. As discussed in detail above, another consequence of this association between relocation funding and post-disaster recovery is that since disaster-based funding is episodic, it may not be aligned with state and community policies, plans, or capacities to implement. Nor are there sufficient resources provided by federal and state agencies in pre-disaster timeframes over the long timescales needed to address the complexities of community-driven relocation. In addition, funding distribution models that are tied to disasters disadvantage areas where property values or population density are low because fewer total resources are available to address major infrastructure needs.

State planning entities such as the Department of Environmental Protection, which created Blue Acres in New Jersey, could play a greater role in community-driven relocation by driving the development of local capacity, plan preparations, and sustained engagements in originating and receiving communities (see Chapter 8). This is particularly important as states can systematically address shortfalls in federal buyout programs, to include creating their own programs or providing targeted assistance and complimentary state funding to better address the additional challenges of community-driven relocation, such as building the local capacity required to write and implement grants, develop buyout and resettlement strategies, and manage them over time.

State-based planning organizations such as GLO or CPRA (particularly the Coastal Advisory Commission on Coastal Protection, Restoration, and Conservation) could play a larger role by working across state agencies, and with other states, leveraging existing procedural systems to create room for discussions of community-driven relocation and to assess how coordinated actions can address shortfalls in state and local government programs and capabilities to act. More and more states, including Louisiana and Florida, have established chief resilience offices that coordinate adaptive governance actions to reduce risks to multiple hazards across all state agencies.

Regional planning commissions already plan for regional changes, such as shifts in population and associated resource needs for infrastructure or transportation. These entities could deepen their focus to address community-driven relocation, either within a state or from one state to another. The ability of regional planning commissions to undertake this type of work varies greatly due to existing staffing, expertise, and financial support needed to assist local governments and communities in addressing the complexities of relocation.

Community-driven relocation will require land-use planning undertaken at multiple scales, from neighborhoods and cities to watersheds, states, and regions, underscoring the value of regional coordination. In the U.S. Gulf Coast, this could be undertaken through the combined efforts of federal, U.S. Gulf Coast states, regional, and metropolitan and municipal planning entities. Such efforts could increase the capacity of local governments and cities by (a) assisting them in assessing natural hazards and climate change-induced risk; (b) conveying the implications of risk and social vulnerability; (c) identifying a network of partners to assist them; (d) developing community goals, objectives, and strategies to address these risks, to include community-driven relocation; (e) facilitating deep and enduring community engagement; (f) making community access to financial support easily accessible, timely, and long-lasting; and (g) assisting communities in developing an implementation strategy tied to a range of governmental and nongovernmental programs, technical assistance measures, and policies that can empower communities to act.

The network of partners would ideally have both institutional and Indigenous knowledge of both external programs and local conditions. It could also serve as a data repository to assist households and communities in relocating and identifying and helping receiving communities. The network could also assist in analyzing the capacity of originating communities to act and the potential of receiving communities to accommodate and accept resettlers (see Chapter 8). By working in both originating and receiving communities, the use of widely recognized land-use planning techniques (e.g., land acquisition, tax increment financing, greenway and park planning, transfer of development rights, capital improvements planning, land suitability analysis, cluster development) and participatory processes (e.g., collaborative planning, alternative dispute resolution, social learning, facilitation) could "serve as an incentive or a pull force, guiding development away from the risk towards areas of lower physical vulnerability" (Bukvic et al., 2022, p. 10).

There is also room for expanded involvement of nonprofit organizations and public-private organizations in planning and implementing relocation programs and policies. An important opportunity exists to deepen the reach of these organizations by bringing the larger philanthropic entities together, with an equivalent program focused on community-driven relocation to coordinate the various initiatives and complement municipal and state efforts. Partnerships with, and funding from, private foundations could facilitate the work of these nonprofit organizations, exemplifying the power of governance.

SUMMARY

This chapter provides an overview of the current framework of policy, funding, and planning as it relates to community-driven relocation. It highlights the limits of the traditional episodic, disaster-based approach to community resilience and the need for an integrated systems-based approach to supporting community relocation, where appropriate. This requires a coordinated, adaptive governance approach that addresses both the root causes of vulnerability and the critical needs of originating and receiving communities in the evolving relocation process. The next chapter describes specific policy challenges to community-driven relocation and ongoing and potential innovative solutions to those challenges, many of which draw directly from the framework laid out in this chapter. Finally, Chapter 11 contains recommendations for how to improve the process of community-driven relocation for those intending to pursue this option.

CONCLUSIONS

Conclusion 9-1: While federal agencies have many of the tools (e.g., funding, capacity) needed to help communities resettle under existing laws, and there are existing programs (e.g., the Federal Emergency Management Agency's Building Resilient Infrastructure and Communities and the Department of Housing and Urban Development's Community Development Block Grant Program) that have facilitated individual households and neighborhoods to relocate, there is currently no interagency coordination to enable community-driven relocation planning at the scale required to address the level of risks in the U.S. Gulf Coast. As a result, the existing programs are difficult for households and communities to navigate.

Conclusion 9-2: Most federal funding that can be used for relocation is available after a disaster occurs. This post-disaster, episodic funding format limits the capacity to plan for community-driven relocation at all levels of government.

Conclusion 9-3: States have some funding and capacity to assist with community-driven relocation, provided there is financial support from the federal government. States are closer to the communities in need of relocation and are in a position to provide more flexible and creative solutions than the federal government (e.g., relieving communities of the burden of providing matching funds, and making sure that those relocating will have suitable housing). While various state agencies in the Gulf region have supported particular relocations (e.g., Louisiana's

Office of Community Development's involvement with Pecan Acres or Isle de Jean Charles), no Gulf state has a comprehensive program to prioritize and serve all of the households and communities that potentially are seeking to relocate.

Conclusion 9-4: Regional entities within states and spanning states could help facilitate relocations within a given region, but no regional entity in the Gulf region has taken on this role.

Conclusion 9-5: While larger municipalities such as Travis County and Harris County in Texas are in a position to facilitate buyouts, most municipalities have limited resources to assist with relocations, and some municipal governments may be reluctant to facilitate relocation that erodes their tax base. Sub-municipal communities, neighborhoods, and individual households wishing to relocate typically must rely on their municipalities to apply for state and federal relocation assistance.

Conclusion 9-6: Targeted relocation planning funding, irrespective of individual disasters, needs to address community development and well-being, and encourage coordination between state and regional planning entities as well as municipalities. Central to this work is the co-creation of approaches alongside originating and receiving communities wherein land-use planning and community preparedness planning are mandatory investments.

Conclusion 9-7: Moving from a disaster-recovery model to an overall community relocation regime could entail evaluating the potential requirements to transition from a primarily competitive grant-making process to a process that places an increased emphasis on providing year-round funding and ongoing assistance to underresourced and at-risk communities to develop and implement risk reduction strategies, including long-term relocation planning.

10

Challenges and Opportunities for Policy

This chapter discusses the following:

- Challenges of the existing approach to community-driven relocation related to
  - Communications and responsibilities relating especially to buyout programs and environmental hazard risk
  - The role of insurance in community-driven relocation
  - Issues related to household eligibility for existing buyout and relocation-related programs
  - Issues related to program complexity, buyout process duration, and post-buyout requirements
  - Economic justice issues including benefit-cost analysis (BCA), outdated cost determinations, funding match requirements, and replacement housing costs and safety
- Opportunities for innovations under the existing legal framework related to knowledge sharing and learning, reducing barriers to obtaining grants, addressing the cost-effectiveness criterion, and implementing other solutions that improve the fairness of current practices related to community-driven relocation
- Lessons that can be learned from New Zealand and Fiji related to national policies that address relocation

INTRODUCTION

In the previous chapter, the committee discussed the complex web of policies, programs, and funding involved in pursuing community-driven relocation. This chapter follows closely from the framework laid out in Chapter 9 to describe the challenges that arise as a result of this web and some potential solutions, which are further defined in recommendations made in Chapter 11. In this chapter, the committee provides an overview of the numerous challenges that households, local and state governments, as well as other community stakeholders face when navigating the relocation process; discusses ongoing innovations to the current system aimed at addressing some of these challenges; and summarizes two international community relocation case studies with lessons learned. The challenges fit into five overarching categories:

1. lack of clarity of responsibility between individual households and government (at various levels);
2. uneven access to and perverse incentives created by current flood insurance systems;
3. funding delays and uncertainties created by unclear and inconsistent eligibility requirements and a patchwork of eligibility criteria;
4. program designs that are too complex and long for homeowners and communities; and
5. economic requirements and determinations that place specific individuals and groups at a disadvantage.

The discussion of each of these categories includes issues of fairness, with examples of innovations to increase fairness in the community-driven relocation process. This chapter also reflects many of the concerns the committee heard from community members at information-gathering sessions over the course of the study.

CHALLENGES OF THE EXISTING APPROACH

This section looks at some of the challenges around the relocation process, and the disaster response system more generally, as it currently stands in the United States. Areas of challenge examined here include communications and responsibilities, insurance, the relationship between disaster funds appropriations and determinations of household eligibility, program complexity, and a lack of economic justice. Many of these areas have been discussed in previous chapters; here, the committee gives a detailed picture of these particular challenges to lay the groundwork for envisioning more effective and equitable approaches.

Communication Challenges

As discussed in Chapter 7, there is limited communication and transparency about the voluntary buyout process among agencies and between agencies, leaders, and residents. Sentiments from Kevin McKinney of Flood Victims of Richmond at the committee's first workshop in Houston, Texas,[1] echoed this limited communication:

> *I think that our government and elected officials need to educate the public and we need to hold our elected officials accountable for this [...] we need to educate our communities at least somehow in the buyout program process and tell them there is hope.*

In some cases, communication about these programs has been poor, which can impede participation in voluntary relocation programs (National Academies of Sciences, Engineering, and Medicine, 2022c). Lessons learned from buyout practices (e.g., those described throughout this chapter, particularly in the section titled Opportunities for Innovation Under the Existing Legal Framework) undertaken by one community have not been effectively shared with other communities, which further highlights the lack of policy learning from relocations efforts in the United States (Greer & Binder, 2017). Since inclusivity, timing, and consistency have been communication challenges in previous relocation efforts (Bragg et al., 2021), policies encouraging effective communication may increase community dialogue about relocation efforts and could help frame and communicate relocation projects to residents (de Vries, 2020). At the committee's information-gathering session on property acquisitions,[2] Courtney Wald-Wittkop, Blue Acres program manager, commented on the importance of communicating at the individual homeowner level as well as at the community level throughout the buyout process:

> *I think we also learned that, you know, when we talk about flooding, it's a people problem, right? This is where people are living, and it's largely their biggest investment. And so, we have to recognize that flooding doesn't just happen to individuals. It happens to communities as a whole. So, the conversation about where buyouts happen is maybe one-on-one with the homeowner, the sort of planning for buyouts and what can you do in terms of restoration after the fact; all of that needs to have a community-level*

---

[1]Comments made to the committee on June 8, 2022, during a public information-gathering session in Texas. More information is available at https://www.nationalacademies.org/event/06-08-2022/managed-retreat-in-the-us-gulf-coast-region-workshop-1

[2]Comments made to the committee on December 13, 2022, during a virtual public information-gathering session. More information is available at https://www.nationalacademies.org/event/12-13-2022/managed-retreat-in-the-us-gulf-coast-region-perspectives-and-approaches-to-property-acquisitions-challenges-and-lessons-learned

focus. And we need to consistently say that these buyout programs are community oriented. They need to be involved.

Communication and Flood Risk Disclosure

The communication of risk between buyers, sellers, and governmental bodies is also an essential element of successful community-driven relocation. Disclosing flood risk, communicating and socializing flood risk to the public, and keeping the public informed of the latest science driving flood risks are key factors in keeping people out of harm's way (Environmental, Social, and Governance Initiative, 2019). The process of buying and selling houses lacks transparency as the federal government (Scata, 2018) and many states do not have statutory or regulatory requirements that a seller disclose a property's flood vulnerability to a buyer (Evans & Baeder, 2022; Frank, 2021; Henstra & Thistlethwaite, 2018; The Wharton School of the University of Pennsylvania, 2019). This is changing in some states, with New York, for example, recently passing legislation that requires that sellers inform buyers if the property is in a flood risk area or has experienced flood damage (New York State, 2023). Another example is the bill proposed in Harris County after Hurricane Harvey that requires a seller to post a disclosure notice for residential property regarding floodplains, flood pools, floodways, or reservoirs (Texas SB 339). This lack of communication and transparency is a challenge to relocation in that market drivers, such as housing demand and broader real estate development, pass on flood risks to residential buyers, who are unaware of property risks. As a result, people continue to buy homes in flood-prone areas, many of them unknowingly placing a household's safety and financial security at risk (Frank, 2021; Hino & Burke, 2021). The need to equip communities with the information needed to "assess their climate risks" is highlighted as an objective in the National Climate Resilience Framework (White House, 2023, p. 17). The flipside of disclosing a property's flood risk (as described in Chapter 9) is that it can contribute to a market-driven retreat wherein people who cannot afford to move are trapped in a home with decreasing market value. Kelly Main, executive director of Buy-In Community Planning, described this phenomenon at the committee's webinar and suggested that buyout programs should be a safety net for people in this situation.[3]

Communication and Insurance

Additional challenges around communication arise around the role of insurance. Growing insurance crises, such as those in Louisiana and Florida, where premiums increase and insurers withdraw, have affected residents'

[3]Ibid.

ability to maintain coverage (Frank, 2023; Ubert, 2017). When homeowners understand their potential flood risk, they are more likely to incorporate flood risk adaptation measures; similarly, when proper incentives are provided, housing demand within a floodplain can be reduced (Hemmati et al., 2021). Notably, although premium increases and insurer withdrawals can effectively minimize housing demand in floodplains, they can also disproportionately force lower-income residents out of their community and away from their jobs and social networks, potentially placing them in a more economically and socially precarious situation, despite having moved out of a floodplain.

Flood Risk Responsibility

Beyond communicating risks, the responsibility to manage those risks is shared by residents and government bodies. Research about risk management in non-U.S. countries (Snel et al., 2021; Hegger et al., 2017; Valois, Bouchard et al., 2020) suggests that there is a broader acknowledgment of the need for a shared responsibility between the government and homeowners, yet homeowners are reluctant to accept this responsibility (Snel et al., 2021). This shift in responsibility from government bodies to homeowners is occurring due to (a) an increase in risks requiring all actors (government, private sector, households) to engage; (b) a lack of governmental resources such as finances and labor availability for enabling and implementing mitigation programs; (c) limited beneficiaries of risk reduction due to government policies; (d) rising physical and mental health impacts to the individual or household; (e) conflicting timescales between implementation, current/future value of projects, and governance; and (f) private property rights, where ultimately the homeowner is the sole decision maker (Hegger et al., 2017; Snel et al., 2021; Valois, Bouchard et al., 2020). A clear understanding of the government's role and responsibility to communicate risks and a homeowner's understanding of their role and responsibility for household decision making are both critical to a transparent and equitable relocation process.

However, in many cases in the Gulf region and beyond, communication around risk and recovery needs between government and homeowners remains disconnected because of ineffective engagement and communication processes (Chapter 7). To address this disconnect, governments could increase residents' flood risk awareness; improve the accessibility and timeliness of financial support; inform community members about and provide technical support for relocation options; and enact policies that aim to reduce flood risk, such as requiring new development to account for flood risk, requiring sellers to disclose flood risk, and requiring insurance providers to stipulate that homeowners build back to more resilient standards—examples of efforts to increase risk awareness from seller to buyer include New York State and Harris County, Texas, as described above. Other opportunities for the government to improve on flood risk communication can occur during the reclassification of regulatory floodplains.

The establishment of trusted communication channels between government bodies and homeowners could foster lasting relationships and result in effective communication and long-term transparency of process. As such, homeowners would be better positioned to assert responsibility for learning about and acting on their risks, including seeking out potential solutions that are available to reduce those risks (e.g., grants, financial aid); actively participating in engagement processes; using insurance, flood risk disclosure, and other market drivers that might impact the real estate market; and participating in collaborative processes to foster collective agency.

The Role of Insurance

Disaster insurance plays a critical role in recovery and securing financial resilience to disasters. Without insurance, most households lack sufficient savings to cover emergency expenses and the cost of rebuilding after a disaster. According to recent survey, over 10 percent of U.S. homeowners lack homeowners' insurance, an increase from around 5–8 percent a few years prior (Fields, 2023). Residents, especially those in poverty and of low socioeconomic status, who cannot afford costly disaster insurance (i.e., flood or earthquake) may have more difficulty recovering after disasters as a result (Substance Abuse and Mental Health Services Administration, 2017). Insurance enables households to mitigate damage costs and financial risk, enhancing recovery after disasters, as an inch of flooding can cost upward of $25,000 (Risk Factor, n.d.).[4] In addition, widespread uptake of flood insurance policies improves local economic recovery by increasing visitations to local commercial establishments, while a lack of flood insurance can widen inequalities in the post-disaster setting (Kousky, 2022).

However, the current insurance system also presents barriers to community-driven relocation by encouraging reconstruction to previous standards in the same high-risk locations rather than to improved resilience standards, thereby not addressing future risks. Furthermore, many households struggle to afford insurance premiums, making them more vulnerable when a disaster strikes and, in some cases, ineligible for federal recovery funding (which

[4]Risk Factor draws on data from government agencies including the National Oceanic and Atmospheric Administration, National Aeronautics and Space Administration, and U.S. Geological Survey to produce damage calculations. More information is available at https://help.riskfactor.com/hc/en-us/articles/360058025433-Data-sources-used-to-determine-a-property-s-Flood-Factor

may include a buyout option) that is tied to holding an insurance policy. Data reported by the National Association of Insurance Commissioners place Florida, Louisiana, and Texas in the top five most expensive states according to average homeowners' insurance premiums, with Mississippi coming in sixth (Insurance Information Institute, 2023). The lack of affordability was echoed by Chris Monforton, chief executive officer at Habitat for Humanity Mississippi Gulf Coast and speaker at the committee's virtual Focused Discussion: Gulf Coast Community Stakeholder Perspectives from Mississippi and Alabama.[5]

> *I got my insurance renewal on Saturday, and it doubled. It doubled from $6,000 to $12,000 a year. In Louisiana, there's two companies writing policies now. People are not able to afford it, and it's going to continue getting worse.*[6]

Insurance companies use climate and risk modeling to forecast their future risk and determine whether it is in their best financial interest to continue providing coverage to a given area (Gall, 2023). As a result, multiple large U.S. insurance companies have stopped covering home policies in some states, including California, Florida, and Louisiana (Gall, 2023). Although insurance companies keep their calculations private, pulling out of an area sends a clear message. One impact of this crisis is that states and residents rely more heavily on public wind pools (i.e., insurance coverage for residents and businesses in coastal areas usually for wind damage),[7] such as Citizens Property Insurance in Florida and Louisiana, which are insurers of last resort. These nonprofit organizations were put into place by the state when a severe event made clear that there was insufficient availability or affordability of insurance from the private sector. Although Citizens Property Insurance started as a last resort, it is now the top home insurer in Florida. While insurers of last resort provide coverage, they are typically more expensive for minimal protection (Clow, 2023). Related to housing costs (which include the cost of insurance), the committee also acknowledges that banks are changing lending policies by not lending as much to low-lying areas (i.e., bluelining), and credit rating agencies are assessing bond ratings and costs based on resilience. These changes do not necessarily account for the equity and well-being of households and local governments (Chung, 2019; Keenan & Bradt, 2020).

---

[5]See footnote 2.

[6]Limits in access to insurers through private companies lead people to insurers of last resort, which in Louisiana is Louisiana Citizens.

[7]More information about wind insurance pools is available at https://www.air-worldwide.com/publications/air-currents/2013/How-Coastal-Wind-Insurance-Pools-Can-Own-the-Risk/

Despite these barriers, there are promising practices using the National Flood Insurance Program's (NFIP's) Community Rating System (CRS), as well as new insurance developments. For example, following Hurricanes Ivan and Katrina, which hit the U.S. Gulf Coast in 2004 and 2005, respectively, insurance companies began raising rates and reducing coverage, causing many residents to drop their wind insurance. In response, the director of the Mitigation Resources Division of the Alabama Department of Insurance created a new program called Strengthen Alabama Homes.[8] The program is modeled on the work done by the Insurance Institute for Building and Home Safety, which aims to reduce a property's risk of being damaged or destroyed in a storm by fortifying homes, subsequently making the home less risky for companies to insure. The program is funded by insurance industry fees and has been successful in increasing insurance coverage in Alabama (Berlin, 2023). The NFIP and additional insurance developments that leverage parametric models to fill coverage gaps in high-risk areas and offer immediate relief post-disaster are discussed further in the sections below.

National Flood Insurance Program

Although the Federal Emergency Management Agency (FEMA) is one of the main potential funders for community-driven relocation projects, the NFIP (administered by FEMA) is one of the main reasons people are able to repair homes and businesses following major disasters and in turn to continue to live on the coast, even as it becomes increasingly costly and dangerous.[9] The NFIP was created by Congress in 1968 with the goals of reducing flood impacts by (a) "providing affordable insurance to property owners" who may experience flooding so they could recover quickly and (b) "encouraging communities to adopt and enforce floodplain management regulations" by requiring communities wishing to benefit from NFIP programs to adopt such regulations (FEMA, 2022d; Government Accountability Office [GAO], 2020b). Unfortunately, according to reporting by the *New York Times* in 2020, based on FEMA data, as many as 250,000 insurance policies violate NFIP requirements, and these insured properties account for over 1 billion dollars in flood claims over the past decade (Flavelle & Schwartz, 2020). Furthermore, the NFIP's land-use criteria, which

[8]More information about Strengthen Alabama Homes is available at https://strengthenalabamahomes.com/

[9]FEMA states that any homes or businesses in high-risk flood areas that have mortgages through a government-backed lender are required to have flood insurance (FEMA, 2022c). In many high-risk flood areas, private insurance companies have stopped offering coverage, signaling that the economic risks outweigh the benefits, and yet the NFIP and state subsidies (e.g., in Florida, Texas, and Louisiana) continue to make it feasible for those who can afford insurance to live on the coast.

"set the baseline for building and zoning ordinances" and are required for NFIP eligibility, haven't been updated since 1976 (Rush, 2022). In addition to flood insurance and floodplain management, the NFIP also requires that FEMA identify and map floodplains (FEMA, 2002). Still these maps do not take into account the effects of climate change that have been projected to increase 100-year flood levels in U.S. Gulf Coast counties, with 100-year flood events estimated to occur every 5–30 years (average across U.S. Gulf Coast counties) by the end of the 21st century (Marsooli et al., 2019). Nor do floodplains account for pluvial flooding due to cloudburst events, a growing concern in many communities (see Chapter 2).

Moreover, these subsidized policies do not account for the actual cost of living in high-risk areas, and the NFIP has been criticized for subsidizing insurance rates, thereby incentivizing development in flood-prone areas (Craig, 2019; Knowles & Kunreuther, 2014). This results in repetitive-loss properties that receive multiple claim payouts that far surpass insurance premiums. Repetitive-loss properties accounted for 30 percent of claim payouts between 1978 and 2004 but only about 1 percent of insurance policies (King, 2005). Craig (2019, p. 217) asserts that these properties are evidence of the NFIP facilitating building and rebuilding in risky areas "rather than encouraging property owners to migrate inland." These properties have become political and financial issues in U.S. Gulf Coast states. In 2005, following Hurricanes Katrina, Rita, and Wilma, the NFIP paid out more than it had in all prior years and ended up nearly 17 billion dollars in debt (GAO, 2020b).

This is changing with Risk Rating 2.0, a new FEMA methodology that was implemented in phases between October 2021 and April 2023 that is shifting the program to charge rates that are "[actuarially] sound, equitable, easier to understand, and better reflect a property's flood risk."[10] Across the U.S. Gulf Coast, Risk Rating 2.0 impacted premiums differently. For example, between May 2020 and October 2021, in Louisiana, 16.7 percent of single-family home NFIP policy premiums decreased while 74.3 percent increased by \$0–\$10, 6.8 percent increased by \$10–\$20, and 2.1 percent increased by more than \$20 (FEMA, n.d.). Notably, these changes do not reflect total rate changes as statutory requirements limit increases to 18 percent per year.[11] Risk Rating 2.0 does not currently have any means-tested affordability program and would need Congress to provide that directive. As of April 2023, only 47 of Louisiana's communities participated in the CRS; however, a national voluntary program to reduce premiums by recognizing community floodplain management programs that exceed NFIP

[10]More information about Risk Rating 2.0 is available at https://www.fema.gov/flood-insurance/risk-rating

[11]Ibid.

minimums is underway (FEMA, 2023b). Moreover, none of these participating communities meet the optimal Class 1 designation, which would allow for a 45 percent discount on premiums (FEMA, 2023b).

A recent analysis of over two decades of CRS classes and actions and NFIP flood loss data showed that "participation in CRS is associated with reduced flood damage claims," with percent reduction in claims roughly matching premium discounts (Gourevitch & Pinter, 2023, p. 5). Buyouts and acquisitions and other structural projects such as floodproofing and elevation were among the CRS activities associated with the greatest reduction in claims (Gourevitch & Pinter, 2023). Gourevitch and Pinter (2023, p. 8) suggest that because CRS benefits (in the form of premium discounts) go to individual policyholders, they create "perverse incentives for floodplain development," and a new model, which directs benefits to local governments for further flood mitigation, could be more beneficial.

FEMA estimates that on average, nationwide, only about 35 percent of households in Special Flood Hazard Areas have flood insurance. In comparison, less than 2 percent of those outside this area have flood insurance (FEMA, 2018). There is, however, high regional variation in flood insurance uptake, with take-up rates of NFIP insurance much higher in communities along the Gulf and East coasts (Kousky & Lingle, 2018). However, according to a representative survey of residents from 24 counties on the Texas Gulf Coast affected by Hurricane Harvey, only 23 percent of those whose homes were damaged had flood insurance (Hamel et al., 2017). Hamel et al. (2017) did not report whether or not survey participants lived in a Special Flood Hazard Area. Increasing rates through Risk Rating 2.0 could lead to a drop in policies unless there is a greater emphasis on improving community ratings and optimizing premium discounts. In April 2023, FEMA released data on the difference between the average current cost of insurance and the average risk-based cost of insurance expected by state, county, and ZIP code.[12] The expected increases are an average of $1,124 in Alabama, $1,256 in Florida, $1,091 in Louisiana, $1,279 in Mississippi, and $629 in Texas. In coastal areas in Florida and Louisiana increases are expected to be especially substantial. For instance, Plaquemines Parish, Louisiana, will experience an average increase of 546 percent (and does not participate in CRS), while a 278 percent increase is expected in Collier County, Florida (which does participate in CRS at Class 5 or a 25% discount; see Figure 10-1).[13]

[12]Data by price range or by state, ZIP code, and county level are available at https://www.fema.gov/flood-insurance/work-with-nfip/risk-rating/single-family-home

[13]More information about CRS classes and discounts is available at https://www.fema.gov/floodplain-management/community-rating-system. The list of CRS-eligible communities as of April 1, 2023, is available at https://www.fema.gov/sites/default/files/documents/fema_crs-eligible-communities_042023.pdf

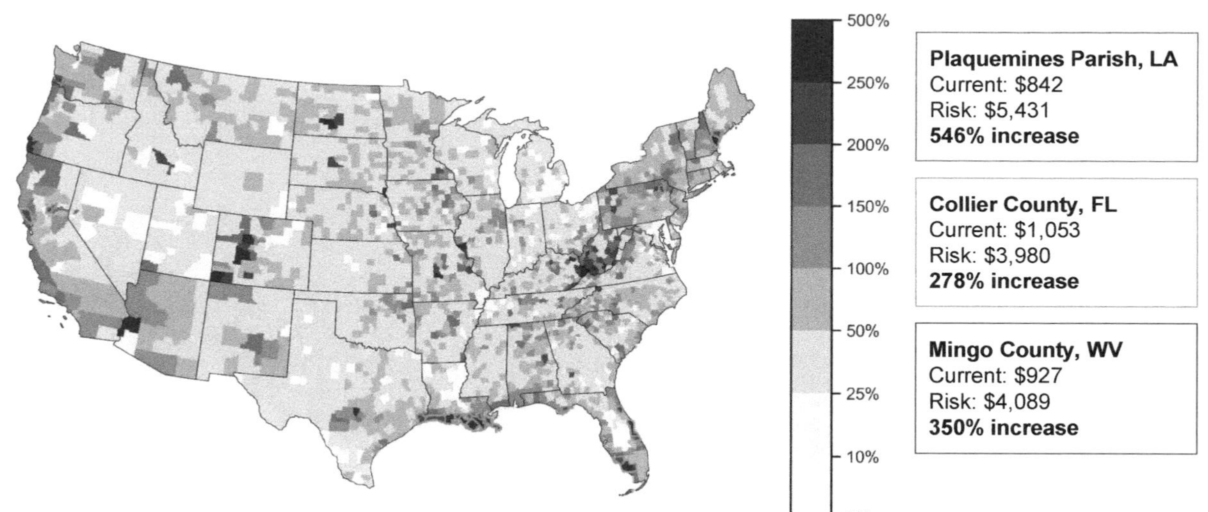

FIGURE 10-1 Percent change in insurance premiums during year one of Risk Rating 2.0 (current to risk based).
SOURCE: Data from https://www.fema.gov/flood-insurance/work-with-nfip/risk-rating/single-family-home

In addition to not being able to afford premiums, many households are not eligible for NFIP insurance (FEMA, 2018), including those located in areas without the required zoning ordinances (FEMA, 2018).[14] Although some are seeking alternative flood insurance from the private market, private insurers are limited due to the catastrophic losses that could be experienced from a flood event and the inability to cover these losses with a premium price that is affordable. Problematically for those outside of NFIP, the FEMA Flood Mitigation Assistance grant program requires individual homeowners to have NFIP policies to be eligible for buyouts (though this requirement is not clearly stated in the statute 42 U.S.C. § 4104c).

Parametric Insurance

Parametric insurance offers new ways of approaching risks.[15] Kousky and team at the Wharton Risk Management and Decision Processes Center at the University of Pennsylvania studied parametric insurance in depth and offered guidance on its value and its challenges. Parametric insurance, unlike traditional insurance, is a form of coverage that pays out when an objective measurement (or "trigger"), such as wind speed or flood levels, indicates a disaster has occurred rather than requiring an assessment of actual damage. The payout amount is predetermined and not linked to the exact cost of damages, enabling quicker, less bureaucratic responses to disasters and making it suitable for covering broader losses such as business interruption during a hurricane. However, this also introduces basis risk, where the payout may not fully cover the actual loss. Despite this, parametric insurance can effectively cover gaps in traditional insurance, provide immediate post-disaster financial assistance, and is being increasingly utilized to improve inclusivity and resilience in underserved communities (Sengupta & Kousky, 2020). In 2018, Louisiana reportedly "signed a three-year parametric policy for named storms with sustained winds of at least 80 miles per hour" (Martinez-Diaz et al., 2020) wherein the payout is 1.25 million dollars per storm (Passy, 2020); other river communities are considering it (Colman, 2020). While the review of varying types of available insurance is beyond the scope of this study, tools such as parametric and blended financial models offer broader resources and therefore broader payor groups (Sengupta & Kousky, 2020). Moreover, these types of policies are not only

[14]To be eligible, the individual must live in a community with ordinances that meet minimum federal requirements to restrict development within Special Flood Hazard Areas (same as 100-year floodplains; see 42 U.S.C. § 4012a). Development in these areas must have flood insurance and must comply with local floodplain management ordinances (42 U.S.C. § 4022).

[15]More information about parametric insurance is available at https://insights-north-america.aon.com/total-cost-of-risk/using-parametric-insurance-to-match-capital-to-climate-risk

for households but also for industries. For example, in the Caribbean, parametric insurance is in place for fisheries (World Bank, 2019a).

Community-Based Parametric Insurance

Community-based parametric insurance is a way of addressing some of the above challenges currently plaguing the U.S. insurance system. A small pilot program was initiated in New York City in early March 2023 to increase equity in flood recovery and support by quickly allocating post-disaster funds for low- and middle-income households (Kousky, 2023). The team represents a public-private partnership including the Environmental Defense Fund (EDF), the New York City Mayor's Office of Climate and Environmental Justice, the Center for New York City Neighborhoods, and St. Bernard Project (a Louisiana-based disaster relief nonprofit) (Kousky, 2023). The motivation behind this initiative was to assist disproportionately affected households in the New York City region who are flood prone and in need of recovery support after a disaster (Kousky & French, 2022). The goal is to enhance financial resilience in the area as "flooding is the costliest natural disaster and the risk is growing," and "low and moderate-income households suffer disproportionately from disasters and recover less quickly than more privileged residents" (EDF, n.d.). Many low- to middle-income households are unaware of potential risks when they first move in (as discussed above), and then are denied post-disaster loans and federal assistance, which are typically inadequate and slowly disseminated (Kousky, 2023).

The cross-sectoral team uses parametric risk transfer to provide quickly accessible and flexible funds from a reinsurance company, Swiss Re, to the Center for New York City Neighborhoods so they can provide small cash grants to pilot neighborhoods immediately following an extreme rainfall flood event. This program provides financial assistance to households while they wait for other slower forms of assistance (Kousky, 2023). The project has four components: deploy innovative insurance pilots, build a community of practice, link research to actionable change, and increase literacy and capacity (EDF, n.d.).

Housing Eligibility Criteria

Disaster appropriations (which are often drawn from for relocation activities) are conditioned by federal and state program guidelines and priorities, including household eligibility requirements. The complex web of agencies and programs that dictate eligibility (see Chapter 9) can be challenging to navigate for households. This section highlights some of the specific challenges associated with eligibility requirements.

Household Eligibility

There is lack of transparency in eligibility criteria about who qualifies for a buyout (Siders, 2019), and those who do not hold clear titles to their homes may not be eligible. For example, rental properties and those in traditional communities where the title is informally handed down following the death of a relative historically have not been eligible (Gotham, 2014; Satter, 2009).

Recently, FEMA implemented a program to allow heirs of property owners to apply with an affidavit of ownership.[16] As applicants (often states) determine mitigation priorities, rental properties are eligible for buyout under the Hazard Mitigation Grant Program (HMGP) if the state in which the structures are located decides to make this an eligible type of project (assuming the structures meet standard eligibility criteria like cost-effectiveness and having a willing seller, i.e., landlord).[17] One example of this was in North Carolina following Hurricane Fran in 1996 (Smith, 2014). In this case, renters were eligible for Uniform Relocation Act assistance. However, in most cases, renters, who are often low-income and non-White due to past discriminatory housing policies, are left out of relocation programs despite making up a substantial proportion of households in floodplains (Dundon & Camp, 2021).

In addition, existing federal funding sources prioritize properties with repetitive or severe repetitive losses as candidates for buyouts on the basis that these are usually more cost-effective (Conrad et al., 1998; Tate et al., 2016; Zavar, 2015). This means that owners whose property has not been repeatedly damaged may not be eligible.

Mobile and Manufactured Homes Eligibility

It is estimated that between 18 and 20 million people in the United States live in mobile or manufactured homes, and 15 percent of these residences are of "high-flood-risk" (National Academies, 2022c; Fadel & Seshadri, 2023). These mobile homes are often overlooked and rarely restored after disasters (Fadel & Seshadri, 2023; Smith, K., 2022). About one-third of these homes are located in mobile home parks where residents "own their housing unit but rent the land underneath" (Sullivan et al., 2022, p. 232). As a result, owners who do not own the land their home sits on face additional challenges since buyout funds require the acquisition

[16]More information about affidavit of ownership for heirs of property owners is available at https://www.fema.gov/press-release/20210902/fema-makes-changes-individual-assistance-policies-advance-equity-disaster

[17]More information about eligibility and priorities for HMGP activities is available at https://www.fema.gov/grants/mitigation/hazard-mitigation/before-you-apply

of the land on which the structure sits (Lubben, 2022). Unless the mobile home park owner agrees to sell the land, the buyout cannot occur (Lubben, 2022; Maryland.gov, n.d.). Such homes are prone to damage from severe weather, and most are not actually mobile, despite their name. Those not meeting alternate location relocation requirements or codes may be abandoned (Smith, K., 2022). Also, there is a stigma associated with mobile home parks, so finding a suitable site for relocation can be challenging. Additionally, mobile homes' values are low (depreciating over time) and rarely qualify for federal funding, such as payments through FEMA (Fadel & Seshadri, 2023). Additionally, mobile home residents are often left out of basic legal protections (Smith, K., 2022). At the committee's first workshop in Houston, Texas,[18] Andy Rumbach, senior fellow at the Urban Institute where he co-leads the Climate and Communities practice area in the Metropolitan Housing and Communities Policy Center, commented,

> *Even in places where they have community involvement, many times the mobile fleets are not involved.*

In Harris County, Texas, FEMA has facilitated buyouts to protect residences from sea level rise, where 357 mobile home units were purchased (Lubben, 2022). Although not necessarily directly tied to flood risk or relocation, other states have developed programs to help protect mobile home residents. One example is Colorado's Mobile Home Park Oversight Program, which, among other responsibilities, handles dispute resolution between park landlords and mobile home owners to keep issues out of the costly court system, and educates residents about mobile home park laws.[19] However, many residents continue to be unaware of this program and its features (Fadel & Seshadri, 2023). Some programs suggest approaches that strengthen rights and legal protections for mobile home residents, enhance statewide databases, and prioritize mobile home residents in short- and long-term disaster planning and recovery (Smith, K., 2022).

Geographic Eligibility

According to FEMA, local officials determine what properties are eligible for buyouts, but usually eligible properties are in Special Flood Hazard Areas and are primary residences.[20] Examples of eligibility determinations include location of the parcel in a floodway, history of flooding, and

[18] See footnote 1.

[19] More information about the Mobile Home Park Oversight Program is available at https://cdola.colorado.gov/mobile-home-park-oversight

[20] More information about the acquisition of property after a flood event is available at https://www.fema.gov/press-release/20230502/fact-sheet-acquisition-property-after-flood-event

insurance coverage with the NFIP. At the community level, property may be determined eligible if there is the potential for it to be used for flood mitigation projects after acquisition (Siders, 2019, Table 3). In addition, the FEMA grants mentioned in Chapter 9 require communities to have hazard mitigation plans (HMPs) to receive funding. However, a six-state study[21] of 176 local comprehensive plans found that many state and local HMPs were not used as a key decision-making mechanism, did not include land-use measures as a risk reduction tool (i.e., avoidance in climate change adaptation language), and were not closely aligned with emerging climate change adaptation plans (Berke et al., 2014; Lyles et al., 2014a,b). This indicates that although these plans are required to obtain federal funding for community relocation, they are not being utilized to their full potential.

Unintended Consequences—Checkerboarding

These eligibility requirements contribute to a checkerboard pattern of existing buyouts wherein some households take a buyout while others stay, leaving vacant homes or vacant lots interspersed between still-inhabited homes. This type of pattern is a major concern in terms of impacts on communities (Atoba et al., 2021; Zavar & Hagelman, 2016). For example, checkerboard buyouts reduce the potential environmental and flood risk reduction benefits that can come from restoring a cluster of plots back to their natural state, creating an unencumbered floodplain (Atoba, 2022; Atoba et al., 2021). Additionally, the cost of upkeep for these sporadic vacant lots throughout still-residential zones can be high, and these lots can become sources of concern for residents left behind if not maintained. Dolores Mendoza, a former resident of Harris County, commented on this at this study's first workshop in Houston, Texas:[22]

> *I moved one year when I was 20 thinking I would love to raise my kids in a new community; I hated it and came back. I came back after a year because I didn't have the community and I wanted it. That's how I want my kids to be. My home was forcibly sold to the county. I moved out on Dec 23rd and it has been vandalized; the county is not coming in to clean it up. The property has a lot of dust in it, people use it to dump things [and] it's full of trash. I'm sorry for my neighbors who are there. Mr. Sánchez can see my house. He sees garbage, an abandoned home, and nothing is being done.*

---

[21]The six coastal states included in this study were California, Florida, Georgia, North Carolina, Texas, and Washington (Lyles et al., 2014a).

[22]See footnote 1.

Methods of reducing checkerboarding include identifying priority areas for acquisition, as has been done by the Harris County Flood Control District (see Chapter 8), and pre-approving contiguous properties for acquisition.

High-Level Analysis of Complexity, Time, and Post-Buyout Requirements

Program Complexity

Current efforts to advance relocation, including associated funding streams and competitive grant programs (i.e., through FEMA, Department of Housing and Urban Development [HUD], U.S. Army Corps of Engineers [USACE]), are highly prescriptive and complex. These programs put little emphasis on local capacity-building assistance. Their rules often fail to account for local needs and conditions. For example, data collected after Hurricane Sandy found that recovery policies were perceived by residents as cumbersome and constantly changing, and that there was a lack of common goals between homeowners and policy makers (Greer & Trainor, 2021).

Because of these difficulties and the complex array of federal programs that may fund relocation described in Chapter 9, it is extremely difficult for a household that wants a buyout or relocation to obtain funding and successfully navigate the process. Individual households generally must rely on their municipality to submit a subgrant application to the state, which then submits an application to FEMA, HUD, or another federal entity (Congressional Research Service, 2023). All of the grant platforms for relocation programs are extremely difficult to use and they are entirely different for each agency (FEMA even has a different platform for HMGP than for Building Resilient Infrastructure and Communities [BRIC]), such that the same information has to be entered on numerous platforms for different grants (GAO, 2022b). Not all municipalities have grant writers able to navigate these platforms. For example, in the first few years of BRIC's existence, underresourced communities often found it very difficult to develop and submit competitive proposals due to a combination of program complexity and limited local government capacity to write successful grant applications (Smith & Vila, 2020). FEMA has recognized this problem, even going so far as to explicitly incorporate the need to reduce the complexity of its assistance programs and "[r]emove barriers to FEMA programs through a people first approach" in its strategic plan (FEMA, 2022e). However, this goal, which is laudable, has not been effectively operationalized. In fact, this goal runs counter to BRIC, one program that is regularly cited as overly complex, leading to many underresourced communities choosing not to apply for this type of federal aid (Smith & Vila, 2020; Vila et al., 2022).

This problem can be addressed in two ways. First, program complexity, particularly among FEMA's hazard mitigation and disaster recovery programs, needs to be reduced. Widely cited program sticking points, like, for instance, the reliance on BCA to determine project eligibility, need to be simplified. (This suggestion is made recognizing that "cost-effectiveness" determinations do not necessarily require the use of this data-intensive, time-consuming tool.) Research by RAND analyzing FEMA's BCA methodology and subsequent equity challenges supports this assertion and recommends, in order to simplify the application process, that FEMA "replace BCA with a simpler measure of cost-effectiveness" and "establish a minimum cost threshold or other criteria for a full BCA" (Miller et al., 2023, p. 70). (BCA and RAND's recommendations are discussed in more detail in the next section.)

Second, FEMA and other stakeholders could expand the provision of technical assistance to underresourced communities, to include helping them to assess their risk, develop HMPs to identify potential relocation projects, refine project scope, write project applications, and implement these projects over time. Research by RAND about social equity in BRIC suggests close partnerships between FEMA and subapplicants that include "context-sensitive nuance," and FEMA-paid consultants who are able to provide technical assistance, with "state hazard mitigation officers or emergency management agencies [playing an] important role" (Clancy et al., 2022, p. 43). Finucane (2023) noted that more information is needed to understand the specific barriers communities face while applying for BRIC to help determine what type of support is optimal and for whom, and that new mechanisms, such as BRIC funding indirect and direct administrative costs up front for lower-income communities, need to be explored. While FEMA is attempting to expand the delivery of BRIC Direct Technical Assistance (DTA),[23] a larger nationwide commitment to this effort is merited. It is noteworthy that "the White House launched a new Community-Driven Relocation Subcommittee as part of the White House National Climate Task Force in August 2022," co-led by FEMA and the U.S. Department of the Interior.[24] This subcommittee could form the basis for a coordinating entity among various agencies involved with climate migration.[25]

[23]More information about the delivery of BRIC DTA is available at https://www.fema.gov/grants/mitigation/building-resilient-infrastructure-communities/direct-technical-assistance

[24]More information about the White House National Climate Task Force in August 2022 is available at https://www.whitehouse.gov/briefing-room/statements-releases/2022/08/01/fact-sheet-10-ways-the-biden-harris-administration-is-making-america-resilient-to-climate-change/

[25]More information on FEMA efforts advancing community-driven relocation is available at https://www.fema.gov/fact-sheet/fema-efforts-advancing-community-driven-relocation

FEMA and HUD could streamline funding programs and make them more user-friendly. They could also support capacity building from the ground up to allow communities to meaningfully address their needs. While states could act as a linchpin, most do not have a strategy to build capacity and address inequities. Finally, limited pre-event land-use planning (both process-based planning as well as physical, including home, site, neighborhood, and regional scales) hampers relocation efforts, and so further support for pre-event planning (within existing policies) could help municipalities to prepare.

Buyout Process Duration

The average timeframe from the application for a buyout to the actual sale is over five years (Weber & Moore, 2019). One study comparing the risk recovery ratios of FEMA's HMGP program and HUD's Community Development Block Grant (CDBG) Program found that acquisitions carried out by CDBG on average took longer than those carried out by HMGP (all applications were submitted in 2009; CDBG acquisitions were not completed until 2014, compared to 2011 for HMGP; Muñoz & Tate, 2016). It is important to note that HUD's CDBG Program is specifically aimed at assisting low- to moderate-income people, and according to this study, participants had to wait longer for home acquisitions to be completed compared to HMGP participants. However, the opposite (that FEMA HMGP funding is slower than HUD CDBG funding) was reported by participants at the committee's webinar, Perspectives and Approaches to Property Acquisitions: Challenges and Lessons Learned.[26] During the waiting period, residents are in limbo and still face disaster risks in potentially unsafe homes. Residents may find that rebuilding in the same space is faster than waiting for funding for a buyout and reduces personal financial impacts, such as simultaneous monthly mortgage and rental payments.

A transitional housing plan that accounts for resident cost burdens and preferences can be a useful element in a relocation strategy (see the case study on Japan in Chapter 3). However, the post-Hurricane Katrina approach in 2005, wherein FEMA rapidly purchased and distributed inexpensive travel trailers of varying sizes for emergency shelter, proved to be unsustainable (Hany Abulnour, 2014). The poor quality of these units, resulting from their cheap materials and rushed production, rendered them inconvenient to the federal government and unsatisfactory to the occupants, who had to endure high relative costs, a relatively short lifespan of the structure, and a detrimental indoor health environment. Moreover, the use of these trailers far exceeded the original 18-month expectation, with

[26]See footnote 2.

a significant population of 60,000 people still living in these temporary homes two years following the disaster (Hany Abulnour, 2014).

In contrast, the "Katrina cottage" emerged as a successful housing solution for some. These homes feature a compact 27.8 m^2 layout assembled from affordable, durable, and lightweight prefabricated timber panels built for hurricane conditions They are designed to withstand high winds and moisture and, coupled with cost-effectiveness intended for permanent residency, offered a practical alternative to FEMA's temporary trailers (Hany Abulnour, 2014). Some states built these cottages faster than others (e.g., by mid-2009 Mississippi had built over 500 where Louisiana had built none) and the program was not without its difficulties (Gogola, 2012). Another example of fast-paced permanent housing recovery that applies a community-based approach is the Lower Rio Grande Rapid Recovery Re-Housing Program (RAPIDO),[27] which prioritizes a swift and efficient rehousing process while ensuring resilience and cultural appropriateness. This approach encompasses pre-disaster preparation and local-focused strategies, and emphasizes community empowerment. RAPIDO's innovative model includes temporary-to-permanent housing transformations that are both cost-effective and sustainable, aligning with the needs and preferences of affected communities. This ensures a seamless transition for families from immediate post-disaster scenarios to stable, long-term housing situations.

Delayed timelines can also impact the number of people a state can help with its allotted funding. Michael Johnson, public assistance officer at the Alabama Emergency Management Agency, noted this in the committee's webinar, Perspectives and Approaches to Property Acquisitions: Challenges and Lessons Learned, explaining that cost estimates for a buyout program (including the removal and acquisition of properties) might be higher by the time the project is carried out compared to the original estimate.[28] This results in the state being unable to cover all of its expenses and/or less work getting done with the same amount of money. This sentiment was echoed by Chris Monforton, chief executive officer, Habitat for Humanity of the Mississippi Gulf Coast, based in Ocean Springs, Mississippi, who described two challenges with grants:

1. The unpredictability of prices makes it difficult to know how much to apply for: "We told [HUD ...] hey, it's like we need to build in a 30 percent contingency just to replace a roof because [of ...] the fluctuation and prices of roofing materials, and then let alone

[27]More information about RAPIDO is available at http://www.rapidorecovery.org/the-idea
[28]See footnote 2.

availability of materials those entities or agencies that are left with implementing."

2. The inflexibility of agency program administrators limits opportunities: "Some of these tend to be very bureaucratic and what they know is what is familiar, not what is actually possible. [...] Oftentimes [it] is very narrow when [...] there's much more potential [...] and flexibility than maybe what is [...] immediately being communicated."[29]

Although there can be a tradeoff between rapidly carrying out a buyout program and ensuring a deliberate process, this tradeoff can be avoided by conducting the necessary preparatory work outside of the funding opportunity. For example, as described in the below section on BCA, the municipality and state could pre-identify houses and infrastructure that merit a buyout and obtain the necessary clearances so that when a household decides to start a buyout, they do not have to wait. The process of obtaining these clearances could also be streamlined (see Chapter 8, "Relocation Site Planning" section). Another method of reducing the duration of the relocation process was pursued by the Hazard Eligibility and Local Projects Act, proposed in Houston (National Academies, 2022c), which would allow Harris County, Texas, to immediately fund buyouts after a storm and then request reimbursement from FEMA afterward (P.L. 117-332).

To mitigate the challenges posed by the compressed timeline of development activities in a rapid post-disaster buyout program, it is important to improve the design of planning processes and institutional structures following disasters, as suggested by Olshansky et al. (2012), and to do as much preemptive planning and preparation as possible. The accelerated pace of disaster recovery necessitates efficient resource mobilization, effective interagency communication, and adaptation of existing systems to expedite the process (Olshansky et al., 2012). While quick decision making and action planning are crucial, they can also undermine transactional transparency, accountability, and public trust. For example, the rapid pace of post-disaster environments often results in an information deficit, which fuels the spread of rumors and mistrust toward government assistance efforts, often outpacing the ability of institutions to provide accurate, clarifying information. Moreover, the pressure to act swiftly increases the likelihood of errors, which can have amplified consequences due to time constraints. To address this, Olshansky et al. (2012) propose the development of decentralized decision-making frameworks and enhanced coordination among organizations to minimize the adverse effects.

[29]Ibid.

New Jersey's Blue Acres program[30] is an example of a program that reduces the timeframe by indicating that if a property floods up to a certain extent during a disaster, the owner will not be allowed to rebuild. It also stipulates that the owner can apply for a buyout at any time, including before the flood, and the buyout will immediately happen after the flood; in this case, the owner is allowed to stay in the home until the next flood. (This program is discussed in relation to federal grant money in Chapter 3.) Another example is from the North Carolina following Hurricane Floyd. To speed up the process, no BCA was used. FEMA Region 4 co-located with the North Carolina Division of Emergency Management to approve projects face-to-face, writing applications in anticipation of future funding. Funding for the acquisition of 600 homes was approved one week after the storm (Smith, 2014). This example is described in more detail in the section below that discusses the cost-effectiveness criterion and buyout eligibility.

Other issues regarding the duration and timing of the current buyout process described at the National Academies acquisitions webinar include people dropping out of buyouts after initially agreeing to them, and investors buying properties in the floodplain and selling them to unsuspecting newcomers.[31] This was reflected by Kathy Hopkins in a public information gathering session, manager of the Flood Mitigation Assistance and State Flood Grant Programs at the Texas Water Development Board, where she described the issue of timing in buyout programs:

> *The time period is so long that we saw a whole bunch of investors come in and buy out the properties and they're not interested in acquisition; they're interested in making money, so they'll keep the properties and sell them to homeowners that are not knowledgeable to the fact their home is in a Special Flood Hazard Areas. It's been a big challenge the last couple of years trying to purchase those properties before investors come in.*

Because of the long timeline, during this time, many interested homeowners revert to making the needed repairs and withdrawing from the program. Recent efforts to alleviate this burden have resulted in rapid buyouts in Kentucky, following the Eastern Kentucky floods in 2022. Within six months, FEMA had awarded 29.9 million dollars to buy and remove 173 homes.[32] Although funding has been awarded quickly, delays may still be experienced by the homeowners moving forward in finalizing agreements and receiving the funding.

---

[30]More information about the Blue Acres Program is available at https://dep.nj.gov/blueacres/

[31]See footnote 2.

[32]More information about the rapid buyouts in Kentucky is available at https://content.govdelivery.com/landing_pages/42025/35c63a32d9a866677b68f2f4916088cb

Post-Buyout Requirements

Once a FEMA buyout occurs, the home must be destroyed or relocated outside of the floodplain (42 U.S.C. § 5170c(b)(2)(B); 44 C.F.R. § 80.19). This can be emotionally difficult for the former homeowners (see Chapter 6) or for some unacceptable (e.g., Farbotko, 2018); during a tour of Isle de Jean Charles, committee members saw that a resident had a sign on their property insisting they would stay. Following acquisition and demolition or relocation, the property must be maintained as open space in perpetuity and belongs to the municipality. Additional options include relying on the county/parish, a quasi-governmental entity, or a nonprofit (42 U.S.C. § 5170c(b)(2)(B); 44 C.F.R. § 80.19). Local governments can lease buyout lands to nearby homeowners to maintain the land over time assuming the property owner uses that land in accordance with FEMA rules and regulations (Smith et al., 2023).

Highly prescriptive and administratively challenging federally funded buyout programs make it difficult for state and local governments to address the myriad individual-level challenges widely recorded in the buyout literature. As discussed throughout the past chapters, these challenges include the length of time it takes to develop and administer a buyout, the financial situation among low-income participants, the failure to identify suitable replacement housing, and deep place attachment, which often leads to uneven levels of participation among community residents.

The committee notes that local governments can impede relocation. Local officials may be unwilling to discuss the risks facing the community, engage in pre-event relocation planning, or participate in buyout programs. In the committee's judgment, state-run buyout programs can be used to gain local government support for community-driven relocation, but this puts some local governments at risk of losing significant parts of their jurisdiction as discussed in Shi et al. (2023) and Chapter 8.

Economic Justice

Benefit-Cost Analysis

Congress requires FEMA to make decisions on buyouts based on cost-effectiveness, a term that could conceivably encompass a range of values. But FEMA has chosen to use a fairly limited BCA that does not quantify values such as environmental justice. Which is to say, FEMA's decisions on whether to acquire property through a buyout are, by agency policy, based primarily on this benefit-cost calculus (C.F.R. Part 80), with the agency defining benefits as the projected future losses and costs as the cost of acquisition and the maintenance costs (Tate et al., 2016). HUD, on the other hand, has integrated more social and environmental factors into its decision-making process and has not relied so stringently on the BCA.

While it is an important part of disaster response, the BCA process and methodology can be controversial (Institute of Medicine, 2013; Kind et al., 2017; Naussbam, 2000). One challenge to the relocation process introduced by the use of the BCA is the inequitable distribution of funds. The use of BCA in flood risk management, both by USACE and FEMA, has led to inequitable distribution of funds to protect higher-value properties (McGee, 2021; Pape, 2021). When a house has a high value, the benefit of relocation is calculated to be higher, because it is only based on the home price and not on the vulnerability of the owners or equitable outcomes (Junod et al., 2021). Thus, BCA can privilege buyouts of high-value property over buyouts in low-income neighborhoods. For example, Louisiana's Road Home Program, a federally funded program, was efficacious for higher-income families but not low-income families because the program provided a grant for either the pre-storm value or the cost of repairs—whichever was less; in many cases for low-income residents, this was the former, and they were therefore left to cover a higher percentage of rebuilding costs on their own (Adelson et al., 2022). Clancy et al. (2022, p. 48) suggest mechanisms that could help reduce disadvantages faced by underserved populations when applying for BRIC funding including "[establishing] a set-aside for underserved populations, similar to the current tribal set-aside" and developing a "formula approach that identifies a certain amount of resources to be directed toward communities that are unable to compete effectively in the current design of the national competition." Further discussion of the methods that can be and are being used to address the challenges laid out in this section can be found in the section below, titled "Addressing the Cost-Effectiveness Criterion and Buyout Eligibility."

Outdated Cost Determinations

Another barrier to community-driven relocation is the enormous difficulty of determining the amount of financial and other resources that will be required. For example, the cost of relocating Newtok, Alaska, was estimated as 80 to 130 million dollars by USACE prior to relocation; but how USACE arrived at this amount is not clear (USACE, 2006; see Chapter 3). The financial costs associated with specific past disasters are often used to develop probabilities and estimates of the cost of future events. Basing financial cost estimates on experience with past disasters is a fundamental error given the extent to which disasters are becoming larger (e.g., Hurricanes Maria and Harvey) and population density in some areas is increasing (Smith, 2022). Additionally, estimates must be adjusted to fit the appropriate timeframes. This means that cost determinations need to account for changes in the cost of acquisitions, demolitions, and other relocation processes between the time funds are applied for to when those actions will be carried out.

Funding Match Requirements

> *If it's a substantial funding amount, there is always a match required, and you know our cities can't pay for the match.*[33]

As described in the above quote, buyouts require nonfederal matching funds from communities (and in some states, individual property owners), which can be difficult for low-income communities (Ristroph, 2021; Smith & Vila, 2020). For example, FEMA buyout programs typically require a 25 percent match from the state (e.g., 42 U.S.C. § 5133(h)). For tribal communities, for example, federal money is their main source of funding, so they struggle to come up with the nonfederal match, and their general fund is often not enough (Ristroph, 2021). There are some exceptions to this requirement, including the Swift Current Initiative, launched in 2022 with Infrastructure Act funding, where the cost share is 10 percent for buildings located in socially vulnerable communities.[34] Also, Community Development Block Grant Disaster Recovery (CDBG-DR) Program funds may be used as a match for FEMA programs if the activity is eligible under CDBG-DR (GAO, 2022b), but in other cases, federal funds from one entity may not serve as the required match for another entity (Smith, 2011). Some states (e.g., North Carolina) cover all or some of the nonfederal match (Smith et al., 2013). Texas has also worked to cover a portion of the local match requirement through a grant and loan program called Flood Infrastructure Fund,[35] administered by the Texas Water Development Board, and using funds associated with Hurricane Harvey-related FEMA public assistance and Hazard Mitigation Assistance funds.[36] Kathy Hopkins of the Texas Water Development Board also described efforts to create annual

---

[33]Comments made to the committee during a virtual public information-gathering session. More information is available at https://www.nationalacademies.org/event/03-30-2023/virtual-focus-group-mississippi-and-alabama-gulf-coast-community-stakeholder-perspectives-on-managed-retreat

[34]More information is available at https://www.fema.gov/press-release/20220321/president-biden-vice-president-harris-fema-announce-flood-mitigation

[35]More information about the Flood Infrastructure Fund is available at https://www.twdb.texas.gov/financial/programs/fif/index.asp

[36]More information about Hurricane Harvey-related funds used for matching nonfederal cost share requirements is available at https://recovery.texas.gov/hurricane-harvey/recovery-funds/index.html

funding for these programs through legislative action.[37] The committee acknowledges the inequities among states with some having much more political will for and funding from the coast; therefore, they will be more likely to have or find the capital for these programs.

However, this leaves the underlying problem of some communities not applying to federal grants in the first place due to a lack of capacity. One study showed that an Alaska Native Village had to acquire and spend nearly $200,000 to develop a competitive funding application for relocating 21 homes (Bureau of Indian Affairs, 2020). In short, wealthier communities seem better able to navigate this complex and biased system and have more capacity to come up with matching funds (Mitsova et al., 2019). At the National Academies webinar featuring speakers from Mississippi and Alabama,[38] Casi (KC) Callaway, chief resilience officer for Alabama, said,

> *I see all these problems and also see solutions, but bringing it together and making it happen is such a challenge, and all of our cities, I feel, are out there operating as individual communities on their own [...] and a 20 or 25 percent match on a project is a lot—often too much. But it's 20 or 25 of a 100, and making a difference and prioritizing spending that money is just huge. So how can we figure out how to get [...] the 20 percent match needed? How can we create allies with more non-traditional partners, or [...] nonprofits or businesses, so that we can actually make some of these differences. There are lots of businesses out there that would donate a percentage of their time to get the rest of the money. There are tradeoffs, and there are opportunities. We just got to think about [projects, partners, and funding] a little bit differently.*

Furthermore, Clancy et al. (2022) recommended adjusting the technical criteria for BRIC, which gives additional points to those subapplications that cover an increased nonfederal cost share. By extension, this places lower-income communities who cannot meet the full nonfederal cost share at a disadvantage because they cannot receive these additional points.

Replacement Housing Costs

Another frequently discussed challenge within the current system for relocation is that money received from a buyout is often not enough to purchase a new house (especially one in a safe area; Smith, 2014). Perla

[37]See footnote 2.
[38]See footnote 33.

Garcia, a resident from Houston's Allen Field neighborhood and National Academies workshop participant,[39] noted,

> *Since the beginning, we have maintained that we will not sell to Harris County because we knew there were going to be many complications [...] They do not want to give enough of what is currently on the market for the properties [...] we are not receiving sufficient support nor help; they want us to ask for loans. Also, because our houses have not been valued at the current market rate, we are receiving an assessment from 2017, which is not benefitting or helping us much.*

Similar concerns were heard in this study's Mississippi and Alabama webinar[40] where Barbara Weckesser, head of Concerned Citizens of Cherokee Subdivision in Pascagoula, Mississippi, said of her neighborhood,

> *There's been several that said well, with relocating, am I going to have enough funds through this [...] buyout to go, relocate, and live somewhere else?*

Pre-disaster fair market value may work as a baseline for replacement costs in middle- and upper-income communities where houses are more likely to be maintained and property values may remain high but may not work well for lower-income communities. For example, when Newtok, Alaska, participated in the 2019 HMGP buyout for seven homes, the maximum house valuation was $140,000. But new homes in remote Alaska can easily cost $500,000. FEMA does have a program that provides up to $31,000 toward the replacement housing differential, but this is often not enough (FEMA, 2020a). At the study's second workshop in St. Petersburg, Florida,[41] Chelsea Nelson, resident of Madeira Beach, commented on how FEMA appraisals also affect residents' ability to recover following a disaster:

> *We have a lot of issues with the FEMA rule where, you know, you can check your FEMA value on the property appraiser website, right? And it's always a fun task because, you know, your house might be worth whatever it is on Realtor.com, but FEMA says your house is worth $100,000. And so, you are allowed to have $50,000 of that to renovate or have damage before you have to become flood compliant. $50,000 might sound like a*

[39]See footnote 1. This is also discussed in more detail on page 8 of the proceedings for this workshop; see National Academies (2022c).

[40]See footnote 33.

[41]Comments made to the committee on July 12, 2022, during a public information-gathering session in Florida. More information is available at https://www.nationalacademies.org/event/07-12-2022/managed-retreat-in-the-us-gulf-coast-region-workshop-2

> *lot, but if you have a damaged roof, if you get flooded and you need a new kitchen, or your flooring is damaged, the $50,000 goes really quickly.*

Research suggests that relocation for low-income communities after disasters happens less frequently than for upper- and middle-class communities, and is associated with reduced or inadequate support from federal programs (Muñoz & Tate, 2016; Rivera et al., 2022). One study suggested that the lack of relocation was due to FEMA denying many low-income residents recovery funds due to pre-existing damage to their property (Rivera et al., 2022). Another study of Lumberton, North Carolina, found that among residents who received funds from the FEMA HMGP, recipients with lower-value property and those living in neighborhoods where many homes are mortgaged were less likely to choose to relocate (Seong et al., 2021). Seong et al. (2021) describe their findings as consistent with the literature, "which finds that homeowners of lower socioeconomic status face greater financial constraints to relocation and are therefore more likely to remain in their disaster-affected properties" (p. 15). Concerns for the feasibility of one buyout program were reflected by Darnell Ozenne's (Black United Fund of Texas) testimony at the committee's first workshop in Houston, Texas:[42]

> *The thing is certain people wanted to participate in the program, but it was a lowball factor of the market value. It was during Ike that we found that the buyout program was a viable option. But it was lowballing and giving people the value of what their homes are at that time. That was the biggest concern with a lot of the people that you know were older, maybe their kids took over the homes and wanted to get rid of the homes. So those were the things that were keeping that program not a viable option in our community.*

Replacement Housing Safety

Though it provides funding for buyouts, FEMA does not ensure that participants will relocate to safe areas (McGhee et al., 2020). FEMA's regulations on acquisition do not require relocation out of hazard-prone areas (44 C.F.R. § Part 80). Elliott et al. (2021) found that the decision to relocate due to flood risks is largely influenced by social and economic circumstances, with affluent homeowners tending to remain closer to their original flood-prone residences and their social networks, while less privileged homeowners tend to relocate further away. It underscores the fact that resettlement, particularly among wealthier neighborhoods, doesn't

[42]See footnote 1.

necessarily result in diminished flood risk, indicating a complex interplay of factors beyond flood risk in relocation decisions.

Adding requirements to buyout funding that participants relocate to land outside of the flood hazard area can help to mitigate this problem. It is also important to utilize planning—and, in particular, land suitability analysis—to identify suitable areas for relocation as a method for ensuring people relocate to safe areas. This topic is discussed in more detail in Chapter 8. Furthermore, as is also discussed in greater detail in Chapter 8, there is no system to support receiving communities in systematically preparing to receive increasing numbers of climate migrants (Junod et al., 2023).

OPPORTUNITIES FOR INNOVATION UNDER THE EXISTING LEGAL FRAMEWORK

It is important to highlight how states and agencies have come up with programs within the existing laws to avoid some of the challenges outlined above. In an article examining buyout programs in the United States, Greer and Binder (2017) found that over time, programs did not reflect an iterative process to enable policy learning. One suggestion they propose is to utilize "after-action reports" to detail program design, processes and components, challenges, and lessons learned, which could help with learning from one program to the next. The committee drew from strategies outlined in this section for several of the recommendations in Chapter 11.

Knowledge Sharing and Institutional and Peer-to-Peer Learning

Knowledge sharing—the processes by which groups exchange expertise and learning with one another—is a powerful method for overcoming some of the barriers present in the current system for relocation. The recent White House *National Climate Resilience Framework* (2023, p. 29) asserts that knowledge sharing in the context of community-driven relocation is an opportunity for action:

> *Evaluate community-driven relocation programs to improve policies over time. Evaluating relocation programs and processes and facilitating knowledge sharing between communities considering or undergoing relocation is critical to understanding and improving their effectiveness. Federal agencies should evaluate their acquisition and regulatory tools that facilitate relocation, including buyout programs, the transfer of development rights, leasebacks, land swaps, and conservation land trusts, as well as ongoing Tribal relocation demonstration projects.*

Additionally, the Denali Commission, a federal agency that operates only in Alaska and is responsible for community development, was able to "borrow" workers from other agencies (e.g., Transportation, Interior) who were considered "on detail" for a certain period of time. These borrowed workers contributed to planning for community relocation. As a result, the Newtok Planning Group was able to broker knowledge sharing among community groups and experts for a successful relocation exercise (Bronen & Chapin, 2013; Ristroph, 2021).

The value of this type of knowledge sharing between communities was echoed by Kelli Cunningham, director of Terrebonne Parish Consolidated Government Housing and Human Services Department, at this study's third workshop in Houma, Louisiana[43]:

> *[R]ather than us reinventing the wheel, why don't we look at other communities who are doing it well? [...] We talked about cousin communities or sister communities and things like that. Let's look at what other communities have done. It may not be a community in South Louisiana. It may be a community in Hawaii or wherever. But what have they done to make sure that if they are hit by something so substantial, that they're not going to have to build from the ground up again? And that's what we need to really look at is, how do we move forward, because we may or may not get hit by another Hurricane Ida. This may be our one time; however, let's make sure that we don't lose everything. Again, I really think that's the most important takeaway.*

Another example of knowledge sharing and learning is "Charlotte-Mecklenburg's peer-to-peer program in which past buyout participants share their experience with eligible households" that are considering participating in buyouts (Shi et al., 2022, p. 11). The program's incorporation of participatory budgeting empowers community members to actively contribute to investment decisions, shaping recovery efforts to align with community priorities. Complementing this approach, the provision of comprehensive resources such as flood risk assessments, community guidebooks, and an online flood risk mapping tool facilitates informed decision making by residents, equipping them with valuable insights into the buyout process and enabling them to assess their own risk levels while accessing information on successful projects (Shi et al., 2022). (Learning and knowledge sharing specifically through originating and receiving community partnerships is discussed further in Chapter 8.)

[43]Comments made to the committee on July 28, 2022, during a public information-gathering session in Louisiana. More information is available at https://www.nationalacademies.org/event/07-28-2022/managed-retreat-in-the-us-gulf-coast-region-workshop-3-part-2

Reducing Barriers to Obtaining Grants

Writing grants can require significant capacity and funding, and there are a handful of ongoing initiatives working to help communities overcome this barrier. In Alaska, the Denali Commission funded relocation coordinators to help communities apply for grants and coordinate relocation (Denali Commission, 2019). The Bureau of Indian Affairs annual climate resilience grant (referenced in Chapter 9) has a category to fund relocation coordinators. Tribal relocation coordinators will lead implementation, manage local teams, and act as the main point of contact, while also facilitating financial and technical support for tribal strategies and matching communities with appropriate federal resources.[44] FEMA provides funding in the form of "project scoping" (previously called "advanced assistance")[45] for municipalities, tribes, and states to do the preparatory work needed for Flood Mitigation Assistance grant program funding (e.g., outreach to residents, assessments, engineering design); however, FEMA's grant application platform and management for project scoping can be difficult to navigate (Smith & Vila, 2020). In a national survey of state hazard mitigation officers, researchers found that very few communities applied for advanced assistance grants and that more research is needed to understand the accessibility of these grants (Smith & Vila, 2020).

In December 2022, HUD issued a request for information for HUD's CDBG-DR Rules, Waivers, and Alternative Requirements (HUD, 2022). The current structure of CDBG-DR was found to be unsuitable for addressing urgent housing needs in disaster-stricken areas. The program's complexity imposed substantial barriers for grantees unfamiliar with its intricacies, and the expensive engagement of consultants fell short in adequately bolstering capacities (Nebraska Department of Economic Development, 2023). Within the December 2022 request, HUD proposed a "universal notice" that would allow the agency to create semi-permanent and uniform guidance with the goal of reducing barriers to funding access, allowing entities to recover faster from disasters and build resilience against future disasters. Streamlining the waiver and alternative requirement process can ease capacity and time burdens on applicants, speeding up the delivery of funding to grantees.

FEMA is also working on providing grant management assistance (including management of the application process) through BRIC's DTA program, which provides underresourced communities with access to FEMA assistance personnel, including federal staff and consultants (FEMA,

[44]More information about the relocation of tribal communities affected by climate change is available at https://www.indiangaming.com/interior-commits-135m-to-support-relocation-of-tribal-communities-affected-by-climate-change/

[45]More information about project scoping is available at https://www.fema.gov/sites/default/files/documents/fema_fy21-fma-project-scoping_fact-sheet.pdf

2023b). As outlined by Smith and Nguyen (2023), one way to bolster the DTA program is to identify faculty and engagement experts at land grant universities, minority serving institutions, and other institutions that possess the skills and interest to serve on a national cadre of individuals who will assist underresourced communities in writing and implementing hazard mitigation assistance grants, including those tied to buyouts. North Carolina State University recently received funding to begin working toward this goal.[46] The intent is to provide ongoing assistance like that found with agricultural extension agents who are widely recognized and trusted providers of information. This is consistent with the GAO-22-106037 recommendation to provide or fund relocation advisory services for property owners (GAO, 2022c). This can help to reduce the red-taped, complex nature of receiving federal grants and provide a more flexible mechanism.

In addition, the Disaster Survivors Fairness Act of 2022 (H.R. 8416) requires FEMA to establish a universal application for disaster survivors that crosses federal agencies. This application could be a model for a universal application for relocation. This grant platform could go through the existing grants.gov, which could be simplified to become more user-friendly. Given the different priorities and rules of the different agencies, the new application process could still be quite long. Still, given the overlap between the agencies and the lack of clarity and understanding about who must complete what application for what program, a single application could be more efficient. As discussed in Chapter 11 and below, "navigators" could help applicants complete these applications. State and tribe applicants could have first priority for funding, followed by municipalities that are not included in a state application, followed by individual households that have not been included in a municipal application. This process would facilitate collaboration between states and historically marginalized groups in prioritizing where relocation, including buyouts, occurs. The lead agency (i.e., the disbursing agency) could route the completed application to the best-fitting program, which could go back to the applicant with a request for any additional information needed to complete the application. One agency would likely need to be designated as the lead agency for updating and maintaining the application system (GAO, 2022b). This would reduce the burden on the public by simplifying the application process. Allowing funds from other federal agencies to be used as matching funds demonstrates that a municipality works to pool resources and is vested in the project.

[46]More information about grants to North Carolina State University is available at https://coastalresilience.ncsu.edu/expertise/gsmith5/

Addressing the Cost-Effectiveness Criterion and Buyout Eligibility

As discussed above in the challenges section, while BCA is important, a focus on improving overall spatial quality and environmental and social quality at larger scales would both reduce inequities in who is eligible for buyouts and increase the community-wide benefits. After Hurricane Floyd, North Carolina negotiated with FEMA to bypass the use of BCA (as discussed in the "Program Complexity" section). Instead, a flood depth/damage proxy was used to determine cost-effectiveness, a key buyout eligibility criterion. Because determining the benefit-to-cost ratio for projects of this size (more than 600 homes) can take months, this proxy helped to speed up the time typically associated with writing a buyout (Smith, 2014). A buyout program in Austin, Texas (discussed further in the next section) chose to diversify its benefit-cost criteria by using "a matrix when deciding where to do a buyout—including cost effectiveness, permitting feasibility, and potential for habitat restoration and public open space" (Shi et al., 2022, p. 10).

The Office of Management and Budget (OMB) provides regulatory guidance to government agencies on BCA through Circular A-4[47] and A-94[48] (see Chapter 11), although each agency can refine this guidance to suit their needs. Some agencies are modifying OMB's original guidance in ways that make for a more equitable process around BCA, accounting for a broader array of costs and benefits (as Austin, Texas, did). As mentioned above, HUD is making refinements to the original guidance that allow for an evaluative approach that moves beyond BCA. In 2021, USACE released a policy directive called "Comprehensive Documentation of Benefits in Decision Document,"[49] which elevated the integration of other social effects, regional economics, and environmental issues into the decision-making process, although the implementation of this directive has been minimal. In April 2023, OMB itself released proposed updates to its A-4[50] and A-94[51] guidelines for federal regulatory analysis in response to President Biden's Executive Order on Modernizing Regulatory Review. These

[47]More information about Circular A-4 is available at https://obamawhitehouse.archives.gov/omb/circulars_a004_a-4/

[48]More information on Circular A-94 is available at https://obamawhitehouse.archives.gov/omb/circulars_a094

[49]More information about the "Comprehensive Documentation of Benefits in Decision Document" is available at https://planning.erdc.dren.mil/toolbox/library/MemosandLetters/ComprehensiveDocumentationofBenefitsinDecisionDocument_5January2021.pdf

[50]More information about the A-4 updates is available at https://www.federalregister.gov/documents/2023/04/07/2023-07364/request-for-comments-on-proposed-omb-circular-no-a-4-regulatory-analysis

[51]More information about the A-94 updates is available at https://www.federalregister.gov/documents/2023/04/07/2023-07179/public-comment-on-guidelines-and-discount-rates-for-benefit-cost-analysis-of-federal-programs

proposed updates notably include clear recommendations for the analysis of distributional impacts from federal regulations and spending, as well as the specific use of equity weights in BCA. Additionally, Clancy et al. (2022, p. 47) recommend shifting from a BCA model for BRIC, which "favors physical assets and projects in more-densely populated communities," to one that "incorporates benefits for underserved populations, such as potential for improving public health, expanding recreational opportunities, or increasing economic development potential." Implementation of these fundamental changes in federal decision-making processes will have deep and far-reaching implications for social and environmental justice.

To the extent that "cost-effectiveness" must be a component of relocation, one method of reducing the inequities created by FEMA's current use of BCA is to pre-approve properties for acquisition. In other words, relocation would be deemed "cost-effective" for anyone living in a flood-prone area. Such a model would more closely align with the Dutch method of BCA, which analyzes costs and benefits at a larger scale rather than at the parcel level focused on in analysis by U.S. agencies (see Chapter 3). This method is also suggested in GAO 22-106037 Flood Mitigation (GAO, 2022c). Considerations based on habitability or location in flood-prone areas that do not require BCA could reduce the length of the acquisition process, thereby reducing the dropout rate of participants and getting them into new homes more quickly. One way to include risk assessments in this process, as recommended in a RAND study assessing BRIC, is to incorporate FEMA's National Risk Index tool (accounting for its limitations) into deliberations and prioritizations for funding proposals (Clancy et al., 2022). To the extent that FEMA does not act, states and local governments could consider adopting state- or locally run buyout programs like those found in New Jersey; Tulsa, Oklahoma; and Charlotte, North Carolina; which draw from a combination of FEMA funding and local funds raised via stormwater fees (see Chapter 9).

Additional Efforts to Increase Fairness in Buyouts

Some state and municipal programs have taken measures to increase fairness regarding who participates in buyouts and to ensure that residents are able to navigate the process and get new homes. Examples in this section describe efforts to address fairness in regard to challenges such as new housing costs, renter eligibility, timing in the decision to relocate, and residential assistance during the buyout process. Adding to previous examples, this array of innovations underscores the importance of making fairness a policy priority. For example, Austin, Texas, has applied the provisions of the Uniform Relocation Assistance and Real Property Acquisition Policies Act of 1970 (URA) to relocations under its buyout program to "help owners bridge the cost between their old and new home" (Shi et al., 2022, p. 7). Participation in the buyout program is voluntary, meaning that participants would not ordinarily be eligible to receive the assistance outlined in the URA, but Austin's Watershed Protection Department (which administers Austin's buyout program) uses its own funding to provide this additional assistance. As a result, Austin helps families find a new house within the city by financing the difference in price between the home subject to the buyout and a new home. This assistance also enables renters to participate in buyouts. The city also uses leasebacks, in which the government buys the home and the resident is able to lease it, effectively extending the time residents have to move. This can be particularly useful for older residents (Shi et al., 2022).

Other measures have also been taken. Austin pays for relocation advisors to assist residents in navigating the buyout process; similarly, New Jersey's Blue Acres program has experts who help homeowners overcome hurdles. These "navigators," as described in Recommendation 9, could also assist households with title clearance (see Household Eligibility section) by referring households to title agencies willing to work at reduced rates or whose work could be subsidized by FEMA grants. Harris County, where Houston is located, uses social vulnerability analysis to prioritize buyouts among poorer, more vulnerable neighborhoods. To ensure that there is adequate funding for buyouts and to ensure local programs address many of the identified shortfalls in federal buyout programs, Charlotte-Mecklenburg, North Carolina, assesses a stormwater fee to all development, while New Jersey applies a 6 percent corporate business tax to raise funds (Shi et al., 2022).

LESSONS TO BE LEARNED FROM OUTSIDE THE UNITED STATES

There are many lessons to be learned from communities that have experienced relocation, including international communities (Smith & Saunders, 2022), but these lessons often go unmarked (Greer & Binder, 2017; Smith et al., 2023). Increasingly, scholars and practitioners are discussing the potential of existing programs associated with the acquisition of hazard-prone housing (buyouts) as a means to accomplish the larger aim of community-driven relocation (Freudenburg et al., 2016; Hino et al., 2017; Mach et al., 2019). This section serves to outline lessons that could be learned from completed buyout and community relocation experiences and policies outside the United States. These cases are included in this chapter and not in Chapter 3 because we offer them as a way of thinking about the broader implications of federal policies or plans rather than as contained examples of relocation.

Buyouts as Part of a National Policy Framework in New Zealand

New Zealand's National Adaptation Plan addresses relocation as an adaptive strategy (New Zealand, 2022). The approaches taken to buyouts in New Zealand provide a number of important lessons (Smith, Saunders et al., 2021). Nationally funded buyouts in New Zealand are not tied to a program explicitly dedicated to this objective. Rather, the process is predicated on incorporating buyouts, and associated funding, with a new or existing national policy framework. For instance, following the Christchurch Earthquake, the Canterbury Earthquake Recovery Authority was created through special legislation to coordinate recovery efforts, serving as the national vehicle through which buyout funds flowed.[52] Among the most effective and publicly contentious policies were the rules governing the identification of buyback properties. The Canterbury Earthquake Recovery Authority designated certain parcels as falling within "red-zoned" areas in which damaged properties could not be rebuilt, which could lead to questions about the "voluntary" nature of the program (Smith & Saunders, 2022). Understood from a risk reduction standpoint, this allowed for the large-scale assemblage of contiguous parcels, strongly influencing the geographic distribution of the more than 6,000 purchased parcels (Smith & Saunders, 2022). In New Zealand, buyback rules have also been incorporated into the Resource Management Act 1991, which enables existing land-use rights to be removed for land-use planning purposes. The Building Act 2004 allows for the removal of buildings when they are determined to pose a potential danger through injury, death, or damage to another property, while the Public Works Act 1981 allows for the purchase of property when necessary to site public works projects (Smith & Saunders, 2022).

In each case, this allowed the New Zealand government to develop rules that reflected local conditions on the ground, which has the potential to address one of the major shortcomings of U.S. buyout policy, which involves highly complex, prescriptive rules (Smith & Saunders, 2022). The policies put in place allowed for greater program flexibility. However, the lack of pre-established rules in New Zealand has, in some cases, led to long implementation timeframes, a common problem often also found in a number of U.S. communities (as described above).

The Christchurch example also highlights the linkage between buyouts and land-use planning strategies and laws, including the required development of "regeneration plans" (i.e., post-buyout open space management

[52] The Canterbury Earthquake Recovery Authority was disestablished on April 18, 2016, "as the Government transitions from leading the recovery, to establishing long-term, locally-led recovery and regeneration arrangements." More information is available at https://www.dpmc.govt.nz/our-programmes/greater-christchurch-recovery-and-regeneration/greater-christchurch-group/roles-and-responsibilities/disestablishment-cera

plans), something that is not required in the United States—a lack that often leads to suboptimal uses of the resulting open space (Smith et al., 2023). Community decision making, in collaboration with local government and other stakeholders, can drive open space management plans and might include the construction of commemorative sites for those who relocated, the development of areas that can absorb floodwaters and protect adjacent human settlements, and places for recreational use that make communities a better place to live. The lack of a clear and enduring coupling of buyouts and proactive land-use planning strategies in the United States remains a major problem (Smith et al., 2023). One potential drawback has been noted: a review of the process undertaken in Christchurch also suggests that the speed of the large-scale buyback program ignored key elements of sound participatory planning processes (Johnson & Mamula-Seadon, 2014).

Lessons learned from the New Zealand managed retreat strategy highlight the importance of an adopted managed retreat strategy at the federal level that allows for flexibility across cases and avoids highly complex, prescriptive rules that might make it difficult for buy-in into the relocation process. Additionally, clear communication of regeneration plans and the use of post-buyout open spaces is essential in promoting open space management in the United States, where resulting open spaces are used in an optimal manner rather than as vacant open spaces.

Threshold-Based Relocation Assistance in Fiji

Following the development of the Planned Relocation Guideline in 2018,[53] the Fijian government has developed Standard Operating Procedures that include a procedure for culturally sensitive negotiation with villages considering relocation as well as a process for determining whether and where to move.[54] Because most of Fiji's lands are held traditionally through customary title, which cannot be bought or sold, relocation is a sensitive issue used only as a last resort (see Chapters 5 and 6 for further discussion of place attachment and reasons for resistance to migration), brokered through the ministry responsible for overseeing customary lands (Ministry of iTaukei Affairs). A request for relocation assistance must come from the village headman (the locally elected liaison to the Fijian government). This initiates a process where the Fijian Taskforce on Relocation and Displacement (a taskforce of Fijian agencies with specialization in various

[53]More information about the Planned Relocation Guideline is available at https://www.refworld.org/docid/5c3c92204.html

[54]More information about Standard Operating Procedures for planned relocation in the Republic of Fiji is available at https://fijiclimatechangeportal.gov.fj/ppss/standard-operating-procedures-for-planned-relocation-in-the-republic-of-fiji/

aspects of relocation consisting of individuals trained to collect data in a culturally sensitive manner) assesses the status of the community. Ninety percent of current residents must agree to relocate, and the Taskforce must find that the village meets the threshold of uninhabitability set out in the Standard Operating Procedures (based on geographic threat and deteriorated living conditions). In the case that these requirements are not met, the Taskforce will assist with protect-in-place measures. If relocating, the Taskforce helps the community negotiate with those who control potential receiving areas so that the relocating community gains the right to live on the new land. The new site must be approved by 60 percent of those in the relocating community. The Taskforce assists with funding and guiding the relocation process and conducts monitoring and evaluation after the relocation.

The Fijian threshold-based approach provides some valuable lessons for the current U.S. approach, especially in the approach of assessing residents' perspectives on the need to relocate. Data are collected in a manner that is culturally sensitive, to ensure that a "true" threshold represents the will of the majority for both the origin and destination communities. Given the diverse nature of U.S. communities, a culturally sensitive approach will ensure that the needs of marginalized groups are adequately researched and considered before the process of relocation even begins.

SUMMARY

This chapter has outlined the numerous challenges that households and communities face when they seek to relocate. First, it expands on the point made in Chapter 9 that there is not a clear, easy-to-navigate method for a household to apply for state or federal assistance. Participation in buyouts sponsored by FEMA or HUD (the most common buyout funders) requires the involvement of state and local governments, even though many local governments cannot meet the matching funds requirements and lack the capacity to apply for assistance. Those who do not own traditional single-family homes (including renters and mobile home residents) have little recourse. Insurance has compounded the problem by allowing the rebuilding of homes when relocation could be a better option, even while insurance is unavailable or unaffordable for many households. Participation in buyouts is further compounded by the inequities resulting from the benefit-cost analysis used to determine who has a house worthy of being bought out, the long timeframes for the process, and the lack of parity between the buyout purchase price and the cost of a comparable home outside of harm's way. Furthermore, this lack of parity, coupled with the absence of a requirement that residents relocate outside of recognized hazard areas, can lead people (especially from lower-income households) to move to another environmentally hazardous area. As was discussed further in Chapter 8, there is often no overarching framework for designating areas for buyouts and "reprogramming" the land afterward to provide for flood mitigation and other community benefits, with the result of a checkerboard pattern of buyouts.

There are lessons to be learned from other countries that have provided for buyouts as well as from state agencies that have stepped up to reduce some of the burdens in federal processes. There are ways that the federal government could reduce burdens even without substantial changes in the law, including through better coordination and the use of a uniform application where "navigators" provide assistance with the application process. In Chapter 11, the committee makes recommendations for how to address many of the challenges described in this and previous chapters, some of which stem from the innovative approaches laid out in the previous two sections.

CONCLUSIONS

Conclusion 10-1: Both government and households are responsible for understanding risks and options to reduce those risks, including buyouts. However, disparities in access to, and understanding of, risk-related data for households and the inability of governments to effectively communicate this risk can create a disconnect between both parties, impeding households from making informed decisions.

Conclusion 10-2: While emerging parametric insurance programs offer additional recovery options for underresourced households recovering after a disaster, the National Flood Insurance Program and other insurers providing coverage in high-risk areas may inadvertently contribute to rebuilding in high-risk areas. Additional research and piloting of community-based parametric insurance is needed to understand whether and how this option could be applied more broadly.

Conclusion 10-3: Buyout eligibility challenges—such as rulemaking, heirs' property rights, renter support, housing typologies (mobile or manufactured), and geographic designation within a floodplain—can contribute to the unintended consequence of "checkerboarding," which may limit community capacities for providing maximum ecological and community benefit with newly vacated land.

Conclusion 10-4: Obtaining funding for a buyout is a complex, time-consuming process that often exceeds the capacity of communities, especially underresourced ones, to act. It requires communities to write an approved hazard mitigation plan, which also takes time and a certain level of capacity and funding, especially if this task is undertaken by a contractor, which is often the case. The complexity of the buyout process also greatly exceeds the adequacy of federal and state resources available to help households and communities navigate the process. Although some assistance programs exist (e.g., the Federal Emergency Management Agency's Advanced Assistance Program), they tend to be underutilized.

Conclusion 10-5: As the current buyout system is designed for people who can afford the time it takes and the cost of comparable housing, not enough assistance is being provided to vulnerable individuals, households, and communities in need of relocation. The Federal Emergency Management Agency's use of benefit-cost analysis unfairly limits the ability of poorer housing and neighborhoods to participate in buyouts. Considering the safety and habitability of residents' current housing to determine buyout eligibility would help to make the process more fair/equitable.

Conclusion 10-6: Multiple sources of funding may be needed for relocation. It is challenging to combine different funding streams because different agencies and programs (e.g., the Federal Emergency Management Agency's Hazard Mitigation Grant Program and the Department of Housing and Urban Development's Community Development Block Grant Program) have different rules and timeframes, and federal funds from one entity may or may not serve as the required match for another entity. Nonfederal match requirements prevent some poorer communities from being able to participate in buyout grants.

Conclusion 10-7: Efforts to reduce the multi-year duration of buyouts, from application to relocation, can help to reduce deterrents for both participants and program administrators to participate in and facilitate buyout programs.

Conclusion 10-8: The committee is unaware of any written requirement in current federally funded relocation efforts to ensure that residents relocate to safer areas or that they have enough funds from the buyout to afford a home of comparable size outside of recognized hazardous areas. Furthermore, there is a lack of federal funding to purchase land for resettlement and construct replacement housing where needed.

11

Recommendations for Community-Driven Relocation Efforts in the Gulf Region and Beyond

This chapter is based on the content and conclusions within this report and contains the committee's recommendations concerning community-driven relocation. Although this study focused on the Gulf Coast of Mexico region, the committee came to a consensus that these recommendations could be applied to communities in other U.S. regions that are or will be compelled to relocate individuals, communities, and infrastructure away from environmentally high-risk places. The committee's recommendations are grouped under three domains rather than by individual chapters to highlight and build upon the key evidence that appears across the report. These domains are as follows:

1. Centering Well-Being (Recommendation 1): This domain addresses the inherent interconnections between community resilience, climate adaptation, and individual and community well-being. Addressing the traumas, stressors, and dearth of resources, and enhancing individual and collective efficacy are all critical prerequisites to providing a foundation for communities to participate in community-driven relocation projects equitably and effectively. Bolstering individual and organizational capacity for well-being in climate-threatened communities is a priority for public health and climate adaptation across the nation.
2. Developing and Sustaining Local Collaborations (Recommendations 2–7): Communication, participation, and engagement are critical elements that need fostering and enhancing among communities at risk/originating communities, receiving communities,

government, and other groups whose participation is necessary to the relocation process. Collaboration in support of community-driven relocation necessitates better integration with ongoing planning efforts at federal, state, regional, and local levels, as well as purposeful capacity building for originating and receiving communities.

3. Strengthening Preparations for Community-Driven Relocation (Recommendations 8–13): Strengthening federal agency preparations includes establishing hazard mitigation "navigators" and community resilience/adaptation extension agents, deepening local capacities, improving acquisition payments, reassessing benefit-cost analysis (BCA) processes, and streamlining funding and interagency collaborations.

Each domain and recommendation contain introductory and supportive text. This text cross-references the conclusions that support each recommendation, as well as the chapters that more broadly link the recommendations to the content of the report. Additionally, the supportive text discusses pathways toward implementation and provides examples of relevant programs and efforts to learn from and to consider partnering with going forward.

The following recommendations align with a series of federal reports that consider relocation as an adaptation strategy to build a more climate resilient nation while also fostering and enhancing community well-being, and the inherent relationship between the two. The U.S. Congress was tasked with multilateral engagement in mitigation of, and adaptation to migration as a result of climate change in *The White House Report on the Impact of Climate Change on Migration* (2021).[1] The Department of the Interior's *Climate Action Plan* (2021) recognizes relocation as part of a "whole-of-government approach" (p. 2),[2] while the Department of Housing and Urban Development's (HUD's) *Climate Resilience Implementation Guide for Community Driven Relocation* provides a step-by-step guide for communities that want to relocate.[3] Finally, the first ever White House *National Climate Resilience Framework* ("Framework") identifies

[1]*The White House Report on the Impact of Climate Change on Migration* is available at https://www.whitehouse.gov/wp-content/uploads/2021/10/Report-on-the-Impact-of-Climate-Change-on-Migration.pdf

[2]More information about the Department of the Interior's *Climate Action Plan* is available at https://www.sustainability.gov/pdfs/doi-2021-cap.pdf

[3]More information about HUD's *Climate Resilience Implementation Guide for Community Driven Relocation* is available at https://files.hudexchange.info/resources/documents/Climate-Resilience-Implementation-Guide-Community-Driven-Relocation.pdf

specific opportunities for funding, supporting, expediting, and evaluating community-driven relocation.[4]

CENTERING WELL-BEING

Healthy communities are a prerequisite to effective and equitable community-driven relocation projects (see Conclusions 2-2, 6-1, 6-2, 6-3, and 9-6). In communities where relocation is being considered, or has already occurred, or where the threat of additional displacement due to environmental hazards exists, understanding local mindsets and analysis of environmental change and risk can help improve understanding of existing collective emotional, cultural, and social perceptions that may affect risk communication and adaptation responses (see Conclusion 7-1). The implementation of this approach entails broad, sustained participation by diverse stakeholders to assess community understandings and potential response to local climate risks (see Conclusion 7-2).

Health care practitioners can collaborate with community stakeholders across sectors to continually refine the relocation process as a community-driven adaptation strategy and bolster capacity for social and emotional well-being, mental health, and related social trust and collective efficacy in climate-threatened communities (see Chapters 6 and 7). Investment in durable, participatory, and co-created strategies and communal capacity is a key part of that commitment, including the reimbursement of mental health clinicians and provider systems to be partners that train, coach, and support community groups through collaborative action that includes evidence-supported task-shared approaches (see Conclusion 6-3). This can be greatly facilitated through multi-level governance, including coastal resilience/adaptation funding and coordination by the federal government (see Conclusion 9-6).

RECOMMENDATION 1: The U.S. Department of Health and Human Services (HHS) Office of Climate Change and Health Equity and Office of the Assistant Secretary for Mental Health and Substance Use should support and coordinate efforts across HHS and other agencies with the following objectives:

- **Accelerate adoption of task-shared approaches to community mental health care, especially in high climate-impacted areas (e.g., through establishment of payment mechanisms, such as assistance from the Health Resources and Services**

[4]More information about the White House *National Climate Resilience Framework* is available at https://www.whitehouse.gov/wp-content/uploads/2023/09/National-Climate-Resilience-Framework-FINAL.pdf

Administration and scope expansion of Certified Community Behavioral Health Clinics). Such approaches should use evidence-supported mental health care, prevention, and promotion methods that community members and community-based organizations can adopt and directly provide.

- **Facilitate collaborations among federal agencies, programs, and policies that promote well-being and build community capacity to support mental health, effective empowerment, trust, inclusion, equity, and collective efficacy for adapting to environmental challenges.**
- **Facilitate regional coordination of the array of public health, health care, and social and mental health services that are required to support the well-being of originating and receiving communities.**
- **Establish metrics, indicators, and baselines to assess the longitudinal and cross-sectional well-being outcomes of individuals in the context of relocation. These data should be collated with existing data collected by federal agencies (e.g., Centers for Disease Control and Prevention, National Oceanic and Atmospheric Administration) and evaluated regularly to improve adaptation governance.**

DEVELOPING AND SUSTAINING LOCAL COLLABORATIONS

Communities in the Gulf region have a long history of migration and adaptation (see Chapter 4), often compelled by force or dire circumstances, as well as through generational change (e.g., moving up the bayou in Louisiana). Many communities in the region struggle with marginalization, vulnerabilities, and inequities that have deep historical roots, including economic injustices (Chapter 4) that have left some groups distinctly disadvantaged and at the greatest risk of harm from an array of already occurring and expected additional environmental and health challenges (see Conclusion 6-1). Consequently, these communities often lack trust in government-sponsored measures, such as relocation programs (see Conclusions 4-1, 4-2, and 8-5).

Careful understanding of the history and current circumstances of climate-affected communities is essential to the development and execution of community-driven relocation that will be equitable, effective, minimally disruptive, and supportive of community members in adapting their lives and livelihoods through all phases of the transition (see Chapters 4 and 7). At the same time, communities sustain strong traditions, attachments to place, and deep understandings of social-ecological systems they inhabit (see Conclusions 2-2, 5-1, and 6-4). Therefore, it is important to understand how local knowledge and experiences shape perspectives and inform processes of community-driven relocation (see Conclusions 5-1, 7-3, and 7-4).

RECOMMENDATION 2: Planning for community-driven relocation should incorporate local perspectives about the histories, impacts, and perceptions of displacements and forced relocations, as well as generational traditions.

- **Federal and state agencies (e.g., Federal Emergency Management Agency [FEMA], Department of Housing and Urban Development, U.S. Army Corps of Engineers, U.S. Environmental Protection Agency, the Centers for Disease Control and Prevention, state historic preservation and cultural resource agencies) should institute systematic, Gulf-wide community-informed local investigations on how past and current patterns of resilience and adaptation and relevant policies influence attitudes and behaviors toward relocation and resettlement.**
- **Emergency management and disaster recovery agencies (e.g., FEMA and regional and state counterparts), local public works agencies (e.g., water, power, drainage, flood protection), mental and behavioral health care institutes, and transportation planning entities (e.g., local and regional) should reevaluate their plans, expenditures, and strategies to account for discriminatory policies and practices that have exacerbated vulnerabilities, and should institute plans (e.g., the Justice40 Initiative) to redress inequities that have undermined the resilience of communities most likely to face relocation.**

There are several examples of efforts and initiatives to evaluate and create equitable processes and outcomes that agencies could draw from. For example, the Office of Management and Budget (OMB) recently opened a public notice for comments on changes to its A-4 and A-94 policies on benefit-cost analysis to increase and advance equity.[5] Additionally, the National Sea Grant Office along with the National Weather Service and the National Oceanic and Atmospheric Administration's (NOAA's) Office for Coastal Management conducted service equity assessments that gave recommendations for supporting Equity Assessment Teams.[6] Concerning implementation, the recent initiative of the U.S. Environmental Protection

[5]More information about OMB's draft for public review about Circular A-4 is available at https://www.whitehouse.gov/wp-content/uploads/2023/04/DraftCircularA-4.pdf. More information about OMB's draft for public review about Circular A-94 is available at https://www.whitehouse.gov/wp-content/uploads/2023/04/CircularA94.pdf

[6]More information about NOAA's Equity Assessment Teams is available at https://oes.gsa.gov/collaborations/noaa-equity-assessment/

Agency (EPA), Environmental Justice Thriving Communities Technical Assistance Centers, in partnership with the U.S. Department of Energy, could resource programs that collaborate with communities in planning and developing policies for community-driven relocation.[7]

These actions will likely result in more effective communication and engagement with local populations and aid in resourcing ongoing preservation of place-based, traditional cultural practices throughout the relocation process. Furthermore, this approach recognizes the need to carry out community-driven relocation as a process that may unfold over many years and involve multiple generations, and potentially include heritage rights or return rights to homelands (see Conclusion 8-8).

Collaborative Planning with Communities

Effective community participation is critical to a successful relocation effort, and a shared understanding of risks is a necessary basis for planning (see Conclusions 2-1 and 7-1). Planning involves an assessment of local natural hazard and climate risks, an assessment of the capabilities of stakeholder groups, the creation of clear and equitable engagement processes, and the identification of appropriate measures to be taken to reduce risk and adapt to a changing climate (see Chapters 8 and 9). Such an assessment can be the basis for a dynamic and responsive plan of communication about risk that addresses the concerns and incorporates other feedback expressed by those affected (see Conclusion 7-1). In turn, community participation in, and knowledge of, risk awareness and options to reduce household risks—such as relocation—becomes stronger (see Conclusion 10-1).

There is still much to learn about how to best use community knowledge and feedback in a planned relocation process, and what works well in some communities may not work well in others (Chapter 7). Yet, without community co-production, relocation efforts have high potential for failure. Thus, beyond risk communication, deep, sustained participation by local communities (from both originating and receiving areas; see Conclusion 8-9) and engagement with their knowledge systems and adaptive capacities is essential for success in community relocation (see Chapter 7).

RECOMMENDATION 3: Agencies that assist communities with relocation (e.g., Department of Housing and Urban Development, Federal Emergency Management Agency, U.S. Army Corps of Engineers, U.S. Department of Agriculture, and state resilience and community

[7]More information about EPA's initiative, Environmental Justice Thriving Communities Technical Assistance Centers, is available at https://www.epa.gov/environmentaljustice/environmental-justice-thriving-communities-technical-assistance-centers

development offices) should foster meaningful partnerships to develop and execute relocation plans in collaboration with communities, including decisions about timing and pace of the relocation process. These agencies should

- **develop a consistent co-creation process and work with each community to establish specific communication requirements that include face-to-face interactions; and**
- **work with locally trusted community-based organizations to build understanding, trust, and enduring relationships with communities to carry out adaptation.**

There is no one formula for a successful community-driven relocation; instead, there is only the criterion that community members are moving according to their wishes. Community members may consider slowly adjusting community boundaries (e.g., Huslia, Alaska); taking a staggered relocation approach where some families move first, followed by others (e.g., Newtok, Alaska); planning for temporary post-disaster evacuation (e.g., planning for temporary post-disaster evacuation to inland communities following hurricanes); or not moving together as a community but rather moving as individual households or groups based on kinship or social ties.

As an example of implementing Recommendation 3, community organizations and other entities involved in relocation decisions and efforts could establish a Community Knowledge Forum to facilitate the sharing and retention of knowledge and perspectives from community members, making sure to include people of all demographic backgrounds and representatives from nonprofit and community-based organizations and faith-based institutions (see Conclusions 5-1, 7-3, and 7-4).

Household-level planning may take the form of housing counseling services regarding the type and cost of replacement housing relative to a household's financial standing, the identification of housing stock available in receiving areas that meet household needs, transition funding and how to access financial support, and individually tailored counseling services based on the unique demographic of each household involved in the process of relocating (see Chapters 8 and 10).

Collaborative Regional Planning

Due to the lack of proactive adaptation planning at the regional, state, municipal, and neighborhood scales to prepare receiving and originating communities, community members are often left to find their own way (see Conclusions 8-1, 9-3, 9-4, and 9-6). This lack of pre- and post-relocation planning can result in ad hoc movements where people end up resettling in similarly hazardous areas (see Conclusions 8-2 and 10-8), and low-resource communities are strained by either an influx of new residents (in receiving communities; see Conclusion 8-4) or a loss of tax base (in originating communities; see Conclusion 8-6). Land left vacant in originating communities after relocation has the potential to offer sustained benefits for the community (e.g., floodwater retention areas, habitat for essential species). However, without proper planning, the vacated land is often not effectively managed—be it to include, for example, the creation of commemorative spaces, recreational assets, enhanced ecosystem services, or flood risk reduction measures—and the opportunities for such services may be lost (see Conclusions 8-7 and 10-3).

RECOMMENDATION 4: Regional planning entities alongside local public works, planning, and housing authorities, and departments involved in relocation, resilience, and climate adaption efforts should

- **account for community-driven relocation (originating and receiving communities) in their planning efforts (e.g., land-use plans, hazard mitigation plans, and economic plans);**
- **revise and assess relocation strategies based on current and projected climate data and traditional ecological knowledge; and**
- **conduct land suitability analysis to identify suitable receiving areas, and in doing so, to work with communities to raise their own capacities to understand land suitability.**

These actions could directly involve community members with social and natural scientists, landscape architects, land-use planners, and other design professionals in the development and management planning of vacated spaces that advance community-driven plans, such as ecological restoration, greenways, parks and recreational activity fields, environmental education sites, water retention areas, fish/wildlife habitat enhancement, and commemorative sites (e.g., cemeteries or memorial grounds; see Conclusions 8-7 and 8-8). Working alongside professionals in this way will grow community capacities to envision, adapt, and determine their futures, while informing planners of the diverse cultural-ecological knowledge, values, practices, and community assets with implications for local decision making (see Chapter 7).

Collaborative Federal Planning

Federal involvement is also critical to successful collaborations between regional entities, local government, and local communities. Collaborative planning that is cross-jurisdictional can guide appropriate adaptation investments in receiving areas and disinvestments in maladaptation in originating areas (see Chapter 8). Additionally, partnering with trusted community organizations can facilitate conversations with originating and receiving communities about the entire relocation process and avoidance of duplication and maladaptation (e.g., simultaneous buyouts and investment in high-hazard areas; see Chapter 9).

RECOMMENDATION 5: Federal agencies should engage with local governments and regional planning entities to support community-driven relocation planning across originating and receiving communities. Federal and local government collaborations with regional planning entities should

- **work with originating communities to establish threshold agreements for consolidation and regionalization of local governments and tax bases as residents relocate;**
- **share data about priority receiving communities and assess the impacts of regional population shifts to aid in planning;**
- **modify federal grant programs (e.g., Building Resilient Infrastructure and Communities, Flood Mitigation Assistance grant program, Hazard Mitigation grant program) to include making the programming of open space an eligible Federal Emergency Management Agency-funded activity; and**
- **modify federal and other relocation funding guidelines to include a requirement that households relocate outside Special Flood Hazard Areas and, in turn, work with communities to broaden understanding of what Special Flood Hazard Areas mean to household-level risks.**

Cross-Sector Collaborations and Capacity Building

Cross-sector collaborations have the potential to build adaptive capacities for all entities involved in community-driven relocation through mechanisms such as knowledge sharing (see Chapter 10) and the pooling of resources (Chapter 7).

RECOMMENDATION 6: State agencies, regional planning entities, professional associations, and academic-community partnerships (e.g., land and sea grant universities, minority serving institutions) should provide targeted capacity building and training initiatives to assist state and local governments in planning for community-driven relocation.

Capacity-building efforts could include training about how to plan for and implement community-driven relocation, including implementing the plan integration for resilience scorecard concept referenced in Chapter 9, to ensure that community-driven relocation efforts align with other community goals and projects found in other local plans. This effort would also include training and advising on how to reprogram and manage post-relocation land for optimal community and ecological benefit (see Chapter 8).

Investing in Receiving Communities

The ability of a receiving community to meet the immediate needs of resettlers (e.g., housing, employment, health care, education, transportation) is a critical component of community-driven relocation, and the availability of necessary resources is a central criterion for suitability. Even in communities with currently sufficient resources, rapid growth patterns challenge the adequacy of those resources (Chapters 8 and 10).

> **RECOMMENDATION 7: Federal government agencies, U.S. Gulf Coast state governments, and regional planning entities should increase investments in preparing receiving communities for new residents (e.g., infrastructure, energy system capacity, broadband, schools, water supply).**

Such investments could take the form of subsidies for communities that are already receiving people from areas of environmental risk and, additionally, incentives for communities willing to prepare to receive people. For example, HUD could set aside a percentage of its Community Development Block Grant funding for communities that agree to receive relocating communities, and the Federal Emergency Management Agency (FEMA) could do a similar set-aside for its Building Resilient Infrastructure and Communities funding, including prioritizing technical planning assistance grants for communities facing relocation (see Chapter 9). Subsidies and incentives could be tied to land-use plans that do not develop environmentally high-hazard areas, and that disinvest from housing stock and businesses in such areas, including areas with episodic and slow onset disasters (e.g., drought, subsidence) due to environmental change. Complementing these subsidies and incentives should be additional investments in nature-based solutions to restore ecological systems and enhance ecosystem services that further reduce flood risks (see Conclusion 8-7). Collaborators such as the Nature Conservancy, the Trust for Public Land, local land banks, and community-based organizations could complement the work of local governments and regional planning commissions.

STRENGTHENING PREPARATIONS FOR COMMUNITY-DRIVEN RELOCATION

Community-driven relocation relies on federal agency leadership and coordination, which can help to anticipate and prepare for the scale of the threat and its pending transformational changes (see Chapter 9). Recognizing the availability of, and high confidence in, climate risks in the U.S. Gulf Coast region (see Chapter 2), systematic federal screening of regions likely to warrant some degree of relocation is an important next step.

> **RECOMMENDATION 8: The Federal Emergency Management Agency should, outside of a disaster timeframe, pre-approve properties for acquisition (conduct a single National Environmental Policy Act/National Historic Preservation Act clearance on all such contiguous properties in a flood-prone area) and deem relocation as "cost-effective" in pre-identified communities.**

This action would facilitate community-wide relocation efforts by increasing efficiency (see Chapter 10) and raise the potential for ecosystem benefits, which come from returning contiguous parcels back to nature (see Chapter 8). This recommendation was also suggested in Government Accountability Office (GAO) report GAO 22-106037 Flood Mitigation.

Technical and Planning Assistance

Technical support provided at the federal level is not sufficient to help households and communities secure funding for and complete community relocation (see Chapter 9).[8] A lack of technical support impacts community relocation timeframes and limits who is able to participate in the planning and implementation of the relocation project (Conclusion 10-4).

> **RECOMMENDATION 9: In the short term, federal agencies (e.g., Federal Emergency Management Agency, U.S. Army Corps of Engineers, Department of Housing and Urban Development) should fund application and implementation assistance through the establishment of hazard mitigation "navigators." The funding and implementation of navigators should be a part of long-term recovery plans and hazard mitigation plans. These navigators would**

[8]As described in Chapter 9 and in the Key Terms (Appendix D), "technical support" (or assistance) is "programs, activities, and services provided by federal agencies to strengthen the capacity of grant recipients and to improve their performance of grant functions" (GAO, 2020b, p. 3).

- **provide the technical assistance needed to help communities apply for and implement a relocation strategy (e.g., through collective buyout programs); and**
- **provide household- and neighborhood-level planning assistance throughout the relocation process.**

Funding for navigators could be part of administrative costs disbursed to local governments (i.e., states, parishes, counties, municipalities) or as part of grants or awards to community-based organizations, and accompanied by sustained support (e.g., financial, human resources). Navigators would help expedite the application and reimbursement process for households and other intended entities, and would be similar to health care navigators who assist with healthcare.gov enrollment but help communities displaced by climate change to know what funding they can apply for and help them apply. To streamline implementation, navigators could be embedded in existing system-level infrastructure and draw from existing models such as land and sea grant university extension programs, NOAA Climate Adaptation Partnerships/Regional Integrated Sciences and Assessments, and FEMA's Building Resilient Infrastructure and Communities Direct Technical Assistance. Moreover, navigators could be community members who contribute to workforce growth while serving local needs. If FEMA does not establish a program for hazard mitigation navigators, funding for this position should be classified as technical support and reimbursable.

Beyond the "navigators" who work with individual households in New Jersey and Austin (described in Chapter 10), navigators should be available to help a whole neighborhood or community that wants to move together. This requires providing this type of assistance over the long timescales typically associated with buyouts and more complex community-wide relocation programs. Navigators could be the first step in developing a national cadre of resilience/adaptation extension agents trained in relocation planning and implementation who can share lessons learned and help connect originating and receiving communities. The FEMA-funded national cadre of individuals to assist underresourced communities, mentioned in Chapter 10, is an example of faculty and engagement experts at institutions who provide a consistent touchpoint for communities and households involved in community-driven relocation.

Taking Advantage of Innovative Strategies to Reduce Complexities and Rethink Priorities

Governance, policy, and funding mechanisms that have the potential to assist in community-driven relocations are hampered by their episodic nature (e.g., post-disaster, annual competitions) and minimal cross-agency, cross-jurisdictional, and cross-sector coordination, resulting in a complex maze that many communities struggle to navigate (Conclusions 8-3, 9-1, 9-2, 9-7, 10-6, and 10-7). However, there are innovative ways to reduce these complexities under existing structures (see Chapters 9 and 10 for examples). The following recommendations align with FEMA's efforts to offer more aid to underresourced communities through the Direct Technical Assistance program[9] and the Community Disaster Resilience Zones Act of 2022, the latter of which mandates the identification of communities that are most vulnerable to disasters and enables communities to partner with government and the private sector for funding and technical assistance.[10]

RECOMMENDATION 10: Federal agencies that provide relocation funding (e.g., Federal Emergency Management Agency, Department of Housing and Urban Development) should assess the benefits of annual funding to pre-disaster mitigation programs. Actions to improve adaptive capacity should include

- **analyzing regulatory and programmatic barriers for converting pre-disaster mitigation programs to include annualized funding for developing adaptive capacities, including relocation; and**
- **evaluating potential requirements to transition from a primarily competitive grant-making process to a process that provides ongoing assistance to underresourced communities to develop and implement risk reduction strategies using a distribution formula that prioritizes the highest climate risk areas.**

These actions reflect initial steps for funding agencies to provide a means for state and local governments and communities to build the necessary capacity and expertise to facilitate relocation efforts (see Conclusion 9-7). Interagency coordination and streamlining of the funding application process is also urgently needed (see Chapter 9) and is discussed in the next recommendation.

RECOMMENDATION 11: Agencies that offer funding for relocation planning, including infrastructure needs (such as Federal Emergency Management Agency [FEMA], U.S. Army Corps of Engineers, Department of Housing and Urban Development), should streamline the

[9]More information about FEMA's Direct Technical Assistance program is available at https://www.fema.gov/grants/mitigation/building-resilient-infrastructure-communities/direct-technical-assistance/communities

[10]More information about the Community Disaster Resilience Zones Act is available at https://www.fema.gov/flood-maps/products-tools/national-risk-index/community-disaster-resilience-zones

process of obtaining relocation funding, including reimbursements, through the following actions.

In the short term:

- Agencies should coordinate eligibility criteria and timing of requests for proposals.
- Agencies should align the timing of grant delivery and the duration of grants across federal agencies so that applicants have the maximum amount of time to fulfill the grant requirements.
- FEMA should allow people with National Flood Insurance Program coverage, whose homes have received a certain level of damage, to apply directly for a buyout rather than going through the state and then FEMA's hazard mitigation program.
- Agencies should allow funds from partnering agencies to be used as matching funds to the main federal source (i.e., the disbursing agency). States should also provide funding matches to communities for grants that require a nonfederal partner.
- The Council on Environmental Quality should convene agencies to develop a memorandum of understanding to coordinate construction, utility provision, and the environmental review process under the National Environmental Protection Act for relocations at the scale of a neighborhood or larger.
- Agencies should create an interagency mechanism, such as a single relocation grant application platform (e.g., the Universal Application for Disaster Survivors), that is accessible by states, tribes, municipalities, and households, and establishes a process to triage the applications and direct them to the most appropriate agency. The process should include step-by-step communication with the applicant for transparency and tracking.

In the longer term:

- Agencies should develop and maintain, across jurisdictions, an information clearinghouse connecting users to existing and new resources necessary to conduct a relocation program. This repository should be controlled by an operations center that includes the services of skilled consultants, planners, mediators, and stakeholders who have experience dealing with diverse interests and navigating issues that arise during cross-stakeholder discussions about relocation.

Together these actions can help to ease the burden on communities seeking funding for relocation. Examples and further descriptions of these actions can be found throughout the report. States helping communities meet nonfederal match requirements include Alaska's Division of Homeland

Security and Emergency Management and North Carolina's State Acquisition and Relocation Fund (SARF), the latter of which is described in Chapter 9. The use of a memorandum of understanding to streamline efforts is described in Chapter 8, while a universal grant application platform is elaborated on in Chapter 10. The recommendation to allow people with National Flood Insurance Program coverage to apply directly for a buyout is also suggested in GAO-22-106037 Flood Mitigation.

Ensuring Equity

FEMA's current BCA process (the method federal agencies use to calculate buyout amounts) privileges wealthier households and can limit who is able to participate in relocation programs (see Conclusions 10-3 and 10-5). To create or support federal grant programs that can make community-driven relocation more equitable and accessible to underresourced communities, including renters, the following actions should be pursued by relevant federal agencies (e.g., FEMA, HUD).

RECOMMENDATION 12: The Federal Emergency Management Agency (FEMA), through the leadership and engagement of the Office of Information and Regulatory Affairs of the Office of Management and Budget, should revise its benefit-cost analysis process. This should include

- **developing a rubric that accounts for a community's qualitative values, characteristics, and root causes of vulnerability, such as social cohesion, social capital, political disenfranchisement, linguistic isolation, and collective efficacy, among others; and**
- **extending FEMA's recent temporary revisions to the benefit-cost analysis for the fiscal 2022 application cycle of Building Resilient Infrastructure and Communities and the Flood Mitigation Assistance grant program.**

Revising BCA processes can help to reduce the inequitable distribution of funds available for relocation efforts and to elevate the consideration of social and ecological elements (see Chapter 10).

RECOMMENDATION 13: Federal programs involved with community-driven relocation (e.g., Federal Emergency Management Agency, U.S. Army Corps of Engineers, Department of Housing and Urban Development) should

- **increase acquisition payments to property owners so they can afford a comparable home in a safe location;**

- **provide relocation assistance to renters, and mobile or manufactured homes; and**
- **use management costs to support buyout grant offers to property owners above typical pre-disaster fair market values.**

Agencies could base the buyout price not on the home's market value before the most recent disaster leading to the buyout but on the market value of a similar house in the closest safe area, as suggested in GAO 22-106037 Flood Mitigation (see Chapter 10). Another method of increasing acquisition payments to property owners is for FEMA to provide vouchers that can be payable to the owners of property that the relocating individuals and families acquire. These would help to close the gap between acquisition payments and the cost of replacement housing for lower-income households (Conclusion 10-5). Such vouchers should also go to lessees to avoid exacerbating historic income disparities. At minimum, renters and those without a title should be able to get "navigation" assistance and/or counseling during the process of relocation (Conclusion 10-4). To the extent that FEMA does not act, states could provide funding for the purchasing of new housing outside Special Flood Hazard Areas, including the floodplain and flood-prone areas (as North Carolina did through SARF; see Chapter 9).

In addition to eliminating cost-effective requirements and ensuring that residents have sufficient funds to purchase or rent housing elsewhere, agencies involved in buyouts, for example, could voluntarily adhere to the Uniform Relocation Act, even if it traditionally has not applied to FEMA property acquisitions other than rental units with tenants. This has been successfully done with Austin's Watershed Protection Department buyout program (see Chapter 10). While states can choose to include rental housing as an eligible type under hazard mitigation assistance grants, they often decide not to pursue this strategy and focus on the buyout of owner-occupied housing instead.

References

Adams, H. (2016). Why populations persist: Mobility, place attachment and climate change. *Population and Environment*, *37*, 429–448.

Adams, V., Van Hattum, T., & English, D. (2009). Chronic disaster syndrome: Displacement, disaster capitalism, and the eviction of the poor from New Orleans. *American Ethnologist*, *36*(4), 615–636. https://doi.org/10.1111/j.1548-1425.2009.01199.x

Adelson, J., Webster, R. A., Hammer, D., & Chou, S. (2022). The Road Home program shortchanged low-income homeowners in Louisiana. New data proves it. *The Advocate*. https://www.theadvocate.com/baton_rouge/news/hurricane/how-louisianas-road-home-program-shortchanged-the-poor/article_12934aed-0900-55dd-af30-c8f1826f96d2.html

Adger, W. N. (2003). Social capital, collective action, and adaptation to climate change. *Economic Geography*, *79*(4), 387–404. https://doi.org/https://doi.org/10.1111/j.1944-8287.2003.tb00220.x

Adger, W. N., Barnett, J., Brown, K., Marshall, N., & O'Brien, K. (2013). Cultural dimensions of climate change impacts and adaptation. *Nature Climate Change*, *3*(2), 112–117. https://doi.org/10.1038/nclimate1666

Adger, W. N., de Campos, R. S., & Mortreux, C. (2018). Mobility, displacement and migration, and their interactions with vulnerability and adaptation to environmental risks. *Routledge handbook of environmental displacement and migration* (pp. 29–41). Routledge.

Adger, W. N., Dessai, S., Goulden, M., Hulme, M., Lorenzoni, I., Nelson, D. R., Naess, L. O., Wolf, J., & Wreford, A. (2009). Are there social limits to adaptation to climate change? *Climatic Change*, *93*(3), 335–354.

Adler, P. S., & Kwan, S. W. (2002). Social capital: Prospects for a new concept. *The Academy of Management Review*, *27*(1), 17–40. https://doi.org/10.2307/4134367

Agnew Beck Consulting. (2011). *Relocation report: Newtok to Mertarvik*.

Aiken, C. S. (2003). *The cotton plantation South since the Civil War*. Baltimore, Maryland: John Hopkins University Press. https://doi.org/10.1353/book.72150

Airriess, C. A., & Clawson, D. L. (1991). Versailles: A Vietnamese enclave in New Orleans, Louisiana. *Journal of Cultural Geography*, *12*(1), 1–13. https://doi.org/10.1080/08873639109478416

Airriess, C. A., Li, W., Leong, K. J., Chen, A. C.-C., & Keith, V. M. (2008). Church-based social capital, networks and geographical scale: Katrina evacuation, relocation, and recovery in a New Orleans Vietnamese American community. *Geoforum, 39*(3), 1333–1346. https://doi.org/https://doi.org/10.1016/j.geoforum.2007.11.003

Ajibade, I., Sullivan, M., & Haeffner, M. (2020). Why climate migration is not managed retreat: Six justifications. *Global Environmental Change: Human and Policy Dimensions, 65,* 102187. https://doi.org/10.1016/j.gloenvcha.2020.102187

Albert, S., Bronen, R., Tooler, N., Leon, J., Yee, D., Ash, J., Boseto, D., & Grinham, A. (2018). Heading for the hills: Climate-driven community relocations in the Solomon Islands and Alaska provide insight for a 1.5°C future. *Regional Environmental Change, 18*(8), 2261–2272. https://doi.org/10.1007/s10113-017-1256-8

Albrecht, G., Sartore, G., Connor, L., Higginbotham, N., Freeman, S., Kelly, B., Stain, H., Tonna, A., & Pollard, G. (2007). Solastalgia: The distress caused by environmental change. *Australasian Psychiatry: Bulletin of Royal Australian and New Zealand College of Psychiatrists, 15*(1), S95–S98. https://doi.org/10.1080/10398560701701288

Aldrich, D. P. (2012). *Building resilience: Social capital in post-disaster recovery.* University of Chicago Press.

Aldrich, D. P., & Meyer, M. A. (2015). Social capital and community resilience. *American Behavioral Scientist, 59*(2), 254–269. https://doi.org/10.1177/0002764214550299

Alexander, K. S., Ryan, A., & Measham, T. G. (2012). Managed retreat of coastal communities: Understanding responses to projected sea level rise. *Journal of Environmental Planning and Management*, *55*(4), 409–433.

Allison, E. H., & Ellis, F. (2001). The livelihoods approach and management of small-scale fisheries. *Marine Policy, 25*(5), 377–388. https://doi.org/https://doi.org/10.1016/S0308-597X(01)00023-9

Almedom, A. M. (2005). Social capital and mental health: An interdisciplinary review of primary evidence. *Social Science & Medicine, 61*(5), 943–964. https://doi.org/10.1016/j.socscimed.2004.12.025

American Map Company. (1931). Lynchings by states and counties in the United States, 1900-1931: (data from Research Department, Tuskegee Institute); cleartype county outline map of the United States. American Map Company. Library of Congress Geography and Map Division. https://www.loc.gov/item/2006636636/

American Red Cross. (2017). *Superstorm Sandy five-year update.* https://www.redcross.org/content/dam/redcross/imported-pdfs/sandy-five-year-update.pdf

Amundsen, H. (2015). Place attachment as a driver of adaptation in coastal communities in Northern Norway. *Local Environment, 20*(3), 257–276.

Ancelet, B. J., Edwards, J., & Pitre, G. (1991). *Cajun country.* University Press of Mississippi.

Anderson, R. B. (2022). The taboo of retreat: The politics of sea level rise, managed retreat, and coastal property values in California. *Economic Anthropology, 9*(2), 284–296. https://doi.org/10.1002/sea2.12247

Anguelovski, I., Connolly, J. J. T., Pearsall, H., Shokry, G., Checker, M., Maantay, J., Gould, K., Lewis, T., Maroko, A., & Roberts, J. T. (2019). Why green "climate gentrification" threatens poor and vulnerable populations. *Proceedings of the National Academy of Sciences, 116*(52), 26139–26143. https://doi.org/doi:10.1073/pnas.1920490117

Anisi, A. (2020). *Addressing challenges in climate change adaptation: Learning from the Narikoso Community Relocation in Fiji* (Policy Brief No. 84). Toda Peace Institute. https://toda.org/policy-briefs-and-resources/policy-briefs/addressing-challenges-in-climate-change-adaptation-learning-from-the-narikoso-community-relocation-in-fiji.html

Anton, C. E., & Lawrence, C. (2014). Home is where the heart is: The effect of place of residence on place attachment and community participation. *Journal of Environmental Psychology*, *40*, 451–461. https://doi.org/https://doi.org/10.1016/j.jenvp.2014.10.007

Aranda, E., & Rivera, F. I. (2016). Puerto Rican families in Central Florida: Prejudice, discrimination, and their implications for successful integration. *Women, Gender, and Families of Color, 4*(1), 57–85. https://doi.org/10.5406/womgenfamcol.4.1.0057

Armitage, D., Berkes, F., Dale, A., Kocho-Schellenberg, E., & Patton, E. (2011). Co-management and the co-production of knowledge: Learning to adapt in Canada's Arctic. *Global Environmental Change, 21*(3), 995–1004. https://doi.org/https://doi.org/10.1016/j.gloenvcha.2011.04.006

Arreola, D. D. (2002). *Tejano South Texas: A Mexican American cultural province.* University of Texas Press. https://doi.org/10.7560/705104

Askland, H. H., & Bunn, M. (2018). Lived experiences of environmental change: Solastalgia, power and place. *Emotion, Space and Society, 27*, 16–22. https://doi.org/https://doi.org/10.1016/j.emospa.2018.02.003

Atif, N., Nazir, H., Sultan, Z. H., Rauf, R., Waqas, A., Malik, A., Sikander, S., & Rahman, A. (2022). Technology-assisted peer therapy: A new way of delivering evidence-based psychological interventions. *BMC Health Services Research, 22*(1), 842. https://doi.org/10.1186/s12913-022-08233-6

Atkins, P. W. B., Wilson, D. S., & Hayes, S. C. (2019). *Prosocial: Using evolutionary science to build productive, equitable, and collaborative groups.* Context Press/New Harbinger Publications. https://psycnet.apa.org/record/2019-59377-000

Atoba, K. O. (2022). A proactive approach for the acquisition of flood-prone properties in advance of flood events. In S. Brody, Y. Lee, & B. Kothuis (Eds.), *Coastal flood risk reduction: The Netherlands and the U.S. Upper Texas Coast* (pp. 303–316). https://doi.org/10.1016/B978-0-323-85251-7.00022-6

Atoba, K. O., Brody, S. D., Highfield, W. E., Shepard, C. C., & Verdone, L. N. (2020). Strategic property buyouts to enhance flood resilience: A multi-criteria spatial approach for incorporating ecological values into the selection process. *Environmental Hazards, 20*(3), 229–247. https://doi.org/10.1080/17477891.2020.1771251

Aune, K. T., Gesch, D., & Smith, G. S. (2020). A spatial analysis of climate gentrification in Orleans Parish, Louisiana post-Hurricane Katrina. *Environmental Research, 185*, 109384. https://doi.org/https://doi.org/10.1016/j.envres.2020.109384

Badullovich, N., Grant, W. J., & Colvin, R. M. (2020). Framing climate change for effective communication: A systematic map. *Environmental Research Letters, 15*(12), 123002.

Bankston, C. L., & Zhou, M. (2021). Involuntary migration, context of reception, and social mobility: The case of Vietnamese refugee resettlement in the United States. *Journal of Ethnic and Migration Studies, 47*(21), 4797–4816. https://doi.org/10.1080/1369183X.2020.1724411

Barcus, H. R., & Brunn, S. D. (2010). Place elasticity: Exploring a new conceptualization of mobility and place attachment in rural America. *Geografiska Annaler: Series B, Human Geography, 92*(4), 281–295. https://doi.org/10.1111/j.1468-0467.2010.00353.x

Bard Center for Environmental Policy. (2012, February 16). Climate change communication: The role of the messenger. *The Official Blog of the Bard Center for Environmental Policy.* https://www.bard.edu/cep/blog/?p=1485

Barra, M. P. (2021). Good sediment: Race and restoration in coastal Louisiana. *Annals of the American Association of Geographers, 111*(1), 266–282. https://doi.org/10.1080/24694452.2020.1766411

Barra, M. P., Hemmerling, S. A., & Baustian, M. M. (2020). A model controversy: Using environmental competency groups to inform coastal restoration planning in Louisiana. *The Professional Geographer, 72*(4), 511–520. https://doi.org/10.1080/00330124.2020.1777574

Barrios, R. E. (2014). 'Here, I'm not at ease': Anthropological perspectives on community resilience. *Disasters, 38*(2), 329–350. https://onlinelibrary.wiley.com/doi/pdfdirect/10.1111/disa.12044?download=true

Barry, J. M. (1998). *Rising tide: The Great Mississippi Flood of 1927 and how it changed America.* Simon & Schuster.

Bates, P. D., Quinn, N., Sampson, C., Smith, A., Wing, O., Sosa, J., Savage, J., Olcese, G., Neal, J., Schumann, G., Giustarini, L., Coxon, G., Porter, J. R., Amodeo, M. F., Chu, Z., Lewis-Gruss, S., Freeman, N. B., Houser, T., Delgado, M., . . . Krajewski, W. F. (2021). Combined modeling of US fluvial, pluvial, and coastal flood hazard under current and future climates. *Water Resources Research, 57*(2), Article e2020WR028673. https://doi.org/10.1029/2020WR028673

Baum, F., MacDougall, C., & Smith, D. (2006). Participatory action research. *Journal of Epidemiology and Community Health, 60*(10), 854–857. https://doi.org/https://doi.org/10.1136%2Fjech.2004.028662

Beckfield, J., Booker, D., Bowie, K., Castro, B., DeMyers, C., Evrard, D. A., Theard-Lewis, A., & Ulama, D. (2022). How the Gulf Coast can lead the energy transition. *The Roosevelt Project.* https://ceepr.mit.edu/wp-content/uploads/2022/12/2022-The-Roosevelt-Project-Gulf-Coast-Case-Study.pdf

Belkin, G. (2020). Leadership for the social climate. *New England Journal of Medicine, 382*(21), 1975–1977.

Belkin, G., & McCray, C. (2019). ThriveNYC: Delivering on mental health. *American Journal of Public Health, 109*(S3), S156–S163.

Ben Dor, T. K., Salvesen, D., Kamrath, C., & Ganser, B. (2020). Floodplain buyouts and municipal finance. *Natural Hazards Review, 21*(3), 1–17.

Benedetto, K. M., & Trepanier, J. C. (2020). Climatology and spatiotemporal analysis of North Atlantic rapidly intensifying hurricanes (1851–2017). *Atmosphere, 11*(3), 291. https://www.mdpi.com/2073-4433/11/3/291

Bentham, W., Vannoy, S. D., Badger, K., Wennerstrom, A., & Springgate, B. F. (2011). Opportunities and challenges of implementing collaborative mental health care in post-Katrina New Orleans. *Ethnicity & Disease, 21*(3 Suppl 1), S1–S37.

Berke, P., Kates, J., Malecha, M., Masterson, J., Shea, P., & Yu, S. (2021). Using a resilience scorecard to improve local planning for vulnerability to hazards and climate change: An application in two cities. *Cities, 119*, 103408.

Berke, P., Lyles, W., & Smith, G. (2014). Impacts of federal and state mitigation policies on local land use policy. *Journal of Planning Education and Research, 34*(1), 60–76. https://doi.org/10.1177/0739456X135170

Berke, P., Malecha, M. L., Yu, S., Lee, J., & Masterson, J. H. (2019). Plan integration for resilience scorecard: Evaluating networks of plans in six US coastal cities. *Journal of Environmental Planning and Management, 62*(5), 901–920.

Berke, P., Newman, G., Lee, J., Combs, T., Kolosna, C., & Salvesen, D. (2015). Evaluation of networks of plans and vulnerability to hazards and climate change: A resilience scorecard. *Journal of the American Planning Association, 81*(4), 287–302. https://doi.org/10.1080/01944363.2015.1093954

Berkes, F., Colding, J., & Folke, C. (2000). Rediscovery of traditional ecological knowledge as adaptive management. *Ecological Applications, 10*(5), 1251–1262.

Berkes, F., & Ross, H. (2013). Community resilience: Toward an integrated approach. *Society & Natural Resources, 26*(1), 5–20. https://doi.org/10.1080/08941920.2012.736605

Berlin, C. (2023, May 24). *An Alabama program helps residents stormproof their homes. Louisiana wants to copy it.* New Orleans Public Radio. https://www.wwno.org/coastal-desk/2023-05-24/an-alabama-program-helps-residents-stormproof-their-homes-louisiana-wants-to-copy-it

Best, K. B., Jouzi, Z., Islam, M. S., Kirby, T., Nixon, R., Hossan, A., & Nyiawung, R. A. (2023). Typologies of multiple vulnerabilities and climate gentrification across the East Coast of the United States. *Urban Climate, 48*, 101430. https://doi.org/10.1016/j.uclim.2023.101430

Bethel, M. B., Brien, L. F., Esposito, M. M., Miller, C. T., Buras, H. S., Laska, S. B., Philippe, R., Peterson, K. J., & Parsons Richards, C. (2014). Sci-tek: A GIS-based multidisciplinary method for incorporating traditional ecological knowledge into Louisiana's coastal restoration decision-making processes. *Journal of Coastal Research, 30*(5), 1081–1099.

Bhattarai, A., & Fowers, A. (2022). For low-income parents, no day care often means no pay. *Washington Post.* https://www.washingtonpost.com/business/2022/02/22/child-care-covid-inequality/

Biesecker, M., & Bajak, F. (2017). Hurricane Harvey: Floodwaters 'caused chemical spill' at Houston's dirtiest toxic waste plant. *The Independent.* https://www.independent.co.uk/news/world/americas/hurricane-harvey-latest-houston-chemical-plant-toxic-spill-floodwater-us-oil-recovery-superfund-epa-a7954586.html

Biggs, R., Schlüter, M., & Schoon, M. (2015). *Principles for building resilience: Sustaining ecosystem services in social-ecological systems.* Cambridge University Press. https://doi.org/https://doi.org/10.1017/CBO9781316014240

Biglan, A., Johansson, M., Van Ryzin, M., & Embry, D. (2020). Scaling up and scaling out: Consilience and the evolution of more nurturing societies. *Clinical Psychology Review, 81*, 101893. https://doi.org/10.1016/j.cpr.2020.101893

Bilskie, M. V., Hagen, S.C., Medeiros, S., Kidwell, D., Buckel, C., & Passeri, D. (2018). *NCCOS ecological effects of sea level rise in the northern Gulf of Mexico (EESLR-NGOM): Simulated return period stillwater elevation (NCEI Accession 0170340).* [Data set]. NOAA National Centers for Environmental Information. https://doi.org/10.7289/V54B2ZKR

Binder, S. B. (2013). *Resilience and postdisaster relocation: A study of New York's home buyout plan in the wake of Hurricane Sandy.* Quick Response Grant Program, Natural Hazards Center, University of Colorado at Boulder. https://hazards.colorado.edu/uploads/quick_report/binder_2013.pdf

Binder, S. B., & Greer, A. (2016). The devil is in the details: Linking home buyout policy, practice, and experience after Hurricane Sandy. *Politics and Governance, 4*(4), 97–106. https://www.cogitatiopress.com/politicsandgovernance/article/view/738

Binder, S. B., Ritchie, L. A., Bender, R., Thiel, A., Baker, C. K., Badillo, E., Goodfellow, S., Kulp, B., & Weir, P. (2020). Limbo: The unintended consequences of home buyout programmes on peripheral communities. *Environmental Hazards, 19*(5), 488–507. https://doi.org/10.1080/17477891.2020.1714537

Bisschop, L. C. J., Strobl, S., & Viollaz, J. S. (2018). Getting into deep water: Coastal land loss and state–corporate crime in the Louisiana bayou. *The British Journal of Criminology, 58*(4), 886–905. https://doi.org/10.1093/bjc/azx057

Bittle, J. (2023). *The great displacement: Climate change and the next American migration.* Simon & Schuster.

Blaine, T., Canney, J., Collins, C., Kline, J., & Locke, R. (2022). *Climate change, migration and the risk of conflict in growing urban centers.* United States Institute of Peace. https://www.usip.org/publications/2022/06/climate-change-migration-and-risk-conflict-growing-urban-centers

Blake, E. S., Kimberlain, T. B., Berg, R. J., Cangialosi, J. P., & Beven II, J. L. (2013). *Tropical Cyclone Report: Hurricane Sandy.* National Hurricane Center. https://www.nhc.noaa.gov/data/tcr/AL182012_Sandy.pdf

Blakeman, H. (2023). *Prioritizing receiving communities: Reducing environmental, social, and economic risk as people migrate from the coast.* Council of Educators in Landscape Architecture. https://doi.org/10.13140/RG.2.2.17065.36963

Blakeman, H., Birch, T., & Grandy, G. (2022). *Addressing climate migration strategically to improve social, environmental, and economic resilience* [Conference session]. ASLA 2022 Conference on Landscape Architecture, San Francisco, CA, United States. https://www.researchgate.net/publication/373041471_Addressing_Climate_Migration_Strategically_to_Improve_Social_Environmental_and_Economic_Resilience

Bloemen, P., Reeder, T., Zevenbergen, C., Rijke, J., & Kingsborough, A. (2018). Lessons learned from applying adaptation pathways in flood risk management and challenges for the further development of this approach. *Mitigation and Adaptation Strategies for Global Change*, *23*, 1083–1108. Spring Nature Switzerland.

Bloemen, P. J., Hammer, F., van der Vlist, M. J., Grinwis, P., & van Alphen, J. (2019). DMDU into practice: Adaptive delta management in the Netherlands. In V. A. W. J. Marchau, W. E. Walker, P. J. T. M. Bloemen, & S. W. Popper (Eds.), *Decision making under deep uncertainty: From theory to practice* (pp. 321–351).

Boege, V., & Rakova, U. (2019). *Climate change-induced relocation: Problems and achievements—the Carterets case* (Policy Brief No. 33). Toda Peace Institute. https://toda.org/policy-briefs-and-resources/policy-briefs/climate-change-induced-relocation-problems-and-achievements-the-carterets-case.html

Boege, V., & Shibata, R. (2020). *Climate change, relocation and peacebuilding in Fiji: Challenges, debates, and ways forward* (Policy Brief No. 97). Toda Peace Institute. https://toda.org/policy-briefs-and-resources/policy-briefs/climate-change-relocation-and-peacebuilding-in-fiji-challenges-debates-and-ways-forward.html

Bondy, R. E. (1938). The town that the Red Cross built. *The Red Cross Courier*, 3–12.

Boonstra, W. J. (2016). Conceptualizing power to study social-ecological interactions. *Ecology and Society*, *21*(1). https://doi.org/http://dx.doi.org/10.5751/ES-07966-210121

Boothroyd, R. I., Flint, A. Y., Lapiz, A. M., Lyons, S., Jarboe, K. L., & Aldridge II, W. A., (2017). Active involved community partnerships: Co-creating implementation infrastructure for getting to and sustaining social impact. *Translational Behavioral Medicine, 7*(3), 467–477. https://doi.org/10.1007/s13142-017-0503-3

Borsa, G. (2020). Vunidogoloa: What can we learn from climate change relocation? https://www.kth.se/blogs/hist/2020/01/vunidogoloa-what-can-we-learn-from-climate-change-relocation/

Bostrom, A. (2017). Mental models and risk perceptions related to climate change. *Oxford research encyclopedia of climate science*. https://doi.org/10.1093/acrefore/9780190228620.013.303

Bourgeois, M., Chapiesky, K., Landry, L., Lightner, J., & Marx, J. (2016). *Louisiana shrimp: Fishery management plan*. Louisiana Department of Wildlife and Fisheries. https://www.wlf.louisiana.gov/assets/Resources/Publications/Marine_Fishery_Management_Plans/2016_Shrimp_Fishery_Management_Plan.pdf

Bower, E. R., Badamikar, A., Wong-Parodi, G., & Field, C. B. (2023). Enabling pathways for sustainable livelihoods in planned relocation. *Natural Climate Change*, *13*, 919–926. https://doi.org/10.1038/s41558-023-01753-x

Braga, B., & Elliott, D. (2023). *The effect of climate migrants on the financial well-being of receiving communities*. Urban Institute. https://www.urban.org/research/publication/effect-climate-migrants-financial-well-being-receiving-communities

Bragg, R. (2000). Vietnamese refugees in New Orleans find a little peace. *The New York Times*. https://www.nytimes.com/2000/10/02/us/vietnamese-refugees-in-new-orleans-find-a-little-peace.html

Bragg, W. K., Gonzalez, S. T., Rabearisoa, A., & Stoltz, A. D. (2021). Communicating managed retreat in California. *Water*, *13*(6), 781. https://doi.org/10.3390/w13060781

Brasher, K., & Wiseman, J. (2008). Community wellbeing in an unwell world: Trends, challenges, and possibilities. *Journal of Public Health Policy*, *29*(3), 353–366. https://doi.org/10.1057/jphp.2008.16

Brasseaux, C. A. (1987). *The founding of New Acadia: The beginnings of Acadian life in Louisiana, 1765-1803*. LSU Press.

___. (1992). *Acadian to Cajun: Transformation of a people, 1803–1877*. University Press of Mississippi.

Bromhead, H. (2022, April 4). "Managed retreat" is a terrible way to talk about responding to climate change. *Slate*. https://slate.com/technology/2022/04/managed-retreat-climate-change-language.html

Bronen, R. (2014). Choice and necessity: Relocations in the Arctic and South Pacific. *Forced Migration Review*, *45*. https://ora.ox.ac.uk/objects/uuid:f91e8fa5-fd5d-4f96-ad39-02a072588c25

___. (2021). Rights, resilience and community-led relocation: Creating a national governance framework. *Harbinger*, *45*, 25–45. https://socialchangenyu.com/harbinger/rights-resilience-and-community-led-relocation/

Bronen, R., & Chapin III, F. S. (2013). Adaptive governance and institutional strategies for climate-induced community relocations in Alaska. *Proceedings of the National Academy of Sciences*, *110*(23), 9320–9325. https://doi.org/10.1073/pnas.1210508110

Brown, B. B., & Perkins, D. D. (1992). Disruptions in place attachment. In I. Altman & S. M. Low (Eds.), *Place attachment* (pp. 279–304). Springer. https://doi.org/10.1007/978-1-4684-8753-4_13

Brown, H., Abdallah, S., & Townsley, R. (2017). *Understanding local needs for wellbeing data measures and indicators*. Happy City, what works wellbeing. https://whatworkswellbeing.org/resources/understanding-local-needs-for-wellbeing-data/

Brown, J. T. (2014). *The Hurricane Sandy rebuilding strategy: In brief* (CRS Report No. R43396). Congressional Research Service. https://crsreports.congress.gov/product/details?prodcode=R43396

Brown, S. K. (1993). Valmeyer designs its destiny. St. Louis Post-Dispatch, A-1.

Brown, T. C., Bankston, W. B., Forsyth, C. J., & Berthelot, E. R. (2011). Qualifying the boom-bust paradigm: An examination of the off-shore oil and gas industry. *Sociology Mind*, *1*(3), 96.

Browning, C. R., & Cagney, K. A. (2002). Neighborhood structural disadvantage, collective efficacy, and self-rated physical health in an urban setting. *Journal of Health and Social Behavior*, *43*(4), 383–399.

Bruyère, C., Rasmussen, R., Gutmann, E., Done, J., Tye, M., Jaye, A., Prein, A., Mooney, P., Ge, M., & Fredrick, S. (2017). *Impact of climate change on Gulf of Mexico hurricanes*. NCAR tech note. NCAR/TN535.

Bukvic, A., & Owen, G. (2017). Attitudes towards relocation following Hurricane Sandy: Should we stay or should we go? *Disasters*, *41*(1), 101–123. https://doi.org/doi:10.1111/disa.12186

Bukvic, A., Whittemore, A., Gonzales, J., & Wilhelmi, O. (2022). Understanding relocation in flood-prone coastal communities through the lens of place attachment. *Applied Geography*, *146*, 102758. https://doi.org/10.1016/j.apgeog.2022.102758

Bulkeley, H. (2000). Common knowledge? Public understanding of climate change in Newcastle, Australia. *Public Understanding of Science*, *9*(3), 313–333. https://doi.org/10.1177/096366250000900301

Bullard, R. D. (1983). Solid waste sites and the black Houston community. *Sociological Inquiry*, *53*(2-3), 273–288.

___. (2000). *Dumping in Dixie: Race, class, and environmental quality* (3rd edition). Westview Press.

Bullard, R. D., & Wright, B. (2009). Race, place and the environment in post-Katrina New Orleans. *Race, place and environmental justice after Hurricane Katrina: Struggles to reclaim, rebuild and revitalize New Orleans and the Gulf Coast* (pp. 19–48). Routledge.

___. (2012). *The wrong complexion for protection: How the government response to disaster endangers African American communities*. New York University Press.

Bureau of Indian Affairs. (2020). *The unmet infrastructure needs of tribal communities and Alaska Native Villages in process of relocating to higher ground as a result of climate change*. https://www.bia.gov/sites/default/files/dup/assets/bia/ots/tcrp/Informational_Report.pdf

___. (2022). *BIA Branch of Tribal Climate Resilience 2022 annual awards summary*. https://www.bia.gov/sites/default/files/dup/inline-files/award_summary_0.pdf

Bureau of Ocean Energy Management. (2023). *Oil and gas—Gulf of Mexico*. https://www.boem.gov/regions/gulf-mexico-ocs-region/oil-and-gas-gulf-mexico

Burke, G., & Dearen, J. (2010, August 25). Gulf waste heads to landfills, some with problems. *San Diego Union Tribune*. https://www.sandiegouniontribune.com/sdut-gulf-waste-heads-to-landfills-some-with-problems-2010aug25-story.html

Burley, D., Jenkins, P., Laska, S., & Davis Giardina, T. (2007). Place attachment and environmental change in Coastal Louisiana. *Organization & Environment, 20*, 347–366. https://doi.org/10.1177/1086026607305739

Burley, D. M. (2010). *Losing ground: Identity and land loss in coastal Louisiana*. University Press of Mississippi.

Butler, W., Holmes, T., Jackson, A., Lange, Z., Melix, B., & Milordis, A. (2021). *Addressing climate driven displacement: Planning for sea level rise in Florida's coastal communities and affordable housing in inland communities in the face of climate gentrification*. https://coss.fsu.edu/collins/wp-content/uploads/sites/28/2022/02/Butler-Jackson-Holmes-et-al.-2021-Final-LCI-Report-Climate-Gentrification-Updated-min.pdf

Butler-Ulloa, D. M. (2022). *Climate displacement, migration and relocation in the United States: Resistance, restoration and resilience in the coastal south* (Publication No. 29323594) [Doctoral dissertation, University of Massachusetts Boston]. ProQuest Dissertations Publishing. https://www.proquest.com/dissertations-theses/climate-displacement-migration-relocation-united/docview/2710980853/se-2?accountid=152665

Cagney, K. A., Sterrett, D., Benz, J., & Tompson, T. (2016). Social resources and community resilience in the wake of Superstorm Sandy. *PLoS ONE, 11*(8), e0160824. https://doi.org/10.1371/journal.pone.0160824

Callaway, E. (2021). Ancient footprints could be oldest traces of humans in the Americas. *Nature*, 597(7878), 601–602.

Campbell, J. R. (2022). *Climate change, population mobility and relocation in Oceania: Part I: Background and concepts* (Policy Brief No. 131). Toda Peace Institute. https://toda.org/policy-briefs-and-resources/policy-briefs/climate-change-population-mobility-and-relocation-in-oceania-part-i-background-and-concepts.html

Capio, C. M., Sit, C. H. P., & Abernethy, B. (2014). Physical well-being. In A.C. Michalos (Ed.), *Encyclopedia of quality of life and well-being research* (pp. 4805–4807). Springer, Dordrecht. https://doi.org/10.1007/978-94-007-0753-5_2166

Carey, J. (2020). Managed retreat increasingly seen as necessary in response to climate change's fury. *Proceedings of the National Academy of Sciences, 117*(24), 13182–13185. https://doi.org/10.1073/pnas.2008198117

Carlo, N. (2020). *Arctic observing: Indigenous peoples' history, perspectives, and approaches for partnership*. University of Alaska Fairbanks, Center for Arctic Policy Studies. https://www.uaf.edu/caps/our-work/Carlo_Arctic-Observing_Indigenous-Peoples-History_CAPS_5MAR2020.pdf

Carp, J. (2008). "Ground-truthing" representations of social space using Lefebvre's conceptual triad. *Journal of Planning Education and Research, 28*(2), 129–142.

Carse, A., & Lewis, J. A. (2020). New horizons for dredging research: The ecology and politics of harbor deepening in the southeastern United States. *Wiley Interdisciplinary Reviews: Water, 7*(6), e1485.

Carter, J. (2010). Protocols, particularities, and problematising Indigenous 'engagement' in community-based environmental management in settled Australia. *Geographical Journal, 176*(3), 199–213.

___. (2017). Superfund sites and the floods of Hurricane Harvey: Foreseeable or an "act of God"? *Union of Concerned Scientists' The Equation.* https://blog.ucsusa.org/jacob-carter/superfund-sites-and-the-floods-of-hurricane-harvey-foreseeable-or-an-act-of-god/

Carter, J. E. (1991). Niobrara, Nebraska: The town too tough to stay put! *Nebraska History, 72,* 144–149.

Carter, L., Dow, K., Hiers, K., Kunkel, K. E., Lascurain, A., Marcy, D., Osland, M., & Schramm, P. (2018). Southeast. In D.R. Reidmiller, C.W. Avery, D.R. Easterling, K.E. Kunkel, K.L.M. Lewis, T.K. Maycock, & B.C. Stewart (Eds.) *Impacts, risks, and adaptation in the United States: Fourth national climate assessment, Volume 2* (pp. 743–808). U.S. Global Change Research Program.

Carter, L. M., Jones, J. W., Berry, L., Burkett, V., Murley, J. F., Obeysekera, J., Schramm, P. J., & Wear, D. (2014). Chapter 17: Southeast and the Caribbean. In J. M. Melillo, T. C. Richmond, & G. W. Yohe (Eds.) *Climate change impacts in the United States: The Third National Climate Assessment* (pp. 367–417). https://doi.org/10.7930/JON-P22CB

Case, A., & Deaton, A. (2021). *Deaths of despair and the future of capitalism.* Princeton University Press.

Casey, E. S. (1997). Smooth spaces and rough-edged places: The hidden history of place. *The Review of Metaphysics, 51*(2), 267–296. http://www.jstor.org/stable/20130200

Cash, A., Chapple, K., Debpsky, N., Elias, R. R., Krnjaic, M., Manji, S., & Montano, H. (2020). *Climate change and displacement in the US –A review of the literature.* SPARCC. https://www.sparcchub.org/wp-content/uploads/2020/04/Climate-and-Displacement-Lit-Review-6.19.2020.pdf

Cash, D. W., Clark, W. C., Alcock, F., Dickson, N. M., Eckley, N., Guston, D. H., Jäger, J., & Mitchell, R. B. (2003). Knowledge systems for sustainable development. *Proceedings of the National Academy of Sciences, 100*(14), 8086–8091. https://doi.org/10.1073/pnas.1231332100

Cattell, V. (2001). Poor people, poor places, and poor health: The mediating role of social networks and social capital. *Social Science & Medicine, 52*(10), 1501–1516. https://doi.org/10.1016/s0277-9536(00)00259-8

Center for Biological Diversity. (2021). *Toxic waters: How offshore fracking pollutes the Gulf of Mexico.* https://www.biologicaldiversity.org/campaigns/fracking/pdfs/Toxic-Waters-offshore-fracking-report-Center-for-Biological-Diversity.pdf

Centers for Disease Control and Prevention (CDC). (2022). *CDC's Building Resilience Against Climate Effects (BRACE) framework.* https://www.cdc.gov/climateandhealth/BRACE.htm

___. (2023). *Emotional well-being: How does social connectedness affect health?* https://www.cdc.gov/emotional-wellbeing/social-connectedness/affect-health.htm

Centers for Disease Control and Prevention & Agency for Toxic Substances Disease Registry (CDC/ATSDR). (2022). Environmental Justice Index. https://www.atsdr.cdc.gov/placeandhealth/eji/index.html

Chaffin, B. C., Gosnell, H., & Cosens, B. A. (2014). A decade of adaptive governance scholarship: Synthesis and future directions. *Ecology and Society, 19*(3). https://www.jstor.org/stable/26269646

Chakraborty, A., Kaza, N., Knaap, G., & Deal, B. (2011). Robust plans and contingent plans. *Journal of the American Planning Association, 77*(3), 251–266. https://doi.org/10.1080/01944363.2011.582394

Chamlee-Wright, E., & Storr, V. H. (2009). "There's no place like New Orleans": Sense of place and community recovery in the Ninth Ward after Hurricane Katrina. *Journal of Urban Affairs, 31*(5), 615–634. https://doi.org/10.1111/j.1467-9906.2009.00479.x

Chapra, S. C., Boehlert, B., Fant, C., Bierman, V. J. J., Henderson, J., Mills, D., Mas, D. M. L., Rennels, L., Jantarasami, L., Martinich, J., Strzepek, K. M., & Paerl, H. W. (2017). Climate change impacts on harmful algal blooms in U.S. freshwaters: A screening-level assessment. *Environmental Science & Technology, 51*(16), 8933–8943. https://doi.org/https://doi.org/10.1021/acs.est.7b01498

Charles, A., Loucks, L., Berkes, F., & Armitage, D. (2020). Community science: A typology and its implications for governance of social-ecological systems. *Environmental Science & Policy*, 106, 77–86. https://doi.org/10.1016/j.envsci.2020.01.019

Cheng, F. (2021). Is compulsory managed retreat our future? *New America*. https://www.newamerica.org/future-land-housing/briefs/is-compulsory-managed-retreat-our-future/

Chibanda, D., Weiss, H. A., Verhey, R., Simms, V., Munjoma, R., Rusakaniko, S., Chingono, A., Munetsi, E., Bere, T., Manda, E., Abas, M., & Araya, R. (2016). Effect of a primary care–based psychological intervention on symptoms of common mental disorders in Zimbabwe: A randomized clinical trial. *JAMA, 316*(24), 2618–2626. https://doi.org/10.1001/jama.2016.19102

Chung, C. S. (2019). Rising tides and rearranging deckchairs: How climate change is reshaping infrastructure finance and threatening to sink municipal budgets. *Georgetown Environmental Law Review, 32*, 165. http://papers.ssrn.com/abstract=3452590

Citizens Research Council of Michigan. (2020). Government consolidation: A historically unpopular solution to local fiscal strain. https://crcmich.org/government-consolidation-a-historically-unpopular-solution-to-local-fiscal-strain

City of Buffalo. (2018, January 1). *Mayor Brown joined with the Puerto Rico Hurricane Maria relief fund to announce a new* [Press Release]. https://www.buffalony.gov/CivicAlerts.aspx?AID=175

___. (2019, February 15). *Mayor Byron W. Brown delivers his thirteenth state of the city address*. https://www.buffalony.gov/CivicAlerts.aspx?AID=342

City of Houston. (2016). *Community land trust business plan*. https://www.houstontx.gov/council/committees/housing/20170201/community-land-trust.pdf

City of Norfolk. (2016). *Norfolk Vision 2100*. https://www.norfolk.gov/DocumentCenter/View/27768/Vision-2100---FINAL?bidId=

___. (2023). *Building a better Norfolk: A zoning ordinance for the 21st century*. https://www.norfolk.gov/DocumentCenter/View/35581/Adopted-Zoning-Ordinance

City of St. Petersburg. (2023). *Generations of growth*. https://www.stpete.org/visitors/history.php

Clancy, N., Finucane, M. L., Fischbach, J. R., Groves, D. G., Knopman, D., Patel, K. V., & Dixon, L. (2022). *The building resilient infrastructure and communities mitigation grant program: Incorporating hazard risk and social equity into decisionmaking processes*. RAND Corporation. https://doi.org/10.7249/RR-A1258-1

Clark, J. M. H. (2017). Pedro Alonso Niño. *Dictionary of Caribbean and Afro–Latin American biography*. Oxford University Press. https://doi.org/10.1093/acref/9780199935796.001.0001

Clark-Ginsberg, A., Chandra, A., & Becerra-Ornelas, A. (2023). *Capacities of health systems in climate migrant receiving communities*. Urban Institute. https://www.urban.org/research/publication/capacities-health-systems-climate-migrant-receiving-communities

Clayton, S., Devine-Wright, P., Stern, P. C., Whitmarsh, L., Carrico, A., Steg, L., Swim, J., & Bonnes, M. (2015). Psychological research and global climate change. *Nature Climate Change*, *5*(7), 640–646. https://doi.org/10.1038/nclimate2622

Clayton, S., Manning, C., Speiser, M., & Hill, A. N. (2021). *Mental health and our changing climate: Impacts, inequities, responses*. ecoAmerica. https://ecoamerica.org/mental-health-and-our-changing-climate-2021-edition/

Climigration Network. (2021). *Lead with listening: A guidebook for community conversations on climate migration*. https://www.climigration.org/guidebook

Clow, C. (2023, October 4). As insurers flee disaster-prone areas, homeowners turn to 'last resort' insurers. *HousingWire*. https://www.housingwire.com/articles/as-insurers-flee-disaster-prone-areas-homeowners-turn-to-last-resort-insurers/

Coastal Alabama Partnership. (2022). Brief of Coastal Alabama Partnership as amicus curiae in support of appellants (Nos. 21-1086 & 21-1087). In the Supreme Court of the United States, on appeal from and writ of certiorari to the Northern District of Alabama. https://www.supremecourt.gov/DocketPDF/21/21-1086/222326/20220502151205793_211086%20Coastal%20Alabama%20Partnership%20Amicus%20Brief.pdf

Coastal Protection and Restoration Authority (CPRA). (2023a). *Fiscal Year 2024 Annual Plan: Integrated ecosystem restoration and hurricane protection in coastal Louisiana* https://coastal.la.gov/our-plan/annual-plan/

___. (2023b). *Louisiana's comprehensive master plan for a sustainable coast*. https://coastal.la.gov/our-plan/2023-coastal-master-plan/

Coenders, M., Gijsberts, M., & Scheepers, P. (2017). Resistance to the presence of immigrants and refugees in 22 countries. In M. Gijsberts & L. Hagendoorn (Eds.), *Nationalism and Exclusion of Migrants* (pp. 97–120). Routledge.

Cohen, D. A., Inagami, S., & Finch, B. (2008). The built environment and collective efficacy. *Health Place, 14*(2), 198–208. https://doi.org/10.1016/j.healthplace.2007.06.001

Cohen, D. T. (2018). *60 million live in the path of hurricanes*. U.S. Census Bureau. https://www.census.gov/library/stories/2018/08/coastal-county-population-rises.html

Cohen, S., Janicki-Deverts, D., & Miller, G. E. (2007). Psychological stress and disease. *JAMA*, *298*(14), 1685–1687. https://doi.org/10.1001/jama.298.14.1685

Coleman, J. S. (1998). Social capital in the creation of human capital. *American Journal of Sociology*, *94*. https://doi.org/https://doi.org/10.1086/228943

Collini, R. C., Carter, J., Auermuller, L., Engeman, L., Hintzen, K., Gambill, J., Johnson, R. E., Miller, I., Schafer, C., & Stiller, H. (2022). *Application guide for the 2022 Sea Level Rise Technical Report*. National Oceanic and Atmospheric Administration Office for Coastal Management, Mississippi–Alabama Sea Grant Consortium (MASGP-22-028), and Florida Sea Grant (SGEB 88). https://oceanservice.noaa.gov/hazards/sealevelrise/noaa-nos-techrpt02-globalregional-SLR-scenarios-US-application-guide.pdf

Colman, Z. (2020). Insurance for when FEMA fails. *Politico*. https://www.politico.com/news/agenda/2020/07/14/climate-change-fema-insurance-341816.

Colten, C. E. (2005). *An unnatural metropolis: Wresting New Orleans from nature*. LSU Press.

___. (2014). *Southern waters: The limits to abundance*. LSU Press.

___. (2017). Environmental management in coastal Louisiana: A historical review. *Journal of Coastal Research*, *33*(3), 699–711.

___. (2021). As inland becomes coastal: Shifting equity and flood risk in the Amite River Basin (USA). *Global Environment*, *14*(3), 475–504. https://doi.org/10.3197/ge.2021.140303

Colten, C. E., & Giancarlo, A. (2011). Losing resilience on the Gulf Coast: Hurricanes and social memory. *Environment: Science and Policy for Sustainable Development*, *53*(4), 6–19.

Colten, C. E., Grismore, A. A., & Simms, J. R. Z. (2015). Oil spills and community resilience: Uneven impacts and protection in historical perspective. *Geographical Review*, *105*(4), 391–407.

Colten, C. E., Hay, J., & Giancarlo, A. (2012). Community resilience and oil spills in coastal Louisiana. *Ecology and Society*, *17*(3). https://www.jstor.org/stable/26269063

Colten, C. E., Simms, J. R. Z., Grismore, A. A., & Hemmerling, S. A. (2018). Social justice and mobility in coastal Louisiana, USA. *Regional Environmental Change*, *18*(2), 371–383.

Comardelle, C., Dardar, T., Jessee, N., Naquin, A., Parfait-Dardar, S., & Philippe, R. (2020, October 11). Resisting the oblivion of eco-colonialism: A conversation with Tribal leaders from Louisiana's Gulf Coast. *Anthropocene Curriculum*. https://www.anthropocene-curriculum.org/contribution/resisting-the-oblivion-of-eco-colonialism

Comeaux, M. (1978). Louisiana's Acadians: The environmental impact. In G. Conrad (Ed.), *Cajuns and their history and culture* (pp. 142–160). Center for Louisiana Studies.

Compton, M. T., & Shim, R. S. (2015). The social determinants of mental health. *Focus*, *13*(4), 419–425. https://doi.org/10.1176/appi.focus.20150017

Conde, C., & Lonsdale, K. (2005). *Engaging stakeholders in the adaptation process* (UNDP Adaptation Policy Framework Technical Paper 2). UNDP. https://www4.unfccc.int/sites/NAPC/Country%20Documents/General/apf%20technical%20paper02.pdf

Congressional Research Service. (2023). *Flood buyouts: Federal funding for property acquisition* (CRS Insight No. IN11911). https://crsreports.congress.gov/product/pdf/IN/IN11911

Connell, J., & Coelho, S. (2018). Planned relocation in Asia and the Pacific. *Forced Migration Review*. https://www.fmreview.org/GuidingPrinciples20/connell-coelho

Conrad, D. R., McNitt, B., & Stout, M. (1998). *Higher ground: A report on voluntary buyouts in the nation's floodplains. A common ground solution serving people at risk, taxpayers and the environment*. National Wildlife Federation. https://www.nwf.org/Educational-Resources/Reports/1998/07-01-1998-Higher-Ground

Convery, I., Carroll, B., & Balogh, R. (2014). Flooding and schools: Experiences in Hull in 2007. *Disasters*, *39*(1), 146–165. https://doi.org/10.1111/disa.12091

Cook Hale, J. W., Hale, N. L., & Garrison, E. G. (2019). What is past is prologue: Excavations at the Econfina Channel site, Apalachee Bay, Florida, USA. *Southeastern Archaeology*, *38*(1), 1–22. https://doi.org/10.1080/0734578X.2018.1428787

Cope, M. R., Slack, T., Blanchard, T. C., & Lee, M. R. (2013). Does time heal all wounds? Community attachment, natural resource employment, and health impacts in the wake of the BP Deepwater Horizon disaster. *Social Science Research*, *42*(3), 872–881. https://doi.org/https://doi.org/10.1016/j.ssresearch.2012.12.011

Cornish, F., Breton, N., Moreno-Tabarez, U., Delgado, J., Rua, M., de-Graft Aikins, A., & Hodgetts, D. (2023). Participatory action research. *Nature Review Methods Primers*, *3*, 34. https://doi.org/10.1038/s43586-023-00214-1

Cottier, F., Flahaux, M. L., Ribot, J., Seager, R., & Ssekajja, G. (2022). Framing the frame: Cause and effect in climate-related migration. *World Development*, *158*, 106016.

Coultas, C. L., & Gross, E. R. (1975). Distribution and properties of some tidal marsh soils of Apalachee Bay, Florida. *Soil Science Society of America Journal*, *39*(5), 914–919.

Court, C., Ferreira, J., Popicki, A., Qiao, X., & Saha, B. (2021). *Quantifying the socio-economic impacts of harmful algal blooms in Southwest Florida in 2018*. University of Florida Economic Impact Analysis Program. https://fred.ifas.ufl.edu/DEStudio/PDF/HarmfulAlgalBlooms072621.pdf

Cowles, A. G. H. (2021). *Effects of historical land-use change on surface runoff and flooding in the Amite River Basin, Louisiana, USA using coupled 1D/2D HEC-RAS–HEC-HMS hydrological modeling* (Publication Number 5325) [Master's thesis, Louisiana State University]. LSU Scholarly Repository. https://repository.lsu.edu/gradschool_theses/5325

Craig, D., & Davies, M. (2005). Ethical relationships for biodiversity research and benefit-sharing with indigenous peoples. *Macquarie Journal of International and Comparative Environmental Law*, *2*(2), 31–74.

Craig, R. K. (2019). Coastal adaptation, government-subsidized insurance, and perverse incentives to stay. *Climatic Change*, *152*(2), 215–226.

Crimmins, A., Balbus, J., Gamble, J. L., Beard, C. B., Bell, J. E., Dodgen, D., Eisen, R. J., Fann, N., Hawkins, M. D., Herring, S. C., Jantarasami, L., Mills, D. M., Saha, S., Sarofim, M. C., Trtanj, J., & L. Ziska (Eds.). (2016). *The impacts of climate change on human health in the United States: A scientific assessment.* U.S. Global Change Research Program. https://health2016.globalchange.gov/

Cruz, J., White, P. C. L., Bell, A., & Coventry, P. A. (2020). Effect of extreme weather events on mental health: A narrative synthesis and meta-analysis for the UK. *International Journal of Environmental Research and Public Health, 17*(22), 8581. https://doi.org/10.3390/ijerph17228581

Cunsolo, A., & Ellis, N. R. (2018). Ecological grief as a mental health response to climate change-related loss. *Nature Climate Change*, *8*(4), 275–281. https://doi.org/10.1038/s41558-018-0092-2

Cunsolo, A., Harper, S. L., Ford, J. D., Landman, K., Houle, K., & Edge, V. L. (2012). "From this place and of this place:" Climate change, sense of place, and health in Nunatsiavut, Canada. *Social Science & Medicine*, *75*(3), 538–547. https://doi.org/10.1016/j.socscimed.2012.03.043

Cunsolo, A., Harper, S. L., Minor, K., Hayes, K., Williams, K. G., & Howard, C. (2020). Ecological grief and anxiety: The start of a healthy response to climate change? *The Lancet Planetary Health, 4*(7), e261–e263. https://doi.org/https://doi.org/10.1016/S2542-5196(20)30144-3

Curato, N., Dryzek, J. S., Ercan, S. A., Hendriks, C. M., & Niemeyer, S. (2017). Twelve key findings in deliberative democracy research. *Daedalus*, *146*(3), 28–38. https://doi.org/10.1162/DAED_a_00444

Curtis, K. J., Fussell, E., & DeWaard, J. (2015). Recovery migration after Hurricanes Katrina and Rita: Spatial concentration and intensification in the migration system. *Demography*, *52*(4), 1269–1293. https://doi.org/10.1007/s13524-015-0400-7

Cushing, F. H. (1896). Exploration of ancient key dwellers' remains on the Gulf Coast of Florida. *Proceedings of the American Philosophical Society*, *35*(153), 329–448. http://www.jstor.org/stable/983594

Cutter, S. L., Barnes, L., Berry, M., Burton, C., Evans, E., Tate, E., & Webb, J. (2008). A place-based model for understanding community resilience to natural disasters. *Global Environmental Change*, 18(4), 598-606. https://doi.org/https://doi.org/10.1016/j.gloenvcha.2008.07.013

Cutter, S. L., & Emrich, C. T. (2006). Moral hazard, social catastrophe: The changing face of vulnerability along the hurricane coasts. *The Annals of the American Academy of Political and Social Science*, *604*, 102–112. http://www.jstor.org/stable/25097783

Dahl, K. A., Fitzpatrick, M. F., & Spanger-Siegfried, E. (2017). Sea level rise drives increased tidal flooding frequency at tide gauges along the U.S. East and Gulf Coasts: Projections for 2030 and 2045. *PLoS ONE*, *12*(2), Article e0170949. https://doi.org/10.1371/journal.pone.0170949

Dahl, K. A., Spanger-Siegfried, E., Caldas, A., & Udvardy, S. (2017). Effective inundation of continental United States communities with 21st century sea level rise. *Elementa: Science of the Anthropocene, 5*. https://doi.org/10.1525/elementa.234

Dalbom, C., Hemmerling, S. A., & Lewis, J. A. (2014). *Community resettlement prospects in Southeast Louisiana: A multidisciplinary exploration of legal, cultural, and demographic aspects of moving individuals and communities.* Tulane Institute on Water Resources Law and Policy. https://thewaterinstitute.org/publications/community-resettlement-prospects-in-southeast-louisiana

Dalziel, P., Saunders, C., & Saunders, J. (2018). From economic growth to wellbeing economics. In P. Dalziel, C. Saunders, & J. Saunders (Eds.), *Wellbeing economics: The capabilities approach to prosperity* (pp. 1–21). Springer International Publishing. https://doi.org/10.1007/978-3-319-93194-4_1

Dandy, J., Horwitz, P., Campbell, R., Drake, D., & Leviston, Z. (2019). Leaving home: Place attachment and decisions to move in the face of environmental change. *Regional Environmental Change*, *19*(2), 615–620. https://doi.org/10.1007/s10113-019-01463-1

Dangendorf, S., Hendricks, N., Sun, Q., Klinck, J., Ezer, T., Frederikse, T., Calafat, F. M., Wahl, T., & Törnqvist, T. E. (2023). Acceleration of US Southeast and Gulf coast sea-level rise amplified by internal climate variability. *Nature Communications*, *14*(1), 1935. https://doi.org/10.1038/s41467-023-37649-9

Dannenberg, A. L., Frumkin, H., Hess, J. J., & Ebi, K. L. (2019). Managed retreat as a strategy for climate change adaptation in small communities: Public health implications. *Climatic Change*, *153*(1), 1–14. https://doi.org/10.1007/s10584-019-02382-0

Dartnell, L. (2020). *Origins: How the Earth made us*. Bodley Head.

Dasandi, N., Graham, H., Hudson, D., Mikhaylov, S. J., vanHeerde-Hudson, J., & Watts, N. (2021). *How do different frames affect public support for climate change policy: Evidence from a multi-country conjoint study*. SocArXiv. https://doi.org/10.31235/osf.io/372pk

Davenport, C., & Robertson, C. (2016). Resettling the first American 'climate refugees'. *New York Times*. https://www.nytimes.com/2016/05/03/us/resettling-the-first-american-climate-refugees.html

Davis, B. K. (2021). *New Orleans' Katrina: History and law of yesteryear in force today*. Yhorst Kimble Publishing LLC. https://books.google.com/books?id=VLluzgEACAAJ

Davis, J. E. (2017). *The Gulf: The making of an American sea*. Liveright Publishing.

Davis, M. (2014). Foreword: Sittin' on the porch with a shotgun. In A. Fontenot, C. M. Reese, & M. Sorkin (Eds.), *New Orleans under reconstruction*. Verso Books.

Dawson, R. J., Ball, T., Werritty, J., Werritty, A., Hall, J. W., & Roche, N. (2011). Assessing the effectiveness of non-structural flood management measures in the Thames Estuary under conditions of socio-economic and environmental change. *Global Environmental Change*, *21*(2), 628–646.

De Bruijn, H., de Bruijne, M., & ten Heuvelhof, E. (2015). The politics of resilience in the Dutch 'Room for the River'-project. *Procedia Computer Science*, *44*, 659–668.

de Haan, L., & Zoomers, A. (2005). Exploring the frontier of livelihoods research. *Development and Change*, *36*(1), 27–47. https://doi.org/https://doi.org/10.1111/j.0012-155X.2005.00401.x

de Sherbinin, A., Grace, K., McDermid, S., van der Geest, K., Puma, M. J., & Bell, A. (2022). Migration theory in climate mobility research. *Frontiers in Climate*, *4*. https://doi.org/10.3389/fclim.2022.882343

De Silva, M. J., McKenzie, K., Harpham, T., & Huttly, S. R. (2005). Social capital and mental illness: A systematic review. *Journal of Epidemiology and Community Health*, *59*(8), 619–627. https://doi.org/10.1136/jech.2004.029678

de Vries, D., & Frasier, J. (2012). Citizenship rights and voluntary decision making in post-disaster U.S. floodplain buyout mitigation program. *International Journal of Mass Emergencies and Disasters*, *30*(1), 1–33. https://journals.sagepub.com/doi/abs/10.1177/028072701203000101

de Vries, G. (2020). Public communication as a tool to implement environmental policies. *Social Issues and Policy Review*, *14*(1), 244–272.

DeDecker, B. (2015, March). Hidden Louisiana: Bayou St. Malo. *Antigravity*. https://antigravitymagazine.com/column/hidden-louisiana-bayou-st-malo/

Del Angel, D. C., Yoskowitz, D., Bilskie, M. V., & Hagen, S. C. (2022). A socioeconomic dataset of the risk associated with the 1% and 0.2% return period stillwater flood elevation under sea-level rise for the Northern Gulf of Mexico. *Data*, 7(6), 71. https://www.mdpi.com/2306-5729/7/6/71

Delaney, D. (1998). Race, place, and the law, 1836–1948. *University of Texas Press.*

Delta Programme Commissioner. (2014). *The 2015 Delta Programme working on the delta. The decisions to keep the Netherlands safe and liveable* (English version). Ministry of Infrastructure and the Environment, Ministry of Economic Affairs, Dutch National Government.

DeMiglio, L., & Williams, A. (2008). A sense of place, a sense of well-being. In J. Eyles (Ed.), *Sense of place, health and quality of life* (pp. 35–50). Routledge.

Denali Commission. (2019). *Denali Commission fiscal year 2020 draft work plan.* (84 FR 38604). https://www.federalregister.gov/documents/2019/08/07/2019-16914/denali-commission-fiscal-year-2020-draft-work-plan

Department of Housing and Urban Development (HUD). (2016). *National Disaster Resilience Competition: Grantee profiles.* https://www.hud.gov/sites/documents/NDRCGRANTPROF.PDF

___. (2019). *Allocations, common application, waivers, and alternative requirements for Community Development Block Grant Mitigation grantees.* https://www.federalregister.gov/documents/2019/08/30/2019-18607/allocations-common-application-waivers-and-alternative-requirements-for-community-development-block

___. (2022). *Request for information for HUD's Community Development Block Grant Disaster Recovery (CDBG-DR) rules, waivers, and alternative requirements.* https://www.federalregister.gov/documents/2022/12/20/2022-27547/request-for-information-for-huds-community development-block-grant-disaster-recovery-cdbg-dr-rules

___. (2023a). *Climate resilience implementation guide: Community driven relocation.* https://www.hudexchange.info/resource/6789/climate-resilience-implementation-guide-community-driven-relocation/

___. (2023b). *Community Development Block Grant Disaster Recovery.* https://www.hud.gov/sites/dfiles/CPD/documents/CDBG-Disaster-Recovery-Overview.pdf

Dermansky, J. (2020). Hurricane Laura's aftermath: Miles of oil sheen in Louisiana's Wetlands. *DeSmog.* https://www.desmog.com/2020/09/09/hurricane-laura-aftermath-miles-oil-sheen-louisiana-wetlands/

Deyle, R. E., Chapin, T. S., & Baker, E. J. (2008). The proof of the planning is in the platting: An evaluation of Florida's hurricane exposure mitigation planning mandate. *Journal of the American Planning Association*, 74(3), 349–370. https://doi.org/10.1080/01944360802229612

Di Liberto, T. (2021, May 21). *A foot of rain causes flash flood emergency in Louisiana during mid-May 2021.* National Oceanic and Atmospheric Administration. https://www.climate.gov/news-features/event-tracker/foot-rain-causes-flash-flood-emergency-louisiana-during-mid-may-2021

Diaz, R. J., & Solow, A. (1999). *Ecological and economic consequences of hypoxia: Topic 2 report for the integrated assessment on hypoxia in the Gulf of Mexico* (No. 16). U.S. Department of Commerce, National Oceanic and Atmospheric Administration, Coastal Ocean Program. https://repository.library.noaa.gov/view/noaa/21436

Dietz, T., Ostrom, E., & Stern, P. C. (2003). The struggle to govern the commons. *Science*, *302*(5652), 1907–1912. https://www.science.org/doi/10.1126/science.1091015

Din, G. C.(1980). "Cimarrones" and the San Malo Band in Spanish Louisiana. *Louisiana History: The Journal of the Louisiana Historical Association*, *21*(3), 237–262. http://www.jstor.org/stable/4232005

___. (1988). *The Canary Islanders of Louisiana.* Louisiana State University Press.

Diouf, S. A. (2014). *Slavery's exiles: The story of the Americans*. New York University Press.

Disaster Relief Appropriations Act, Pub. L. No. 113-2 § 1, 127 STAT. 4, 36 (2013).

Dobson, J. E., Spada, G., & Galassi, G. (2020). Global choke points may link sea level and human settlement at the last glacial maximum. *Geographical Review*, *110*(4), 595–620. https://doi.org/10.1080/00167428.2020.1728195

Dormon, J. H. (1977). The persistent specter: Slave rebellion in territorial Louisiana. *Louisiana History: The Journal of the Louisiana Historical Association*, *18*(4), 389–404. http://www.jstor.org/stable/4231728

Drew, R. B., & Jakabovics, A. (2023). *Housing markets and climate migration*. Urban Institute. https://www.urban.org/research/publication/housing-markets-and-climate-migration

Drew, R. B., & Temsamani, A. (2023). *Policy brief: Preparing receiving communities for climate migrations*. Enterprise Community Partners. https://www.enterprisecommunity.org/resources/policy-brief-preparing-receiving-communities-climate-migrations

Dryzek, J. S., Bächtiger, A., Chambers, S., Cohen, J., Druckman, J. N., Felicetti, A., Fishkin, J. S., Farrell, D. M., Fung, A., Gutmann, A., Landemore, H., Mansbridge, J., Marien, S., Neblo, M. A., Niemeyer, S., Setälä, M., Slothuus, R., Suiter, J., Thompson, D., & Warren, M. E. (2019). The crisis of democracy and the science of deliberation. *Science*, *363*(6432), 1144–1146. https://doi.org/doi:10.1126/science.aaw2694

Du, W., FitzGerald, G. J., Clark, M., & Hou, X.-Y. (2010). Health impacts of floods. *Prehospital and Disaster Medicine*, *25*(3), 265–272. https://doi.org/10.1017/s1049023x00008141

Dumaru, P., Dau, I., Koroiwaqa, I., Caginitoba, A., Radway, C., & Mangubhai, S. (2020). *Climate resilient mobility: An integrated vulnerability assessment of Koro Island, Lomaiviti Province*. The University of the South Pacific and the Wildlife Conservation Society. https://repository.usp.ac.fj/12850/

Dundon, L. A., & Abkowitz, M. (2021). Climate-induced managed retreat in the U.S.: A review of current research. *Climate Risk Management*, *33*, 100337. https://doi.org/10.1016/j.crm.2021.100337

Dundon, L. A., & Camp, J. S. (2021). Climate justice and home-buyout programs: Renters as a forgotten population in managed retreat actions. *Journal of Environmental Studies and Sciences*, *11*(3), 420–433. https://doi.org/10.1007/s13412-021-00691-4

Easterling, D. R., Arnold, J., Knutson, T., Kunkel, K., LeGrande, A., Leung, L. R., Vose, R., Waliser, D., & Wehner, M. (2017). Precipitation change in the United States. *Climate science special report: Fourth National Climate Assessment*, *1*, 207–230. U.S. Global Change Research Program. https://doi.org/10.7930/J0H993CC

Economic Research Service. (2022). *Rural poverty & well-being*. U.S. Department of Agriculture. https://www.ers.usda.gov/topics/rural-economy-population/rural-poverty-well-being/

Edelenbos, J., Van Buuren, A., Roth, D., & Winnubst, M. (2017). Stakeholder initiatives in flood risk management: Exploring the role and impact of bottom-up initiatives in three 'Room for the River' projects in the Netherlands. *Journal of Environmental Planning and Management*, *60*(1), 47–66. https://doi.org/10.1080/09640568.2016.1140025

Eder, M., Tobin, J. N., Proser, M., & Shin, P. (2012). Special issue introduction: Building a stronger science of community-engaged research. *Progress in Community Health Partnerships: Research, Education, and Actions*, 6(3), 227–230. Johns Hopkins University Press. https://doi.org/10.1353/cpr.2012.0040

Edwards, J. B. (2013). The logistics of climate-induced resettlement: Lessons from the Carteret Islands, Papua New Guinea. *Refugee Survey Quarterly*, *32*(3), 52–78. http://www.jstor.org/stable/45054964

Eiroa-Orosa, F. J. (2020). Understanding psychosocial wellbeing in the context of complex and multidimensional problems. *International Journal of Environmental Research and Public Health*, *17*(16). https://doi.org/10.3390/ijerph17165937

Elliott, J. R., Brown, P. L., & Loughran, K. (2020). Racial inequities in the federal buyout of flood-prone homes: A nationwide assessment of environmental adaptation. *Socius: Sociological Research for a Dynamic World, 6*. https://doi.org/10.1177/2378023120905439

Elliott, J. R., Loughran, K., & Brown, P. L. (2021). Divergent residential pathways from flood-prone areas: How neighborhood inequalities are shaping urban climate adaptation. *Social Problems, 70*(4), 869–892. https://doi.org/10.1093/socpro/spab059

Environmental Defense Fund (EDF). (n.d.). *Inclusive insurance: Promoting the post-flood financial resilience of low and moderate income households*. https://www.edf.org/inclusive-insurance.

___. (2021). *Harnessing nature to reduce Gulf Coast flood and chemical exposure risk*. https://www.edf.org/gulf-coast-flood-and-chemical-exposure-risk

Environmental Integrity Project. (2017). *Port Arthur, Texas: The end of the line for an economic myth*. Environmental Integrity Project. https://environmentalintegrity.org/wp-content/uploads/2017/02/Port-Arthur-Report.pdf

Environmental Law Institute. (n.d.). *Floodplain buyout case studies*. https://www.eli.org/sustainable-use-land/floodplain-buyout-case-studies

Environmental Protection Agency Office of Inspector General. (2004, September 30). *Review of actions at Escambia Treating Company Site, Pensacola, Florida*. (Ombudsman Report No. 2004-P-00032). https://www.epaoig.gov/sites/default/files/2015-12/documents/20040930-2004-p-00032.pdf

Equal Justice Initiative. (2017). *Lynching in America: Confronting the legacy of racial terror* (Edition No. 3). https://eji.org/reports/lynching-in-america/

Ethridge, R., & Shuck-Hall, S. M. (2009). *Mapping the Mississippian shatter zone: The colonial Indian slave trade and regional instability in the American South*. University of Nebraska Press. https://doi.org/10.2307/j.ctt1dgn4d8

Eugene, N. (2017, August 31). After Katrina, I fled to Houston. Now I'm reliving the nightmare. *Vox*. https://www.vox.com/first-person/2017/8/31/16229956/katrina-survivor-new-orleans-harvey-houston

European Spatial Planning Observation Network. (2017). *Comparative analysis of territorial governance and spatial planning systems in Europe*. https://www.espon.eu/planning-systems.

Evans, D. D., & Baeder, L. (2022). *Estimating undisclosed flood risk in real estate transactions*. Milliman. https://www.milliman.com/en/insight/Estimating-undisclosed-flood-risk-in-real-estate-transactions

Eyer, J., Dinterman, R., Miller, N., & Rose, A. (2018). The effect of disasters on migration destinations: Evidence from Hurricane Katrina. *Economics of Disasters and Climate Change, 2*(1), 91–106. https://doi.org/10.1007/s41885-017-0020-3

Fadel, L., & Seshadri, M. (2023, June 19). *Of the Americans living in mobile homes, 3 million of them reside in high flood areas* [Radio broadcast]. NPR. https://www.npr.org/2023/06/19/1183040896/of-the-americans-living-in-mobile-homes-3-million-of-them-reside-in-high-flood-a'

Fang, Z., Dolan, G., Sebastian, A., & Bedient, P. B. (2014). Case study of flood mitigation and hazard management at the Texas Medical Center in the wake of Tropical Storm Allison in 2001. *Natural Hazards Review, 15*(3). https://doi.org/10.1061/(ASCE)NH.1527-6996.0000139

Faragher, J. M. (2005). *A great and noble scheme: The tragic story of the expulsion of the French Acadians from their American homeland*. W.W. Norton & Company, Inc.

Farbotko, C. (2018, June 13). *No retreat: Climate change and voluntary immobility in the Pacific Islands*. Migration Policy Institute. https://www.migrationpolicy.org/article/no-retreat-climate-change-and-voluntary-immobility-pacific-islands

Farr, M., Davies, R., Davies, P., Bagnall, D., Brangan, E., & Andrews, H. (2020). *A map of resources for co-producing research in health and social care* [Version No. 1.2]. National Institute for Health Research (NIHR) ARC West and People in Health West of England. https://arc-w.nihr.ac.uk/publications/a-map-of-resources-for-co-producing-research-in-health-and-social-care/

Federal Emergency Management Agency (FEMA). (n.d.). *Risk Rating 2.0: Projected premium changes by state [Interactive map]*. Esri. https://www.arcgis.com/apps/dashboards/44d08581aaf14f39bc0da5d02f378007

___. (2002). *National Flood Insurance Program: Program description*. Federal Insurance and Mitigation Administration. https://www.fema.gov/doc/plan/prevent/floodplain/nfipdescrip.doc

___. (2016). *State mitigation planning key topics bulletins: Mitigations strategy*. https://www.fema.gov/sites/default/files/2020-06/fema-state-mitigation-strategy-planning-bulletin_10-26-2016_0.pdf

___. (2017). *Pre-disaster recovery planning guide for local governments*. https://www.fema.gov/sites/default/files/2020-07/pre-disaster-recovery-planning-guide-local-governments.pdf

___. (2018). *An affordability framework for the National Flood Insurance program*. Department of Homeland Security, Federal Emergency Management Agency.

___. (2020a). *Addendum to the hazard mitigation assistance*. https://www.fema.gov/sites/default/files/2020-07/fy15_hma_addendum.pdf

___. (2020b). *Public Assistance Program and policy guide* (FP 104-009-2). https://www.fema.gov/assistance/public

___. (2021a). *Building community resilience with nature-based solutions: A guide for local communities*. https://www.fema.gov/sites/default/files/documents/fema_riskmap-nature-based-solutions-guide_2021.pdf

___. (2021b). *3 years long, 3 years strong: New Jersey's successful approach to purchasing homes along Sandy's flooded path*. https://www.fema.gov/case-study/3-years-long-3-years-strong-new-jerseys-successful-approach-purchasing-homes-along

___. (2022a). *Flood insurance*. https://www.fema.gov/flood-insurance

___. (2022b). *Flood insurance and FEMA assistance*. https://www.fema.gov/fact-sheet/flood-insurance-and-fema-assistance

___. (2022c). *2022-2026 FEMA strategic plan: Building the FEMA our nation needs and deserves*. https://www.fema.gov/about/strategic-plan

___. (2023a). *Community rating system*. https://www.fema.gov/floodplain-management/community-rating-system

___. (2023b). *Hazard mitigation assistance program and policy guide* (FP-206-21-0001). https://www.fema.gov/grants/mitigation

___. (2023c). *Hurricane Ian assistance exceeds $4.5 billion; Thousands of survivors affected by Hurricane Nicole register for assistance*. [Press Release] https://www.fema.gov/press-release/20230109/hurricane-ian-assistance-exceeds-45-billion-thousands-survivors-affected

___. (2023d). *Local mitigation planning handbook*. https://www.fema.gov/sites/default/files/documents/fema_local-mitigation-planning-handbook_052023.pdf

___. (2023e). *Mitigation minute for May 2, 2023*. https://content.govdelivery.com/landing_pages/42025/35c63a32d9a866677b68f2f4916088cb

___. (2023f). *National preparedness goal*. https://www.fema.gov/emergency-managers/national-preparedness/goal

___. (2023g). *National Risk Index: Explore the map*. https://hazards.fema.gov/nri/map

Feld, S., & Basso, K. H. (1996). *Senses of place*. School of American Research Press.

Felipe Pérez, B., & Tomaselli, A. (2021). Indigenous peoples and climate-induced relocation in Latin America and the Caribbean: Managed retreat as a tool or a threat? *Journal of Environmental Studies and Sciences*, *11*, 352–364. https://doi.org/10.1007/s13412-021-00693-2

Feller, S. C., Castillo, E. G., Greenberg, J. M., Abascal, P., Van Horn, R., Wells, K. B., & University of California, Los Angeles Community Translational Science Team Public Health Reports. (2018). Emotional well-being and public health: Proposal for a model national initiative. *Public Health Reports*, *133*(2), 136–141. https://doi.org/10.1177/0033354918754540

Festing, H. (2023, January 3). *Newsletter: A year of support for frontline communities*. Anthropocene Alliance. https://anthropocenealliance.org/a-year-of-support-for-frontline-communities/

Fiedler, K., Forgas, J. P., & Crano, W. D. (2021). *The psychology of populism: The tribal challenge to liberal democracy*. Routledge.

Field, C. B., Barros, V., Stocker, T. F., Qin, D., Dokken, D. J., Ebi, K. L., Mastrandrea, M. D., Mach, K. J., Plattner, G. K., Allen, S. K., Tignor, M., & Midgley, P. M. (Eds.). (2012). *Managing the risks of extreme events and disasters to advance climate change adaptation*. International Panel on Climate Change (IPCC). Cambridge University Press. https://www.ipcc.ch/report/managing-the-risks-of-extreme-events-and-disasters-to-advance-climate-change-adaptation/

Fields, S. (2023, August 23). *More Americans are going without homeowners insurance. That could spell trouble*. Marketplace. https://www.marketplace.org/2023/08/29/homeowners-insurance-risk/

Finucane, M. L., Clancy, N., Parker, A. M., Paige, J. W., Patel, K. V., Tierney, D., Wilson, M. T., Wilcox, P., Reese, T., Williams, J., Reimer, J. R., Goode, T., Morales, S., & Harding, A. (2023). *An initial methodology for evaluating social equity performance in disaster mitigation grants: The Building Resilient Infrastructure and Communities Program*. RAND Corporation. https://doi.org/10.7249/RRA2145-1

Flavelle, C. (2022, November 10). Here's where the U.S. is testing a new response to climate hazards. *The New York Times*. https://www.nytimes.com/2022/11/02/climate/native-tribes-relocation-climate.html

Flavelle, C., & Belleme, M. (2021, September 1). Climate change is bankrupting America's small towns. *The New York Times*. https://www.nytimes.com/2021/09/02/climate/climate-towns-bankruptcy.html

Flavelle, C., & Healy, J. (2023, June 1). Arizona limits construction around Phoenix as its water supply dwindles. *The New York Times*. https://www.nytimes.com/2023/06/01/climate/arizona-phoenix-permits-housing-water.html

Flavelle, C., & Schwartz, J. (2020, April 9). Cities are flouting flood rules. The cost: $1 billion. *The New York Times*. https://www.nytimes.com/2020/04/09/climate/fema-flood-insurance.html

Florida Department of Law Enforcement. (2023). *Update: Florida medical examiners commission Hurricane Ian deaths*. https://www.fdle.state.fl.us/News/2023/February/Update-Florida-Medical-Examiners-Commission-Hurric

Flower Garden Banks National Marine Sanctuary. (2023). *Basic current patterns in the Gulf of Mexico, including the Loop Current*. Office of National Marine Sanctuaries, National Oceanic and Atmospheric Association. https://flowergarden.noaa.gov/about/naturalsetting.html

Fogelson, R., Sturtevant, W.C., & Smithsonian Institution. (2004). *Handbook of North American Indians. Volume 14: Southeast*. United States Government Printing Office.

Folke, C., Hahn, T., Olsson, P., & Norberg, J. (2005). Adaptive governance of social-ecological systems. *Annual Review of Environment and Resources*, *30*(1), 441–473. https://doi.org/10.1146/annurev.energy.30.050504.144511

Foote, I. (2022). A taking timebomb: Loss of access takings as a barrier to managed retreat from sea level rise. *Minnesota Journal of Law, Science & Technology, 23*(2). https://scholarship.law.umn.edu/mjlst/vol23/iss2/4/

Forsyth, T. (2013). Community-based adaptation: A review of past and future challenges. *Wiley Interdisciplinary Reviews: Climate Change, 4*(5), 439–446. https://wires.onlinelibrary.wiley.com/doi/abs/10.1002/wcc.231

Frank, T. (2021, February 2). Home sales need better disclosure of flood risk, experts say. *Scientific American*. https://www.scientificamerican.com/article/home-sales-need-better-disclosure-of-flood-risk-experts-say/

___. (2023, May 10). Flood insurance rates will soar in some areas, FEMA says. *E&E News*. https://www.eenews.net/articles/flood-insurance-rates-will-soar-in-some-areas-fema-says/

Frankenberger, T., Mueller, M., Spangler, T., & Alexander, S. (2013). *Community resilience: Conceptual framework and measurement feed the future learning agenda*. Westat. https://agrilinks.org/sites/default/files/resource/files/FTF%20Learning_Agenda_Community_Resilience_Oct%202013.pdf

Fresque-Baxter, J. A., & Armitage, D. (2012). Place identity and climate change adaptation: A synthesis and framework for understanding. *WIREs Climate Change, 3*(3), 251–266. https://doi.org/10.1002/wcc.164

Freudenberg, R., Calvin, E., Tolkoff, L., & Brawley, D. (2016). *Buy-in for buyouts: The case for managed retreat from flood zones*. Lincoln Institute of Land Policy. https://www.lincolninst.edu/sites/default/files/pubfiles/buy-in-for-buyouts-full.pdf

Frey, W. (2021). *Mapping America's diversity with the 2020 Census*. Brookings Institution. https://www.brookings.edu/research/mapping-americas-diversity-with-the-2020-census/

Frijters, P., & Krekel, C. (2021). *A handbook for wellbeing policy-making: History, theory, measurement, implementation, and examples*. Oxford University Press.

Fulton, B. D., Scheffler, R. M., Sparkes, S. P., Auh, E. Y., Vujicic, M., & Soucat, A. (2011). Health workforce skill mix and task shifting in low income countries: A review of recent evidence. *Human Resources for Health, 9*(1), 1–11. https://doi.org/10.1186/1478-4491-9-1

Fussell, E., Curtis, K.J., & DeWaard, J. (2014). Recovery migration to the City of New Orleans after Hurricane Katrina: A migration systems approach. *Population and Environment, 35*(3), 305–322. https://doi.org/10.1007/s11111-014-0204-5

Gaillard, F. (2007). After the storms: Tradition and change in Bayou La Batre. *The Journal of American History, 94*(3), 856–862. http://archive.oah.org/special-issues/katrina/Gaillard.html

Gall, M. (2023, June 7). Why insurance companies are pulling out of California and Florida, and how to fix some of the underlying problems. *The Conversation*. https://theconversation.com/why-insurance-companies-are-pulling-out-of-california-and-florida-and-how-to-fix-some-of-the-underlying-problems-207172

Garden State Preservation Trust. (2018, June 12). *Meeting Minutes*. Statehouse Annex Meeting Room 16. https://www.nj.gov/gspt/pdf/pdf/MeetingMinutes/June12018MeetingMinutes.pdf

Garrison, E. G., & Cook Hale, J. W. (2020). "The early days"–underwater prehistoric archaeology in the USA and Canada. *The Journal of Island and Coastal Archaeology, 16*(1), 27–45. https://doi.org/10.1080/15564894.2020.1783399

Gaspar, C. (2007). *GISCorps volunteer teaches GIS to Gulf Coast community design studio team in Biloxi, MS*. GISCorps. https://www.giscorps.org/biloxi_022/#

Gaventa, J. (2006). Finding the spaces for change: A power analysis. *IDS Bulletin*, 37(6), 23–33. https://doi.org/10.1111/j.1759-5436.2006.tb00320.x

George, C. (2018). The world's largest medical city is ready for the storm. *Texas Medical Center News*. https://www.tmc.edu/news/2018/07/the-worlds-largest-medical-city-is-ready-for-the-storm/

Georgetown Climate Center. (2020). *Moving forward: A guide to state and local action on climate equity and resilience.* https://www.georgetownclimate.org/files/MRT/GCC_20_FULL-3web.pdf

Geronimus, A. T., Hicken, M., Keene, D., & Bound, J. (2006). "Weathering" and age patterns of allostatic load scores among blacks and whites in the United States. *American Journal of Public Health*, *96*(5), 826–833. https://doi.org/10.2105/ajph.2004.060749

Ghezelloo, Y., Kondo, T., Maly, E., Stanley, M., & Meyer, M. (2023). Rationale and processes of residential buyout programs: A review on buyout regulations and consequences in Japan and the US. *Japan Architectural Review*, *6*(1), e12344. https://doi.org/10.1002/2475-8876.12344

Ghorbani, P., & Wolf, C. (2018). *Home buyouts in New York State: Strategies for maximizing homeowner participation.* Lincoln Institute of Land Policy. https://www.lincolninst.edu/publications/other/case-study-home-buyouts-in-new-york-state

Ghosh, A. K., Demetres, M. R., Geisler, B. P., Ssebyala, S. N., Yang, T., Shapiro, M. F., Setoguchi, S., & Abramson, D. (2022). Impact of hurricanes and associated extreme weather events on cardiovascular health: A scoping review. *Environmental Health Perspectives*, *130*(11), 116003. https://doi.org/10.1289/ehp11252

Gibbs, M. T. (2016). Why is coastal retreat so hard to implement? Understanding the political risk of coastal adaptation pathways. *Ocean & Coastal Management*, *130*, 107–114. https://doi.org/https://doi.org/10.1016/j.ocecoaman.2016.06.002

Gilman, H. R. (2019). We decide! Theories and cases in participatory democracy. *Political Science Quarterly*, *134*(3), 571–573. https://doi.org/10.1002/polq.12948

Glorioso, R. S., & Moss, L. A. G. (2007). Amenity migration to mountain regions: Current knowledge and a strategic construct for sustainable management. *Social Change*, *37*(1), 137–161. https://doi.org/10.1177/004908570703700108

Goddard, I., & Sturtevant, W. C. (Eds.). (1996). *Handbook of North American Indians. Volume 17: Languages.* Smithsonian Institution Scholarly Press.

Gogola, T. (2012). *Katrina cottages: Years late and $1 million over budget.* New Orleans Public Radio. https://www.wwno.org/latest-news/2012-05-04/katrina-cottages-years-late-and-1-million-over-budget

Goldstein, E. A. (2013, October 29). *Post-Sandy floodplain buyout programs are taking off in the New York region.* Natural Resources Defense Council. https://www.nrdc.org/bio/eric-goldstein/post-sandy-floodplain-buyout-programs-are-taking-new-york-region

Gomez, L. E., & Bernet, P. (2019). Diversity improves performance and outcomes. *Journal of the National Medical Association*, *111*(4), 383–392. https://doi.org/10.1016/j.jnma.2019.01.006

Google Earth. (2023). Isle de Jean Charles, Louisiana, 29°23'39"N 90°28'25"W. https://earth.google.com/web/search/Isle+de+Jean+Charles,+LA/@29.40611415,-90.47644019,-2.61320997a,9848.76718144d,35y,-10.9951822h,34.77168086t,0r/data=CigiJgokCWjLlJZQcj1AES2AkylTYT1AGWsAmkonm1bAIVIYC9IDo1bAOgMKATA

Gosman, R., & Botchwey, N. (2013). *Community engagement: Challenges & tools from the planner's perspective* [Applied Research Paper, School of City & Regional Planning, College of Architecture, Georgia Institute of Technology]. https://repository.gatech.edu/server/api/core/bitstreams/c350d462-7125-4a2b-bf31-31f05e622f7b/content

Gotham, K. F. (2014). Reinforcing inequalities: The impact of the CDBG Program on Post-Katrina rebuilding. *Housing Policy Debate*, *24*(1), 192–212. https://doi.org/10.1080/10511482.2013.840666

Gould-Werth, A., Abbott, S., & Openchowski, E. (2023, January 26). *What is social infrastructure, and how does it support economic growth in the United States?* Washington Center for Equitable Growth. https://equitablegrowth.org/what-is-social-infrastructure-and-how-does-it-support-economic-growth-in-the-united-states/

Gourevitch, J. D., Kousky, C., Liao, Y., Nolte, C., Pollack, A. B., Porter, J. R., & Weill, J. A. (2023). Unpriced climate risk and the potential consequences of overvaluation in US housing markets. *Nature Climate Change*, *13*, 250–257. https://doi.org/10.1038/s41558-023-01594-8

Gourevitch, J. D., & Pinter, N. (2023). Federal incentives for community-level climate adaptation: An evaluation of FEMA's Community Rating System. *Environmental Research Letters*, *18*(3), 034037. https://doi.org/10.1088/1748-9326/acbaae

Government Accountability Office (GAO). (2009). *Alaska Native villages: Limited progress has been made on relocating villages threatened by flooding and erosion* (Report No. GAO-09–551). https://www.gao.gov/products/gao-09-551

___. (2014). *2013 Sequestration: Agencies reduced some services and investments, while taking certain actions to mitigate effects* (Report No. GAO-14-244). https://www.gao.gov/assets/gao-14-244.pdf

___. (2020a). *Climate change: A climate migration pilot program could enhance the nation's resilience and reduce federal fiscal exposure* (Report No. GAO-20-488). https://www.gao.gov/products/gao-20-488

___. (2020b). *National Flood Insurance Program: Fiscal exposure persists despite property acquisitions* (Report No. GAO-20-508). https://www.gao.gov/assets/gao-20-508.pdf

___. (2020c). *Grants management: Agencies provided many types of technical assistance and applied recipients' feedback* (Report No. GAO-20-580). https://www.gao.gov/products/gao-20-580

___. (2021). *FEMA flood maps: Better planning and analysis needed to address current and future flood hazards* (Report No GAO-22-104079). https://www.gao.gov/assets/d22104079.pdf

___. (2022a). *Alaska Native issues: Federal agencies could enhance support for Native village efforts to address environmental threats* (Report No. GAO-22-104241). https://www.gao.gov/assets/gao-22-104241.pdf

___. (2022b). *Disaster recovery: Actions needed to improve the federal approach* (Report No. GAO-23-104956). https://www.gao.gov/products/gao-23-104956

___. (2022c). *Flood mitigation: Actions need to improve use of FEMA property acquisitions* (Report No. GAO-22-106037). https://www.gao.gov/products/gao-22-106037

Governor's Office of Storm Recovery (GOSR). (2015). *NY Rising Buyout and Acquisition Program policy manual*. New York State. https://stormrecovery.ny.gov/sites/default/files/uploads/po_20150415_buyout_and_acquisition_policy_manual_final_v3.pdf

___. (2017). *NY Rising housing program relocation policy for Uniform Relocation Act tenant fact sheet*. New York State. https://stormrecovery.ny.gov/sites/default/files/crp/community/documents/20170720_URATenant_FINAL_0.pdf

___. (2021). *NY Rising infrastructure program policy manual*. New York State. https://hcr.ny.gov/system/files/documents/2023/07/20210909_infrapolicymanual_v4.0_final_0.pdf

Graff Zivin, J., Liao, Y., & Panassié, Y. (2023). How hurricanes sweep up housing markets: Evidence from Florida. *Journal of Environmental Economics and Management*, *118*, 102770. https://doi.org/10.1016/j.jeem.2022.102770

Graham, C. (2017). *Happiness for all? Unequal hopes and lives in pursuit of the American dream*. Princeton University Press.

___. (2023). *The power of hope: How the science of well-being can save us from despair.* Princeton University Press.

Gramling, B., & Brabant, S. (1986). Boomtowns and offshore energy impact assessment: The development of a comprehensive model. *Sociological Perspectives*, *29*(2), 177–201. https://doi.org/10.2307/1388958

Granberry, J. (2011). *The Calusa: Linguistic and cultural relationships*. The University of Alabama Press.

Grannis, J. (2021). *Community land = community resilience: How community land trusts can support urban affordable housing and climate initiatives*. Georgetown Climate Center. https://www.adaptationclearinghouse.org/resources/community-land-community-resilience-how-community-land-trusts-can-support-urban-affordable-housing-and-climate-initiatives.html

Greer, A., & Binder, S. B. (2017). A historical assessment of home buyout policy: Are we learning or just failing? *Housing Policy Debate*, *27*(3), 372–392. https://doi.org/10.1080/10511482.2016.1245209

Greer, A., Binder, S. B., & Zavar, E. (2022). From hazard mitigation to climate adaptation: A review of home buyout program literature. *Housing Policy Debate*, *32*(1), 152–170. https://doi.org/10.1080/10511482.2021.1931930

Greer, A., & Trainor, J. (2021). A system disconnected: Perspectives on post-disaster housing recovery policy and programs. *Natural Hazards*, *106*, 1–24. https://doi.org/10.1007/s11069-020-04463-1

Gregory, J. (2005). *The southern diaspora: How the great migration of black and white southerners transformed America*. University of North Carolina Press.

Grismore, A. (2018). *Natural resources-based conflicts in coastal Louisiana: A multi-faceted social and ecological setting* (Publication No. 4767) [Doctoral Dissertation, Louisiana State University]. LSU Scholarly Repository. https://repository.lsu.edu/gradschool_dissertations/4767

Grothmann, T., & Reusswig, F. (2006). People at risk of flooding: Why some residents take precautionary action while others do not. *Natural Hazards*, *38*, 101–120. https://doi.org/10.1007/s11069-005-8604-6

Gulf of Mexico Alliance. (2021). *Governors' action plan number iv for healthy & resilient coasts 2021-2026*. https://gulfofmexicoalliance.org/what-we-do/governors-action-plan/

Gulf of Mexico Division. (2022). *2022 Annual Report protecting and preserving the Gulf of Mexico*. U.S. Environmental Protection Agency. https://www.epa.gov/system/files/documents/2022-12/GMD2022AR%20FINAL_0.pdf

Gulf Regional Planning Commission (GRPC), Mississippi-Alabama Sea Grant Consortium, and NOAA Coastal Services Center. (2013). *Plan for opportunity: Summary report on resiliency for the MS Gulf Coast*. https://grpc.com/wp-content/uploads/2018/04/Final_-A_ResilientGC2.pdf

Gurney, G. G., Blythe, J., Adams, H., Adger, W. N., Curnock, M., Faulkner, L., James, T., & Marshall, N. A. (2017). Redefining community based on place attachment in a connected world. *Proceedings of the National Academy of Sciences*, 114(38), 10077–10082. https://doi.org/10.1073/pnas.1712125114

Gustin, G. (2017, September 2). Harvey Floods batter Texas farms, stranding cattle and destroying crops. *Inside Climate News*. https://insideclimatenews.org/news/02092017/hurricane-harvey-texas-farms-climate-change-cotton-cattle-longhorns-ranches-photos/

Haasnoot, M. (2013). *Anticipating change: Sustainable water policy pathways for an uncertain future* [Doctoral dissertation, University of Twente]. https://doi.org/10.3990/1.9789036535595

Haasnoot, M., Brown, S., Scussolini, P., Jimenez, J. A., Vafeidis, A. T., & Nicholls, R. J. (2019). Generic adaptation pathways for coastal archetypes under uncertain sea-level rise. *Environmental Research Communications*, *1*(7), 071006. https://doi.org/10.1088/2515-7620/ab1871

Haasnoot, M., Kwakkel, J. H., Walker, W. E., & ter Maat, J. (2013). Dynamic adaptive policy pathways: A method for crafting robust decisions for a deeply uncertain world. *Global Environmental Change*, *23*(2), 485–498. https://doi.org/10.1016/j.gloenvcha.2012.12.006

Haer, T., Botzen, W. J. W., & Aerts, J. C. J. H. (2016). The effectiveness of flood risk communication strategies and the influence of social networks—Insights from an agent-based model. *Environmental Science & Policy*, *60*, 44–52. https://doi.org/https://doi.org/10.1016/j.envsci.2016.03.006

Hale, J. W. C., Davis, D. S., & Sanger, M. C. (2023). Evaluating the archaeological efficacy of bathymetric LiDAR across oceanographic contexts: A case study from Apalachee Bay, Florida. *Heritage*, *6*(2), 928–945. https://www.mdpi.com/2571-9408/6/2/51

Hall, G. M. (1992). *Africans in colonial Louisiana: The development of Afro-Creole culture in the eighteenth-century.* LSU Press.

Hamel, L., Wu, B., Brodie, M., Sim, S.-C., & Marks, E. (2017). *An early assessment of Hurricane Harvey's impact on vulnerable Texans in the Gulf Coast Region: Their voices and priorities to inform rebuilding efforts.* Kaiser Family Foundation and Episcopal Health Foundation. https://www.kff.org/mental-health/report/an-early-assessment-of-hurricane-harveys-impact-on-vulnerable-texans-in-the-gulf-coast-region-their-voices-and-priorities-to-inform-rebuilding-efforts/

Hamilton, D. R., Gavagan, T., Smart, K., Weller, N., Upton, L. A., Havron, D. A., Fishkind, A., Persse, D., Shank, P., Shah, U. A., & Mattox, K. (2009). Houston's medical disaster response to Hurricane Katrina: Part 2: Transitioning from emergency evacuee care to community health care. *Annals of Emergency Medicine*, *53*(4), 515–527. https://doi.org/https://doi.org/10.1016/j.annemergmed.2008.10.024

Hamilton, R. (2010). The Huddled Masses. *The Texas Tribune*. https://www.texastribune.org/2010/08/30/five-years-houstonians-conflicted-about-katrina/

Hanna, C. J., White, I., & Glavovic, B. (2019). Managed retreat in practice: Mechanisms and challenges for implementation. *Oxford research encyclopedia of natural hazard science.* https://doi.org/10.1093/acrefore/9780199389407.013.350

___. (2020). The uncertainty contagion: Revealing the interrelated, cascading uncertainties of managed retreat. *Sustainability, 12*(2), 736. https://doi.org/10.3390/su12020736

Hany Abulnour, A. (2014). The post-disaster temporary dwelling: Fundamentals of provision, design and construction. *HBRC Journal*, *10*(1), 10–24. https://doi.org/10.1016/j.hbrcj.2013.06.001

Hardoon, D., Hey, N., & Brunetti, S. (2020). *Wellbeing evidence at the heart of policy*. What Works Wellbeing. https://whatworkswellbeing.org/resources/wellbeing-evidence-at-the-heart-of-policy/

Hardwick, S. W. (2002). *Mythic Galveston: Reinventing America's third coast.* Baltimore: JHU Press.

Harrington-Abrams, R. (2022). *Towards greater transparency and accountability in decision-making for planned relocation. Climate crisis and displacement: From commitment to action.* Forced Migration Review. www.fmreview.org/climate-crisis

Harris, A. (2019). *At $60 million a mile, the Keys may abandon some roads to sea rise rather than raise them.* WUSF Public Media. https://wusfnews.wusf.usf.edu/environment/2019-12-07/at-60-million-a-mile-the-keys-may-abandon-some-roads-to-sea-rise-rather-than-raise-them

Harris County Flood Control District. (2023). *Home buyout program*. https://www.hcfcd.org/Activity/Additional-Programs/Home-Buyout-Program

Hartwig, R. P., & Wilkinson, C. (2010). *Hurricane Katrina: The five-year anniversary*. Insurance Information Institute. https://www.iii.org/sites/default/files/1007Katrina5Anniversary.pdf

Hauer, M. E. (2017). Migration induced by sea-level rise could reshape the U.S. population landscape. *Nature Climate Change*, 7(5), 321–325. https://doi.org/10.1038/nclimate3271

Hauer, M. E., Evans, J. M., & Mishra, D. R. (2016). Millions projected to be at risk from sea-level rise in the continental United States. *Nature Climate Change*, 6(7), 691–695. https://doi.org/10.1038/nclimate2961

Hawai'i Coastal Zone Management Program. (2019). *Assessing the feasibility and implications of managed retreat strategies for vulnerable coastal areas in Hawai'i.* https://files.hawaii.gov/dbedt/op/czm/ormp/assessing_the_feasibility_and_implications_of_managed_retreat_strategies_for_vulnerable_coastal_areas_in_hawaii.pdf

Hay, R. (1998). Sense of place in developmental context. *Journal of Environmental Psychology, 18*(1), 5-29. https://doi.org/https://doi.org/10.1006/jevp.1997.0060

Hayes, K., Blashki, G., Wiseman, J., Burke, S., & Reifels, L. (2018). Climate change and mental health: Risks, impacts and priority actions. *International Journal of Mental Health Systems, 12*(28). https://doi.org/10.1186/s13033-018-0210-6

Heart of Louisiana. (2023). *Bayou region.* https://heartoflouisiana.com/regions/bayou-region/

Hedden, A. (2020). Where the oil goes: Communities across the Gulf Coast grapple with impacts of oil and gas. *Carlsbad Current-Argus.* https://www.currentargus.com/story/news/local/2020/05/08/oil-prices-natural-gas-market-us-economy-permian-basin/5132895002/

Hegger, D. L. T., Mees, H. L. P., Driessen, P. P. J., & Runhaar, H. A. C. (2017). The roles of residents in climate adaptation: A systematic review in the case of the Netherlands. *Environmental Policy and Governance, 27*(4), 336–350. https://doi.org/https://doi.org/10.1002/eet.1766

Helmer, M. R., Chamberlain, E. L., & Mehta, J. M. (2023). A centennial perspective on archeological research trends and contemporary needs for a vanishing Mississippi Delta. *The Holocene, 33*(3), 355–365. https://doi.org/10.1177/09596836221138328

Hemmati, M., Mahmoud, H. N., Ellingwood, B. R., & Crooks, A. T. (2021). Unraveling the complexity of human behavior and urbanization on community vulnerability to floods. *Scientific Reports, 11*(1), 20085.

Hemmerling, S. A. (2017). A Louisiana coastal atlas: Resources, economies, and demographics. *LSU Press.*

Hemmerling, S. A., Barra, M., Bienn, H. C., Baustian, M. M., Jung, H., Meselhe, E., Wang, Y., & White, E. (2020). Elevating local knowledge through participatory modeling: Active community engagement in restoration planning in coastal Louisiana. *Journal of Geographical Systems, 22*(2), 241–266. https://doi.org/10.1007/s10109-019-00313-2

Hemmerling, S. A., Barra, M., & Bond, R. H. (2020). Adapting to a smaller coast: Restoration, protection, and social justice in coastal Louisiana. In S. Laska (Ed.), *Louisiana's response to extreme weather* (pp. 113–144). Springer. https://doi.org/10.1007/978-3-030-27205-0_5.

Hemmerling, S. A., DeMyers, C. A., & Parfait, J. (2021). Tracing the flow of oil and gas: A spatial and temporal analysis of environmental justice in coastal Louisiana from 1980 to 2010. *Environmental Justice, 14*(2), 134–145. https://www.liebertpub.com/doi/10.1089/env.2020.0052

Henderson, K. (2022). *The crisis of low wages in the US. Who makes less than $15 an hour in 2022.* Oxfam America. https://www.oxfamamerica.org/explore/research-publications/the-crisis-of-low-wages-in-the-us/

Hennick, C. (2014). *A tale of two neighborhoods.* U.S. Green Building Council. http://plus.usgbc.org/a-tale-of-two-neighborhoods/

Henry, J. M., & Bankston, C. L. (2002). *Blue collar bayou: Louisiana Cajuns in the new economy of ethnicity.* Bloomsbury Academic.

Henstra, D., & Thistlethwaite, J. (2018). *Buyer beware: Evaluating property disclosure as a tool to support flood risk management* [Policy Brief No. 131]. Centre for International Governance Innovation. https://www.cigionline.org/publications/buyer-beware-evaluating-property-disclosure-tool-support-flood-risk-management/

Hermans, T. H. J., Malagón-Santos, V., Katsman, C. A., Jane, R. A., Rasmussen, D. J., Haasnoot, M., Garner, G. G., Kopp, R. E., Oppenheimer, M., & Slangen, A. B. A. (2023). The timing of decreasing coastal flood protection due to sea-level rise. *Nature Climate Change, 13*, 359–366. https://doi.org/10.1038/s41558-023-01616-5

Hernández, D., & Swope, C. B. (2019). Housing as a platform for health and equity: Evidence and future directions. *American Journal of Public Health*, *109*(10), 1363–1366. https://doi.org/10.2105/ajph.2019.305210

Hersher, R. (2018). *Wisconsin reservation offers a climate success story and a warning* [Radio broadcast]. NPR. https://www.npr.org/2018/08/15/632335735/wisconsin-reservation-offers-a-climate-success-story-and-a-warning

Hickey, F. (2022). *Building capacity to receive: How four communities in the U.S. are preparing for climate driven in-migration* [Masters Paper, University of North Carolina Chapel Hill]. https://doi.org/10.17615/wz5e-t549

Hickman, C., Marks, E., Pihkala, P., Clayton, S., Lewandowski, R. E., Mayall, E. E., Wray, B., Mellor, C., & van Susteren, L. (2021). Climate anxiety in children and young people and their beliefs about government responses to climate change: A global survey. *The Lancet Planetary Health*, *5*(12), 863–873. https://doi.org/10.1016/S2542-5196(21)00278-3

Highfield, W., & Brody, S. (2017). Determining the effects of the FEMA Community Rating System program on flood losses in the United States. *International Journal of Disaster Risk Reduction*, *21*, 396–404. https://doi.org/10.1016/j.ijdrr.2017.01.013

Hikichi, H., Sawada, Y., Tsuboya, T., Aida, J., Kondo, K., Koyama, S., & Kawachi, I. (2017). Residential relocation and change in social capital: A natural experiment from the 2011 Great East Japan Earthquake and Tsunami. *Science Advances*, *3*(7), e1700426. https://doi.org/10.1126/sciadv.1700426

Hino, M., & Burke, M. (2021). The effect of information about climate risk on property values. *Proceedings of the National Academy of Sciences*, *118*(17), e2003374118. https://www.pnas.org/doi/full/10.1073/pnas.2003374118

Hino, M., Field, C. B., & Mach, K. J. (2017). Managed retreat as a response to natural hazard risk. *Nature Climate Change*, *7*(5), 364–370. https://doi.org/10.1038/nclimate3252

Hoeft, T. J., Fortney, J. C., Patel, V., & Unützer, J. (2018). Task-sharing approaches to improve mental health care in rural and other low-resource settings: A systematic review. *Journal of Rural Health*, *34*(1), 48–62. https://doi.org/10.1111/jrh.12229

Hoffman, P. E. (2002). *Florida's frontiers*. Indiana University Press.

Hogg, T. L., Stanley, S. K., O'Brien, L. V., Wilson, M. S., & Watsford, C. R. (2021). The Hogg Eco-Anxiety Scale: Development and validation of a multidimensional scale. *Global Environmental Change*, *71*, 102391. https://doi.org/https://doi.org/10.1016/j.gloenvcha.2021.102391

Holland, C. (2023, February 16). *Centering frontline communities*. Ecotrust. https://ecotrust.org/centering-frontline-communities/

Holt-Lunstad, J. (2022). Social connection as a public health issue: The evidence and a systemic framework for prioritizing the "social" in social determinants of health. *Annual Review of Public Health*, *43*, 193–213. https://doi.org/10.1146/annurev-publhealth-052020-110732

Hori, M., & Schafer, M. J. (2010). Social costs of displacement in Louisiana after Hurricanes Katrina and Rita. *Population and Environment*, *31*(1/3), 64–86. http://www.jstor.org/stable/40587574

House, K. (2021). Can Michigan become a climate haven? Duluth is already planning. *Bridge Michigan*. https://www.bridgemi.com/michigan-environment-watch/can-michigan-become-climate-haven-duluth-already-planning

Housing Matters. (2022, January 31). *Why cities need to prepare for climate migration*. Urban Institute. https://housingmatters.urban.org/feature/why-cities-need-prepare-climate-migration

Houston-Galveston Area Council. (n.d.). *Our Great Region 2040*. http://www.ourregion.org/download/OurGreatRegion2040-FINAL.pdf

Howard, B., & Morris, T. (2019). *Tribal Technology Assessment: The state of internet service on tribal lands (2019)*. American Indian Policy Institute, Arizona State University. https://aipi.asu.edu/sites/default/files/tribal_tech_assessment_compressed.pdf

Howe, C., Anderson, K., Siders, A. R., Ristroph, B., Spidalieri, K., Li, J., Burns, W., Warner, E. K., Tanana, H., & Vizcarra, H. (2021). Chapter 24: Climate change. *Law of Environmental Protection*. Environmental Law Institute. https://www.eli.org/law-environmental-protection

Hu, M. D., Lawrence, K. G., Gall, M., Emrich, C. T., Bodkin, M. R., Jackson, W. B., MacNell, N., Kwok, R. K., Engel, L. S., & Sandler, D. P. (2021). Natural hazards and mental health among US Gulf Coast residents. *Journal of Exposure Science & Environmental Epidemiology, 31*(5), 842–851. https://doi.org/10.1038/s41370-021-00301-z

Hudson, C. (1997). *Knights of Spain, warriors of the sun: Hernando de Soto and the South's ancient chiefdoms*. University of Georgia Press.

Hurlbert, J. S., Haines, V. A., & Beggs, J. J. (2000). Core networks and tie activation: What kinds of routine networks allocate resources in nonroutine situations? *American Sociological Review, 65*(4), 598–618. https://doi.org/10.2307/2657385

Hwang, J., & McDaniel, T.W. (2022). Racialized reshuffling: Urban change and the persistence of segregation in the twenty-first century. *Annual Review of Sociology, 48*, 397–419. https://doi.org/10.1146/annurev-soc-030420-014126

Iceland, J., Sharp, G., & Timberlake, J. M. (2012). Sun belt rising: Regional population change and the decline in black residential segregation, 1970–2009. *Demography, 50*(1), 97–123. https://doi.org/10.1007/s13524-012-0136-6

Immediate Action Workgroup. (2009). *Immediate Action Workgroup: Recommendations to the governor's subcabinet on climate change*. https://www.denali.gov/wp-content/uploads/2018/10/Reccomendations-to-the-Governors-Subcabinet-on-Climate-Change.pdf

Institute of Medicine. (2013). *Environmental decisions in the face of uncertainty*. The National Academies Press. https://doi.org/doi:10.17226/12568

Insurance Information Institute. (2023). *Facts + Statistics: Homeowners and renters insurance*. https://www.iii.org/fact-statistic/facts-statistics-homeowners-and-renters-insurance

Intergovernmental Panel on Climate Change (IPCC). (2014a). Climate change 2014: Impacts, adaptation, and vulnerability. Part A: Global and sectoral aspects. Contribution of Working Group II to the Fifth Assessment Report of the Intergovernmental Panel on Climate Change. In C. B. Field, V. R. Barros, D. J. Dokken, K. J. Mach, M. D. Mastrandrea, T. E. Bilir, M. Chatterjee, K. L. Ebi, Y. O. Estrada, R. C. Genova, B. Girma, E. S. Kissel, A. N. Levy, S. MacCracken, P. R. Mastrandrea, and L. L. White (Eds.), *Contribution of Working Group II to the Fifth Assessment Report of the Intergovernmental Panel on Climate Change* (pp. 1–32). Cambridge University Press.

___. (2014b). *Climate change 2014: Synthesis report*. Contribution of Working Groups I, II and III to the Fifth Assessment Report of the Intergovernmental Panel on Climate Change. https://www.ipcc.ch/site/assets/uploads/2018/02/SYR_AR5_FINAL_full.pdf

___. (2019). FAQs chapter 7. In P. R. Shukla, J. Skea, E. Calvo Buendia, V. Masson-Delmotte, H.-O. Pörtner, D. C. Roberts, P. Zhai, R. Slade, S. Connors, R. van Diemen, M. Ferrat, E. Haughey, S. Luz, S. Neogi, M. Pathak, J. Petzold, J. Portugal Pereira, P. Vyas, E. Huntley, K. Kissick, M. Belkacemi, J. Malley (Eds.), *Climate Change and Land: An IPCC special report on climate change, desertification, land degradation, sustainable land management, food security, and greenhouse gas fluxes in terrestrial ecosystems*. https://www.ipcc.ch/srccl/faqs/faqs-chapter-7/

Internal Displacement Monitoring Centre (IDMC). (2022). Climate change 2022: Impacts, adaptation and vulnerability. Contribution of Working Group II to the Sixth Assessment Report of the Intergovernmental Panel on Climate Change. Cambridge University Press. https://doi.org/10.1017/9781009325844

___. (2023). 2021 global report on internal displacement. https://www.internal-displacement.org/publications/2021-global-report-on-internal-displacement

Internal Displacement Monitoring Centre & Norwegian Refugee Council. (2023). *Global report on internal displacement*. https://www.internal-displacement.org/global-report/grid2023

Inwood, J. F. J. (2011). Constructing African American urban space in Atlanta, Georgia. *Geographical Review, 101*(2), 147–163. http://www.jstor.org/stable/41303620

Iuchi, K. (2023). Adaptability of low-income communities in postdisaster relocation. *Journal of the American Planning Association*, 1–16. https://doi.org/10.1080/01944363.2022.2133781

Jacquet, J. B., & Stedman, R. C. (2014). The risk of social-psychological disruption as an impact of energy development and environmental change. *Journal of Environmental Planning and Management*, *57*(9), 1285–1304. https://doi.org/10.1080/09640568.2013.820174

Jan Goossen, W. (2018). *Interview—The Dutch make room for the river*. https://www.eea.europa.eu/signals/signals-2018-content-list/articles/interview-2014-the-dutch-make

Jarden, A., & Roache, A. (2023). What is wellbeing? *International Journal of Environmental Research and Public Health*, *20*(6). https://doi.org/10.3390/ijerph20065006

Jenkins, P. (2016). *A sense of place at risk: Perspectives of residents of coastal Louisiana on nonstructural risk reduction strategies*. Oxfam America. Oxfam, Boston, MA.

Jessee, N. (2021). Tribal leaders raise 'serious concerns' about plans to turn their shrinking Louisiana island home into a 'sportsman's paradise'. *DeSmog*. https://www.desmog.com/2021/07/23/isle-de-jean-charles-tribe-louisiana-sportsmans-paradise/

___. (2022). Reshaping Louisiana's coastal frontier: Managed retreat as colonial decontextualization. *Journal of Political Ecology*, *29*(1). https://doi.org/10.2458/jpe.2835

Johannessen, M., & Goldweit-Denton, D. (2020). *The Green Dot Effect: Neighborhood recovery after Hurricane Katrina*. Columbia University. https://centerforspatialresearch.github.io/conflict_urbanism_sp2020/2020/05/06/Johannessen.html

Johnson, D. A. (2015). History of regional planning. *International Encyclopedia of the Social & Behavioral Sciences (Second Edition)*, 141–145. https://doi.org/https://doi.org/10.1016/B978-0-08-097086-8.74069-4

Johnson, L., & Mamula-Seadon, L. (2014). Transforming governance: How national policies and organizations for managing disaster recovery evolved following the 4 September 2010 and 22 February 2011 Canterbury earthquakes. *Earthquake Spectra*, *30*(1), 557– 605.

Johnson, L. A., & Olshansky, R. B. (2017). *After great disasters: An in-depth analysis of how six countries managed community recovery*. Lincoln Institute. http://www.lincolninst.edu/publications/books/after-great-disasters

Johnson, M. (2005). Addressing housing needs in the post Katrina Gulf Coast. *Thurgood Marshall Law Review, 31*, 327.

Jones, S. C., Ruppert, T., Deady, E., Payne, H., Pippin, J. S., Huang, L.-Y., & Evans, J. M. (2019). Roads to nowhere in four states: State and local governments in the Atlantic Southeast facing sea-level rise. *Columbia Journal of Environmental Law*, 44(1), 67–136. https://doi.org/10.7916/cjel.v44i1.806

Jones, T. L. (2018). Black community in flood-prone New Roads area feels pushback from white neighborhood over relocation site. *The Advocate*. https://www.theadvocate.com/baton_rouge/news/article_ee6b7b88-95db-11e8-a52e-cb57c9ecb7d0.html

Juhola, S., & Käyhkö, J. (2023). Maladaptation as a concept and a metric in national adaptation policy-Should we, would we, could we? *PLOS Climate*, *2*(5), e0000213.

Junod, A., Rivera, F., Rogin, A., & Morales-Burnett, J. (2023). *Climate migration and receiving community institutional capacity in the US Gulf Coast*. Urban Institute. https://www.urban.org/research/publication/climate-migration-and-receiving-community-institutional-capacity-us-gulf-coast

Junod, A. N., Martín, C., Marx, R., & Rogin, A. (2021). *Equitable investments in resilience: A review of benefit-cost analysis in federal flood mitigation infrastructure*. Urban Institute. https://www.urban.org/sites/default/files/publication/104302/equitable-investments-in-resilience.pdf

Kaetz, J. P. (2023). Bayou La Batre. *Encyclopedia of Alabama*. https://encyclopediaofalabama.org/article/bayou-la-batre/

Kai, N. (2015). Black Seminoles: The maroons of Florida. *African and Black Diaspora: An International Journal*, *8*, 1–12. https://doi.org/10.1080/17528631.2015.1027331

Kaiser Family Foundation. (2023). Status of state Medicaid Expansion Decisions Interactive Map. https://www.kff.org/medicaid/issue-brief/status-of-state-medicaid-expansion-decisions-interactive-map/

Kalra, V. S., & Kapoor, N. (2009). Interrogating segregation, integration and the community cohesion agenda. *Journal of Ethnic and Migration Studies*, *35*(9), 1397–1415. https://doi.org/10.1080/13691830903125893

Karlamangla, A. S., Singer, B. H., & Seeman, T. E. (2006). Reduction in allostatic load in older adults is associated with lower all-cause mortality risk: MacArthur studies of successful aging. *Psychosomomatic Medicine Journal of Behavioral Medicine*, *68*(3), 500–507. https://doi.org/10.1097/01.psy.0000221270.93985.82

Kawachi, I., Kim, D., Coutts, A., & Subramanian, S. (2004). Commentary: Reconciling the three accounts of social capital. *International Journal of Epidemiology*, *33*(4), 682–690. https://doi.org/10.1093/ije/dyh177

Keenan, J. M. (2019). *Destination Duluth: Competitive economic development in the age of climigration* [Conference session]. 2019 Global Shifts Colloquium: A Changing Climate, A Changing World. University of Pennsylvania, Philadelphia, PA. http://dx.doi.org/10.5281/zenodo.5247182

Keenan, J. M., & Bradt, J. T. (2020). Underwaterwriting: From theory to empiricism in regional mortgage markets in the U.S. *Climatic Change*, *162*(4), 2043–2067. https://doi.org/10.1007/s10584-020-02734-1

Keenan, J. M., Hill, T., & Gumber, A. (2018). Climate gentrification: From theory to empiricism in Miami-Dade County, Florida. *Environmental Research Letters*, *13*(5). https://doi.org/10.1088/1748-9326/aabb32

Keller Reeves, C. (1985). *The Choctaw before removal.* University Press of Mississippi, Choctaw Heritage Press.

Kemp, C. G., Petersen, I., Bhana, A., & Rao, D. (2019). Supervision of task-shared mental health care in low-resource settings: A commentary on programmatic experience. *Global Health: Science and Practice*, 7(2), 150–159. https://doi.org/10.9745/ghsp-d-18-00337

Kempton, W. M., Boster, J. S., & Hartley, J. A. (1995). *Environmental values in American culture*. MIT Press.

Kennicutt, M. C. (2017). Water quality of the Gulf of Mexico. In C. Ward (Ed.), *Habitats and biota of the Gulf of Mexico: Before the Deepwater Horizon oil spill* (pp. 55–164). Springer. https://doi.org/10.1007/978-1-4939-3447-8_2

Kerry Smith, V., & Whitmore, B. (2020). Coastal amenities and income stratification. *Economics Letters*, *192*, 109241. https://doi.org/10.1016/j.econlet.2020.109241

Khalil, M. B., & Jacobs, B. C. (2021). Understanding place-based adaptation of women in a post-cyclone context through place attachment. *Environmental Development*, *39*, 100644.

Khatibi, F. S., Dedekorkut-Howes, A., Howes, M., & Torabi, E. (2021). Can public awareness, knowledge and engagement improve climate change adaptation policies? *Discover Sustainability*, *2*(1), 18. https://doi.org/10.1007/s43621-021-00024-z

Kianicka, S., Buchecker, M., Hunziker, M., & Müller-Böker, U. (2006). Locals' and tourists' sense of place: A case study of a Swiss Alpine village. *Mountain Research and Development*, *26*. https://doi.org/10.5167/uzh-2621

Kidd, V., & Tilchin, R. (n.d.). *Community land trust: Houston, TX*. Results for America. https://catalog.results4america.org/case-studies/clt-houston

Kiel, K. A., & Williams, M. (2007). The impact of Superfund sites on local property values: Are all sites the same? *Journal of Urban Economics*, *61*(1), 170–192. https://doi.org/10.1016/j.jue.2006.07.003

Kind, J., Wouter Botzen, W.J., & Aerts, J.C. (2017). Accounting for risk aversion, income distribution and social welfare in cost-benefit analysis for flood risk management. *Wiley Interdisciplinary Reviews: Climate Change*, *8*(2), e446.

King, M., Smith, A., & Gracey, M. (2009). Indigenous health part 2: The underlying causes of the health gap. *Lancet, 374*(9683), 76–85. https://doi.org/10.1016/s0140-6736(09)60827-8

King, R. (2005). *Federal flood insurance: The repetitive loss problem*. Congressional Research Service. https://sgp.fas.org/crs/misc/RL32972.pdf

Kinniburgh, F., Simonton, M. G., & Allouch, C. (2015). *Come heat and high water: Climate risk in the southeastern U.S. and Texas*. Risky Business. https://riskybusiness.org/site/assets/uploads/2015/09/Climate-Risk-in-Southeast-and-Texas.pdf

Klijn, F., de Bruin, D., de Hoog, M., Jansen, S., & Sijmons, D. (2013). Design quality of room-for-the-river measures in the Netherlands: Role and assessment of the quality team (Q-team). *International Journal of River Basin Management*, *11*, 287–299.

Klopotek, B. (2011). *Recognition odysseys: Indigeneity, race, and federal Tribal recognition policy in three Louisiana Indian communities*. Duke University Press.

Knabb, R. D., Rhome, J. R., & Brown, D. P. (2023). *Tropical Cyclone Report: Hurricane Katrina*. 2023 National Hurricane Center. https://www.nhc.noaa.gov/data/tcr/AL122005_Katrina.pdf

Kniffen, F. B., Gregory, H. F., & Stokes, G. A. (1994). *The historic Indian Tribes of Louisiana: From 1542 to the present*. LSU Press.

Knight Foundation. (2020). *The 100 Million Project: Full topline results*. https://knightfoundation.org/reports/the-100-million-project/

Knight, V. J. (2009). *The search for Mabila: The decisive battle between Hernando de Soto and Chief Tascalusa*. University of Alabama Press.

Knobloch, D. M. (2005). Moving a community in the aftermath of the great 1993 Midwest flood. *Journal of Contemporary Water Research & Education*, *130*(1), 41–45.

Knowles, S. G., & Kunreuther, H. C. (2014). Troubled waters: The National Flood Insurance Program in historical perspective. *Journal of Policy History*, *26*(3), 327–353. https://doi.org/10.1017/S0898030614000153

Kobel, R. (2015). For vulnerable barrier islands, a rush to rebuild on U.S. Coast. *Yale School of the Environment 360*. https://e360.yale.edu/features/for_vulnerable_barrier_islands_a_rush_to_rebuild_on_us_coast

Kohrt, B. A., Ottman, K., Panter-Brick, C., Konner, M., & Patel, V. (2020). Why we heal: The evolution of psychological healing and implications for global mental health. *Clinical Psychology Review*, *82*, 101920.

Koslov, L. (2016). The case for retreat. *Public Culture*, *28*(2), 359–387. https://doi.org/10.1215/08992363-3427487

Koslov, L., Merdjanoff, A., Sulakshana, E., & Klinenberg, E. (2021). When rebuilding no longer means recovery: The stress of staying put after Hurricane Sandy. *Climatic Change*, *165*(3). https://doi.org/10.1007/s10584-021-03069-1

Kousky, C. (2022). *Understanding disaster insurance: New tools for a more resilient future*. Island Press. https://islandpress.org/books/understanding-disaster-insurance

___. (2023). A new pilot launches to support equitable flood recovery in NYC. *Environmental Defense Fund.* https://blogs.edf.org/markets/2023/03/01/a-new-pilot-launches/

Kousky, C., & French, K. (2022). *Inclusive insurance for climate-related disasters: A roadmap for the United States.* Ceres. https://www.ceres.org/resources/reports/report-inclusive-insurance-climate-related-disasters.

Kousky, C., & Lingle, B. (2018). The 3 maps that explain residential flood insurance purchases. *Resources.* https://www.resources.org/archives/the-3-maps-that-explain-residential-flood-insurance-purchases/

Kousky, C., & Michel-Kerjan, E. (2017). Examining flood insurance claims in the United States: Six key findings. *The Journal of Risk and Insurance*, *84*(3), 819–850. http://www.jstor.org/stable/26483841

Kramer, D. (2016). Norfolk: A case study in sea-level rise. *Physics Today*, *69*(5), 22–25. https://doi.org/10.1063/pt.3.3163

Kroll-Smith, J. S., & Couch, S. R. (1993). Technological hazards: Social responses as traumatic stressors. *International handbook of traumatic stress syndromes*, 79–91.

Krupnik, I. (2022). *Handbook of North American Indians, Volume 1: Introduction.* Smithsonian Institution Scholarly Press.

Kühne, O., & Koegst, L. (2023). The multiple causes of coastal land loss in Louisiana—An overview. *Land loss in Louisiana: A neopragmatic redescription*, 19–33. https://doi.org/10.1007/978-3-658-39889-7_3

Kundnani, A. (2007). Integrationism: The politics of anti-Muslim racism. *Race and Class*, *48*(4), 24–44.

Kuta, S. (2022). Federal flood maps are outdated because of climate change, FEMA Director says. *Smithsonian Magazine.* https://www.smithsonianmag.com/smart-news/federal-flood-maps-are-outdated-because-of-climate-change-fema-director-says-180980725/

Kyne, D. (2023). Storm surge risk assessment in coastal communities in the Rio Grande Valley: An application of GIS-based spatial multicriteria decision analysis with analytical hierarchy process. *Journal of Coastal Research*, *39*(3), 471–483. https://doi.org/10.2112/JCOASTRES-D-22-00011.1

Lachance, P. F. (1994). The formation of a three-caste society: Evidence from wills in antebellum New Orleans. *Social Science History*, *18*(2), 211–242. https://doi.org/10.2307/1171266

Lagomasino, D., Fatoyinbo, T., Castañeda-Moya, E., Cook, B. C., Montesano, P. M., Neigh, C. S. R., Corp, L. A., Ott, L. E., Chavez, S., & Morton, D. C. (2021). Storm surge and ponding explain mangrove dieback in southwest Florida following Hurricane Irma. *Nature Communications*, *12*(4003). https://doi.org/https://doi.org/10.1038/s41467-021-24253-y

Lambert, C. E., Holley, J. R., McComas, K. A., Snider, N. P., & Tucker, G. K. (2021). Eroding land and erasing place: A qualitative study of place attachment, risk perception, and coastal land loss in southern Louisiana. *Sustainability*, *13*(11), 6269. https://www.mdpi.com/2071-1050/13/11/6269

Lamond, J. E., Joseph, R. D., & Proverbs, D. G. (2015). An exploration of factors affecting the long term psychological impact and deterioration of mental health in flooded households. *Environmental Research*, *140*, 325–334. https://doi.org/10.1016/j.envres.2015.04.008

Lander, E. S., & Mallory, B. (2021). *Indigenous traditional ecological knowledge and federal decision making.* Executive Office of the President Office of Science and Technology Policy and Council on Environmental Quality.

Lane, R. R., Paul Kemp, G., & Day, J. W. (2018). A brief history of Delta formation and deterioration. In J. W. Day & J. Erdman (Eds.), *Mississippi Delta restoration: Pathways to a sustainable future* (pp. 11–27). Springer International Publishing. https://doi.org/10.1007/978-3-319-65663-2_2

Latulippe, N., & Klenk, N. (2020). Making room and moving over: Knowledge co-production, Indigenous knowledge sovereignty and the politics of global environmental change decision-making. *Current Opinion in Environmental Sustainability*, *42*, 7–14. https://doi.org/10.1016/j.cosust.2019.10.010

Lawrance, D. E., Thompson, R., Fontana, G., & Jennings, N. (2021). *The impact of climate change on mental health and emotional wellbeing: Current evidence and implications for policy and practice* (Briefing Paper No 36). Grantham Institute. https://spiral.imperial.ac.uk/bitstream/10044/1/88568/9/3343%20Climate%20change%20and%20mental%20health%20BP36_v6.pdf

Lazrus, H., Maldonado, J., Blanchard, P., Souza, M. K., Thomas, B., & Wildcat, D. (2022). Culture change to address climate change: Collaborations with Indigenous and Earth sciences for more just, equitable, and sustainable responses to our climate crisis. *PLoS Climate*, *1*(2), p.e0000005.

Le Strat, A., and Menser, M. (2022). *Democratizing public services*. Rosa Luxemburg Stiftung.

Lee, D. B. (2022). Chitimacha Tribe of Louisiana. *64 Parishes*. https://64parishes.org/entry/chitimacha-tribe-of-louisiana

Lee, H., Calvin, K., Dasgupta, D., Krinner, G., Mukherji, A., Thorne, P., Trisos, C., Romero, J., Aldunce, P., Barrett, K., Blanco, G., Cheung, W. W. L., Connors, S. L., Denton, F., Diongue-Niang, A., Dodman, D., Garschagen, M., Geden, O., Hayward, B., . . . Zommers, Z. (2023). Summary for policymakers. *Climate change 2023: Synthesis report. Contribution of Working Groups I, II and III to the sixth assessment report*, 1–34. Intergovernmental Panel on Climate Change. https://doi.org/10.59327/IPCC/AR6-9789291691647.001

Lee, J. Y., & Van Zandt, S. (2019). Housing tenure and social vulnerability to disasters: A review of the evidence. *Journal of Planning Literature*, *34*(2), 156–170. https://doi.org/10.1177/0885412218812080

Lehmann, R. (2020). Do no harm: Managing retreat by ending new subsidies. *R Street Policy Study*. https://www.rstreet.org/research/do-no-harm-managing-retreat-by-ending-new-subsidies/

Leibbrand, C., Massey, C., Alexander, J. T., & Tolnay, S. (2019). Great Migration's great return? An examination of second-generation return migration to the South. *Social Science Research*, *81*, 117–131. https://doi.org/10.1016/j.ssresearch.2019.03.009

Leiserowitz, A. (2006). Climate change risk perception and policy preferences: The role of affect, imagery, and values. *Climatic Change*, *77*(1-2), 45–72.

Leland, S., & Thurmaier, K. (2005). When efficiency is unbelievable: Normative lessons from 30 years of city–county consolidations. *Public Administration Review*, *65*(4), 475–489.

LeMenager, S. (2014). *Living oil: Petroleum culture in the American century*. OUP USA.

Lemos, M. C., & Morehouse, B. J. (2005). The co-production of science and policy in integrated climate assessments. *Global Environmental Change*, *15*(1), 57–68. https://doi.org/10.1016/j.gloenvcha.2004.09.004

Leong, K. J., Airriess, C. A., Li, W., Chen, A. C.-C., & Keith, V. M. (2007). Resilient history and the rebuilding of a community: The Vietnamese American community in New Orleans East. *The Journal of American History*, *94*(3), 770–779. https://doi.org/10.2307/25095138

Lessans, J. (2022). *With new incentives, Harris County hopes to gain buy-in for buyouts*. Rice University Kinder Institute. https://kinder.rice.edu/urbanedge/new-incentives-harris-county-hopes-gain-buy-buyouts

Letki, N. (2008). Does diversity erode social cohesion? Social capital and race in British neighbourhoods. *Political Studies*, *56*(1), 99–126. https://doi.org/10.1111/j.1467-9248.2007.00692.x

Li, J., & Spidalieri, K. (2021). Home is where the safer ground is: The need to promote affordable housing laws and policies in receiving communities. *Journal of Environmental Studies and Sciences*, *11*, 682–695. https://doi.org/10.1007/s13412-021-00702-4

Lichter, D. T., Parisi, D., & Taquino, M. C. (2015). Toward a new macro-segregation? Decomposing segregation within and between metropolitan cities and suburbs. *American Sociological Review*, *80*(4), 843–873. https://doi.org/10.1177/0003122415588558

Lim, J. R. (2022). Why people adopt climate change adaptation and disaster risk reduction behaviors: Integrated model of risk communication and results from hurricanes, floods, and wildfires. *Bulletin of the American Meteorological Society*, *103*(10), E2440–E2469. https://doi.org/https://doi.org/10.1175/BAMS-D-21-0087.1

Lin, N. (2000). Inequality in social capital. *Contemporary Sociology*, *29*(6), 785–795. https://doi.org/10.2307/2654086

Lindell, M. K., & Perry, R. W. (2012). The protective action decision model: Theoretical modifications and additional evidence. *Risk analysis: An official publication of the Society for Risk Analysis*, *32*(4), 616–632. https://doi.org/10.1111/j.1539-6924.2011.01647.x

Lochner, K., Kawachi, I., & Kennedy, B. P. (1999). Social capital: A guide to its measurement. *Health & Place*, *5*(4), 259–270.

Loewen, J. (2005). *Sundown towns: A hidden dimension of American racism*. The New Press.

Logan, T. M., Anderson, M. J., & Reilly, A. C. (2023). Risk of isolation increases the expected burden from sea-level rise. *Nature Climate Change*, *13*, 397–402. https://doi.org/10.1038/s41558-023-01642-3

Louisiana Office of Community Development (LA-OCD). (2020). *Resettlement of Isle de Jean Charles*. https://isledejeancharles.la.gov/sites/default/files/public/IDJC-Background-and-Overview-1-28-21.pdf

___. (2021). *Community master planning and program development for the Isle de Jean Charles Resettlement: Phase 2 report*. https://isledejeancharles.la.gov/sites/default/files/public/IDJC_Phase2Report_7-21-21.pdf

Louisiana Office of the Governor. (2023, October 18). *Gov. Edwards Joins Former Residents of Pecan Acres to Celebrate Completion of New Resilient Neighborhood of Audubon Estates*. https://gov.louisiana.gov/index.cfm/newsroom/detail/4294

Louisiana Watershed Initiative. (n.d.). *Statewide Buyout Program*. https://watershed.la.gov/buyouts

Low, S. M., & Altman, I. (1992). Place attachment. In I. Altman, & S. M. Low, (Eds.), *Place attachment. human behavior and environment, vol 12* (pp. 1–12). Springer. https://doi.org/10.1007/978-1-4684-8753-4_1

LSU AgCenter. (2012). *Racial and ethnic groups in the Gulf of Mexico region: Asians*. Research Report 117. Baton Rouge. https://www.lsuagcenter.com/~/media/system/3/0/e/e/30eeed5170ea8fabada44a411a55b3fb/rr117racialandethnicgroupsinthegulfofmexicoregiona.pdf

Lubben, A. (2022). Houston's solution to climate change is to force low-income people to move. *Vice*. https://www.vice.com/en/article/k7bp5e/houston-mobile-home-buyout-flood-risks

Luchi, K., & Mutter, J. (2020). Governing community relocation after major disasters: An analysis of three different approaches and its outcomes in Asia. *Progress in Disaster Science*, 6, 100071. https://doi.org/https://doi.org/10.1016/j.pdisas.2020.100071

Lyles, W., Berke, P., & Smith, G. (2014a). A comparison of local hazard mitigation plan quality in six states, USA. *Landscape and Urban Planning*, *122*, 89–99. https://doi.org/10.1016/j.landurbplan.2013.11.010

___. (2014b). Do planners matter? Examining factors driving incorporation of land use approaches into hazard mitigation plans. *Journal of Environmental Planning and Management*, *57*(2), 792–811.

Lyons, K. (2022, November 8). How to move a country: Fiji's radical plan to escape rising sea levels. *The Guardian*. https://www.theguardian.com/environment/2022/nov/08/how-to-move-a-country-fiji-radical-plan-escape-rising-seas-climate-crisis

Macchi, V. (2015). Half a world away, Vietnamese build lives on the American Bayou. *VOA*. https://projects.voanews.com/all-over-the-map/vietnamese-bayou/

Mach, K. J., Kraan, C. M., Hino, M., Siders, A. R., Johnston, E. M., & Field, C. B. (2019). Managed retreat through voluntary buyouts of flood-prone properties. *Science Advances*, *5*(10), 1–9. https://doi.org/10.1126/sciadv.aax8995

Mach, K. J., & Siders, A. R. (2021). Reframing strategic, managed retreat for transformative climate adaptation. *Science*, *372*(6548), 1294–1299. https://doi.org/doi:10.1126/science.abh1894

Mack, J. (2018, December 10). See map of all U.S. counties by median household income. *MLive*. https://www.mlive.com/news/2018/12/see-map-of-all-us-counties-by-median-household-income.html

MacLeod, K. K. (2016). The unsaid of the Grand Dérangement: An analysis of outsider and regional interpretations of Acadian history. *The Graduate History Review*, *5*(1). https://journals.uvic.ca/index.php/ghr/article/view/13572

Macrotrends. (2023). *Washington DC Metro Area population trends 1950–2023*. https://www.macrotrends.net/cities/23174/washington-dc/population

Madumere, N. (2017). Public enlightenment and participation—A major contribution in mitigating climate change. *International Journal of Sustainable Built Environment*, *6*(1), 9–15. https://doi.org/10.1016/j.ijsbe.2016.10.003

Mahan, L. (2013). *Come hell or high water: The battle for Turkey Creek* [Documentary]. https://leahmahan.com/comehellorhighwater/

Maldonado, J. K. (2019). *Seeking justice in an energy sacrifice zone: Standing on vanishing land in coastal Louisiana*. Routledge.

Maldonado, J. K., Marino, E., & Iaukea, L. (2020). Reframing the language of retreat. *Eos*, *101*(10.1029). https://doi.org/10.1029/2020EO150527

Maldonado, J. K., Shearer, C., Bronen, R., Peterson, K., & Lazrus, H. (2014). The impact of climate change on tribal communities in the US: Displacement, relocation, and human rights. *Climate change and Indigenous peoples in the United States: Impacts, experiences and actions*, 601–614. https://link.springer.com/chapter/10.1007/978-3-319-05266-3_8

Maly, E., Kondo, T., Banda, M., & Iuchi, K. (2018). The role of residential buyouts in post-disaster housing recovery support: A comparison of recent cases from Japan and the United States. *International Planning History Society Proceedings*, *18*(1), 48–54.

Mann, C. C. (2011). *1493: Uncovering the new world Columbus created*. Vintage Books.

Manning-Broome, C., Dubinin, J., & Jenkins, P. (2015). *View from the Coast: Local perspectives and policy recommendations on flood-risk reduction in south Louisiana*. [Policy report]. Center for Planning Excellence.

Marandi, A., & Main, K. L. (2021). Vulnerable city, recipient city, or climate destination? Towards a typology of domestic climate migration impacts in US cities. *Journal of Environmental Studies and Sciences*, *11*(3), 465–480. https://doi.org/10.1007/s13412-021-00712-2

Marks, B. (2012). The political economy of household commodity production in the Louisiana shrimp fishery. *Journal of Agrarian Change*, *12*(2-3), 227–251.

Marré, A. W., & Weber, B. A. (2010). Assessing community capacity and social capital in rural America: Lessons from two rural observatories. *Community Development*, *41*(1), 92–107. https://doi.org/10.1080/15575331003661099

Marshall, N. A., Park, S. E., Adger, W. N., Brown, K., & Howden, S. M. (2012). Transformational capacity and the influence of place and identity. *Environmental Research Letters*, *7*(3), 034022. https://doi.org/10.1088/1748-9326/7/3/034022

Marsooli, R., Lin, N., Emanuel, K., & Feng, K. (2019). Climate change exacerbates hurricane flood hazards along US Atlantic and Gulf Coasts in spatially varying patterns. *Nature Communications*, *10*(1), Article 3785. https://doi.org/10.1038/s41467-019-11755-z

Martikainen, P., Bartley, M., & Lahelma, E. (2002). Psychosocial determinants of health in social epidemiology. *International Journal of Epidemiology*, *31*(6), 1091–1093. https://doi.org/10.1093/ije/31.6.1091

Martín, C., Gilbert, B., Teles, D., & Theodos, B. (2019). *Housing recovery and CDBG-DR: A review of the timing and factors associated with housing activities in HUD's Community Development Block Grant for Disaster Recovery Program*. HUD Office of Policy Development and Research. https://www.huduser.gov/portal/sites/default/files/pdf/HousingRecovery_CDBG-DR.pdf

Martín, C., & Williams, A. (2021). *A federal policy and climate migration briefing for federal executive and legislative officials*. Urban Institute. https://www.urban.org/research/publication/federal-policy-and-climate-migration-briefing-federal-executive-and-legislative-officials

Martinez-Diaz, L., Sidner, L., & Sengupta, R. (2020). Importing a good idea to the U.S.: Parametric insurance and climate-related risks. *World Resources Institute*. https://www.wri.org/insights/importing-good-idea-us-parametric-insurance-and-climate-related-risks

Maryland.gov. (n.d.). *Frequently asked questions (FAQs): FEMA funded residential property voluntary flood buyouts*. https://mdem.maryland.gov/Documents/Buyout%20FAQ.pdf

Masquelier, A. (2006). Why Katrina's victims aren't refugees: Musings on a "dirty" word. *American Anthropologist*, *108*(4), 735–743. http://www.jstor.org/stable/4496516

Massey, D. (1994). *Space, place and gender*. Polity Press.

Masterson, V. A. (2016). *Sense of place and culture in the landscape of home: Understanding social-ecological dynamics on the Wild Coast, South Africa* [Doctoral dissertation, Stockholm Resilience Centre, Stockholm University].

Masterson, V. A., Stedman, R. C., Enqvist, J., Tengö, M., Giusti, M., Wahl, D., & Svedin, U. (2017). The contribution of sense of place to social-ecological systems research: A review and research agenda. *Ecology and Society*, *22*(1). https://www.jstor.org/stable/26270120

Mayer, B., Running, K., & Bergstrand, K. (2015). Compensation and community corrosion: Perceived inequalities, social comparisons, and competition following the Deepwater Horizon oil spill. *Sociological Forum*, *30*(2), 369–390.

Mayor's Office of Housing Recovery Operations. (2017). *Completing the Build It Back Program*. https://www.nyc.gov/assets/housingrecovery/downloads/pdf/2017/october_2017_build_it_back_progress_update.pdf

Mayseless, O. (2020). The development of care. In L. A. Jensen (Ed.), *The Oxford handbook of moral development: An interdisciplinary perspective* (pp. 9–26). Oxford Library of Psychology. https://doi.org/10.1093/oxfordhb/9780190676049.013.2

Mazzocchi, F. (2006). Western science and traditional knowledge. Despite their variations, different forms of knowledge can learn from each other. *EMBO Reports*, *7*(5), 463–466. https://doi.org/10.1038/sj.embor.7400693

McClain, R. (2003, June 20). *In Louisiana rice: Rain helps fight saltwater intrusion*. Farm Progress. https://www.farmprogress.com/corn/in-louisiana-rice-rain-helps-fight-saltwater-intrusion

McClure, S., Oths, K., Agomo, C., Foster, P. P., Krieg, R., Lichtenstein, B., Pruitt, S., Hosangadi, D., Trotochaud, M., & Radcliffe, O. (2022). *Building a ground game: How to conduct a community needs assessment and launch a CHW workforce development coalition*. Johns Hopkins Center for Health Security.

McCormick, S. (2009). *Mobilizing science: Movements, participation, and the remaking of knowledge*. Temple University Press.

___. (2012). After the cap: Risk assessment, citizen science and disaster recovery. *Ecology and Society*, *17*(4).

McEwen, B. S. (1998). Stress, adaptation, and disease: Allostasis and allostatic load. In S. M. McCann, J. M. Lipton, E. M. Sternberg, G. P. Chrousos, P. W. Gold, & C. C. Smith (Eds.), *Molecular aspects, integrative systems, and clinical advances* (pp. 33–44). New York Academy of Sciences.

McEwen, B. S., & Seeman, T. (1999). Protective and damaging effects of mediators of stress. Elaborating and testing the concepts of allostasis and allostatic load. *Annals of the New York Academy of Sciences*, *896*, 30–47. https://doi.org/10.1111/j.1749-6632.1999.tb08103.x

McGee, K. (2021). A place worth protecting: Rethinking cost-benefit analysis under FEMA's flood-mitigation programs. *The University of Chicago Law Review*, *88*, 1925.

McGhee, D. (2017). *Were the post-Sandy Staten Island buyouts successful in reducing national vulnerability?* [Master's project, Duke University]. https://hdl.handle.net/10161/14168

McGhee, D. J., Binder, S. B., & Albright, E. A. (2020). First, do no harm: Evaluating the vulnerability reduction of post-disaster home buyout programs. *Natural Hazards Review*, *21*(1), 05019002. https://doi.org/10.1061/(ASCE)NH.1527-6996.0000337

McKee, J. O., & Schlenker, J. A. (1980). *The Choctaws: Cultural evolution of a Native American Tribe*. University Press of Mississippi.

McLaughlin, R., Edwards, R., & Ruppert, T. (2018). *Living with sea level rise on the upper Texas coast: Public policy concerns and comparisons to Texas*. Houston Endowment. https://gomaportal.tamucc.edu/slr/whitePaper_SLRPolicy.pdf

Mcleod, E., Bruton-Adams, M., Förster, J., Franco, C., Gaines, G., Gorong, B., James, R., Posing-Kulwaum, G., Tara, M., & Terk, E. (2019). Lessons from the Pacific Islands—Adapting to climate change by supporting social and ecological resilience. *Frontiers in Marine Science*, *6*. https://doi.org/10.3389/fmars.2019.00289

McMichael, A., McMichael, C., Berry, H., & Bowen, K. (2010). Climate-related displacement: Health risks and responses. In J. McAdam (Ed.), *Climate change and population displacement: Multidisciplinary perspectives* (pp. 191–220). Hart Publishing Ltd. https://doi.org/10.1017/S0922156512000428

McMichael, C., Dasgupta, S., Ayeb-Karlsson, S., & Kelman, I. (2020). A review of estimating population exposure to sea-level rise and the relevance for migration. *Environmental Research Letters*, *15*(12), 123005. https://doi.org/10.1088/1748-9326/abb398

McTarnaghan, S., Morales-Burnett, J., & Marx, R. (2022). *Urban resilience: From global vision to local practice, executive summary of the final outcome evaluation of the 100 Resilient Cities Program*. Urban Institute. https://www.urban.org/research/publication/urban-resilience-global-vision-local-practice

Meadow, A. M., Ferguson, D. B., Guido, Z., Horangic, A., Owen, G., & Wall, T. (2015). Moving toward the deliberate coproduction of climate science knowledge. *Weather, Climate, and Society*, *7*(2), 179–191. https://doi.org/10.1175/WCAS-D-14-00050.1

Mehta, J., & Skipton, T. (2019, September 27). Rising seas threaten hundreds of Native American heritage sites along Florida's Gulf Coast. *The Conversation*. https://theconversation.com/rising-seas-threaten-hundreds-of-native-american-heritage-sites-along-floridas-gulf-coast-118500

Melish, J. P. (1998). *Disowning slavery: Gradual emancipation and "race" in New England, 1780–1860, Ithaca and London*. Cornell University Press.

Meltzer, G. Y., Merdjanoff, A. A., & Abramson, D. M. (2021). Adverse physical and mental health effects of the Deepwater Horizon oil spill among Gulf Coast children: An environmental justice perspective. *Environmental Justice*, *14*(2), 124–133. https://doi.org/10.1089/env.2020.0046

Mendelssohn, I. A., Byrnes, M. R., Kneib, R. T., & Vittor, B. A. (2017). Coastal Habitats of the Gulf of Mexico. In C. H. Ward (Ed.), *Habitats and Biota of the Gulf of Mexico: Before the Deepwater Horizon Oil Spill*. Springer, New York, NY. https://doi.org/10.1007/978-1-4939-3447-8_6

Mercer, J., Kelman, I., Taranis, L., & Suchet-Pearson, S. (2010). Framework for integrating Indigenous and scientific knowledge for disaster risk reduction. *Disasters*, *34*(1), 214–239. https://doi.org/10.1111/j.1467-7717.2009.01126.x

Meyer-Arendt, K. J. (1987). *Resort evolution along the Gulf of Mexico littoral: Historical, morphological, and environmental aspects* [Dissertation, Louisiana State University].

Miller, B. M., Clancy, N., Ligor, D. C., Kirkwood, G., Metz, D., Koller, S., & Stewart, S. (2023). *The cost of cost-effectiveness: Expanding equity in Federal Emergency Management Agency Hazard Mitigation Assistance Grants.* RAND Corporation. https://www.rand.org/pubs/research_reports/RRA2171-1.html

Milnes, T., & Haney, T. J. (2017). 'There's always winners and losers': Traditional masculinity, resource dependence and post-disaster environmental complacency. *Environmental Sociology, 3*(3), 260–273. https://doi.org/10.1080/23251042.2017.1295837

Minemyer, P. (2017). How Texas Medical Center used the lessons from Tropical Storm Allison to prepare for Hurricane Harvey. *Fierce Healthcare.* https://www.fiercehealthcare.com/population-health/hurricane-harvey-texas-medical-center-houston-methodist-disaster-planning

Minovi, D. (2021). Toxic floodwaters on the Gulf Coast and beyond: Commentary on the public health implications of chemical releases triggered by extreme weather. *Environmental Justice, 14*(2), 105–109. https://doi.org/10.1089/env.2020.0051

Misdary, R. (2022). How the Sandy-era buyout program turned bustling Staten Island communities into vacant overgrown lots. *Gothamist.* https://gothamist.com/news/how-sandy-era-buyout-program-staten-island-communities-vacant-lots

Mississippi-Alabama Sea Grant Consortium. (2021). *Stories from the Alabama waterfront: Preserving the oral histories of Bayou La Batre.* https://storymaps.arcgis.com/stories/7e91d589406f4ed2828c1b5504998c3b

Mississippi Encyclopedia. (2023). Harrison County. https://mississippiencyclopedia.org/entries/harrison-county/

Mississippi Regional Economic Analysis Project. (2023). *Gulfport-Biloxi MSA vs. Mississippi comparative trends analysis: Population growth and change, 1969–2021.* https://mississippi.reaproject.org/analysis/comparative-trends-analysis/population/tools/80970000/280000/

Misuri, A., Moreno, V.C., Quddus, N., & Cozzani, V. (2019). Lessons learnt from the impacts of Hurricane Harvey on the chemical and process industry. *Reliability Engineering & System Safety, 190*, 106521.

Mitchell, D. J. (2023). Aging and shrinking: 3 in 4 Louisiana parishes have seen more deaths than births recently. *The Advocate.* https://www.theadvocate.com/baton_rouge/news/how-many-louisiana-parishes-are-aging-and-shrinking/article_d9fccc6a-2285-11ee-bcb0-37179e444131.html

Mitchell, S. A. (1861). Map of the United States, and territories [Map]. Library of Congress Geography and Map Division. https://www.loc.gov/item/99447041/

Mitsova, D., Escaleras, M., Sapat, A., Esnard, A.-M., & Lamadrid, A. J. (2019). The effects of infrastructure service disruptions and socio-economic vulnerability on hurricane recovery. *Sustainability, 11*(2), 516. https://www.mdpi.com/2071-1050/11/2/516

Miyasada, A., & Maly, E. (2021). Impacts of collective housing relocation in the Ogatsu area of Ishinomaki City after the 2011 Great East Japan Earthquake and Tsunami. *IOP Conference Series: Earth and Environmental Science, 630*(1), 012014. https://doi.org/10.1088/1755-1315/630/1/012014

Moder, U., & Otieno, V. W. (2022, August 12). Tapping into the power of young people for climate action. *United Nations Development Programme.* https://www.undp.org/blog/tapping-power-young-people-climate-action

Morello-Frosch, R., & Obasogie, O. K. (2023). The climate gap and the color line - Racial health inequities and climate change. *New England Journal of Medicine, 388*(10), 943–949. https://doi.org/10.1056/NEJMsb2213250

Morgan, M. G., Fischhoff, B., Bostrom, A., & Atman, C. J. (2002). *Risk communication: A mental models approach.* Cambridge University Press.

Morris, A. M., & Diaz, L. (2020). Reimagining housing: Affordability crisis and its role in disaster resilience and recovery. In S. Laska (Ed.), *Louisiana's response to extreme weather: A coastal state's adaptation challenges and successes* (pp. 241–259). Springer International Publishing. https://doi.org/10.1007/978-3-030-27205-0_9

Morris, C. (2012). *The big muddy: An environmental history of the Mississippi and its peoples from Hernando de Soto to Hurricane Katrina*. Oxford University Press.

Morrissey, J., & Oliver-Smith, A. (2013). *Perspectives on non-economic loss and damage: Understanding values at risk from climate change*. Loss & Damage in Vulnerable Countries, United Nations University. https://doi.org/10.13140/RG.2.1.1668.1041

Moser, S. C. (2007). Communication strategies to mobilize the climate movement. In J. Isham & S. Waage (Eds.), *Ignition: What you can do to fight global warming and spark a movement* (pp. 161-174). Island Press.

Moser, S. C., & Dilling, L. (Eds.). (2007). *Creating a climate for change: Communicating climate change and facilitating social change*. Cambridge University Press.

Moskwa, E., Bardsley, D. K., Weber, D., & Robinson, G. M. (2018). Living with bushfire: Recognising ecological sophistication to manage risk while retaining biodiversity values. *International Journal of Disaster Risk Reduction, 27*, 459–469. https://doi.org/https://doi.org/10.1016/j.ijdrr.2017.11.010

Motiva. (2020). *North America's largest refinery*. https://www.motiva.com/About/What-We-Do/Refining

Moulton, A. A., & Machado, M. R. (2019). Bouncing forward after Irma and Maria: Acknowledging colonialism, problematizing resilience and thinking climate justice. *Journal of Extreme Events, 6*(1).

Mulkern, A. C. (2021, November 5). Managed retreat: Unpopular, expensive and not going away. *ClimateWire*. https://www.eenews.net/articles/managed-retreat-unpopular-expensive-and-not-going-away/

Muñoz, C. E., & Tate, E. (2016). Unequal recovery? Federal resource distribution after a Midwest flood disaster. *International Journal of Environmental Research and Public Health, 13*(5). https://doi.org/10.3390/ijerph13050507

Murphy, M., Lando, J., Kieszak, S., Sutter, M., Noonan, G., Brunkard, J., & McGeehin, M. (2013). Formaldehyde levels in FEMA-supplied travel trailers, park models, and mobile homes in Louisiana and Mississippi. *Indoor Air, 23*(2), 134–141.

Nathan, A. (2019, July 15). Climate is the newest gentrifying force and its effects are already reshaping cities. *Science in the News Blog*. https://sitn.hms.harvard.edu/flash/2019/climate-newest-gentrifying-force-effects-already-re-shaping-cities/

National Academies of Sciences, Engineering, and Medicine (National Academies). (2016). *Attribution of extreme weather events in the context of climate change*. The National Academies Press. https://doi.org/https://doi.org/10.17226/21852

___. (2017). *Communities in action: Pathways to health equity*. The National Academies Press. https://doi.org/10.17226/24624

___. (2018a). *Improving health research on small populations: Proceedings of a workshop*. The National Academies Press. https://doi.org/10.17226/25112

___. (2018b). *Understanding the long-term evolution of the coupled natural-human coastal system: The future of the U.S. Gulf Coast*. The National Academies Press. https://doi.org/doi:10.17226/25108

___. (2019a). *Building and measuring community resilience: Actions for communities and the Gulf Research Program*. The National Academies Press. https://doi.org/10.17226/25383

___. (2019b). *Taking action against clinician burnout: A systems approach to professional well-being*. The National Academies Press. https://doi.org/10.17226/25521

___. (2021). *Enhancing community resilience through social capital and connectedness: Stronger together!* The National Academies Press. https://doi.org/10.17226/26123

___. (2022a). *Communities, climate change, and health equity—state-level implementation: Proceedings of a workshop—in brief*. The National Academies Press. https://doi.org/doi:10.17226/26693

___. (2022b). *Engaging socially vulnerable communities and communicating about climate change–related risks and hazards*. The National Academies Press. https://doi.org/10.17226/26734

___. (2022c). *Environmental challenges and prospects for community relocation in Houston and Port Arthur, Texas: Proceedings of a workshop*. The National Academies Press. https://doi.org/10.17226/26701

___. (2022d). *Relocation and other climate adaptations on Florida's Gulf Coast: Proceedings of a workshop—in brief*. The National Academies Press. https://doi.org/10.17226/26736

___. (2022e). *Structural racism and rigorous models of social inequity: Proceedings of a workshop*. The National Academies Press. https://doi.org/10.17226/26690

___. (2023a). *Assisted resettlement and community viability on Louisiana's Gulf Coast: Proceedings of a workshop*. The National Academies Press. https://doi.org/10.17226/26774

___. (2023b). *Strengthening equitable community resilience: Criteria and Guiding Principles for the Gulf Research Program's Enhancing Community Resilience (EnCoRe) initiative*. The National Academies Press. https://doi.org/10.17226/26880

National Archives. (n.d.). *Dawes Rolls*. Native American Heritage. https://www.archives.gov/research/native-americans/dawes/tutorial/intro.html

National Association of Realtors. (2006). *The impact of hurricanes on housing and economic activity: A case study for Florida*. https://www.nar.realtor/reports/the-impact-of-hurricanes-on-housing-and-economic-activity-a-case-study-for-florida

National Fish and Wildlife Foundation. (2018). *National Coastal Resilience 2018 Grant Slate*. https://www.nfwf.org/sites/default/files/coastalresilience/Documents/2018grantslate.pdf

National Institutes of Health. (2011). *Principles of community engagement: Clinical and Translational Science Awards Consortium Community Engagement Key Function Committee task force on the Principles of Community Engagement* (2nd ed.). https://atsdr.cdc.gov/communityengagement/pdf/PCE_Report_508_FINAL.pdf

National Ocean Service. (2021). *What is high tide flooding?* https://oceanservice.noaa.gov/facts/high-tide-flooding.html

National Oceanic and Atmospheric Administration (NOAA). (n.d.). *Harmful algal blooms: Tiny organisms with a toxic punch*. https://oceanservice.noaa.gov/hazards/hab/

___. (2013). *State of the coast: National coastal population report, population trends from 1970 to 2020*. https://aambpublicoceanservice.blob.core.windows.net/oceanserviceprod/facts/coastal-population-report.pdf

___. (2022). *Pilot project builds Tribal climate and disaster resilience in Louisiana*. https://www.noaa.gov/news-release/pilot-project-builds-tribal-climate-and-disaster-resilience-in-louisiana

National Oceanic and Atmospheric Administration National Centers for Environmental Information. (2023). *U.S. billion-dollar weather and climate disasters*. https://www.ncei.noaa.gov/access/billions/

National Oceanic and Atmospheric Administration Office for Coastal Management. (2012). *State coastal boundaries*. National Oceanic and Atmospheric Administration. https://coast.noaa.gov/data/czm/media/StateCZBoundaries.pdf

National Weather Service. (2022). Weather fatalities 2021 and 2022 [Table]. https://www.weather.gov/hazstat/

Ndugga, N. & Artiga, S. (2023, April 21). Disparities in health and health care: 5 key questions and answers. *KFF*. https://www.kff.org/racial-equity-and-health-policy/issue-brief/disparities-in-health-and-health-care-5-key-question-and-answers/

Nebraska Department of Economic Development. (2023, February 21). *RE: HUD, CDBG-DR RFI – Rules, Waivers, and Alternative Requirements Docket No. FR-6336-N-01; Document Number: 2022-27547* [Press release]. https://coscda.org/wp-content/uploads/2023/03/Nebraska-DED-HUD-RFI_CDBG-DR-Rules-Waivers-Alt-Req-FR-6336-N-01.pdf

Needham, H. F., Brown, D. P., & Carter, L. M. (2012). *Impacts and adaptation options in the Gulf Coast.* Center for Climate and Energy Solutions. https://www.c2es.org/document/impacts-and-adaptation-options-in-the-gulf-coast/

Nelson, E. S., Peles, A., & Melton, M. A. (2020). Foodways and community at the Late Mississippian site of Parchman Place. *Southeastern Archaeology*, *39*(1), 29–50. https://doi.org/10.1080/0734578X.2019.1689740

Nelson, J., & Grubesic, T. (2018). The implications of oil exploration off the Gulf coast of Florida. *Journal of Marine Science and Engineering*, 6(2), 30. MDPI AG. http://dx.doi.org/10.3390/jmse6020030

Nelson, M., Ehrenfeucht, R., Birch, T., & Brand, A. (2022). Getting by and getting out: How residents of Louisiana's frontline communities are adapting to environmental change. *Housing Policy Debate*, *32*(1), 84–101.

Neumann, J. E., Emanuel, K., Ravela, S., Ludwig, L., Kirshen, P., Bosma, K., & Martinich, J. (2015). Joint effects of storm surge and sea-level rise on US Coasts: New economic estimates of impacts, adaptation, and benefits of mitigation policy. *Climatic Change*, *129*(1-2), 337–349. https://doi.org/10.1007/s10584-014-1304-z

New Jersey Department of Community Affairs. (2013, April 29). *Community Development Block Grant Disaster Recovery action plan.* https://www.nj.gov/dca/announcements/pdf/CDBG-DisasterRecoveryActionPlan.pdf

New Orleans Regional Planning Commission. (n.d.). *Louisiana Watershed Initiative.* https://www.norpc.org/environment/projects/lwi/

New York State. (2023). *Assembly Bill A1967.* https://www.nysenate.gov/legislation/bills/2023/A1967

New Zealand. (2022). *Adapt and thrive: Building a Climate-resilient New Zealand. New Zealand's First National Adaptation Plan.* Ministry for the Environment. https://environment.govt.nz/publications/aotearoa-new-zealands-first-national-adaptation-plan/

Nguyen, M. T., & Salvesen, D. (2014). Disaster recovery among multiethnic immigrants: A case study of Southeast Asians in Bayou La Batre (AL) after Hurricane Katrina. *Journal of the American Planning Association*, *80*(4), 385–396. https://doi.org/10.1080/01944363.2014.986497

Niven, R. J., & Bardsley, D. K. (2013). Planned retreat as a management response to coastal risk: A case study from the Fleurieu Peninsula, South Australia. *Regional Environmental Change*, *13*(1), 193–209. https://doi.org/10.1007/s10113-012-0315-4

Norris, F. H., Stevens, S. P., Pfefferbaum, B., Wyche, K. F., & Pfefferbaum, R. L. (2008). Community resilience as a metaphor, theory, set of capacities, and strategy for disaster readiness. *American journal of community psychology*, 41(1-2), 127 -150. https://doi.org/10.1007/s10464-007-9156-6

Norström, A. V., Cvitanovic, C., Löf, M. F., West, S., Wyborn, C., Balvanera, P., Bednarek, A. T., Bennett, E. M., Biggs, R., de Bremond, A., Campbell, B. M., Canadell, J. G., Carpenter, S. R., Folke, C., Fulton, E. A., Gaffney, O., Gelcich, S., Jouffray, J.-B., Leach, M., . . . Österblom, H. (2020). Principles for knowledge co-production in sustainability research. *Nature Sustainability*, *3*(3), 182–190. https://doi.org/10.1038/s41893-019-0448-2

North Carolina Department of Public Safety. (2019, October 15). *State awards supplements to local governments for buyout of properties flooded by Hurricane Matthew* [Press release]. https://www.ncdps.gov/news/press-releases/2019/10/15/state-awards-supplements-local-governments-buyout-properties%C2%A0flooded

North Carolina Department of Public Safety & North Carolina Emergency Management. (2023). *State Acquisition and Relocation Fund (SARF)*. https://www.nctreasurer.com/dps-1-2023/download?attachment

North Carolina Office of Recovery and Resiliency. (2023). *Strategic Buyout Program manual*. https://www.rebuild.nc.gov/homeowners-and-landlords/strategic-buyout-program

Nussbaum, M. C. (2000). The costs of tragedy: Some moral limits of cost-benefit analysis. *The Journal of Legal Studies*, *29*(S2),1005–1036.

NYC Build It Back. (2018). *New York City Build It Back single-family acquisition, buyout, cooperative relocation and resettlement incentives policy manual*. Equal Housing Opportunity. https://www.nyc.gov/assets/housingrecovery/downloads/pdf/2018/build_it_back_acquisition_relocation_and_buyout_policy_manual_v2.0.pdf

Oberg, A., Flagg, J., Clay, P. M., Colburn, L. L., & McCay, B. (2016). Surviving Sandy: Identity and cultural resilience in a New Jersey fishing community. In K. O'Neill & D. Van Abs (Eds.), *Taking chances: The coast after Hurricane Sandy* (pp. 122–142). Rutgers University Press.

O'Donnell, T. (2022). Managed retreat and planned retreat: *A systematic literature review. Philosophical Transactions of the Royal Society B: Biological Sciences*, 377(1854), 20210129. https://doi.org/10.1098/rstb.2021.0129

Office for Coastal Management. (2023a). Coastal County Snapshots. https://coast.noaa.gov/digitalcoast/tools/snapshots.html

___. (2023b). Coastal Flood Exposure Mapper: Gulf of Mexico. https://coast.noaa.gov/floodexposure/#-9725012,3188145,7z/eyJiIjoiZGFyayJ9

___. (2023c). Sea Level Rise and Coastal Flooding at 1': Gulf of Mexico. https://coast.noaa.gov/slr/

___. (2023d). Sea Level Rise Viewer: Gulf of Mexico Vulnerability, 2' Water Level. https://coast.noaa.gov/slr/#/layer/vul-soc/2/-9785443.24747092/3371743.335002211/7/satellite/none/0.8/2050/interHigh/midAccretion

Office of Inspector General. (2004). *Review of actions at Escambia treating company site, Pensacola, Florida* (Report No. 2004-P-00032). U.S. Environmental Protection Agency. https://www.epaoig.gov/report-review-actions-escambia-treating-company-site-pensacola-florida

Office of Science and Technology Policy (OSTP). (2021, November 15). *White House commits to elevating Indigenous knowledge in federal policy decisions* [Press release]. White House. https://www.whitehouse.gov/ostp/news-updates/2021/11/15/white-house-commits-to-elevating-indigenous-knowledge-in-federal-policy-decisions/

___. (2022, December 1). *White House releases first-of-a-kind Indigenous Knowledge Guidance for Federal Agencies* [Press release]. Council on Environmental Quality, White House. https://www.whitehouse.gov/ceq/news-updates/2022/12/01/white-house-releases-first-of-a-kind-indigenous-knowledge-guidance-for-federal-agencies/

Office of the Assistant Secretary for Preparedness and Response. (2016). *2017–2022 health care preparedness and response capabilities*. https://aspr.hhs.gov/HealthCareReadiness/HPP/Documents/2017-2022%20Health%20Care%20Preparedness%20and%20Response%20Capabilities.pdf

Office of the Prime Minister, Republic of Fiji. (2023). *Standard Operating Procedure for planned relocation in the Republic of Fiji*. https://fijiclimatechangeportal.gov.fj/wp-content/uploads/2023/04/Standard-Operating-Procedures-for-Planned-Relocation-in-the-Republic-of-Fiji-1.pdf

O'Hare, W. (2017). *2020 Census faces challenges in rural America*. University of New Hampshire Carsey School of Public Policy. https://carsey.unh.edu/publication/2020-census

Okada, T., Haynes, K., Bird, D., van den Honert, R., & King, D. (2014). Recovery and resettlement following the 2011 flash flooding in the Lockyer Valley. *International Journal of Disaster Risk Reduction*, *8*, 20–31. https://doi.org/https://doi.org/10.1016/j.ijdrr.2014.01.001

Okonta, P. (2018). Race-based political exclusion and social subjugation: Racial gerrymandering as a badge of slavery. *Columbia Human Rights Law Review*, *49.2*(1). https://hrlr.law.columbia.edu/files/2018/07/PatriciaOkontaRaceBasedPo.pdf

Oliver-Smith, A. (2009). Climate change and population displacement: Disasters and diasporas in the twenty-first century. In S. A. Crate & M. Nuttall (Eds.), *Anthropology and climate change* (pp. 116–136). https://www.scopus.com/inward/record.uri?eid=2-s2.0-80055065372&partnerID=40&md5=9c52dd69ff06366b5b8cd09aac460624

Olshansky, R. B., Hopkins, L. D., & Johnson, L. A. (2012). Disaster and recovery: Processes compressed in time. *Natural Hazards Review*, *13*(3), 173–178.

Olshansky, R. B., & Johnson, L. A. (2010). *Clear as mud: Planning for the rebuilding of New Orleans*. American Planning Association.

Olsson, P., Gunderson, L. H., Carpenter, S. R., Ryan, P., Lebel, L., Folke, C., & Holling, C. S. (2006). Shooting the rapids: Navigating transitions to adaptive governance of social-ecological systems. *Ecology and Society*, *11*(1). https://www.jstor.org/stable/26267806

Oppenheimer, M., Campos, M., Warren, R., Birkmann, J., Luber, G., O'Neill, B., & Takahashi, K. (2014). Emergent risks and key vulnerabilities. *Climate change 2014: Impacts, adaptation, and vulnerability. Part A: Global and sectoral aspects: Contribution of Working Group II to the fifth assessment report*, 1039–1099. Intergovernmental Panel on Climate Change. Cambridge University Press. https://www.ipcc.ch/report/ar5/wg2/

Oppenheimer, M., Glavovic, B. C., Hinkel, J., Van De Wal, R., Magnan, A. K., Abd-Elgawad, A., Cai, R., Cifuentes-Jara, M., DeConto, R. M., Ghosh, T., Marzeion, B., Meyssignac, B., & Sebesvari, Z. (2019). Sea level rise and implications for low-lying islands, coasts and communities. *IPCC special report on the ocean and cryosphere in a changing climate*. Cambridge University Press. https://www.ipcc.ch/srocc/chapter/chapter-4-sea-level-rise-and-implications-for-low-lying-islands-coasts-and-communities/

Ortiz, G., Schultheis, H., Novack, V., & Holt, A. (2019). *A perfect storm: Extreme weather as an affordable housing crisis multiplier.* Center for American Progress. https://www.americanprogress.org/article/a-perfect-storm-2/

Osborne, M., Sankey, K., & Wilson, B. (2007). *Social capital, lifelong learning and the management of place: An international perspective*. Taylor & Francis.

Osburn, K. M. B. (2014). *Choctaw resurgence in Mississippi: Race, class, and nation building in the Jim Crow South, 1830-1977*. University of Nebraska Press.

Ostler, J. (2015). *Genocide and American Indian history*. Oxford University Press.

Ostrom, E. (1990). *Governing the commons: The evolution of institutions for collective actions*. Cambridge University Press. https://doi.org/https://doi.org/10.1017/CBO9780511807763

Oxfam. (2012). *Coping with disaster: A vital region at risk and a moment of opportunity, social vulnerability and climate hazards in the Gulf Coast*. Oxfam America in the Gulf Coast. http://svm.oxfamamerica.org.s3.amazonaws.com/OxFam/publications/SVM%20II%20Full%20Report%20from%20Oxfam%20America.pdf

Page, S. (2017, August 30). Houston's toxic Superfund sites are underwater and leaking. *Think Progress*. https://archive.thinkprogress.org/houston-toxic-superfund-sites-209bb800b38d/

Pandve, H. T., Deshmukh, P. R., Pandve, R. T., & Patil, N. R. (2009). Role of youth in combating climate change. *Indian Journal of Occupational and Environmental Medicine*, *13*(2), 105. https://doi.org/10.4103/0019-5278.55130

Pape, E. (2021). *Improving benefit-cost analyses for rural areas*. Headwater Economics. https://headwaterseconomics.org/equity/improving-benefit-cost-analyses/

Parfait, J. R. (2019). *The effects of forced migration on the Houma of Louisiana*. [Masters thesis, Louisiana State University].

Parker, H. (2022). *Army Corps greenlights Louisiana's $2.2 billion sediment diversion to combat land loss*. WWNO—New Orleans Public Radio. https://www.wwno.org/post/army-corps-greenlights-louisiana-s-22-billion-sediment-diversion-combat-land-loss-0

Parker, K. H., Menasce, J., & Minkin, R. (2020). *How the Coronavirus outbreak has—and hasn't—changed the way Americans work*. Pew Research Center. https://www.pewresearch.org/social-trends/2020/12/09/how-the-coronavirus-outbreak-has-and-hasnt-changed-the-way-americans-work/

Parker, L. E., McElrone, A. J., Ostoja, S. M., & Forrestel, E. J. (2020). Extreme heat effects on perennial crops and strategies for sustaining future production. *Plant Science, 295*(110397). https://doi.org/10.1016/j.plantsci.2019.110397

Passy, J. (2020). This 'incredibly powerful' home-insurance policy will make payouts even if your property isn't damaged. *Market Watch*. https://www.marketwatch.com/story/this-powerful-home-insurance-policy-it-pays-out-even-if-your-property-isnt-damaged-2020-01-17

Patel, V. (2012). Global mental health: From science to action. *Harvard Review of Psychiatry, 20*, 6–12.

Patel, V., Weobong, B., Weiss, H. A., Anand, A., Bhat, B., Katti, B., Dimidjian, S., Araya, R., Hollon, S. D., King, M., Vijayakumar, L., Park, A. L., McDaid, D., Wilson, T., Velleman, R., Kirkwood, B. R., & Fairburn, C. G. (2017). The Healthy Activity Program (HAP), a lay counsellor-delivered brief psychological treatment for severe depression, in primary care in India: A randomised controlled trial. *Lancet, 389*(10065), 176–185. https://doi.org/10.1016/S0140-6736(16)31589-6

Peacock, W. G., Killian, C. D., & Bates, F. L. (1987). The effects of disaster damage and housing aid on household recovery following the 1976 Guatemalan earthquake. *International Journal of Mass Emergencies & Disasters, 5*(1), 63–88.

Pender County. (2019). *Memorandum of Agreement for State Acquisition Relocation Funds (SARF)*. https://pendercountync.civicweb.net/document/17716/Memorandum%20of%20Agreement%20for%20State%20Acquisition%20R.pdf?handle=3BDD9988835746CCA29498C3B08F7FAD

Perdue, T. (2012). The legacy of Indian removal. *The Journal of Southern History, 78*(1), 3–36. http://www.jstor.org/stable/23247455

Pew Research Center. (2018). *The public, the political system and American democracy*. https://www.pewresearch.org/politics/2018/04/26/the-public-the-political-system-and-american-democracy/

___. (2019). *For local news, Americans embrace digital but still want strong community connection*. https://www.pewresearch.org/journalism/2019/03/26/for-local-news-americans-embrace-digital-but-still-want-strong-community-connection/

Phelps, D. A. (1957). The Chickasaw, the English, and the French 1699–1744. *Tennessee Historical Quarterly, 16*(2), 117–133. http://www.jstor.org/stable/42621333

Picou, S., & Gill, D. (1996). The Exxon Valdez oil spill and chronic psychological stress. *American Fisheries Society Symposium, 18*.

Pierre-Louis, K. (2019). Want to escape global warming? These cities promise cool relief. *The New York Times*. https://www.nytimes.com/2019/04/15/climate/climate-migration-duluth.html

___. (2021). How rising groundwater caused by climate change could devastate coastal communities. *MIT Technology Review*. https://www.technologyreview.com/2021/12/13/1041309/climate-change-rising-groundwater-flooding

Pinter, N. (2021a). The lost history of managed retreat and community relocation in the United States. *Elementa: Science of the Anthropocene, 9*(1). https://doi.org/10.1525/elementa.2021.00036

___. (2021b). True stories of managed retreat from rising waters. *Issues in Science and Technology, 37*(4), 64–73. https://issues.org/true-stories-managed-retreat-rising-waters-pinter/

___. (2022). *Managed retreat and community relocation in North America*. Paper presented at the Managed Retreat Forum: Global Lessons for Success. https://www.nationalacademies.org/event/04-08-2022/international-forum-on-managed-retreat-global-lessons-for-success

Pinter, N., Ishiwateri, M., Nonoguchi, A., Tanaka, Y., Casagrande, D., Durden, S., & Rees, J. (2019). Large-scale managed retreat and structural protection following the 2011 Japan tsunami. *Natural Hazards*, *96*(3), 1429–1436. https://doi.org/10.1007/s11069-019-03602-7

Pinter, N., & Rees, J. C. (2021). Assessing managed flood retreat and community relocation in the Midwest USA. *Natural Hazards*, *107*(1), 497–518. https://doi.org/10.1007/s11069-021-04592-1

Pisor, A. C., Basurto, X., Douglass, K. G., Mach, K. J., Ready, E., Tylianakis, J. M., Hazel, A., Kline, M. A., Kramer, K. L., Lansing, J. S., Moritz, M., Smaldino, P. E., Thornton, T. F., & Jones, J. H. (2022). Effective climate change adaptation means supporting community autonomy. *Nature Climate Change*, *12*(3), 213–215. https://doi.org/10.1038/s41558-022-01303-x

Plyer, A. (2016). *Facts for features: Katrina impact New Orleans*. The Data Center. https://www.datacenterresearch.org/reports_analysis/census-2010/

Pope, K. (2023). Climate migrants find a home in the Great Lakes Region. *Yale Climate Connections*. https://yaleclimateconnections.org/2023/07/climate-migrants-find-a-home-in-the-great-lakes-region/

Porter, L., Rickards, L., Verlie, B., Bosomworth, K., Moloney, S., Lay, B., Latham, B., Anguelovski, I., & Pellow, D. (2020). Climate justice in a climate changed world. *Planning Theory & Practice*, *21*(2), 293–321. https://doi.org/10.1080/14649357.2020.1748959

Portes, A. (1998) Social capital: Its origins and applications in modern sociology. *Annual Review of Sociology*, *24*, 1–24.

Potenza, A. (2017). Toxic waste seeps from a Houston Superfund site after Harvey's floods. *The Verge*. https://www.theverge.com/2017/9/29/16385568/hurricane-harvey-superfund-site-houston-dioxin-cancer-chemicals

Prabhakar, A., & Mallory, B. (2022). *Memorandum for heads of federal departments and agencies: Guidance for federal departments and agencies on Indigenous knowledge*. Executive Office of the President Office of Science and Technology Policy and Council on Environmental Quality.

Putnam, R. D. (1993a). *Making democracy work*. Princeton University Press.

___. (1993b). The prosperous community. *The American Prospect*, *4*(13). http://www.philia.ca/files/pdf/ProsperousCommunity.pdf

___. (1995). Bowling alone: America's declining social capital. *Journal of Democracy*, *6*(1), 65–78.

Quay, R. (2010). Anticipatory governance. *Journal of the American Planning Association*, *76*(4), 496–511. https://doi.org/10.1080/01944363.2010.508428

Rabalais, N. N., & Turner, R. E. (2019). Gulf of Mexico hypoxia: Past, present, and future. *Limnology and Oceanography Bulletin*, *28*(4), 117–124. https://doi.org/https://doi.org/10.1002/lob.10351

Radley, D. C., Baumgartner, J. C., Collins, S. R., Zephyrin, L., & Schneider, E. C. (2021). *Achieving racial and ethnic equity in US health care*. The Commonwealth Fund. https://www.commonwealthfund.org/publications/scorecard/2021/nov/achieving-racial-ethnic-equity-us-health-care-state-performance

Raff, J. (2022). *Origin: A genetic history of the Americas*. Hachette Book Group.

Rakodi, C., & Lloyd-Jones, T. (2002). *Urban livelihoods: A people-centred approach to reducing poverty* (1st ed.). Routledge. https://doi.org/https://doi.org/10.4324/9781849773805

Ramkumar, M., Menier, D., & Kumaraswamy, K. (2019). Coastal zone management during changing climate and rising sea level: Transcendence of institutional, geographic, and subject field barriers is the key. In M. Ramkumar, R. A. James, D. Menier, & K. Kumaraswamy (Eds.), *Coastal zone management* (pp. 1–12). Elsevier. https://doi.org/https://doi.org/10.1016/B978-0-12-814350-6.00001-X

Randolph, N. (2021). Pipeline logic and culpability: Establishing a continuum of harm for sacrifice zones. *Frontiers in Environmental Science*, *9*. https://doi.org/10.3389/fenvs.2021.652691

Ranganathan, M., & Bratman, E. (2019). From urban resilience to abolitionist climate justice in Washington, DC. *Antipode*, *53*(1), 115–137.

Ranghieri, F., & Ishiwatari, M. (2014). *Learning from megadisasters: Lessons from the Great East Japan Earthquake*. World Bank Publications.

Ravenstein, E. G. (1885). The laws of migration. *Journal of the Statistical Society of London*, *48*(2), 167–235. https://doi.org/10.2307/2979181

___. (1889). The laws of migration. *Journal of the Royal Statistical Society*, *52*(2), 241–305. https://doi.org/10.2307/2979333

REACH NOLA. (n.d.). *The REACH NOLA mental health infrastructure and training project*. https://aims.uw.edu/sites/default/files/ReachNOLA.pdf

Reckien, D., Magnan, A. K., Singh, C., Lukas-Sithole, M., Orlove, B., Schipper, E. L. F., & Coughlan de Perez, E. (2023). Navigating the continuum between adaptation and maladaptation. *Nature Climate Change*, *13*(9), 907–918. https://doi.org/10.1038/s41558-023-01774-6

Reconstruction Agency. (2023). *Status of reconstruction and reconstruction efforts*. Government of Japan. https://www.reconstruction.go.jp/english/topics/Progress_to_date/English_April_2023_genjoutorikumi.pdf

Reidmiller, D. R., Avery, C. W., Easterling, D. R., Kunkel, K. E., Lewis, K. L. M., Maycock, T. K., & Stewart, B. C. (Eds.) (2018). *Impacts, Risks, and Adaptation in the United States: Fourth National Climate Assessment, Volume II*. U.S. Global Change Research Program. https://doi.org/10.7930/NCA4.2018

Renfro, A. (2022). *Battered by recent hurricanes, Southwest Louisiana benefits from new coastal restoration projects*. Restore the Mississippi River Delta. https://mississippiriverdelta.org/battered-by-recent-hurricanes-southwest-louisiana-benefits-from-new-coastal-restoration-projects/

Renn, P. (2020). Education's ecosystems: Learning through life. *Education and Culture*, *36*(2). https://docs.lib.purdue.edu/eandc/vol36/iss2/art5

Rentschler, J., Klaiber, C., Tariverdi, M., Desjonqueres, C., & Mercadante, J. (2021). *Frontline: Preparing healthcare systems for shocks from disasters to pandemics*. The World Bank. http://documents.worldbank.org/curated/en/932971618251523386/Frontline-Preparing-Healthcare-Systems-for-Shocks-from-Disasters-to-Pandemics

Reséndez, A. (2016). *The other slavery: The uncovered story of Indian enslavement*. Houghton Mifflin Harcourt.

Reuben, A., Manczak, E. M., Cabrera, L. Y., Alegria, M., Bucher, M. L., Freeman, E. C., Miller, G. W., Solomon, G. M., & Perry, M. J. (2022). The interplay of environmental exposures and mental health: Setting an agenda. *Environmental Health Perspectives*, *130*(2), 25001. https://doi.org/10.1289/EHP9889

Riabova, L., & Skaptadóttir, U. D. (2003). Social capital and community capacity building. In R.O. Rasmussen & N. E. Koroleva (Eds.), *Social and environmental impacts in the north: Methods in evaluation of socio-economic and environmental consequences of mining and energy production in the Arctic and Sub-Arctic* (pp. 437–447). Springer. https://doi.org/10.1007/978-94-007-1054-2

Richardson, J., Gough, M., & Puentes, R. (2003). *Is home rule the answer? Clarifying the influence of Dillon's rule on growth management*. The Brookings Institution. https://www.brookings.edu/articles/is-home-rule-the-answer-clarifying-the-influence-of-dillons-rule-on-growth-management/

Riggs, E. (2020). Regionalization: Five key takeaways with resources! *The Environmental Finance Blog*. https://efc.web.unc.edu/2020/03/18/regionalization-five-key-takeaways-with-resources/

Rijkswaterstaat. (2019). *Room for the River program completed.* https://www.rijkswaterstaat.nl/nieuws/2019/03/ruimte-voor-de-rivierprogramma-afgerond.aspx

Risk Factor. (n.d.). *Learn about the benefits of having flood insurance.* https://help.riskfactor.com/hc/en-us/articles/360048256113-Learn-about-the-benefits-of-having-flood-insurance

Risk Management Solutions, Inc. (2013, October). *Modeling Sandy: A high-resolution approach to storm surge* (RMS White Paper).

Ristroph, B. (2019). New site for Newtok Village [Photograph]

___. (2020). Coast of Newtok, Alaska [Photograph].

Ristroph, E. B. (2019). Fulfilling climate justice and government obligations to Alaska Native villages: What is the government role? *William & Mary Enviornmental Law and Policy Review*, *43*(2). https://ristroph.files.wordpress.com/2019/07/fulfilling-climate-justice-and-government-obligations-to-anvs-2.pdf

___. (2021). Navigating climate change adaptation assistance for communities: A case study of Newtok Village, Alaska. *Journal of Environmental Studies and Sciences*, *11*(3), 329–340. https://doi.org/10.1007/s13412-021-00711-3

___. (2023). *Using traditional knowledge to inform planned relocation for Pacific Islands communities.* Pacific Resilience Partnership. https://www.resilientpacific.org/en/resources/using-traditional-knowledge-inform-planned-relocation-pacific-islands-communities

Ristroph, E. B., & Robards, M. (2019). Preparing for the aftermath of drilling on Arctic lands. *LSU Journal of Energy Law & Resources*, *8*, 155.

Rivera, D. Z., Jenkins, B., & Randolph, R. (2022). Procedural vulnerability and its effects on equitable post-disaster recovery in low-income communities. *Journal of the American Planning Association*, *88*(2), 220–231. https://doi.org/10.1080/01944363.2021.1929417

Robards, M. D., Huntington, H. P., Druckenmiller, M., Lefevre, J., Moses, S. K., Stevenson, Z., Watson, A., & Williams, M. (2018). Understanding and adapting to observed changes in the Alaskan Arctic: Actionable knowledge co-production with Alaska Native communities. *Deep Sea Research Part II: Topical Studies in Oceanography*, 152, 203–213. https://doi.org/10.1016/j.dsr2.2018.02.008

Robert Wood Johnson Foundation. (2018). Advancing well-being in an inequitable world: Moving from measurement to action. https://www.rwjf.org/en/insights/our-research/2019/01/advancing-well-being-in-an-inequitable-world.html

Robinson, C., Dilkina, B., & Moreno-Cruz, J. (2020). Modeling migration patterns in the USA under sea level rise. *PLoS ONE*, *15*(1), e0227436. https://doi.org/10.1371/journal.pone.0227436

Ross, M. H. (2018). *Slavery in the North: Forgetting history and recovering memory.* University of Pennsylvania Press.

Rossi, M. (2019, August 7). Some northern cities could be reborn as 'climate havens'. *Yale Climate Connections.* https://yaleclimateconnections.org/2019/08/some-northern-cities-could-be-reborn-as-climate-havens/

Rudowitz, R., Drake, P., Tolbert, J., & Damico, A. (2023). *How many uninsured are in the coverage gap and how many could be eligible if all states adopted the Medicaid expansion?* KFF. https://www.kff.org/medicaid/issue-brief/how-many-uninsured-are-in-the-coverage-gap-and-how-many-could-be-eligible-if-all-states-adopted-the-medicaid-expansion/

Rush, E. (2015). Leaving the sea: Staten Islanders experiment with managed retreat. *Urban Omnibus*, *11.* https://urbanomnibus.net/2015/02/leaving-the-sea-staten-islanders-experiment-with-managed-retreat/

___. (2022). I would have never bought this home if I knew it flooded. *New York Times.* https://www.nytimes.com/2022/04/11/opinion/climate-change-flooding.html

Ryan, E., Owen, S., Lawrence, J., Glavovic, B., Robichaux, L., Dickson, M., Kench, P. S., Schnider, P., Bell, R., & Blackett, P. (2022). Formulating a 100-year strategy for managing coastal hazard risk in a changing climate: Lessons learned from Hawke's Bay, New Zealand. *Environmental Science & Policy*, *127*, 1–11.

Salvesen, D., BenDor, T. K., Kamrath, C., & Ganser, B. (2018). *Are floodplain buyouts a smart investment for local governments*. University of North Carolina Policy Collaboratory. https://coastalreview.org/wp-content/uploads/2018/09/Project-Report-Floodplain-Buyout1.pdf

Sampson, R. J., Raudenbush, S. W., & Earls, F. (1997). Neighborhoods and violent crime: A multilevel study of collective efficacy. *Science*, 277(5328), 918–924. https://doi.org/10.1126/science.277.5328.918

Sand-Fleishman, M. (2019). *Circumventing the next Trail of Tears: Re-approaching planning and policy for the climatologically displaced Indigenous communities of coastal Louisiana* [Doctoral dissertation, Cornell University]. ProQuest Dissertations Publishing. https://ecommons.cornell.edu/items/c32a73bb-222a-459f-bc09-e053673f27ed

Sandifer, P. A., Knapp, L. C., Collier, T. K., Jones, A. L., Juster, R.-P., Kelble, C. R., Kwok, R. K., Miglarese, J. V., Palinkas, L. A., Porter, D. E., Scott, G. I., Smith, L. M., Sullivan, W. C., & Sutton-Grier, A. E. (2017). A conceptual model to assess stress-associated health effects of multiple ecosystem services degraded by disaster events in the Gulf of Mexico and elsewhere. *GeoHealth, 1*(1), 17–36. https://doi.org/https://doi.org/10.1002/2016GH000038

Santella, N., Steinberg, L. J., & Sengul, H. (2010). Petroleum and hazardous material releases from industrial facilities associated with Hurricane Katrina. *Risk Analysis: An International Journal, 30*(4), 635–649.

Satter, B. (2009). *Family properties: Race, real estate, and the exploitation of Black urban America*. Henry Holt and Company, LLC.

Sayers, D. O. (2015). *A desolate place for a defiant people*. University of Florida Press.

Scally, C. P., & Burnstein, E. (2020). Rural communities need better data. *Urban Wire*. https://www.urban.org/urban-wire/rural-communities-need-better-data

Scannell, L., & Gifford, R. (2010). Defining place attachment: A tripartite organizing framework. *Journal of Environmental Psychology*, *30*(1), 1–10. https://doi.org/10.1016/j.jenvp.2009.09.006

Scata, J. (2019). Home buyers face stacked deck to learn of past floods. *Natural Resources Defense Council*. https://www.nrdc.org/bio/joel-scata/home-buyers-face-stacked-deck-learn-past-floods

Schiefer, D., & van der Noll, J. (2016). The essentials of social cohesion: A literature review. *Social Indicators Research, 132(2*), 579-603. https://doi.org/10.1007/s11205-016-1314-5

Schipper, E. L. F. (2020). Maladaptation: When adaptation to climate change goes very wrong. *One Earth*, *3*(4), 409–414. https://doi.org/https://doi.org/10.1016/j.oneear.2020.09.014

Schleifstein, M. (2023). More than $2 billion approved for unprecedented Louisiana coastal restoration project. *NOLA*. https://www.nola.com/news/environment/226-billion-approved-for-louisiana-restoration-project/article_36981094-a27d-11ed-83c2-0774b86d13e7.html

Schneider, B. (2012). Participatory action research, mental health service user research, and the Hearing (our) Voices projects. *International Journal of Qualitative Methods*, *11*(2), 152–165. https://doi.org/10.1177/160940691201100203

Schneider, S. (2008). Who's to blame? (Mis) perceptions of the intergovernmental response to disasters. *Publius: The Journal of Federalism*, *38*(4), 715–738.

Schwab, J. (2014). *Planning for post-disaster recovery: Next generation* (PAS Report No. 576). American Planning Association.

Schwartz, J., & Tabuchi, H. (2020). When hurricanes lead to industrial fires, minority neighborhoods can take a hit. *New York Times*. https://www.nytimes.com/2020/08/27/climate/hurricane-laura-fire-pollution.html

Schwartz, S. B. (2015). *Sea of storms: A history of hurricanes in the Greater Caribbean from Columbus to Katrina*. Princeton University Press.

Scott, J. (2014). Move, or wait for the flood and die: Protection of environmentally displaced populations through a new relocation law. *Florida A&M University Law Review*, *9*(2), 369–391. https://commons.law.famu.edu/famulawreview/vol9/iss2/6

Seamon, D. (2015). *A geography of the lifeworld (Routledge Revivals): Movement, rest and encounter*. Routledge.

Sebastian, A. (2022). Compound flooding. In S. Brody, Y. Lee, & B. B. Kothuis (Eds.), *Coastal flood risk reduction* (pp. 77–88). Elsevier. https://doi.org/10.1016/B978-0-323-85251-7.00007-X

Seeman, T. E., McEwen, B. S., Rowe, J. W., & Singer, B. H. (2001). Allostatic load as a marker of cumulative biological risk: MacArthur studies of successful aging. *Proceedings of the National Academy of Sciences*, *98*(8), 4770–4775. https://doi.org/doi:10.1073/pnas.081072698

Semali, L. M., & Kincheloe, J. L. (1999). *What is indigenous knowledge? Voices from the academy* (1st ed.). Routledge. https://doi.org/10.4324/9780203906804

Sempier, T. T., Swann, D. L., Emmer, R., Sempier, S. H., Schneider, M., & Thompson, J. (2021). *Coastal Community Resilience Index: A community self-assessment (revised)* (MASGP-21-055). National Oceanic and Atmospheric Administration.

Sen, A. (1983). Poor, relatively speaking. *Oxford Economic Papers*, *35*(2), 153–169. http://www.jstor.org/stable/2662642

___. (1999). *Development as freedom*. Anchor Books.

Sengupta, R., & Kousky, C. (2020). *Parametric insurance for disasters*. Wharton Risk Management and Decision Processes Center. https://esg.wharton.upenn.edu/wp-content/uploads/2023/07/Parametric-Insurance-for-Disasters_Sep-2020.pdf

Seong, K., Losey, C., & Van Zandt, S. (2021). To rebuild or relocate? Long-term mobility decisions of Hazard Mitigation Grant Program (HMGP) recipients. *Sustainability*, *13*(16), 8754. https://www.mdpi.com/2071-1050/13/16/8754

Setyawan, K. (2021). Isle de Jean Charles residents see new homes for 1st time. *U.S. News & World Report*. https://www.usnews.com/news/best-states/louisiana/articles/2021-04-10/isle-de-jean-charles-residents-see-new-homes-for-1st-time

___. (2022). *Pilot project with Louisiana Indigenous Tribe aims to build climate resilience*. New Orleans WWNO 89.9 Public Radio. https://www.wwno.org/coastal-desk/2022-12-08/pilot-project-with-louisiana-indigenous-tribe-aims-to-build-climate-resilience

Shadroui, T. (2022). Environmental justice considerations in managed retreat. *Vibrant Environment Blog*. https://www.eli.org/vibrant-environment-blog/environmental-justice-considerations-managed-retreat

Sharma-Wallace, L., Velarde, S. J., & Wreford, A. (2018). Adaptive governance good practice: Show me the evidence! *Journal of Environmental Management*, *222*, 174–184. https://doi.org/https://doi.org/10.1016/j.jenvman.2018.05.067

Sharp, J. (2022, May 12). Climate change is endangering the health of communities living near chemical facilities. *MedCity News*. https://medcitynews.com/2022/05/climate-change-is-endangering-the-health-of-communities-living-near-chemical-facilities/

Shen, S., & Ristroph, E. B. (2020). The relationship between climate vulnerability and disaster declarations: A case study of flood-prone indigenous communities in Alaska. *Natural Hazards Review*, *21*(1), 05019004. https://ascelibrary.org/doi/10.1061/%28ASCE%29NH.1527-6996.0000341

Sheng, Y. P., Yang, K., & Paramygin, V. A. (2022). Predicting compound coastal inundation in 2100 by considering the joint probabilities of landfalling tropical cyclones and sea-level rise. *Environmental Research Letters*, *17*(4), 044055.

Sherrieb, K., Norris, F. H., & Galea, S. (2010). Measuring capacities for community resilience. *Social Indicators Research*, *99*(2), 227–247. https://doi.org/10.1007/s11205-010-9576-9

Shi, L., Butler, W., Holmes, T., Thomas, R., Milordis, A., Ignatowski, J., Mahid, Y., & Aldag, A. M. (2023). Can Florida's coast survive its reliance on development? *Journal of the American Planning Association*, 1–17. https://doi.org/10.1080/01944363.2023.2249866

Shi, L., Fisher, A., Brenner, R. M., Greiner-Safi, A., Shepard, C., & Vanucchi, J. (2022). Equitable buyouts? Learning from state, county, and local floodplain management programs. *Climatic Change*, *174*(3), 29. https://doi.org/10.1007/s10584-022-03453-5

Shi, L., & Moser, S. (2021). Transformative climate adaptation in the United States: Trends and prospects. *Science*, *372*(6549), eabc8054. https://doi.org/10.1126/science.abc8054

Shi, L., & Varuzzo, A. (2020). Surging seas, rising fiscal stress: Exploring municipal fiscal vulnerability to climate change. *Cities*, *100*(102658), 1–13.

Shidhaye, R., Murhar, V., Gangale, S., Aldridge, L., Shastri, R., Parikh, R., Shrivastava, R., Damle, S., Raja, T., Nadkarni, A., & Patel, V. (2017). The effect of VISHRAM, a grassroots community-based mental health programme, on the treatment gap for depression in rural communities in India: A population-based study. *The Lancet Psychiatry*, *4*(2), 128–135. https://doi.org/https://doi.org/10.1016/S2215-0366(16)30424-2

Shultz, J. M., Rechkemmer, A., Rai, A., & McManus, K. T. (2019). Public health and mental health implications of environmentally induced forced migration. *Disaster Medicine and Public Health Preparedness*, *13*(2), 116–122. https://doi.org/10.1017/dmp.2018.27

Siders, A. R. (2018). Social justice implications of US managed retreat buyout programs. *Climatic Change*, *152*(2), 239–257. https://link.springer.com/article/10.1007/s10584-018-2272-5

___. (2019). Managed retreat in the United States. *One Earth*, *1*(2), 216–225. https://doi.org/https://doi.org/10.1016/j.oneear.2019.09.008

Siders, A. R., & Ajibade, I. (2021). Introduction: Managed retreat and environmental justice in a changing climate. *Journal of Environmental Studies and Sciences*, *11*, 287–293. https://doi.org/10.1007/s13412-021-00700-6

Siders, A. R., Hino, M., & Mach, K. J. (2019). The case for strategic and managed climate retreat. *Science*, *365*(6455), 761–763. https://doi.org/doi:10.1126/science.aax8346

Siebentritt, M., Halsey, N., & Stafford-Smith, M. (2014). *Regional climate change adaptation plan for the Eyre Peninsula*. Eyre Peninsula Integrated Climate Change Agreement Committee. https://cdn.environment.sa.gov.au/environment/docs/ep-regional-climate-change-adaptation-plan.pdf

Siegrist, M., & Árvai, J. (2020). Risk perception: Reflections on 40 years of research. *Risk Analysis*, *40*(S1), 2191–2206.

Simms, J. R. Z. (2017). "Why would I live anyplace else?": Resilience, sense of place, and possibilities of migration in coastal Louisiana. *Journal of Coastal Research*, *33*(2), 408–420. https://doi.org/10.2112/JCOASTRES-D-15-00193.1

Simms, J. R. Z., Waller, H. L., Brunet, C., & Jenkins, P. (2021). The long goodbye on a disappearing, ancestral island: A just retreat from Isle de Jean Charles. *Journal of Environmental Studies and Sciences*, *11*(3), 316–328. https://doi.org/10.1007/s13412-021-00682-5

Singla, D. R., Kohrt, B. A., Murray, L. K., Anand, A., Chorpita, B. F., & Patel, V. (2017). Psychological treatments for the world: Lessons from low- and middle-income countries. *Annual Review of Clinical Psychology*, *13*(1), 149–181. https://doi.org/10.1146/annurev-clinpsy-032816-045217

Sipe, N., & Vella, K. (2014). Relocating a flood-affected community: Good planning or good politics? *Journal of the American Planning Association*, *80*(4), 400–412. https://doi.org/10.1080/01944363.2014.976586

Skinner, V. (2022). Census data: Louisiana's population in decline. *The Center Square*. https://www.thecentersquare.com/louisiana/article_4b58dafc-8795-11ed-9027-57ad769d5e78.html

Sluyter, A., Watkins, C., Chaney, J. P., & Gibson, A. M. (2015). *Hispanic and Latino New Orleans: Immigration and identity since the eighteenth century*. Louisiana State University Press.

Smith, A. B. (2022, January 24). 2021 U.S. billion-dollar weather and climate disasters in historical context. *Beyond the Data.* https://www.climate.gov/news-features/blogs/beyond-data/2021-us-billion-dollar-weather-and-climate-disasters-historical

Smith, G., & Vila, O. (2020). A national evaluation of state and territory roles in hazard mitigation: Building local capacity to implement FEMA Hazard Mitigation Assistance Grants. *Sustainability, 12*(10013), 1–18. https://doi.org/10.3390/su122310013

Smith, G. P. (2011). *Planning for post-disaster recovery: A review of the United States disaster assistance network.* Island Press. https://www.researchgate.net/publication/323644236_Planning_for_Post-Disaster_Recovery_A_Review_of_the_United_States_Disaster_Assistance_Network

Smith, G. P. (2014). Applying hurricane recovery lessons in the United States to climate change adaptation: Hurricanes Fran and Floyd in North Carolina, USA. In B. C. Glavovic & G. P. Smith (Eds.), *Adapting to climate change: Lessons from natural hazards planning* (pp. 193–229). Springer Netherlands. https://doi.org/10.1007/978-94-017-8631-7_9

Smith, G. P., Anderson, A., & Perkes, D. (2021). New urbanism and the hazard transect overlay district: Improving the integration of disaster resilience and design in coastal areas. *Landscape Journal: Design, Planning, and Management of the Land, 40*(1), 35–47. https://www.muse.jhu.edu/article/800818

Smith, G. P., Fox, A., Klondike, T., Black, A., Henkel, C., Vaughn, B., Biswas, C., Bhattarai, S., & Gyawali, S. (2023). *Open space management guide: Building community capacity to program FEMA-funded housing buyout land.* North Carolina State University.

Smith, G. P., Lyles, W., & Berke, P. (2013). The role of the state in building local capacity and commitment for hazard mitigation planning. *International Journal of Mass Emergencies and Disasters, 32*, 178–203.

Smith, G. P., & Nguyen, M. T. (2021). University-public partnerships for disaster recovery: Promoting community resilience through research, teaching, and engagement. *Journal of Community Engagement and Scholarship, 14*(1), 1c. https://doi.org/10.54656/NPFV8067

___. (2023). Applying the results of a U.S.-based national resilient design education study in the field and the classroom during disaster recovery operations. *International Journal of Mass Emergencies & Disasters, 41*(1), 150–163. https://doi.org/10.1177/02807270231173656

Smith, G. P., & Saunders, W. (2022). A comparative review of hazard-prone housing acquisition laws, policies and programs in the United States and Aotearoa New Zealand: Implications for improved practice. In S. S. Kuo, J. T. Marshall, & R. Rowberry (Eds.), *The Cambridge handbook of disaster law and policy* (pp. 250–269). Cambridge University Press.

Smith, G. P., Saunders, W., Vila, O., Gyawali, S., Bhattarai, S., & Lawdley, E. (2021). A comparative analysis of hazard-prone housing acquisition programs in US and New Zealand communities. *Journal of Environmental Studies and Sciences, 11*(3), 392–403. https://doi.org/10.1007/s13412-021-00689-y

Smith, H. (2015). People are still living in FEMA's toxic Katrina trailers — and they likely have no idea. *Grist.* https://grist.org/politics/people-are-still-living-in-femas-toxic-katrina-trailers-and-they-likely-have-no-idea/

Smith, K. (2022). *Mobile home residents face higher flood risk.* Headwater Economics. https://headwaterseconomics.org/natural-hazards/mobile-home-flood-risk/

Smith, M. (2022). This hurricane-ravaged town has waited years for long-term aid. It could happen again. *ProPublica.* https://www.propublica.org/article/lake-charles-waits-years-for-long-term-federal-aid

Snel, K. A., Priest, S. J., Hartmann, T., Witte, P. A., & Geertman, S. C. (2021). 'Do the resilient things': Residents' perspectives on responsibilities for flood risk adaptation in England. *Journal of Flood Risk Management, 14*(3), e12727.

Snel, K. A., Witte, P. A., Hartmann, T., & Geertman, S. C. (2020). The shifting position of homeowners in flood resilience: From recipients to key-stakeholders. *Wiley Interdisciplinary Reviews: Water*, *7*(4), e1451.

Sorice, M. G., Rajala, K., Brown, B. L., Masterson, V. A., & Fuhlendorf, S. D. (2023). Relationship with the land as a foundation for ecosystem stewardship. *Frontiers in Ecology and the Environment*, *21*(6), 282–288. https://doi.org/https://doi.org/10.1002/fee.2651

South Alabama Regional Planning Commission. (2022). *2022 Comprehensive Economic Development Strategy (CEDS)*. https://storymaps.arcgis.com/stories/7d0bd2c6d5f64e8189279647be70e295

Spanger-Siegfried, E., Dahl, K., Caldas, A., Udvardy, S., Cleetus, R., Worth, P., & Hammer, N. H. (2017). *When rising seas hit home hard choices ahead for hundreds of US coastal communities*. Union of Concerned Scientists. https://www.ucsusa.org/resources/when-rising-seas-hit-home#ucs-report-downloads

Spidalieri, K., & Bennett, A. (2020a). *Georgetown Climate Center's managed retreat toolkit*. Georgetown Climate Center. https://www.georgetownclimate.org/adaptation/toolkits/managed-retreat-toolkit/about-this-toolkit.html

___. (2020b). *Louisiana land trust resettlement projects*. Georgetown Climate Center, Managed Retreat Toolkit. https://www.adaptationclearinghouse.org/resources/louisiana-land-trust-resettlement-projects.html

___. (2020c). *Louisiana Strategic Adaptations for Future Environments (LA SAFE)*. Georgetown Climate Center, Managed Retreat Toolkit. https://www.adaptationclearinghouse.org/resources/louisiana-strategic-adaptations-for-future-environments-la-safe-adaptation-strategies.html

___. (2020d). *Social/equity: Community engagement and equity*. Georgetown Climate Center, Managed Retreat Toolkit. https://www.georgetownclimate.org/adaptation/toolkits/managed-retreat-toolkit/social-equity-community-engagement-and-equity.html

Spidalieri, K., Smith, I., Grannis, J., Li, J., Love, A., Arroyo, V., & Hamilton, L. A. (2020a). *Managing the retreat from rising seas: Lessons and tools from 17 case studies*. Georgetown Climate Center. https://www.georgetownclimate.org/files/MRT/GCC_20_FULL-3web.pdf

___. (2020b). *Managing the retreat from rising seas: Staten Island, New York: Oakwood Beach Buyout Committee and Program*. Georgetown Climate Center. https://www.georgetownclimate.org/files/MRT/GCC_20_Oakwood-4web.pdf

Springgate, B. F., Wennerstrom, A., Meyers, D., Vannoy, S. D., Bentham, W., & Wells, K. B. (2011). Building community resilience through mental health infrastructure and training in Post-Katrina New Orleans. *Ethnicity & Disease*, *21*(301), S1. https://www.ncbi.nlm.nih.gov/pmc/articles/PMC3731130/

Statkewicz, M. D., Talbot, R., & Rappenglueck, B. (2021). Changes in precipitation patterns in Houston, Texas. *Environmental Advances*, *5*, 100073. https://doi.org/https://doi.org/10.1016/j.envadv.2021.100073

Stedman, R. C. (1999). Sense of place as an indicator of community sustainability. *The Forestry Chronicle*, *75*(5), 765–770. https://doi.org/10.5558/tfc75765-5

___. (2003). Is it really just a social construction?: The contribution of the physical environment to sense of place. *Society & Natural Resources*, *16*(8), 671–685. https://doi.org/10.1080/08941920309189

Stedman, R. C., & Ingalls, M. (2014). Topophilia, biophilia and greening in the red zone. In K.G. Tidball & M. E. Krasny (Eds.), *Greening in the red zone: Disaster resilience and community greening* (pp. 129–144). Springer Dordrecht. https://doi.org/10.1007/978-90-481-9947-1_10

Stege, M. H. N. (2017). Atoll habitability thresholds. In W. Leal Filho & J. Nalau (Eds.), *Limits to climate change adaptation* (pp. 381–399). Springer. https://doi.org/10.1007/978-3-319-64599-5_21

Stepenuck, K. F., & Green, L. T. (2015). Individual-and community-level impacts of volunteer environmental monitoring: A synthesis of peer-reviewed literature. *Ecology and Society*, *20*(3). https://www.jstor.org/stable/26270236

Stevens, C., Tosatti, E., Ayer, L., Barnes-Proby, D., Belkin, G., Lieff, S., & Martineau, M. (2020). *Helpers in plain sight: A guide to implementing mental health task sharing in community-based organizations*. RAND Corporation. https://doi.org/10.7249/TL317

Strauss, B. H., Kulp, S., & Levermann, A. (2015). Carbon choices determine US cities committed to futures below sea level. *Proceedings of the National Academy of Sciences*, *112*(44), 13508–13513. https://doi.org/10.1073/pnas.1511186112

Stults, M. (2017). Integrating climate change into hazard mitigation planning: Opportunities and examples in practice. *Climate Risk Management*, *17*, 21–34. https://doi.org/10.1016/j.crm.2017.06.004

Substance Abuse and Mental Health Services Administration. (2017). *Greater impact: How disasters affect people of low socioeconomic status*. Disaster Technical Assistance Center Supplemental Research Bulletin. https://www.samhsa.gov/sites/default/files/dtac/srb-low-ses_2.pdf

Sullivan, E., Makarewicz, C., & Rumbach, A. (2022). Affordable but marginalized: A socio-spatial and regulatory analysis of mobile home parks in the Houston metropolitan area. *Journal of the American Planning Association*, *88*(2), 232–244. https://doi.org/10.1080/01944363.2021.1952477

Suykens, C. B. R., Tarlock, D., Priest, S. J., Doorn-Hoekveld, W. J., & Van Rijswick, H. F. M. W. (2019). Sticks and carrots for reducing property-level risks from floods: An EU–US comparative perspective. *Water International*, *44*(5), 622–639.

Swartsell, N. (2021, January 26). *Cincinnati as climate change haven? Some transplants and city officials think so*. 91.7 WVXU. https://www.wvxu.org/environment/2021-01-26/cincinnati-as-climate-change-haven-some-transplants-and-city-officials-think-so

Swartz, J. M., Cardenas, B. T., Mohrig, D., & Passalacqua, P. (2022). Tributary channel networks formed by depositional processes. *Nature Geoscience*, *15*, 216–221. https://doi.org/https://doi.org/10.1038/s41561-022-00900-x

Sweet, W., Park, J., Marra, J., Zervas, C., & Gill, S. (2014). *Sea level rise and nuisance flood frequency changes around the United States* (Report No. NOS CO-OPS 073). National Atmospheric and Oceanic Administration. https://tidesandcurrents.noaa.gov/publications/NOAA_Technical_Report_NOS_COOPS_073.pdf

Sweet, W. V., Hamlington, B. D., Kopp, R. E., Weaver, C. P., Barnard, P. L., Bekaert, D., Brooks, W., Craghan, M., Dusek, G., Frederikse, T., Garner, G., Genz, A. S., Krasting, J. P., Larour, E., Marcy, D., Marra, J. J., Obeysekera, J., Osler, M., Pendleton, M., . . . Zuzak, C. (2022). *Global and regional sea level rise scenarios for the United States: Updated mean projections and extreme water level probabilities along U.S. coastlines* (NOAA Technical Report No. 01). National Oceanic and Atmospheric Administration. https://oceanservice.noaa.gov/hazards/sealevelrise/noaa-nos-techrpt01-global-regional-SLR-scenarios-US.pdf

Tabuchi, H., Popovich, N., Migliozzi, B., & Lehren, A. W. (2018, February 6). Floods are getting worse, and 2,500 chemical sites lie in the water's path. *The New York Times*. https://www.nytimes.com/interactive/2018/02/06/climate/flood-toxic-chemicals.html

Tate, E., Strong, A., Kraus, T., & Xiong, H. (2016). Flood recovery and property acquisition in Cedar Rapids, Iowa. *Natural Hazards*, *80*(3), 2055–2079. https://doi.org/10.1007/s11069-015-2060-8

Taylor, J., & Turner, R. J. (2002). Perceived discrimination, social stress, and depression in the transition to adulthood: Racial contrasts. *Social Psychology Quarterly*, *65*(3), 213–225. https://doi.org/10.2307/3090120

Tee Lewis, P. G., Chiu, W. A., Nasser, E., Proville, J., Barone, A., Danforth, C., Kim, B., Prozzi, J., & Craft, E. (2023). Characterizing vulnerabilities to climate change across the United States. *Environment International*, *172*, 107772. https://doi.org/https://doi.org/10.1016/j.envint.2023.107772

Teirstein, Z. (2021, April 8). Retreat from coastlines? Politicians don't want to talk about it. *Grist*. https://grist.org/climate/retreat-from-coastlines-politicians-dont-want-to-talk-about-it/

Texas Real Estate Research Center. (2022). *Population data for Houston-The Woodlands-Sugar Land, TX*. Texas A&M University. https://www.recenter.tamu.edu/data/population#!/msa/Houston-The_Woodlands-Sugar_Land%2C_TX

Thatcher, C. A., Brock, J. C., & Pendleton, E. A. (2013). Economic vulnerability to sea-level rise along the northern US Gulf Coast. *Journal of Coastal Research*, *63*(10063), 234–243.

Thiri, M. A. (2022). Uprooted by tsunami: A social vulnerability framework on long-term reconstruction after the Great East Japan earthquake. *International Journal of Disaster Risk Reduction*, *69*, 102725. https://doi.org/https://doi.org/10.1016/j.ijdrr.2021.102725

Thomas, C. C., Huber, C., Skrabis, K., & Sidon, J. (2016). *Estimating the economic impacts of ecosystem restoration—methods and case studies*. United States Geological Survey.

Thomas Tobin, C. S., & Hargrove, T. W. (2022). Race, lifetime SES, and allostatic load among older adults. *The Journals of Gerontology: Series A*, *77*(2), 347–356. https://doi.org/10.1093/gerona/glab160

Thomas Tobin, C. S., Robinson, M. N., & Stanifer, K. (2019). Does marriage matter? Racial differences in allostatic load among women. *Preventive Medicine Reports*, *15*, 100948. https://doi.org/10.1016/j.pmedr.2019.100948

Thompson, P. R., Widlansky, M. J., Hamlington, B. D., Merrifield, M. A., Marra, J. J., Mitchum, G. T., & Sweet, W. (2021). Rapid increases and extreme months in projections of United States high-tide flooding. *Nature Climate Change*, *11*(7), 584–590. https://doi.org/10.1038/s41558-021-01077-8

Thornton, T. F. (2008). *Being and place among the Tlingit*. University of Washington Press.

Thornton, T. F., & Bhagwat, S. A. (2021). *The Routledge handbook of Indigenous environmental knowledge*. Routledge International.

Thornton, T. F., & Manasfi, N. (2010). Adaptation--genuine and spurious: Demystifying adaptation processes in relation to climate change. *Environment and Society*, *1*(1), 132–155. https://doi.org/10.3167/ares.2010.010107

Titus, J. G. (2023). Population in floodplains or close to sea level increased in US but declined in some counties—especially among Black residents. *Environmental Research Letters*, *18*(3), 034001. https://doi.org/10.1088/1748-9326/acadf5

Tolnay, S. E. (2003). The African American "Great Migration" and beyond. *Annual Review of Sociology*, *29*, 209–232. http://www.jstor.org/stable/30036966

Tolnay, S. E., & Beck, E. M. (1995). *Festival of violence: An analysis of Southern lynchings, 1882–1930*. University of Illinois Press.

Tonn, G., & Czajkowski, J. (2022). Evaluating the risk and complexity of pluvial flood damage in the US. *Water Economics and Policy*, 8(03), 2240002. https://doi.org/10.1142/S2382624X2240002

Törnqvist, T. E., Cahoon, D. R., Morris, J. T., & Day, J. W. (2021). Coastal wetland resilience, accelerated sea-level rise, and the importance of timescale. *AGU Advances*, *2*(1), e2020AV000334. https://doi.org/10.1029/2020AV000334

Törnqvist, T. E., Jankowski, K. L., Li, Y.-X., & González, J. L. (2020). Tipping points of Mississippi Delta marshes due to accelerated sea-level rise. *Science Advances*, *6*(21), eaaz5512. https://doi.org/10.1126/sciadv.aaz5512

Törnqvist, T. E., Wallace, D. J., Storms, J. E. A., Wallinga, J., van Dam, R. L., Blaauw, M., Derksen, M. S., Klerks, C. J. W., Meijneken, C., & Snijders, E. M. A. (2008). Mississippi Delta subsidence primarily caused by compaction of Holocene strata. *Nature Geoscience, 1*(3), 173–176. https://doi.org/10.1038/ngeo129

Traphagen, K., & Traill, S. (2014). *How cross-sector collaborations are advancing STEM learning*. Noyce Foundation. https://smile.oregonstate.edu/sites/smile.oregonstate.edu/files/stem_ecosystems_report_execsum_140128.pdf

Tronquet, C. (2015). From Vunidogoloa to Kenani: An insight into successful relocation. In F. Gemenne, C. Zickgraf, & D. Ionesco (Eds.), *The state of environmental migration 2015* (pp. 121–142). International Organization for Migration. http://labos.ulg.ac.be/hugo/wp-content/uploads/sites/38/2017/11/The-State-of-Environmental-Migration-2015-121-142.pdf

Trust for America's Health. (2021). *The impact of chronic underfunding on America's public health system*. https://www.tfah.org/report-details/publichealthfunding2020/

Tuan, Y.-F. (1980). The significance of the artifact. *Geographical Review, 70*(4), 462–472. https://doi.org/10.2307/214079

Tucker, D. T. (2018). *Managed retreat: Transparency may improve U.S. home buyout programs*. The Stanford Woods Institute for the Environment. https://sustainability.stanford.edu/news/transparency-may-improve-us-home-buyout-programs

Turner, R. E., & McClenachan, G. (2018). Reversing wetland death from 35,000 cuts: Opportunities to restore Louisiana's dredged canals. *PLoS ONE, 13*(12), e0207717. https://doi.org/10.1371/journal.pone.0207717

Ubert, E. (2017). Investigating the difference in policy responses to the 2004 and 2005 hurricane seasons and homeowner insurance crises in Florida and Louisiana. *Socio-Economic Review, 15*(4), 691–715. https://doi.org/10.1093/ser/mwx013

Ueland, J., & Warf, B. (2006). Racialized topographies: Altitude and race in Southern cities. *Geographical Review, 96*(1), 50–78. http://www.jstor.org/stable/30034004

Uhler, B. (2015). *Lower-income households moving to inland California from coast*. Legislative Analyst's Office. https://lao.ca.gov/LAOEconTax/article/Detail/133

Ujang, N. (2012). Place attachment and continuity of urban place identity. *Procedia-Social and Behavioral Sciences, 49*, 156–167.

Uniform Relocation Assistance and Real Property Acquisition Policies Act of 1970, as amended, 42 U.S.C. § 4601 et seq. (1970). https://www.govinfo.gov/app/details/COMPS-1432#

Union of Concerned Scientists (UCS). (2016). *Toward climate resilience: A framework and principles for science-based adaptation*. https://www.ucsusa.org/resources/toward-climate-resilience

___. (2017). *Tracing fossil fuel companies' contributions to temperature increase and sea level rise*. https://www.ucsusa.org/sites/default/files/attach/2017/10/gw-accountability-factsheet.pdf

___. (2018). *Underwater: Rising seas, chronic floods, and the implications for US coastal real estate*. https://www.ucsusa.org/sites/default/files/attach/2018/06/underwater-analysis-full-report.pdf

United Nations. (n.d.). Communicating on climate change. *Climate Action*. https://www.un.org/en/climatechange/communicating-climate-change

___. (2023). *State of the world's Indigenous Peoples: Indigenous Peoples' access to health services*. https://www.un.org/development/desa/indigenouspeoples/wp-content/uploads/sites/19/2018/03/The-State-of-The-Worlds-Indigenous-Peoples-WEB.pdf

United Nations Development Programme (UNDP). (2016). *Tulele Peisa, Papua New Guinea: Equator initiative case study series*. https://www.equatorinitiative.org/wp-content/uploads/2017/05/case_1473429470.pdf

___. (2021). *Uncertain times, unsettled lives: Shaping our future in a transforming world.* https://www.undp.org/egypt/publications/human-development-report-2021-22-uncertain-times-unsettled-lives-shaping-our-future-transforming-world

___. (2022). *Human development report 2021-22.* http://report.hdr.undp.org

United Nations Environment Programme. (2018, September 6). *Toxic algal bloom continues to suffocate Florida's Gulf Coast.* https://www.unep.org/news-and-stories/story/toxic-algal-bloom-continues-suffocate-floridas-gulf-coast

United Nations International Children's Emergency Fund (UNICEF). (2015). *Unless we act now: The impact of climate change on children.* https://www.unicef.org/reports/unless-we-act-now-impact-climate-change-children

___. (2021). *The climate crisis is a child rights crisis: Introducing the Children's Climate Risk Index.* https://www.unicef.org/reports/climate-crisis-child-rights-crisis

United States Geological Survey Texas Water Science Center Gulf Coast Program. (n.d.). *Texas Gulf Coast groundwater and land subsidence: Over forty years of research in the Houston-Galveston region.* https://txpub.usgs.gov/houston_subsidence/#Publications

University of North Carolina Center for Community Capital. (2018). *Weathering the storm: Affordable housing in New Orleans 12 years after Katrina.* https://communitycapital.unc.edu/2018/06/weathering-the-storm-affordable-housing-in-new-orleans-12-years-after-katrina/

Urban Land Institute. (2021). *On safer ground: Floodplain buyouts and community resilience.* Urban Land Institute. https://knowledge.uli.org/en/Reports/Research%20Reports/2021/On%20Safer%20Ground%20Floodplain%20Buyouts%20and%20Community%20Resilience

U.S. Army Corps of Engineers (USACE). (2006). *Alaska Village Erosion Technical Assistance Program: An examination of erosion issues in the communities of Bethel, Dillingham, Kaktovik, Kivalina, Newtok, Shishmaref, and Unalakleet.* http://www.cakex.org/virtual-library/2970

___. (2016). *Planning bulletin: Clarification of existing policy for USACE participation in nonstructural flood risk management and coastal storm damage reduction measures* (PB No. 2016-01). https://planning.erdc.dren.mil/toolbox/library/pb/PB2016_01.pdf

___. (2022). *Final environmental impact statement for the proposed Mid-Barataria sediment diversion project Plaquemines Parish, Louisiana.* https://www.mvn.usace.army.mil/Missions/Regulatory/Permits/Mid-Barataria-Sediment-Diversion-EIS/

U.S. Army Corps of Engineers & Texas General Land Office. (2021). *Coastal Texas Protection and Restoration Feasibility Study: Final report.* https://www.glo.texas.gov/coastal-grants/projects/usace-coastal-texas-protection-restoration-feasibility-study.html

U.S. Census Bureau. (n.d.). ACS demographic and housing estimates [Table]. https://data.census.gov/table?q=population&g=010XX00US_310XX00US45300&tid=ACSDP5Y2020.DP05

___. (2019). *Coastline America.* https://www.census.gov/content/dam/Census/library/visualizations/2019/demo/coastline-america.pdf

___. (2020). 2020 Census Demographic Data Map Viewer: Population density. https://mtgisportal.geo.census.gov/arcgis/apps/MapSeries/index.html?appid=2566121a73de463995ed2b2fd7ff6eb7

___. (2021a). American Community Survey 5-year estimates: Census Reporter Profile page for Bayou La Batre, AL. http://censusreporter.org/profiles/16000US0104684-bayou-la-batre-al/

___. (2021b). Historical population change data (1910–2020). https://www.census.gov/data/tables/time-series/dec/popchange-data-text.html

___. (2022). Annual resident population estimates for metropolitan and micropolitan statistical areas and their geographic components for the United States: April 1, 2020 to July 1, 2022 (CBSA-EST2022). https://www.census.gov/data/tables/time-series/demo/popest/2020s-total-metro-and-micro-statistical-areas.html

___. (2023a). QuickFacts: St. Petersburg city, Florida. https://www.census.gov/quickfacts/fact/table/stpetersburgcityflorida/POP060210

___. (2023b). State population totals and components of change: 2020-2022. https://www.census.gov/data/tables/time-series/demo/popest/2020s-state-total.html

U.S. Department of Commerce. (1972). *1970 Census of population and housing: Census tracts: Tampa-St. Petersburg, FLA. Standard Metropolitan Statistical Area.* Social and Economic Statistics Administration, U.S. Census Bureau. https://www2.census.gov/prod2/decennial/documents/39204513p21ch7.pdf

U.S. Department of the Interior (DOI). (2022a). *Biden-Harris Administration makes $135 million commitment to support relocation of Tribal communities affected by climate change* [Press release]. https://www.doi.gov/pressreleases/biden-harris-administration-makes-135-million-commitment-support-relocation-tribal

___. (2022b). *Bipartisan Infrastructure Law and Annual Awards Program to support Tribal climate resilience and ocean and coastal management planning for federally recognized Tribes and authorized Tribal organizations.* https://www.bia.gov/sites/default/files/dup/inline-files/fy22_tribal_climate_resilience_rfp_508_1.pdf

U.S. Energy Information Administration. (2023). Top 10 U.S. refineries operable capacity [Table]. https://www.eia.gov/energyexplained/oil-and-petroleum-products/refining-crude-oil-refinery-rankings.php

U.S. Environmental Protection Agency (EPA). (n.d.). *Climate impacts in the Southeast.* https://19january2017snapshot.epa.gov/climate-impacts/climate-impacts-southeast_.html

___. (2019a). *EPA Superfund Permanent and Temporary Relocation.* https://www.epa.gov/superfund/contaminated-media-superfund-sites

___. (2019b). *2019 Environmental Justice Small Grants Program: Project summaries by EPA region.* https://www.epa.gov/system/files/documents/2021-12/2019-environmental-justice-small-grants-program-summaries_2.pdf

___. (2021a). *Gulf of Mexico Division: 2021 annual report.* https://www.epa.gov/system/files/documents/2023-06/GMP2021AR_FINAL_0.pdf

___. (2021b). *Climate change and social vulnerability in the United States: A focus on six impacts* (430-R-21-003).

___. (2022a). *Climate adaptation and harmful algal blooms.* https://www.epa.gov/arc-x/climate-adaptation-and-harmful-algal-blooms

___. (2022b). *Learn about environmental justice.* https://www.epa.gov/environmentaljustice/learn-about-environmental-justice

___. (2023). *Climate equity.* https://www.epa.gov/climateimpacts/climate-equity

U.S. Federal Government. (2023). U.S. Climate Resilience Toolkit Climate Explorer. https://crt-climate-explorer.nemac.org/faq/

U.S. Department of Health and Human Services. (n.d.). *Social cohesion.* Office of Disease Prevention and Health Promotion. https://health.gov/healthypeople/priority-areas/social-determinants-health/literature-summaries/social-cohesion

Valois, P., Bouchard, D., Talbot, D., Caron, M., Renaud, J. S., Gosselin, P., & Jacob, J. (2020). Adoption of flood-related preventive behaviours by people having different risks and histories of flooding. *Natural Hazards, 102*, 1155–1173.

Valois, P., Tessier, M., Bouchard, D., Talbot, D., Morin, A. J. S., Anctil, F., & Cloutier, G. (2020). Monitoring the evolution of individuals' flood-related adaptive behaviors over time: Two cross-sectional surveys conducted in the Province of Quebec, Canada. *BMC Public Health*, *20*(1), 1643.

van Alphen, S. (2020). Room for the river: Innovation, or tradition? The case of the Noordwaard. In C. Hein (Ed.), *Adaptive strategies for water heritage* (pp. 308–323). Springer Cham. https://doi.org/10.1007/978-3-030-00268-8

van Valkengoed, A., & Steg, L. (2019). *The psychology of climate change adaptation*. Cambridge University Press. https://doi.org/10.1017/9781108595438

van Veelen, P. C. (2016). Adaptive planning for resilient coastal waterfronts. *A+ BE| Architecture and the Built Environment*, *6*(19), 1–248.

van Vuuren, D. P., Edmonds, J., Kainuma, M., Riahi, K., Thomson, A., Hibbard, K., Hurtt, G. C., Kram, T., Krey, V., Lamarque, J. F., & Masui, T. (2011). The representative concentration pathways: An overview. *Climatic Change*, *109*, 5–31. https://doi.org/10.1007/s10584-011-0148-z

Van Zandt, S., Peacock, W. G., Henry, D. W., Grover, H., Highfield, W. E., & Brody, S. D. (2012). Mapping social vulnerability to enhance housing and neighborhood resilience. *Housing Policy Debate*, *22*(1), 29–55. https://doi.org/10.1080/10511482.2011.624528

Vandenbeld, A., & MacDonald, J. (2013). Fostering community acceptance of managed retreat in New Zealand. *Climate adaptation futures*, 161–166.

Veettil, A. V., & Mishra, A. (2020). Water security assessment for the contiguous United States using water footprint concepts. *Geophysical Research Letters*, *47*(7), e2020GL087061. https://doi.org/https://doi.org/10.1029/2020GL087061

Vella, S.-L. C., & Pai, N. B. (2019). A theoretical review of psychological resilience: Defining resilience and resilience research over the decades. *Archives of Medicine and Health Sciences*, *7*(2), 233–239.

Vila, O., Smith, G., Cutts, B., Samata, G., & Samiksha, B. (2022). Equity in FEMA Hazard Mitigation Assistance Programs: The role of State Hazard Mitigation Officers. *Environmental Science and Policy*, *136*, 632–641. https://doi.org/10.1016/j.envsci.2022.07.027

Vock, D. C. (2021). Climate migrants are on the move: Which cities need to plan for population booms? *Planning Magazine*. https://www.planning.org/planning/2021/winter/climate-migrants-are-on-the-move/

Vogels, E. A. (2021a). *Digital divide persists even as Americans with lower incomes make gains in tech adoption*. Pew Research Center. https://www.pewresearch.org/fact-tank/2021/06/22/digital-divide-persists-even-as-americans-with-lower-incomes-make-gains-in-tech-adoption/

___. (2021b). *Some digital divides persist between rural, urban and suburban America*. Pew Research Center. https://www.pewresearch.org/fact-tank/2021/08/19/some-digital-divides-persist-between-rural-urban-and-suburban-america/

Vogels, E. A., Perrin, A., Rainie, L., & Anderson, M. (2020). *53% of Americans say the Internet has been essential during the COVID-19 outbreak*. https://www.pewresearch.org/internet/2020/04/30/53-of-americans-say-the-internet-has-been-essential-during-the-covid-19-outbreak/

Vos, S. R., Clark-Ginsberg, A., Puente-Duran, S., Salas-Wright, C. P., Duque, M. C., Herrera, I. C., Maldonado-Molina, M. M., Castillo, M. N., Lee, T. K., Garcia, M. F., Fernandez, C. A., Hanson, M., Scaramutti, C., & Schwartz, S. J. (2021). The family crisis migration stress framework: A framework to understand the mental health effects of crisis migration on children and families caused by disasters. *New Directions for Child and Adolescent Development*, *2021*(176), 41–59. https://doi.org/10.1002/cad.20397

Walshe, R. A., & Nunn, P. (2012). Integration of Indigenous knowledge and disaster risk reduction: A case study from Baie Martelli, Pentecost Island, Vanuatu. *International Journal of Disaster Risk Science*, *3*(4), 185–194. https://doi.org/10.1007/s13753-012-0019-x

Walters, E. (2018). "It's our form of apartheid": How Galveston stalled public housing reconstruction in the 10 years after Ike. *Texas Tribune*. https://www.texastribune.org/2018/04/16/galveston-public-affordable-housing-hurricane-ike/

Wamsler, C. (2017). Stakeholder involvement in strategic adaptation planning: Transdisciplinarity and co-production at stake? *Environmental Science & Policy*, *75*, 148–157. https://doi.org/10.1016/j.envsci.2017.03.016

Wamsler, C., & Bristow, J. (2022). At the intersection of mind and climate change: Integrating inner dimensions of climate change into policymaking and practice. *Climatic Change*, *173*(1), 1–22.

Wamsler, C., Osberg, G., Osika, W., Henderson, H., & Mundaca, L. (2021). Linking internal and external transformation for sustainability and climate action: Towards a new research and policy agenda. *Global Environmental Change*, *71*, 102373.

Wang, G., Zhou, X., Wang, K., Ke, X., Zhang, Y., Zhao, R., & Bao, Y. (2020). GOM20: A stable geodetic reference frame for subsidence, faulting, and sea-level rise studies along the coast of the Gulf of Mexico. *Remote Sensing*, *12*(3), 350. https://www.mdpi.com/2072-4292/12/3/350

Wang, H.-H., Charoenmuang, M., Knobloch, N. A., & Tormoehlen, R. L. (2020). Defining interdisciplinary collaboration based on high school teachers' beliefs and practices of STEM integration using a complex designed system. *International Journal of STEM Education*, *7*(1), 3.

Warburg, J., & Metcalf, G. (2015, July 28). From catastrophe to renaissance. *The Urbanist: Learning from New Orleans*. https://www.spur.org/publications/urbanist-article/2015-07-28/catastrophe-renaissance

Ward, G. M., Ward, A. K., & Harris, P. M. (2023). Gulf Coast rivers of the Southeastern United States. In M. D. Delong, T. D. Jardine, A. C. Benke, & C. E. Cushing (Eds.), *Rivers of North America* (2nd ed., pp. 124–175). Academic Press. https://doi.org/10.1016/B978-0-12-818847-7.00003-3

Waring, T. M., Kline Ann, M., Brooks, J. S., Goff, S. H., Gowdy, J., Janssen, M. A., Smaldino, P. E., & Jacquet, J. (2015). A multilevel evolutionary framework for sustainability analysis. *Ecology and Society*, *20*(2).

Wasem, R. E. (2009). *Cuban migration to the United States: Policy and trends*. Congressional Research Service, Library of Congress. https://apps.dtic.mil/sti/citations/ADA501411

Water Resources Mission Area. (2021, April 2). Overview of water quality in principal aquifers, 2013-2021. U.S. Geological Survey. https://www.usgs.gov/media/images/overview-water-quality-principal-aquifers-2013-2021

Watts, N., Amann, M., Arnell, N., Ayeb-Karlsson, S., Belesova, K., Berry, H., Bouley, T., Boykoff, M., Byass, P., Cai, W., Campbell-Lendrum, D., Chambers, J., Daly, M., Dasandi, N., Davies, M., Depoux, A., Dominguez-Salas, P., Drummond, P., Ebi, K. L., . . . Costello, A. (2018). The 2018 report of the Lancet Countdown on health and climate change: shaping the health of nations for centuries to come. *Review*, *392*(10163), P2479–P2514. https://doi.org/10.1016/S0140-6736(18)32594-7

Weber, A., & Moore, R. (2019). *Going under: Long wait times for post-flood buyouts leave homeowners underwater*. Natural Resources Defense Council. https://doi.org/10.13140/RG.2.2.36060.82560

Weintrobe, S. (2021). *Psychological roots of the climate crisis: Neoliberal exceptionalism and the culture of uncare*. Bloomsbury Publishing. https://doi.org/10.1080/00207578.2021.1967160

Weisman, B. R. (2014). The background and continued cultural and historical importance of the Seminole wars in Florida. *FIU Law Review*, *9*(2), 391–404. https://doi.org/10.25148/lawrev.9.2.14

Welch, C. (2019, October 23). Climate change has finally caught up to this Alaska village. *National Geographic*. https://www.nationalgeographic.com/science/article/climate-change-finally-caught-up-to-this-alaska-village?loggedin=true&rnd=1699269354180

Wells, K. B., Jones, L., Chung, B., Dixon, E. L., Tang, L., Gilmore, J., Sherbourne, C., Ngo, V. K., Ong, M. K., Stockdale, S., Ramos, E., Belin, T. R., & Miranda, J. (2013a). Community-partnered cluster-randomized comparative effectiveness trial of community engagement and planning or resources for services to address depression disparities. *Journal of General Internal Medicine*, *28*(10), 1268–1278. https://doi.org/10.1007/s11606-013-2484-3

Wells, K. B., Springgate, B. F., Lizaola, E., Jones, F., & Plough, A. (2013b). Community engagement in disaster preparedness and recovery: A tale of two cities—Los Angeles and New Orleans. *Psychiatric Clinics of North America*, *36*(3), 451–466. https://doi.org/https://doi.org/10.1016/j.psc.2013.05.002

Wendland, T. (2020). *Water ways: Dutch cities are letting the water in*. New Orleans Public Radio. https://pulitzercenter.org/reporting/water-ways-dutch-cities-are-letting-water

The Wharton School of the University of Pennsylvania. (2019). *Digital dialogue no. 2: Improving flood risk disclosure*. Environmental, Social and Governance Initiative. https://esg.wharton.upenn.edu/engagement/digital-dialogues/improving-flood-risk-disclosure/

White, L. (2022). *Managed retreat: An introduction and exploration of policy options*. The American Meteorological Society. https://doi.org/10.1175/managed-retreat-2022

White, R. (2018). *Life at the fenceline: Understanding cumulative health hazards in environmental justice communities*. Coming Clean, The Environmental Justice Health Alliance for Chemical Policy Reform, and The Campaign for Healthier Solutions. https://ej4all.org/assets/media/documents/Life%20at%20the%20Fenceline%20-%20English%20-%20Public.pdf

White House. (2022). *Guidance for federal departments and agencies on Indigenous knowledge*. https://www.whitehouse.gov/ceq/news-updates/2022/12/01/white-house-releases-first-of-a-kind-indigenous-knowledge-guidance-for-federal-agencies/

___. (2023). *National Climate Resilience Framework*. https://www.whitehouse.gov/wp-content/uploads/2023/09/National-Climate-Resilience-Framework-FINAL.pdf

Wildcat, D. R. (2013). Introduction: Climate change and Indigenous peoples of the USA. In J.K. Maldonado, R. Pandya, & B. Colombi (Eds.), *Climate change and Indigenous peoples in the United States* (pp. 1–7). Springer, Cham. https://doi.org/10.1007/978-3-319-05266-3_1

Williams, D. R., & Vaske, J. J. (2003). The measurement of place attachment: Validity and generalizability of a psychometric approach. *Forest Science*, *49*(6), 830–840. https://doi.org/10.1093/forestscience/49.6.830

Wirz, C. D., Brossard, D., Curtis, K., & Block, P. (2022). The risk of relocation: Risk perceptions and communication surrounding the tradeoffs between floods and economic opportunities in Iquitos, Peru. *Journal of Risk Research*, 1–16. https://doi.org/10.1080/13669877.2022.2077413

WMBB. (2021a, July 21). Freeport is working on multi-million dollar improvement project. *My Panhandle*. https://www.mypanhandle.com/news/freeport-is-working-on-multi-million-dollar-improvement-project/

___. (2021b, September 21). Sewer line improvements will allow more Walton population growth. *My Panhandle*. https://www.mypanhandle.com/news/sewer-line-improvements-will-allow-more-walton-population-growth/

Wolf, E. R. (1982). *Europe and the people without history.* University of California Press.

Wollenberg, E., Edmunds, D., & Buck, L. (2000). Using scenarios to make decisions about the future: Anticipatory learning for the adaptive co-management of community forests. *Landscape and Urban Planning*, *47*(1-2), 65–77. https://doi.org/10.1016/S0169-2046(99)00071-7

Woodruff, S., Meerow, S., Stults, M., & Wilkins, C. (2018). Adaptation to resilience planning: Alternative pathways to prepare for climate change. *Journal of Planning Education and Research*, *42*, 64–75.

Woodson, L., Frankenberger, T., Smith, L., Langworthy, M., & Presnall, C. (2016). *The effects of social capital on resilience capacity: Evidence from Ethiopia, Kenya, Uganda, Niger, and Burkina Faso.* International Livestock Research Institute, TANGO International. https://www.fsnnetwork.org/sites/default/files/Report%204%20-%20The%20Effects%20of%20Social%20Capital%2018Feb2016.pdf

Wooltorton, S., Collard, L., & Horwitz, P. (2017). The land still speaks: Ni, Katitj! *Philosophy Activism Nature*, *13*, 57–67. https://ro.ecu.edu.au/ecuworkspost2013/5040

World Bank. (2019a). Innovative fisheries insurance benefits Caribbean fisherfolk. *World Bank News.* https://www.worldbank.org/en/news/feature/2019/09/20/innovative-fisheries-insurance-benefits-caribbean-fisherfolk

___. (2019b, November 20). International symposium on managed retreat as counter measures against disasters with a diversity/gender perspective. *World Bank News.* https://www.worldbank.org/en/news/feature/2019/11/20/international-symposium-on-managed-retreat-as-counter-measures-against-disasters-with-a-diversity-gender-perspective-drmhubtokyo

World Health Organization. (1946). Preamble. *Constitution of the World Health Organization.* WHO.

World Population Review. (2023). Population of counties in Mississippi. https://worldpopulationreview.com/states/mississippi/counties

Wrathall, D. (2015). *Differentiated migration as community disassembly: Perspectives on catastrophic disturbances in livelihood systems* (UNU-EHS Working Paper Series No.18). United Nations University Institute of Environment and Human Security.

Yeoman, B. (2023). As climate change erodes land and health, one Louisiana tribe fights back. *Food & Environment Reporting Network.* https://thefern.org/2023/05/after-a-series-of-climate-disasters-a-young-chief-helps-a-louisiana-tribe-find-its-way-forward/

Yin, J. (2023). Rapid decadal acceleration of sea level rise along the US East and Gulf Coasts during 2010–22 and its impact on hurricane-induced storm surge. *Journal of Climate*, *36*(13), 4511–4529. https://doi.org/10.1175/JCLI-D-22-0670.1

Yu, S., Brand, A. D., & Berke, P. (2020). Making room for the river: Applying a plan integration for resilience scorecard to a network of plans in Nijmegen, the Netherlands. *Journal of the American Planning Association*, 1–14.

Yua, E., Raymond-Yakoubian, J., Daniel, R. A., & Behe, C. (2022). A framework for co-production of knowledge in the context of Arctic research. *Ecology & Society*, *27*(1), Article 34. https://doi.org/10.5751/ES-12960-270134

Zacks, M. (2019). Florida mullet. *Southeastern Geographer*, *59*(1), 14–39.

Zammitti, A., Russo, A., Santisi, G., & Magnano, P. (2021). Personal values in relation to risk intelligence: Evidence from a multi-mediation model. *Behavioral Sciences (Basel, Switzerland)*, *11*(8), 109. https://doi.org/10.3390/bs11080109

Zaninetti, J. M., & Colten, C. E. (2012). Shrinking New Orleans: Post-Katrina population adjustments. *Urban Geography*, *33*(5), 675–699.

Zanotti, L., Carothers, C., Apok, C. A., Huang, S., Coleman, J., & Ambrozek, C. (2020). Political ecology and decolonial research: Co-production with the Iñupiat in Utqiaġvik. *Journal of Political Ecology*, *27*(1), 43–66.

Zavar, E. (2015). Residential perspectives: The value of floodplain-buyout open space. *Geographical Review, 105*(1), 78–95. https://doi.org/10.1111/j.1931-0846.2014.12047.x

___. (2019). An analysis of floodplain buyout memorials: Four examples from central U.S. floods of 1993–1998. *GeoJournal, 84*(1), 135–146. https://www.jstor.org/stable/48699977

___. (2022, December 13). Managed retreat in the U.S. Gulf Coast Region: Perspectives and approaches to property acquisitions: Challenges and lessons learned [Webinar presentation].

Zavar, E., & Fischer, L. A. (2021). Fractured landscapes: The racialization of home buyout programs and climate adaptation. *Current Research in Environmental Sustainability, 3*, 100043. https://doi.org/https://doi.org/10.1016/j.crsust.2021.100043

Zavar, E., & Hagelman III, R. R. (2016). Land use change on U.S. floodplain buyout sites, 1990–2000. *Disaster Prevention and Management, 25*(3), 360–374. https://doi.org/10.1108/DPM-01-2016-0021

Zhang, H. (2020, December 23). For coastal farmers, climate change rubs salt in their wounds. *Scienceline*. https://scienceline.org/2020/12/for-coastal-farmers-salt-in-their-wounds/

Zhou, X., Wang, G., Wang, K., Liu, H., Lyu, H., & Turco, M. J. (2021). Rates of natural subsidence along the Texas coast derived from GPS and tide gauge measurements (1904-2020). *Journal of Surveying Engineering, 174*(4). https://ascelibrary.org/doi/abs/10.1061/%28ASCE%29SU.1943-5428.0000371

Zhu, L., Goodman, L., & Zhu, J. (2022). The Community Reinvestment Act meant to combat redlining's effects. 45 years later, black homebuyers are still significantly underserved. *Urban Wire*. https://www.urban.org/urban-wire/community-reinvestment-act-meant-combat-redlinings-effects-45-years-later-black

Zou, Y., Stock, A., Davidson, R., Nozick, L., Trainor, J., & Kruse, J. (2020). Perceived attributes of hurricane-related retrofits and their effect on household adoption. *Natural Hazards, 104*(1), 201–224.

Zurba, M., Petriello, M. A., Madge, C., McCarney, P., Bishop, B., McBeth, S., Denniston, M., Bodwitch, H., & Bailey, M. (2022). Learning from knowledge co-production research and practice in the twenty-first century: Global lessons and what they mean for collaborative research in Nunatsiavut. *Sustainability Science, 17*(2), 449–467. https://doi.org/10.1007/s11625-021-00996-x

Zurich. (2013). *European floods: Using lessons learned to reduce risks*. Zurich Insurance Company Ltd. https://www.zurich.com/en/knowledge/topics/flood-resilience/european-floods-using-lessons-learned-to-reduce-risks

Zuzak, C., Goodenough, E., Stanton, C., Mowrer, M., Sheehan, A., Roberts, B., McGuire, P., & Rozelle, J. (2023). *National Risk Index technical documentation*. Federal Emergency Management Agency. https://www.fema.gov/sites/default/files/documents/fema_national-risk-index_technical-documentation.pdf

Zuzak, C., Mowrer, M., Goodenough, E., Burns, J., Ranalli, N., & Rozelle, J. (2022). The National Risk Index: Establishing a nationwide baseline for natural hazard risk in the US. *Natural Hazards, 114*(2), 2331–2355. https://doi.org/10.1007/s11069-022-05474-w

APPENDIXES C AND D REFERENCE LIST

Albrecht, G., Sartore, G., Connor, L., Higginbotham, N., Freeman, S., Kelly, B., Stain, H., Tonna, A., & Pollard, G. (2007). Solastalgia: The distress caused by environmental change. *Australasian Psychiatry: Bulletin of Royal Australian and New Zealand College of Psychiatrists, 15*(1), S95–S98. https://doi.org/10.1080/10398560701701288

Anderson, R. N., & Rosenberg, H. M. (1998). Age standardization of death rates: implementation of the year 2000 standard. *National vital statistics reports: from the Centers for Disease Control and Prevention, National Center for Health Statistics, National Vital Statistics System, 47*(3), 1–20.

Armitage, D., Berkes, F., Dale, A., Kocho-Schellenberg, E., & Patton, E. (2011). Co-management and the co-production of knowledge: Learning to adapt in Canada's Arctic. *Global Environmental Change*, *21*(3), 995–1004. https://doi.org/10.1016/j.gloenvcha.2011.04.006

Baum, F., MacDougall, C., & Smith, D. (2006). Participatory action research. *Journal of Epidemiology and Community Health*, *60*(10), 854–857. https://doi.org/https://doi.org/10.1136%2Fjech.2004.028662

Berg, R. (2009). *Tropical Cyclone Report: Hurricane Ike* (Report No. AL092008). National Hurricane Center. https://www.nhc.noaa.gov/data/tcr/AL092008_Ike.pdf

___. (2013). *Tropical Cyclone Report: Hurricane Isaac* (Report No. AL092012). National Hurricane Center. https://www.nhc.noaa.gov/data/tcr/AL092012_Isaac.pdf

Berkes, F., Colding, J., & Folke, C. (2000). Rediscovery of traditional ecological knowledge as adaptive management. *Ecological Applications*, *10*(5), 1251–1262.

Beven II, J. L. (2014). *Tropical Cyclone Report: Hurricane Frances*. National Hurricane Center. https://www.nhc.noaa.gov/data/tcr/AL062004_Frances.pdf

Beven II, J. L., & Berg, R. (2018). *Tropical Cyclone Report: Hurricane Nate*. National Hurricane Center. https://www.nhc.noaa.gov/data/tcr/AL162017_Nate.pdf

Beven II, J. L., Hagen, A., & Berg, R. (2022). *Tropical Cyclone Report: Hurricane Ida* (Report No. AL092021). National Hurricane Center. https://www.nhc.noaa.gov/data/tcr/AL092021_Ida.pdf

Beven II, J. L., & Kimberlain, T. B. (2009). *Tropical Cyclone Report Hurricane Gustav* (Report No. AL072008). National Hurricane Center. https://www.nhc.noaa.gov/data/tcr/AL072008_Gustav.pdf

Blake, E., Berg, R., & Hagen, A. (2020). *Tropical Cyclone Report: Hurricane Zeta* (Report No. AL282020). National Hurricane Center. https://www.nhc.noaa.gov/data/tcr/AL282020_Zeta.pdf

Blake, E. S., & Zelinsky, D. A. (2018). *National Hurricane Center Tropical Cyclone Report: Hurricane Harvey* (Report No. AL092017). National Hurricane Center. https://www.nhc.noaa.gov/data/tcr/AL092017_Harvey.pdf

Brasher, K., & Wiseman, J. (2008). Community wellbeing in an unwell world: Trends, challenges, and possibilities. *Journal of Public Health Policy*, *29*(3), 353–366. https://doi.org/10.1057/jphp.2008.16

Bucci, L., Alaka, L., Hagen, A., Delgado, S., & Beven, J. (2023). *Tropical Cyclone Report: Hurricane Ian* (Report No. AL092022). National Hurricane Center. https://www.nhc.noaa.gov/data/tcr/AL092022_Ian.pdf

Butler-Ulloa, D. M. (2022). *Climate displacement, migration and relocation in the United States: Resistance, restoration and resilience in the coastal south* (Publication No. 29323594) [Doctoral dissertation, University of Massachusetts Boston]. ProQuest Dissertations Publishing. https://www.proquest.com/dissertations-theses/climate-displacement-migration-relocation-united/docview/2710980853/se-2?accountid=152665

Cangialosi, J. P., & Berg, R. (2020). *National Hurricane Center Tropical Cyclone Report Hurricane Delta* (Report No. AL282020). National Hurricane Center. https://www.nhc.noaa.gov/data/tcr/AL262020_Delta.pdf

Cangialosi, J. P., Latto, A. S., & Berg, R. (2018). *Tropical Cyclone Report: Hurricane Irma* (Report No. AL112017). National Hurricane Center. https://www.nhc.noaa.gov/data/tcr/AL112017_Irma.pdf

Cattell, V. (2001). Poor people, poor places, and poor health: the mediating role of social networks and social capital. *Social Science & Medicine*, *52*(10), 1501–1516. https://doi.org/10.1016/s0277-9536(00)00259-8

Centers for Disease Control and Prevention (CDC). (n.d.). Climate and Health Program Heat and Health Tracker. Heat exposure data. https://ephtracking.cdc.gov/Applications/heatTracker/

___. (2022). *CDC's Building Resilience Against Climate Effects (BRACE) framework*. https://www.cdc.gov/climateandhealth/BRACE.htm

___. (2023). CDC PLACES. https://www.cdc.gov/places

Centers for Disease Control and Prevention & Agency for Toxic Substances Disease Registry (CDC/ATSDR). (2022a). CDC/ATSDR Social Vulnerability Index Interactive Map 2020. Database St. Petersburg, Florida. https://www.atsdr.cdc.gov/placeandhealth/svi/interactive_map.html

___. (2022b). Environmental Justice Index. https://www.atsdr.cdc.gov/placeandhealth/eji/index.html

___. (2022c). *Technical Documentation for the Environmental Justice Index 2022*. https://www.atsdr.cdc.gov/placeandhealth/eji/docs/EJI-2022-Documentation-508.pdf

___. (2023). Social Vulnerability Index Interactive Map 2020. https://www.atsdr.cdc.gov/placeandhealth/svi/interactive_map.html

Chaffin, B. C., Gosnell, H., & Cosens, B. A. (2014). A decade of adaptive governance scholarship: Synthesis and future directions. *Ecology and Society, 19*(3). https://www.jstor.org/stable/26269646

Cohen, D. A., Inagami, S., & Finch, B. (2008). The built environment and collective efficacy. *Health Place, 14*(2), 198–208. https://doi.org/10.1016/j.healthplace.2007.06.001

Copp, D. (2020, October 29). Zeta leaves wind damage, power outages in Lafourche and Terrebonne. *Houma Today*. https://www.houmatoday.com/story/news/2020/10/29/zeta-leaves-wind-damage-power-outages-lafourche-and-terrebonne/6054941002/

Dahl, K. A., Spanger-Siegfried, E., Caldas, A., & Udvardy, S. (2017). Effective inundation of continental United States communities with 21st century sea level rise. *Elementa: Science of the Anthropocene, 5*. https://doi.org/10.1525/elementa.234

Eiroa-Orosa, F. J. (2020). Understanding psychosocial wellbeing in the context of complex and multidimensional problems. *International Journal of Environmental Research and Public Health, 17*(16). https://doi.org/10.3390/ijerph17165937

Garcia-Buckalew, B. (2022, August 25). The Backstory: Five years ago this week, Hurricane Harvey brought catastrophic flooding to Texas. *KVUE ABC*. https://www.kvue.com/article/news/local/texas/hurricane-harvey-catastrophic-flooding-texas-five-years-ago/269-0a738956-e387-4b81-aaa2-1ed6115caef4

Garnham, J. P. (2020). Still recovering from Harvey, Texans in Beaumont and Port Arthur are now preparing for a new hurricane during the pandemic. *Texas Tribune*. https://www.texastribune.org/2020/08/26/hurricane-laura-beaumont-port-arthur-texas/

Genova, R. C., Girm, B., Kissel, E. S., Levy, A. N., MacCracken, S., Mastrandrea, P. R., & White, L. L. (Eds.), *Contribution of Working Group II to the Fifth Assessment Report of the Intergovernmental Panel on Climate Change* (pp. 833–868). Cambridge University Press.

Gisclair, C. (2012, September 5). Darkness lingers locally in Hurricane Isaac. *The Houma Times*. https://www.houmatimes.com/news/darkness-lingers-locally-in-hurricane-isaac/

Gould-Werth, A., Abbott, S., & Openchowski, E. (2023, January 26). *What is social infrastructure, and how does it support economic growth in the United States?* Washington Center for Equitable Growth. https://equitablegrowth.org/what-is-social-infrastructure-and-how-does-it-support-economic-growth-in-the-united-states/

Government Accountability Office. (2020). *National flood insurance program: Fiscal exposure persists despite property acquisitions* (Report No. GAO-20-508). https://www.gao.gov/assets/gao-20-508.pdf

Hartwig, R. P., & Wilkinson, C. (2010). *Hurricane Katrina: The five year anniversary*. Insurance Information Institute. https://www.iii.org/sites/default/files/1007Katrina5Anniversary.pdf

Hazard Aware. (2022). *Hazard Impact Statement*. https://www.hazardaware.org/Default.aspx

Holland, C. (2023, February 16). *Centering frontline communities.* Ecotrust. https://ecotrust.org/centering-frontline-communities/

Intergovernmental Panel on Climate Change (IPCC). (2014). *Climate change 2014: Impacts, adaptation, and vulnerability: Part A: Global and sectoral aspects.* Contribution of Working Group II to the Fifth Assessment Report of the Intergovernmental Panel on Climate Change. Cambridge University Press. https://www.ipcc.ch/report/ar5/wg2/

___. (2022). *Summary for policymakers.* In H.-O. Pörtner, D. C. Roberts, E. S. Poloczanska, K. Mintenbeck, M. Tignor, A. Alegría, M. Craig, S. Langsdorf, S. Löschke, V. Möller, A. Okem (Eds.), *Climate Change 2022: Impacts, Adaptation and Vulnerability* (pp. 3–33). Contribution of Working Group II to the Sixth Assessment Report of the Intergovernmental Panel on Climate Change. Cambridge University Press. https://www.ipcc.ch/report/ar6/wg2/downloads/report/IPCC_AR6_WGII_SummaryForPolicymakers.pdf

Jarden, A., & Roache, A. (2023). What is wellbeing? *International Journal of Environmental Research and Public Health, 20*(6). https://doi.org/10.3390/ijerph20065006

Johnson, D. A. (2015). *Regional planning, history of international encyclopedia of the social & behavioral sciences (Second Edition),* 141–145. https://doi.org/10.1016/B978-0-08-097086-8.74069-4

Karlamangla, A. S., Singer, B. H., & Seeman, T. E. (2006). Reduction in allostatic load in older adults is associated with lower all-cause mortality risk: MacArthur studies of successful aging. *Psychosomatic Medicine Journal of Behavioral Medicine, 68*(3), 500–507. https://doi.org/10.1097/01.psy.0000221270.93985.82

Knabb, R. D., Rhome, J. R., & Brown, D. P. (2023). *Tropical Cyclone Report Hurricane Katrina.* 2023 National Hurricane Center. https://www.nhc.noaa.gov/data/tcr/AL122005_Katrina.pdf

Lander, E. S., & Mallory, B. (2021). *Indigenous traditional ecological knowledge and federal decision making.* Executive Office of the President Office of Science and Technology Policy and Council on Environmental Quality.

Lawrence, M. B., & Cobb, H. D. (2005). *Tropical Cyclone Report: Hurricane Jeanne.* National Hurricane Center. https://www.nhc.noaa.gov/data/tcr/AL112004_Jeanne.pdf

Manisalidis, I., Stavropoulou, E., Stavropoulos, A., & Bezirtzoglou, E. (2020). Environmental and health impacts of air pollution: A review. *Front Public Health, 8*(14). https://doi.org/10.3389/fpubh.2020.00014

Martikainen, P., Bartley, M., & Lahelma, E. (2002). Psychosocial determinants of health in social epidemiology. *International Journal of Epidemiology, 31*(6), 1091–1093. https://doi.org/10.1093/ije/31.6.1091

Masterson, V. A., Stedman, R. C., Enqvist, J., Tengö, M., Giusti, M., Wahl, D., & Svedin, U. (2017). The contribution of sense of place to social-ecological systems research: A review and research agenda. *Ecology and Society, 22*(1). https://www.jstor.org/stable/26270120

McEwen, B. S., & Seeman, T. (1999). Protective and damaging effects of mediators of stress. Elaborating and testing the concepts of allostasis and allostatic load. *Annals of the New York Academy of Sciences, 896,* 30–47. https://doi.org/10.1111/j.1749-6632.1999.tb08103.x

Meadow, A. M., Ferguson, D. B., Guido, Z., Horangic, A., Owen, G., & Wall, T. (2015). Moving toward the deliberate coproduction of climate science knowledge. *Weather, Climate, and Society,* 7(2), 179–191. https://doi.org/10.1175/WCAS-D-14-00050.1

National Academies of Sciences, Engineering, and Medicine. (2017). *Communities in action: Pathways to health equity.* The National Academies Press. https://doi.org/10.17226/24624

___. (2019). *Building and measuring community resilience: Actions for communities and the Gulf Research Program.* The National Academies Press. https://doi.org/10.17226/25383

___. (2022). *Structural racism and rigorous models of social inequity: Proceedings of a workshop*. The National Academies Press. https://doi.org/10.17226/26690

Nuwer, D. S. (2017, July 11). Hurricane Katrina. *Mississippi Encyclopedia*. Center for Study of Southern Culture.

Office for Coastal Management. (n.d.a). Coastal County Snapshots: Special flood hazard. National Oceanic and Atmospheric Administration. https://coast.noaa.gov/digitalcoast/tools/snapshots.html

___. (n.d.b). Coastal County Snapshots: People at risk. National Oceanic and Atmospheric Administration. https://coast.noaa.gov/digitalcoast/tools/snapshots.html

___. (n.d.c). Coastal Flood Exposure Mapper. National Oceanic and Atmospheric Administration. https://coast.noaa.gov/digitalcoast/tools/flood-exposure.html

___. (2023). Coastal County Snapshots: Special flood hazard. National Oceanic and Atmospheric Administration. https://coast.noaa.gov/digitalcoast/tools/snapshots.html

Pasch, R. J., Berg, R., Roberts, D. P., & Papin, P. P. (2020). *National Hurricane Center Tropical Cyclone Report: Hurricane Laura* (Report No. AL132020). National Hurricane Center. https://www.nhc.noaa.gov/data/tcr/AL132020_Laura.pdf

Putnam, R. D. (1993). The prosperous community. *The American Prospect*, *4*(13). http://www.philia.ca/files/pdf/ProsperousCommunity.pdf

Ramkumar, M., Menier, D., & Kumaraswamy, K. (2019). Coastal zone management during changing climate and rising sea level: Transcendence of institutional, geographic, and subject field barriers is the key. In M. Ramkumar, R. A. James, D. Menier, & K. Kumaraswamy (Eds.), *Coastal zone management* (pp. 1–12). Elsevier. https://doi.org/https://doi.org/10.1016/B978-0-12-814350-6.00001-X

Razzano, T. (2022, September 29). Hurricane Ian: Scenes from St. Petersburg after the storm. *Patch*. https://patch.com/florida/stpete/hurricane-ian-scenes-st-petersburg-after-storm

Sampson, R. J., Raudenbush, S. W., & Earls, F. (1997). Neighborhoods and violent crime: A multilevel study of collective efficacy. *Science*, *277*(5328), 918–924. fhttps://doi.org/10.1126/science.277.5328.918

Scannell, L., & Gifford, R. (2010). Defining place attachment: A tripartite organizing framework. *Journal of Environmental Psychology*, *30*(1), 1–10. https://doi.org/10.1016/j.jenvp.2009.09.006

Schiefer, D., & van der Noll, J. (2016). The essentials of social cohesion: A literature review. *Social Indicators Research*, *132*(2), 579-603. https://doi.org/10.1007/s11205-016-1314-5

Seeman, T. E., McEwen, B. S., Rowe, J. W., & Singer, B. H. (2001). Allostatic load as a marker of cumulative biological risk: MacArthur studies of successful aging. *Proceedings of the National Academy of Sciences*, *98*(8), 4770–4775. https://doi.org/doi:10.1073/pnas.081072698

Spanger-Siegfried, E., Dahl, K., Caldas, A., Udvardy, S., Cleetus, R., Worth, P., & Hammer, N. H. (2017). *When rising seas hit home hard choices ahead for hundreds of US coastal communities*. Union of Concerned Scientists. https://www.ucsusa.org/resources/when-rising-seas-hit-home#ucs-report-downloads

Tessendorf, S. (2012, November 8). Non-stationarity: New vocabulary for a changing climate. *The Globe Program Scientists' Blog*. https://www.globe.gov/explore-science/scientists-blog/archived-posts/sciblog/index.html_p=1471.html

U.S. Census Bureau. (2021a). Quick facts - United States. https://www.census.gov/quickfacts/fact/table/US/HSG445221

___. (2021b). Quick facts—St. Petersburg city, Florida; Mobile County, Alabama; Harrison County, Mississippi; Lafourche Parish, Louisiana; Terrebonne Parish, Louisiana; Port Arthur city, Texas. https://www.census.gov/quickfacts/fact/table/stpetersburgcityflorida,mobilecountyalabama,harrisoncountymississippi,lafourcheparishlouisiana,terrebonneparishlouisiana,portarthurcitytexas/FIPS

___. (2021c). American Community Survey 2021 5-year estimates: Income in the past 12 months. https://data.census.gov/table?q=S1901&g=050XX00US01097,22057,22109,28047_160XX00US1263000,4858820&tid=ACSST5Y2021.S1901

___. (2021d). American Community Survey 2021 5-year estimates: Educational Attainment. https://data.census.gov/table?q=S1501&g=050XX00US01097,22057,22109,28047_160XX00US1263000,4858820&tid=ACSST5Y2021.S1501

___. (2021e). American Community Survey 2021 5-year estimates: Households and Families. https://data.census.gov/table?q=S1101:+HOUSEHOLDS+AND+FAMILIES&g=050XX00US01097,22057,22109,28047_160XX00US1263000,4858820&tid=ACSST5Y2021.S1101

___. (2021f). American Community Survey 2021 5-year estimates: Household Type by Units in Structure. https://data.census.gov/table?q=UNITS+IN+STRUCTURE&g=050XX00US01097,22057,22109,28047_160XX00US1263000,4858820&tid=ACSDT5Y2021.B11011

___. (2021g). American Community Survey 2021 5-year estimates: Selected characteristics of health insurance coverage in the United States. https://data.census.gov/table?q=health+insurance+coverage+status+&g=010XX00US&tid=ACSST5Y2021.S2701

___. (2021h). American Community Survey 2021 1-year estimates: Hispanic or Latino origin. https://data.census.gov/table?q=B03003:+HISPANIC+OR+LATINO+ORIGIN

___. (2021i). American Community Survey 2021 1-year estimates: Race. https://data.census.gov/table?q=race&tid=ACSDT1Y2021.B02001

___. (2020). 2020: Decennial Census Demographic and housing characteristics. https://data.census.gov/table?q=race&g=160XX00US4858820&tid=DECENNIALDHC2020.P8

U.S. Environmental Protection Agency (EPA). (n.d.). Environmental Justice Screening and Mapping Tool. https://ejscreen.epa.gov/mapper/

___. (2019). *2019 Environmental Justice Small Grants Program: Project summaries by EPA region.* https://www.epa.gov/system/files/documents/2021-12/2019-environmental-justice-small-grants-program-summaries_2.pdf

___. (2022). *Learn about environmental justice.* https://www.epa.gov/environmentaljustice/learn-about-environmental-justice

___. (2023a). *Climate equity.* https://www.epa.gov/climateimpacts/climate-equity

___. (2023b). *Particulate Matter (PM2.5) Trends.* https://www.epa.gov/air-trends/particulate-matter-pm25-trends

Vella, S.-L. C., & Pai, N. B. (2019). A theoretical review of psychological resilience: Defining resilience and resilience research over the decades. *Archives of Medicine and Health Sciences*, 7(2), 233–239.

Wallach, D. (2016, September 13). 8 years ago, Hurricane Ike powered through Southeast Texas. *Beaumont Enterprise.* https://www.beaumontenterprise.com/news/weather/article/8-years-ago-Hurricane-Ike-powered-through-9219448.php

Wamsler, C. (2017). Stakeholder involvement in strategic adaptation planning: Transdisciplinarity and co-production at stake? *Environmental Science & Policy*, *75*, 148–157. https://doi.org/10.1016/j.envsci.2017.03.016

Wilson, X. A. (2012, October 1). Flood prevention: Officials say work diminished Isaac's damage. *Houma Today.* https://www.houmatoday.com/story/news/2012/10/01/flood-prevention-officials-say-work-diminished-isaacs-damage/27029634007/

Wyatt, M., & Mamone, D. (2021, September 6). Terrebonne, Lafourche residents remain without power, limited cell service after Hurricane Ida. *The Acadiana Advocate*. https://www.theadvocate.com/acadiana/news/weather_traffic/terrebonne-lafourche-residents-remain-without-power-limited-cell-service-after-hurricane-ida/article_f08ded78-0f46-11ec-8d36-3fb648294a3b.html

Yan, H., & Chavez, N. (2017, August 31). Harvey aftermath: Death toll rises; so do the floodwaters. *CNN*. https://www.cnn.com/2017/08/30/us/harvey-texas-louisiana/index.html

Zullo, R., & King, N. (2008, September 5). More than four days after Gustav, no shelters in Terrebonne. *Houma Today*. https://www.houmatoday.com/story/news/2008/09/05/more-than-four-days-after-gustav-no-shelters-in-terrebonne/26486331007/

Appendix A

Committee Members

JANICE BARNES (*Co-Chair*, she/her/hers), founder of Climate Adaptation Partners, a New York City-based woman-owned business, focuses on planning, advocacy, and partnership-building for climate adaptation. With technical training in architecture and organizational behavior, she helps clients to critically evaluate their risk tolerances and possible adaptation pathways given current and expected hazard exposures and link these to appropriate design and financing or funding options. Working from the intersection of climate change and public health, Barnes links environmental, social, and economic indicators to advance resilience principles and connect knowledge across communities. She co-chairs the New York State Energy Research and Development Authority's Climate Impact Assessment Health and Safety Technical Working Group, oversees the New York City Panel on Climate Change 4th Assessment, and serves on the board of the Florida Institute for Built Environment Resilience. She also teaches Public Health, Climate Change, and Cities in a shared appointment at the University of Pennsylvania with Perelman School of Medicine and Weitzman School of Design. Barnes previously led global resilience for Perkins+Will, working with 24 offices across multiple countries to advance resilience in concert with in-country initiatives, and co-chaired the American Institute of Architects National Resilience Working Group. She has a Ph.D. and an M.S. from the University of Michigan, a Master of Architecture from Tulane University, a B.A. from the University of Tennessee, and a certificate in municipal finance from the University of Chicago and in geographic information systems from the University of California, Davis. She values teams' collective contributions to broaden transdisciplinary practices. Her message settles on a shared truth about the responsibilities to act on climate change as its implications are increasingly understood: #WeCantUnknowThis.

TRACIE T. SEMPIER (*Co-Chair*, she/her/hers) is the coastal resilience engagement specialist for the Mississippi-Alabama Sea Grant Consortium. She works with local communities, state and federal agencies, nonprofit organizations, businesses, coastal managers, residents, and K–12 audiences to decrease the negative effects of disasters (natural, technological, and biological) on families, communities, and the environment. Sempier is also the VORTEX-SE engagement coordinator, for which she is creating a model for regional extension programming focused on severe weather, synthesizing research findings to inform application at the local level, and working to create safe sheltering options for vulnerable populations. She is the lead for the Gulf of Mexico Climate and Resilience Community of Practice, for which she utilizes existing networks to build connections with target audiences. Sempier has professional experience in education/outreach with various audiences in formal and informal learning environments. She is a recipient of the Gulf Guardian Award and the Spirit of Community Award for her work on resilience issues in the Gulf of Mexico, and is the recipient of a three-year grant from the Gulf Research Program to fund the Gulf of Mexico Climate and Resilience CoP as it forms an Advisory Committee on Equity to help the CoP consider different points of view and advise on how to engage new partners to include a more inclusive and diverse membership. Sempier earned a B.S. in marine science and biology from the University of Alabama, an M.S. in science and mathematics education at Oregon State University, and a Ph.D. in curriculum and instruction from Mississippi State University.

KAYODE O. ATOBA (he/him/his) is an associate research scientist at the Institute for a Disaster Resilient Texas at Texas A&M University. He is a mentor and an alumnus of the William Averette Anderson Fund, the first interdisciplinary organization in the United States focused on increasing the number of underrepresented persons in the field of disaster research and planning. Atoba's research draws on the broader theory of urban planning and hazard resiliency to propose best mitigation and adaptation strategies, and environmental policies that reduce hazard impacts. His research uses quantitative and geospatial methodologies to identify the interactions between the built environment and natural hazards. Atoba's recent work addresses issues related to property acquisition and buyouts as nonstructural mitigation strategies to reduce flood hazard impacts. He has frequently made statements on hazard mitigation through his website and his LinkedIn profile. Atoba has also published multiple journal articles and book chapters on hazard mitigation and environmental hazards. One of his recently co-authored article, "Buy Them Out Before They Are Built: Evaluating the Proactive Acquisition of Vacant Land in Flood-Prone Areas," in *Environmental Conservation*, emphasizes the benefits of buying flood-prone property before it is flooded. He has also published buyouts research in other journals such as *Climate Risk Management*, *Environmental Hazards, and Sustainability*, as well as in a book chapter published by Elsevier. He participated in an expert workshop that was one source for the publication "Property Buyouts Can Be an Effective Solution for Flood-Prone Communities: Improved Federal Policy on Funding and Planning Would Deliver Better Long-Term Outcomes." Atoba has an M.S. in geographic information systems from Sam Houston State University and a Ph.D. in urban and regional science from Texas A&M University.

GARY S. BELKIN (he/him/his) is director, Billion Minds Project at Columbia University, and chair, COP^2 (cop2.org). A psychiatrist who approaches mental health as a building block of social policy and progress, he recently founded Billion Minds as a "think-action tank." The intention of Billion Minds is to link mental health to problems of great scale, and to safeguarding sustainable societies through a humane social climate. COP^2 was one outcome of that work—a global network aligned about converging growing activity and learning on climate-psychological resilience connections and putting them to global scale. An initial effort from that was completing an implementation roadmap, launched at COP28, for global-sized efforts and campaigns, such as the Race to Resilience, to incorporate the goal of building capacity to promote psychological resilience within the goal of the Sharm El Sheikh Adaptation Agenda to increase the climate resilience of four billion people by 2030. Belkin is also the former executive deputy commissioner in the New York City Department of Health and Mental Hygiene where he led the Division of Mental Hygiene and its development and implementation of the innovative New York City-wide public mental health initiative, ThriveNYC. Before joining city government, he was medical director for behavioral health across the Health and Hospitals Corporation of the City of New York, and served as founding editor-in-chief of the open access journal *Global Mental Health*. As director of the New York University's Program in Global Mental Health, Belkin partnered with other groups globally to test and scale community-led models of mental health promotion and access in less resourced countries that are now widely used.

DEBRA M. BUTLER (she/her/hers) is the executive director of the American Society of Adaptation Professionals. Her transdisciplinary research focuses on climate displacement, migration, and resettlement on the U.S. Gulf Coast. Butler has collaborated with Indigenous and placed-based communities in Louisiana, Alabama, Mississippi, and Sancti Spiritus, Cuba to examine dynamics of adaptation and resilience in ecological and human communities. Butler was awarded research fellowships from the National Academies of Sciences' Engineering, and Medicine's Gulf Research Science Policy Program, National Science Foundation-Integrative Graduate Education and Research Traineeship, and the Harte Research Institute at Texas A&M University-Corpus Christi. Butler's commitment to Gulf communities is reflected in her service on numerous not-for-profit boards and community organizations including the Climigration Network, Stone Living Lab, and Rising Voices Center for Indigenous and Earth Sciences-National Center for Atmospheric Research. As a National Academies' Gulf Research policy fellow, she worked with the U.S. Environmental Protection Agency (Region IV Gulf of Mexico Program) with climate-impacted ecological and cultural restoration projects in Turkey Creek, Mississippi; with the the Poarch Band of Creek Indians; and in Dauphin Island, Alabama. Butler has earned an M.B.A. in international business from Brandeis University, an Ed.M. from Harvard Graduate School of Education, and a Ph.D. in environmental studies from the University of Massachusetts-Boston. She is a Gulf Coast native.

CRAIG E. COLTEN (he/him/his) is professor emeritus at Louisiana State University. His principal training is in historical geography, with foci on human adaptation to environmental conditions and settlement geography. Colten's recent research has focused on hazards and community resilience in the Gulf Coast, adaptation to environmental change, and environmental migration as an adaptive strategy. He is senior advisor at the Water Institute of the Gulf, a fellow of the American Association of Geographers, and recipient of the association's 2022 Gilbert White Distinguished Public Service Honor. Colten held the Carl O. Sauer Professorship at Louisiana State University and received a Rainmaker Award from the university. He has received a Landhaus Fellowship with the Rachel Carson Center in Munich. Previously, Colten was on the faculty at Texas State University, was a senior project manager for PHR Environmental Consultants in the D.C. area, held several positions with the Illinois Department of Energy and Natural Resources, and served as the chair of the Isle de Jean Charles Resettlement Project Academic Advisory Committee. He has reported to academic and applied audiences at professional conferences that the absence of community relocation considerations is a shortcoming in current Louisiana state coastal restoration projects. Colten has authored and co-authored articles in academic publications with the viewpoint that current Louisiana state coastal restoration projects do not adequately take into consideration community relocation. He has also authored several books, with the most recent one entitled *State of Disaster: A Historical Geography of Louisiana's Land Loss Crisis*. Colten has a Ph.D. in geography from Syracuse University.

KATHERINE J. CURTIS (she/her/hers) is professor of community and environmental sociology and associate director of the Center for Demography and Ecology at the University of Wisconsin–Madison. Her work is centered in demography and extends to spatial, environmental, rural, and applied demography, and focuses on two central themes: population-environment interactions (most centrally the relationship between demographic, economic, and environmental forces) and spatial and temporal dimensions of social and economic inequality (most centrally historical and local forces perpetuating racial disparities). In her work, Curtis adopts place-based theoretical frameworks and employs advanced spatial and spatiotemporal statistical approaches to analyze questions about inequality, which has profound and far-reaching impacts on population well-being. Professional service and awards include Diversity Committee of the Rural Sociological Society, Program Committee of the Population Association of America, associate editor of *Rural Sociology*, editorial board of *Spatial Demography*, and National Experiment Station Section Excellence in Multistate Research Award (W4001 Multistate Research Project on the Social, Economic and Environmental Causes and Consequences of Demographic Change in Rural America, past chair). She earned her Ph.D. in sociology at the University of Washington.

HARRIET FESTING[1] (she/her/hers) is co-founder and executive director of the Anthropocene Alliance (A2), a Florida-based nonprofit that combats climate change and environmental abuse by building grassroots coalitions in the communities most affected by flooding, toxic waste, wildfires, drought, and heat. A2 has more than 250 member-communities in 41 U.S. states and territories. She spent her time working for UK government leading research and advising ministers on public attitudes about energy and climate change policy. Festing was director of fundraising for His Royal Highness Prince Charles's Foundation for urban design and architecture in London. Prior to founding A2, she worked for the Center for Neighborhood Technology in Chicago where she undertook ground-breaking research on urban flooding in the United States. Festing's research won several awards, led to state legislation, and preceded the National Academies of Sciences, Engineering, and Medicine publication *Framing the Challenge of Urban Flooding in the United States*, on which committee she was a member. A2 has released two policy statements on climate migration, *A10-Point Platform (and Anti-Platform) on Climate Change* and *The Great American Climate Migration: A Roundtable Discussion by Grassroots Leaders*, both of which take the viewpoint that climate change is disproportionately affecting low-income and marginalized communities. A2 is also a signatory to a white paper

[1]Until December 2022.

produced by the Coastal Flood Resilience Project that recommends specific policy actions to be undertaken by the federal government, including the creation and funding of a federal Coastal Community Relocation Assistance Program. Her work with A2 advances community transformation by building grassroots coalitions in the communities most badly affected by climate change, including current work in Port Arthur, Texas, helping community leaders to survey their residents to see what climate migration might look like for this community. Festing has an M.Phil. in business economics from the University of London.

LYNN R. GOLDMAN (she/her/hers), a pediatrician and epidemiologist, is the Michael and Lori Milken Dean and professor of environmental and occupational health at the Milken Institute School of Public Health at the George Washington University. She was previously professor of environmental health sciences at the Bloomberg School of Public Health; assistant administrator for toxic substances at the U.S. Environmental Protection Agency, where she directed the Office of Chemical Safety and Prevention; and chief of the division of Environmental and Occupational Disease Control at the California Department of Public Health. Goldman is a member of the National Academy of Medicine and serves on the National Academies of Sciences, Engineering, and Medicine's Environmental Health Matters Initiative. She formerly chaired the board for the Association of Schools and Programs of Public Health and has served in advisory capacities to the Centers for Disease Control and Prevention, the National Institutes of Health, the Food and Drug Administration, and MITRE. Goldman holds a B.S. and an M.S. from the University of California, Berkeley; an M.D. from the University of California, San Francisco; and an M.P.H. from Johns Hopkins University. She completed a pediatric residency at the University of California, San Fransisco's Benioff Children's Hospital in Oakland. She serves as a trustee for the Environmental Defense Fund.

E. BARRETT RISTROPH (she/her/hers) is owner of Ristroph Law, Planning, and Research, which provides services at a reasonable cost to tribes, communities, and agencies related to natural resources, hazard mitigation, government, and climate change adaptation and relocation. She is a lawyer, planner, mediator, evaluator, and researcher based in south Louisiana and sometimes Alaska. Her work has included assisting Newtok Village, Alaska, with relocating to Mertarvik; establishing a climate change program for an Alaskan inter-tribal organization; assisting tribes with hazard mitigation and adaption planning; working with the National Oceanic and Atmospheric Administration on environmental review for Louisiana coastal restoration projects; and working on reports for international agreements related to environmental and human rights issues. She volunteers her time to various coalitions on adaptation and has served as a mentor through the Louisiana Bar Association and the American Society of Adaptation Professionals. She holds a Ph.D in adaptation planning and a J.D. She is a frequent presenter at conferences on the experience of Newtok residents and has published articles such as "Strategies for Planned Community Relocation: A Case Study of Newtok Village, Alaska" in the *Journal of Environmental Studies and Sciences*.

CATHERINE L. ROSS (she/her/hers) is Regents Professor Emeritus of City and Regional Planning and Civil and Environmental Engineering and Georgia Power Professor of Excellence at the Georgia Institute of Technology. Her work includes a multi-disciplinary focus on resilience, analytics, transportation impact assessment, Mobility-as-a-Service, and performance management. She was the first executive director of the Georgia Regional Transportation Authority and deputy director of Georgia Tech's Tier 1 Center for Transportation System Productivity and Management. Ross is an internationally renowned scholar and a global thought leader, author of *Megaregions Planning for Global Competitiveness*, and co-author of *Health Impact Assessment in the United States and the Inner City*. She is chairman of the board of the Auto Club Group (American Automobile Association) and a board member of the Health Effects Institute. She has extensive private-sector experience, serving previously as president of the Association of Collegiate Schools of Planning, president of Catherine Ross and Associates, and vice president of Euquant.

GAVIN P. SMITH (he/him/his) is a professor in the Department of Landscape Architecture and Environmental Planning at North Carolina State University. His research focuses on hazard mitigation, disaster recovery, and climate change adaptation and the integration of research and practice through deep community engagement. Smith's current research includes assessing the state of disaster resilient design education at U.S. universities; analyzing a national survey assessing the role of states in building the capacity of local governments to implement hazard mitigation grants; and conducting a comparative assessment of hazard-prone housing acquisition programs in the United States, New Zealand, and Australia. He has developed a graduate certificate program in disaster resilient policy, engineering, and design and is helping to coordinate a university-wide effort focused on disaster resilience spanning research, teaching, and engagement-related activities. Smith is the author of *Planning for Post-Disaster Recovery: A Review of the United States Disaster Assistance Framework* and served as the co-editor of the text *Adapting to Climate Change: Lessons from Natural*

Hazards Planning. He has received funding from several jurisdictions—including Louisiana; Queensland, Australia; the U.S. Virgin Islands; and the U.S. Department of Homeland Security—for advising on hazard adaptation and mitigation strategies, coastal management, and disaster response. Smith has written numerous peer reviewed journal articles, book chapters, and practice-oriented reports that address hazard mitigation and disaster recovery issues. Recent articles discuss lessons from buyouts and their application to managed retreat strategies, development of a hazard overlay districts to adapt to climate change-induced hazards, and a governance-based approach to improve recovery outcomes. He holds a Ph.D. in urban and regional planning from Texas A&M University.

NATALIE L. SNIDER (she/her/hers) is currently serving as a science integrator at the University of Maryland Center for Environmental Science Integration and Application Network. Until recently, Snider was the associate vice president for climate resilient coasts and watersheds for the Environmental Defense Fund (EDF). Her work centers on building just climate resilience through the adaptation, transition, and transformation of the socioecological system, focusing on governance and adaptive management, to meet the challenges of climate change impacts to coastal and riverine ecosystems and communities. Snider previously worked at Louisiana Coastal Protection and Restoration Authority, leading efforts on the Louisiana Coastal Master Plan, and as the science director at the Coalition to Restore Coastal Louisiana. She has received a Champion of Inspiration award from the National Conference on Volunteering and Service, a Make a Difference Day Award from USA Today, a Women in Conservation Award from the National Audubon Society, and a Coastal Stewardship Award from the Coalition to Restore Coastal Louisiana. Snider has actively engaged with the challenge of climate change through tweets and blogs, including "4 Ways to Reduce Disproportionate Flood Risk and Build Resilience for All Communities" and "Building Climate Resilience Requires a Whole-of-Government Approach. Here's How Louisiana Is Making It Happen" on EDF's blog; she has also co-authored the article "Eroding Land and Erasing Place: A Qualitative Study of Place Attachment, Risk Perception, and Coastal Land Loss in Southern Louisiana" in *Sustainability* and "Responding to Flood Risk in Louisiana: The Roles of Place Attachment, Emotions and Location" in *Natural Hazards*. She has a B.S. in wildlife and fisheries management and an M.S. in oceanography and coastal sciences, both from Louisiana State University, and a Ph.D. in marine and estuarine environmental sciences from the University of Maryland.

COURTNEY S. THOMAS TOBIN (she/her/hers) is an associate professor in community health sciences and associate dean for equity, diversity, and inclusion at the Fielding School of Public Health and a faculty associate of the Ralph J. Bunche Center for African American Studies at the University of California, Los Angeles (UCLA). As a medical sociologist, she integrates traditional sociological theories with perspectives from public health, social psychology, medicine, and the biological sciences to examine the social, psychological, and biological (i.e., biopsychosocial) pathways that contribute to the health and longevity of Black Americans. Her research program makes conceptual and empirical contributions to three interrelated areas of inquiry: (a) psychosocial pathways to embodiment, including the interconnections between mental and physical health; (b) health risks and resources across the life course; and (c) racialized stress and coping processes among Black Americans. She was a University of California President's Postdoctoral Fellow in public health and psychology prior to joining the faculty at UCLA. She holds a B.S. in psychology from Xavier University of Louisiana and a Ph.D. in sociology from Vanderbilt University.

Appendix B

Public Info Session Participants

WORKSHOP #1 PART 1: BUYOUTS AND OTHER FORMS OF STRATEGIC RELOCATION IN GREATER HOUSTON

RAY BELTRAN, Community Engagement Coordinator, Harris County, Precinct 1
PERLA GARCIA, Coalition for Environment, Equity, and Resilience
MARCUS GLENN, Black United Fund of Texas
PAMELA GRAHAM, Resident of Port Arthur, Texas
DAVID GRIFFIN, JR., Resident of Port Arthur, Texas
DEBORAH JANUARY-BEVERS, President and Chief Executive Officer, Houston Wilderness
CLEO JOHNSON-McLAUGHLIN, President, Black United Fund of Texas
BARBARA McINTYRE, Coalition for Environment, Equity, and Resilience
KEVIN McKINNEY, Flood Victims of Richwood
DARNELL OZENNE, Black United Fund of Texas
SUSAN ROGERS, Associate Professor and Director of the Community Design Resource Center, University of Houston College of Architecture
SHIRLEY RONQUILLO, Co-Founder and Community Activist, Houston Department of Transformation
ANDREW RUMBACH, Associate Professor of Landscape Architecture and Urban Planning, Texas A&M University at College Station

MARCIAL SANCHEZ, Coalition for Environment, Equity, and Resilience
RYAN SLATTERY, Senior Advisor of Sustainability and Resilience, Houston Mayor's Office
ELIZABETH VAN HORN, Urban Planner, Harris County Public Health
SHANNON VAN ZANDT, Professor, Landscape Architecture and Urban Planning, Texas A&M University at College Station
CAROLYN WHITE, Urban Planner, Harris County Public Health

WORKSHOP #1 PART 2: STRATEGIC RELOCATION AND ENVIRONMENTAL PERCEPTION: COMMUNITY PERSPECTIVES FROM PORT ARTHUR, TEXAS

TIFFANY ANDERSON, Resident of Port Arthur, Texas
CLYDE DIXON, Resident of Port Arthur, Texas
HILTON KELLEY, Founder and Director, Community In-Power and Development Association Inc.
LINDA KELLEY, Community In-Power and Development Association Inc.
L. MARIE KELLEY, Community In-Power and Development Association Inc.
WARREN KELLEY, Community In-Power and Development Association Inc.
LANDY PATIN, Resident of Port Arthur, Texas
OCTAVIA SANDERS, Resident of Port Arthur, Texas
MICHELLE SMITH, Community In-Power and Development Association Inc.

WORKSHOP #2: OPPORTUNITIES & CHALLENGES OF CLIMATE ADAPTATION ON FLORIDA'S GULF COAST

JOSEPH AYALA,[1] Research Assistant, Student, Columbia Climate School
ALEJANDRO BRITO, Resident of St. Petersburg, Florida
HILARY L. BRUNO, Assistant Director, Community Development, Pasco County
KENNETH BRYANT, Founder and Chief Executive Officer of Minority Health Coalition of Pinellas, Inc.
CARMELA CRUZ, Resident of St. Petersburg, Florida
GETULIO GONZALEZ-MULATTIERI, Resident of St. Petersburg, Florida
EUGENE HENRY, Community Hazard Mitigation, ISO/Verisk

[1]At the time of the workshop, Joseph Ayala worked as an associate program manager at the CLEO Institute.

TISHA HOLMES, Assistant Professor, Department of Urban & Regional Planning, Florida State University
BETTY JEAN-JEREMIE,[2] Executive Director, Governing Council for Mercy Focus
DAYNA LAZARUS, Housing Technical Advisor, Florida Housing Coalition
RUSSELL MEYER, Executive Director, Florida Council of Churches
LEROY MOORE, Senior Vice President/Chief Operating Officer, Tampa Housing Authority
JERRY MURPHY, Murphy Consulting and Faculty Consultant, Institute of Food and Agricultural Sciences, University of Florida
CHELSEA NELSON, Resident of Madeira Beach, Florida
SIDNEY PERSON, Resident of St. Petersburg, Florida
ELISEO SANTANA, Resident of St. Petersburg, Florida
MARILENA SANTANA, Resident of St. Petersburg, Florida
TREVOR TATUM, Resident of St. Petersburg, Florida
CHRIS UEJIO, Associate Professor, Department of Geography, Florida State University
ANTWAUN WELLS, Resident of St. Petersburg, Florida
FLORENCE WRIGHT, Resident of St. Petersburg, Florida

WORKSHOP #3 PART 1: COMMUNITY VIABILITY AND ENVIRONMENTAL CHANGE IN COASTAL LOUISIANA

CHIEF ROMES ANTOINE, Avoyel-Taensa Tribe
JAY CLUNE, President, Nicholls State University
WINDELL CUROLE, General Manager, South Lafourche Levee District
ELDER CHIEF SHIRELL PARFAIT DARDAR, Grand Caillou/Dulac Band of Biloxi-Chitimacha-Choctaw and Chair, Louisiana Governor's Commission on Native Americans
ELDER THERESA DARDAR, Pointe-au-Chien Indian Tribe, Lafourche/Terrebonne Parish
ALESSANDRA JEROLLEMAN, Community Resilience Specialist and Applied Researcher, Lowlander Center
GARY LAFLEUR, President, Barataria-Terrebonne National Estuary Foundation, and Professor, Biological Sciences, Nicholls State University
CHIEF ALBERT NAQUIN, Jean Charles Choctaw Nation
CHIEF DEVON PARFAIT, Grand Caillou/Dulac Band of Biloxi-Chitimacha-Choctaw

[2] At the time of the workshop, Betty Jean-Jeremie worked as a climate equity program manager at the CLEO Institute.

ELDER ROSINA PHILIPPE, Atakapa-Ishak/Chawasha Tribe and President of the First Peoples' Conservation Council

WORKSHOP #3 PART 2: ASSISTED RESETTLEMENT AND RECEIVING COMMUNITIES IN LOUISIANA

GENIE ARDOIN, Resident of Houma, Louisiana
BETTE BILLIOT, The United Houma Nation Indigenous Tribe
BETH BUTLER, Executive Director, A Community Voice
KELLI CUNNINGHAM, Director, Terrebonne Parish Housing and Human Services
JESSICA DOMANGUE, Terrebonne Parish Councilwoman, Houma District 5
PAT FORBES, Executive Director, Louisiana Office of Community Development
JONATHAN FORET, Executive Director, South Louisiana Wetlands Discovery Center
MARK GOODSON, Principal, Planning and Resilience Practice Lead, CSRS
DEE KNOWLES,[3] Resident of Southern Louisiana
CYNDI NGUYEN, Executive Director, Vietnamese Initiatives in Economic Training
SAM OLIVER, Executive Director, Acadiana Center for the Arts
THADDEUS (MIKE) PELLEGRIN, Resident of Houma, Louisiana
CHRIS PULASKI, Director of Planning and Zoning, Terrebonne Parish Consolidated Government
CINDY ROBERTSON, Director, micah 6:8
BONNIE THERIOT, Resident of Houma, Louisiana
MARK VANLANDINGHAM, Professor of Sociology and Director of the Center for Studies of Displaced Populations, Tulane University
SHANA WALTON, Toups Professor of Cultural Studies, Department of English, Modern Languages, and Cultural Studies, Nicholls State University
CHERRY WILMORE, Resident of Houma, Louisiana
SHERRY WILMORE, Resident of Houma, Louisiana

PERSPECTIVES AND APPROACHES TO PROPERTY ACQUISITIONS: CHALLENGES AND LESSONS LEARNED

LAURA DHUWE, Chief of Mitigation, Florida Division of Emergency Management

[3]At the time of the workshop, Dee Knowles worked as a community liaison at micah 6:8.

JEFFREY GIERING, Section State Hazard Mitigation Office, Hazard Mitigation Technical Services, Lousiana Governor's Office of Homeland Security and Emergency Preparedness

JANA HENDERSON, Mitigation Office Director, Mississippi Emergency Management Agency

KATHY HOPKINS, Manager, Flood Mitigation Assistance and State Flood Grant Programs, Texas Water Development Board

MICHAEL JOHNSON, Public Assistance Officer, Alabama Emergency Management Agency

KELLY MAIN, Executive Director, Buy-in Community Planning

SABRINA SIMMS, Supervisory Grants Management Specialist, Federal Emergency Management Agency Region 4

COURTNEY WALD-WITTKOP, Program Manager, New Jersey Department of Environmental Protection: Office of Climate Resilience, and New Jersey's Blue Acres Program

ELYSE ZAVAR, Associate Professor, Department of Emergency Management and Disaster Science, University of North Texas

VIRTUAL FOCUSED DISCUSSION: MISSISSIPPI AND ALABAMA GULF COAST COMMUNITY STAKEHOLDER PERSPECTIVES ON MANAGED RETREAT

CASI (KC) CALLAWAY, Chief Resilience Officer, City of Mobile, Alabama

DERRICK EVANS, Turkey Creek Community Initiatives in Gulfport, Mississippi

SARA GUICE, Director, Land Trust for the Mississippi Coastal Plain

GORDON JACKSON, Board President, Steps Coalition

CAROLYN MARTIN, Planning and Grants Administrator, City of Ocean Springs Community Development

CHRIS MONFORTON, Chief Executive Officer, Habitat for Humanity of the Mississippi Gulf Coast

JANE NGUYEN, Program Manager and Community Health Worker, Boat People SOS, Biloxi, Mississippi

DAVID PERKES, Professor and Director, Gulf Coast Community Design Studio College of Architecture, Art and Design, Mississippi State University

NICOLE TAYLOR, Planner/Geographic Information Systems Analyst, South Alabama Regional Planning Commission

BARBARA WECKESSER, Head of Concerned Citizens of Cherokee Subdivision and Resident of Pascagoula, Mississippi

Appendix C

Community Profiles

SUMMARY

This appendix presents the community profiles of select cities along the Gulf Coast: St. Petersburg, Florida; Mobile County and the community of Bayou La Batre, Alabama; Harrison County and the community of Turkey Creek, Mississippi; southeast Louisiana (Lafourche and Terrebonne Parishes); and Port Arthur, Texas. These profiles focus on unique aspects and critical vulnerabilities of these communities, such as sociodemographic characteristics, abilities, flood and heat risks, environmental justice indexes, and notable recent disasters. This appendix serves as a valuable resource as coastal communities grapple with compounding challenges induced by environmental hazards.

DEFINITIONS AND CONCEPTS FOR PROFILE CHARACTERISTICS

Health

A population's physical and mental health can increase its vulnerability to climate and environmental hazards, so understanding the incidence of certain diseases and health conditions is a key component of a community's profile. The data and images in this section are obtained from the Centers for Disease Control and Prevention (CDC) PLACES interactive map.[1] Prevalence data come from CDC's Behavioral Risk Factor Surveillance System.[2] Age-adjusted[3] incidence rates are reported so that rates can be compared across cities (Anderson & Rosenberg, 1998).

Environmental Justice Index

The U.S. Environmental Protection Agency (EPA) defines environmental justice as "the fair treatment and meaningful involvement of all people regardless of race, color, national origin, or income with respect to the development, implementation and enforcement of environmental laws, regulations and policies" (CDC/Agency for Toxic Substances and Disease Registry [ATSDR], 2022, p. 5). It is therefore important to be able to examine demographic and environmental factors in concert. EPA created environmental justice indexes (EJIs)[4] at a census tract level to combine demographic factors (low-income and people of color populations) with a single environmental factor (e.g., particulate matter, ozone, traffic proximity, hazardous waste proximity). The EJI is a location-specific tool for assessing environmental burdens in relation to human health and equity. It assigns a score to each community, helping health officials identify and address areas most at risk due to factors like poverty, race, ethnicity, and pre-existing health conditions. This aids in prioritizing support for the most affected communities (CDC/ATSDR, 2022c). These environmental indicators reflect potential air and water quality issues, among other things. For example, ozone and particulate matter have harmful impacts on respiratory and cardiovascular health and are associated with diseases such as asthma and cardiovascular events (Manisalidis et al., 2020). A higher EJI means that a census tract has

---

[1]More information is available at https://experience.arcgis.com/experience/22c7182a162d45788dd52a2362f8ed65

[2]CDC's Behavioral Risk Factor Surveillance System is "the nation's premier system of health-related telephone surveys that collect state data about U.S. residents regarding their health-related risk behaviors, chronic health conditions, and use of preventive services." More information is available at https://www.cdc.gov/brfss/index.html

[3]Age-adjusted rates account for the age of a specific population, adjusting rates so that they represent what the rates would be if the "population under study had the same age distribution as the 'standard' population." More information is available at https://health.mo.gov/data/mica/CDP_MICA/AARate.html

[4]EJI "uses data from the U.S. Census Bureau, the U.S. Environmental Protection Agency, the U.S. Mine Safety and Health Administration, and the U.S. Centers for Disease Control and Prevention to rank the cumulative impacts of environmental injustice on health for every census tract. Census tracts are subdivisions of counties for which the Census collects statistical data. EJI ranks each tract on 36 environmental, social, and health factors and groups them into three overarching modules and ten different domains" (CDC/ATSDR, 2022c). More information about EJI is available at https://www.atsdr.cdc.gov/placeandhealth/eji/index.html. More information about EPA's tool EJScreen is available at https://ejscreen.epa.gov/mapper/

more residents that are low income and/or people of color, and/or have a higher environmental indicator value.[5] Each index, representing a distinct aspect of environmental quality or impact, is evaluated separately within each city. These indexes can be used to compare census tracts and identify areas with higher environmental and economic burdens (CDC/ATSDR, 2022c).

National Oceanic and Atmospheric Administration's (NOAA's) Coastal Flood Exposure Mapper

One component of flood risk projection is profile maps that come from the NOAA Coastal Flood Exposure Mapper.[6] The tool allows users to select a hazard layer (options include coastal flood hazard composite, high tide flooding, Federal Emergency Management Agency [FEMA] flood zones, tsunami, storm surge, sea level rise [SLR]), societal exposure (options include, for example, population density, poverty rates, elderly, employees), infrastructure exposure (development, critical facilities, development patterns), and ecosystem exposure (natural areas and open space, potential pollution sources, natural protection, wetland potential). In this appendix, poverty rates and flood hazard zones are displayed in separate maps because when one is superimposed over the other, it is difficult to see both statistics. When areas with high poverty rates are also flood hazard zones, it indicates that vulnerable populations are also at risk of being impacted by flooding.

Projected Flood Risk and Extreme Heat

The Union of Concerned Scientists (UCS) conducted an analysis of coastal property in the United States at risk of SLR using data from Dahl, Spanger-Siegfried et al. (2017), Spanger-Siegfried et al. (2017), and the Zillow Transaction and Assessment Database.[7] More information about their analysis can be found under the "About this Analysis" tab of the footnoted website. Projected extreme heat was taken from the National Integrated Heat Health Information System.[8]

---

[5]More information about what EJI means is available at https://www.epa.gov/ejscreen/ej-and-supplemental-indexes-ejscreen

[6]More information about NOAA's Coastal Flood Exposure Mapper is available at https://coast.noaa.gov/digitalcoast/tools/flood-exposure.html

[7]More information is available at https://ucsusa.maps.arcgis.com/apps/MapSeries/index.html?appid=cf07ebe0a4c9439ab2e7e346656cb239

[8]More information about the National Integrated Heat Health Information System is available at www.Heat.gov

Social Vulnerability Index (SVI)

Social vulnerability can be defined as the factors (e.g., poverty, lack of access to transportation, crowded housing) that "may weaken a community's ability to prevent human suffering and financial loss in a disaster."[9] In order to assist emergency response planners and public health officials in identifying "communities that will most likely need support before, during, and after a hazardous event," CDC and ATSDR created the SVI.[10]

Population and Sociodemographics

Table C-1 summarizes relevant census data for the six Gulf Coast communities: city of St. Petersburg, Florida; Mobile County, Alabama; Harrison County, Mississippi; Lafourche Parish, Louisiana; Terrebonne Parish, Louisiana; and the city of Port Arthur, Texas. Sociodemographics data of these places are compared with national averages for the United States, including analysis of race and ethnicity, income and poverty, education, families and living arrangements, housing, residential mobility factor, transportation, and disability. The information for cells marked "Not Available" was not captured by the census.

COMMUNITY PROFILE: ST. PETERSBURG, FLORIDA

Social Vulnerability Index

The 2020 national overall SVI score for Pinellas County, Florida, was 0.7247 where possible scores range from 0 (lowest vulnerability) to 1 (highest vulnerability). This score indicates a medium to high level of vulnerability (see Figure C-1).

[9]More information is available at https://www.atsdr.cdc.gov/placeandhealth/svi/fact_sheet/fact_sheet.html

[10]In order to determine social vulnerability, the CDC/ATSDR SVI ranks every census tract on 16 social factors pulled from U.S. Census data. The 16 factors fit into four themes: socioeconomic status, household characteristics, racial and ethnic minority status, and housing type and transportation. Each tract is then given a ranking for each of these four themes and an overall ranking, which indicate a census tract's SVI.

TABLE C-1 Population Sociodemographics

	St. Petersburg	Mobile County	Harrison County	Lafourche Parish	Terrebonne Parish	Port Arthur	National
Population	258,245	414,620	207,382	97,677	110,100	55,757	329,725,481
Pop Density (persons/ square mile)	4,178.7	337.4	212.5	66.28	52.93	727.0	93.8
Age 65+	20.2%	16.3%	16.0%	15.6%	14.6%	12.7%	16.8%
Race (2021 1-year estimates)[a]							
American Indian and Alaska Native	0.2%	0.4%	1.0%	1.9%	5.1%	0.6%	1.0%
Asian	3.3%	2.2%	2.7%	0.7%	1.2%	6.5%	5.8%
Black or African American	20.1%	36.1%	22.3%	12.0%	17.1%	42.2%	12.1%
Native Hawaiian/ Pacific Islander	0.02%	0.0%	0.1%	0.0%	0.0%	0.1%	0.2%
Other	2.0%	1.9%	0.9%	1.7%	0.2%	3.6%	7.2%
Two or more	9.5%	3.5%	10.8%	6.5%	9.1%	4.1%	12.6%
White	64.5%	55.9%	62.3%	76.9%	67.3%	43.0%	61.2%
Ethnicity: Hispanic or Latino	8.4%	3.1%	5.7%	4.6%	5.6%	32.2%	18.8%

(continued)

TABLE C-1 Continued

	St. Petersburg	Mobile County	Harrison County	Lafourche Parish	Terrebonne Parish	Port Arthur	National
Income and Poverty[b]							
Median household income	$64,375	$51,169	$51,590	$58,747	$57,940	$42,933	$69,021
Per capita income	$41,493	$27,942	$27,664	$30,552	$29,885	$22,557	$37,638
Persons in poverty	12.4%	17.6 %	17.9%	15.7%	17.8%	25.8%	12.6%
Education (age 25+)							
High school graduate +	93.5%	87.9%	89.0%	80.9%	81.1%	77.5%	88.9%
Bachelor's degree +	38.8%	23.9%	24.5%	17.3%	16.5%	10.9%	33.7%
Families & Living Arrangements							
Household size (persons)	2.26	2.58	2.56	2.51	2.59	2.71	2.60
Households with children <18	21.1%	30.3%	30.2%	29.1%	30.4%	Not available	30.6%
Multi-generational households	2.2%	3.4%	3.5%	4.22%	4.59%	Not available	3.4%

Non-English spoken at home	12.6%	4.4%	6.4%	11.1%	8.5%	33.9%	21.7%
Housing							
Median gross rent	$1,251	$916	$958	$816	$913	$859	$1,163
Occupancy rate	80.9%	Not available	Not available	89.2%	89.2%	81.0%	88.8%
Types of Structures							
Single unit	59.4%	74.5%	67.1%	75.3%	73.4%	70.2%	67.6%
Multi-unit	38.0%	18.1%	13.6%	8.3%	12.0%	28.3%	26.4%
Mobile home	2.6%	7.2%	11.8%	16.3%	14.6%	1.5%	5.9%
Boat, RV, van, etc.	0.08%	0.2%	7.5%	0.2%	0.3%	0.0%	0.1%
Residential Mobility Factors							
Owner-occupied unit rate	62.7%	63.5%	58.1%	77.7%	72.7%	57.1%	64.6%
Same house as 1 year ago	85.5%	88.2%	81.0%	89.2%	88.0%	90.6%	86.6%
Transportation							
Minutes to work	23.6	25.7	23.7	28.5	25.5	23.2	26.8
No vehicle available	7.7%	5.2%	6.2%	7.5%	9.0%	10.4%	8.0%
Disability (under age 65)	9.4%	9.1%	12.9%	17.1%	16.9%	11.0%	8.7%

(*continued*)

TABLE C-1 Continued

	St. Petersburg	Mobile County	Harrison County	Lafourche Parish	Terrebonne Parish	Port Arthur	National
No Health Insurance	10.3%	11.4%	14.3%	6.7%	7.2%	29.1%	8.8%

NOTE: Demographic statistics come from the American Community Survey (ACS) 2021 5-year estimates unless otherwise noted.

[a]2021 1-year estimates were reported for race and ethnicity because these variables were revised in 2020 for all areas except for race in Port Arthur. See https://www.census.gov/library/stories/2021/08/improved-race-ethnicity-measures-reveal-united-states-population-much-more-multiracial.html. For Port Arthur, Texas, 2021 ACS statistics were not available for race so 2020 Decennial Census data were used.

[b]Income is reflected in 2021 inflation-adjusted dollars over the past 12 months.

SOURCES:

U.S. Census Bureau. (2021a). Quick facts—United States. https://www.census.gov/quickfacts/fact/table/US/HSG445221

___. (2021b). Quick facts—St. Petersburg city, Florida; Mobile County, Alabama; Harrison County, Mississippi; Lafourche Parish, Louisiana; Terrebonne Parish, Louisiana; Port Arthur city, Texas. https://www.census.gov/quickfacts/fact/table/stpetersburgcityflorida,mobilecountyalabama,harrisoncountymississippi,lafourcheparishlouisiana,terrebonneparishlouisiana,portarthurcitytexas/FIPS

___. (2021c). American Community Survey 2021 5-year estimates: Income in the past 12 months. https://data.census.gov/table?q=S1901&g=050XX00US01097,22057,22109,28047_160XX00US1263000,4858820&tid=ACSST5Y2021.S1901

___. (2021d). American Community Survey 2021 5-year estimates: Educational attainment. https://data.census.gov/table?q=S1501&g=050XX00US01097,22057,22109,28047_160XX00US1263000,4858820&tid=ACSST5Y2021.S1501

___. (2021e). American Community Survey 2021 5-year estimates: Households and families. https://data.census.gov/table?q=S1101:+HOUSEHOLDS+AND+FAMILIES&g=050XX00US01097,22057,22109,28047_160XX00US1263000,4858820&tid=ACSST5Y2021.S1101

___. (2021f). American Community Survey 2021 5-year estimates: Household type by units in structure. https://data.census.gov/table?q=UNITS+IN+STRUCTURE&g=050XX00US01097,22057,22109,28047_160XX00US1263000,4858820&tid=ACSDT5Y2021.B11011

___. (2021g). American Community Survey 2021 5-year estimates: Selected characteristics of health insurance coverage in the United States. https://data.census.gov/table?q=health+insurance+coverage+status+&g=010XX00US&tid=ACSST5Y2021.S2701

___. (2021h). American Community Survey 2021 1-year estimates: Hispanic or Latino origin. https://data.census.gov/table?q=B03003:+HISPANIC+OR+LATINO+ORIGIN

___. (2021i). American Community Survey 2021 1-year estimates: Race. https://data.census.gov/table?q=race&tid=ACSDT1Y2021.B02001

___. (2020). 2020: Decennial Census demographic and housing characteristics. https://data.census.gov/table?q=race&g=160XX00US4858820&tid=DECENNIALDHC2020.P8

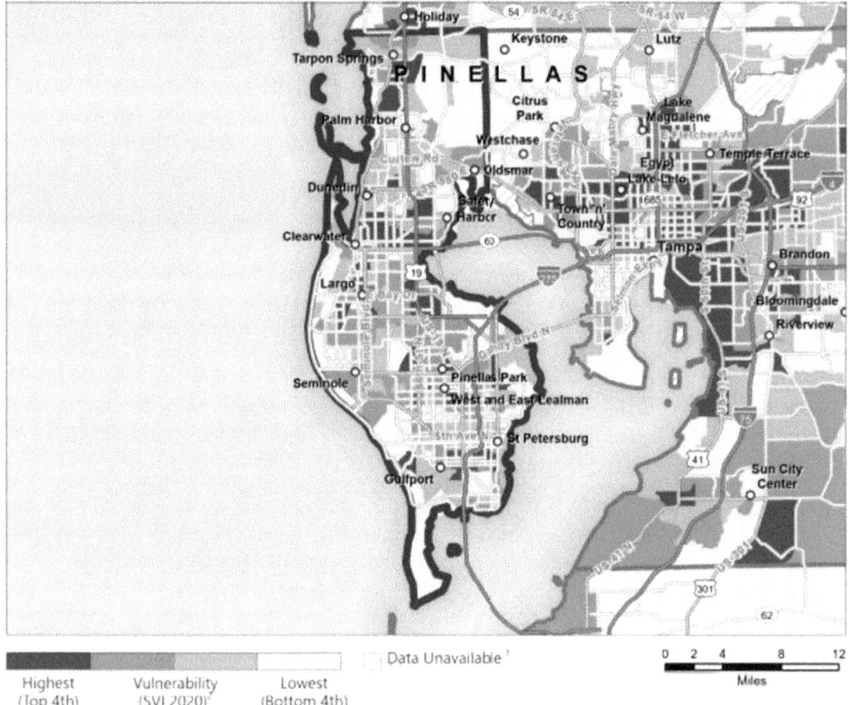

FIGURE C-1 The 2020 national overall Social Vulnerability Index for Pinellas County, Florida.
SOURCE: CDC/ATSDR. (2023). CDC/ATSDR Social Vulnerability Index Interactive Map 2020. https://www.atsdr.cdc.gov/placeandhealth/svi/interactive_map.html

Health

In St. Petersburg,[11] the estimated age-adjusted[12] prevalence of asthma among adults aged 18+ was 9.1 percent (confidence interval [CI]: 9.0, 9.1) in 2020. This is below the national average[13] of 10 percent, but south St. Petersburg has several census tracts with an asthma incidence rate above

[11]To view maps of the city's prevalence rate of health risk factors, visit the CDC PLACES website at https://experience.arcgis.com/experience/22c7182a162d45788dd52a2362f8ed65

[12]Age-adjusted is reported in the text. Only crude prevalence rate was provided by CDC PLACES.

[13]CDC PLACES reports both the tract and place level national averages and legends. The national average is reflected in the legend and reported in the text on this page and in the following health maps.

the national average. The highest incidence is found around the Child Park neighborhood and the area just north of Lake Maggiore.

The estimated age-adjusted prevalence of coronary heart disease among adults age 18+ was 5.7 percent (CI: 5.6, 5.7) in 2020, below the national average of 7.1 percent. Like asthma, there are high rates of heart disease in the neighborhoods north of Lake Maggiore, with one census tract showing an incidence rate of 9.4 percent. Another area of high incidence (8.4%) is seen along Riviera Bay and Grande Bayou.

The estimated age-adjusted prevalence of adults aged 18+ who reported their mental health as "not good" for 14 or more days out of the past 30 was 16.0 percent (CI: 15.9, 16.2) in 2020. This is slightly higher than the national average of 15.1 percent. Like asthma and heart disease, some of the highest incidence rates of poor mental health in St. Petersburg can be found around Child Park and Lake Maggiore. One census tract reports an incidence rate of over 21 percent.

The estimated age-adjusted prevalence of fair or poor health among adults aged 18 years and older was 33.1 percent (CI: 29.7, 37.0) in 2020, almost double the national average of 15.8 percent (see Figure C-2).

Current Flood Risk

NOAA's Coastal County Snapshot[14] for Special Flood Hazard in Pinellas County reports that 35.6 percent of county land falls within the 100-year floodplain where just over 30 percent of the county's population resides. Almost 34 percent of the population over age 65 lives in the 100-year floodplain and almost 27 percent of this population is in poverty (see Figure C-3). According to FEMA and U.S. Geological Survey (USGS) data, 16.4 percent of critical facilities (schools, police and fire stations, and medical facilities) in Pinellas County are located within the 100-year floodplain, including 31 schools and 17 fire stations (see Figure C-4), and almost a quarter of Pinellas County businesses (almost 12,000), meaning that many community services, revenues, and salaries are at risk. Since 1991, over 12,000 flood insurance claims totaling 152 million dollars have been made in Pinellas County, with over 35 million dollars in National Flood Insurance Program payouts between 2016 and 2020. Although 95 percent of development inside the 100-year floodplain existed by 1996, the other 5 percent (3.5 square miles) was added between 1996 and 2016. Although homes

[14]NOAA's Coastal County Snapshot tool uses data from multiple complex datasets to give communities a snapshot of their county's resilience and risk "in terms of flood hazards, critical facilities, jobs, businesses, and more" (Office for Coastal Management, 2023). The tool provides snapshots in four different areas: marine economy, total coastal economy, SLR, and special flood hazard. More information is available at https://coast.noaa.gov/digitalcoast/tools/snapshots.html

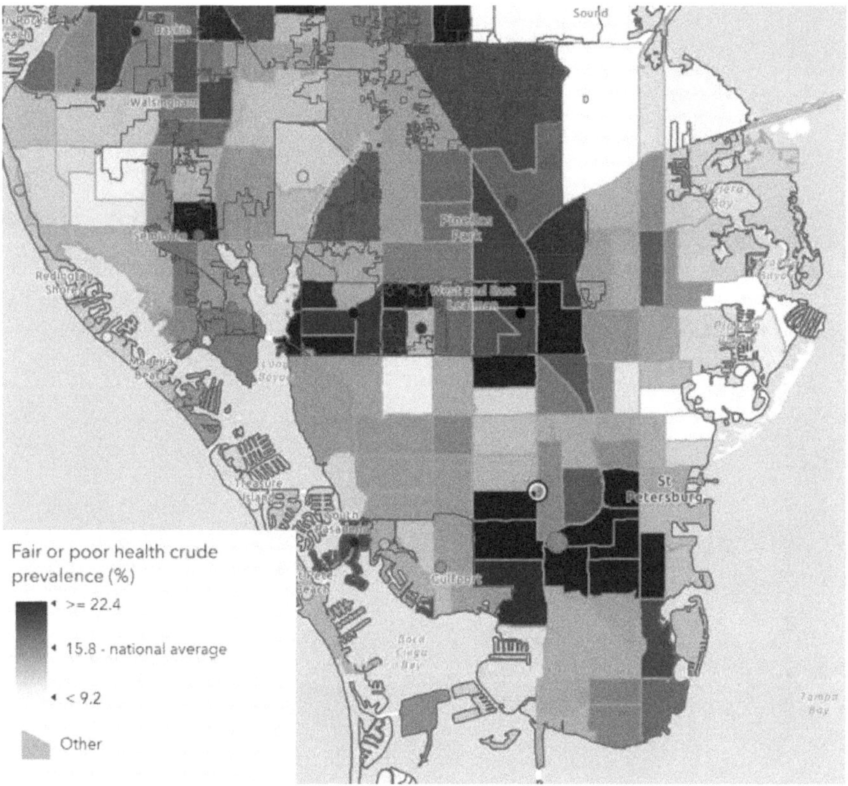

FIGURE C-2 The prevalence of adults aged 18+ who reported fair or poor health in 2020 in St. Petersburg, Florida.
SOURCE: CDC. (2023). CDC PLACES. https://www.cdc.gov/places

built since 2015 "are likely to be built to a more hazard resilient code," this only accounts for a very small proportion of homes in St. Petersburg (Hazard Aware, 2022).

Projected Flood Risk and Extreme Heat

By 2035, 256 homes (<1%), home to 471 people, are projected to be at risk of chronic inundation[15] in St. Petersburg (see Figure C-5). Together, these homes are valued at just under 130 million dollars and contribute over 2.1 million dollars to the local property tax base. By 2100, 19,383

[15]Chronic inundation means that "tidal flooding occurs 26 times per year, or on average, about twice a month" (Spanger-Siegfried et al., 2017).

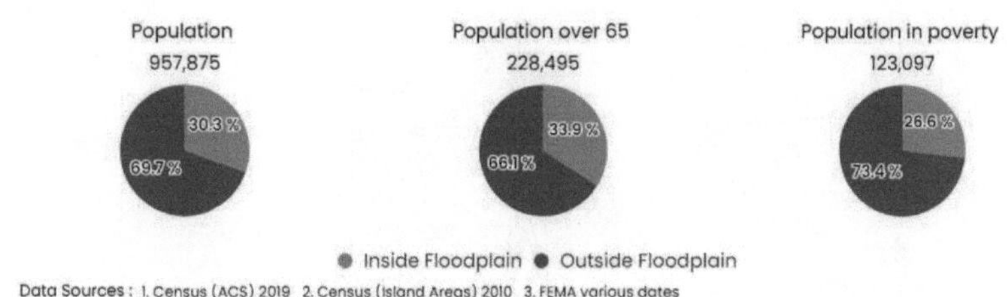

FIGURE C-3 Percentages of people that live in the floodplain in Pinellas County, Florida.
SOURCE: Office for Coastal Management. (n.d.a). Coastal County Snapshots: Special flood hazard. National Oceanic and Atmospheric Administration. https://coast.noaa.gov/digitalcoast/tools/snapshots.html

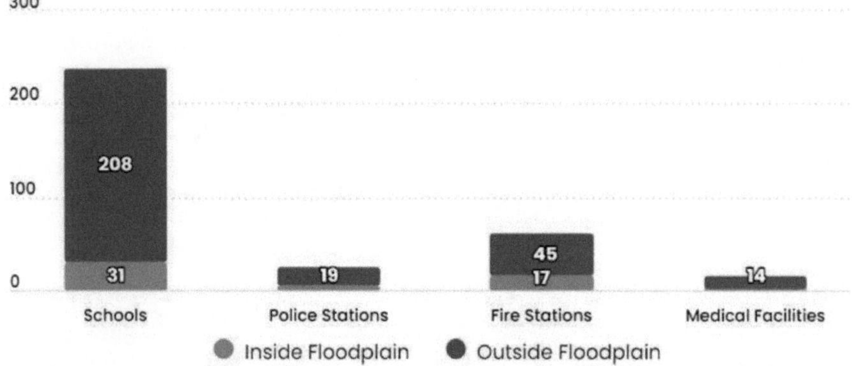

FIGURE C-4 Critical facilities in the 100-year floodplain in Pinellas County, Florida.
SOURCE: Office for Coastal Management. (n.d.a). Coastal County Snapshots: Special flood hazard. National Oceanic and Atmospheric Administration. https://coast.noaa.gov/digitalcoast/tools/snapshots.html

homes (11%) with 35,665 residents will be at risk of chronic inundation. These homes are valued at almost 5 billion dollars and contribute over 74 million dollars to the local property tax base.[16]

The first map in Figure C-5 shows critical facilities (hospitals, schools, fire and police stations, etc.) and "areas prone to flooding from one or more of the following hazards: high tide flooding; high risk (1% annual chance for A and V zones) and moderate risk (0.2% annual chance) flooding (designated by the Federal Emergency Management Agency); storm surge

[16]UCS Rising Seas' website uses 2014 National Climate Assessment SLR scenarios. The moderate SLR scenario assumes 1 foot global average SLR by 2035 and 4 feet by 2100.

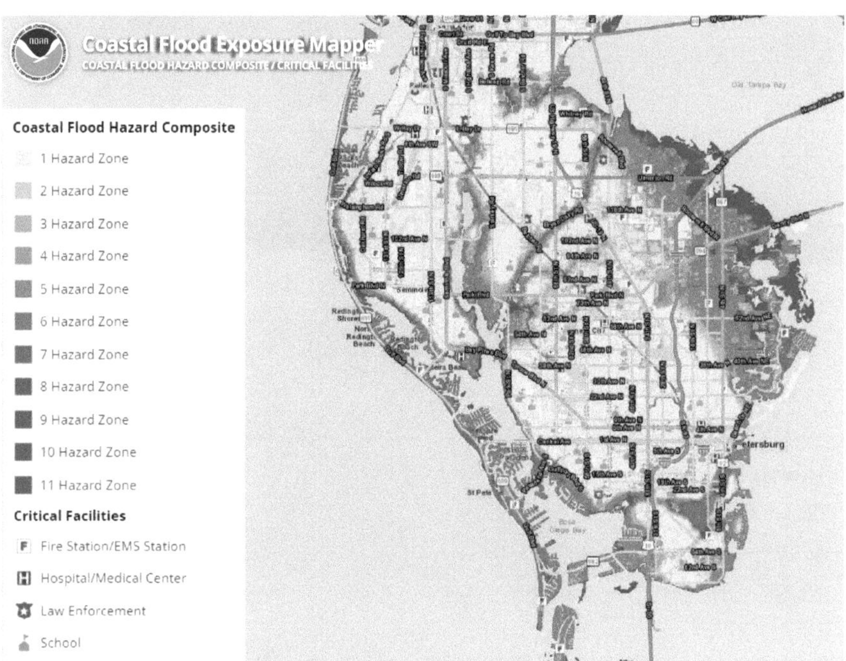

FIGURE C-5 Risk analysis and poverty in St. Petersburg, Florida.
NOTES: NOAA's Coastal Flood Exposure Mapper allows users to select a hazard layer (options include coastal flood hazard composite, high tide flooding, FEMA flood zones, tsunami, storm surge, SLR), societal exposure (options include population density, poverty, elderly, employees), infrastructure exposure (development, critical facilities, development patterns), and ecosystem exposure (natural areas and open space, potential pollution sources, natural protection, wetland potential). Poverty rates and flood hazard zones are displayed in separate maps because when one is superimposed over the other, it is difficult to see both statistics. When areas with high poverty rates are also flood hazard zones, it indicates that vulnerable populations are also at risk of being impacted by flooding.
SOURCE: Office for Coastal Management. (n.d.c). Coastal Flood Exposure Mapper. National Oceanic and Atmospheric Administration. https://coast.noaa.gov/digitalcoast/tools/flood-exposure.html

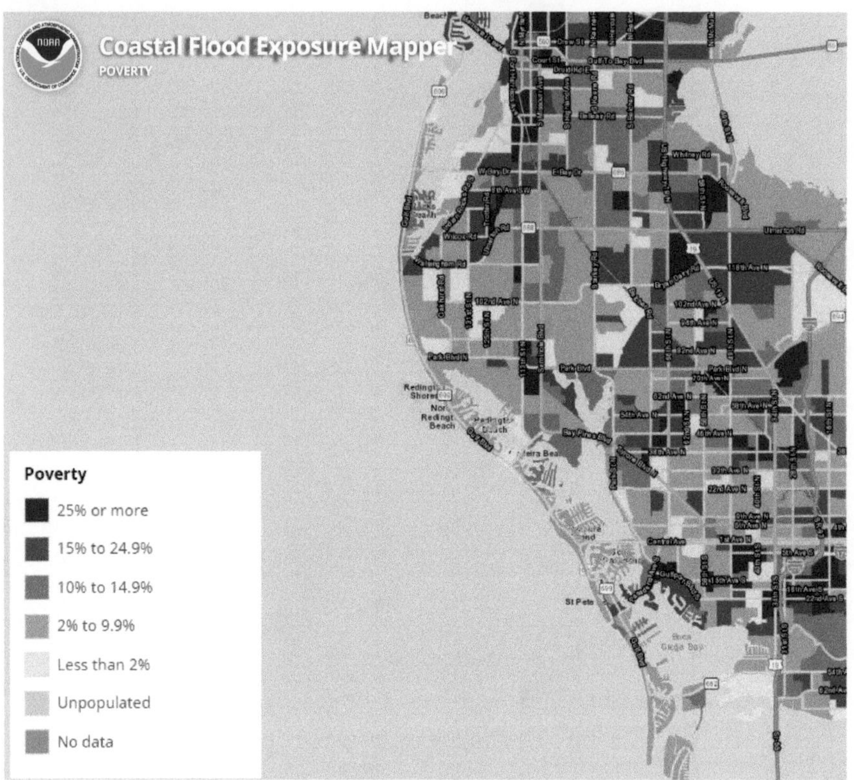

FIGURE C-5 Continued

for category 1 through category 3 hurricanes; sea level rise scenarios of 1, 2, and 3 feet; tsunami run-up zones (for high risk areas). The darker red color on the map indicates more flood hazard zones for that area" (Office for Coastal Management, n.d.b).

The second map in Figure C-5, based on 2014–2018 American Community Survey (ACS) five-year estimates, shows the "percentage of people living below the poverty line for census block groups in or near coastal flood-prone areas (e.g., four-person family with annual cash income below $23,283). People in poverty may not have adequate resources to prepare for or respond to hazards. Their limitations may include substandard housing, lack of transportation to evacuate, lack of social support systems, and incomes that limit their ability to afford temporary lodging, relocation, or housing improvements" (Office for Coastal Management, n.d.b).

National Integrated Heat Health Information System

- **Days above 90F:** Projected number of days (based on Representative Concentration Pathway [RCP] 8.5)[17] with temperature over 90F in 2050 = 145 (compared to 75 days per year on average from 1976 to 2005)
- **Extreme heat days:** Projected number of days per year warmer than the top 1 percent historically in 2050 = 66 (compared to four per year from 1976 to 2005)

Environmental Justice Indexes

The graph below[18] shows where St. Petersburg falls in relation to the rest of the state and nation by using a percentile for various EJIs within state and national contexts. For example, St. Petersburg's EJI for ozone levels is in the 82nd percentile for the state of Florida and 71st for the nation as a whole. This means that only about 18 percent of the population of Florida lives in a block group with a higher EJI for ozone than the average person in St. Petersburg (see Figures C-6 and C-7). Almost 30 percent of the U.S. population lives in a block group with a higher EJI for ozone than the average person in St. Petersburg. In general, the higher the percentile,

[17]RCPs of an 8.5 emissions scenario from the Fourth National Climate Assessment. RCPs capture a range of potential greenhouse gas emissions pathways and associated atmospheric concentration levels through the year 2100.

[18]This information was obtained by using the EPA EJ Screener (https://ejscreen.epa.gov/mapper/). To access, click the "Reports" icon in the upper left-hand corner; click "Select City"; search for the city name in the text box in the upper right-hand corner; and click on city map area. To generate a pdf of the standard report, click "EJScreen Community Report" in the pop-up box.

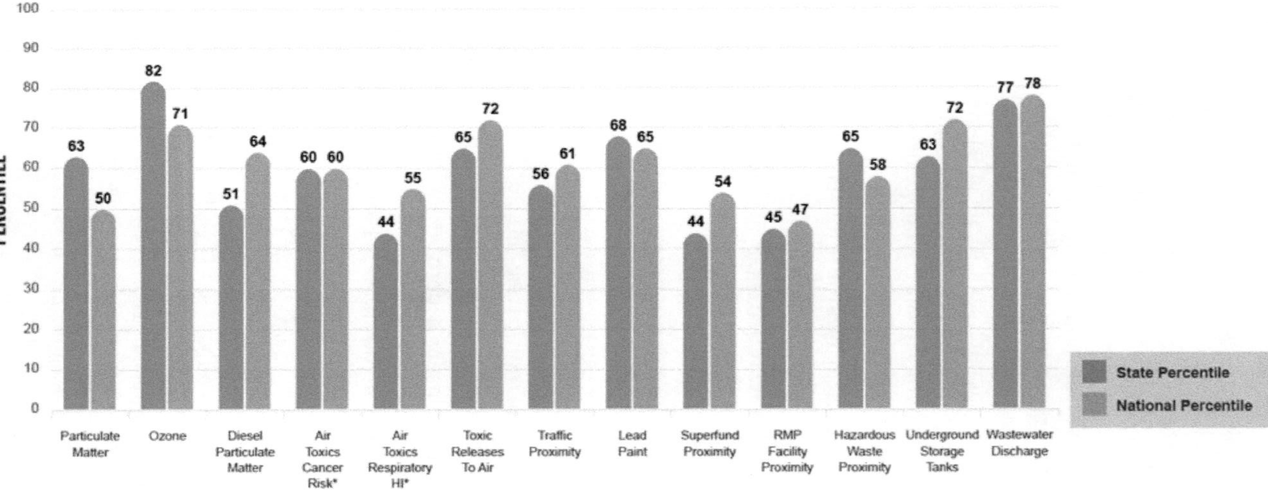

FIGURE C-6 Environmental Justice Index for St. Petersburg, Florida, compared to the state and nation.
NOTE: "The years for which the data are available, and the methods used, vary across these indicators. Important caveats and uncertainties apply to this screening-level information, so it is essential to understand the limitations on appropriate interpretations and applications of these indicators. Please see EJScreen documentation for discussion of these issues before using reports."
SOURCE: EPA. (n.d.). Environmental Justice Screening and Mapping Tool. https://ejscreen.epa.gov/mapper/

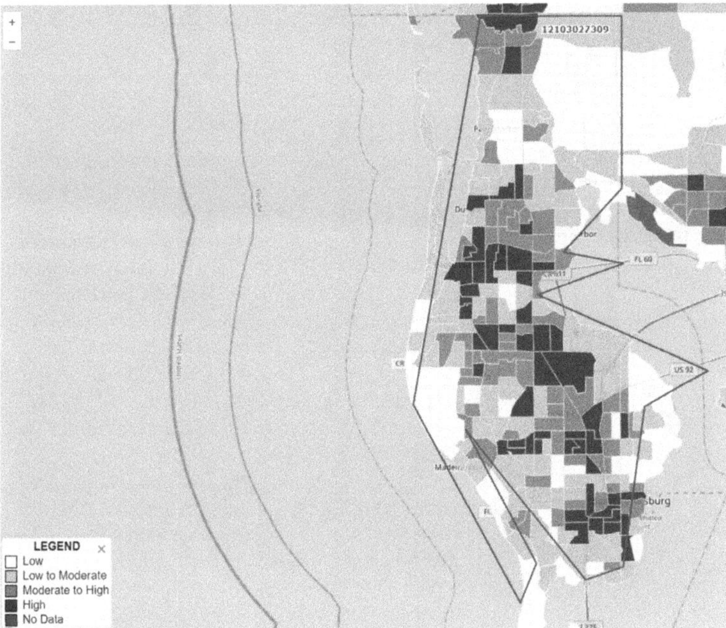

FIGURE C-7 The Environmental Justice Index rank for Pinellas County, Florida. SOURCE: CDC. (n.d.). Climate and Health Program Heat and Health Tracker. Heat exposure data. https://ephtracking.cdc.gov/Applications/heatTracker/

the more vulnerable the selected area is compared to the rest of the state and nation. St. Petersburg is close to the 50th percentile in the nation for particulate matter 2.5 ("fine inhalable particles, with diameters that are generally 2.5 micrometers and smaller"; U.S. Environmental Protection Agency, 2023), ozone (a greenhouse gas composed of three atoms of oxygen), diesel particulate matter, air toxics cancer risk, toxic releases to air, traffic proximity, lead paint, proximity to hazardous waste, underground storage tanks, and wastewater discharge.

Notable Recent Disasters Since 2000

St. Petersburg has been affected by five federally declared disasters[19] since the year 2000. Table C-2 below lists each of these disasters in reverse

[19]A major disaster declaration is made by the president for any natural event "that the president believes has caused damage of such severity that it is beyond the combined capabilities of state and local governments to respond." Following a major declaration, FEMA's Individual, Public, and Hazard Mitigation Assistance programs may be available to the affected state. More information is available at https://www.fema.gov/pdf/media/factsheets/dad_disaster_declaration.pdf

TABLE C-2 Hurricanes Impacting St. Petersburg, Florida, That Led to Federal Disaster Declarations Since 2000

Storm	Landfall Date	Damage and Impact	Federal Response
Hurricane Ian[a]	September 28, 2022	• 87 mph winds (Pinellas County) • Storm surge (Pinellas County) - 2–4 ft • 172,000 lost power (30% of county) • St. Petersburg - minor damage, mainly trees, power lines • Direct fatalities in Florida - 66 • Indirect fatalities in Florida - 90 • Storm surge fatalities in Florida - 41 • Total damages in the United States - $112.9 billion • Total damages in Florida - $109.5 billion	• September 23, 2022 - President issued a major disaster declaration • Individual assistance - >$1 billion to >380,000 Florida residents • SBA - $1.68 billion in low-interest loans • NFIP - $2.29 billion in claims • Public assistance - $552 million • FEMA's Transitional Sheltering Assistance Program - $647 million, >70,000 households, 4,500 in hotels • FEMA Direct Lease - 313 apartment homes • 366 families in temporary housing (more being built)
Hurricane Irma[b,c,d]	September 10, 2017	• Power outages, flooding, property, boat, and infrastructure damage • Closed roads, bridges, destroyed homes and businesses • 87% lost power, up to 7 days (Pinellas County) • Initial public property damage - >$10 million • Pinellas County residential losses - >$448 million • Displaced 200,000 jobs • Fatalities in Florida - 7 • Total damages in the United States - >$50 billion	• September 4, 2017 - Governor requested expedited disaster declaration • September 10, 2017 - President issued a major disaster declaration • Public assistance - >$2.45 billion for >7,900 projects • Resilience initiatives - >$35 million for 299 projects • HMGP - >$565 million for future prevention • FEMA and Florida Division of Emergency Management streamlined public assistance grant approval process • Individual assistance - >$1 billion for >780,000 individuals • NFIP - >$982 million • SBA - >$1.4 billion

TABLE C-2 Continued

Storm	Landfall Date	Damage and Impact	Federal Response
Hurricane Jeanne[i]	September 26, 2004	• Roof damage, toppled light poles, bridge flooding • >2.5 million lost power • 5–9 inches of rain • Direct fatalities in Florida - 3 • Total damages in the United States - >$7.6 billion	• President requested $7.1 billion for Jeanne and Ivan relief • Total request for Jeanne, Ivan, Charley, Frances - $12.2 billion • $600 million for road and highway repairs
Hurricane Frances[e]	September 5, 2004	• Widespread destruction - flooding, infrastructure, homes, businesses • Storm surge (Pinellas County) - 6 ft; homes flooded with 2 ft water • Storm surge (St. Petersburg, Tampa) - 2–4 ft • Direct fatalities in the United States - 7 • Direct fatalities in Florida - 5 • Indirect fatalities in the United States - 43 • Indirect fatalities in Florida - 32 • Insured property damage in the United States - >$4.4 billion • Insured property damage in Florida - >$4.1 billion • Total damages in the United States - $9 billion	• >1.2 million Floridians applied for aid, >$4.3 billion approved • Individual assistance - >$1.14 billion • Emergency response and protective measures - >$1.1 billion • SBA - >$1.4 billion • Public assistance - >$559 million • Housing inspections - >872,000 • 15,000+ manufactured units used for shelter • Lodging, rental, home repairs - >$187 million • Personal property repairs, medical expenses - >$215 million • Low-interest repair loans - >$313 million • Funds for local governments, nonprofits - >$130 million • Volunteers served >2.8 million meals • Disaster Medical Assistance Teams treated >1,400 patients

(continued)

TABLE C-2 Continued

Storm	Landfall Date	Damage and Impact	Federal Response
Hurricane Charley[f,g,h]	August 13, 2004	• >1.4 million residents evacuated • >2 million people lost power • Emergency shelters for >100,000 individuals • Fatalities in Florida - 27 • Damage to fire and police stations - limited response • Total damages in the United States - $15.4 billion • Insured losses - $6.8 billion	• August 13, 2004 - President issued a major disaster declaration • Federal assistance - $3 billion for >280,000 individuals • Housing assistance - $59 million • 12 Disaster Recovery Centers established • Assisted ~19,000 individuals • Medical teams treated ~3,000 patients • FEMA supplies - 1.2 million L of water, 8.1 million lbs. of ice, 2 million meals/snacks

NOTE: FEMA = Federal Emergency Management Agency, HMGP = Hazard Mitigation Grant Program, NFIP = National Flood Insurance Program, SBA = Small Business Administration.

[a]https://www.fema.gov/press-release/20230221/fema-assistance-hurricane-ian-survivors-surpasses-1-billion-biden-harris

[b]https://www.fema.gov/sites/default/files/2020-03/FEMA4337DRFL_Expedited.pdf

[c]https://www.fema.gov/press-release/20220829/florida-rebuilding-resilience-after-hurricane-irma

[d]https://www.fema.gov/sites/default/files/2020-07/mat-report_hurricane-irma_florida.pdf standard

[e]https://www.claimsjournal.com/news/southeast/2005/03/07/52202.htm

[f]https://georgewbush-whitehouse.archives.gov/news/releases/2004/08/20040827-9.html

[g]https://georgewbush-whitehouse.archives.gov/news/releases/2004/08/20040827-9.html

[h]https://www.fema.gov/sites/default/files/2020-08/fema488_mat_report_hurricane_charley_fl.pdf

[i]https://georgewbush-whitehouse.archives.gov/news/releases/2004/09/20040927-10.html

SOURCES: Beven II, J. L. (2014). *Tropical Cyclone Report: Hurricane Frances*. National Hurricane Center. https://www.nhc.noaa.gov/data/tcr/AL062004_Frances.pdf

Bucci, L., Alaka, L., Hagen, A., Delgado, S., & Beven, J. (2023). *Tropical Cyclone Report: Hurricane Ian* (Report No. AL092022). National Hurricane Center. https://www.nhc.noaa.gov/data/tcr/AL092022_Ian.pdf

Cangialosi, J. P., Latto, A. S., & Berg, R. (2018). *Tropical Cyclone Report: Hurricane Irma* (Report No. AL112017). National Hurricane Center. https://www.nhc.noaa.gov/data/tcr/AL112017_Irma.pdf

Lawrence, M. B., & Cobb, H. D. (2005). *Tropical Cyclone Report: Hurricane Jeanne*. National Hurricane Center. https://www.nhc.noaa.gov/data/tcr/AL112004_Jeanne.pdf

Razzano, T. (2022, September 29). Hurricane Ian: Scenes from St. Petersburg after the storm. *Patch*. https://patch.com/florida/stpete/hurricane-ian-scenes-st-petersburg-after-storm

chronological order and briefly describes the damage and impact caused by each, along with the federal response. Additionally, limited data were available on Pinellas County's evacuation plans and the damage and impact assessed on the city of St. Petersburg. There was also limited information found on FEMA's response to Hurricane Jeanne.

Throughout the years, the government's response to hurricanes impacting Florida, from Hurricane Ian in 2022 to Hurricane Jeanne in 2004, has experienced substantial progress in scope, effectiveness, and support offered. As weather events have become increasingly devastating, the government has assigned additional resources, funds, and personnel to facilitate relief and recovery measures. For instance, the federal government's, and FEMA's, response to Hurricane Ian was considerably more comprehensive compared to the response for Hurricane Jeanne, with billions of dollars allocated to relief funds and a more comprehensive deployment of resources. In addition, the process approving disaster relief has improved, as seen in the more streamlined public assistance grant approval process after Hurricane Irma. This progress highlights the federal government's commitment to adapting to the growing challenges posed by climate disasters, with an enhanced emphasis on resilience, reduction, and readiness. FEMA's aid initiatives have broadened to encompass not only immediate relief and assistance but also long-term recovery and disaster prevention. In addition, federal response efforts have become more comprehensive, encompassing a range of support measures such as emergency shelter, medical assistance, temporary housing, and financial assistance for individuals and businesses. As is outlined throughout this report, primarily in Chapter 9, while several aspects of disaster recovery have seen significant advancements, federal response has yet to fully incorporate the potential for relocation as an integral component of disaster recovery.

COMMUNITY PROFILE: MOBILE COUNTY AND COMMUNITY OF BAYOU LA BATRE, ALABAMA

Social Vulnerability Index

The 2020 national overall SVI score for Mobile County was 0.7947 where possible scores range from 0 (lowest vulnerability) to 1 (highest vulnerability; see Figure C-8). A score of 0.7947 indicates a high level of vulnerability.

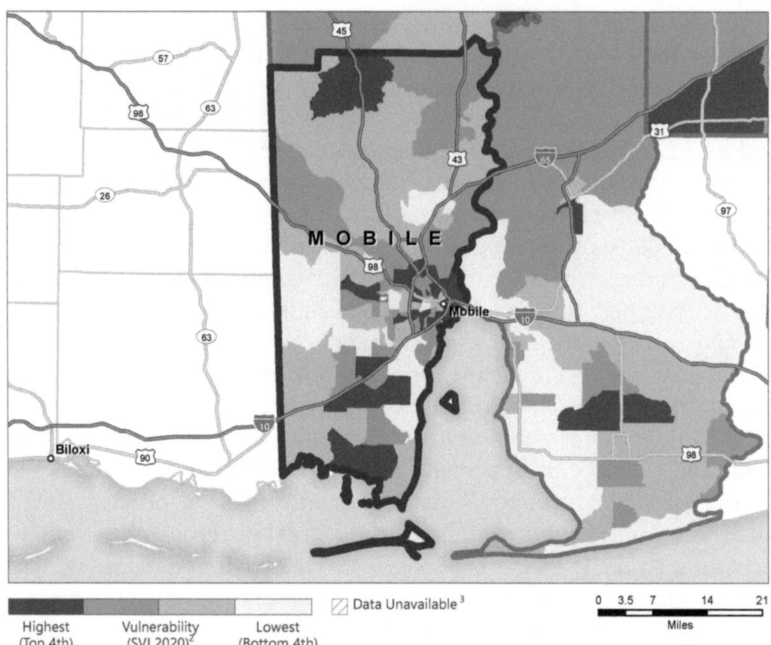

FIGURE C-8 The 2020 national overall Social Vulnerability Index for Mobile County, Alabama.
SOURCE: CDC/ATSDR. (2023). Social Vulnerability Index Interactive Map 2020. https://www.atsdr.cdc.gov/placeandhealth/svi/interactive_map.html

Health

For Mobile County,[20] the estimated age-adjusted[21] prevalence of asthma among adults age 18+ was 10.3 percent (CI: 9.8, 10.7) in 2020. This is around the national average[22] of 10 percent. The highest incidences of asthma found in the northeastern regions of Mobile County are in Mt. Vernon (11.6%), Prichard (12.5%), Muvico (12.3%), Theodore (11.7%), and Chickasaw City (11.5%).

The estimated age-adjusted prevalence of coronary heart disease among adults age 18+ was 6.8 percent (CI: 6.3, 7.3) in 2020. This is right below the national average of 7.1 percent. Like asthma, there are high rates of heart disease in the northeast regions of Mobile County. One of the areas

[20]See footnote 11.
[21]See footnote 12.
[22]See footnote 13.

with the highest rate of incidence (8.9%) is seen south of Bayou La Batre in the neighborhoods inclusive of Dauphin Island.

The estimated age-adjusted prevalence of adults aged 18+ who reported their mental health as "not good" for 14 or more days out of the past 30 was 16.9 percent (CI: 15.8, 18.0) in 2020. This is higher than the national average of 15.1 percent. Similar to asthma and heart disease, some of the highest incidence rates of poor mental health in Mobile County, Alabama, can be found northeast of the county, which includes Theodore (18.2%), Prichard (19.0%), Chickasaw (19.5%), Movico (18.3%), and Mt. Vernon (18.3%).

The estimated age-adjusted prevalence of fair or poor health among adults aged 18 years and older was 17.5 percent (CI: 15.7, 19.4) in 2020, which is higher than the national average of 16.3 percent (see Figure C-9).

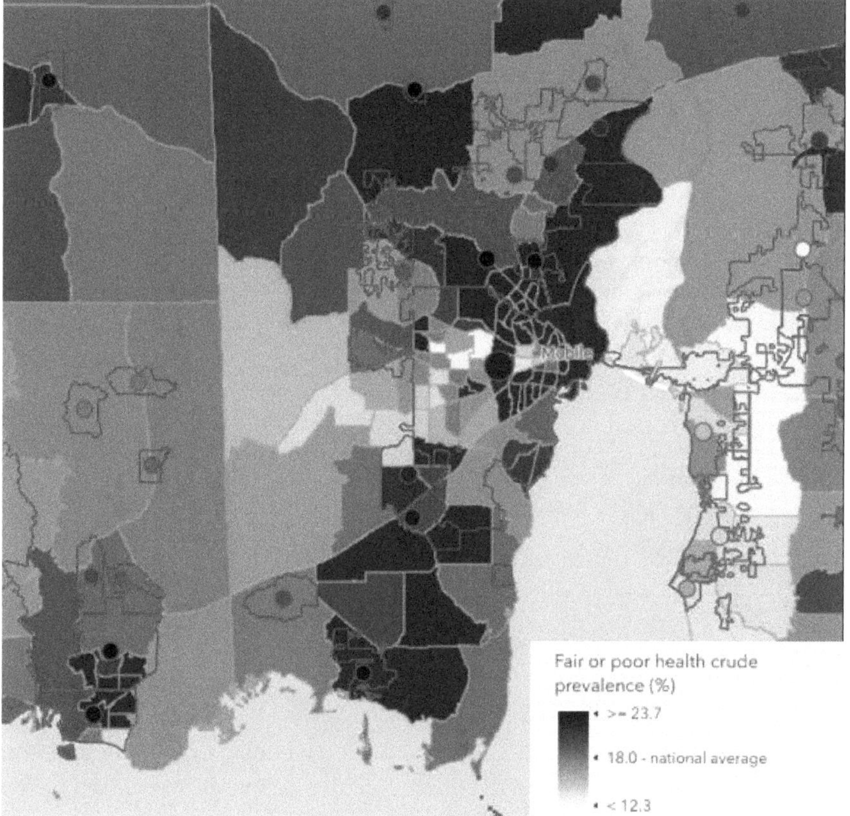

FIGURE C-9 The prevalence of adults aged 18+ who reported fair or poor health in 2020 in Mobile County, Alabama.
SOURCE: CDC. (2023). CDC PLACES. https://www.cdc.gov/places

Current Flood Risk

NOAA's Coastal County Snapshot[23] for Special Flood Hazard in Mobile County reports that 21.8 percent of county land falls within the 100-year floodplain where 13.6 percent of the county's population resides. Of the population residing in the projected floodplain region, 12.9 percent of that population is over the age of 65, and 13.7 percent of the population is in poverty (see Figure C-10). According to FEMA and USGS data, 4.7 percent of critical facilities (schools, police and fire stations, and medical facilities) in Mobile County are located within the 100-year floodplain, including two schools and six fire stations (see Figure C-11), and a little over 10 percent of Mobile County businesses (1,598), meaning that many community services, revenues, and salaries are at risk. Since 1991, over 10,000 flood insurance claims totaling over 315 million dollars have been made in Mobile County, with over 10 million dollars in National Flood Insurance Program payouts between 2016 and 2020. Although 94.4 percent of development inside the 100-year floodplain existed already in 1996, the other 5.6 percent (1.06 square miles) was added between 1996 and 2016.

Projected Flood Risk and Extreme Heat

By 2035, 317 homes (2.93% of the community's homes), home to 580 people, are projected to be at risk of chronic inundation[24] in Bayou La Batre. Together, these homes are valued at a little over 72 million dollars and contribute over $625,000 to the local property tax base. By 2100, 1,797

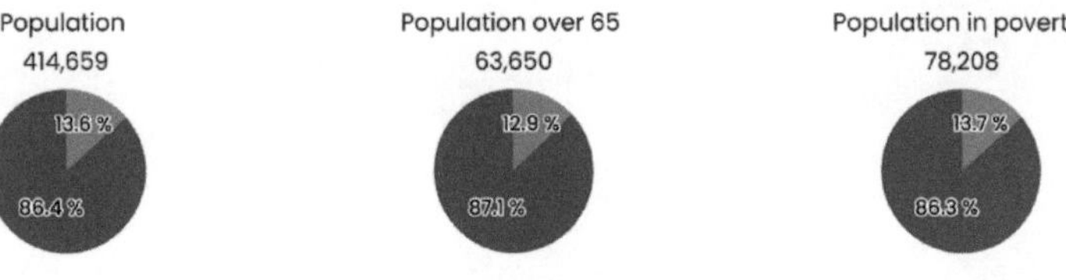

FIGURE C-10 Percentages of people that live in the floodplain in Mobile County, Alabama.
SOURCE: Office for Coastal Management. (2023). Coastal County Snapshots: Special flood hazard. National Oceanic and Atmospheric Administration. https://coast.noaa.gov/digitalcoast/tools/snapshots.html

[23]See footnote 14.
[24]See footnote 15.

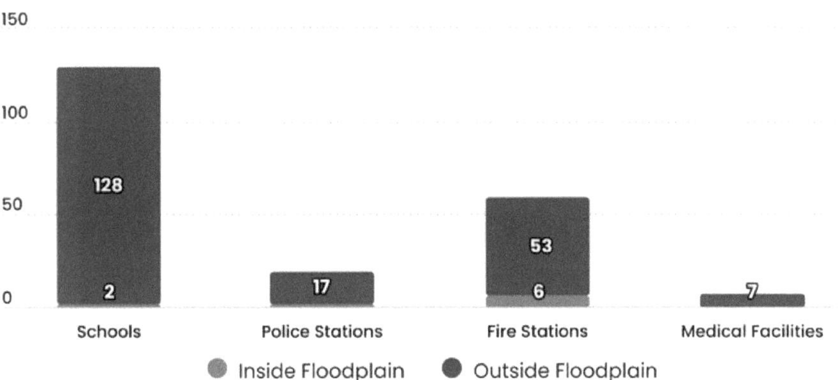

FIGURE C-11 Critical facilities in the 100-year floodplain in Mobile County, Alabama.
SOURCE: Office for Coastal Management. (2023). Coastal County Snapshots: Special flood hazard. National Oceanic and Atmospheric Administration. https://coast.noaa.gov/digitalcoast/tools/snapshots.html

homes (17%) with 3,289 residents will be at risk of chronic inundation. These homes are valued at almost 378 million dollars and contribute over 2.8 million dollars to the local property tax base.[25]

Figure C-12's map (left) shows critical facilities (hospitals, schools, fire and police stations, etc.) and "areas prone to flooding from one or more of the following hazards: high tide flooding; high risk (1% annual chance for A and V zones) and moderate risk (0.2% annual chance) flooding (designated by Federal Emergency Management Agency); storm surge for category 1 through category 3 hurricanes; sea level rise scenarios of 1, 2, and 3 feet; tsunami run-up zones (for high risk areas). The darker red color on the map indicates more flood hazard zones for that area" (Office for Coastal Management, n.d.b).

Figure C-12's map (right), based on 2014–2018 ACS five-year estimates, shows the "percentage of people living below the poverty line for census block groups in or near coastal flood-prone areas (e.g., four-person family with annual cash income below $23,283). People in poverty may not have adequate resources to prepare for or respond to hazards. Their limitations may include substandard housing, lack of transportation to evacuate, lack of social support systems, and incomes that limit their ability to afford temporary lodging, relocation, or housing improvements" (Office for Coastal Management, n.d.b).

[25]See footnote 16.

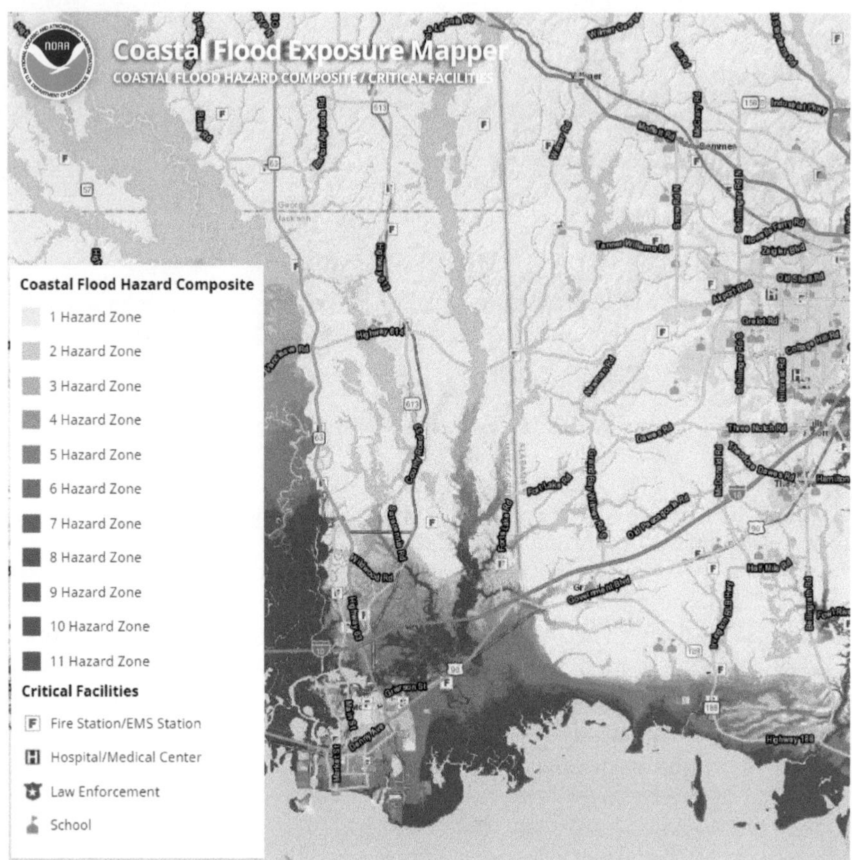

FIGURE C-12 Risk analysis and poverty in Mobile County, Alabama.
NOTES: NOAA's Coastal Flood Exposure Mapper allows users to select a hazard layer (options include coastal flood hazard composite, high tide flooding, FEMA flood zones, tsunami, storm surge, SLR), societal exposure (options include population density, poverty, elderly, employees), infrastructure exposure (development, critical facilities, development patterns), and ecosystem exposure (natural areas and open space, potential pollution sources, natural protection, wetland potential). Poverty rates and flood hazard zones are displayed in separate maps because when one is superimposed over the other, it is difficult to see both statistics. When areas with high poverty rates are also flood hazard zones, it indicates that vulnerable populations are also at risk of being impacted by flooding.
SOURCE: Office for Coastal Management. (n.d.c). Coastal Flood Exposure Mapper. National Oceanic and Atmospheric Administration. https://coast.noaa.gov/digitalcoast/tools/flood-exposure.html

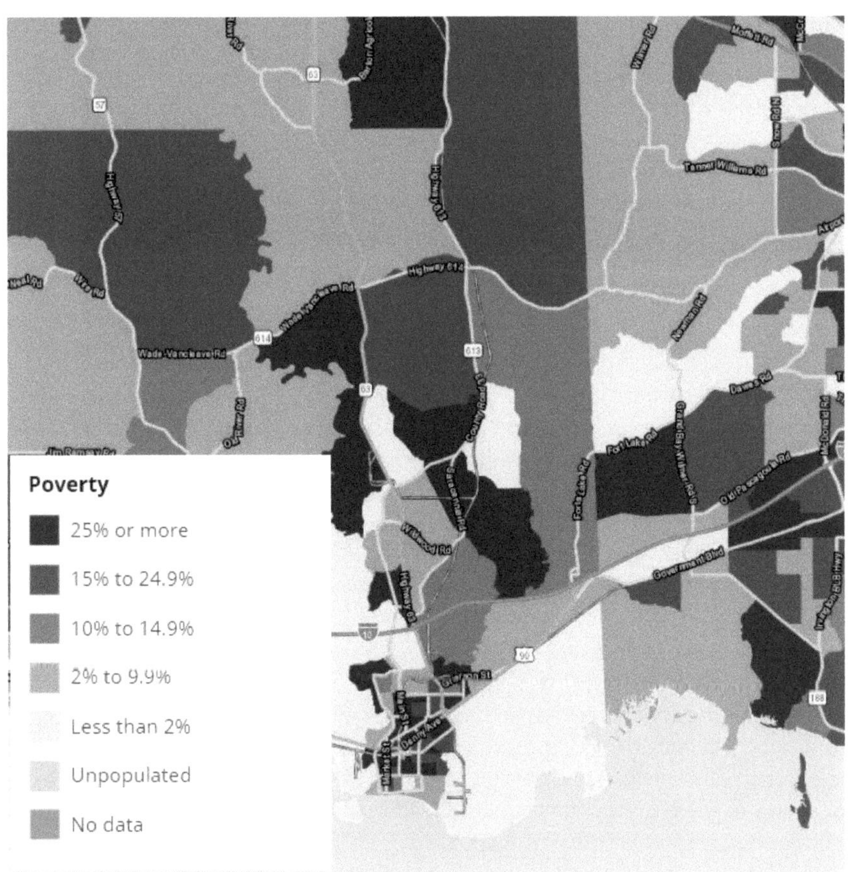

FIGURE C-12 Continued

National Integrated Heat Health Information System

- **Days above 90F:** Projected number of days (based on RCP 8.5)[26] with temperature over 90F in 2050 = 121 (compared to 71 days per year on average from 1976 to 2005)
- **Extreme heat days:** Projected number of days per year warmer than the top 1 percent historically in 2050 = 32 (compared to four per year from 1976 to 2005)

Environmental Justice Indexes

Figure C-13[27] shows where Mobile County falls in relation to the rest of the state and nation by using a percentile for various EJIs within state and national contexts (see also Figure C-14). For example, Mobile County's EJI for hazardous waste proximity is in the 82nd percentile when compared to the rest of the state of Alabama, and in the 73rd percentile for the rest of the country. This means that only about 18 percent of the population of Alabama lives in a block group with a higher EJI for hazardous waste proximity than the average person in Mobile County. Almost 30 percent of the U.S. population lives in a block group with a higher EJI for hazardous waste proximity than the average person in Mobile County. Mobile County is close to the 60th percentile in the nation for particulate matter; ozone; diesel particulate matter; risks associated with air toxins leading to cancer and respiratory issues, as indicated by the hazard index (HI); toxic releases to air; traffic proximity; lead paint; superfund proximity; proximity to facilities with a Risk Management Plan (RMP) for handling hazardous substances; and proximity to hazardous waste, underground storage tanks, and wastewater discharge.

Notable Recent Disasters Since 2000

Table C-3 below provides information for some of the most impactful hurricane disasters (all of which were federally declared major disasters[28]) since 2000 in Alabama, including the storm's impact, damage, and federal response. Throughout these disasters FEMA has worked closely with the Alabama Emergency Management Agency (AEMA) to identify local partners to distribute funds and resources from federal programs to affected communities.

The two largest hurricane disasters in Alabama since the year 2000 were Hurricane Katrina and Hurricane Ivan. These two hurricanes had the

[26]See footnote 17.
[27]See footnote 18.
[28]See footnote 19.

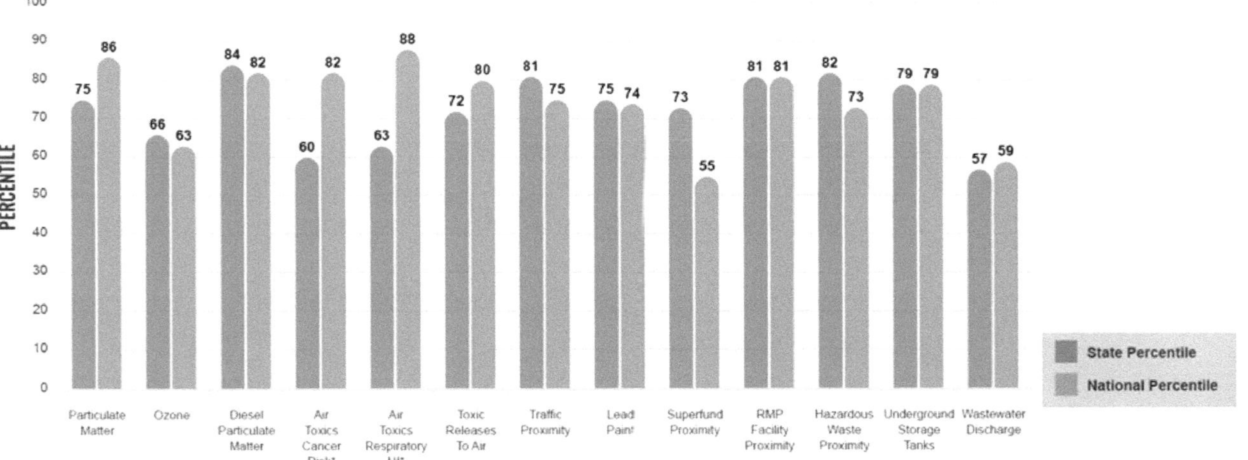

FIGURE C-13 Environmental Justice Index for Mobile County, Alabama, compared to the state and nation.
NOTE: The years for which the data are available, and the methods used, vary across these indicators. Important caveats and uncertainties apply to this screening-level information, so it is essential to understand the limitations on appropriate interpretations and applications of these indicators. Please see EJScreen documentation for discussion of these issues before using reports.
SOURCE: EPA. (n.d.). Environmental Justice Screening and Mapping Tool. https://ejscreen.epa.gov/mapper/

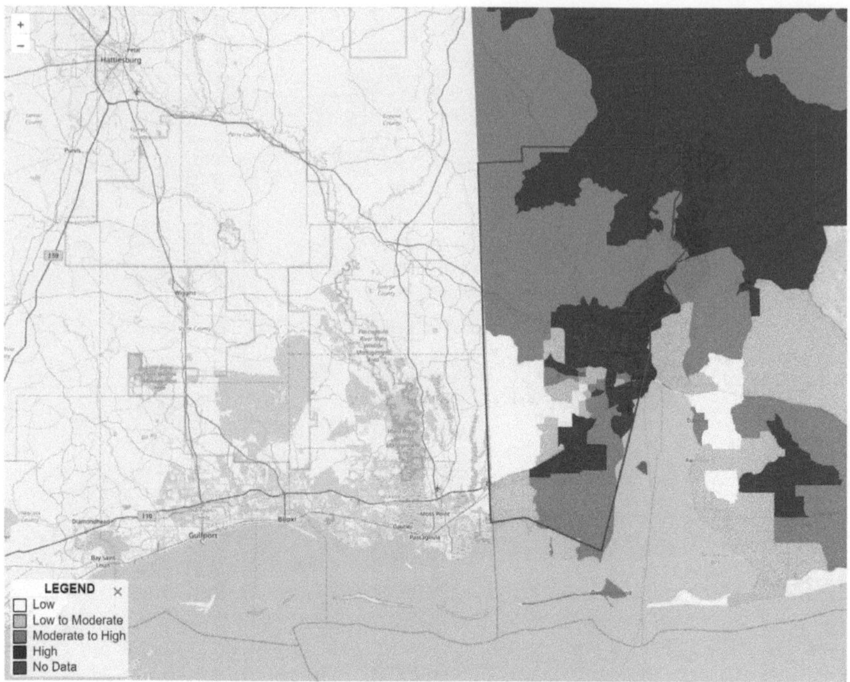

FIGURE C-14 The Environmental Justice Index rank for Mobile County, Alabama. SOURCE: CDC. (n.d.). Climate and Health Program Heat and Health Tracker. Heat exposure data. https://ephtracking.cdc.gov/Applications/heatTracker/

highest wind speeds, largest number of power outages to Alabama, and overall highest costs to the state. FEMA played a crucial role in coordinating and providing assistance to affected areas. It worked in partnership with state and local authorities to assess damage, provide emergency resources, and support recovery efforts. However, for some of these disasters there was no information on FEMA aid programs. This is particularly the case for Hurricane Ida, which was the most current hurricane, compounding the damage from the previous year's hurricanes. Some of the funding provided from FEMA for Hurricane Ida recovery was disbursed in an effort to meet the aid need for Hurricane Zeta and Hurricane Sally recovery, underscoring how much greater the current need is for aid.

There has been an increased focus in disaster preparedness for AEMA and the local government of Alabama. AEMA has worked on enhancing its resource management strategies, including stockpiling necessary supplies, pre-positioning assets and equipment, and ensuring effective coordination

TABLE C-3 Hurricanes Impacting Mobile County, Alabama, That Led to Federal Disaster Declarations Since 2000

Storm	Landfall Date	Damage and Impact	Federal Response
Hurricane Ida	August 29, 2021	• Storm surge - 2–4 ft • Rainfall - >10 inches • 35 tornadoes in the United States; 7 in Alabama • Indirect fatalities in the United States - 2 • 16 billion barrels of oil removed • Total damages in the United States - $75 billion	• August 28, 2021 - Governor declared state of emergency • U.S. Coast Guard and National Guard - search and rescue • HUD - $189.5 million
Hurricane Zeta[a,b,c,d]	October 28, 2020	• >400,000 lost power • 110 mph winds caused widespread damage • Storm surge - 6–10 ft • Total fatalities in Alabama - 1 • Total fatalities in the United States - 5 • Total damages in Alabama - >$840 million	• October 29, 2020 - Governor requested expedited major disaster declaration • November 24, 2020 - state withdrew request • December 1, 2020 - state requested individual assistance • December 10, 2020 - President issued a major disaster declaration • HUD - $501 million • Internal Revenue Service - Provided tax filing relief • >642,600 cubic yards of debris collected • Housing assistance - >$20 million • Other needs assistance - >$9.4 million • NFIP - >$3.5 million • SBA - $5.7 million • Public assistance - >$54 million • HMGP - >$250,000

(continued)

TABLE C-3 Continued

Storm	Landfall Date	Damage and Impact	Federal Response
Hurricane Sally[e,f,g,h]	September 16, 2020	• 105 mph winds • Rainfall - 30 inches • Storm surge - 7–9 ft • Direct fatalities in Alabama - 1 • Indirect fatalities in Alabama - 2 • Total damages in the United States - $7.3 billion • Total damages in Alabama - $1.5 million	• September 17, 2020 - Governor requested an expedited major disaster declaration • September 20, 2020 - President issued a major disaster declaration • Housing assistance - >$71.6 million • Other needs assistance - >$24.8 million • Public assistance - >$263.7 million • SBA - $109.8 million • NFIP - >$74.2 million • HMGP - $592,000
Hurricane Katrina[i,j]	August 28, 2005	• 80–145 mph winds • Storm surge - 10–15 ft, destroyed homes • Indirect fatalities in Alabama - 2 • >656,000 lost power • Oil spills along Gulf Coast • Tornadoes in Alabama - 4	• August 29, 2005 - President issued a major disaster declaration. • Disaster aid - $5.2 million • Created 5 Disaster Recovery Centers • CDBG Disaster Action Plan - $74 million • NFIP - $260 million
Hurricane Ivan[k,l,m]	September 16, 2004	• 120 mph winds • Storm surge - 10–15 ft • Tornadoes in Alabama - 8 • >489,000 lost power • Total damages in the United States - >$18.8 billion	• September 16, 2004 - President issued a major disaster declaration • HMGP - >$3 million • Food stamps - >$37 million • Individual assistance - $169 million for recovery • Temporary housing and repairs - $99.5 million • SBA - $73.4 million • NFIP - $59.1 million • 3 Disaster Recovery Centers opened, assisting ~50,000 residents

TABLE C-3 Continued

NOTE: CDBG = Community Development Block Grant, FEMA = Federal Emergency Management Agency, HMGP = Hazard Mitigation Grant Program, HUD = U.S. Department of Housing and Urban Development, NFIP = National Flood Insurance Program, SBA = Small Business Administration.

[a]https://www.fema.gov/press-release/20210212/federal-assistance-alabamas-zeta-recovery-tops-31-million

[b]https://adeca.alabama.gov/cdbg-disaster-recovery/hurricanes-sally-and-zeta/

[c]https://www.irs.gov/newsroom/irs-announces-tax-relief-for-hurricane-zeta-victims

[d]https://www.fema.gov/sites/default/files/documents/PDAReport_FEMA4573DR-AL.pdf

[e]https://www.weather.gov/mob/Sally

[f]https://www.fema.gov/press-release/20210318/federal-aid-tops-260-million-alabama-recovery-hurricane-sally

[g]https://www.fema.gov/disaster/4563

[h]https://www.fema.gov/sites/default/files/documents/PDAReport_expedited_FEMA4563DR-AL.pdf

[i]https://www.disastercenter.com/Katrina%20Alabama.html

[j]https://georgewbush-whitehouse.archives.gov/reports/katrina-lessons-learned/chapter5.html

[k]https://www.weather.gov/mob/ivan

[l]https://www.claimsjournal.com/news/southeast/2005/01/18/49787.htm

[m]https://georgewbush-whitehouse.archives.gov/news/releases/2004/09/20040916-1.html

SOURCES: Beven II, J. L., Hagen, A., & Berg, R. (2022). *Tropical Cyclone Report: Hurricane Ida* (Report No. AL092021). National Hurricane Center. https://www.nhc.noaa.gov/data/tcr/AL092021_Ida.pdf

Blake, E., Berg, R., & Hagen, A. (2020). *Tropical Cyclone Report: Hurricane Zeta* (Report No. AL282020). National Hurricane Center. https://www.nhc.noaa.gov/data/tcr/AL282020_Zeta.pdf

of resources between various response agencies and organizations. This has included the positioning of resources at locations of anticipated highest need. On behalf of the governor of Alabama, there have been preemptive declarations of emergency to help facilitate the distribution of aid throughout the state. Furthermore, AEMA is focused on making improvements to its communication systems and early warning systems to aid in accurate and timely information about approaching hurricanes and evacuation plans.

COMMUNITY PROFILE: HARRISON COUNTY AND COMMUNITY OF TURKEY CREEK, MISSISSIPPI

Social Vulnerability Index

The 2020 national overall SVI score for Harrison County was 0.9217 where possible scores range from 0 (lowest vulnerability) to 1 (highest

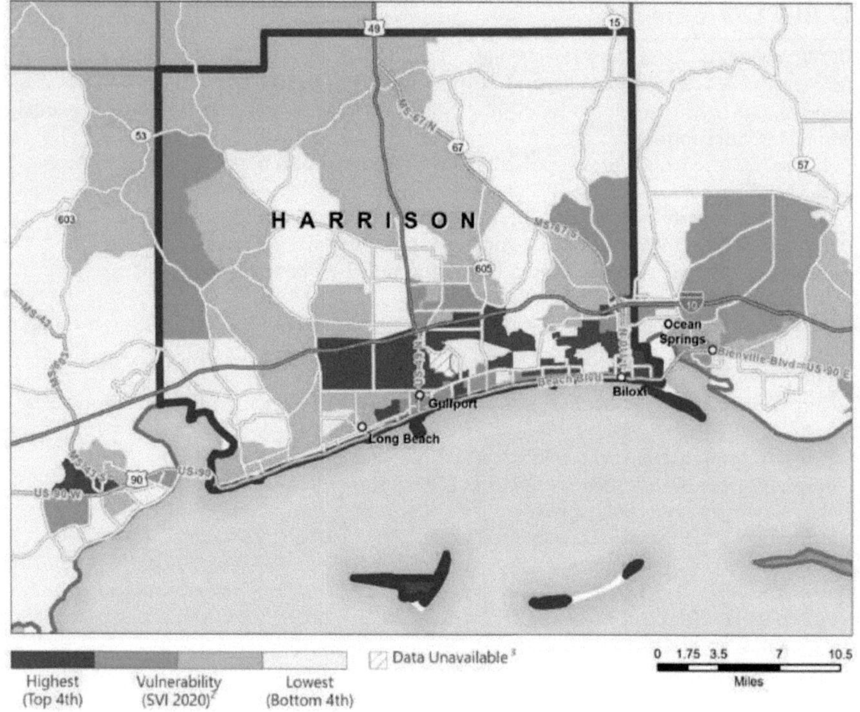

FIGURE C-15 The 2020 national overall Social Vulnerability Index for Harrison County, Mississippi.
SOURCE: CDC/ATSDR. (2023). Social Vulnerability Index Interactive Map 2020. FL. https://www.atsdr.cdc.gov/placeandhealth/svi/interactive_map.html

vulnerability; see Figure C-15). A score of 0.9217 indicates a high level of vulnerability.

Health

For Harrison County,[29] the estimated age-adjusted[30] prevalence of asthma among adults age 18+ was 9.3 percent (CI: 9.0, 9.7) in 2020. This is just below the national average[31] of 10 percent. The highest incidence

[29]See footnote 11.
[30]See footnote 12.
[31]See footnote 13.

of asthma found in the southwest regions of Harrison County are in tracts near Gulfport (12.7%) and Biloxi (10.9%).

The estimated age-adjusted prevalence of coronary heart disease among adults age 18+ was 6.5 percent (CI: 5.9, 7.0) in 2020. This is right below the national average of 7.1 percent. There are high rates of heart disease in the southeast regions of Harrison County. One of the areas with the highest rate of incidence is Henderson Point (7.3%).

The estimated age-adjusted prevalence of adults aged 18+ who reported their mental health as "not good" for 14 or more days out of the past 30 was 15.2 percent (CI: 14.3, 16.0) in 2020. This is similar to the national average of 15.1 percent. Some of the highest incidence rates of poor mental health in Harrison County can be found around the city of Gulfport.

The estimated age-adjusted prevalence of fair or poor health among adults aged 18 years and older was 18.3 percent (CI: 16.2, 20.7) in 2020, almost 3 percent higher than the national average of 15.8 percent (see Figure C-16).

Current Flood Risk

NOAA's Coastal County Snapshot[32] for Special Flood Hazard in Harrison County reports that 19.6 percent of county land falls within the 100-year floodplain where 26 percent of the county's population resides. Of the population residing in the projected floodplain region, 27.6 percent of that population is over the age of 65, and 28.5 percent of the population is in poverty (see Figure C-17). According to FEMA and USGS data, 9.1 percent of critical facilities (schools, police and fire stations, and medical facilities) in Harrison County are located within the 100-year floodplain, including seven schools and four fire stations (see Figure C-18), and a little over 13 percent of Harrison County businesses (1,148), meaning that many community services, revenues, and salaries are at risk. Since 1991, over 14,287 flood insurance claims totaling 1 billion dollars have been made in Harrison County; all of these National Flood Insurance Program payouts were made between 2001 and 2005. Although 88.4 percent of development inside the 100-year floodplain existed already in 1996, the other 11.6 percent (2.59 square miles) was added between 1996 and 2016.

Projected Flood Risk and Extreme Heat

Under the National Climate Assessment's moderate SLR scenario,[33] by 2035, 17 homes (0.1% of the community's homes), home to 35 people,

[32]See footnote 14.
[33]See footnote 16.

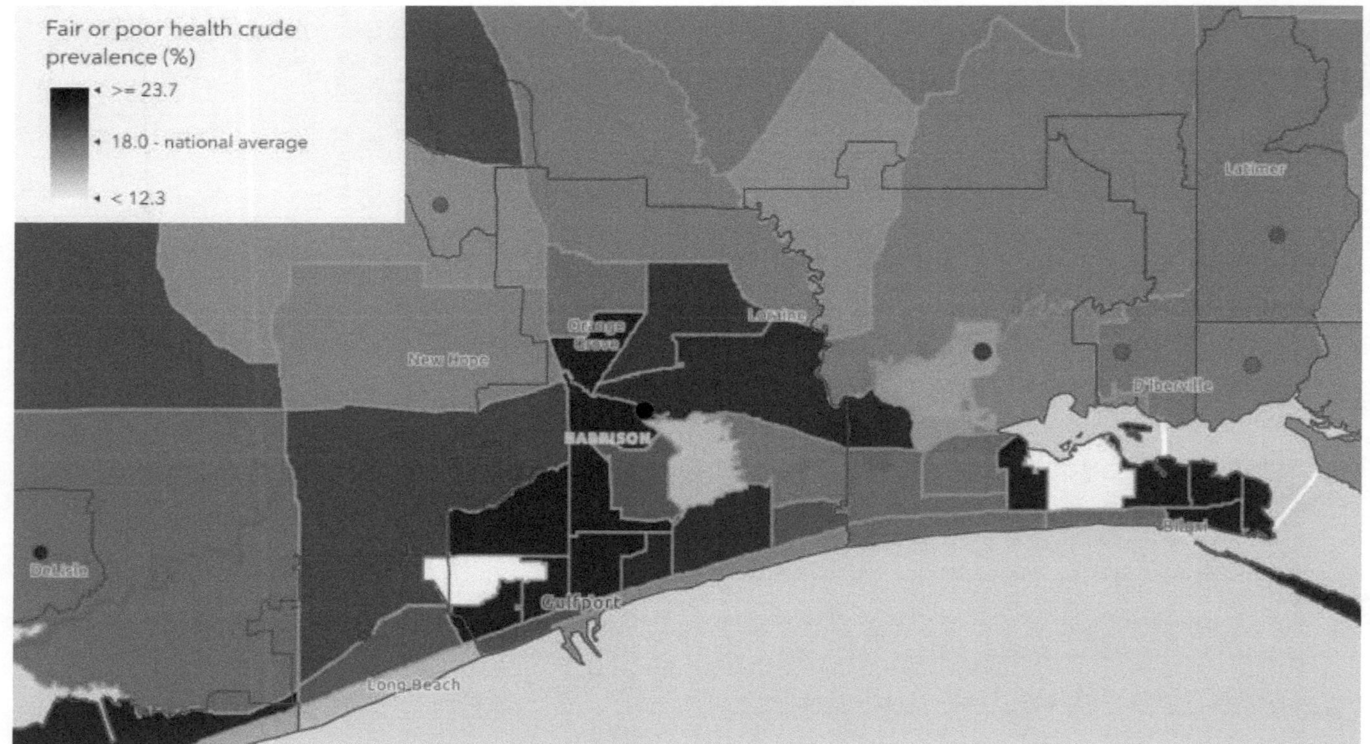

FIGURE C-16 The prevalence of adults aged 18+ who reported fair or poor health in 2020 in Harrison County, Mississippi.
SOURCE: CDC. (2023). CDC PLACES. https://www.cdc.gov/places

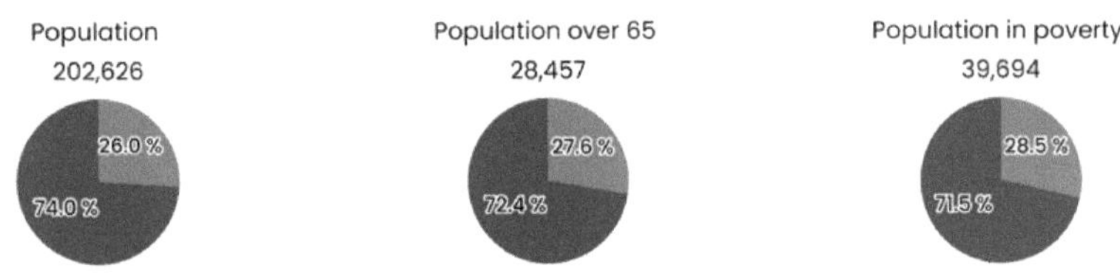

FIGURE C-17 Percentages of people that live in the floodplain in Harrison County, Mississippi.
SOURCE: Office for Coastal Management. (n.d.a). Coastal County Snapshots: Special flood hazard. National Oceanic and Atmospheric Administration. https://coast.noaa.gov/digitalcoast/tools/snapshots.html

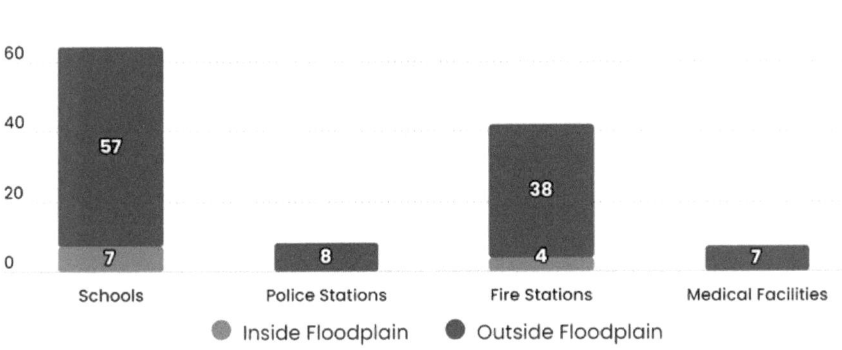

FIGURE C-18 Critical facilities in the 100-year floodplain in Harrison County, Mississippi.
SOURCE: Office for Coastal Management. (n.d.a). Coastal County Snapshots: Special flood hazard. National Oceanic and Atmospheric Administration. https://coast.noaa.gov/digitalcoast/tools/snapshots.html

are projected to be at risk of chronic inundation[34] in Harrison County. Together, these homes are valued at a little over 2 million dollars and contribute over $32,000 to the local property tax base. By 2100, 171 homes (1%) with 349 residents will be at risk of chronic inundation. These homes are valued at over 23 million dollars and contribute over $281,000 to the local property tax base.

Figure C-19's map shows critical facilities (hospitals, schools, fire and police stations, etc.) and "areas prone to flooding from one or more of the following hazards: high tide flooding; high risk (1% annual chance for A

[34] See footnote 15.

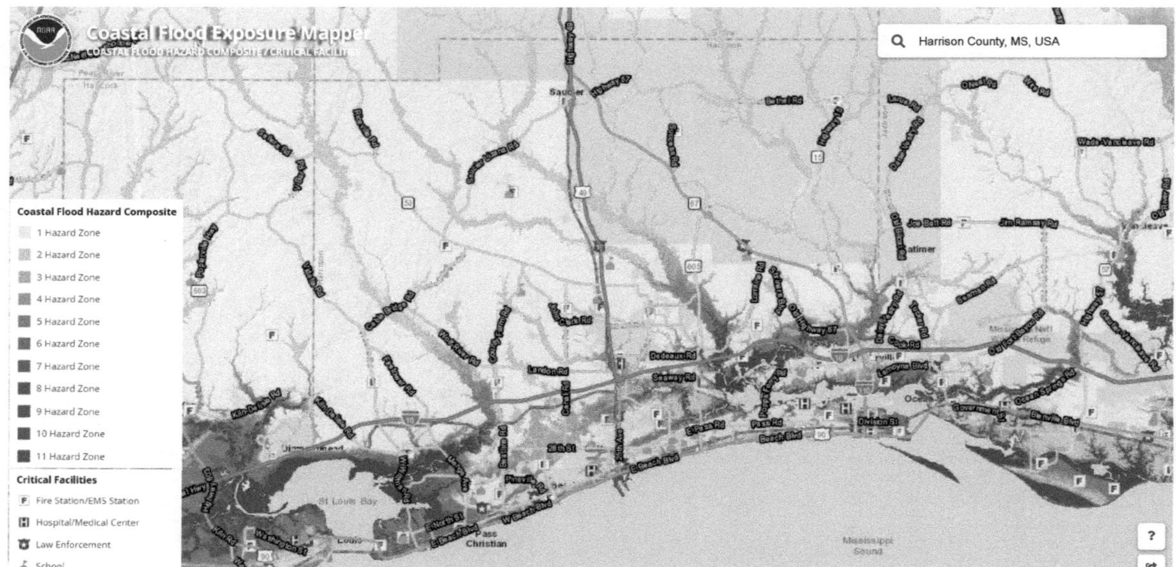

FIGURE C-19 Critical facilities prone to flooding in Harrison County, Mississippi.
NOTES: NOAA's Coastal Flood Exposure Mapper allows users to select a hazard layer (options include coastal flood hazard composite, high tide flooding, FEMA flood zones, tsunami, storm surge, SLR), societal exposure (options include population density, poverty, elderly, employees), infrastructure exposure (development, critical facilities, development patterns), and ecosystem exposure (natural areas and open space, potential pollution sources, natural protection, wetland potential). Poverty rates and flood hazard zones are displayed in separate maps because when one is superimposed over the other, it is difficult to see both statistics. When areas with high poverty rates are also flood hazard zones, it indicates that vulnerable populations are also at risk of being impacted by flooding.
SOURCE: Office for Coastal Management. (n.d.c). Coastal Flood Exposure Mapper. National Oceanic and Atmospheric Administration. https://coast.noaa.gov/digitalcoast/tools/flood-exposure.html

and V zones) and moderate risk (0.2% annual chance) flooding (designated by FEMA); storm surge for category 1 through category 3 hurricanes; sea level rise scenarios of 1, 2, and 3 feet; tsunami run-up zones (for high risk areas). The darker red color on the map indicates more flood hazard zones for that area" (Office for Coastal Management, n.d.b).

Figure C-20's map, based on 2014–2018 ACS five-year estimates, shows the "percentage of people living below the poverty line for census block groups in or near coastal flood-prone areas (e.g., four-person family with annual cash income below $23,283). People in poverty may not have adequate resources to prepare for or respond to hazards. Their limitations may include substandard housing, lack of transportation to evacuate, lack of social support systems, and incomes that limit their ability to afford temporary lodging, relocation, or housing improvements" (Office for Coastal Management, n.d.b).

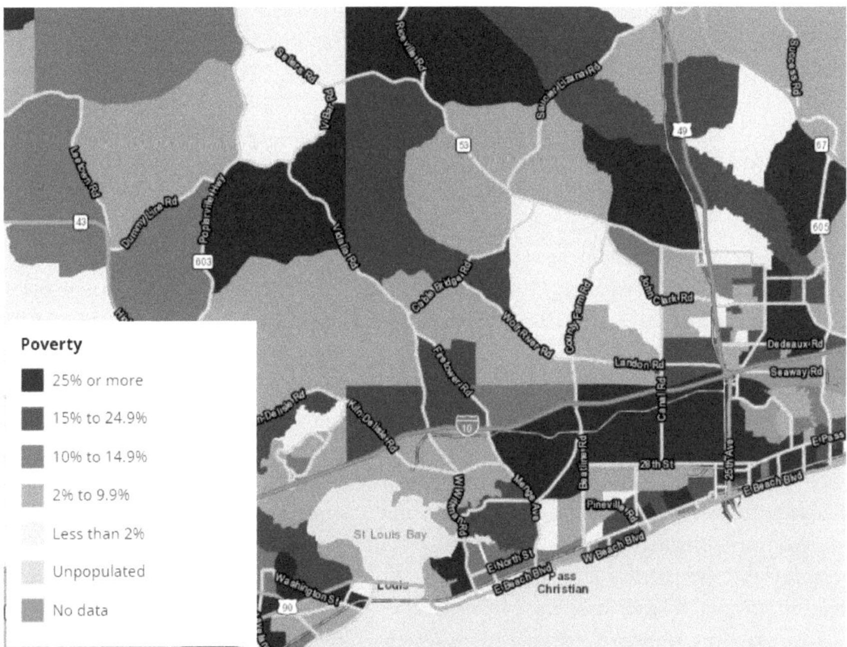

FIGURE C-20 People living below the poverty line in Harrison County, Mississippi.
SOURCE: Office for Coastal Management. (n.d.c). Coastal Flood Exposure Mapper. National Oceanic and Atmospheric Administration. https://coast.noaa.gov/digitalcoast/tools/flood-exposure.html

National Integrated Heat Health Information System

- **Days above 90F:** Projected number of days (based on RCP 8.5)[35] with temperature over 90F in 2050 = 118 (compared to 66 days per year on average from 1976 to 2005)
- **Extreme heat days:** Projected number of days per year warmer than the top 1 percent historically in 2050 = 33 (compared to four per year from 1976 to 2005)

Environmental Justice Indexes

Figure C-21[36] shows where Harrison County falls in relation to the rest of the state and nation by using a percentile for various EJIs within state and national contexts (see also Figure C-22). For example, Harrison County's EJI for proximity to a superfund site is in the 76th percentile for the state of Mississippi and 74th for the nation as a whole. This means that only about 24 percent of the population of Mississippi lives in a block group with a higher EJI for proximity to a superfund site than the average person in Harrison County. Similarly, 26 percent of the U.S. population lives in a block group with a higher EJI for proximity to a superfund site than the average person in Harrison County. In general, the higher the percentile, the more vulnerable the selected area is compared to the rest of the state and nation. Harrison County is approximately at or above the 50th percentile in the nation in particulate matter, ozone, diesel particulate matter, air toxics cancer risk, air toxics respiratory HI, toxic releases to air, traffic proximity, superfund proximity, RMP facility proximity, proximity to hazardous waste, and underground storage tank.

Notable Recent Disasters Since 2000

The hurricane data provided gives a snapshot of each event's impact, damage, and federal response. However, there was a lack of data on federal hurricane relief efforts beyond the dollars obligated for individual assistance, public assistance, and/or Hazard Mitigation Grant Program (HMGP) assistance. There was also an absence of data on insurance payouts outside the National Flood Insurance Program, and non-monetary federal assistance, such as manpower and resources from federal agencies like FEMA.

Between 2000 and the present day, Mississippi has been struck by several notable hurricanes, including Hurricane Ida (2021), Hurricane Zeta (2020), Hurricane Nate (2017), Hurricane Isaac (2012), and Hurricane

[35]See footnote 17.

[36]See footnote 18.

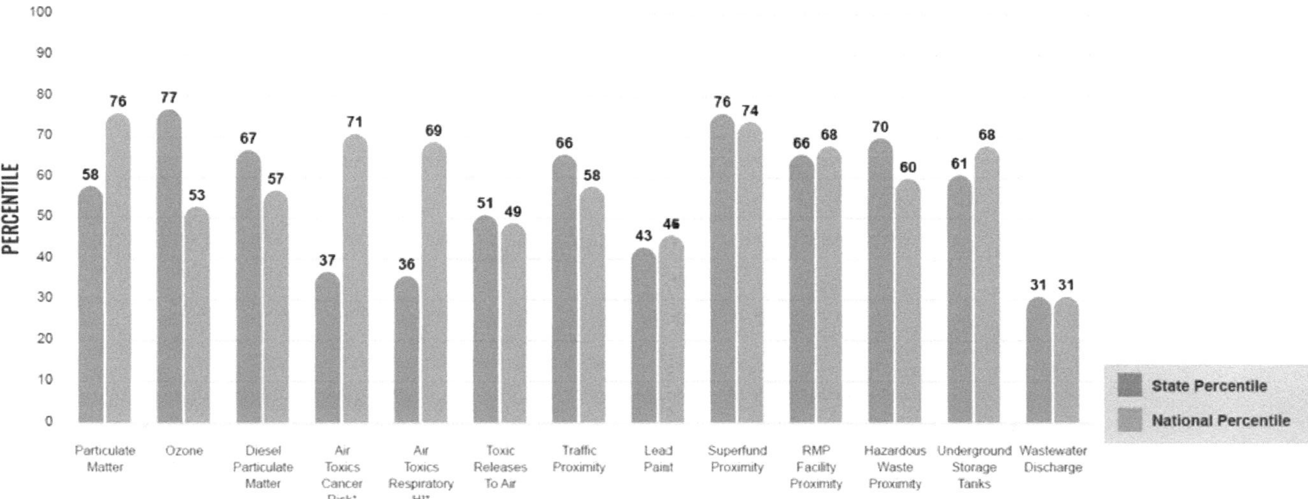

FIGURE C-21 Environmental Justice Index for Harrison County, Mississippi, compared to the state and nation.
NOTE: The years for which the data are available, and the methods used, vary across these indicators. Important caveats and uncertainties apply to this screening-level information, so it is essential to understand the limitations on appropriate interpretations and applications of these indicators. Please see EJScreen documentation for discussion of these issues before using reports.
SOURCE: EPA. (n.d.). Environmental Justice Screening and Mapping Tool. https://ejscreen.epa.gov/mapper/

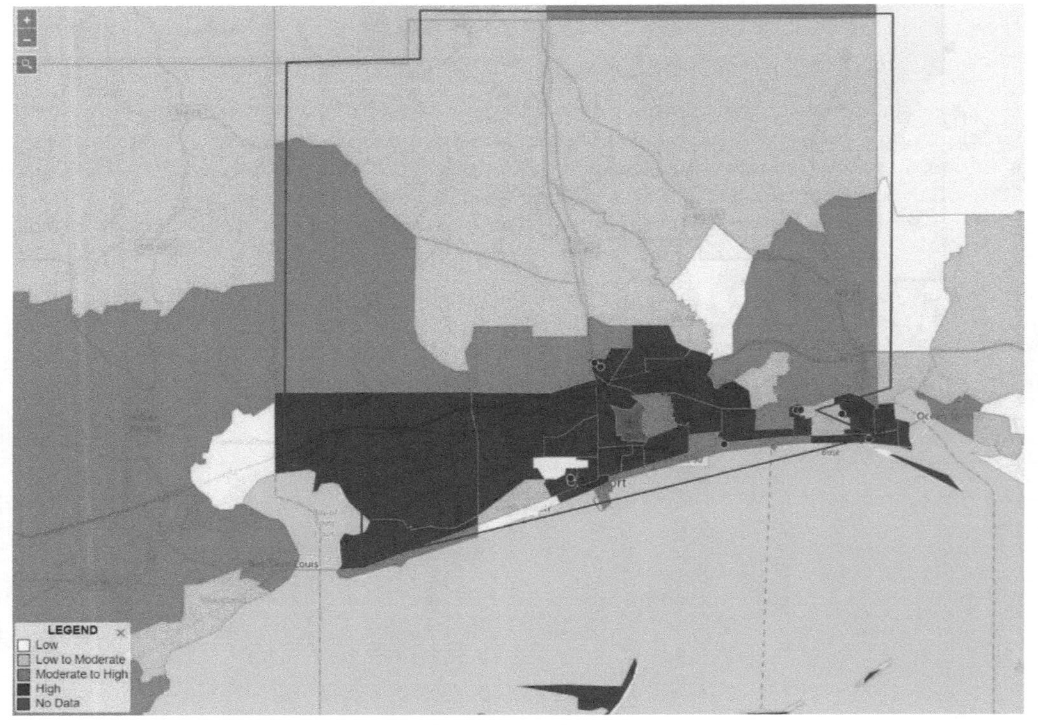

FIGURE C-22 The Environmental Justice Index rank for Harrison County, Mississippi. Harrison County has areas with low to high environmental justice indexes.
SOURCE: CDC. (n.d.). Climate and Health Program Heat and Health Tracker. Heat exposure data. https://ephtracking.cdc.gov/Applications/heatTracker/

Katrina (2005), each of which were federally declared disasters (see Table C-4).[37] These storms resulted in varying degrees of damage, with Hurricane Katrina causing the most devastation, including over 238 fatalities and 186.3 billion dollars in total U.S. damages. The federal response to these disasters has varied, with assistance ranging from millions to billions of dollars to support housing, public assistance grants, and other needs. The impact of these storms on Mississippi has been significant, with power outages, storm surges, heavy rainfall, and tornadoes causing widespread destruction and loss of life.

Over the years, the federal government's response to hurricanes in Mississippi has evolved in several ways, adapting to the severity and impact of each storm. While the amount of aid has generally correlated with the extent of the damage, there has been a growing focus on improving the speed and efficiency of response. Additionally, the federal government has increased its emphasis on preparedness, mitigation, and recovery efforts in order to build resilience against future disasters. Parallel to this, the Mississippi Emergency Management Agency (MEMA) has continually refined its disaster response plans based on experiences from previous hurricanes. It has focused on better pre-disaster planning, including more detailed evacuation plans, and has worked on improving communication with the public during emergencies. The state has also invested in infrastructure upgrades, such as reinforcing levees and improving the resilience of the power grid, to better withstand hurricanes. Additionally, MEMA has worked to ensure more effective coordination with local, federal, and nongovernmental partners for a comprehensive response. It has also focused on improving recovery processes, such as streamlining the application process for disaster assistance, to help residents recover more quickly after a storm.

COMMUNITY PROFILE: SOUTHEAST LOUISIANA (LAFOURCHE AND TERREBONNE PARISHES)

Social Vulnerability Index

The 2020 national overall SVI score for Lafourche Parish scored 0.8033 and Terrebonne Parish 0.86 where possible scores range from 0 (lowest vulnerability) to 1 (highest vulnerability), indicating high vulnerability (see Figures C-23 and C-24).

---

[37]See footnote 19.

TABLE C-4 Hurricanes Impacting Harrison County, Mississippi, That Led to Federal Disaster Declarations Since 2000

Storm	Landfall Date	Damage and Impact	Federal Response
Hurricane Ida[a]	August 29, 2021	• Storm surge - 4–7 ft • Rainfall - >10 inches • 24 tornadoes in the United States; 13 in Mississippi • Direct fatalities in the United States - 55 • Indirect fatalities in the United States - 28 (including 13 from heat exhaustion due to power outages) • Total damages in the United States - $75 billion	• September 29, 2021 - Governor requested a major disaster declaration • October 22, 2021 - President issued a major disaster declaration • Housing assistance - $9.2 million • Other needs assistance - $1.5 million • Approved applications - 2,908 • Public assistance grants - $28.2 million • HMGP obligated - $350,000
Hurricane Zeta[b]	October 28, 2020	• Homes damaged by wind/debris - 10,000 • Storm surge - 6–10 ft • >200,000 lost power • Rainfall - 4–6 inches • Direct fatalities in the United States - 5 • Direct fatalities in Mississippi - 1 • Indirect fatalities in the United States - 2 • Indirect fatalities in Mississippi - 1 • Total damages in the United States - $4.4 billion • Total damages in Mississippi - $635 million	• November 24, 2020 - Governor requested a major disaster declaration • December 31, 2020 - President issued a major disaster declaration • $17.39 million in FEMA assistance • 4,827 individuals and households approved • Housing assistance - $14.4 million • Other needs - $2.99 million • SBA loans - $23.9 million for 877 applicants • NFIP - 829 claims; $11.1 million paid

TABLE C-4 Continued

Storm	Landfall Date	Damage and Impact	Federal Response
Hurricane Nate[c]	October 8, 2017	• Max inundation - 6–9 ft above ground • Rainfall - 3–7 inches • 16 tornadoes across 4 states (including Mississippi) • Total damages in the United States - $225 million • Reported damages - Minor roof, shingle damage, one mobile home destroyed by a tree	• October 27, 2017 - Governor requested a major disaster declaration • November 22, 2017 - President issued a major disaster declaration • Public assistance grants - $11 million • HMGP obligated - $360,000
Hurricane Isaac[d]	August 28, 2012	• Inundation levels - 5–9 ft above ground • River reversal - Mississippi River flowed backward for 24 hours • Surge flooding - Most severe in Harrison County, Mississippi • Rainfall - 10+ inches, caused moderate to record river flooding • Tornadoes - 6 in Mississippi, 3 injuries • Direct fatalities in the United States - 5 • Direct fatalities in Mississippi - 2 • Insured damage - $970 million • NFIP payout - $407 million for surge and inland flooding • Total damages in the United States - $2.35 billion	• August 29, 2012 - Governor requested an expedited major disaster declaration • August 29, 2012 - President issued a major disaster declaration • Housing assistance - $15 million • Other needs assistance - $2.7 million • Individual and housing program - $18 million • Approved assistance requests - 6,664 • Public assistance grants - $41 million

(*continued*)

TABLE C-4 Continued

Storm	Landfall Date	Damage and Impact	Federal Response
Hurricane Katrina[e,f]	August 29, 2005	• Rainfall - 8–10 in • Tidal surge - 20–30 ft, 55 ft sea waves in Mississippi • ~800,000 lost power • Mississippi fatalities - 238 • Total damages in the United States - $186.3 billion • Insured losses - $41.1 billion	• September 2, 2005 - President issued a major disaster declaration • Housing assistance - $877 million • Other needs assistance - $419 million • Approved requests - 274,761 • Public assistance grants - $3 billion

NOTES: FEMA = Federal Emergency Management Agency, HMGP = Hazard Mitigation Grant Program, NFIP = National Flood Insurance Program, SBA = Small Business Administration.

[a]https://www.fema.gov/disaster/4626

[b]https://www.fema.gov/fact-sheet/hurricane-zeta-recovery-update-009

[c]https://www.fema.gov/disaster/4350

[d]https://www.fema.gov/es/disaster/4081

[e]https://www.fema.gov/es/disaster/1604

[f]https://www.fema.gov/disaster-federal-register-notice/initial-notice-301

SOURCES: Berg, R. (2013). *Tropical Cyclone Report: Hurricane Isaac.* National Hurricane Center. https://www.nhc.noaa.gov/data/tcr/AL092012_Isaac.pdf

Beven II, J. L., & Berg, R. (2018). *Tropical Cyclone Report: Hurricane Nate.* National Hurricane Center. https://www.nhc.noaa.gov/data/tcr/AL162017_Nate.pdf

Beven II, J. L., Hagen, A., & Berg, R. (2022). *Tropical Cyclone Report: Hurricane Ida.* National Hurricane Center. https://www.nhc.noaa.gov/data/tcr/AL092021_Ida.pdf

Blake, E., Berg, R., & Hagen, A. (2020). *Tropical Cyclone Report: Hurricane Zeta.* National Hurricane Center. https://www.nhc.noaa.gov/data/tcr/AL282020_Zeta.pdf

Hartwig, R. P., & Wilkinson, C. (2010). *Hurricane Katrina: The five year anniversary.* Insurance Information Institute. https://www.iii.org/sites/default/files/1007Katrina5Anniversary.pdf

Nuwer, D. S. (2017, July 11). Hurricane Katrina. *Mississippi Encyclopedia.* Center for Study of Southern Culture.

Health[38]

In Lafourche Parish, the estimated age-adjusted[39] prevalence of asthma among adults aged 18 and older was slightly lower than the national percentage at 8.3 percent (CI: 7.9, 8.8) in 2020. In Terrebonne Parish, the estimated prevalence of asthma among adults aged 18 and older was 10.0 percent (CI: 9.7, 10.4) in 2020. These compared to a national average[40] of 10.0 percent. This indicates that the prevalence of asthma in Lafourche is

[38]See footnote 11.

[39]See footnote 12.

[40]See footnote 13.

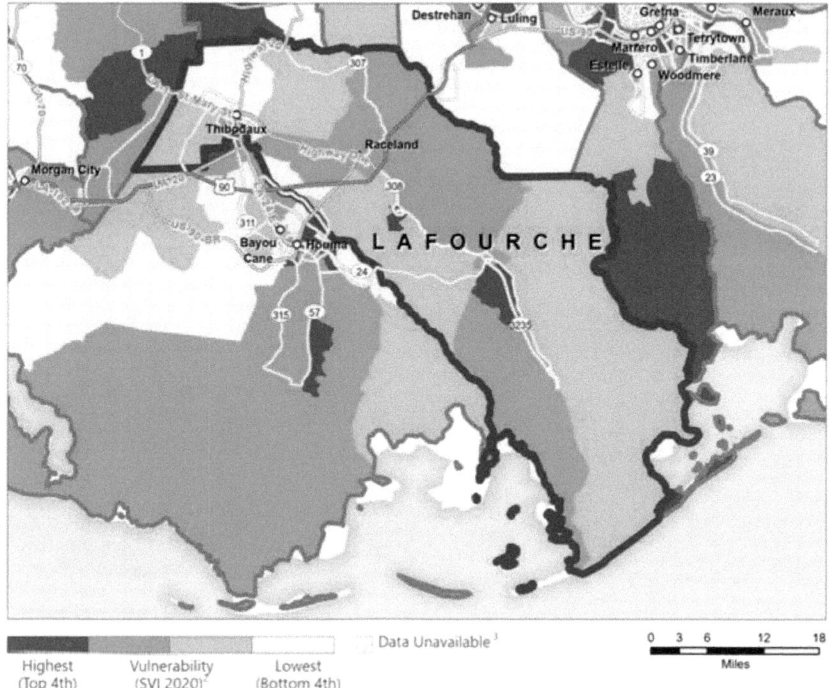

FIGURE C-23 The 2020 national overall Social Vulnerability Index for Lafourche Parish, Louisiana.
SOURCE: CDC/ATSDR. (2023). Social Vulnerability Index Interactive Map 2020. https://www.atsdr.cdc.gov/placeandhealth/svi/interactive_map.html

lower than the national average while in Terrebonne the prevalence is the equivalent.

The estimated age-adjusted prevalence of coronary heart disease among adults aged 18 and older in Lafourche Parish was 7.6 percent (CI: 7.1, 8.0) in 2020. In Terrebonne Parish, the prevalence was slightly lower at 7.5 percent (CI: 7.0, 7.9). Compared to a national average of 6.2 percent, the prevalence of heart disease in both parishes is slightly higher.

The estimated age-adjusted prevalence of adults aged 18+ who reported their mental health as "not good" for 14 or more days out of the past 30 days in Lafourche Parish was 19.3 percent (CI: 18.4, 20.2) in 2020, while the estimated prevalence in Terrebonne Parish was 18.7 percent (CI: 18.0, 19.4). The prevalence of adults with poor mental health across southeast Louisiana is higher than the national average of 15.1 percent.

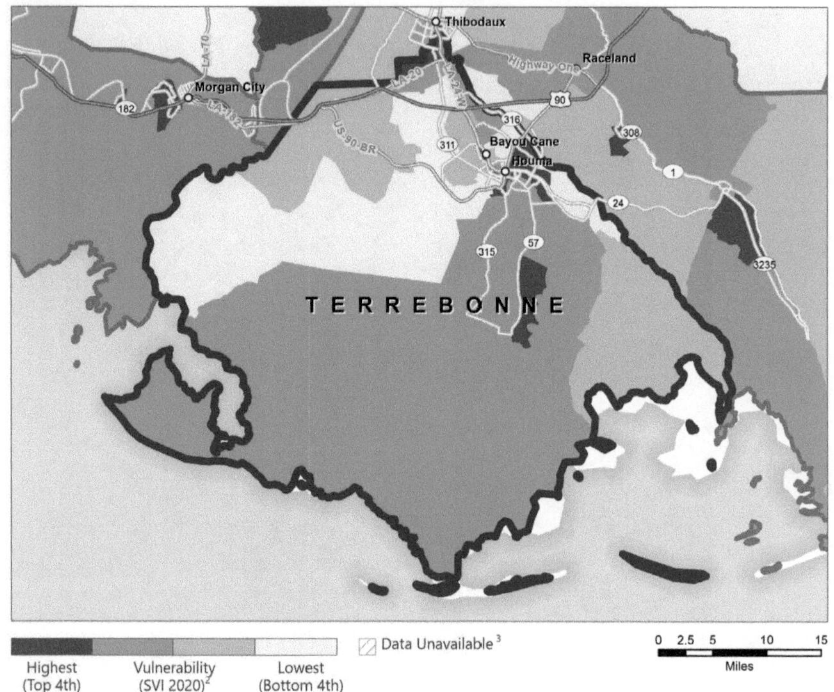

FIGURE C-24 The 2020 national overall Social Vulnerability Index for Terrebonne Parish, Louisiana.
SOURCE: CDC/ATSDR. (2023). Social Vulnerability Index Interactive Map 2020. https://www.atsdr.cdc.gov/placeandhealth/svi/interactive_map.html

In Lafourche Parish, the estimated age-adjusted prevalence of fair or poor health among adults aged 18 years and older was 21.4 percent (CI: 19.6, 23.2) in 2020, while in Terrebonne Parish, the estimated prevalence was 20.8 percent (CI: 19.3, 22.5) in 2020. Compared to the national average of almost 15.8 percent, both Lafourche and Terrebonne Parishes have higher prevalence of adults with fair or poor health (see Figure C-25).

Current Flood Risk

NOAA's Coastal County Snapshot[41] for Special Flood Hazard for Lafourche Parish reveals Lafourche Parish's considerable vulnerability to flooding, with 90.1 percent of its land situated within the designated

[41]See footnote 14.

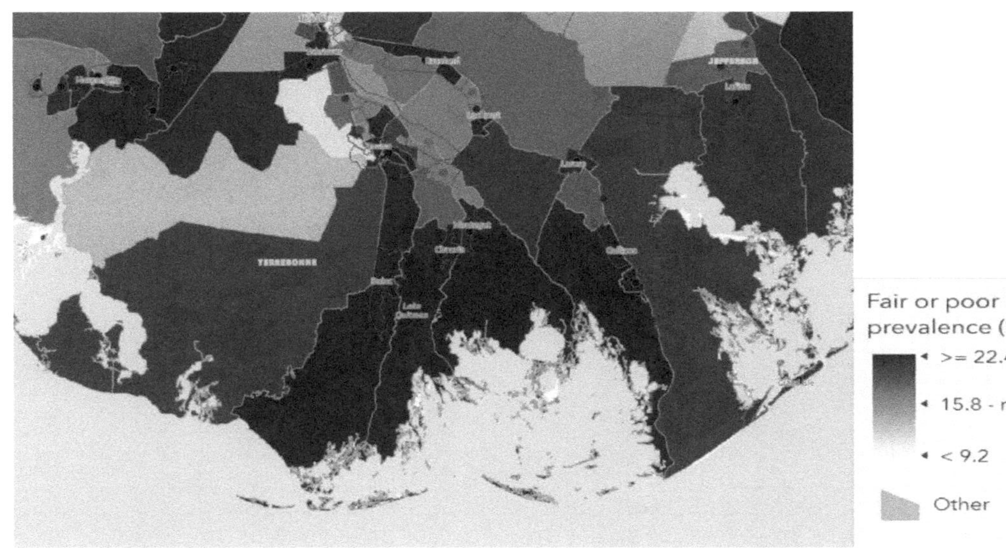

FIGURE C-25 The prevalence of adults aged 18+ who reported fair or poor health in 2020 in Lafourche and Terrebonne Parishes, Louisiana.
SOURCE: CDC. (2023). CDC PLACES. https://www.cdc.gov/places

100-year floodplain. Nearly 63 percent of the parish's population resides in this flood-prone region, including vulnerable segments such as older adults and economically disadvantaged individuals. Specifically, around 60 percent of residents aged 65 and older and approximately 61 percent of those living in poverty are located in the floodplain (see Figure C-26). The flood risk in Lafourche Parish also affects local businesses and critical facilities. Approximately 40 percent of the businesses operating in the parish are located within the 100-year floodplain. The parish experienced an almost 12 percent increase in development between 1996 and 2016, with about 88 percent of the existing development already established in 1996. Moreover, about 41 percent of critical facilities, including 14 schools, three police stations, 12 fire stations, and one medical facility, are situated within the designated 100-year floodplain (see Figure C-27). The financial impact of flooding in Lafourche Parish totals to approximately 51 million dollars in flood insurance claims filed between 1991 and 2020, covering almost 4,000 homes.

NOAA's Coastal County Snapshot for Special Flood Hazard reveals that Terrebonne Parish is highly susceptible to flooding, with 94.5 percent of its land area located within the designated 100-year floodplain. This flood-prone region is home to almost 53 percent of the parish's population, including vulnerable groups such as older adults and economically disadvantaged individuals. Specifically, about 52 percent of residents aged 65 and older reside in the floodplain, while nearly 56 percent of the population live

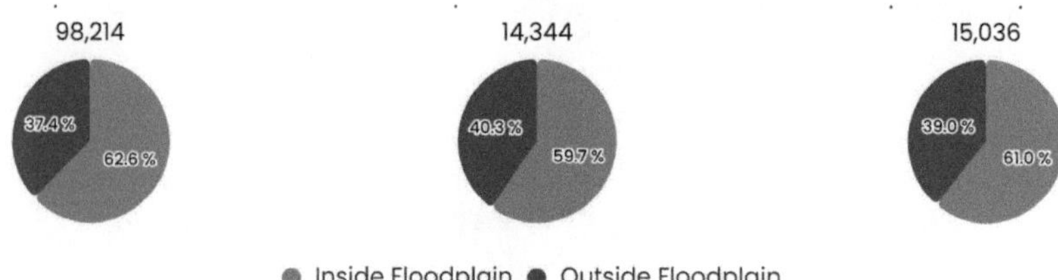

FIGURE C-26 Percentages of people that live in the floodplain in Lafourche Parish, Louisiana.
SOURCE: Office for Coastal Management. (2023). Coastal County Snapshots: Special flood hazard. National Oceanic and Atmospheric Administration. https://coast.noaa.gov/digitalcoast/tools/snapshots.html

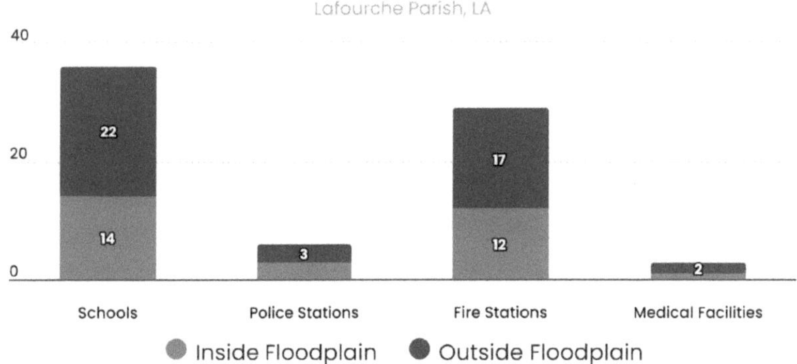

FIGURE C-27 Critical facilities in the 100-year floodplain in Lafourche Parish, Louisiana.
SOURCE: Office for Coastal Management. (2023). Coastal County Snapshots: Special flood hazard. National Oceanic and Atmospheric Administration. https://coast.noaa.gov/digitalcoast/tools/snapshots.html

in poverty (see Figure C-28). The flood risk also affects the local economy, with about 23 percent of the parish's businesses situated within the 100-year floodplain. Between 1996 and 2016, Terrebonne Parish experienced almost a 9 percent increase in development, with about 91 percent of the current development already established in 1996. Critical facilities are not exempt from this risk, as almost 30 percent of these infrastructures, including 11 schools and 12 fire stations, are located within the designated 100-year floodplain (see Figure C-29). The financial toll of flooding in Terrebonne Parish is substantial, with a total of 270 million dollars in flood insurance claims filed between 1991 and 2020, covering approximately 11,000 homes.

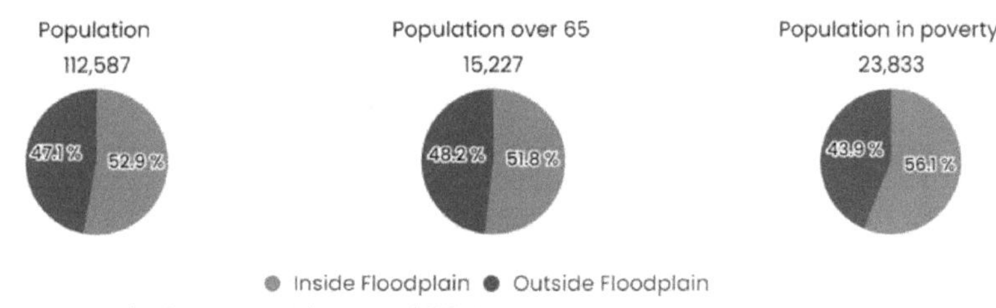

FIGURE C-28 Percentages of people that live in the floodplain in Terrebonne Parish, Louisiana.
SOURCE: Office for Coastal Management. (2023). Coastal County Snapshots: Special flood hazard. National Oceanic and Atmospheric Administration. https://coast.noaa.gov/digitalcoast/tools/snapshots.html

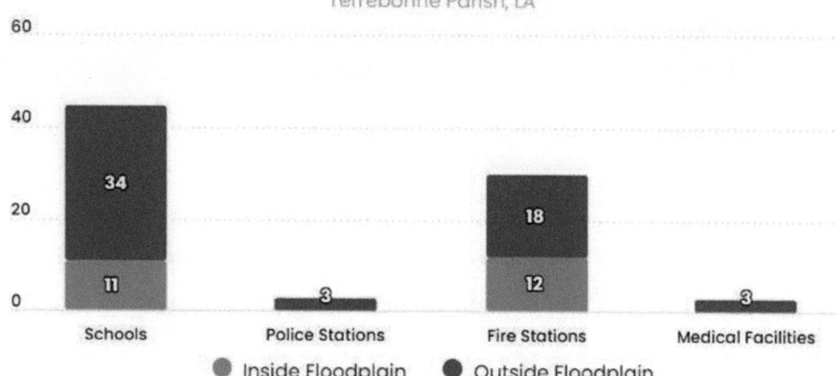

FIGURE C-29 Critical facilities in the 100-year floodplain in Terrebonne Parish, Louisiana.
SOURCE: Office for Coastal Management. (2023). Coastal County Snapshots: Special flood hazard. National Oceanic and Atmospheric Administration. https://coast.noaa.gov/digitalcoast/tools/snapshots.html

Projected Flood Risk and Extreme Heat

Under the National Climate Assessment's moderate SLR scenario,[42] by 2035, Lafourche Parish will see more than 1,500 (34%) of its existing homes at risk of chronic inundation. These homes hold a total worth of more than 120 million dollars, house more than 4,000 residents, and contribute almost $900,000 to the local property tax revenue. By 2100, the number of homes at risk is expected to rise to more than 3,600 (75%). These homes have a total value of almost 300 million dollars, house 9,195 people, and generate more than 2.2 million dollars for the local property tax base.

Similarly, by 2035, in Terrebonne Parish, almost 1,600 existing homes (23%) face the threat of chronic inundation.[43] These homes currently have a combined value of just under 123 million dollars, provide shelter for approximately 4,400 individuals, and generate more than half a million dollars in local property taxes. By 2100, the number of homes at risk increases to almost 4,000 (60%), with a total value of more than 400 million dollars, housing over 11,000 people, and adding more than 2 million dollars to the property tax base.

[42]See footnote 16.
[43]See footnote 15.

The maps in Figures C-30 and C-31 come from the NOAA Coastal Flood Exposure Mapper.[44] The tool allows you to select a hazard layer (options include coastal flood hazard composite, high tide flooding, FEMA flood zones, tsunami, storm surge, SLR), societal exposure (options include population density, poverty, elderly, employees), infrastructure exposure (development, critical facilities, development patterns), and ecosystem exposure (natural areas and open space, potential pollution sources, natural protection, wetland potential). Poverty rates and flood hazard zones are displayed in separate maps because when one is superimposed over the other, it is hard to see both statistics. When areas with high poverty rates are also flood hazard zones, it indicates that vulnerable populations are also at risk of being impacted by flooding.

Figure C-30's map shows critical facilities (hospitals, schools, fire and police stations, etc.) and "areas prone to flooding from one or more of the following hazards: high tide flooding; high risk (1% annual chance for A and V zones) and moderate risk (0.2% annual chance) flooding (designated by the Federal Emergency Management Agency); storm surge for category 1 through category 3 hurricanes; sea level rise scenarios of 1, 2, and 3 feet; tsunami run-up zones (for high risk areas). The darker red color on the map indicates more flood hazard zones for that area" (Office for Coastal Management, n.d.b).

Figure C-31's map, based on 2014–2018 ACS five-year estimates, shows the "percentage of people living below the poverty line for census block groups in or near coastal flood-prone areas (e.g., four-person family with annual cash income below $23,283). People in poverty may not have adequate resources to prepare for or respond to hazards. Their limitations may include substandard housing, lack of transportation to evacuate, lack of social support systems, and incomes that limit their ability to afford temporary lodging, relocation, or housing improvements" (Office for Coastal Management, n.d.b).

National Integrated Heat Health Information System

Lafourche Parish:

- **Days above 90F:** Projected number of days (based on RCP 8.5)[45] with temperature over 90F in 2050 = 120 (compared to 69 days per year on average from 1976 to 2005)

[44] See footnote 6.

[45] See footnote 17.

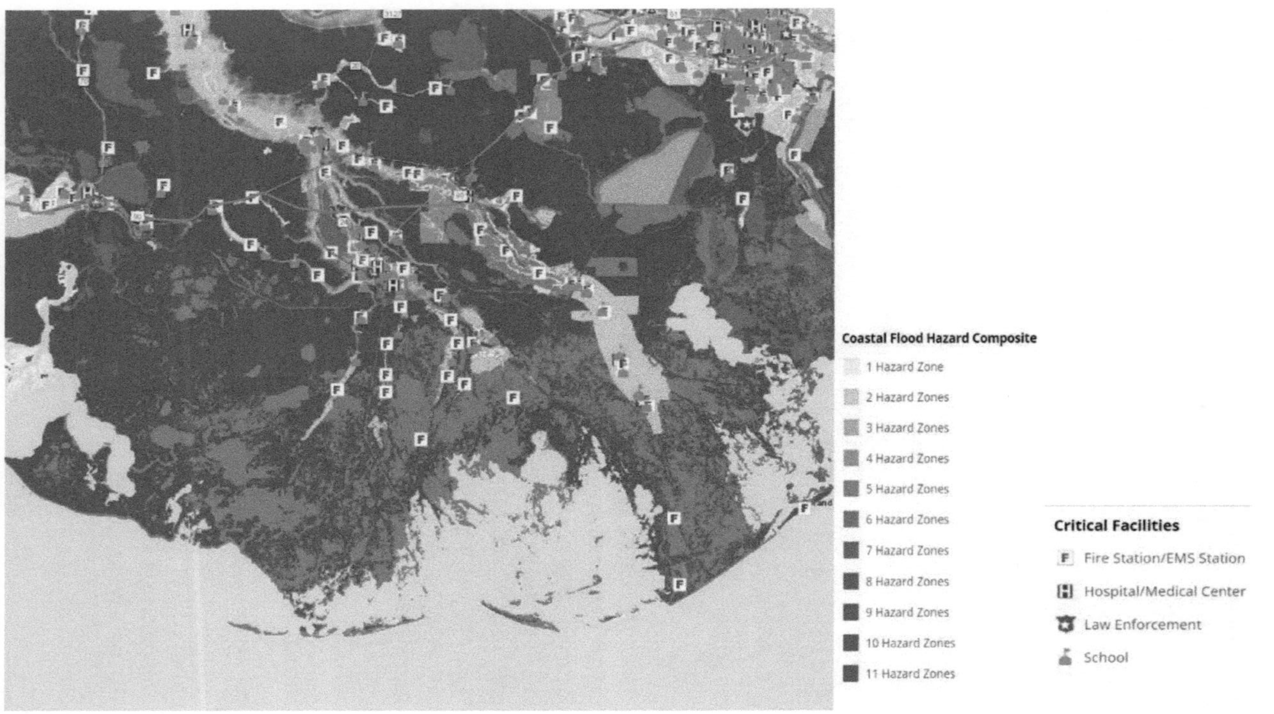

FIGURE C-30 Critical facilities prone to flooding in southeast Louisiana.
NOTE: NOAA's Coastal Flood Exposure Mapper allows users to select a hazard layer (options include coastal flood hazard composite, high tide flooding, FEMA flood zones, tsunami, storm surge, SLR), societal exposure (options include population density, poverty, elderly, employees), infrastructure exposure (development, critical facilities, development patterns), and ecosystem

FIGURE C-30 Continued
exposure (natural areas and open space, potential pollution sources, natural protection, wetland potential). Poverty rates and flood hazard zones are displayed in separate maps because when one is superimposed over the other, it is difficult to see both statistics. When areas with high poverty rates are also flood hazard zones, it indicates that vulnerable populations are also at risk of being impacted by flooding. SOURCE: Office for Coastal Management. (n.d.c). Coastal Flood Exposure Mapper. National Oceanic and Atmospheric Administration. https://coast.noaa.gov/digitalcoast/tools/flood-exposure.html

- **Extreme heat days:** Projected number of days per year warmer than the top 1 percent historically in 2050 = 35 (compared to four per year from 1976 to 2005)

Terrebonne Parish:

- **Days above 90F:** Projected number of days (based on RCP 8.5)[46] with temperature over 90F in 2050 = 122 (compared to 72 days per year on average from 1976 to 2005)
- **Extreme heat days:** Projected number of days per year warmer than the top 1 percent historically in 2050 = 35 (compared to four per year from 1976 to 2005)

Environmental Justice Indexes

Figures C-32 and C-33[47] show where Lafourche and Terrebonne Parishes fall in relation to the rest of the state and nation by using a percentile for various EJIs within state and national contexts (see also Figure C-34). For example, Lafourche Parish's ozone level is in the 70th percentile for the state of Louisiana and in the 59th percentile for the nation. Meanwhile, Terrebonne Parish's ozone level is in the 74th percentile for the state of Louisiana and in the 62nd percentile for the nation. This indicates that 41 percent of the U.S. population lives in a block group with a higher EJI for ozone than the average person in Lafourche Parish, and 38 percent of the U.S. population lives in a block group with a higher EJI for ozone than the average person in Terrebonne Parish. Lafourche Parish ranks close to or above the 50th percentile in the nation for particulate matter, ozone, diesel particulate matter, air toxics cancer risk, air toxics respiratory HI, toxic

[46]See footnote 17.
[47]See footnote 18.

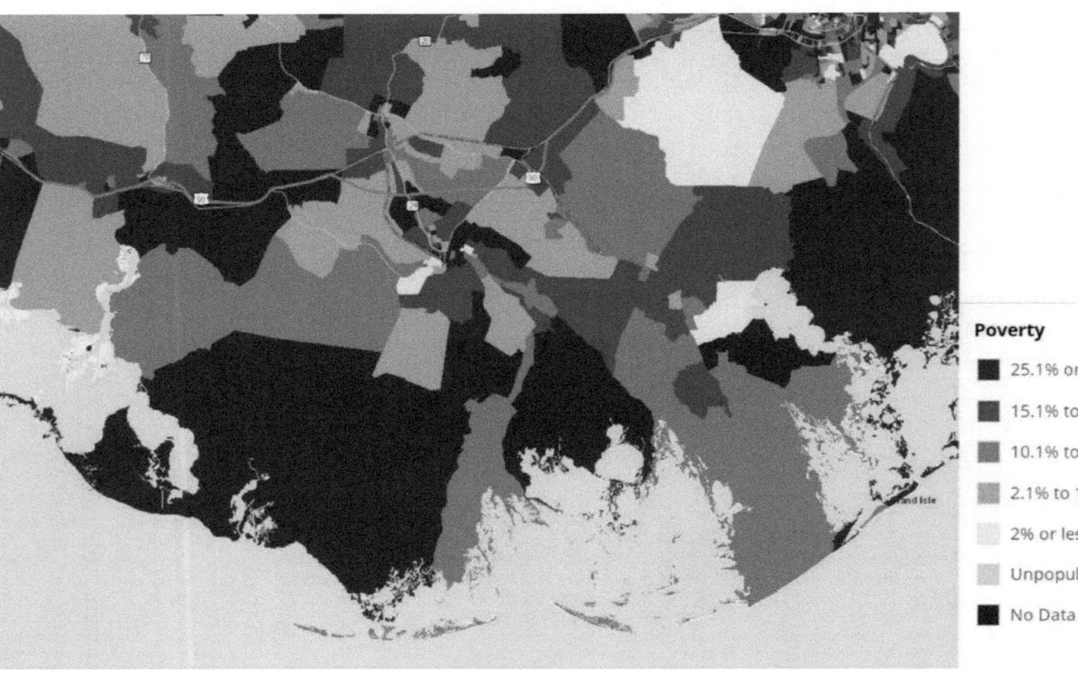

FIGURE C-31 People living below the poverty line in southeast Louisiana.
SOURCE: Office for Coastal Management. (n.d.c). Coastal Flood Exposure Mapper. National Oceanic and Atmospheric Administration. https://coast.noaa.gov/digitalcoast/tools/flood-exposure.html

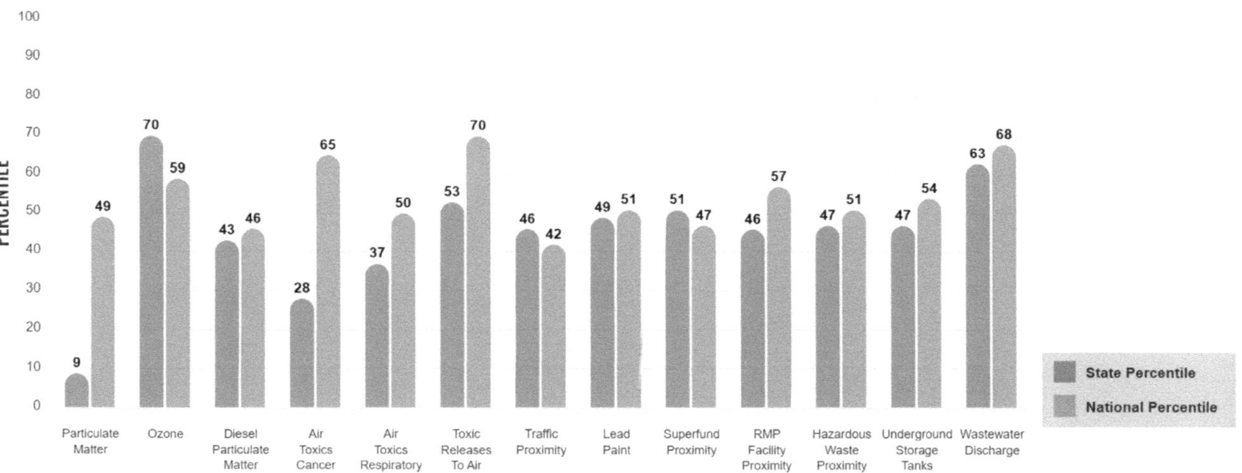

FIGURE C-32 Environmental Justice Index for Lafourche Parish, Louisiana, compared to the state and nation.
NOTE: The years for which the data are available, and the methods used, vary across these indicators. Important caveats and uncertainties apply to this screening-level information, so it is essential to understand the limitations on appropriate interpretations and applications of these indicators. Please see EJScreen documentation for discussion of these issues before using reports.
SOURCE: EPA. (n.d.). Environmental Justice Screening and Mapping Tool. https://ejscreen.epa.gov/mapper/

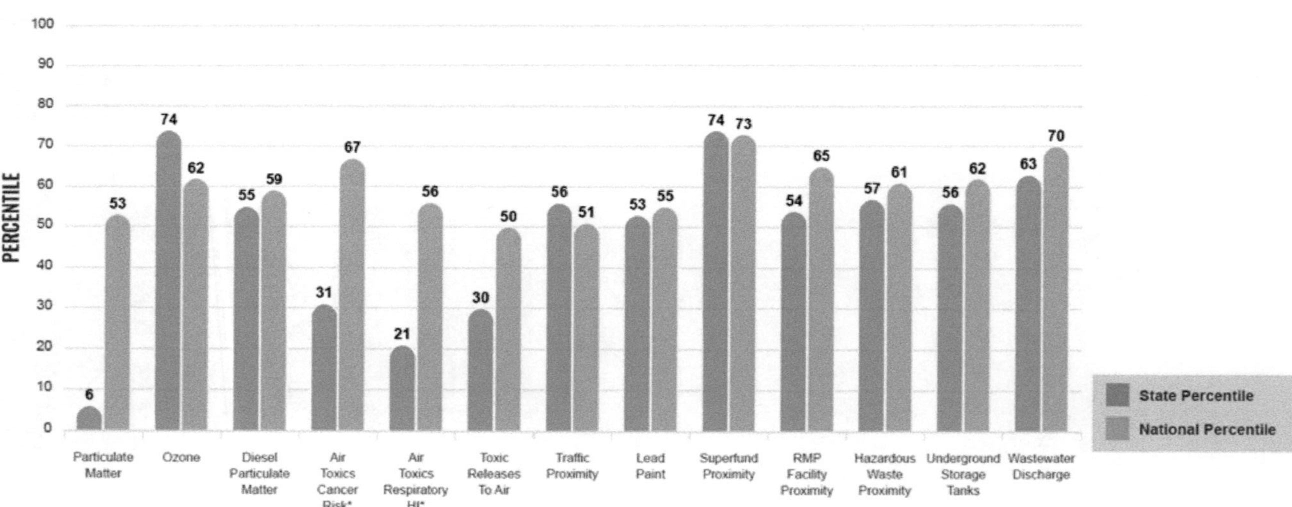

FIGURE C-33 Environmental Justice Index for Terrebonne Parish, Louisiana, compared to the state and nation.
SOURCE: EPA. (n.d.). Environmental Justice Screening and Mapping Tool. https://ejscreen.epa.gov/mapper/

FIGURE C-34 The Environmental Justice Index rank for Lafourche Parish (top) and Terrebonne Parish (bottom), Louisiana. Lafourche Parish has areas with low to high environmental justice indexes and Terrebonne Parish has areas with low to high environmental justice indexes.
SOURCE: CDC. (n.d.). Climate and Health Program Heat and Health Tracker. Heat exposure data. https://ephtracking.cdc.gov/Applications/heatTracker/

releases to air, lead paint, superfund proximity, RMP facility proximity, hazardous waste proximity, underground storage tanks, and wastewater discharge. Terrebonne Parish is approximately at or above the 50th percentile in the nation for particulate matter, ozone, diesel particulate matter, air toxics cancer risk, air toxics respiratory HI, toxic releases to air, traffic proximity, lead paint, superfund proximity, RMP facility proximity, proximity to hazardous waste, underground storage tanks, and wastewater discharge.

Notable Recent Disasters Since 2000

Table C-5 below provides an overview of the significant impacts of hurricanes on Terrebonne and Lafourche Parishes as well as the state of Louisiana as a whole. However, there are data limitations, which include limited information on the federal government's responses to Hurricanes Isaac and Gustav. Since the year 2000, Louisiana has experienced five hurricanes deemed federally declared major disasters,[48] including Hurricanes Ida (2021), Laura (2020), Delta (2020), Zeta (2020), Isaac (2012), Gustav (2008), and Katrina (2005). These storms caused widespread damage, resulting in billions of dollars in property loss and infrastructure damage across the state. The most severe of these hurricanes was Hurricane Katrina, with a total of 186 billion dollars in damages and 41.1 billion dollars in insured damages in the United States (27.8 billion in 2009 dollars in insured damages in Louisiana; Hartwig & Wilkinson, 2010; Knabb et al., 2023). The federal response to these disasters involved major disaster declarations, financial assistance for affected residents, and funding for public infrastructure projects, emergency protective measures, and hazard mitigation programs. The impact of these hurricanes highlights the vulnerability of Terrebonne and Lafourche Parishes to storm surges, flooding, and extreme weather events.

The response to these events has demonstrated the evolving and multifaceted approach of federal, state, and local governments in addressing natural disasters. Federal agencies have played instrumental roles in providing disaster assistance. Over the years, FEMA's efforts and initiatives have broadened over time to include financial assistance, repair grants, housing support, and rental assistance. The federal government has become increasingly proactive in providing aid before and after disasters. This is evidenced by the rapid issuance of major disaster declarations and the allocation of funding for various recovery programs following a hurricane event. Additionally, there has been an emphasis on adopting pre-disaster

[48]See footnote 19.

mitigation measures, such as the HMGP, which can help reduce the impact of future disasters. State governments have consistently responded to these disasters by declaring states of emergency and requesting assistance from the federal government. The coordination between Louisiana's governors and federal authorities has been crucial in securing funding and resources for the affected communities. State-level efforts have also included the allocation of resources to recovery programs and emergency services, such as the National Guard and first responders. At the local level, governments have implemented acquisition initiatives to buy flood-prone properties and encourage homeowners to relocate to safer areas. These programs, along with the development and revision of hazard mitigation plans, demonstrate local governments' commitment to reducing the impact of future disasters on vulnerable communities.

COMMUNITY PROFILE: PORT ARTHUR, TEXAS

Social Vulnerability Index

The 2020 national overall SVI score for Jefferson County, Texas, was 0.9554 where possible scores range from 0 (lowest vulnerability) to 1 (highest vulnerability). A score of 0.9554 indicates a high level of vulnerability (see Figure C-35).

Health

In Port Arthur,[49] the estimated age-adjusted[50] prevalence of asthma among adults age 18+ was 10.7 percent (CI: 10.6, 10.8) in 2020. This is above the national average[51] of 10 percent. Atreco and Pleasure Island have high incidence just north of Sabine Pass. And areas in close vicinity to the Jack Brooks Regional Airport and Groves report lower rates of asthma.

In this area, the estimated age-adjusted prevalence of coronary heart disease among adults aged 18+ was 7.5 percent (CI: 7.4, 7.6) in 2020. This is above the national average of 6.2 percent of crude prevalence of coronary heart disease. Pleasure Island, Port Arthur Reservoir, and Atreco have higher rates of coronary heart disease, and Nederland, Viterbo, Port Neches, and Central Gardens have lower rates of coronary heart disease.

In this area, the estimated age-adjusted prevalence of adults who reported their mental health as "not good" for 14 days or more among adults

[49]See footnote 11.
[50]See footnote 12.
[51]See footnote 13.

TABLE C-5 Hurricanes Impacting Lafourche and Terrebonne Parishes, Louisiana, That Led to Federal Disaster Declarations Since 2000

Storm	Landfall Date	Damage and Impact	Federal Response
Hurricane Ida[a,b,c]	August 29, 2021	• Storm surge - 3–6 ft (Terrebonne); 6–12 ft (Lafourche) • Widespread damage in Louisiana - roofs, trees, power lines, roads • >900,000 lost power; >96% affected in Terrebonne and Lafourche • Medical centers damaged; water supplies lost • Direct fatalities in the United States - 55 • Indirect fatalities in the United States - 32 • Fatalities in Louisiana - 26 • Total damages in the United States - $75 billion • Total damages in Louisiana - $55 billion	• August 26, 2021 - Governor declared a state of emergency • August 29, 2021 - President issued a major disaster declaration • Individual assistance - >$1.2 billion • Repair grants - >$334 million • Rental aid - >$309 million • SBA - $1.28 billion • NFIP - >$640 million • >22,000 survivors advised by mitigation specialists. • Public assistance grants - >$1.6 billion • >1,400 households in temporary FEMA housing • HMGP - >$10.3 million • 40 Disaster Recovery Centers; >76,000 assisted.

TABLE C-5 Continued

Storm	Landfall Date	Damage and Impact	Federal Response
Hurricane Zeta[h,i]	October 28, 2020	• Rainfall - 4–6 inches • Storm surge - 6–8 ft • Mild to severe wind damage to hundreds of homes • Road debris - overturned trucks, trailers, and boats • Tree emergencies - >500 reported, blocking roads and buildings • Nearly 30,000+ homes and businesses lost power • Direct fatalities in the United States - 5 • Indirect fatalities in the United States - 2 • Injuries - 75 documented across multiple states • Total damages in the United States - $4.4 billion • Transportation damages in Louisiana - >$25 million • Crop losses in Louisiana- $576.4 million • Timber losses in Louisiana - >$1.39 billion	• October 26, 2020 - Governor declared a state of emergency • November 24, 2020 - Governor requested a major disaster declaration • January 12, 2021 - President issued a major disaster declaration • January 26, 2021 - Governor requested additional $3 billion in federal funding for unmet needs • Individual housing assistance - >$11.4 million • Other needs assistance - >$2.1 million • Public assistance grants - >$45.4 million • HMGP - >$17.3 million for Lafourche; >$17.6 million for Terrebonne

(continued)

TABLE C-5 Continued

Storm	Landfall Date	Damage and Impact	Federal Response
Hurricane Delta[f,g]	October 10, 2020	• Rainfall - 5–10 inches • Storm surge - 6–9 ft • Direct fatalities in the United States - 2 • Indirect fatalities in the United States - 2, both in Louisiana • Additional damage to homes and businesses that were still in recovery from Hurricane Laura • Temporary roofs were blown away by winds. • Leftover debris piles from Hurricane Laura were blown around, causing roadways and drains to be blocked • Total damages in the United States - $2.9 billion	• October 14, 2020 - Governor John Bel Edwards requested an expedited major disaster declaration • October 16, 2020 - President issued a major disaster declaration • Housing assistance - >$35 million • Other needs assistance - $11 million • Public assistance - >$112 million • HMGP - >$3.7 million
Hurricane Laura[d,e]	August 27, 2020	• Storm surge - 12 to 18 ft • Rainfall - 12 inches • Direct fatalities in the United States - 7 • Direct fatalities in Louisiana - 6 • Indirect fatalities in the United States - 34 • Indirect fatalities in Louisiana - 26 • Wind damage to buildings and trees • 10,000 homes in Louisiana were demolished • Triggered the chemical plant - releasing cloud of toxic smoke • 568,000 power outages • Total damages in the United States - $19 billion • Total damages in Louisiana - $17.5 billion	• August 20, 2020 - Governor John Bel Edwards requested an expedited major disaster declaration • August 28, 2020 - President issued a major disaster declaration • Housing assistance - >$172 million • Other needs assistance - >$69 million • Public assistance - $2.5 billion • HMGP - >$47 million

TABLE C-5 Continued

Storm	Landfall Date	Damage and Impact	Federal Response
Hurricane Isaac[j,k]	August 28, 2012	• Rainfall - >10 inches resulting in flash and river flooding • >59,000 homes damaged • Terrebonne homes damages - >1,500 • Lafourche homes damages - >1,800 • Severe damage reports - 11 homes in Terrebonne, 20 homes in Lafourche • Water intrusion reports - 80 residents in Terrebonne, few in Lafourche • 47% lost power in state; >24,500 in Terrebonne, >34,500 in Lafourche • Deepwater Horizon oiled material resurfaced - >565,000 lbs on coast • Direct fatalities in the United States - 5 • Insured damages in the United States - $970 million • Total damages in the United States - >$2.3 billion	• August 29, 2012 - Governor requested an expedited major disaster declaration • August 29, 2012 - President issued a major disaster declaration • Individual assistance - >$67 million • Public assistance - >$7.6 million • SBA: >$1.4 million • U.S. Department of Agriculture - >$36 million for >86,000 households

(*continued*)

TABLE C-5 Continued

Storm	Landfall Date	Damage and Impact	Federal Response
Hurricane Gustav[m,n,o,p]	September 1, 2008	• Storm surge - 9–10 ft • 2 million evacuated; Terrebonne Parish - 15% stayed, no shelters or medical services • Local levees breached in Terrebonne - >2,500 flooded homes • Terrebonne homes damaged - 197 owner-occupied, 121 rentals • Terrebonne flooded nonresidential structures - 247 • 1.2 million lost power in Louisiana • 11 tornadoes in Louisiana • Fatalities in the United States - 112 • Direct fatalities in Louisiana - 7 • Indirect fatalities in Louisiana - 41 • Insured property damage - >$2.1 billion • Insured property damage in Louisiana - >$2 billion • Uninsured losses in the United States - >$4.6 billion • Terrebonne Parish businesses - lost productivity ($50–100 million), lost revenues ($200–400 million) • Commercial/industrial damages in Terrebonne - $75–225 million	• September 1, 2008 - Governor requested major disaster declaration • September 3, 2008 - President issued a major disaster declaration • FEMA/SBA approved $300 million[l] • Public assistance grants - $34.1 million • Individual assistance - $109 million • Home inspections - ~250,000 • Other needs assistance grants - $33.7 million • SBA - $40.5 million • HMGP - $6 million

TABLE C-5 Continued

Storm	Landfall Date	Damage and Impact	Federal Response
Hurricane Katrina[q,r,s]	August 29, 2005	• Storm surge - 24–28 ft, 20 mi wide • Direct fatalities in the United States - 520 • Indirect fatalities in the United States - 565 • Indeterminate fatalities in the United States - 307 • Fatalities in Louisiana - 986 • Total damages in the United States - $186.3 billion • Insured losses in the United States - $41.1 billion • Insured losses in Louisiana - $25.3 billion • Oil spills from damaged facilities in Southeast Louisiana	• August 29, 2005 - President issued a major disaster declaration • September 8, 2005 - President directed immediate financial assistance • $2,000 emergency relief per affected household • Shelters - 273,000 people • FEMA trailers - 114,000 households • Public assistance - >$2.3 billion • Repair/replacement of fire/police stations - >$100 million • Repair/replacement of schools/universities - >$940 million • Public works projects - >$277 million • Public safety projects - >$201 million • Health care projects - >$96 million • Public infrastructure projects - >$704 million • Debris removal/ emergency measures - $114 million • Structure elevation - $9.5 million • Housing assistance - $5.7 billion

NOTE: FEMA = Federal Emergency Management Agency, HMGP = Hazard Mitigation Grant Program, NFIP = National Flood Insurance Program, SBA = Small Business Administration.

[a]https://ldh.la.gov/news/6308

[b]https://www.fema.gov/fact-sheet/hurricane-ida-numbers-six-months

[c]https://gov.louisiana.gov/index.cfm/newsroom/detail/3374

[d]https://www.fema.gov/disaster/4559

[e]https://www.fema.gov/disaster/4559/notices

[f]https://www.fema.gov/disaster/4570

[g]https://www.fema.gov/disaster/4570/notices

[h]https://gov.louisiana.gov/index.cfm/newsroom/detail/2940

(continued)

TABLE C-5 Continued

[i]https://www.fema.gov/disaster/4577

[j]https://www.fema.gov/sites/default/files/2020-07/craig-fugate_appropriations_testimony_9-25-2012.pdf

[k]https://www.fema.gov/sites/default/files/2020-10/pda-report_fema-4080-dr_la.pdf

[l]Federal response includes Hurricanes Gustav and Ike.

[m]https://www.tpcg.org/files/flooding/GustavIke_Proposed_CDBG_Application_Final.pdf

[n]https://reliefweb.int/report/united-states-america/usa-president-declares-major-disaster-louisiana

[o]http://floods.dotd.la.gov/multimodal/public_works/LaFloods/documents/newsletters/fp_2008dec.pdf

[p]https://www.fema.gov/press-release/20230425/nearly-6-million-mitigation-grants-help-communities-across-la

[q]https://www.fema.gov/pdf/hazard/hurricane/2005katrina/la_progress_report_0810.pdf

[r]https://georgewbush-whitehouse.archives.gov/news/releases/2005/09/20050908-8.html

[s]https://www.datacenterresearch.org/data-resources/katrina/facts-for-impact/

SOURCES: Berg, R. (2013). *Tropical Cyclone Report Hurricane Isaac* (Report No. Al092012). National Hurricane Center. https://www.nhc.noaa.gov/data/tcr/AL092012_Isaac.pdf

Beven II, J. L., Hagen, A., & Berg, R. (2022). *Tropical Cyclone Report: Hurricane Ida* (Report No. AL092021). National Hurricane Center. https://www.nhc.noaa.gov/data/tcr/AL092021_Ida.pdf

Beven II, J. L., & Kimberlain, T. B. (2009). *Tropical Cyclone Report: Hurricane Gustav* (Report No. AL072008). National Hurricane Center. https://www.nhc.noaa.gov/data/tcr/AL072008_Gustav.pdf

Blake, E., Berg, R., & Hagen, A. (2020). *Tropical Cyclone Report: Hurricane Zeta*. National Hurricane Center. https://www.nhc.noaa.gov/data/tcr/AL282020_Zeta.pdf

Cangialosi, J. P., & Berg, R. (2020). *Tropical Cyclone Report: Hurricane Delta* (Report No. AL282020). National Hurricane Center. https://www.nhc.noaa.gov/data/tcr/AL262020_Delta.pdf

Copp, D. (2020, October 29). Zeta leaves wind damage, power outages in Lafourche and Terrebonne. *Houma Today*. https://www.houmatoday.com/story/news/2020/10/29/zeta-leaves-wind-damage-power-outages-lafourche-and-terrebonne/6054941002/

Gisclair, C. (2012, September 5). Darkness lingers locally in Hurricane Isaac. *The Houma Times*. https://www.houmatimes.com/news/darkness-lingers-locally-in-hurricane-isaac/

Hartwig, R. P., & Wilkinson, C. (2010, July). *Hurricane Katrina: The five year anniversary*. Insurance Information Institute. https://www.iii.org/sites/default/files/1007Katrina5Anniversary.pdf

Knabb, R. D., Rhome, J. R., & Brown, D. P. (2023). *Tropical Cyclone Report: Hurricane Katrina*. National Hurricane Center. https://www.nhc.noaa.gov/data/tcr/AL122005_Katrina.pdf

Pasch, R. J., Berg, R., Roberts, D. P., & Papin, P. P. (2020). *Tropical Cyclone Report: Hurricane Laura* (Report No. AL132020). National Hurricane Center. https://www.nhc.noaa.gov/data/tcr/AL132020_Laura.pdf

Wilson, X. A. (2012, October 1). Flood prevention: Officials say work diminished Isaac's damage. *Houma Today*. https://www.houmatoday.com/story/news/2012/10/01/flood-prevention-officials-say-work-diminished-isaacs-damage/27029634007/

Wyatt, M., & Mamone, D. (2021, September 6). Terrebonne, Lafourche residents remain without power, limited cell service after Hurricane Ida. *The Acadiana Advocate*. https://www.theadvocate.com/acadiana/news/weather_traffic/terrebonne-lafourche-residents-remain-without-power-limited-cell-service-after-hurricane-ida/article_f08ded78-0f46-11ec-8d36-3fb648294a3b.html

Zullo, R., & King, N. (2008, September 5). More than four days after Gustav, no shelters in Terrebonne. *Houma Today*. https://www.houmatoday.com/story/news/2008/09/05/more-than-four-days-after-gustav-no-shelters-in-terrebonne/26486331007/

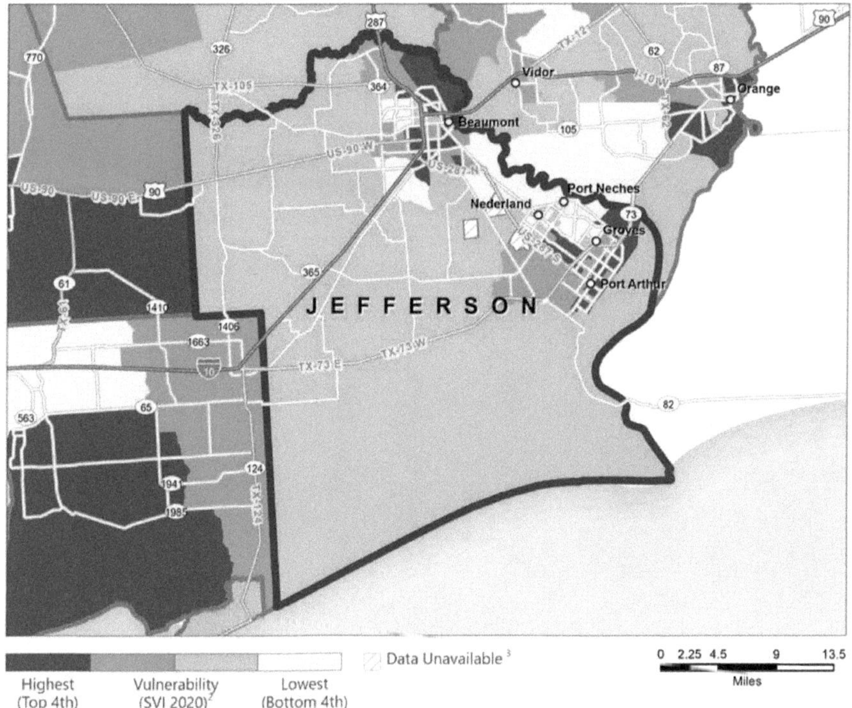

FIGURE C-35 The 2020 national overall Social Vulnerability Index for Jefferson County, Texas.
SOURCE: CDC/ATSDR. (2023). Social Vulnerability Index Map. https://www.atsdr.cdc.gov/placeandhealth/svi/interactive_map.html

18+ was 17.4 percent (CI: 17.2, 17.6) in 2020. This is slightly higher than the national average of 15.1 percent. Like asthma and heart disease, some of the highest incidence rates of poor mental health are in Atreco and along the Sabine Neches Canal. One census tract reports an incidence rate of over 19 percent.

In this area, the estimated age-adjusted prevalence of fair or poor health among adults aged 18 years and older was 28.5 percent (CI: 26.7, 30.5) in 2020, almost 13 percent higher than the national average of 15.8 percent (see Figure C-36).

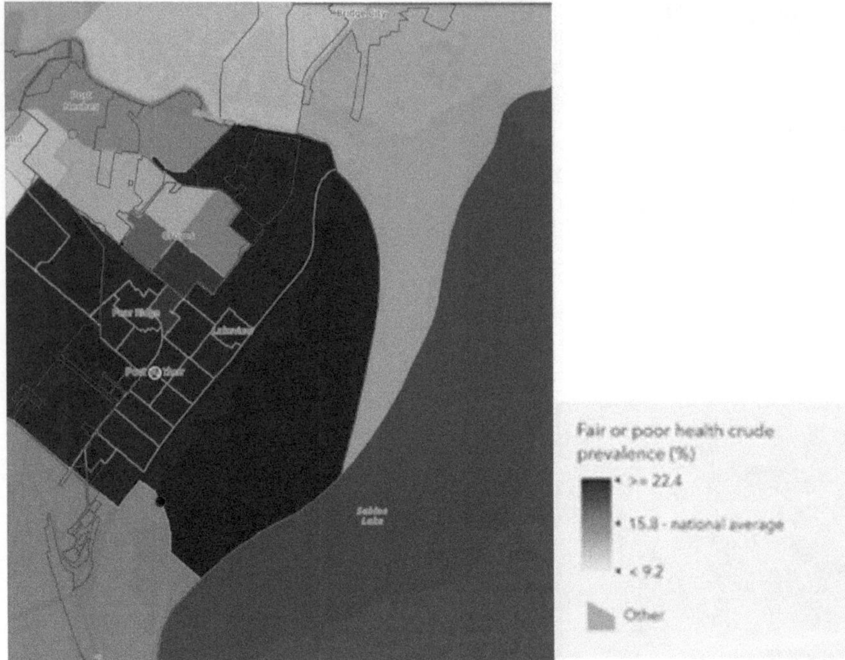

FIGURE C-36 The prevalence of adults aged 18+ who reported fair or poor health in 2020 in Port Arthur, Texas.
SOURCE: CDC. (n.d.). CDC PLACES. https://www.cdc.gov/places

Current Flood Risk

NOAA's Coastal County Snapshot[52] for SLR[53] in Jefferson County reports 1.5 percent of the population resides in low-lying areas (elevation less than 2 feet above sea level). These low-lying areas are prone to flooding and storm surges from severe weather events like hurricanes or heavy rains, making residents vulnerable to property damage and personal injury. Increased population and factors such as age, income, and capabilities can worsen the effects, as not all residents might be adequately prepared (see Figure C-37). Despite these challenges, all of Jefferson County's critical facilities (schools, police and fire stations, and medical facilities) are situated outside of these low-lying areas. Additionally, 0.2 percent of Jefferson County's businesses are situated within low-lying areas that are at an

[52]See footnote 14.

[53]Special Flood Hazard data were not available for Jefferson County from NOAA's Coastal County Snapshots, so SLR data were reported instead.

FIGURE C-37 Population in Jefferson County, Texas, at risk from sea level rise.
SOURCE: Office for Coastal Management. (n.d.a). Coastal County Snapshots: People at risk. National Oceanic and Atmospheric Administration. https://coast.noaa.gov/digitalcoast/tools/snapshots.html

elevation of less than 2 feet above sea level. Approximately 90 percent of the areas inundated at 2 feet of SLR are natural features (see Figure C-38).

Projected Flood Risk and Extreme Heat

By 2035, eight homes in Port Arthur are at risk of becoming chronically inundated,[54] representing less than 1 percent of the community's homes. Today those homes are worth a collective $689,230, house an estimated 18 people, and contribute $9,219 to the local property tax base. By 2100, 62 homes are at risk of becoming chronically inundated in Port Arthur, this represents less than 1 percent of the community's homes. Today those homes are worth a collective 4.8 million dollars, house 141 people, and contribute $92,428 to the local property tax base.

Figure C-39's map shows critical facilities (hospitals, schools, fire and police stations, etc.) and "areas prone to flooding from one or more of the following hazards: high tide flooding; high risk (1% annual chance for A and V zones) and moderate risk (0.2% annual chance) flooding (designated by the Federal Emergency Management Agency); storm surge for category 1 through category 3 hurricanes; sea level rise scenarios of 1, 2, and 3 feet; tsunami run-up zones (for high risk areas). The darker red color on the map indicates more flood hazard zones for that area" (Office for Coastal Management, n.d.a).

Figure C-40's map, based on 2014–2018 ACS five-year estimates, shows the "percentage of people living below the poverty line for census block groups in or near coastal flood-prone areas (e.g., four-person family with annual cash income below $23,283). People in poverty may not have adequate resources to prepare for or respond to hazards. Their limitations may include substandard housing, lack of transportation to evacuate, lack of social support systems, and incomes that limit their ability to afford temporary lodging, relocation, or housing improvements" (Office for Coastal Management, n.d.a).

National Integrated Heat Health Information System

- **Days above 90F:** Projected number of days (based on RCP 8.5)[55] with temperature over 90F in 2050 = 131 (compared to 86 days above 90F per year on average from 1976 to 2005)
- **Extreme heat days:** Projected number of days per year warmer than the top 1 percent historically in 2050 = 32 (compared to four extreme heat days per year from 1976 to 2005)

[54] See footnote 15.

[55] See footnote 17.

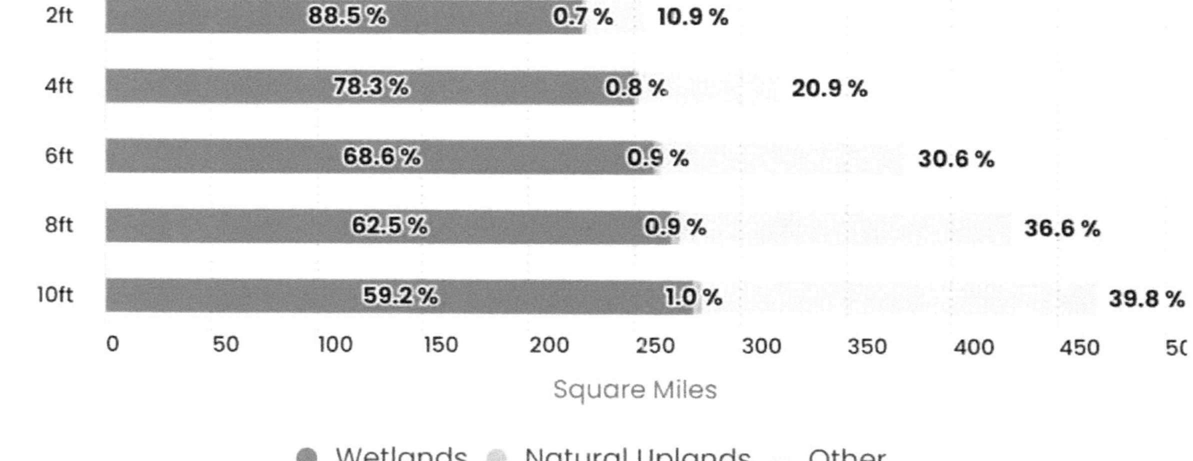

FIGURE C-38 Natural landscapes exposed to inundation in Jefferson County, Texas.
SOURCE: Office for Coastal Management. (n.d.b). Coastal County Snapshots: People at risk. National Oceanic and Atmospheric Administration. https://coast.noaa.gov/digitalcoast/tools/snapshots.html

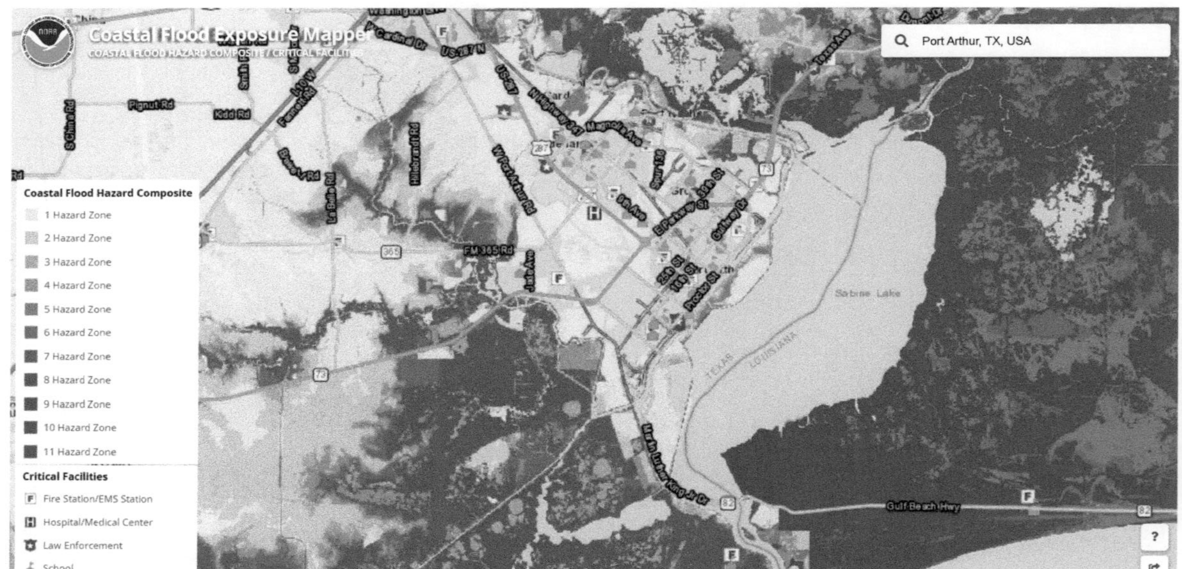

FIGURE C-39 Critical facilities prone to flooding in Port Arthur, Texas.
SOURCE: Office for Coastal Management. (n.d.c). Coastal Flood Exposure Mapper. National Oceanic and Atmospheric Administration. https://coast.noaa.gov/digitalcoast/tools/flood-exposure.html
NOTES: NOAA's Coastal Flood Exposure Mapper allows users to select a hazard layer (options include coastal flood hazard composite, high tide flooding, FEMA flood zones, tsunami, storm surge, SLR), societal exposure (options include population density, poverty, elderly, employees), infrastructure exposure (development, critical facilities, development patterns), and ecosystem exposure (natural areas and open space, potential pollution sources, natural protection, wetland potential). Poverty rates and flood hazard zones are displayed in separate maps because when one is superimposed over the other, it is difficult to see both statistics. When areas with high poverty rates are also flood hazard zones, it indicates that vulnerable populations are also at risk of being impacted by flooding.

FIGURE C-40 People living below the poverty line in Port Arthur, Texas.
SOURCE: Office for Coastal Management. (n.d.c). Coastal Flood Exposure Mapper. National Oceanic and Atmospheric Administration. https://coast.noaa.gov/digitalcoast/tools/flood-exposure.html

Environmental Justice Indexes

Figure C-41[56] shows where Port Arthur falls in relation to the rest of the state and nation by using a percentile for various EJIs within state and national contexts. For example, Port Arthur's air toxics cancer risk (lifetime cancer risk from the inhalation of air toxics) is in the 96th percentile for the state of Texas and 98th for the nation as a whole. This means that only about 4 percent of the population of Texas and 2 percent of the U.S. population live in a block group with higher air toxics cancer risk than the average person in Port Arthur. Port Arthur is approximately at or above 90th percentile in the nation for particulate matter, ozone, air toxics cancer risk, toxic releases to air, superfund proximity, RMP facility proximity, hazardous waste proximity, underground storage tanks, and wastewater discharge. The only EJIs for which Port Arthur is below 80th percentile in the nation are diesel particulate matter and air toxics respiratory HI. High percentiles on almost all EJIs reflect the scale of environmental hazards Port Arthur is dealing with outside of issues related to natural hazards and SLR.

Figure C-42 displays hazardous waste facilities and infrastructure (e.g., generators, transporters, treaters, storers, and disposers of hazardous waste) and flood risk (due to rainfall, riverine flooding, and coastal surge flooding) in Port Arthur.[57] Yellow, orange, and red areas are at 80th percentile or above in the nation for flood risk. The overlap of areas with high flood risk and hazardous waste facilities is another indication of the numerous risks Port Arthur faces (see Figure C-43).

Notable Recent Disasters Since 2000

Port Arthur has been hit by several significant hurricane disasters since 2000, resulting in extensive damage to the city's infrastructure and impacting the livelihood of residents (see Table C-6). The first major hurricane to hit Port Arthur since 2000 was Hurricane Rita in 2005, which caused widespread power outages and flooding throughout the city. The storm left many residents without power for several days, and recovery efforts were slow due to the extent of the damage. In 2008, Hurricane Ike struck Port Arthur, causing significant damage to homes and businesses, and resulting in extensive power outages and widespread flooding. Many lost their homes and struggled to recover from the widespread damage. Hurricane Harvey hit Port Arthur in 2017 and caused unprecedented flooding throughout

---

[56] See footnote 18.

[57] More information is available at https://www.epa.gov/ejscreen/ejscreen-map-descriptions#sites-reporting-to-epa

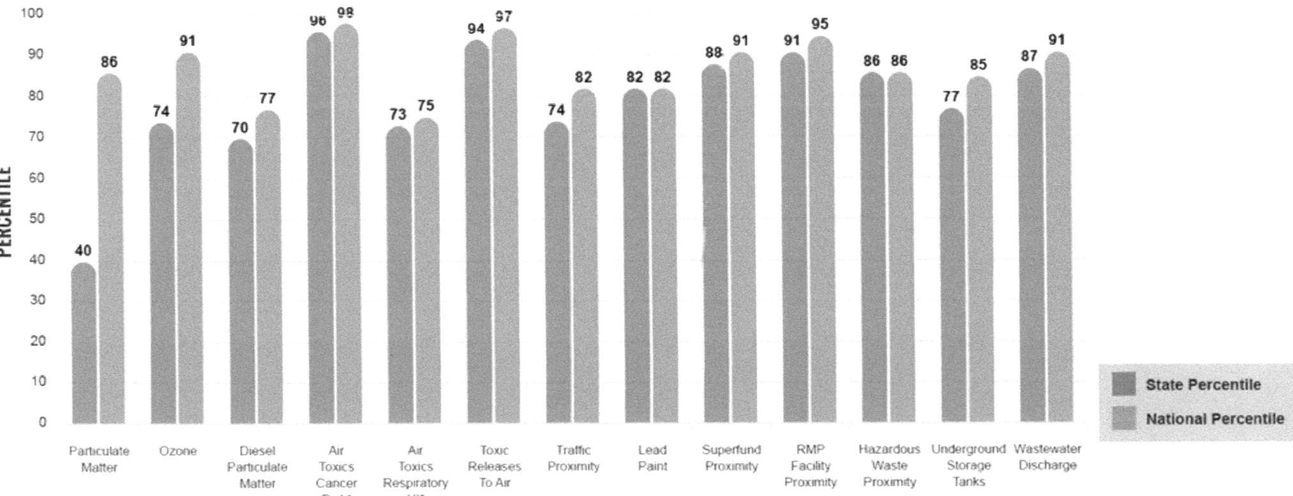

FIGURE C-41 Environmental Justice Index for Port Arthur, Texas, compared to the state and nation.
SOURCE: EPA. (n.d.). Environmental Justice Screening and Mapping Tool. https://ejscreen.epa.gov/mapper/

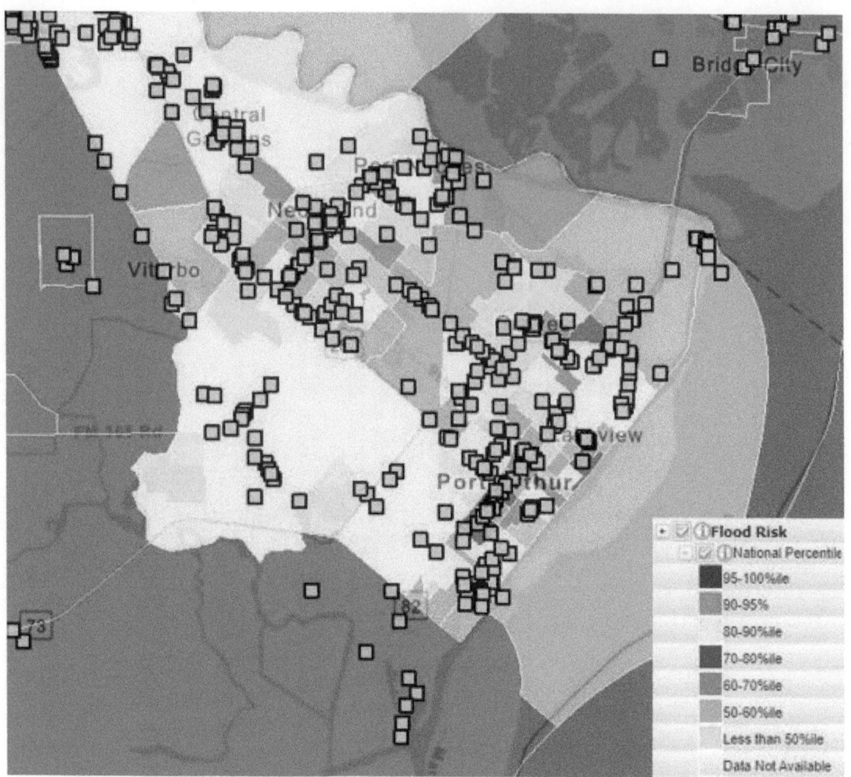

FIGURE C-42 Flood risk and hazardous waste facilities/infrastructure in Port Arthur, Texas.
SOURCE: EPA. (n.d.). Environmental Justice Screening and Mapping Tool. https://ejscreen.epa.gov/mapper/

the city, with many residents having to be rescued from their homes by emergency personnel. The hurricane caused significant damage to the city's infrastructure (i.e., power lines, roads, and bridges), leaving many residents without electricity or access to basic services for several days. Finally, Hurricane Laura impacted Port Arthur in 2020 causing a mandatory evacuation prior to the storm. FEMA and other federal assistance programs supported much of the Gulf region to assuage flooding and storm damages to businesses and infrastructure.

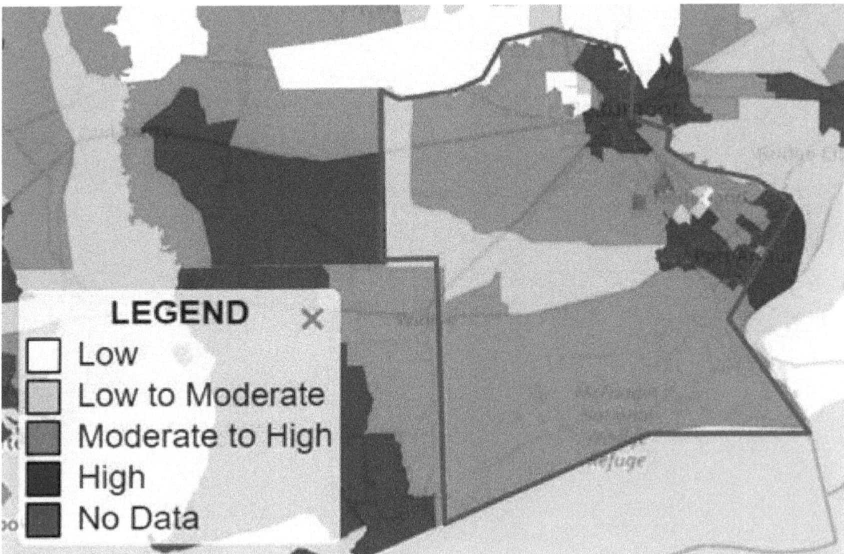

FIGURE C-43 The Environmental Justice Index rank for Jefferson County, Texas. Port Arthur has areas with moderate to high environmental justice indexes.
SOURCE: CDC. (n.d.). Climate and Health Program Heat and Health Tracker: Heat exposure data. https://ephtracking.cdc.gov/Applications/heatTracker/

TABLE C-6 Hurricanes Impacting Port Arthur, Texas, That Led to Federal Disaster Declarations Since 2000

Storm	Landfall Date	Damage and Impact	Federal Response
Hurricane Laura[a,b,c,d]	August 20, 2020	• Severe flooding and COVID-19 impact challenged city's response • Jefferson County saw downed trees, powerlines, poles, damaging homes and businesses • Direct fatalities in the United States - 7 • Indirect fatalities in the United States - 34 • Indirect fatalities in Texas - 8	• September 30, 2020 - Governor requested a major disaster declaration • December 9, 2020 - President issued a major disaster declaration • Individual assistance - $235 million • Housing assistance - $167.5 million • SBA - $608 million • NFIP - $49 million • Public assistance - $426 million • FEMA's Interagency Recovery Coordination managed recovery strategies and resources
Hurricane Harvey[e,f,g,h,i]	August 29, 2017	• Extensive flood damage in Texas - structures, homes, infrastructure • Jefferson County - 110,000 structures flooded • Port Arthur - 26 inches rain, flash floods • Overwhelmed shelters, including nursing homes • Fatalities in Texas - 68; Jefferson - 5 • Total damage in the United States - $125 billion	• August 25, 2017 - Governor requested an expedited major disaster declaration • August 25, 2017 - President issued a major disaster declaration • Coast Guard, FEMA, U.S. Department of Health and Human Services, and the U.S. Geological Survey provided aid during and after Hurricane Harvey • Housing assistance - >$1.2 billion • Other needs assistance - >$413 million • Public assistance - >$2.8 billion • HMGP - >$310 million • NFIP - $8.97 billion • SBA - >$3.4 billion

TABLE C-6 Continued

Storm	Landfall Date	Damage and Impact	Federal Response
Hurricane Ike[j,k,l,m]	September 13, 2008	• 110 mph winds • Storm surge - 25 ft • Port Arthur - power loss, wind damage • 2.6 million lost power in Texas and Louisiana • 10 offshore oil rigs destroyed; pipelines damaged • Direct fatalities in the United States - 21 • Indirect fatalities in Texas - 64 • Total damages in the United States - $29 billion	• September 12, 2008 - President issued a major disaster declaration • Housing/other assistance - $519 million • Public assistance - $602 million • SBA - $584 million • October 2008 - 715,000+ victims registered, 359,000 housing inspections • FEMA faced political pressure, paid $30,000 extra rent for a Disaster Recovery Center extension
Hurricane Rita[n,o,p,q,r]	September 23, 2005	• Significant damage - power outages, major flooding in Port Arthur, Beaumont • Offshore oil platforms damaged, bus fire caused indirect deaths during evacuations • Many Southeastern Texans displaced, stayed in hotels, shelters, etc. • Indirect fatalities in the United States - 100+ • Direct fatalities in Texas - 59 • Indirect fatalities in Texas - 6 • Total damages in the United States - $9.4 billion	• September 23, 2005 - President issued a major disaster declaration • 4,000+ trailer and mobile homes used as temporary homes • ~350,000 home inspections completed • Federal disaster unemployment assistance - $4.6 million • Other needs assistance - $82.1 million • SBA business disaster - $73.5 million • SBA renters/ homeowners - $104.1 million • Individual housing program - $500.2 million • Public assistance projects - $202 million • NFIP - $45.6 million

(continued)

TABLE C-6 Continued

NOTE: FEMA = Federal Emergency Management Agency, HMGP = Hazard Mitigation Grant Program, NFIP = National Flood Insurance Program, SBA = Small Business Administration.

[a]https://abc13.com/port-arthur-hurricane-laura-beaumont-east-texas/6388711/

[b]https://www.fema.gov/sites/default/files/documents/PDAReport_FEMA4572DR-TX.pdf

[c]https://www.fema.gov/press-release/20210825/hurricane-laura-recovery-efforts-through-one-year

[d]https://www.fema.gov/disaster/4572

[e]https://www.lbb.texas.gov/documents/publications/staff_report/2019/5097_hurricane_harvey.pdf

[f]https://www.wikiwand.com/en/Port_Arthur,_Texas

[g]https://www.fema.gov/sites/default/files/2020-03/FEMA4332DRTX_Expedited.pdf

[h]https://www.fema.gov/press-release/20230425/president-donald-j-trump-approves-major-disaster-declaration-texas

[i]https://www.fema.gov/press-release/20230425/historic-disaster-response-hurricane-harvey-texas

[j]https://incidentnews.noaa.gov/incident/7893

[k]https://incidentnews.noaa.gov/incident/7893

[l]https://www.hsdl.org/?view&did=35507

[m]https://www.fema.gov/sites/default/files/2020-09/PDAReport_FEMA-1791-DR-TX.pdf

[n]https://www.panews.com/tag/hurricane-rita-anniversary/

[o]https://www.weather.gov/lch/rita_main

[p]https://reliefweb.int/report/united-states-america/usa-six-months-after-hurricane-rita

[q]https://georgewbush-whitehouse.archives.gov/news/releases/2005/09/20050923-3.html

[r]https://georgewbush-whitehouse.archives.gov/news/releases/2005/09/20050924-7.html

SOURCES: Berg, R. (2009). *Tropical Cyclone Report: Hurricane Ike* (Report No. AL092008). National Hurricane Center. https://www.nhc.noaa.gov/data/tcr/AL092008_Ike.pdf

Blake, E. S., & Zelinsky, D. A. (2018). *National Hurricane Center Tropical Cyclone Report: Hurricane Harvey* (Report No. AL092017). National Hurricane Center. https://www.nhc.noaa.gov/data/tcr/AL092017_Harvey.pdf

Garcia-Buckalew, B. (2022, August 25). The Backstory: Five years ago this week, Hurricane Harvey brought catastrophic flooding to Texas. *KVUE ABC*. https://www.kvue.com/article/news/local/texas/hurricane-harvey-catastrophic-flooding-texas-five-years-ago/269-0a738956-e387-4b81-aaa2-1ed6115caef4

Garnham, J. P. (2020). Still recovering from Harvey, Texans in Beaumont and Port Arthur are now preparing for a new hurricane during the pandemic. *Texas Tribune*. https://www.texastribune.org/2020/08/26/hurricane-laura-beaumont-port-arthur-texas/

Pasch, R. J., Berg, R., Roberts, D. P., & Papin, P. P. (2020). *National Hurricane Center Tropical Cyclone Report: Hurricane Laura* (Report No. AL132020). National Hurricane Center. https://www.nhc.noaa.gov/data/tcr/AL132020_Laura.pdf

Wallach, D. (2016, September 13). 8 years ago, Hurricane Ike powered through Southeast Texas. *Beaumont Enterprise*. https://www.beaumontenterprise.com/news/weather/article/8-years-ago-Hurricane-Ike-powered-through-9219448.php

Yan, H., & Chavez, N. (2017, August 31). Harvey aftermath: Death toll rises; so do the floodwaters. *CNN*. https://www.cnn.com/2017/08/30/us/harvey-texas-louisiana/index.html

Appendix D

Key Terms

Adaptive governance: Adaptive governance is "a range of interactions between actors, networks, organizations, and institutions emerging in pursuit of a desired state for social-ecological systems" (Chaffin et al., 2014, p. 1). Governance in general is the manner and practice of governing.

Allostasis/allostatic load: A psycho-physiological "state" resulting from the body's long-term attempts to maintain physical, mental, emotional, and social equilibrium; a series of continual recalibrations to chronic stresses (McEwen & Seeman, 1999; Seeman et al., 2001). Elevated allostatic load has been linked to increased risk for chronic physical health conditions (e.g., hypertension, cardiovascular disease) and premature mortality (Karlamangla et al., 2006).

Climate adaptation: "The process of adjustment to actual or expected climate and its effect. In human systems, adaptation seeks to moderate or avoid harm or exploit beneficial opportunities. In some natural systems, human intervention may facilitate adjustment to expected climate and its effects" (Intergovernmental Panel on Climate Change [IPCC], 2014, p. 5).

Climate equity: The "goal of recognizing and addressing the unequal burdens made worse by climate change, while ensuring that all people share the benefits of climate protection efforts" (U.S. Environmental Protection Agency [EPA], 2023).

Climate justice: The belief that "[a]ll people—regardless of race, color, national origin, or income—are entitled to equal protection from environmental and health hazards caused by climate change and equal access to the development, implementation, and enforcement of environmental laws, regulations, and policies" (Centers for Disease Control and Prevention, 2022).

Collective efficacy: A form of social capital that encompasses both individual perceptions of social cohesion among neighbors as well as the willingness to intervene on behalf of the "common good." Higher levels of collective efficacy within communities have been linked to more positive health and well-being outcomes (Cohen et al., 2008; Sampson et al., 1997).

Community: "A geographically defined collection of people, at a subnational and substate level of jurisdiction" (National Academies of Sciences, Engineering, and Medicine, 2019, p. 12)—for example, "metropolitan statistical area[s]; rural villages or townships sharing similar environmental, cultural, or political ties; politically bounded places such as counties, cities, water districts, or wards within cities; or culturally defined places such as neighborhoods or street blocks that are greater than an individual household, parcel, or built project" (National Academies, 2019, p. 13).

Community resilience: The capacity of a community to continue its physical and cultural existence in the face of disaster, climate change, and other existential threats.[1] "Key actions that communities could take to build and measure their resilience include: (1) building community engagement and buy-in to develop resilience goals and priorities; (2) accounting for the multiple dimensions of a community—natural, built, social, financial, human, and political—to identify resilience needs and challenges and develop resilience goals" (National Academies, 2019, p. 5).

Co-production: The process of developing knowledge, plans, and strategies through the iterative engagement of at-risk communities, researchers, practitioners, and other groups, whose participation is necessary to the relocation process (see Armitage et al., 2011; Meadow et al., 2015; Wamsler, 2017).

Environmental justice: "[T]he fair treatment and meaningful involvement of all people regardless of race, color, national origin, or income with respect to the development, implementation and enforcement of environmental laws, regulations and policies" (EPA, 2022).

[1]The committee generated this definition.

Federal technical assistance: "[P]rograms, activities, and services provided by federal agencies to strengthen the capacity of grant recipients and to improve their performance of grant functions" (Government Accountability Office, 2020, p. 3).

Frontline community: "Those that experience 'first and worst' the consequences of climate change. These are communities of color and low-income, whose neighborhoods often lack basic infrastructure to support them and who will be increasingly vulnerable as our climate deteriorates" (Holland, 2023).

Indigenous traditional ecological knowledge (ITEK): "[A] body of observations, oral and written knowledge, practices, and beliefs that promote environmental sustainability and the responsible stewardship of natural resources through relationships between humans and environmental systems. It is applied to phenomena across biological, physical, cultural and spiritual systems. [It] has evolved over millennia, continues to evolve, and includes insights based on evidence acquired through direct contact with the environment and long-term experiences, as well as extensive observations, lessons, and skills passed from generation to generation" (Lander & Mallory, 2021, p. 2).

Infrastructure: For the purposes of this report, infrastructure includes both physical infrastructure (e.g., utilities, roads, municipal buildings, health clinics) and social infrastructure ("the policies, resources, and services that ensure people can participate in productive social and economic activities. This includes social services, public education, and healthcare" [Gould-Werth et al., 2023]).

Land subsidence: The sinking of land due to compression of sediments, removal of groundwater or other subsurface fluids, or geologic processes such as faulting or isostatic adjustment.[2]

Land-use planning: A tool used to manage "a variety of influential human activities by controlling and designing the ways in which humans use land and natural resources" (Ramkumar et al., 2019, p. 6). Land-use planning emphasizes collaborative problem solving, process-based techniques, and spatially oriented processes.

Maladaptation: "Actions that may lead to increased risk of adverse climate-related outcomes, including via increased greenhouse gas emissions,

[2]The committee generated this definition.

increased or shifted vulnerability to climate change, more inequitable outcomes, or diminished welfare, now or in the future. Most often, maladaptation is an unintended consequence" (Intergovernmental Panel on Climate Change, 2022, p. 7). More broadly, maladaptation impacts human capacities and may well inadvertently increase vulnerability or exposure to environmental conditions.

Non-stationarity: Natural hazard risk modeling has historically assumed that models can be predicated on an assessment of past hazard history (i.e., stationarity) to inform future hazard risk. In an era of climate change, scientists now recognize that we have entered a period of non-stationarity where we can no longer look to the past to help us predict the future. For example, 100-year floods are happening more frequently, thus becoming 50-year floods (Tessendorf, 2012).

Originating community: Originating community (or origin or sending community) refers to locations demonstrably unsafe or undergoing protracted environmental change, or where a combination of conditions makes them undesirable, and from which populations may flee following disasters or preemptively before such events or depart gradually due to environmental change or undesirable conditions.[3]

Participatory action research (PAR): "Collective, self-reflective inquiry that researchers and participants undertake, so they can understand and improve upon the practices in which they participate and the situations in which they find themselves"; the reflective process of PAR "is directly linked to action, influenced by an understanding of history, culture, and local context and embedded in social relationships" (Baum et al., 2006, p. 854).

Place attachment: The relationship between people, place, and process (Scannell & Gifford, 2010) and "an emotional bond between individuals or groups and their environment which is composed of both dependence and identity components" (Dandy et al., 2019; see also Masterson et al., 2017).

Place-based knowledge: Knowledge that has developed by a community in a particular location that incorporates cultural heritage as well as adaptations to the landscape and ecosystem.[4]

---

[3]The committee generated this definition.
[4]The committee generated this definition.

Psychological resilience: The ability to "bounce back" or overcome adversity and "experience positive outcomes despite an adverse event or situation" (Vella & Pai, 2019, p. 233).

Psychosocial well-being: A "superordinate construct that includes emotional or psychological well-being, as well as social and collective well-being" (Eiroa-Orosa, 2020, p. 1; Martikainen et al., 2002).

Receiving community: Receiving community (or destination community) is a broad term used to describe locations where people are resettling away from a hazardous area. This may include moving to a new jurisdiction or moving within the current jurisdiction to a new location. Ideally receiving communities have a lower climate risk and the necessary physical, economic, institutional, and social infrastructure to accommodate resettlers, although this is not always the case. The term refers to both the jurisdiction to which resettlers move and the social communities into which they must integrate.[5]

Regional planning: "Regional planning may be defined as the integrated management of the economic, social, and physical resources of a spatially bounded area" (Johnson, 2015, p. 141). For example, regional planning may be used to address watershed protection, which affects more than one local jurisdiction. In this report regional planning refers to both intrastate and interstate issues.

Social capital: "[F]eatures of social organization, such as networks, norms, and trust, that facilitate coordination and cooperation for mutual benefit" (Putnam, 1993, p. 2). Social capital has also been defined as the ability to secure resources by virtue of membership in social networks (Cattell, 2001), which can refer to the specific community ties held by individuals or by the broader community as a whole.

Social cohesion: "[A] descriptive, multifaceted and gradual phenomenon attributed to a collective, indicating the quality of collective togetherness" (Schiefer & van der Noll, 2016, p. 595). In reference to communities, social cohesion encompasses the quality of social relations within the community (such as social networks, trust, acceptance of diversity, and participation), the extent to which individuals identify with the community, and their orientation toward the common good (i.e., sense of responsibility, solidarity, compliance to social order; Schiefer & van der Noll, 2016).

---

[5]The committee generated this definition.

Social determinants of health: "[T]he conditions in the environments in which people live, learn, work, play, worship, and age that affect a wide range of health, functioning, and quality-of-life outcomes and risks [. . .] the social determinants of health are: education; employment; health systems and services; housing; income and wealth; the physical environment; public safety; the social environment; and transportation" (National Academies, 2017, p. 100).

Solastalgia: The anxiety of *impending* loss. In contrast to nostalgia—a longing for loss of home or homelands in the past—solastalgia relates to a different set of circumstances—that is, when individuals fear or anticipate being uprooted or removed and separated from long-tenured homes, place, and/or community (Albrecht et al., 2007; Butler-Ulloa, 2022).

Structural inequities: "[T]he systemic disadvantage of one social group compared to other groups with whom they coexist, and the term encompasses policy, law, governance, and culture and refers to race, ethnicity, gender or gender identity, class, sexual orientation, and other domains" (National Academies, 2017, p. 100).

Structural racism: "The public and private policies, institutional practices, norms, and cultural representations that inherently procure unequal freedom, opportunity, value, resources, advantage, restrictions, constraints, or disadvantage for individuals and populations according to their race and ethnicity both across the life course and between generations" (National Academies, 2022, p. 1).

Traditional ecological knowledge (TEK): "[A] cumulative body of knowledge, practice, and belief that evolves by adaptive processes, is handed down through generations by cultural transmission, and centers on the relationships of humans with one another and with their environment" (Berkes et al., 2000).

Traditional population: A self-identified group with long-standing residence in a particular place, with livelihoods and other cultural practices that are intertwined with the local environment and resources. It may be indigenous or have roots in Europe, Africa, Asia, or other parts of the Americas.[6]

Underserved community: A "community with environmental justice concerns and/or vulnerable populations, including people of color, low income,

[6]The committee generated this definition.

rural, tribal, Indigenous, and homeless populations" (EPA, 2019, p. 1), including small communities (under 1,000 people in population) that lack the resources to carry out resilience and public health building efforts.

Well-being: Encompasses "social, economic, environmental, cultural, and political conditions" that communities and individuals identify as essential to "flourish and fulfill their potential" (Brasher & Wiseman, 2008, p. 358). It can be broadly defined as how people feel and how they function physically, socially, and psychologically (Jarden & Roache, 2023).

Appendix E

Gulf Coast Timeline

The U.S. Gulf Coast region has been a place of migration, adaptation, and displacement for hundreds of years. Figure E-1 is a visual timeline that includes some defining moments in the region's history that are critical to understanding deeply rooted community perspectives on displacement and relocation. The timeline identifies early settlements, colonial expansion, plantation slavery, forced removal, and other landmark dates of injustice and immigration. This visual timeline is a supplement to Chapters 3 and 4 but relevant to the report as a whole.

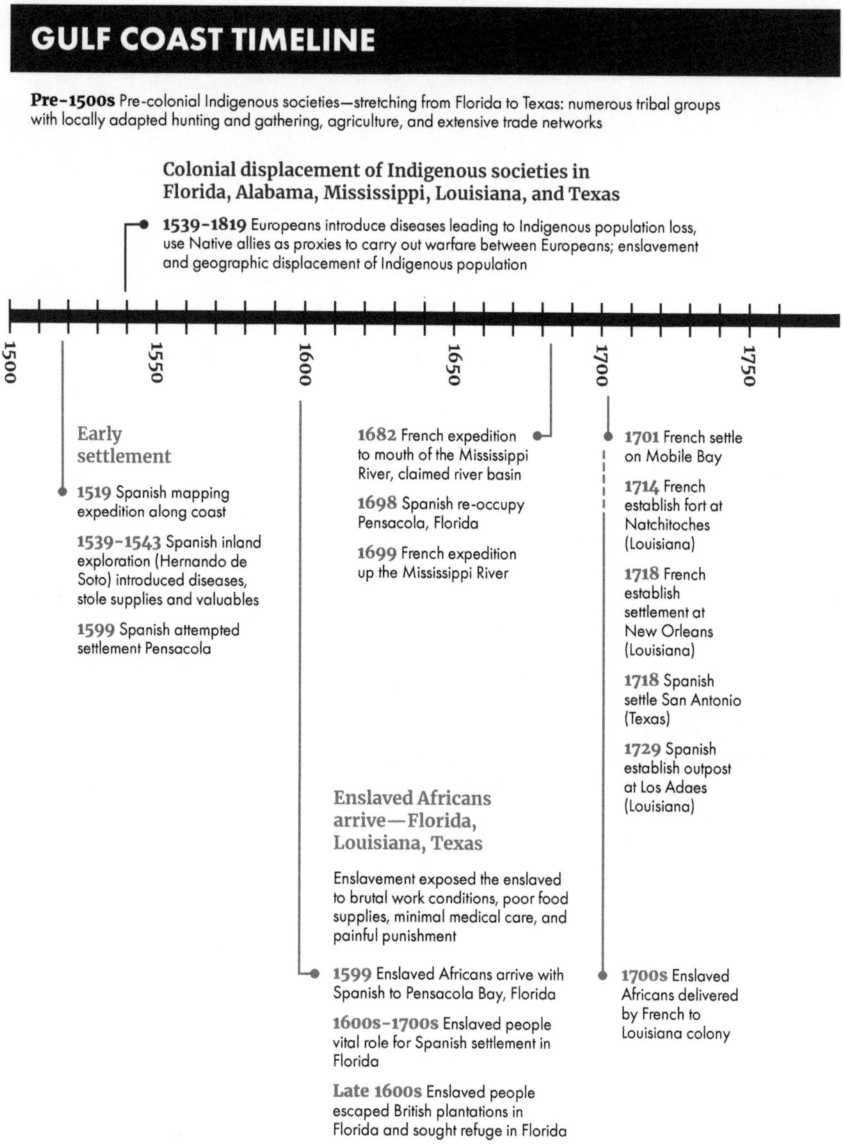

GULF COAST TIMELINE

Pre-1500s Pre-colonial Indigenous societies—stretching from Florida to Texas: numerous tribal groups with locally adapted hunting and gathering, agriculture, and extensive trade networks

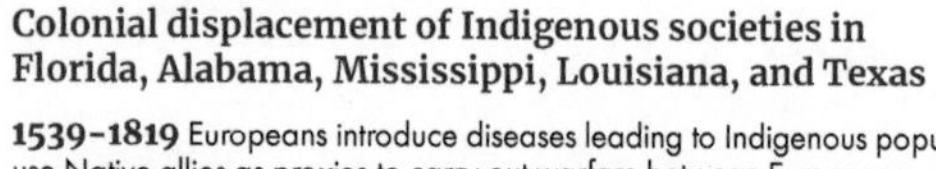

Colonial displacement of Indigenous societies in Florida, Alabama, Mississippi, Louisiana, and Texas

1539–1819 Europeans introduce diseases leading to Indigenous population loss, use Native allies as proxies to carry out warfare between Europeans; enslavement and geographic displacement of Indigenous population

1500 1550 1600 1650 1700 1750

Early settlement

1519 Spanish mapping expedition along coast

1539–1543 Spanish inland exploration (Hernando de Soto) introduced diseases, stole supplies and valuables

1599 Spanish attempted settlement Pensacola

1682 French expedition to mouth of the Mississippi River, claimed river basin

1698 Spanish re-occupy Pensacola, Florida

1699 French expedition up the Mississippi River

1701 French settle on Mobile Bay

1714 French establish fort at Natchitoches (Louisiana)

1718 French establish settlement at New Orleans (Louisiana)

1718 Spanish settle San Antonio (Texas)

1729 Spanish establish outpost at Los Adaes (Louisiana)

Enslaved Africans arrive—Florida, Louisiana, Texas

Enslavement exposed the enslaved to brutal work conditions, poor food supplies, minimal medical care, and painful punishment

1599 Enslaved Africans arrive with Spanish to Pensacola Bay, Florida

1600s–1700s Enslaved people vital role for Spanish settlement in Florida

Late 1600s Enslaved people escaped British plantations in Florida and sought refuge in Florida

1700s Enslaved Africans delivered by French to Louisiana colony

FIGURE E-1 Gulf Coast timeline.
SOURCE: Committee generated.

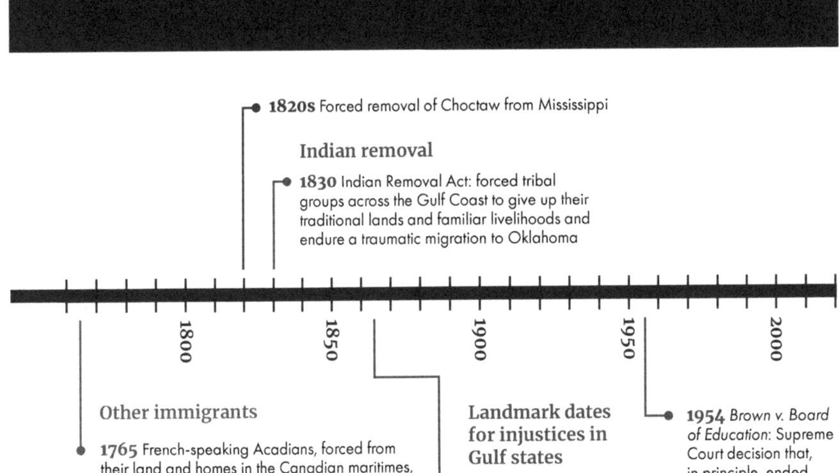

Other immigrants

1765 French-speaking Acadians, forced from their land and homes in the Canadian maritimes, begin arriving in Louisiana

1778 Isleno conscripts from the Canary Islands stationed in Louisiana

1791–1803 Initial Haitian exodus to Louisiana

1940s Bracero program: federal program to recruit thousands of temporary agricultural workers from Mexico into the United States during World War II

1952–1959 Cuban Revolution: Castro overthrew the U.S.-backed Batista regime and established a communist society in Cuba, prompting many Cubans to flee the island for the United States

1975 Vietnamese and Cambodian arrivals begin: thousands of South Vietnamese refugees fled their country after victory by the Viet Cong and many resettled along the Gulf Coast, their arrival in fishing communities was met with mistrust and anti-Asian violence

1800s Cotton plantations in Alabama and Mississippi acquire enslaved Africans

1800s Enslaved Africans brought to work cotton plantations in Texas

1811 Revolt of enslaved people in Louisiana

Landmark dates for injustices in Gulf states

1861 American Civil War begins—Southern states fought to retain slavery

1865 American Civil War ends, slavery abolished across the entire country

1865–1877 Reconstruction: African Americans in the South received right to vote and other limited and temporary rights

1865–1968 Jim Crow Era

- Southern states created restrictions for Black citizens
- Segregation policies were prevalent across the Gulf Coast
- Separate but unequal facilities in education and other public services
- Lynchings, and other acts of violence, became common tools for repression of Black citizens
- Incarceration rates, employment opportunities, and property ownership rights also were intolerant of equal rights for Blacks

1954 *Brown v. Board of Education*: Supreme Court decision that, in principle, ended separate but equal, but only began the protracted process of school integration

1965 Voting Rights Act: federal legislation that began the process of removing Jim Crow era voting restrictions for Blacks in the South

FIGURE E-1 Continued